Critical acclaim f

"Barry delves deep into the political process and describes it with extraordinary intimacy. . . . Most of the major players who people Barry's book still inhabit the stage. His insider account of these men bears directly on the politics of the moment." —*Financial World*

"[Wright's fall] was not a morality play. It was a classic power struggle which Wright lost and his ambitious antagonists won. . . . The quality of Barry's reporting makes most newspaper work seem like the funny papers. . . . Scenes dance on the page as though blocked out by Frank Capra." —*Los Angeles Times*

"An important accomplishment . . ."
—*The New York Times Book Review*

"Holds many fascinations and teaches more than a few lessons . . . Barry raises the curtain on the inside [game] as no other writer is likely to do for a long time." —*National Review*

"This is a riveting portrait, not just of Wright, but of how [Washington] really works . . . Brilliant" —*Business Week*

"John Barry has given us a close-up look at the latest battle for the Hill. It may presage the final push for political dominance in Washington." —*Newsday*

"More than the tragic portrait of a man, it is a running newsreel of the backstage workings of the U.S. House of Representatives during a time of crisis, perhaps the best book on Congress in recent memory." —*USA Today*

"This chronicle of aspiration and defeat is a valuable document, a prodigious work giving a rare picture." —*The Washington Post*

PENGUIN BOOKS

THE AMBITION AND THE POWER

John M. Barry, former Washington editor of *Dun's Business Month*, has written for *The New York Times*, *The Washington Post*, *Esquire*, and *Sports Illustrated*. He has a B.A. from Brown University, did graduate work in history at the University of Rochester, and then coached college football at Tulane. He currently lives in Washington, D.C. *The Ambition and the Power* is his first book.

THE
AMBITION
AND THE
POWER

JOHN M. BARRY

PENGUIN BOOKS

PENGUIN BOOKS
Published by the Penguin Group
Viking Penguin, a division of Penguin Books USA Inc.,
375 Hudson Street, New York, New York 10014, U.S.A.
Penguin Books Ltd, 27 Wrights Lane,
London W8 5TZ, England
Penguin Books Australia Ltd, Ringwood,
Victoria, Australia
Penguin Books Canada Ltd, 2801 John Street,
Markham, Ontario, Canada L3R 1B4
Penguin Books (N.Z.) Ltd, 182–190 Wairau Road,
Auckland 10, New Zealand

Penguin Books Ltd, Registered Offices:
Harmondsworth, Middlesex, England

First published in the United States of America by
Viking Penguin, a division of Penguin Books USA Inc., 1989

Published in Penguin Books 1990

10 9 8 7 6 5 4 3 2 1

Grateful acknowledgment is made for permission to reprint excerpts from the following
copyrighted works:
  "In the Musée des Beaux Arts" from *W. H. Auden: The Collected Poems* edited by Edward
Mendelson. Copyright 1940, renewed 1968 by W. H. Auden. Reprinted by permission of
Random House, Inc., and Faber and Faber Ltd.
  "Chicago" from *Chicago Poems* by Carl Sandburg. Copyright 1916 by Holt, Rinehart and
Winston, Inc., and renewed 1944 by Carl Sandburg. Reprinted by permission of Harcourt
Brace Jovanovich, Inc.

LIBRARY OF CONGRESS CATALOGING IN PUBLICATION DATA
Barry, John M., 1947–
The ambition and the power/John M. Barry.
    p. cm.
  Originally published: New York: Viking, 1989.
  Includes index.
  ISBN 0 14 01.0488 7
  1. Wright, Jim, 1922–   . 2. United States. Congress. House—
Speaker. 3. United States—Politics and government—1981–1989.
4. Corruption (in politics)—United States—History—20th century.
I. Title.
E840.8.W75B37   1990
328.73'0762'092—dc20   90–40356

Printed in the United States of America
Set in Times Roman
Designed by Fritz Metsch

To Brownie

CONTENTS

THE
AMBITION
AND THE
POWER

PROLOGUE
The Will to Power

At ten o'clock on the morning of July 28, 1987, Speaker of the House James Claude Wright, Jr., a Texas Democrat, and House Republican leader Robert Michel, from Illinois, sat down with Carlos Tunnermann Bernheim, the ambassador to the United States from Nicaragua, a country whose Marxist government was supported by the Soviet Union and Cuba. They met in room H-201 of the U.S. Capitol; it was a small conference room belonging to Wright's suite of offices, down the hall from his own. Mounted on one wall were the wide, sweeping horns of a Texas longhorn steer, beside a plaque that read, "Don't tell me it can't be done. Show me how it can." On another was a collage of photographs and political memorabilia. Just the other side of that wall, hundreds of tourists milled about the entrance to the rotunda, waiting to begin tours of the Capitol.

Though he was sixty-four years old, Wright in a way was beginning too. Just six months earlier he had become Speaker, and he had spent those months consolidating his power. Now he was about to exercise it. Wright was about to begin making foreign policy for the United States.

The Constitution reserved foreign-policy making to the President.

But Wright's involvement had been invited. A few days earlier a White House emissary had asked him to join President Ronald Reagan in sponsoring a new, bipartisan diplomatic initiative. The goal, supposedly, was to end the civil war in Nicaragua between the Marxist "Sandinista" government and anticommunist guerrillas, the "contras."

He was interested, but worried that the invitation was a trap. The

White House had created and backed the contras, and several times in the past had very publicly pursued diplomatic initiatives, then suddenly withdrawn its support from them—after Congress, lulled by the apparent diplomatic progress, approved more aid for the contras.

Wright and most of his House Democratic colleagues, who had elected him Speaker, bitterly opposed such aid. If he joined with Reagan in a peace plan it could have enormous impact. Never in history had a President and a Speaker done such a thing. But if the peace initiative turned out to be another administration ploy, if it resulted not in peace but in more war, Wright's authority as Speaker would be destroyed. The perception of power was power. If his Democratic colleagues perceived him as a dupe, a fool, he would have no power. The risk was great.

Still, the White House invitation attracted him. If he had much to lose, he also had much to gain. What greater goal could any public figure seek than to bring peace and end war? What better use for power was there? And, aside from this issue, he had his own policy agenda, a comprehensive agenda which rivaled that of most Presidents; he wanted to elevate the speakership to a new level of power, almost equivalent to the presidency. The lightning bolt of a joint peace initiative would electrify Washington, and go far toward permanently shifting power from the presidency to the speakership. Good works and ambition coincided.

Wright was willing therefore to take the risk, but he was not about to plunge ahead blindly. He would take care, calculate, and proceed only if convinced that a diplomatic initiative had a reasonable chance to succeed. Already his intelligence gathering had begun. In the few days since the White House first approached him, he had talked by phone with several Central American heads of state, and had traveled to Puerto Rico and met with other regional leaders. But the key was the Sandinistas themselves. He needed a better feel for them.

Michel's presence at the meeting involved some calculation by Wright too. The two of them had not yet developed the relationship of absolute trust that Michel—shrewder and tougher than the simple, solid, salt-of-the-earth man he seemed—had shared with Wright's predecessor, Thomas P. "Tip" O'Neill; this would help develop trust. Wright also wanted to present the Sandinistas with a bipartisan front. Lastly, Michel's presence protected Wright's flank; it would prevent anticommunist Republicans from attacking him for meeting privately with Marxists, whom they regarded as enemies of the United States.

Tunnermann, the ambassador, arrived with William Vigil, deputy foreign minister, and a woman translator. In his mid-fifties, Tunnermann was short, dumpy, serious, nervous. It was summer in Washington. As he entered he mopped sweat from his face. Vigil, much younger, was in his twenties, thin, with a scraggly goatee and sharp eyes. The woman, attractive, blond and blue-eyed, ironically had the strongest presence of the three. Nicaragua had once virtually been ruled by the United Fruit Company, backed up by the U.S. Marine Corps. Perhaps that accounted for Tunnermann's nervousness, for Vigil's surliness— there was nothing overt, just a glint in his eye, as if to say that if America had the arrogance of power on its side, he had the arrogance of history on his. Wright shook hands and invited them to sit down. At each seat, atop a tablecloth, were memo pads and pencils and plates of fresh fruit. A waiter hurried over to pour coffee for Wright, but he protested, "Oh, no. Please. Our guests first."

But Wright began with a stern message, barely masked by such courtesies. He explained that he had lived through the who-lost-China attacks on the Democratic Party and the McCarthy period which followed, and warned that he was determined to protect his party from similar charges in Central America. He reminded them that the Sandinistas had promised democracy in 1979 to the Organization of American States and personally to him. "Perhaps military aid to the contras will be extended," Wright observed ominously. He listed the regional foreign-policy and national-security concerns of the United States, and insisted that those concerns could not be compromised. Then he added, "But that gives us a small window of opportunity here."

Michel echoed Wright's words, and warned, "This Speaker, unlike the last Speaker, has pressures on him too. Texas is not like Massachusetts politically." But he too said that he and the Republican Party could support negotiations if progress was rapid and real. He agreed that perhaps a small window for a negotiated settlement did exist.

When they finished, Tunnermann began: "I believe this is the most important conversation I have had in my three years in Washington." He explained that, although his English was good, he wanted to make certain no misunderstandings occurred, no nuances of meaning were lost, and therefore he would use the translator. For the next forty minutes, Wright's eyes were fixed on Tunnermann, watching his expression both while the principals spoke—Wright understood Spanish—and while the words were translated. Then Wright asked, "Do you think it is possible this is one moment in history where we might explore an agreement? Do you feel if there's a good-faith effort made by the United States we could reach one?"

"Yes," Tunnermann instantly replied.

Wright nodded. He had decided to proceed. The meeting was over.

The White House had invited Jim Wright into perhaps the one foreign-policy area closest to Ronald Reagan's heart. Wright would soon dominate it. And that was not the only policy area which he would dominate. He wanted to dominate. He intended to dominate. He wanted to reverse White House policies on issue after issue, but his plans went beyond his policy differences with Reagan; they came from his own ambition and his view of the institutional relationship between Congress and the Executive.

He thought in grand terms, and in a private journal he kept for years, wrote, "We make more mistakes by thinking too small than by thinking too large"; he blamed the failure of Jimmy Carter's presidency on the fact that "he thought too small."

To him, the Speaker, as constitutional head of the Legislative Branch, was in many ways comparable to the President, the head of the Executive; he believed the Speaker could and should focus and mobilize the power of the House to define the national agenda. While still majority leader, he complained to a reporter, "Even up here on the Hill there are those who agree with the saying 'The President proposes and Congress disposes.' I don't think that's true. I think there's a creative role for the Legislative Branch and a leadership role for the Speaker . . . The Congress should not simply react, passively, to recommendations from the President but should come forward with initiatives of its own. Each year I would like to have some congressional initiatives. Not a hundred, not even a dozen. But four or five major items which becomes the congressional agenda."

He intended to dictate that agenda by controlling pathways of power so submerged and labyrinthine that many in Washington did not even know that they existed. Those pathways led to the insides of power, and Wright knew the private passages intimately. More than that, he was willing to use them in ways unlike anyone since fellow Texan and onetime friend Lyndon Johnson. If he succeeded, he would shift the institutional balance of power in Washington; the new balance he sought would allow a Speaker to confront a strong President as a near equal and to dominate a weak President.

There is a simpler way of saying this. The concept of a separation of powers in the federal government does not describe reality. People in Washington do not divide power; they share it. Wright wanted a bigger share. He had waited patiently for power, submerging his own agenda through the forty years of politics it took him to become Speaker; now that he had it he intended to use it.

But even as Wright took charge, as his agenda moved forward and his involvement in Central America increased his visibility and power, the question remained whether his ascendancy of the moment would be just that, momentary, a lunge which overextended and exhausted him, or whether his power would take root, deepen, and grow; whether his triumphs were flashes against the backdrop of a fading presidency, or whether they marked the ascension of someone who might dominate Washington for a decade or more, and leave a legacy behind.

The answer to that question lay within Wright himself. By rising he exposed himself, made himself a target, and exposed his weaknesses. Now those weaknesses would be explored, probed, stressed, tested, to see if they could withstand the pressure. Perhaps his biggest weakness was ambition itself, an ambition dangerously close to hubris. George Miller, a California Democratic congressman, said, "We've got a hedge-clipping service around here. When someone sticks his head up, sooner or later someone else comes around and cuts it off. That goes for Speakers too."

Ambition was acceptable only when it comported with the interests of others. Brian Donnelly, a Democratic congressman from Boston, said, "People talk about 'friends' here. There aren't any friends. The only blood oath I swore was to my district. It's like Sal Tessio in *The Godfather*—the guy who had helped the family for fifty years, but betrayed them when the kid took over. He said, 'I love ya, Michael. It's nothing personal. It's business.' That's what this is like. When they screw you it's not personal, just business. You've got guys here just watching Wright, just sitting and watching. They're setting him up for a fall—for a big fall."

Some Republicans saw more than ambition in Wright's reach for power—they saw evil, saw Wright as a dangerous man willing to do whatever it took to get his way. Dick Cheney had been White House chief of staff under Gerald Ford, and, now a Wyoming congressman, was third-ranking member of the House Republican leadership; he recognized and understood that sometimes one had to use power roughly and brutally. Yet even he believed Wright went too far. Within a few months of Wright's meeting with Tunnermann, Cheney would call Wright "a heavy-handed son of a bitch" who would "break the rules or bend the rules" to win. Other Republicans believed that Wright's relentlessness justified breaking unwritten rules to stop him, and some saw him as a tool to use in their own grasp for power.

One Republican, Georgia congressman Newt Gingrich, had an agenda as ambitious as Wright's and he would cross lines that even Wright would not. Long before Wright met with Tunnermann, Gingrich concluded, "If Wright consolidates his power, he will be a very, very formidable man. We have to take him on early to prevent that."

Gingrich lacked the votes to take him on inside the House, so he planned to leverage his own power by manipulating the media, by using the power of the press against Wright, by turning Wright into a foil for his own aims, his own ambition. Early in Wright's speakership, Gingrich decided on his course of action: he would repeatedly and publicly charge Wright with unethical conduct in the hope of creating enough echoes in the media to force a formal investigation. As Wright was meeting with Tunnermann, Gingrich was launching his attack. At the very moment of Wright's greatest triumph, Gingrich was explaining, "Wright's a useful keystone to a much bigger structure. I'll just keep pounding and pounding on his ethics. There comes a point where it comes together and the media takes off on it, or it dies . . . He's from Texas. He's been in politics over thirty years. An aggressive investigator with subpoena powers might find something."

Then, with an odd tone of respect in his voice, he added, "If Wright survives this ethics thing, he may become the greatest Speaker since Henry Clay."

If Wright survives.

Henry Clay became Speaker in 1811 and was the last Speaker to dominate foreign policy, when he bullied President James Madison into the War of 1812.

Wright believed that right now, *now,* was the moment at which he could alter the balance of forces, affect the outcome of history. He was impatient, almost desperate, to move. As majority leader, he had been forced to hold back. "Wait for a Democratic President, Jimmy," Tip O'Neill had told him, leaning forward and patting him on the knee. "Don't you know we're fighting a rearguard action?"

Betty Wright, his wife, observed, "When he was majority leader he felt helpless, impotent to do anything. It was going to be different when he became Speaker."

Wright declared, "There is no next game to wait for. This is it."

Gingrich and conservatives both inside and outside the House had viewed O'Neill as an enemy. They saw Wright as a threat.

This is a book about power and ambition. Washington lies at the epicenter of power. All force collides here. In Washington resides the power to take money and spend money, the power to decide what people can do and what people cannot do, the power to make a nation strong or weak, the power to wage war or make peace.

The ambition belongs to many men, but none more than to Jim Wright, who burned for a place in history. He would use the 100th Congress of the United States, convened during the bicentennial anniversary of the Constitution, to earn it. He would rise up and fill the sky with lightning bolts, and he would become a target for them.

Both Wright and Gingrich saw historical forces at work, forces which both ran through America's psyche and society and would define its future. Each hoped to influence and channel different elements of those forces to turn them to his own ends, Wright through expanding and exercising the power of the Speaker, Gingrich by destroying Wright.

PART I

THE ASCENSION

A man who becomes prince with the help of the nobles finds it more difficult to maintain his position than one who does so with the help of the people. . . . A man who becomes prince by way of the people stands alone, and has near him either no one or very few not prepared to take orders . . . [but if he becomes prince by way of nobles] he finds himself surrounded by many who believe they are his equals, and because of that he cannot command them the way he wants.

—Machiavelli, *The Prince*

CHAPTER 1

In March 1976 Texas congressman Jim Wright and Craig Raupe, his close friend and senior aide, began a four-hour drive from Wright's suburban Washington home to Keyser, West Virginia, where Wright was scheduled to make a speech for the local congressman. Such speechmaking was routine for Wright. He was generally considered the best orator in the House of Representatives, and over the years dozens of colleagues had invited him to visit their districts and address party gatherings and fund-raisers. He had an ability to make an audience care, to make them believe that they mattered and belonged to something large, and he always left them eager to contribute effort, money, and votes to the local member of Congress.

Wright made these speeches for his own reasons. Thirty years earlier, he had entered politics as a twenty-three-year-old liberal war-hero crusader with, as he once said, a "messianic" impulse, but in his one term of service in the Texas legislature he "soon learned that personal acceptance meant more to legislative success than ideology." So he submerged his messianic impulse and began devoting himself to winning acceptance. Nothing won more acceptance, thus nothing would be more helpful to his own success, than helping a colleague win reelection. His seat on the House Public Works Committee gave him little opportunity to address grand issues, but it gave him considerable opportunity to help colleagues with some extra miles of interstate highways here or airport expansion there. His visits to colleagues' districts were even more important. Any member of Congress could help a colleague legislatively, but sacrificing one's own time and visiting a colleague's constituents—well, that was special. That showed Wright would really work hard to help, and really thought his colleague was important. You could count on Wright.

But Wright did not give up weekend after weekend, travel constantly, inflict on himself strains which hurt his own family—contributing to the destruction half a dozen years before of his first marriage—simply to win acceptance. Acceptance was only a means to an end. All his life Wright had burned to play on the national stage, to rise above the anonymity of being one of 435 members of the House. Ambition burned in him as fiercely as in anyone in Washington; if he hid it better than others, perhaps that was only because it ran deeper in him. Wright sacrificed his personal life in order to spin strands. Meticulously he had begun to gather each strand and weave it into a web designed to yield one thing—power.

Power was defined in the Annunzio rule, as stated by Illinois Democrat Frank Annunzio: "The only thing that counts up here is votes. Everything else is bullshit." Votes, that's where power lay. No matter what one's title, chairman, Speaker, or President, without votes one had nothing. And the trips were the single-best way to gain influence over votes, not only because they counted as a favor but because if a man was sensitive (and Wright was alert to and remembered everything), he could sense a colleague's needs and weaknesses and what his constituents were like, whom his colleague listened to and how best to approach him. Later, when that colleague said, *Gee, Jim, I'd like to vote with you but my district just won't allow it,* Wright could say, *Hell, Frank, I've been to your district. They love you. Besides, I'll bet that union fellow in Springfield, what was his name? Sam Jones? I'll bet Sam would be proud of you supporting this. Lot of votes in that union, aren't there? Maybe you ought to call Sam.* Maybe even Wright would get Sam to call him. So Wright had made these trips routine. This one, though, would not be routine.

This speech was for Harley Staggers, chairman of the Interstate and Foreign Commerce Committee. Although Staggers was neither a legislative nor intellectual leader of the House, his chairmanship gave him weight, and his opinion represented that of many average, middle-of-the-road colleagues.

On the drive to West Virginia, Wright thought about his speech and talked little. Raupe, a rail-thin, hyperactive, and fearless man, drove and kept quiet. The two had been friends since 1949 when Wright was mayor of Weatherford, Texas, and Raupe, who had been fired from one teaching job because of his liberal politics, asked him if he knew where he could find a paycheck until his job teaching political science at Weatherford College began. Wright had given him a job with the town. Raupe had come to Washington as his top aide when Wright won election to the House in 1954, then gone on to greater things—work in Lyndon Johnson's administration, deputy chairman of the Democratic National Committee, and vice president of Eastern Airlines—before falling on alcohol and hard times. Wright had lifted him up, given him a job again, and protected him in it until he straightened himself out, and inscribed on a photograph a few months before, "To Craig—as near as I've ever had to a brother." They were as close as two men got.

Early in the evening they arrived. Keyser, Staggers's hometown, was a coal town near the headwaters of the Potomac River. Just big enough to seem darkly industrial, it had soot-covered, four-story wooden tenements, a couple of blinking traffic lights, three blocks filled with dreary stores, a dozen railroad sidings packed with coal cars, and a high school. Yet the whole town seemed temporary and fragile somehow; its streets ran up to a creek along a mountainside and stopped, dead—as if the earth refused to yield more, as if nature was signifying that it could destroy people's lives with a casual shrug of one cave-in or mudslide. In its fragility and dependence on the earth it was reminiscent of Wright's part of Texas, of the dry, rolling hills that looked pretty but provided no sustenance.

Wright spoke in the town's largest hall, the Moose Lodge. A capacity crowd of several hundred showed up. A few men wore coats and ties, most did not, but they all loved Wright. Despite the long drive home he didn't want to leave until the event ended. It was after eleven before Raupe could get him headed for the car, and they gave Staggers a short ride to his home.

As Staggers got out of the car he invited Wright—not Raupe—inside for a word in private. Members were members and staff was staff and some things were for members only. So what if Raupe was almost Wright's brother? So what if Raupe had been deputy national chairman of the Democratic Party? Raupe waited in the car, huddling up and turning the engine on and off to keep warm. Fifteen minutes. Thirty minutes. Forty-five minutes. Finally Wright came out and they started back to Washington.

Raupe knew better than to ask what had been said. If Wright wanted to tell him he would. It was after midnight. The road was empty, the moon bright, the night like crystal. Just as on the way out, Wright said nothing at first, just sat, shifting back and forth in his seat, staring out the window at the moonlit mountains. Then, abruptly, he turned to Raupe and asked, "What would you think if I were to run for majority leader?"

That's what Staggers had talked to him about. The incumbent majority leader, the floor leader of the Democrats, Thomas P. "Tip" O'Neill, was about to replace retiring Speaker of the House Carl Albert. No one was running against O'Neill for Speaker, but several candidates were already running for majority leader. The post mattered not for what it was but for what it could become; counting O'Neill, ten floor leaders in a row had ascended to Speaker, and the next majority leader would likely be the eleventh.

The question jolted Raupe. Could Wright win it? During the entire four-hour drive home Wright and Raupe talked through the race.

He would have to compete with three far more prominent members. The first was Californian John McFall, the whip, who as third-ranking member of the leadership headed its vote-counting and vote-convincing operation; McFall played the inside game well and, generally popular, had the additional advantage of already being on the leadership ladder. Even more formidable were Philip Burton, another Californian, and Missouri's Richard Bolling. Burton already had an internal political machine and had won election as chairman of the Democratic Caucus, the organization of all House Democrats. Bolling, a brilliant if abrasive man, had served as an intellectual beacon of the House for over a decade. Both were nationally prominent leaders against the Vietnam War, and both had led a decade-long reform movement that had made the House itself more democratic and had taken power from the few, committee chairmen such as Staggers, and given it to the many, the junior members.

At first look, Wright seemed to have no chance against any of them. For one thing, he had been on the wrong side of several issues. Unlike Burton and Bolling—and O'Neill—he had done little to contribute to the reform movement. Indeed, just eighteen months earlier, in the tumultuous Caucus meeting that dismembered the formal seniority system and ousted three aged chairmen, Wright gave an emotional speech defending one of those three, Banking Committee chairman and fellow

Texan Wright Patman. A few years before that he had outraged liberals, who dominated the Democratic Caucus, by sponsoring a resolution supporting Nixon's Vietnam policy. And McFall, Burton, and Bolling had been running hard for the post for almost a year now. Some members had even asked Wright if he was running and he had told them no; they had promptly pledged support to others. Nor would Wright be running from a position of power. He didn't even serve on, much less chair, a prestigious committee. His only formal leadership post was relatively insignificant; he was one of several deputy whips. It seemed an impossible leap from there to Speaker-in-waiting.

Yet an opening for Wright did exist, an opening for a good-old-boy and a moderate. House leadership elections are conducted in rounds, with the candidate getting the fewest votes in each round dropping out until only two remain. Wright's strategy was simple: beat McFall in the first round; in the second round, let Burton and Bolling split the same liberal constituency while Wright picked up everyone else; in the third and final round, lay everything on the line and roll the dice.

On the long ride home, Raupe and Wright went over the prospects in detail. The more they talked, the more possible it looked, although it remained a long shot. If he ran and lost, whoever won—especially Burton if he won—would make his future difficult. Still, Raupe concluded, "I don't think you can win, but I think you should run."

Wright flared at him. He didn't get into things thinking failure. Especially now. The chance to become majority leader!—and then Speaker! The Speaker was second only to the President in power, and in some ways more powerful. All his life he had wanted such a chance. From boyhood he had wanted to be President, had tried twice for the Senate en route to that prize and been disappointed, and only a few years earlier finally, on his fiftieth birthday, had acknowledged to himself for the first time that he would never attain that goal. Now it was as if he could be born all over again, as if everything he had once dreamed of and finally given up on was again possible. Wright grew animated, excited. This was the last chance he would ever have to fulfill his ambitions. He couldn't pass it up. And he would hear no more of failure. He *could* win.

Yet he had seen many a politician humiliated by his own ego. He was not going to get in the race if it would make him look like a fool. Feelers went out, word spread quietly, and he listened, weighed information, evaluated what he was hearing, looked for confirmation of his own assessment that, long shot or not, he had a chance. It came. Members started coming to him, urging him to run. Dan Rostenkowski, a power player without power, was one; Rostenkowski needed a horse to ride for his own ambition. Run, he told him. Others said the same. Go out there and *run*. Later, laughing, Wright said, "I didn't need much convincing."

The House is a live thing, a vital thing, and it moves according to rhythms generated by forces that bind all men and women together—personal ambition, trust, friendship and dislike, anger, the memory of past kindnesses and slights—made more complicated by ideology, by internal, national, and local politics. To succeed in the House a man or woman must be able to read its rhythms, and recognize and understand not only broad obvious currents but the eddies and undertow indicated when another member smiles too quickly or not quickly enough, keeps silent at another's joke or laughs too hard. Even Jack Brooks, a Texas Democrat known for bluntness rather than subtlety, observes, "*Nuance*. It's all *nuance*."

The most obvious force is ideology; it is the easiest to read, the one outsiders can follow, but in a leadership election it is not the most important force. Both Burton and Bolling were liberals, as was the bulk of the Caucus. McFall was a moderate. Wright was running as a moderate, but he had taken plenty of liberal positions in his career. Liberals who based their decision on ideology would not make him their first choice, but he was acceptable.

Closely linked to ideology is geography, a more subtle but more important factor in a leadership race. The interests of one region differ from those of other regions; Republicans and Democrats from Iowa vote the same way on more issues than not, as do Republicans and Democrats from Pennsylvania or Louisiana.

Wright had a geographic advantage. Ever since Jack Garner of Texas became Speaker in 1931, a member from an oil state had served as one of the top House Democrats, while a member from Massachusetts had served as another. In this almost formalized "Boston-Austin connection," whoever was from Massachusetts represented the party's urban element; the Texan, or in Carl Albert's case the Oklahoman, gave conservative and rural Democrats a receptive ear and helped raise campaign contributions from big-spending oilmen. Sam Rayburn and Lyndon Johnson had forged that money connection; in return, Rayburn had demanded pledges of support for oil industry tax breaks before allowing a member to go on the tax-writing Ways and Means Committee.

O'Neill came from Boston, but of the candidates for majority leader only Wright had good connections to the South or Southwest. Electing anyone but him would end the geographic balance which had served Democrats so well. Between geography and ideology, moderates, southerners, and conservatives worried that with O'Neill as Speaker and Burton or Bolling as majority leader, they would be cut out of the loop. McFall was a moderate, but he, too, broke geographic tradition. Wright continued it.

The most important binding force, though, is neither geography nor ideology, but personal relationships. This represents a more complicated standard than friendship.

Members measure one another constantly. The pressure of being judged never abates. And personal relationships depend on something deeper than whether one colleague "likes" another. Talking of a particularly obnoxious member, one man warned, "Don't confuse your judgment of his personality with your judgment of his effectiveness as a member." There are personal things more important than personality. Most important: *is that member reliable?* Reliability offers the only security in politics. Members want it from all their colleagues; they demand it from their leaders.

Few members will lie outright to a colleague, but one must listen more closely to one member's precise phrasing than to another's. There are other measures of reliability too. Suppose a member promises to whip colleagues from his state on an issue. Will he just place a phone call and then forget about it? Will he mention it to them in passing? Or will he track them down on the floor, pull them aside, and sell them? And if he does a selling job, does he lay out the pros and cons fairly, describe the political risks of a vote honestly, or does he distort the issue?

Faulkner wrote, *The past is never over. It isn't even past.* Members do not forget the measure they have taken of their colleagues; that measure is a factor in every vote. Often it is submerged, but it is there. What is the measure of a member? Not his intelligence, but his character. When a junior member, a former Rhodes Scholar, got a seat on a major committee, a subcommittee chairman said, "I'm waiting to find out what that means. I've seen young, smart members who had defects in their character. There's no substitute for character." Wright explains, "The House is like a small town, really. I grew up in a small town. I loved it."

All four men running for majority leader had been measured by their colleagues. The closer they looked at McFall, the farther behind he fell. But Burton, Bolling, and Wright all could win. Morris Udall, a man who chose to pursue the 1976 Democratic presidential nomination instead of the majority leader's race, noted that all three were workaholics, all three were hard to know, and none of them had close friends among their colleagues.

Burton was tall, beefy, and abrasive. The youngest of the four candidates at fifty, and the most junior with twelve years of House service, he had a Lyndon Johnson style, pushy, aggressive; he would corner a member, isolate him, physically tower over him, envelop him, jab his finger at a colleague's chest and demand support. He was a drinker, raucous, a hustler, a wheeler-dealer. He made deals, as opposed to building coalitions. Coalitions survive over time because each element recognizes a commonality of interest. Deals are onetime, one-shot transactions, with no commitment on anyone's part for the future. Recalled Udall, "Burton was a larger-than-life figure with great vitality and immense ambition, who wasn't above using political power to get his way. He'd rather do something a devious way if given a choice, and pit one guy against another."

Burton and his California machine played hardball. After the 1980 census he oversaw California's redistricting, which blatantly gerrymandered Democratic districts around the state and paid off both enemies and friends. Describing the new districts to his California Democratic colleagues, he said, "Some of you are as snug as in your mother's arms. Some of you will have to work harder. And some of you got fucked."

His 1983 funeral drew a huge crowd; one man in attendance looked around and said, "Half are here out of love and respect, and half want to make sure he's dead." Four years after Burton's death, a California congressman who acknowledged supporting Wright against Burton still worried about retribution from the remnants of Burton's machine; he insisted, "You can't identify me."

Burton had made people uneasy in his campaign for and service as Caucus chairman. Before Burton, campaigns for Caucus chairman had been casual. The preceding one had lasted less than twenty-four hours. Burton's campaign lasted for months. He especially focused on winning support from the seventy-five newly elected Democrats in the Watergate class of 1974, calling each of them personally, offering his help and advice, and asking for their support. Burton won easily. (He beat fellow Californian Bernie Sisk, whose top assistant was a young man named Tony Coelho.)

As Caucus chairman, Burton wielded the gavel arrogantly. Once Louisiana's Joe Waggoner sought recognition, shouting, "Mr. Chairman! Mr. Chairman!" Burton simply ignored him. Craig Raupe said, "Let's say the chair is about to rule on a point of order. Members were wondering with Burton, 'Is that bastard gonna rule fairly, or is some kind of deal involved?' "

Burton did have pluses. He was a doer, a mover. Things happened around him. He shook things up, and for decades the House had needed shaking up. It was only after years of anti-Vietnam protests, for example, that the House leadership had allowed any kind of floor vote on it. Burton had a certain charm, too, the charm of a rogue. His political machine produced for its allies, raising money nationally. Those who voted on the basis of getting things done were inclined toward him. The bulk of the California delegation—10 percent of all House Democrats—supported him, and so did most northern liberals. The two most liberal members of the Texas delegation, Jack Brooks and Bob Eckhardt, were for him. Burton was the front-runner.

Richard Bolling was a close second. A onetime protégé of Sam Rayburn's, Bolling had provided the intellectual ammunition for much of the internal House reform movement of the late sixties and early seventies. No one doubted his courage—he had confronted two Speakers, John McCormack and Carl Albert, repeatedly—or his word. A big man physically, like Burton he stood over six feet and weighed over two hundred pounds.

His biggest opponent was his own ego, for his brilliance was more than matched by his arrogance. He disliked certain requirements of being in the leadership, and considered it beneath him to perform such minutiae as stopping in the hall to shake hands with a colleague's constituents. He prided himself on not suffering fools gladly—and let it be known he considered many colleagues fools. It was difficult for him to personally ask for votes, to actually, physically, personally *ask* his colleagues for their help, especially from members he considered his inferiors. He recognized his problem, and told Udall, "I think I'm too arrogant to win."

The fact that Bolling was a serious contender indicated members' uneasiness about Burton, and Bolling drew the anybody-but-Burton vote. He actually got into the race only because he despised Burton and later said, "I wanted to make sure Burton didn't win. That was what I cared about most."

Yet despite their flaws, Burton and Bolling were both big men, with more than physical largeness. Their collisions, head-on, echoed through the House, made it shake. Smaller men got out of their way. But one of those smaller men—physically smaller, tighter, narrower, more private and self-contained—did not. That man was Wright.

Wright knew that members of Congress were "both proud and shy. They want you to come to them."

Minutiae mattered. Members believe one function of the leadership—and to many members it is the most important function—is to service them just as they service constituents. Minutiae measured that service. Wright had thrived on minutiae, had proven his willingness to do little things for colleagues not just on Public Works or on a trip to a district. For years he had learned names and faces of just-elected members so he could greet them by name. Several members recalled that Wright was the first colleague they met when they arrived in Washington; at a reception Wright would be grinning at them with his teeth flashing, coming toward them with hand outstretched, congratulating them on winning.

Where Bolling disdained colleagues as fools, Wright said gently, "We're all fools in our own ways, don't you think?"

Wright's chief allies included the bulk of both the Texas delegation and his colleagues on the Public Works Committee. One's internal power base almost always began with state and committee allies. It differed little from neighborhood and ethnic groups in big cities. One looked after one's own.

Wright also had supporters who had their own reasons to help him, especially Dan Rostenkowski of Chicago. Big, brawny, almost six feet four inches and hulking, husky, he looked like a Bears linebacker— the kind who would smile when he hit someone. A description of him years later by a lobbyist would have been just as apt in 1976: "If you're on his side he takes care of you. If you're not, he tries to kick you to death."

A product of Mayor Richard Daley's Chicago machine, Rostenkowski was a natural politician. His father had been an alderman, and Rostenkowski had turned down a professional baseball contract to play politics. Even after he became Ways and Means chairman in 1981, he kept his post as a Chicago precinct captain and returned to Chicago almost every weekend, often spending half the week there. With his base of support among Illinois Democrats and his infighting ability, he had seemed headed for great power in the House until he derailed himself.

His first problem came at the 1968 Democratic National Convention in Chicago when then–House majority leader Carl Albert could not control the convention. No one could have. Antiwar protests and riots had all but spread from the streets to the convention floor. Albert, a brilliant man, a Rhodes Scholar, stood barely over five feet tall and lacked physical presence, physical power with the gavel. Rostenkowski got an order from Lyndon Johnson in Texas to quiet the convention. He went to the podium and, according to Albert, said it would mean a lot to him if he could preside briefly, here in his hometown. Could he? Albert gave him the gavel; Rostenkowski banged it forcefully, gave the gavel back, and thanked Albert. "If he says any different," Albert later recalled, "he's a liar."

But word got back to Albert that Rostenkowski was bragging he had grabbed the gavel and pounded the convention to order. Rostenkowski denied having said that, but the story circulated widely. In 1970 Albert ran for Speaker. He asked every state delegation for support. Illinois, alone among the big states, did not offer it. "I inquired why and Frank Annunzio told me it was Rostenkowski," he said.

Albert did become Speaker. At the same time, Rostenkowski was working hard to elect Hale Boggs majority leader with the understanding Boggs would make him whip—traditionally, the Speaker allowed the majority leader to choose the whip, although he retained veto power. Boggs won but Albert refused to appoint Rostenkowski whip. Boggs then suggested Tip O'Neill, and Albert appointed him.

Simultaneously, Rostenkowski experienced another bitter disappointment. In addition to seeking the whip job, Rostenkowski was seeking reelection as chairman of the Democratic Caucus. One day before the election, Rostenkowski was unopposed, but also unpopular.

But that afternoon the Texas delegation met. One member said, "Somebody at least should run against the son of a bitch." Another member laughed. "Tiger's not here. Let's run Tiger." He was talking about Olin "Tiger" Teague. The delegation, half in jest and half seriously, organized a candidacy for him. The next day Teague voted for Rostenkowski but beat him.

Instead of being the third-ranking Democrat in the House, the whip, or the fourth-ranking, Caucus chairman, Rostenkowski was rebuffed by both the leadership and his colleagues. He wanted to be something. He was nothing.

Boggs died in a plane crash, and suddenly Tip O'Neill became majority leader, and now, in 1976, was stepping up to Speaker. Rostenkowski believed it could have been, should have been, he stepping up. Albert disputed that: "His colleagues rejected him for Caucus chairman. He could never be elected Speaker. Never." But Rostenkowski believed he could have won, if he had been in the game. Now he wanted to get back into it. Both Burton and Bolling were enemies. Wright was the only other horse around. Rostenkowski urged him to run and worked hard for his election; it was his own future, not just Wright's, he was fighting for, and he would fight brutally.

But most important in this race was Wright himself. Wright would devote everything in his soul to this race. Meticulously, attending to each detail, he would exploit every resource available to him, exhaust himself as well as those around him. In 1961 he had run to fill Lyndon Johnson's Senate seat and finished third of seventy-two candidates, just missing a runoff he would have been favored to win; later he said he learned "just how big a state Texas was. I thought I would get up earlier, go to bed later, give more speeches, shake more hands than anyone else. I did all that but it was like trying to siphon the Gulf of Mexico with a spoon." He had lacked the money for a media campaign; Texas was too large for a personal campaign. But the House was not too large.

He kept in personal touch, personal control of his campaign. There was something tactile about it, as if he spread out his fingers wide and laid hands on his colleagues. Years later he analyzed his style himself: "It's like simultaneously playing chess and Ping-Pong. A lot of what I do isn't calculated in some arcane sense, but a lot of what I say to a member is calculated in ways in which I have only a vague sense myself. I don't think consciously of this strategy or that tactic. Things are too fluid for that. I have goals in mind and pursue those goals." Burton, Bolling, and McFall had been seeking commitments for a year. Wright was far behind. He poured himself into his effort, asking members one by one for support. By summer recess he had sat down privately with 165 colleagues. The Democratic Convention was in New York City that year, and all the candidates for majority leader were in attendance. Each of them campaigned in a way reflecting his own style. Bolling did little more than show the flag, waiting for members to come to him. Burton hosted cocktail parties and draped his big arm around members' shoulders. Wright organized his helpers to track down members and candidates for House seats—especially candidates—and bring them to his room for one-on-one meetings.

Finding people wasn't easy in the crush of an immense convention, with people scattered amid dozens of hotels, distracted by the lights and grit of New York City. Every logistical detail was analyzed, a map made which described traffic patterns and the best routes to and from his hotel. His people would scour the convention area, scour hotels, scour the streets, looking for their quarry; when they found someone they called in so that Wright could be located. By the time the candidate got to Wright's room, Wright would be waiting. He would chat, get to know the person, make him feel as if Wright knew him, then mention his interest in becoming majority leader and offer to help in any way in the candidate's own campaign. It was soft-sell.

But if his one-on-one style was soft-sell, nothing else about his effort was. Shortly after the convention, Wright formally announced his candidacy. Almost simultaneously, he compiled a list of candidates and colleagues who needed election help and who had a good chance of winning—he wasted neither time nor money on candidates who had little chance.

To raise money, he dispatched Craig Raupe and Marshall Lynam, another aide, to Texas. In Houston, they picked up Don Kennard, a state senator; the three chartered a plane and flew to see Arthur Temple, their first target, a multimillionaire who lived in Diboll, a small, isolated East Texas town.

Temple said he didn't think Jim could win but, what the hell, he'd give $500. Lynam said, "To tell you the truth, Arthur, we were hoping you'd help more than that." He pushed forward the list of candidates. "And we'd like you to raise money for these people, not Jim."

Temple shook his head no. Raising money for Wright was one thing, even if he couldn't win. But asking folks for money for somebody they didn't know, somebody who might even be some northern liberal? No.

Raupe assured him that not a single person on the list would embarrass him, even if some might be a bit liberal. Just then the phone rang. Temple answered it, said, "Sure. I can do that . . . sure . . . no problem . . . fine." Then, just before hanging up, he asked, "Say, you got any political money? Good . . . Give me a check for $500 . . . Never mind what it's for. You trust me, don't you? . . . Write it out to—" He grabbed the list and read off the name of a soon-to-be Maryland congresswoman, and later senator. "Barbara Mikulski. M-I-K-U-L-S-K-I . . . No, hell, don't send it to her. Send it to me." Then he turned to Raupe and laughed. "This might be more fun than I thought."

From Diboll, Wright's people split up. Kennard went to see Judge Woodrow Wilson Bean, a descendant of Judge Roy Bean, who refused to help—"I ain't giving to no damn liberals"—but looked over the list anyway and spotted the name of Utah congressman Allen Howe. "Is that the fellow who got arrested for picking up a whore?" Bean asked. Sheepishly Kennard said yes. "Well, that's my kind of man," Bean said, writing the check.

Raupe estimated that they raised $50,000, not insignificant in 1976, although Burton almost certainly raised more.

Wright personally handed the checks to candidates. He did not stop there, gave speeches for them in their districts, and even held Public Works Committee hearings for them there. His competitors also campaigned for colleagues, but Wright did more, worked harder, spent more time. For Allen Ertel in Pennsylvania Wright flew up early one Saturday morning in a driving, drenching rain, spent eighteen hours with him, and gave more than a speech an hour. For Barbara Mikulski in Maryland, he reassured businessmen that she was responsible and solid, not wild-eyed and untrustworthy. In the end, twenty-one of the candidates he campaigned for became freshmen members and he believed all voted for him as majority leader.

Wright worked with equal tenacity inside the House. He and his core supporters met every night to review the latest intelligence; knowing who was leaning one way or another, who had committed to one man or another, meant they could focus efforts—or not waste time—on them. Two, three, four different Wright supporters would talk to a member over a period of days, and then they would repeat precisely what the member had said and decipher his position. Wright learned how many ways people could say no. People would tell him, "Jim, you'd be a great majority leader! Absolutely terrific!" *But that didn't mean the member would vote for him.* "You're the best man in the race! I'll help you any way I can." *But that didn't mean the member would vote for him.* Udall, who had lost an earlier leadership race, advised Wright that unless someone explicitly promised his vote—"in front of witnesses," Udall snorted—then at best he was undecided.

As the number of those undecideds shrank, Wright's people began to draw fine distinctions, and went back to people committed to others. "What about if your man gets knocked out? Will you vote for Wright then, on the second ballot? What about on the third ballot?" They went further than that, suggesting to some members a way they could keep their commitment to another candidate and still support Wright. "When you said you'd support Burton, what *precise* words did you use? Just that you'd vote for him? Good, that's no problem. Keep your commitment. Vote for Burton on the first ballot. Go for Jim after that." There was an undercurrent to that argument: Burton was always doing dirty deals, he'd make that kind of argument himself; so hoist him on his own petard.

Burton pushed just as hard, with his own combination of charm, and his own vision of how to make a deal, how to forge a connection. He visited Missouri's just-elected Harold Volkmer, said he understood he had to support Bolling initially—Bolling came from Missouri—but if Bolling was eliminated, what about then? Burton said, "California and Missouri have a lot in common—" *What? Beach boys? Surfers? What?* "Did you know the bear on the California flag is a Missouri bear?"

Then Wright got a break. Nick Masters, a senior Budget Committee aide, was friendly with Bolling but was doing what he could for Wright. Bolling was arrogant enough to tell him, "Wright can't win. I know that disappoints you. I'll tell you why." Bolling then detailed three Wright weaknesses he and Burton were exploiting. First, oil and natural gas lobbyists—one in particular—were working hard for Wright, so he and Burton were saying Wright was in oil's pocket. They were also reminding liberals of Wright's vote against the 1964 Civil Rights Act. And they spread rumors that not even the Texas delegation supported him wholeheartedly, so why should anyone else?

Masters called Marshall Lynam immediately, and they had breakfast the next day in the cafeteria of the massive Rayburn House Office Building, a building which seems from a distance like an immense, impenetrable block of marble but is honeycombed with corridors. Masters repeated what Bolling had said. Quickly Wright acted on it. His supporters talked up his refusal to sign the "Southern Manifesto," a document signed by all but half a dozen southerners in Congress which denounced the 1954 Supreme Court decision outlawing segregation; his vote for the 1957 Civil Rights Act; his lead efforts for Hawaiian statehood—a racial issue at the time; and the fact that, virtually alone among southerners, he had opposed the expulsion from the House of Harlem congressman Adam Clayton Powell. Next, every Democrat in the Texas delegation, except for Jack Brooks and Bob Eckhardt, who had both committed to Burton before Wright got into the race, signed a strong letter endorsing Wright. Finally, the oil lobbyists were told to back off.

Suddenly things began to break Wright's way. Rostenkowski took him to Chicago to meet Mayor Richard Daley. Daley liked him, called Philadelphia mayor Frank Rizzo and New York mayor Abraham Beame—Wright had been one of only two southerners to support aid for New York City—and asked them to talk to their delegations for Wright. Then, *The Washington Post* linked McFall to "Koreagate," payoffs to members by Koreans. That destroyed his chances although he stayed in the race. And a major breakthrough came in the Kentucky delegation when Wright approached William Natcher, its dean. The two had arrived in Washington one year apart, were both southern, both gentlemanly in their manner. Indeed, Natcher was even more courtly; precise, he kept a daily diary and had not missed a single vote in his over twenty years in Congress. He looked with distaste on Burton's deal-making and Bolling's arrogance, and Wright asked for his support with all the formal courtesy of a southern gentleman asking for the hand of his daughter; Natcher then organized a caucus of the Kentuckians. The next day, all six Kentucky votes belonged to Wright.

Then came the final little things. All four candidates appeared on *Meet the Press*. A reporter asked Wright how he would vote on disciplining Florida congressman Bob Sikes, who had committed financial transgressions. "That's none of your business," Wright replied. It was members' business, and his answer helped him with House insiders. Next, Wright invited the forty-eight newly elected Democrats to a lunch in what turned out to be the only free time the freshmen had before the leadership election. So Wright invited the other candidates to address the luncheon, and gave them gracious introductions. (Wright later told political scientist Robert Peabody, "I didn't want to win by doing things that would make it harder to function as majority leader. I didn't want to sit in the chair. I wanted to perform the job.") Burton talked power politics, and told the freshmen that if they wanted power to organize as a class—that's what had made the class of '74 an immediate force in the House. Most of the class of '74 supported Burton, but Wright immediately recognized Carroll Hubbard—from Kentucky—president of that class. Hubbard said, "I'm for Jim Wright for majority leader, 100 percent."

Meanwhile, Raupe had prevailed upon Larry King, the onetime Wright aide, then–political columnist, and later playwright, to write a column favorable to Wright. The story ran the morning of the majority-leader election, and Raupe made sure that almost three hundred copies of the paper, folded so the story appeared prominently, were hand-delivered to every Democrat in the House.

That morning several papers had stories about the race. The theme in all was the same as *The Washington Post*'s: Would it be Bolling or Burton? Which of the two House giants would win? Might either of them outshine new Speaker O'Neill? As an afterthought, the story mentioned that also in the race were McFall and Wright.

The Caucus convened in the House chamber. Most members had not seen one another in weeks, and they grinned and shook hands, and talked about how good it would be to work with a Democratic President, Jimmy Carter, for a change. Except for each candidate's active supporters, members said little about the majority leader race; three of the four candidates would end up on the wrong side of a fight, and no one wanted to be identified with anyone but the winner. Burton was active, fitful, nervous. So was Bolling. Wright was calm. He had done what he could. He had done *everything* he could. But there was one last thing. A debate erupted over giving the Puerto Rican delegate a vote; Wright was strongly in favor and talked with the man in Spanish. The other candidates went along. Tip O'Neill talked to both Bolling and Burton, inviting whoever of them won to come by for a drink. He didn't talk to Wright.

Charlie Wilson of Texas nominated Wright, and in his speech called himself a "provincial," and recited how hard Wright had worked to get him to vote for aid to New York City. Wilson's speech carried a double message: it made the point that Wright alone of the candidates could get southerners and conservatives to support northern or liberal interests, and it reminded members that Bolling had recently and publicly called most of his colleagues "provincials."

Then came the time to stop talking and vote. The first tally: Burton, 106; Bolling, 81; Wright, 77; McFall, 31. McFall was out. No surprise there, but each candidate had overestimated his own support by ten or so votes. Frantic to compensate, in the few moments between ballots, the floor was electric. Every candidate's supporters tried to figure whom they had lost and get them back, as well as pick up McFall's backers. The next vote's results: Burton, 107; Bolling, 93. Wright had 95. Bolling was out. Only Wright and Burton remained. *And Burton had picked up only one vote,* from 106 to 107, on the second ballot.

Rumors swept the floor. Bolling and his supporters were convinced that Burton switched some of his own votes to Wright to eliminate Bolling, believing Wright would be easy to beat on the third ballot. Burton denied it, and Wright believed that many members had committed to Burton only for the first ballot, and felt free after that. Still, such manipulation seemed in character for Burton and the theory had impact. And O'Neill weighed in indirectly; formally he had no preference, but informally, he clearly did not want Burton as majority leader. The Speaker is supposed to be the boss; loyalty was not Burton's strong suit. Massachusetts's Eddie Boland, Tip's longtime roommate and close friend, had been supporting Bolling; he switched to Wright and made sure every Massachusetts Democrat knew it.

Still, few believed Wright could win. As members marked the final ballot, Rostenkowski saw Ohio's Thomas "Lud" Ashley, a friend and golfing buddy, write down Burton's name and asked, "What'd you do that for?"

"Wright doesn't have a chance," Ashley shrugged, "but if you want me to vote for him I will." He crossed out Burton's name and wrote down Wright's.

The votes were counted in boxes. Charlie Wilson, one of Wright's tally-checkers, was counting his box. Burton was five votes ahead and just one card left was uncounted. Then a voice announced that Wright had won the other box by five votes. It came down to the one uncounted card. Wilson, his hand feeling like a hundred-pound weight, turned it over. Burton had 147 votes. *Wright had 148.* Arkansas congressman Bill Alexander ran out of the room looking for Wright. "You did it!"

he shouted. "You won!" Wright looked at him for a moment in disbelief. And then he let out a yelp.

Members were surging around Wright now, a crowd of them, shaking his hand, whooping, clapping him on the back. Amid the tumult and joy, the new Speaker, Tip O'Neill, pushed forward, he, too, smiling, grinning. "Come on down to the office," he said. "Let's have a drink."

Wright's ambition was back on track.

Almost immediately after Wright's victory, speculation began that Burton would run against him in the future, either for leader or, if something happened to O'Neill, for Speaker. Wright intended to end that speculation, and Burton, for good.

He paid off debts, wooed enemies, and behaved in accordance with the admonition "what goes around, comes around." In that, Congress is unlike the Executive Branch. Policy makers in the Executive usually serve for only two or three years—rarely more than four—and cross paths on few issues; one person can double-cross another and disappear before the victim has an opportunity for vengeance. In Congress members remain for ten years, twenty years, thirty years, and cross paths on every issue; opportunities for revenge are plentiful.

Wright's first debt was to Rostenkowski, who wanted back on the path to power. Wright could not give him the whip job. O'Neill had already promised that to John Brademas, another Rhodes Scholar and the incumbent chief deputy whip who, in case the whip job had become an elective post, had already collected commitments from half the Caucus. So Rostenkowski replaced Brademas as chief deputy whip. (Rostenkowski paid his debts too. Carl Albert asked O'Neill, as a personal favor, to let his protégé Jim Jones, an Oklahoma congressman who had been White House chief of staff under Lyndon Johnson, stay on as one of four deputy whips. Rostenkowski said *no way*. Jones went.)

Wright preferred to build bridges to his enemies. Every week for over half a century the Texas delegation luncheon had gotten together to resolve differences behind closed doors. The resulting unity was one reason for Texas's power. At the first luncheon after Wright's election, when he entered his colleagues sprang to their feet and applauded, shouted, yelled. But there was also tension. Jack Brooks, the most senior member present (he had entered Congress one term before Wright), chaired the luncheon, and he had supported Burton. He and

Wright had long been rivals. Brooks was blunt, tough, and a fierce liberal despite his redneck style; once one of his opponent's supporters called him a communist and he threatened to shoot him if he did it again. He didn't. Brooks had been closer to Rayburn than Wright had, had been the golden boy of the delegation. Rivalry between the two existed, all right. Once a staffer said something nice about Brooks in front of Wright and Wright had exploded, had blasted Brooks, had not even wanted to hear anything good about him. But now Wright wooed him. When one colleague asked Wright, the new majority leader, how the delegation should handle a problem, Wright smiled, stood up, and said, "I'm flattered that you asked me, but I think I ought to defer to my senior colleague, Mr. Brooks."

Wright also tracked Burton's every movement and stayed one step ahead. In the 1978 election, Burton raised money for Democratic candidates, even some in primaries, figuring that helping a primary winner would give him a leg up on Wright. In one Massachusetts race he funneled over $100,000 to a heavily favored candidate who lost to Brian Donnelly. O'Neill had helped Donnelly's opponent, too. But Donnelly was street-smart and tough—he was drafted by the NFL out of Boston University—and grew up breathing bite-spit-scratch-kick Boston politics. (His uncle had been a Boston city councilman and would have become mayor when James Curley went to prison, but O'Neill, then Speaker of the Massachusetts House, had cooperated with Republicans to prevent it by passing a bill that in effect blocked him. When Donnelly arrived in Washington, O'Neill's first words to him were "I'm sorry about what I did to your uncle." Donnelly replied, "Yeah. And thanks for trying to keep me from getting here.")

When Burton tried to make peace with Donnelly, Donnelly said, "Let me tell you something I don't think you know. While you were trying to keep me from getting elected, Jim Wright was raising money for me." *You can count on Wright.* "I told him that however long it takes, he had my vote for Speaker. Do you think I'll screw him for majority leader?"

Later Burton said that at that moment he realized he could never beat Wright, and decided not to challenge him again. Bolling also faded away, contenting himself with the chairmanship of the Rules Committee, which gave him power, then retiring in 1982.

Wright only grew stronger. He earned respect for overseeing Jimmy Carter's complex energy initiatives. Members came to him with personal problems and he helped. If a member had trouble with his committee chairman—if, for example, the chairman kept him from getting on television by cutting off his questions at hearings whenever cameras were present—Wright helped. If a member needed something for his district, Wright helped. And if helping meant mending a fence, Wright was even more eager to help. When Jim Jones wanted to become chairman of the Budget Committee, Wright helped. O'Neill remained neutral and Rostenkowski opposed him; Jones won. Wright grew stronger.

And there was something else. For all Wright's relentless helpfulness, relentless courtesy, a courtesy which could border on obsequy—bending over to pick up a pencil someone else had dropped; pouring coffee for others—tension ran through him and others sensed it. That smile of his, that omnipresent, impossible-to-read killer smile, unnerved people. He seemed a dangerous man, a man not to be trifled with, a man to be handled gently. Several times Wright had almost gotten into fistfights on the floor. Once, when he was sixty, Fortney "Pete" Stark, a liberal California Democrat a generation younger, called him a "cocksucker." Colleagues stepped between them and Wright invited Stark outside; he was serious and later sent word that unless Stark apologized, the next time Wright saw him, wherever that was including on the floor, he would knock him down. Stark apologized. Another time a Republican accused him of unfairness while presiding and Wright came down off the rostrum, furious but grinning, saying, "I'm smiling because if I wasn't I'd punch you in the nose." GOP congressman Dick Cheney, White House chief of staff under Gerald Ford, said, "You get the sense you wouldn't want to cross him."

If Wright's campaign for Speaker began when he won the majority leader race in 1976, it intensified after O'Neill's announcement, before the 1984 election, that he would serve one more term, then retire. But Wright would not ascend automatically. The future of the Democratic Party was at stake.

Ronald Reagan had just humiliated Democratic presidential nominee Walter Mondale, winning forty-nine states. Most Democrats felt the entire party had been shaken, that a thorough reexamination was needed. They grumbled that Wright and O'Neill belonged to an old order that had passed away. Wright, after all, had endorsed Mondale right at his weakest moment, immediately after his New Hampshire primary loss to Gary Hart. He had also scorned Hart's call for "new ideas," implicitly rejecting the need for a reexamination of the party, arguing, "What's wrong with an idea just because it's old? What's good about it because it's new?"

The grumblings against Wright grew louder when, in a confrontation in O'Neill's office shortly after the election, younger colleagues asked how the leadership planned to respond. O'Neill and Wright insisted that nothing need change, and O'Neill bragged that despite Reagan's landslide, Democrats had lost only a dozen House seats and gained in the Senate and in governorships. To one member, "Wright and O'Neill sounded as if they were living in another world."

Talk surfaced about challenging O'Neill's reelection as Speaker. No one seriously believed anyone could defeat him—even opponents were willing to let him retire gracefully—but it would send a warning to O'Neill to open himself to change. It would send a stronger warning to Wright.

Conservative Charlie Stenholm, a Texan whose district included Wright's old hometown of Weatherford, was most serious about opposing O'Neill. In the early 1980s Stenholm had been the one whose hard grunt work forged the boll weevils, conservative and mostly southern Democrats, into a force which had helped Reagan dominate Congress; he played straight-up, look-you-in-the-eye politics and did not get along with Wright. Time after time in those early Reagan days Wright had sat down next to Stenholm on the floor and asked for his help. Time after time Stenholm would shake his head no and say, "Jim, I can't do it." Stenholm's continued and repeated resistance had penetrated deep into Wright: he had wondered in his diary if his inability to influence even Texas colleagues meant that he was a failure as a leader. But now Stenholm's ruminations made Wright angry.

Liberals, meanwhile, talked of returning the party to its roots. That would not challenge O'Neill, but liberals had never felt Wright was one of them. And the most dangerous force at work in the House was a group of twenty to twenty-five pragmatic, generally moderate, younger Democrats who had achieved some prominence. Led by soon-to-be Caucus chairman Richard Gephardt and Tony Coelho, head of the Democratic Congressional Campaign Committee (known as the "D-triple-C"), these members began meeting in September 1984, when it became obvious that Reagan would demolish Mondale. They wanted to plan new directions for the party and the House, and formed a powerful nucleus of inside operators. Often they gathered at either Coelho's or Gephardt's home for security reasons, to keep information from O'Neill and Wright. At one early meeting, some members suggested running Gephardt against O'Neill as a powerful message to Wright.

Gephardt and Coelho had no intention of contesting O'Neill's reelection. Neither believed in confronting the power structure. Gephardt started in politics just out of law school in the mid-sixties, but while his contemporaries were demonstrating in the streets he started at the ward level, rising from within. He had ambition enough, yes, but he was planning to devote his energies to a run for President and would not waste himself in a vain battle inside the House. He was too junior, and while there were enough junior members to cause problems for the leadership, there were not enough to take over. But they remained in a hanging mood.

First to the gallows went Armed Services Committee chairman Melvin Price, challenged by Les Aspin. Price was eighty and feeble, barely able to move about, incapable of running the committee or espousing a party position on crucial issues such as arms control. Aspin was articulate, good-looking, in his forties, a defense expert with a Ph.D. from the Massachusetts Institute of Technology, and an excellent television performer who had massaged the press for years. Aspin had once publicly said that O'Neill was "in a fog. . . . The Democratic Party needs some new leadership and needs it badly." O'Neill despised him. But when the Caucus voted on Price's chairmanship, despite O'Neill's intense efforts to help him, despite the strength of seniority and tradition, Price lost. Some members started saying that Price's ouster showed that the era of automatic promotions—like Wright's stepping up to Speaker—had ended. If Aspin could win with all O'Neill's forces opposing him, what did it mean for Wright?

A dozen different factions—the Stenholm crowd, the hard-core liberals, the Gephardt-Coelho group, and others—were maneuvering for position and debating the future of the party and the House. Sometimes factions within the House move past each other, almost as if wearing blinders; other times they collide; and, sometimes, they come together in a kind of spontaneous combustion. Waiting in the wings in case that spontaneous combustion occurred, waiting to take advantage of any opening, trying to create one, was Danny Rostenkowski.

Rostenkowski had become chairman of Ways and Means, the single most powerful committee in the Congress, after the 1980 election. Back then he had had a choice of that chairmanship or the whip job (Brademas had lost reelection). At the time, Rostenkowski debated the decision with his senior staff. He was a proud man, and many members doubted his intellectual ability to grasp the complexities of economic policy, something demanded of a good Ways and Means chairman. Whip would have been more natural to him: it involved the kind of floor activity, the feeling-touching-handshake-clap-on-the-back-what-can-I-do-for-you politics, that he enjoyed. But he wanted the challenge. *He wanted to show them.*

That wasn't the only reason he chose Ways and Means. As whip, a job sometimes referred to as the assistant majority leader, he would have had to jump over Wright, number two, to become Speaker. That smacked of disloyalty and offended both his sensibilities and those of the House. If he wanted to become Speaker, whip was the wrong choice. And he did want to become Speaker. From Ways and Means, from the outside, he could challenge Wright for it. His and Wright's shared ambition shattered their old alliance.

Rostenkowski wanted instability; O'Neill and Wright wanted stability—O'Neill for a peaceful last term, and Wright to secure the speakership. So O'Neill calmed the waters by making concessions: conservatives and moderates got more representation on key committees, the number of deputy whips doubled from four to eight, a new "Speaker's Cabinet" was organized to include six rank-and-file members who would regularly consult with O'Neill. Wright did not like all this consultation—it limited the power of the Speaker—but grudgingly conceded, "Consultation's all right, as long as they understand we're not taking a vote before we act." But hardest for Wright to swallow was the last concession O'Neill made: beginning in 1986, the Caucus would elect the whip. Speakers had always appointed the whip, and thus controlled him. An election made the whip responsible to the Caucus. Back ten years earlier, when O'Neill was in Wright's position, he had fought the same change. Now he was making the concession, to take effect after his retirement. Wright had no choice but to go along.

The changes only seemed to excite the press, which continued to write stories about the race to succeed O'Neill. It was still almost two years away, but regularly reporters wrote of a likely challenge to Wright from Rostenkowski, and possibly also from John Dingell, chairman of Energy and Commerce. Rostenkowski fostered the speculation. All the talk of a wide-open race increased the chance for one. And the most important legislation in the Congress was going to be tax reform. Taxes moved through Ways and Means. That would be Rostenkowski's show; his strategy would be to ride tax reform to the speakership. The people around Wright grew increasingly impatient—and nervous.

Every day Wright, his top floor aide John Mack, Marshall Lynam, who now administered Wright's office and handled district business, and a handful of other senior staff met for breakfast. They sat at a round table reserved for Wright in an otherwise closed section of the Members' Dining Room in the U.S. Capitol. On January 30, 1985, twenty-two months before the election of the next Speaker, amid eggs, pancakes, and sausage, annoyed by a recent quote from Rostenkowski, Mack said, "Look, it's time to end the bullshit." Mack suggested doing what they had already discussed: a blitzkrieg. Go all out for ten days, then announce backing by enough Democrats to scare any opponent away. But there was risk. If they fell short of an imposing vote count, they would encourage rather than discourage opposition.

Wright agreed. In ten days they would wrap up the race, or open it up.

While the coffee went cold they planned three crucial meetings for that afternoon. At each they would ask colleagues to commit themselves to Wright's election as Speaker. The first meeting would be the regularly scheduled Texas delegation luncheon. Immediately after that, Mack would put together a two o'clock meeting with members virtually certain to support Wright. But the bulk of their energies were spent choosing members to invite to a third meeting, members who were not Wright loyalists but who had influence in the House. If that group committed itself to helping him, the election would be all but over. The psychology of the meeting mattered and they had to select carefully. If the group got together and hemmed and hawed and did not give Wright a commitment, the result could be disastrous. Within hours it would be all over the House and any and every doubt any member had ever entertained about Wright would resurface. The race would be wide open. Mack set that last meeting for three-thirty.

Wright went to the phone on the wall nearest the table—phones are everywhere in the House, an indispensable element of the network of information which moves things—and called Jack Brooks, now the dean of the Texas delegation, to tell him of his plans for that day's luncheon. "It's about time," Brooks replied.

By the time of the delegation luncheon Wright had finished all his preparations. If it seemed quick, it was not. In a way, he had spent ten years plotting the next few hours. At lunch he told his Texas colleagues his plan and asked for their help. All enthusiastically signed on: they believed the speakership belonged to Texas. Rayburn's speakership had spanned seventeen years; before him Cactus Jack Garner had held it.

Wright laid out the criteria for an accurate count. Only one question and one answer mattered. The question was, "Will you make a commitment now to support Wright for Speaker next year?" The only answer that counted was "Yes." Wright told everyone to ask the question gently, without arm-twisting, without even implied arm-twisting. At this point he wanted volunteers, not draftees; if the count didn't look good he had to know. And just asking would apply pressure. They were asking members to pick sides. Are you for Jim Wright? If not, you're against him. *Do you want to be against the next Speaker?* Ask gently; the iron fist lay under the velvet glove.

The Texas delegation lunch began at twelve-thirty and lasted over an hour. At two came the second meeting. As expected, they all added their names to the Wright "Steering Committee" and, like the Texas delegation, left the meeting and began to approach members asking the one key question.

The three-thirty meeting was the one that counted. Twenty members had been invited. Each was his own person, and each had influence. By the time Wright sat down with them they knew what the meeting concerned. Those who did not want to make a commitment were uncomfortable. The election was still nearly two years away. They did not like being pushed so soon, but even hesitation would mark them as enemies. Wright explained his plans and then said, "I sure would like your help."

Two members said nothing, just sat there, silent and uneasy. Their silence was a declaration. But eighteen, one after another, swore fealty to his election effort.

Wright added the eighteen names to his Steering Committee list. In half a day that list had grown to fifty. Within the fifty lay a core group of the dozen closest supporters with whom he kept in constant contact, tracking every eddy and current in the House that could have any impact on his election. But Wright never identified the members of this core group; he wanted each member of the Steering Committee to believe he belonged.

They quickly divided House Democrats by state, region, committee, sex, religion, and, for the most junior members of the House, class. Jewish members would be counted individually by Martin Frost, a Jewish Wright protégé from Dallas, while Mickey Leland, a black from Houston, would help count blacks. As commitments came in, Wright kept track not only of the answer, but to whom the promise of support was made. He wanted to know who was working the hardest for him, who collected the most commitments, who was reliable. Commitments came in rapidly.

Wright had his base now and it was a firm one, an almost impregnable one. He then went on the attack against Rostenkowski directly by asking for commitments from Rostenkowski's own Illinois delegation and his sanctum sanctorum, his Ways and Means Committee. In Illinois, Wright got the immediate commitments of over half the delegation; in Ways and Means he got exactly half. Even Rostenkowski's closest personal allies, people like Marty Russo, a young Chicago Democrat on Ways and Means who had almost a father-son relationship with Rostenkowski, were asked to support Wright. "We wanted to make them say no," said Mack.

Meanwhile, Coelho came out early for Wright—Rostenkowski had helped Coelho early in his career and considered this a betrayal—and let it be known he was running for whip. Making the whip an elective office had given the young turks an attainable goal, one that did not mean revolution, and Coelho identified himself and his campaign with Wright.

On February 5, 1985, three days ahead of schedule, Wright called a news conference in the Rayburn Room, just off the House floor and a few feet from the Speaker's office, to announce that 184 Democrats, almost three-fourths of those in the House, had given him their word that they would vote for him for Speaker.

It was, now, all over but for the shouting.

The Steering Committee disbanded, and Wright hand-wrote a personal note to each person on it, telling each of them, "You went the second mile on my Steering Committee this past week. Your help was magnificent." A week later, as reports continued to trickle in, the count of commitments grew to 215. That was inevitable. The fight was over. Few members wanted to stay outside Wright's tent now. But while the organization went into suspended animation, Wright and Mack never let up. "You quit the day you're elected," Mack observed dryly.

Rostenkowski still hoped. Lingering in that large, powerful body, behind that fill-the-room-up-with-himself style, there in the back corridors of his mind, lay the knowledge that this was it, this was his last chance to be Speaker.

Wright still had weaknesses. But Rostenkowski had greater weaknesses. Members complained that Wright did poorly on television, but Rostenkowski was no better. And Rostenkowski, known for his gruffness, rudeness even with junior members, embarrassed himself when he tried to get chummy. Once he called Jim Moody—who was trying to get on his committee—"Bruce" and a Wright supporter said, "If you're going to run for Speaker, Danny, you're going to have to learn the members' names."

"Whaddaya mean?"

"That was Jim Moody. You thought he was Bruce Morrison, didn't you?"

"Ahhh, that's all right. I'll send him $1,000."

"You better. We already did."

Whenever Rostenkowski made specific noises about running, John Dingell stirred. Wright, early in his blitzkrieg, had talked to Dingell, and Dingell had assured him of support unless another candidate entered the race. Then Dingell himself would run. He and Wright both understood that the only candidate who might enter the race was Rostenkowski. Bad blood ran between him and Dingell. Rostenkowski came from Chicago, Dingell from Detroit, and both were Polish; if both ran they would split the same rust-belt and big-city constituency, helping Wright.

But Rostenkowski did not give up even then and continued to make noises about running. Meanwhile, Wright opposed tax reform, which was Rostenkowski's pride, increasing the bitterness between them.

Finally someone close to Rostenkowski told Mack, "For God's sake, John, this isn't good for anyone. If Wright just plays up to him a little,

Danny will stop all his talk about running. He'll think, 'I can't run against Jim. He's too good a buddy.' He knows he can't win anyway."

But Wright wasn't about to play up to Rostenkowski. Nor would Rostenkowski yield. It became a matter of pride with both of them, although both knew what the final outcome would be. The closer the speakership election came, the more powerful a presence Wright had. Ten straight floor leaders had stepped up to Speaker. Ten straight. Wright seemed certain to be number eleven. No one wanted to cross him now. And Wright kept helping colleagues, raising millions of dollars for them by attending their fund-raisers, by working hard at Democratic Congressional Campaign Committee events, and through his own political action committee.

Up until the House adjourned for the 1986 election, up even until the eve of the meeting when newly elected and reelected Democratic members of the House would caucus to organize themselves for the 100th Congress, up to the last, members most loyal to Rostenkowski, like Marty Russo and his housemate George Miller, refused to give Wright their commitments. Neither did Rostenkowski ever say he wasn't running. He could not bring himself to do it.

On December 8, 1986, in the first meeting of the House Democratic Caucus of the 100th Congress, Jack Brooks nominated Wright for Speaker. Salah Burton, who had been elected three years earlier to fill her husband Philip's seat when he died, seconded the nomination. There were no other nominations. Wright won by acclamation.

Yet even as Wright assumed the speakership, he remained a puzzle to Washington, an unknown quantity. He was complex and self-contained, sentimental and loyal yet also calculating; few colleagues understood him, understood that a passion, an almost desperate impatience, burned in him to transform his beliefs—and they ran deep—into policy. One Democratic colleague unenthusiastically remarked, "I think Wright's strength is at the level of getting new rugs put in members' offices. Maybe he can translate that into legislative victories."

Shortly before Wright took over, Morris Udall visited with him. Udall, greatly respected and immensely popular, might have run against Wright and possibly beaten him, but for Parkinson's disease. The two men had known each other for a quarter of a century, yet even Udall, who believed in a strong speakership, felt it necessary to remind him, "John McCormack was majority leader or Speaker for twenty-five years and there isn't a single policy, a single bill, a single set of actions, identified with him. I hope you don't make that mistake.''

How little even Wright's colleagues knew of him, or understood him, or expected of him. Wright had waited thirty-two long years for power. He intended to use it for more than putting rugs in members' offices.

CHAPTER 2

Jim Wright seemed unimposing and unremarkable physically. He was short of six feet, and by the time he became Speaker his young man's leanness had long since given way to a soft and slightly overlarge stomach; his eyebrows, whose bushy V-slant dominated his facial features and gave him a satanic cast, seemed relatively subdued now that his flaming red hair had gone gray. If he entered a room no magnetism drew people to him.

Yet he had a certain presence in a room. An inner certainty and tightness would make those with whom he was talking yield to him in a subtle way. And those standing near would become aware of him, and cast a glance his way, or tilt an ear. Gradually, in slow ripples, he would dominate more and more space, and more and more people would unconsciously give way to him. If he inhaled deeply to yawn, his soft stomach would suddenly disappear into a barrel chest banded by muscle. In conversation, he might suddenly focus intently; alert to every nuance of wording and facial expression and body language, his concentration would become tactile, like fingers crawling on the skin, disconcerting and intimidating.

His intelligence could be like that too. It devoured information but concentrated less on the vertical than the horizontal; he did not so much penetrate and analyze a single truth, in the way an academic might, as assimilate and weave together seemingly unconnected bits of information. His was a listening, watching, waiting intelligence. Before he became Speaker, colleagues and reporters often confused this aspect of his style with caution. But Wright was not cautious. On the contrary, often he would take risks, dangerous risks, based on a private passion. He calculated and manipulated, as do all those whose goals can be achieved only through the compliance of others, but the calculating and manipulating occurred when he executed his will, rather than as an integral part of his decision-making process.

On the surface, all that showed was an unreadable smile. But there were layers to Wright below the surface, and folds within layers. Beneath all these layers strong passions burned—a loner's desire to be liked, an individualist's pride, a missionary's desire to do good, and an achiever's ambition to leave a mark. These passions intertwined and collided and wound about one another, drove him forward and tugged him sideways and pulled him back. Together they formed a pattern as complex and twisted as an Escher drawing. The twists and collisions within him created a dynamism which could explode without warning. His voice, rich, soothing, not deep but timbrous and resonant, was an orator's voice, and it hinted of something deep and dangerous.

In the small cemetery of Weatherford, Texas, Jim Wright Senior and his wife, Marie, are buried. A rutted dirt road divides the cemetery into an older part, where scraggly pines burned out by the dry heat give a sort of shade, and a newer section which seems less a graveyard than part of the bleached hills that roll south and west for hundreds of miles. The cemetery itself seems part of the unmanicured, hard land thereabouts, a land which bred generations of populists who feared God, loved their country, and hated the banks, a land in which Wright had grown up but which now, all over the nation, was disappearing.

A few yards from his parents' graves, Wright sat in a car and talked softly about them for a moment: "They were very great people. My father had a wonderful flair. I'll never match it . . . I was very fortunate to have had people who believed in me and taught me to believe in myself, told me I could do anything I wanted to, if I was willing to pay the price . . . Mother was a patrician and Dad was an egalitarian. I suppose I inclined toward Dad's view, though I always cherished Mother's belief in us and her insistence we were something special."

He fell silent for a moment, then added, "I always thought I had to work twice as hard as anyone else to get anywhere."

James Claude Wright, Sr., Wright's father, was a large man. Big-shouldered, thickly muscled, and six feet tall early in the century when six feet *was* tall, taller than his son would ever grow to, he moved with the grace of an athlete and had beautiful hands, not delicate but beautifully formed, powerful and symmetrical. He had been a professional boxer, but that career ended when, up in Montana, he watched a man fight who was a contender for a title Wright wanted. Afterwards he thought, laughing, *What the hell do I want to get in the ring with him for?* He was good-natured like that, full of charm.

His wife, Marie Lyster, came from a moneyed and cultured family— her father had some aristocratic blood and was a graduate of Heidelberg University—which disapproved strongly of her marriage. Years later, a relative who was asked "Whatever happened to Marie?" replied with disgust, "She married someone she met at a carnival."

There was more to Wright the elder than that. His charm had a recklessness about it which, along with courage, could take him down dangerous paths. He used the second paycheck of his life to buy a newspaper advertisement attacking the Ku Klux Klan—this in a small Texas town early in the century. Equally dangerous, perhaps more so, was the fact that he was a dreamer.

A salesman, he sold what he called "intangibles," oil leases, or fundraising gimmicks for charities (Easter seal–type gimmicks, buy them and help poor unfortunates), memberships in the Chamber of Commerce, and a dozen other things. He sold ideas. He revered ideas although his formal education ended in the fourth grade. "Any fool," he would say, "can sell a shoe, but ideas—it takes an artist to sell an idea. A man who will steal someone else's idea will steal anything."

A hero in World War I, he rose to captain despite his lack of formal schooling; he loved learning and read voraciously in literature, poetry, and history—his son later called him the best-educated person he had ever known—and he seemed to know everything and be able to tell a story about anything.

His selling put him often on the road, and when he wasn't the family was. They moved constantly, usually after one year in a place, from and to small towns in Texas, Oklahoma, Louisiana, and to big-city Dallas. By the time young Jim got to high school, he had attended nine different schools in nine different towns, small towns, cliquish towns. It was lonely for a young boy trying to find friends, more lonely than the loneliness of the land itself, for his was an exclusive kind of loneliness, that of the new boy excluded.

His rootlessness and outsider status formed him. It made him burn to belong. Other boys had friends; he had to work to make them. He did work to make them. He smiled and learned quickly to give people what they liked, which was someone like themselves, and he began to hide himself a little. Instead of building a wall between himself and others, he constructed a sort-of see-through mirror that allowed him to look out at the world while others, looking in, saw their own reflection.

School came easy to him and he skipped grades. Younger than his classmates, he lied about his age. One year his mother wanted to give him a birthday party and he refused to allow it out of fear the truth would come out. Another time, he told new schoolmates he had just arrived from Fort Worth when he really had come from Dallas. Fort Worth was a "cow town"; it was "where the West began," and was relatively acceptable in a small town. Big-city Dallas was, as Will Rogers said, "where the East petered out"; people from there were foreigners, big-city people. His first ambition was to be a football coach because the coach was, he later wrote, "the most admired man in the community . . . I did whatever Dad wanted me to do, whatever Coach wanted me to do. I wasn't a rebellious person. I wanted to be part of the team."

His father taught him to box; he took to it eagerly, to please his father and because it helped win acceptance and respect. He was good. Boxing let his passion rise to the surface, let all that he contained come out. At thirteen he lied about his age again—saying he was older—to be allowed to enter a tournament; he won it. Yet in one boxing match with a boy who was a friend, in complete control of the fight, he did not move in for the kill; instead, he let up so the boy would not look too bad. Later his father angrily berated him. His mother came to his defense and said, "Jim would rather have a friend than a victim."

If almost desperate to be liked, Jim did not, however, lack confidence. His parents gave him adulation. When he was ten or eleven, his mother started bringing him into the living room when adults visited, and he talked with them and charmed them and had things to say. "His mother thought he was the only perfect man," said his first wife, "Mab," Mary Ethelyn Lemmons, who died a few months before he rose to Speaker.

The parents cared about what the world thought—the children were constantly reminded that something they did "reflects on the entire family," said Jim's sister Mary Wright Connell, the middle of three children. Their reputation, their good name, was the most important thing they had, and so was it for others. Carrying gossip was foul, evil. If one of the children repeated something they had heard, mother or father would say, "How do you know? Are you sure? Did you see it happen? You can't be besmirching people's names."

Yet, paradoxically, there was no pressure to conform per se, no small-town smallness. Honor and being one's own man mattered more than the world's assessment; they were important enough to separate oneself from the group. All the children learned Kipling's poem "If," which included not only the famous line about keeping one's head while others are losing theirs, but more: "If you can trust yourself when all men doubt you . . . If you can dream—and not make dreams your master;/ If you can think—and not make thoughts your aim . . . If you can make one heap of all your winnings/ And risk it on one turn of pitch-and-toss . . . If all men count with you, but none too much . . . If you can fill the unforgiving minute/ With sixty seconds' worth of distance run . . ."

It became Jim's favorite poem; it penetrated him, voiced something he could cling to, and reinforced all that his father taught. Together those teachings gave him a ferocious, potentially devouring kind of pride, a sense of specialness. The paradox of being one's own man while worrying about the world's opinion was resolved in achievement. Achievement mattered, and the house was filled with great expectations for all the children. Wright senior, the nomad who moved from town to town carrying his own roots with him, the man who had been dismissed by his wife's relative as "someone she met at a carnival," the man who sold ideas, taught his children to achieve, to make a mark, to imprint themselves on the world, to match pride with ambition.

The message took. Betty Lee Wright, the youngest child, became a college professor, wrote several textbooks, and designed part of the curriculum taught in Texas high schools. "She didn't do that because of any love of scholarship," said Mary Connell. "She did it because a doctorate was as far as you could go. It was competitiveness."

Mary Connell had other dreams. She started writing poetry as a child and into her fifties still believed her life would be a failure if she did not win the Nobel Prize for Literature. She gave up much of her life to her writing, giving up place and roots, herself moving from town to town, rarely staying anywhere for more than a year and never staying more than two years. She published several books of poetry, and Graham Greene wrote a preface to one, hailing her as a new American discovery. But the achievement and recognition she sought eluded her. With a touch of bitterness she once wrote,

> *The child whose mother lets him yearn,*
> *for excellence, celebrity,*
> *or love, is done a dirty turn.*
> *Why cannot each: contented be*
> *with mannered love? accept advice?*
> *and hope next summer turns out nice?*

Young Jim had passion for achievement too. Seeking acceptance, burning to belong, he channeled his energy and contempt for limits into achievement rather than rebellion.

After all, his mother said he was the only perfect man. Though he had skipped grades, he was easily an academic star. Though he was two full years younger than his schoolmates, and smaller, he could whip them in a fight. He made his own rules. At thirteen he had claimed to be fourteen to enter that boxing tournament, and had won it, beating sixteen-year-olds. In the Army Air Corps, impatient to get into action, he picked up a phone, impersonated a senior officer, and ordered clerks to process his papers. He was the only perfect man. Rules didn't apply to him. Besides, they were innocent, harmless violations. Impatient, he respected no limits. "I always wanted to do things *before*," he said. "I wanted to be the youngest to do this, the first to do that."

There was a taut balance in him. Passionate, impatient, burningly impatient, capable, proud, and enormously self-confident, he was also insecure, desperate for approval, yearning to belong. If the balance shifted for a moment, he might career in one direction before recovering his footing.

Politics.

The populism that grew out of the hot, baked land called for economic change. It had done so for decades, going back to the Greenback movement after the Civil War, growing into the Populist Party in the 1880s, whose ideas were incorporated by the William Jennings Bryan faction of the Democratic Party and ultimately became law under Teddy Roosevelt and Woodrow Wilson. This same populism also took on an angry moralistic fervor epitomized in Prohibition.

Jim Wright's family believed in economic populism, but not just a hatred of the banks, of big business. The Wright family's politics were tempered by tolerance. Mary Connell recalled, "The only prejudice we had was against Baptists who believed you would go to hell if you drank, danced, smoked, or played cards."

Indeed, Wright senior loathed all prejudice—economic, racial, or social. His finances went up and down, and when he was one of the richest men in town, he demanded that the schools allow children to wear jeans so poor kids would not be embarrassed by their clothes. He despised signs of wealth, despised what so many in his profession of sales revered. In Oklahoma, children in public school had to buy their textbooks, and he railed against the injustice of that. "If a child can't get educated," he asked, "how can he ever improve himself?"

Religion mattered, but the children were taught a loving, forgiving God. Jim followed his father to different churches every week. Once, when Jim was making fun of Holy Rollers who claimed to hear God, his father told him to turn on the radio, then turn it off. "Do you hear the music now, Jim?" he asked. "Do you think they stopped playing or you just can't hear it?" Tolerance and equality were burned into young Jim.

The Depression burned itself into him too. The family moved in with his paternal grandparents, then sold, one by one, their belongings, including their car. His father, the traveling salesman, had to travel by train and bus. Meanwhile, home, day after day, Wright would look out the window and see his grandfather trudge up the walk with stooped shoulders after not finding work. Years later Wright recalled the scene: "There is hardly a greater shock to the nervous system than a feeling of uselessness."

Politics became the air he breathed. Politics meant jobs, or the lack of jobs, pride, or the lack of pride. Everywhere Wright looked was pain. He came to "love"—his word—Roosevelt in an almost concrete way. It all mixed together and formed a set of populist political values that differed from the values of the northern, urban left.

Wright grew up without the kind of class consciousness and critical societal analysis of an intellectual. Instead, he believed in a creative, vital, dynamic kind of equality which built things, made them flower. He had that booster spirit, that booster, builder, can-do, positive-thinker spirit which historian Daniel Boorstin identified as a basic trait of America. He accepted rather than questioned the rhetorical assumptions about America, and later declared that the goal of the American revolution, rather than destroying an aristocracy and replacing it "with a dictatorship of the proletariat, . . . has been to expand the aristocracy through universal opportunity and absolute equality before the law."

By the time he was a teenager, his need to belong and his pride were already mature passions. His political passion—ideological values—was defining itself. The passion for achievement, raw ambition, had developed too. And now he was finding his focus in politics, in what he later called his "messianic impulse."

At fifteen, he was addressing rallies for gubernatorial candidate Ernest Thompson, who had served in World War I with his father. A boy, he stood before, controlled, hundreds of men and women, filling them up with the need for change. He felt power over those crowds, felt his words wash over the crowd and return to him in waves of laughter, or anger, or warmth—whatever effect he sought. The crowds loved him, this precocious boy, loved him. He stirred them up. (He was an orator, perhaps the last of his kind. In the coming years of television, how important would it be for a politician to move a crowd?) The power and the crowd's embrace intoxicated him. "It's heady wine," he later said. "You never get used to it."

Politics. Where else could one make the kind of mark one could there? Where else could one feel the approval of thousands and thousands? *Politics.* His high school yearbook predicted he would be in Congress in 1955. When Jim and his soon-to-be wife Mab started dating before the war—they married in 1942, when he was on leave—he told her he planned to run for Congress in ten years.

Wright's sister Mary dreamed of the Nobel Prize. Wright wanted to be President.

There is an old photograph of Jim Wright, Jr., as a youth, leaning against a car with a girl on his arm. His eyes look into the distance, not at her, and he has a lean, brooding, sensual quality. He is smiling, but the smile communicates isolation and tension, not warmth. He could be James Dean in that photograph, twenty years before James Dean. By then he was almost fully formed and his blood ran fast. But there were still lessons he would learn that would thicken the mask he had begun to wear to please people, add further layers of complexity, and begin the process of compromise.

He volunteered for the army the day after Pearl Harbor, dropping out of the University of Texas (he never finished college), and served in the Pacific as a navigator on a bomber. Immediately after the war his political career began. He first became embroiled defending free speech at the University of Texas, and helping organize a group of young liberals whose agenda included a world police force, medical care for the elderly, anti-lynching laws, and an end to the poll tax. In 1946 he ran for the state legislature from Parker County and, at twenty-three, won his first election.

The youngest, and perhaps the most driven and the most liberal, member of the Texas House, he felt as invulnerable and certain as youth itself, led a fight to tax big oil companies to pay for roads and schools, and tried to help blacks. Then came his 1948 reelection campaign. Two opponents faced him. One was Eugene Miller, a former state legislator, a gambler who reportedly had run big-money card games in Austin. Miller hit Wright with gut punches and kicks to the groin; it was a streetfight with no rules. Miller called him a communist dupe and said Wright wanted "every uppity nigra with a high school diploma" to go to the University of Texas Law School. Then, three weeks before the election, someone shot Miller. Wright went to the hospital to give blood for him.

In the hospital Miller told people that Wright had nothing to do with the shooting—directly. But he said "commies" and maybe Wright's "henchmen" had shot him. Some people believed he expected to live and was trying to exploit the shooting politically. Others believed he was accusing Wright of murder. Rumors swept Parker County. *Was Wright a murderer?*

At first Wright did nothing, believing no one could credit such a charge. Then a farmer said he had heard Wright shooting a pistol in a field. *Maybe he was practicing.* Wright said he had been banging nails, putting up campaign signs. At a campaign rally his remaining opponent, Floyd Bradshaw, said he had received a bomb threat if he didn't withdraw. *Were the communists behind Wright?*

Wright grew suddenly desperate. He wanted to win, wanted desperately to win—enough to compromise principle. It was the first such compromise of his political life. He took out a last-minute newspaper ad saying he supported the "Southern way of life," saying he "despised communism . . . I believe in the Southern tradition of segregation and have strongly resisted any and all efforts to destroy it."

He lost by thirty-eight votes. The loss stunned him, and, at least for the moment, embittered him. The taint of murder quickly died away: though the crime was never solved, Texas Rangers found nothing implicating Wright, and did find evidence that Miller had been killed for welshing on big-money gambling debts. But Wright thought bitterly, *What did he need politics for? Who needed all this pain, for people who would reject him? The hell with them. He would get rich instead.*

By then one of his father's ideas had struck gold. Before the war, he had started a company called the National Trades Day Association, which helped small-town merchants run promotions with games and bingo and boxing matches and raffles and sales. It boomed with the rest of the post-war economy. At its peak, more towns had had a "trade day" promotion than there were counties in the United States. The Wrights were rich.

In the late 1940s the son bought 25 percent of the family business from the father and they continued to build it; money poured in, and net profits reached $1,000 a day. Friends tried to interest him in running for mayor of Weatherford. He declined, and to punctuate the decision took a train to Chicago on business; the filing deadline for the mayor's race would pass while he was away. But if getting on the train punctuated his decision, it also gave him time to do nothing but think and watch the country, watch the country, watch the country. Mile after mile on his way north he thought about the sales meeting he was going to. *Was that what he wanted to do with his life? Just make money?*

At one stop he got off and telephoned a friend. "Can you file my papers?" he asked. "I'm going to run."

At twenty-six he became the youngest mayor in Texas. But the memory of his earlier loss remained with him. He hid himself, now more than ever. It was nothing new. He had been that way in school as a boy. After the war, before going into business with his father, he had worked as a salesman and before each appointment had told himself, *I'm going to like this person, I wish him well, and he's going to like me.* But he had always told people exactly what he thought about politics. *Look where that had gotten him.* Now a veil descended over him fully, a smiling cordial front that reflected his control over himself; now the see-through mirror fell firmly into place; the mask locked into place. He kept himself private even from himself. With his wife, Mab, even, the veil rarely lifted.

Meanwhile, as mayor, he did things. Damn the law. He was the law. When the gas utility threatened to cut off service to poorer neighborhoods, he told them, fine, but they wouldn't be able to service the rest of the city either. When one milk distributor advertised misleadingly, he told the distributor he could not sell in Weatherford unless the ads were corrected. He had no legal authority for these things, but he had power and he did them. His proudest moment came when he bought a reservoir from the Texas & Pacific railroad and assured a water supply to the city. He was a doer who could make something grow, a builder. He became the youngest president ever of the Association of Texas Mayors.

Politics was his life now. There had been a moment after that one reelection defeat when he had considered both the ministry and a lay job with the Presbyterians. Mab had wanted him to preach. He was a lay preacher at a small church in Granbury, twenty miles from Fort Worth. She later recalled, "He did that for me, not for him. I wanted to marry a minister. But after a while he told me, 'Don't you think a politician is like a minister?' "

Business gave him even less satisfaction than the ministry. He was prospering—and secretive. "He never let me know how much money he was making," Mab recalled. "That was part of his manipulation, having his finger on everything." But she was convinced he was making over $70,000 a year. He wasn't thirty yet, in the early 1950s. Congressmen then made $12,500.

At thirty-one, in 1954, he ran for the United States House of Representatives against Congressman Wingate Lucas, a conservative supported by Fort Worth newspaper owner Amon Carter. It was a dirty campaign. Mail-fraud charges were filed against the Wrights' promotion company with the Post Office (and dropped after the campaign). Wright fought back. Years earlier, when Wright was just returned from the war and full of himself and his own future, he had introduced himself to Carter at a picnic. Carter had snubbed him. Wright never forgot. The day before the election Wright ran a full-page ad in Carter's paper: "You have at last met a man, Mr. Carter, who is not afraid of you, who will not bow his knee to you, and come running like a simpering pup at your beck and call."

There was a self-righteousness in that language, and ego, but it also struck a populist chord. Jim Wright romped to victory. He was thirty-one when he was elected, right on track with the prediction in his high school yearbook—in Congress in 1955—on track to power.

He had been the youngest legislator, the youngest mayor, one of the youngest congressmen. The House at first seemed only another stepping-stone. When mail came from Texas but from outside the district, instead of referring it to the proper member his office took care of it. And he let people throughout the state know of his interest in something higher. But he also followed Speaker Sam Rayburn's advice, "Go along to get along." Though from the first Wright sought the largest stage and wanted a seat on the Foreign Affairs Committee, he took a Public Works Committee assignment at Rayburn's "suggestion." There was little grand about Public Works, so he made it grand. The water projects, highways, and later synthetic fuels which the press castigated as pork he boasted about as investments in America.

At the same time, some of the verities of politics were driven home to him. Desegregation loosed passions that could destroy a young southern Congressman as easily as snapping one's fingers. He showed courage in refusing to sign the "Southern Manifesto," which denounced the 1954 Supreme Court decision on integration; fewer than ten southern colleagues refused. But during his first term he also said the Supreme Court had "erred in judgment . . . I feel that segregation could be ideally maintained without discrimination, that it is possible for facilities to be equal while being separate."

Once during that first term he faced a large audience in a small-town high school gym. He wanted to talk about schools and roads and building the nation when a woman hissed, "What are you gonna do about them niggers?" He ignored the question but she interrupted again. *"What are you gonna do about them niggers?"*

"I was born out here myself," he told her. "I know how you feel."

He sounded sympathetic but then gently, gently, began to bring the crowd around. Tolerance was a good Christian thing, wasn't it? And the Supreme Court had decided and the law was the law and they had elected him to uphold the law. It was as far as a liberal could go in the South then. The mask bit deeper into his flesh. Afterwards, driving home with Craig Raupe, he sighed, "I'm awful tired of people."

On policy matters, he began to make a mark despite his junior status. He hated debt—proud, like his father he wanted to owe no one, and called interest "enslavement." The Depression had made him fear debt too. He had taken out a mortgage for his first house, but paid it off in four years. This visceral dislike of debt translated itself into policy when it came to financing the interstate highway system. A commission had recommended issuing bonds to pay for it. He persuaded Eisenhower to support instead a pay-as-you-go gasoline tax, which became law. He also offered a plan, which attracted press attention but nothing else, to pay off the national debt by 1 percent a year. It was borrowing he opposed, not spending. According to a 1979 study, Fort Worth had the highest per capita federal spending of any district in the nation.

Inside the House he won respect for his knowledge, reliability, and work habits. Outside he was attracting some attention and the larger, national stage beckoned to him. Then Lyndon Johnson became Vice President, vacating a Senate seat. Wright said, "Johnson is the only man of whom I ever had the sense 'This fellow can outsmart me.' "

But this was Wright's chance, this was the larger stage, this was what he had been maneuvering for. He was the first to announce for the seat in a 1961 special election. More than seventy others followed suit.

He poured himself into the race. In the last few days it was close, so close. His campaign needed more money desperately, and borrowed it. The race was open to members of both parties: the top two finishers would face each other in a runoff. Almost all the candidates were Democrats. Wright came in third. In the runoff, Republican John Tower won.

It was a shattering experience. He wasn't the youngest, the fastest-moving, the meteor anymore. He had *lost,* even though, since the Senate race had been an off-year special election, the House seat remained his.

Most politicians would have let creditors wait until they held fund-raisers to pay off the campaign debt. But Wright hated owing favors more than debt. Once he ended a relationship with a supporter who pressed him too hard, snapping, "I wear no man's collar!" So he used almost $70,000 of his personal funds to pay what the campaign owed. That forced him to sell a ranch he loved for part of the money, and take out personal bank loans for the rest. The ranch was his oasis; he could go there and touch the soil and watch things grow. A quarter century later he said, "Not a day goes by that I don't regret selling that." With the ranch gone, owing the banks, he felt locked in a jail. The House seat meant little to him.

Wright went to see Johnson and asked for an ambassadorship, some place where he could act as his own agent and influence policy. Johnson refused, saying, "You think you're frustrated? Who else in Washington do you think is frustrated?"

Wright turned even more inward. The roots of the mask went deeper and deeper into the skin. "He is a controlled man," Mab said. "You do not know what he is thinking. I learned that over a period of years, not immediately. I never knew if something upset him because his reaction was always to laugh."

He did not want to leave public life. He voted against the 1964 Civil Rights Act. A yes vote could have been political death in the South. *The first principle of statesmanship is to get elected,* went the saying. But he voted for every other piece of civil rights legislation.

Still more frustration came, more rejection. The Senate seat came up again in 1966. This time the money had to come first. He thought he could raise it without any big-money contributors and made a televised statewide appeal for ten-dollar donations. But it yielded little. He did not run. Reality finally penetrated. His naivete about money finally vanished.

If he had been quiet about politics with Mab before, now he grew silent. To find out what was happening, she had to invite Raupe or a few congressmen to dinner; they would tell her the latest political gossip. Only ambition saved him from bitterness. He began to look for influence in other directions, doing more speaking trips to colleagues' districts, and at every opportunity involving himself nationally. When Hubert Humphrey ran for President, Wright traveled the country speaking for him. After the 1968 election, troubled by the disarray in the Democratic Party, he wrote a book-length report on rebuilding it through aggressive outreach in colleges and developing a base of small donors. (Republicans later did both, leaving the Democrats to spend much of the 1980s trying to catch up.) But his views arrived unsolicited at the Democratic National Committee; party professionals ignored them.

He was in his forties. His intensity still burned, but to what end? His hobbies were all lonely, personal pursuits. Some required absolute concentration: flying, boxing—he trained into his fifties and once planned an exhibition match with then–heavyweight champion Joe Frazier (Speaker John McCormack vetoed it, calling it undignified). Other hobbies—writing, four books and his own speeches, painting, gardening—produced something. He explained, "I am alert to the inexorable movement of the hand on the clock, the pages on the calendar . . . What do you have after two hours of golf? If I spend two hours in the garden I have something to show for it."

Mab and he drifted apart. "Jim said to me, 'Why can't you be like Lady Bird is to Lyndon?'" she recalled. "Well, she subjugated her life to Lyndon. I didn't want to do that." Jim no longer seemed quite so marvelous to her, and she resented that he seemed to be performing when he came home just as he did inside the House. "He has to be all things to all people," she said. "Even to me he wanted to appear as I thought he was. I had Jim on a pedestal but when it got to the point where I couldn't see him that way, that's where I think our marriage fell apart."

A lowly rung on the leadership ladder opened. Jack Brooks was giving up his job as one of four deputy whips, men who counted votes for the leadership and persuaded members to vote for leadership positions. Did Wright want it? The leadership would prefer a Texan, and Brooks would help him get it. Brooks said, "I wasn't willing to take the time away from my family. Jim was."

In 1969 Mab asked him to move out and they began a two-year legal separation. It was a far, far cry from the way his career had started out. Not even his wife respected him as she once had. *And he had wanted to be President of the United States?* What a mockery of his dreams.

A secretary named Betty Hay had started working for him in 1965. They were the same age and he started seeing her. Betty had had a hard life. Growing up poor in St. Louis, her mother abandoned by her father when she was an infant, as a teen-ager she had danced in shows while her mother looked for work. She was tough, independent, would not take guff from anybody, had herself been a loner, had a brief failed marriage of her own, even sadly considered herself a failure. They were drawn to each other. At first, Wright did not want to marry again. Mab and his children still had to be supported. They never fought over that. "He's a kind man," Mab said. He was still in debt. Every move he had made to escape it, every chance, every roll of the dice, had turned out badly and buried him further.

For all his inwardness, he still wanted someone or something to confide in, and he began keeping a journal. In it he wrote, "My finances are in shambles. With what unbelievable folly have I so long ignored them and let them drift? In my 30th year I was the richest young man in town. In my 50th, well I'm driving a 10 year old car, owe so god-awful much money I'll need luck to pay it off. But I will, somehow I will."

How could he give anything to a new wife? But, after his divorce became final in 1972, he and Betty did marry. Speaking of that time years later, Betty told *The Washington Post,* "Men feel like a failure, too."

It was a telling remark. At their age, they would not have children. He had long since abandoned the family business, which at one time had seemed capable of growing into a multimillion-dollar corporation, but had deteriorated as his father began to drink heavily. All he and Betty would have was his career, his success, his fulfillment. But what was his career?

On his fiftieth birthday he reviewed his life in his journal. For the first time he admitted, formally, that he never would be President. He tried to reconcile himself to that failure, assuring himself he had accomplished much and claiming to feel relief at giving up his dream. But his words rang with hollow and wintry tones. Soon, inevitably, he would become chairman of Public Works, but that accomplishment seemed to mock him, mock everything he had once dreamed of being and doing.

That career was . . . not what he had dreamed of. And he began to wonder about his children and his new wife. He loved Betty. He often carried an album of pictures of her under his arm and bored people with them. Suppose he dropped dead—what could he leave anyone? Nothing. Not a goddamn thing. Rayburn had died penniless but also childless and wifeless. *Men feel like a failure, too.* Didn't Betty deserve a little comfort? Didn't his kids deserve something? Didn't he at least deserve to get this terrible weight off his back? His decision to pay off, from personal funds, that $70,000 Senate campaign debt had created that weight. His net worth, $129,000 when he entered Congress at age thirty-one, fell to $68,000 at age fifty-three. Inflation shrank that figure by half again. It could turn a man bitter. And if not exactly bitter, didn't his family, well, deserve more? His wife had had nothing all her life. He wanted to give her something. And didn't he deserve something?

There was a businessman named George Mallick whom Wright had become closer to since his remarriage. His first wife, Mab, had been popular. Many people in Fort Worth were cool to Betty. Only the Mallicks welcomed her warmly, took to her, and she to them. The two couples became close. And Mallick began to help Wright improve his financial situation.

Then came the majority leader race. Suddenly all that he had abandoned hope of achieving seemed once again possible.

*   *   *

Betty had started working for the Public Works Committee seven years before their marriage, which protected her from antinepotism rules. After their marriage, she declined all promotions and merit raises. But when Wright became majority leader, the press attacked her for working for Congress. It angered him, but she quit her $24,000-a-year job although they needed the money.

Enter J.D. Williams. "J.D.," as everyone called him, became very interested in Wright's welfare. J.D. was a lobbyist who had worked for Democratic senator Bob Kerr of Oklahoma. Kerr had not had a good reputation. Of J.D., even California Democratic congressman Tony Coelho, who was perhaps the premier fund-raiser since Lyndon Johnson, said, "I don't have a very high opinion of his crowd."

Whoever had power, Williams wanted access to. "J.D.'s done so many favors," said one Wright aide, "when he comes to you with a problem, he knows exactly what he wants you to do. If you can do it, you do it."

Williams pointed out to Wright a loophole in the campaign financing law that allowed him to transfer campaign funds to personal use. (The law was later changed.) Wright listened and decided to, in his own mind, pay himself back for the personal funds he had used earlier to pay his Senate campaign debt. He wasn't naive about money anymore. He invited lobbyists to a fund-raiser, told them the purpose, and raised $98,000. Half went to pay taxes, half to pay off personal debts. For the first time in over a decade, he could hold his head above water without having to stand on tiptoes. He could breathe. Shortly before the fund-raiser, perhaps with it in mind, he told a reporter with the *Dallas Times-Herald,* "When I started out as a young man I was a real purist. I took no contribution of more than $100 and nothing from people affected by legislation. But, hell, after a while you see everyone is affected one way or another. You can't raise any money like that. My position now is if the law says it's all right, I'll take the money. I've complied with the law."

It was a far different standard from that with which he had entered politics. Privately, to a few select colleagues, Wright complained about new restrictions on members' outside earnings. And he was ambivalent about and frustrated in Congress. The title "majority leader" sounded good, but he had less real power than he would have had as chairman of Public Works. In October 1979, he wrote in his journal, "I've seldom felt quite so despondent about this job. I seriously—truly more seriously than ever before—contemplate retiring from this well-nigh impossible task."

Of course he stayed; the messianic impulse still burned. And a 1980 poll of his colleagues named him the most-respected member of the House, more so than the Speaker. But the House was changing. The 1974 and 1976 elections had brought in an entirely different kind of member: reformers, whose views of government were shaped by Vietnam and Watergate. They distrusted it. They distrusted and were independent of authority. They came from suburbs and subdivisions. Few were professional politicians; many had never run for office before. They disdained Rayburn's advice of "Go along to get along."

Wright came to government with a vision and a purpose: to use the government as a tool in building the nation. The junior members were angry at what government had done. They were not visionaries, but managers.

Simultaneously, a sort of new anger had taken hold of Wright, a sense that the world was treating him unfairly. There wasn't a damned thing wrong with going out and making money per se, he told some colleagues. The only thing wrong was if you capitalized on your office.

His finances improved under Mallick's guidance, and later the two families formed a closely held company. Mallick did nothing illegal; he even got IRS rulings stipulating that some things he was doing were all right. True, those same things might not look good on the front page of *The Washington Post*. But why would they ever come out?

Wright left all that to Mallick, and concentrated on what, despite his occasional ambivalence, he loved, what he had always wanted to do, what he was good at: moving policy.

In the ten years waiting to become Speaker, loyally waiting for O'Neill to retire, Wright's view of the House crystallized. "The House is the institution closest to the people," he said. "Every member who ever served in it was elected. That cannot be said of the presidency or the Senate. The House is the raw essence of the nation."

His view gave the House authority. And the Speaker was the leader of the House. He believed that the Speaker's authority was derived from the nation itself. Like the President's.

His style developed too. Asked if, like O'Neill, he believed that "all politics is local," he replied, "I don't know what that means. If it means that each person is affected by what we do in Washington and that politicians must keep in mind that what they do has consequences, yes, I agree." But if it's juxtaposed against ideas? If it defines a process wherein local interests triumph over national themes? "No. I don't agree with that." Still, policy must touch ground with individuals: "Politicians should have a 'friends list.' I don't believe anyone motivated by a desire for revenge, with an enemies list, deserves to have power. You do kindnesses for your friends. Never forget what you owe them. In politics, that's an increasing number of people. Too many to do favors for. The only way you can repay them is to help the corporate body, and that helps them."

But, as the list grows, who knows who are the real friends? And who knew the real Jim Wright?

As he waited to become Speaker, he wrote an "affirmation" which he carried in his pocket and pondered daily until it became, he said, "ingrained." In it he described his rigid self-control, his mask, and inadvertently hinted at a volcano of ambition and insecurity rumbling beneath that self-control. It hinted at a powerful, unreadable man of contained, explosive passion.

It began: "This is the day the Lord has made; I shall be glad and rejoice in it . . . I shall surely not let others upset me, nor rob me of my serenity. No person can take from me my inner peace, for I shall quietly, calmly, gently, pleasantly hold onto it—for it is mine, a gift of God, and with it I can do anything . . . I shall be open to new things, new thoughts, new truths that I can learn from other people . . . I have performed well in the past, and I fully expect success in the future . . . I deserve to have happiness, career success, and economic security . . . The Lord wants me to have them . . . Because I like and respect myself, I am not adversely affected by the attitudes of others. If they think they do not like me, it is because they do not know me."

But how could they know him? *The mask.* All politicians wear masks, but Wright never took it off. In his own journal he described himself as "secretive." Republican leader Bob Michel said, "When you go on trips, you spend six, seven days with your colleagues, you get to know them, talk about your family, your kids. Wright never talks about his kids. In fact, I don't even know if he has kids." Former Texas congressman Bob Eckhardt, after forty years of working with Wright, said, "I don't know if he has kids either." (He has four.) His friend Craig

Raupe noted, "Jim can go to a social event and charm people but that's work for him, that's hard work. . . . If you've had two or three moments of real intimacy with him, that's a lot."

At times Wright almost seemed to keep secrets from himself, pretend problems were not problems, deny realities. His wife, Betty, said, "He talks about his childhood as if everything was always perfect but I wonder. His father was an alcoholic but he never talks about that. I learned that from his sisters, not from him."

There was something chilling in this element of the man. Yet if he was a mystery, if he hid himself sometimes even from himself, then behind the mirror, behind the relentless smile, a relentless drive and a relentless passion still burned. He was the last of an era, the last man to rise to power whose beliefs had been forged by the Depression, the last who had first experienced political triumph seeing his words electrify a crowd at a county fair.

His colleagues would soon learn about him.

CHAPTER 3

Action, not talk, would define his speakership; by acting he would define the agenda, force others to react to him, exercise power. Even before the 1986 election returned control of the Senate to the Democrats, Wright was preparing immediate, decisive action for the next, the 100th, Congress to take. He wanted a definitive, quick victory over the administration to signal to the press, the public, and the White House itself that a new era had begun. So he talked with Jim Howard, chairman of the Public Works and Transportation Committee, about having a major bill ready for floor action within forty-eight hours of the House's convening.

Such action would be unprecedented. Each separate Congress consists of the two-year cycle between elections, beginning with the first Congress in 1789, and is identified by a number. The 89th Congress, for example, existed in 1965 and 1966. Each new Congress usually takes weeks to organize itself as members get new committee and subcommittee assignments, staff changes jobs, and agendas are redefined. Legislation which does not become law in one Congress must start all over, often with an entirely new series of hearings and "markups," the committee sessions in which bills are actually written. So it takes weeks before any significant legislation reaches the floor. Asking Howard to report out a bill immediately infringed on his and his entire committee's prerogatives. Most chairmen would react angrily, refusing to be bullied.

But Wright had picked his man carefully. Wright had been the first colleague Howard had met when he arrived in Congress twenty-two years earlier when Wright, in a red vest and with a southern accent, had come over to him at a reception and introduced himself. Howard, from New Jersey, had wondered, "Who the hell is this?" But they had hit it off, and had also served on Public Works together until Wright became majority leader. Even though Howard ran perhaps the most bipartisan committee in Congress and his Republicans might not like being used as pawns in a battle against their President, Howard agreed to Wright's request.

The first bill would be numbered HR-1 ("HR" stands for House of Representatives; Senate bills have an "S" prefix), and would be the Clean Water bill, a nine-year authorization to spend $20 billion. The bill symbolized to Wright both Reagan's disdain for Congress and his insistence on an ideological position regardless of the merits. Congress had passed it in 1986 by a combined 504–0 vote, but then–Senate majority leader Bob Dole, the Kansas Republican, had delayed sending it to the White House long enough to allow Reagan to pocket-veto it. (If the President fails to sign or veto a bill within ten days after receiving it, it becomes law unless, as in this case, Congress has adjourned; then his failure to sign it kills, or pocket-vetoes, the bill.) Reagan did not want to hurt Republicans in the election, so he did not announce his position until after it.

Even as Wright was talking to Howard, he was also wooing Robert C. Byrd, who would soon reassume his post as Senate majority leader and who, like Wright in the House although not with the same power, controlled the Senate floor schedule. Byrd and O'Neill had gotten along poorly, and all but their most formal and pro forma communications had occurred at the staff level. As a result, House and Senate Democrats had rarely acted in concert. Wright would work to improve that.

Of average height but always stiffly erect, his white hair in a pompadour, Byrd had a way of bobbing his head that was almost a nervous tic. Born Cornelius Sale, Jr., raised in West Virginia coalfields, he lost both parents at age ten when his mother died and his father abandoned him. Byrd hated his father's name and gave it up, taking his uncle's instead. He had a pride that could turn deeply bitter—at twenty-four he joined the Klan and five years later was still proselytizing for it—and an insecurity that drove him, that never left him. Valedictorian of his high school class, he pumped gas after graduating; determined to better himself, he waited twelve more years to go to college. After being elected to the United States Senate he went to law school at night; speaking on the Senate floor in 1987 he declared, "I know no one likes me around here."

He first won election to the state legislature by going from town to town and playing the fiddle, entertaining people, performing for them, doing things for them. His one political message was his belief in the New Deal. In the Senate he studied the arcane rules until he mastered floor procedures better than anyone—on a trip to Central America he brought books not on the region but on Senate procedures—and served his colleagues, took care of their wants. He had a Uriah Heep–like way of doing little things for others, from holding a door open to scheduling legislation to accommodate a colleague's travel schedule. That suited his colleagues, who did not want a leader who might overshadow them, and Byrd reassured them, never pushed himself out front, explaining, "I don't think our party needs a superstar." He was cautious, often willing to defer to the White House. Wright believed the speakership was useful only because it let him act, gave him a position from which to reify his will; he used his position as a tool. Byrd seemed more interested in a state of being than a state of action; being majority leader, being in the Senate, that was its own reward. His own colleagues were unenthusiastic about his performance, and he beat back a challenge to his leadership partly by letting it be known he would trade in his post in the 101st Congress for the chairmanship of the Appropriations Committee.

Wright had to work with him, however, and treated him with deference and courtesy. He understood Byrd's background, understood rural poverty, understood the way it could turn a spirit mean. If Byrd had started his political career going from hamlet to hamlet playing the fiddle for folks, Wright understood that too. As a courtesy, Wright called on Byrd to discuss his plans, and then extended another courtesy. The Democratic Party was given equal time each year to respond to the President's State of the Union speech. This year Wright controlled that time; in the past, the party had put together prepackaged, glitzy responses which Wright disliked. His views were confirmed in a discussion with Lawrence Grossman, president of NBC News, who told him that the Democratic responses "don't serve the viewers or the Democrats. I think you're much better off talking about the issues. So are we." Wright had decided to respond himself and now graciously offered to share the time with Byrd. Byrd accepted. Already he and

Wright were getting along better, much better, than had he and O'Neill.

Byrd was also enthusiastic about Wright's idea of a quick start, to demonstrate that the Democrats were in command and could govern the country. They agreed to talk often and hold regular meetings between the joint—both House and Senate—Democratic leadership. They agreed on other priorities too, especially on trade legislation. The House had passed a sweeping, omnibus trade bill in the last Congress with an overwhelming 295 votes. Wright had been the force behind it, and behind melding the work of a dozen committees into one package, but Bob Dole, again at White House request, had blocked Senate action.

Wright did not talk about taxes with Byrd, but in the rounds of meetings with House colleagues Wright held preparatory to taking over as Speaker, he repeatedly discussed the need to raise taxes. Reagan had inherited a national debt, built up over 191 years, of $800 billion; in his first six years in office it grew to almost $2.3 trillion. Jimmy Carter's highest budget deficit was $73 billion. Reagan's highest reached $221 billion. It wasn't as if spending cuts hadn't been made. Domestic spending had been cut over 20 percent and the deficit had still gone up, because of $660 billion worth of tax cuts. Wright thought the budget deficit had to come down and that some spending cuts were possible, but that taxes had to go up too. Tax reform had dropped the top income tax rate from 50 percent to 38 percent for 1987, and scheduled it to drop to 28 percent in 1988. The rich needed no more tax cuts, he believed, and he wanted to freeze the top rate at 38 percent. *Didn't that make sense? Not raising taxes, just not giving any more tax cuts?* His leadership colleagues listened and worried about Mondale's loss of forty-nine states. Mondale had called for tax increases; Reagan had rejected them. But no one raised any objection. Wright gave Rostenkowski notice of his plans too. Speakers traditionally deferred to chairmen; they did not fight them. Wright would not defer but was giving fair warning of his wants.

On December 8, 1986, the Democratic Caucus met in the House chamber in private, with the doors to the galleries sealed, to elect its leaders for the next Congress. After his nomination—technically, the Speaker was elected by the whole House—Wright spoke to his colleagues.

"Now we have the mantle of leadership passed to each of us and to all of us," he said forcefully, with determination. "This is a time when

I believe the legislative branch of government, with united leadership in the House and Senate, can renew its rightful role as the major initiator of policy for the United States. The people who wrote the Constitution two hundred years ago never intended that the elected Congress would be passive, just merely reactive, supine and complacent to an all-powerful Executive. That is not the vision they had for us. They expected their chosen representatives in Congress to be leaders, to face the truth, willing to confront the nation's problems and unafraid to act. We do not seek confrontation. We prefer bipartisan consensus. But we will not shrink from the legislative action that is necessary where prolonged inaction has been causing problems to fester and the American people to suffer."

Then he added a warning: "I think [the American people] expect us to be honest about the national debt, to have the guts to look truth in the eye."

After his nomination, he rode one of the many elevators near the floor up to the press gallery. Reporters peppered him with questions. What about the budget deficit? they asked. Wright gave a lengthy explanation of the issue. They pressed him for more specifics, and he said, "Instead of giving additional tax cuts to the wealthiest people in this country, we should stretch out or postpone any future tax cuts to the top brackets until we get our fiscal house in order."

That comment set off the first firestorm of his speakership. It would not be the last. Within moments, reporters were contacting other politicians for a response. The overwhelming majority of Democrats agreed—privately—and privately, so did many Republicans, that tax increases were necessary. But Republicans attacked.

The New York Times, The Wall Street Journal, The Washington Post, all ran stories quoting GOP leaders condemning the proposal. Senate Republican leader Bob Dole, who himself had earlier called for tax increases, said, "There they go again. The Democrats are up to their old tax tricks." GOP presidential candidate Congressman Jack Kemp said, "Mr. Wright has confirmed the worst fears of the American people. He has revealed once again that the national leadership of the Democratic Party is concerned with tax hikes first, the worker, saver, and investor last." Treasury Secretary Jim Baker said, "This is nothing more than a general tax increase. It would break a compact that Congress and the Executive Branch made with the American people. We would be totally and unalterably opposed to that."

Democrats backed away too. Lloyd Bentsen, Wright's old Texas colleague and the new chairman of the Senate Finance Committee, told reporters, "It would be a political impossibility to pass a tax increase of any kind without the active support of the President." Rostenkowski said only, "It's something I have to discuss with my committee."

The stories all implied that Wright was politically naive. O'Neill had based Democratic political strategy on the premise that, although taxes were necessary, Congress would not act unless Reagan called for them first. O'Neill was not going to subject Democrats to "tax and spend" charges again.

Privately, Democrats worried about Wright's comment too. Byrd asked him, "Do you have to use the word 'tax'?" And a House Democrat who actively supported tax increases complained, "He's modeled himself after Walter Mondale. If you want to do something like that, you plan it, you orchestrate it, you get a message out. You don't just shoot your mouth off. Now he's made it harder to raise taxes, not easier."

There had been no plan, no coordinated attack on the issue. Wright had simply answered a question. In his new role as Speaker, the symbolic head of the Democratic Party, he had identified the whole party with it. He was stunned by the response, and the criticism. As majority leader he had been frustrated by his inability to get the press to repeat his views. That was no longer a problem. The day after the storm broke, Wright's office issued a statement limiting his proposal to families making over $150,000 a year. The qualification did little to calm things.

As the press stirred, Rostenkowski confided to an ally, "We're going to have a rough time."

In essence, Wright wanted to govern the country from the House. That required overawing the Senate and confronting and defeating the White House. Such ambition soared so high as to seem almost laughable. And yet he intended to succeed, by transforming the House into a disciplined weapon, a phalanx which he could hurl at his enemies. To do that, he had to change the way the House had operated for three-quarters of a century, ever since 1910. Back then, Speaker Joe Cannon, a Republican, had tremendous powers, among them the power to appoint all chairmen and all members of committees, which gave him dictatorial control over the House. His rigid dictatorship became a national issue while he mocked his opponents, declaring, "Behold

Mr. Cannon, the Beelzebub of Congress! Gaze on this noble form! Me, the Beelzebub! Me! The Czar!'' The House finally rose against its czar, stripped the speakership of power to appoint members to committees— giving it to Ways and Means—created the seniority system, made chairmen kings, and allowed Rayburn later to say, ''You can control the floor without being Speaker.''

But chairmen soon became the target of wrath. Rayburn's personal force had kept them somewhat in check and responsive to the Caucus, but he died in 1961. His successors John McCormack and Carl Albert could not control them, and junior members grew restive. Simultaneously, party discipline was breaking down; junior members increasingly owed their elections not to party machinery but to their own fundraising and their abilities to communicate on television. (Rayburn despised television and would not allow televised hearings; once he responded on radio to a televised speech by Eisenhower.) Pressure for reform intensified and reform came, gradually at first, explosively in 1974 with the dismantling of the formal seniority system.

The most obvious result of the reforms was the decentralization of power. Over one hundred relatively junior members won new powers as subcommittee chairmen, and each one tried to expand his or her authority. Jurisdictional overlap made legislating unruly and complex. Members who lacked any formal power base learned to influence policy through the media. Political scientist Norman Ornstein observed that in 1963 only twenty-six members had press secretaries; by the 100th Congress virtually all 435 did.

Yet the same reforms that seemed to atomize power also vastly strengthened the Speaker's hand. The revolt had been not against the Speaker, but against chairmen. A phrase from English history, ''King and Commons,'' describes the 1974 winners: the Speaker and the Caucus won, while chairmen, the nobility, lost. The Speaker gained the power to appoint Rules Committee members, to set deadlines for committees to report out legislation—so chairmen could not block his will and the will of the Caucus—and other procedural weapons. Ways and Means lost the power to make members' committee assignments; that went to the Democratic Steering and Policy Committee, and the Speaker dominated that committee. Carl Albert did not even try to avail himself of his new powers. O'Neill was much, much stronger, but under him the House still ran loosely. The nuts and bolts of the place rattled; O'Neill had not turned the screws. Wright intended to bring the power of the speakership full circle; he would turn the screws. That required building an internal political machine which would dominate the inner workings of the House.

Wright had another, contradictory goal: to return the House to the kind of collegial, bipartisan place which it had been when he himself arrived, in the days when the harshest thing one member said about another was John McCormack's comment that he held a colleague "in minimal high regard." Wright, in private, talked of Rayburn constantly; it was not simply Rayburn's strength he craved, but the respect and even love Rayburn had earned from members in both parties. But the House had become an increasingly bitter, partisan body. That had nothing to do with Wright. The preceding Congress had been the most partisan, when measured either by voting statistics or vituperation, in at least a quarter century. Wright never recognized that his determination to succeed, and his willingness to turn the screws, conflicted with his wish for collegiality, or that ramming an agenda through the House would inflame not only Republicans but those Democrats whose influence was undermined by his wants. He could take power—perhaps—but he could not make people love him.

Wright's first step was to take physical possession of his surroundings. The United States Capitol sprawls over what is formally named Jenkins Hill but is known as Capitol Hill. The Capitol overlooks and dominates Washington; the Capitol itself is a private city, as jealous of its prerogatives as any independent kingdom, home of thirty thousand souls. No tax is charged on meals eaten here, on postcards bought here, no tribute paid to any government outside itself; it is home to its own architects, its own medical corps, its own carpenters, its own restaurant system, its own police force, its own engineers, its own gift shops, its own telephone system, its own television network, its own postal service. The Capitol building itself, dominated by the dome, flanked by columns, laced with great halls, and haunted by history, is an oriental, byzantine maze of curved, painted ceilings, offices hidden within folds of corridors, spiraling stairways, and rooms that do not exist on blueprints.

Lord of all this is the Speaker of the House, first officer of all the Capitol, who, though ceding command of one-half the complex to the Senate majority leader, either directly or indirectly controls the House side, controls virtually every room, every hallway, every closet in one-half of the Capitol building and five massive office buildings which cover the entire southern side of Capitol Hill. Control over real estate provides more than symbolic evidence of the Speaker's power: it *is* power, because information is power and proximity to the floor of the House chamber affects the flow of information. Only on the floor do members who do not serve on the same committee, or whose offices do not occupy the same corridor, see each other and exchange information; if it takes twenty minutes to get to and from one's office, information goes unheard. Only the leadership and a handful of the chairmen and ranking members of the most powerful committees have space in the Capitol itself, close to the floor, in addition to offices in the buildings across the street, where the other four hundred–plus members must sit.

Wright was not shy about taking control. In December 1986, even before formally becoming Speaker, he moved from his old first-floor Capitol offices to O'Neill's vacated ones; but he did more, adding to O'Neill's space in the Capitol, seizing real estate, wrapping his offices about the House chamber like a coiling python. The House chamber sits on the second floor of the Capitol, and every second-floor office except for one—belonging to Rostenkowski—on the entire east front, on the House side, of this immense, blocks-long building belongs to the Speaker. Along the corridor that runs from the entrance to the rotunda, down past a private conference room, past staff offices, past his reception area, his outer office, his personal secretary's office, past his own inner office, winding through the Rayburn Room, where tables and chairs and couches form a dozen little private corners for members to huddle with lobbyists or the press, all those offices are his. His demesne continued, winding around the corner—past the one intrusion into his space, room H-208, Rostenkowski's office—past stairwells and elevators to more staff offices, down finally to another private, "ceremonial" office of his own just off the House floor where the corridor intersects with the Speaker's Lobby, an ornate hallway and meeting area outside the House chamber lined with portraits of past Speakers and plush leather armchairs and Associated Press and United Press International news tickers and racks of newspapers from around the country. But there was more. On the third floor, across a corridor from the galleries overlooking the chamber, sits H-324, the Thomas P. O'Neill Room, a large, two-storied, townhouse-size complex (complete with a spiral staircase in the back of the room and a regular staircase in the front), the upper story rabbit-warrened with staff space, the lower story used for meetings. Wright took that space from the whip's office and moved into it the staff of the Democratic Steering and Policy Committee, staff who answered to him and who under O'Neill had occupied space a quarter of a mile away. Down below, down on the first floor across from the Members' Dining Room, was H-122, the Speaker's Dining Room. And, immediately below the House chamber, down an iron-balustraded staircase, Wright took from the Rules Committee another room, H-128, a room with a special history for him, the room Rayburn had used and from which he had run the House; the room once called the "Board of Education." There Rayburn and intimates had met each day to drink bourbon and educate one another about the internal happenings of the House; Wright had been privileged to visit this room as a junior congressman but, unlike Texans Jack Brooks, chairman of the Government Operations Committee, and Lloyd Bentsen, chairman of the Senate Finance Committee, had not frequented it because Wright had not been a special Rayburn protégé. Now the room belonged to Wright. He had still more—his regular congressional office across the street in the Longworth Building. And finally, across the hall from the House chamber, closest to the floor of any office, sat the parliamentarian; though nonpartisan and trusted by Republicans, he served at the pleasure of the Speaker and helped him control the floor.

All this—the real estate, the people who occupied the real estate—extended Wright's person, served as outposts of information and operation, of thought and intelligence, of eyes and ears; they were the coils and nerve endings of Wright's rule.

If Wright's offices entwined loosely about the outside of the House, the Speaker's Rostrum, a stiff spine of order around which activity revolves, pierced its heart. From the galleries, the floor of the House of Representatives resembles an amphitheater. Even when empty, a subtle tension, an electricity fills the chamber. The echoes of history resonate within. Thick tan leather seats lie in neat rows which slope from a height near the back down to the well of the House. On each side of the chamber, substituting for part of one row of seats, stand long tables used by floor managers of legislation. Unlike the Senate, seats are all unassigned and belong to whoever fills them; members drift back and forth between the Democratic side (at the right of the Speaker) and the Republican side (at the left of the Speaker), and when the House is full, members mill about in the aisles, put their feet up on the back of the chair in front of them, talk in small clusters behind the brass railings that mark off the floor, until the chamber fills with a constant buzz of their conversations, conversations which, no matter how seemingly casual, all have purpose, and which create background noise that sounds like an orchestra warming up.

Two marble columns on each side of the rostrum anchor the chamber, and the huge American flag draped behind it infuses it with color. The Speaker's high-backed chair resembles a throne, and its authority flows down over the layers of clerks and parliamentarians and functionaries who sit beneath it. The Senate has nothing like it; indeed, in the Senate the majority leader controls events from the floor, and the most junior senators have the penance rather than the honor of presiding. Just below the rostrum on the right are volumes of *Hind's Precedents, Cannon's Precedents, Deschler's Precedents,* and *The Rules and Manual of the 100th Congress.* To the left on the rostrum is a copying machine; farther left, where members would enter from the men's room and shoeshine stand across the Speaker's Lobby, lie small white towels along with a stack of the daily "Calendar of the House of Representatives."

Above the chamber, light streams through an eagle's talons adorning a great, fake skylight; bas-relief sculptures of history's great lawmakers line the walls above the galleries—all in profile except for Moses, whose full face stares directly at the Speaker. And if from the galleries the chamber seems chaotic, all confusion and largeness, the members as fragmented as passengers in a railroad station, from the rostrum it appears small and intimate—as intimate and as difficult to control as a bedroom, where passion can erupt and where people reveal themselves in petty betrayals or jealousies or courage or honor.

Wright used staff as an extension of himself, as executors of his will, not as advisers. As with most politicians, loyalty was the first requisite for employment. Indeed, only one senior member of his majority-leader staff had finished a four-year major college at all, although as Speaker he added alumni of Yale, Princeton, and Dartmouth. Staff worked for Wright, period; they had no agendas of their own, were not plotting ways to advance their own careers. Under O'Neill, accounts of private meetings in the Speaker's office would appear in print twenty-four hours later. O'Neill would shrug and say, "These walls have ears." Under Wright the leaks disappeared.

His chief aides were John Mack and Marshall Lynam. Lynam had the title of chief of staff, his own office, outer office, and personal secretary, all located near Wright, far from the floor. Tall, lean, white-bearded, only a few years younger than Wright, he handled Wright's personal business and constituent services, but nothing legislative, and had worked for Wright for thirty years. Wright dominated him as he dominated almost everyone about him. Lynam's wife, Eddie, more than once told Wright's first wife, Mab, "Marshall just can't take it anymore. He hates it." But he did take it, did Wright's bidding, did all the little things in anticipation of his bidding. Like Wright, he was secretive even with those around him. And he seemed to enjoy power, could be imperious with those below him, and, as Wright took over, said with relish, "This place will be disciplined like the members wouldn't believe."

Mack, in his early thirties, had the title of executive director of the Democratic Steering and Policy Committee. He occupied one desk among seven in H-209, at one end of the Speaker's Lobby and next to the Speaker's ceremonial office, which Mack used at will, closing the door. He was stronger than Lynam; he did not confront Wright—only his former aide Raupe had ever stood in Wright's face and said, "God-dammit, Jim, you can't do that"—but he could turn Wright in the way a tugboat turns an ocean liner, and he often interjected his own judgment between an order from Wright and executing it. He also had more power than Lynam; power emanated from the floor.

Quick with a smile, a good old boy with a beer belly—a good golfer and better with a shotgun shooting trap or ducks—Mack had an easy, open way with members, joking or even jousting with the younger ones physically, the way high school boys wrestle good-naturedly in the halls. He handled members and legislation, seeing to it that things which were supposed to happen did happen, and, mostly, he listened. He gave out nothing. For all his outgoing manner, there was a brooding depth to him. Few people recognized it and fewer penetrated it. He had a past.

As a teenager he had dropped out of college and gone to work in a convenience store. Nineteen years old, he married and was suddenly promoted to store manager. The company called him back from his honeymoon to work the late shift, and he found himself already trapped by the world. Nineteen years old and trapped. In one inexplicable moment he exploded and beat and slashed a woman customer, a stranger, with a hammer and knife, left her unconscious and fled.

She lived. It was a horrible, brutal, violent crime, and he went to jail.

The jailers called him a "model prisoner." The county sheriff said he was a special case. The psychiatrist chosen by the prosecutor said keeping him in jail served no purpose. His brother was married to Wright's daughter, who had known him since his high school days and told her father he was really a good kid. Wright wrote the parole board that he would give John a job. Mack was paroled, having served twenty-seven months, and opened mail and filed things for Wright, the lowliest job in the office, at $9,000 a year. He doubled his salary working at night part time as a telephone magazine subscription salesman; his voice had a gentle, persistent, seductive quality. In the office too he did well, and after a few years graduated to helping with the office computer system. Then he ran the system. He had talent, intelligence, and Wright was giving him a chance. He was growing, stretching. When Raupe, the former deputy chairman of the Democratic Party, Eastern Airlines vice president, and political science professor, once and for all quit working for Wright in 1979, quit his job as chief floor assistant to the majority leader, he recommended Mack as his replacement. It was an extraordinary suggestion.

There was discussion in the office about the propriety of Mack doing the new job. He couldn't even vote. But, was he not rehabilitated? If he was, why shouldn't he get a chance? If Mack had grown before, now he blossomed. From behind his bulk his eyes sparkled with intelligence; his mind soaked up knowledge—of procedures, of legislation, of who wanted what, and of whom to trust. He could read men, read their motives, read where they were going. Who, after all, could fool him, considering the places of the soul he had visited? Mack owed Wright his life. And Wright trusted him as he did few men. When Wright became Speaker, Mack was thirty-two and had worked for him for his entire adult life. At that same time anonymous letters about his past went to reporters and House staff. Mack wanted to resign to save Wright embarrassment. Wright talked him out of it. Once Mack told a man who admired Wright, "You like him. I love him."

But Mack was only staff. The distance between staff and members was insurmountable. Staff did not put their ass on the line in elections. Staff could not vote on the floor. Staff, except for half a dozen leadership aides like Mack, could not even walk onto the floor; in meetings staff often stood while members sat. Members, and only members, were princes.

*　*　*

Perhaps no society in the twentieth century, not even the Senate, so resembles feudalism as the House of Representatives. Members *are* princes. The title "members" signifies both their uniqueness and their equality; like feudal lords, everything in the Capitol, from the elevator operators who respond instantly to "Members Only" buttons to the Library of Congress, exists to serve them. Everyone has his or her own agenda and lives by the saying *No permanent friends, no permanent enemies, only permanent interests*. Even if a member lacks the power base of a chairman, if he or she simply works harder than anyone else, or has expertise, or is well respected, then that member has power in the House. Television, access to campaign funds, and the decline of party organization—all of which were interrelated and reinforced one another—further increases each member's independence. *The only blood oath I ever swore was to my constituents*. That service is repaid: In 1986 more than 98 percent of House incumbents seeking reelection won, although, including retirements, turnover was at the postwar average. Senators are much more vulnerable to defeat. Each member of the House and everyone who has ever been a member of the House was elected to that position; that is not true of the Senate, the presidency, or the vice presidency. Also unlike the Senate, semipermanent relationships develop where a more powerful member may look after another in exchange for fealty. The Speaker is the most powerful member, but not the only one who can offer protection.

The key to controlling members lies in form and structure; through form and structure, one can control substance. The most important element of form is procedure; of structure, the whip organization. Parliamentary procedure is dry, technical, and mundane; but, like the coils of a rope, it can constrain or even strangle. Procedure is part of the minutiae of politics which the press and public do not understand; the insiders understand. John Dingell, a creature of the institution who came to Washington when he was five years old with his congressman father, then worked as a page, then inherited his father's seat, once told the Rules Committee, "If I let you write substance and you let me write procedure, I'll screw you every time."

Procedure is the primary shield against power, whether for individuals against the state in the due process clause of the Constitution, or for minorities in Congress. The Constitution stipulates that the House and

Senate will write their own "rules," their own procedures, and the two bodies are radically different.

The Senate majority leader, like the Speaker of the House, does control legislative scheduling, but one senator can wreak havoc on the Senate floor. He or she can block any legislation with the endless debate called a filibuster; closing it off, "cloture," requires the votes of sixty senators. Other senatorial courtesies include the informal "hold" a senator can put on legislation or nominations; a hold blocks floor action indefinitely. And senators can offer any amendment, no matter how irrelevant, to almost any legislation.

The floor of the House is controlled by the Speaker, who has the power of recognition—he may even ask, "For what purpose does the gentleman rise?" Depending on the answer, he may recognize the member or not. But even more crucial are the standing rules of the House and the House Rules Committee.

In each Congress, the two most partisan votes are the first two: the first elects the Speaker and the second adopts a set of standing rules—each party offers a nominee for Speaker and a package of standing rules—and both will govern the House for two years. For example, according to the Democrat-written rules for the 100th Congress, although Republicans controlled 41 percent of House seats, Democrats hold a two-thirds-plus-one advantage, nine Democrats to four Republicans, on the Rules Committee. Since the 1974 reforms, the Speaker has had the power to appoint personally, with Caucus approval, all Democrats on Rules. And Rules writes a specific rule covering floor handling of almost every piece of major legislation.

The rule for the bill dictates several things, most important being which different parts of a package, if any, will be voted on separately and what amendments can be offered. The House (the Senate has no comparable procedure) first debates and votes on the rule for a bill, and only later on the bill itself. Because of the constitutional mandate that the House write its own rules, House rules take precedence over the law, even over the Constitution itself. In procedure lies power.

Process. Suppose there are two bills. One is very, very popular; the other is somewhat unpopular. Suppose the Speaker has Rules link the two bills together, and only allows members one vote—they either take both bills or reject both bills. The unpopular bill passes. *Process.* The rules of the House require a committee to have a quorum before voting out legislation, but suppose less than a quorum attends a certain meeting, suppose hardly any Republicans, and the committee votes out a bill anyway, and the Speaker has the Rules Committee waive the standing rules of the House. *Process.* Suppose a law—the law of the land, something the House itself has passed, the Senate has passed, the President has signed into law; *this is the law*—requires the House to allow a vote on a certain issue. Suppose the Speaker asks the Rules Committee to write a House rule that voids the law. *The rule takes precedence over the law.* Procedure is power.

When Wright took over from O'Neill, all the Democrats on Rules were returning, including chairman Claude Pepper. Several had served on the committee for all of O'Neill's ten years as Speaker; some had served even longer. Wright didn't care about their seniority. Nor did personalities interest him. But power did, having them heed him did. A few came to see him privately to assure him of loyalty and ask to be reappointed. Wright wanted that little investiture ceremony; they would ask, and he would grant. But he wanted them to ask. Not all of them did. "Some of them had got to thinking they were on Rules through the divine right of kings," Wright said. "That was a little foolish. I just wanted them to remember they were the Speaker's appointees."

He delayed telling them he would reappoint them, until some began to wonder. Rules was one of three "exclusive" committees, meaning that members served only on it. Anyone removed and placed on other committees would start dead-last in seniority, would go from being one of nine members on one of the most important committees in Congress to number twenty-five or thirty in seniority on a lesser one. Finally, a few days before the organizing Caucus in which Wright would formally name Rules members, he hosted a luncheon for committee Democrats. He explained that he intended to use the committee as a tool, and sometimes they would have to obey the leadership. Then he said, "I assume you all want to be reappointed."

There was a still moment. They would not forget again whose appointees they were.

The Rules Committee gave Wright control over the form of legislation on the floor. He needed control over structure as well, beginning with the leadership. This was more delicate. He did not appoint the majority leader or the whip. They were elected. (The whip had always been appointed, until now. One of O'Neill's 1984 concessions had been to allow the Caucus to elect the whip.) And being elected meant that the majority leader and whip had their own constituencies.

Still, Thomas S. Foley, the majority leader from Spokane, Washington, was loyal. He had, unopposed, stepped up to majority leader from the whip job, but he still owed Wright for it; Wright had made the phone call after the 1980 election telling him he would be appointed whip. That had taken guts on Wright's and O'Neill's part: Foley had been reelected with only 51 percent of the vote, which could have made it difficult for him to side with the leadership on tough issues. Foley appreciated the vote of confidence and had proven his loyalty over the years. He was not the kind of man to rock the boat anyway.

He played the role of *consigliore,* counselor, adviser to the Speaker, handled the floor and responded to Republicans on it, and arranged the legislative schedule—no minor task—subject to the Speaker's approval. Large, bulky, tall, and heavy, with big hands and a big head, despite his size he seemed out of touch with his body. Even his walk seemed awkward, lumbering, with no spring to his step. Each foot landed, flat, and stuck to the ground, until it seemed he remembered consciously to lift it for the next step. He was a creature of the mind, brilliant, judicious, and analytical. He had perspective where Wright was passionate, and his office reflected him. It held several thousand dollars' worth of stereo equipment; when alone, he would play classical music, capable of piercing events of the moment and rolling around inside his mind. The office was laid out like a living room, with a small desk, no larger than what a child might have in a bedroom, against a window; Foley's job was to listen and he believed that a large desk, which conveyed authority and served as moat between listener and visitor, interfered with people speaking freely. He did not impose himself; he listened. He was content as majority leader. "I'm not personally interested in or entertained by court politics," he said. "There's only one king, the Speaker."

Tony Coelho, the newly elected whip from California, was different. He understood loyalty well enough and said, "There's only one leader." But he also said, "I'm a political entrepreneur." Coelho did not wait for something to happen; he made it happen. Few members—few people—had his intensity. He could look at someone, get up in someone's face, challenge him. Like Lyndon Johnson, he played the game at close range, challenging by physical proximity, pushing, invading, using the physical discomfort of proximity as a weapon. He took nothing for granted. His victory in the whip race was locked up early, but after the November election he had called every Democrat in the House and asked him or her to recommit to him. Coelho had even asked his campaign manager, Vic Fazio, who had replied, "You can't be serious. I'm your campaign manager." Coelho had said, "Answer the question."

In 1984, Coelho had led the insurgents who demanded that O'Neill change the way he ran the House. As Democratic Congressional Campaign Committee chairman from 1981 to 1986, he had become intimate with colleagues' districts and problems, had given colleagues money, and was particularly close to the younger, more impatient members elected with his help while at the DCCC. Although Coelho was only forty-four, with only four terms in Congress behind him, Rostenkowski had tried to get him to run for majority leader against Foley, using him as a foil in his own plans to run for Speaker against Wright; for well over a year, rumor had him running against Foley for majority leader. Instead, Coelho had trounced two other candidates in the whip race, winning almost two-thirds of the vote on the first ballot. He had already told friends—word had spread quickly—that he did not intend to wait ten years to become Speaker. His explanation that he had meant only that he might sometime leave the House fell short of quieting the undercurrents he had created. He also picked ambitious people for his own staff. "Some people think my staff is all sharks," he said. "I like strong people." Some *were* sharks: one Coelho aide said, "Tony's the only one of these guys who's won a contested [internal] election in ten years. Foley never won one at all."

Foley had been the last appointed whip. Coelho was the first elected one. The difference was stark: Coelho owed the membership for his job, and Foley owed Wright. It mattered because the whip headed a powerful organization, the only real organization inside the Congress.

The whip organization had two jobs: to provide intelligence by counting votes, and to execute policy by convincing members to vote with the leadership. The organization included a chief deputy whip, ten deputy whips—just four years earlier there had been only four, but O'Neill had doubled that number as a concession to insurgents and Wright added two more—twenty-two whips elected by region, and forty-five at-large whips. They met every Thursday morning in H-324, the big townhouse two-storied room across from the House chamber, whose second floor was used for Steering and Policy staff. Between forty and sixty members would show up at a given meeting; the leadership sat at the front of the room, the members facing them in rows like in a lecture hall. The organization was designed to reach into every crevice of the Caucus, and even, delicately, to some Republicans.

The whip meetings began in 1969 at Rostenkowski's suggestion to undermine, not enhance, the Speaker's power. Rostenkowski's idea was to go over the legislative schedule for the following week with a handful of members. Colleagues who wanted to know what was happening had to come to them on the floor. "We became an exclusive group of guys," Rostenkowski said. At the time, he was Caucus chairman and talked whip Hale Boggs, who was running for majority leader, into holding the meetings. Back then, Boggs's wife, Lindy, got up at four-thirty in the morning to bake pastries for them. Much was discussed besides the schedule. Speaker John McCormack was not invited and did not attend.

Wright would not allow any such undermining of his authority; he intended to control this organization himself, to burn into everyone's mind that, make no mistake, *he* was king, that *he,* Wright, held power now, that *he,* Wright, was the one who made the decisions. And those in the House who wanted to share in his power had to recognize that fact.

The chief deputy whip was now the most senior slot appointed by the Speaker. With it went an office in the Capitol, prominence in Washington, and a step onto the leadership ladder which could lead to bigger steps. The choice would also send an important signal from Wright to the membership. O'Neill asked him to keep alive the Boston-Austin connection, the fifty-year history of a leadership team including both Massachusetts and an oil state, by naming Brian Donnelly, from Dorchester, a working-class Boston area. Donnelly served on Ways and Means and was as savvy and tough a politician as there was in the House. This was the same Donnelly whom Wright had helped win a primary in 1978 while Philip Burton was helping his opponent, the same Donnelly who started his House career at war with O'Neill, for O'Neill had decades earlier kept Donnelly's uncle from becoming mayor of Boston. But Donnelly and O'Neill had learned to get along. O'Neill was convinced Wright would appoint him.

Another candidate was Steny Hoyer. Forty-eight years old, Hoyer, along with Coelho and Richard Gephardt, had led the group of House insurgents seeking internal changes after the 1984 election, but he had simultaneously worked to maintain relations with O'Neill and Wright. He had gone out of his way to do that. A Wright aide said, "Steny carried water for Wright for two years." He worked hard, particularly in organizing the Democratic Congressional Dinner, which would bring in $2.3 million in early 1987. (Wright offered him the chairmanship of the DCCC; Hoyer declined, not wanting to leave his family as often as that would require.) Hoyer had even opposed electing the whip, preferring to keep the position an appointive one, and believed in a strong speakership. Coelho urged Wright to name Hoyer. Not long before Wright made his choice, Hoyer came out to Wright's home in McLean where they spent two hours in private. Wright's wife, Betty, was convinced Hoyer would get it. She was glad. Hoyer had always seemed so nice.

But Hoyer was not already active as a deputy whip. Wright wanted to promote from within that organization. He was determined to let members know that being part of the organization meant work, but that unlike under O'Neill, who played personal favorites, work would be rewarded. And the *Baltimore Sun* printed a story saying Hoyer was the choice. That annoyed Wright, made him wonder if someone was trying to use the press to make something happen. Finally, Wright's aide John Mack weighed in. Mack liked Hoyer, liked him a lot, and Mack and Coelho were close friends—close enough that some people worried that Mack's loyalties were split. They were wrong; Mack served Wright first. When Wright and Mack sat down to talk over the appointment, Mack warned, "Members are going to see Steny as Coelho's man, not yours." *Coelho's man, not yours.* Then Mack suggested David Bonior.

Bonior? Bonior was no one's man, but everyone respected him. Bearded—one of the very few in Congress—divorced, a former Big Ten quarterback at Iowa, Bonior had a deceptively laid-back quality that made him easy to talk to. Yet underneath the surface affability lay a toughness. Elected in 1976, he had repeatedly risked his political life back home by voting against antibusing legislation, and had supported tax increases even though a state senator in his district had been recalled for that reason. He served on the Rules Committee, and a Speaker can never have too many friends on Rules. Bonior was the right age, just forty-two, a Vietnam veteran, and came from Michigan. The Midwest had no representation in the leadership. Bonior was also a deputy whip already. More than that, he had run the Democrats' efforts to kill funding of the Nicaraguan contras. He had lost on the issue, but had run the operation so well—orchestrating the media and lobbying by outside groups—that Coelho planned to model all his whip task forces on Bonior's approach.

Bonior also had his own constituency in the House, his own loyalists. He had assembled them in preparation for running for Caucus chairman in case a vacancy occurred there. (It didn't.) His constituency was precisely where Wright was weakest, among younger members and liberals opposed to Reagan's Central America policy. Those activists still resented Wright's having helped to pass Reagan's package of aid to El Salvador in 1982. At the time, liberals had grumbled that if Wright kept it up he would never become Speaker, while Republican Henry Hyde called Wright's action a profile in courage. Wright and Bonior had opposed each other then, but Bonior had sent Wright a handwritten note telling him to ignore his critics, adding that "I know you did what you believe was the right thing and it took courage to do it."

The relationship between Bonior and Wright was part of the weave in the House fabric. Over the years members cross paths over and over; those criss-crossed pathways form a web. Wright had talked to Bonior. Would he be a team-player? *Yes,* Bonior replied excitedly. *Yes.*

Wright did not tell Coelho of his choice. It was no accident. He also neither consulted nor informed Coelho about the selection of the ten deputy whips. Californian Norman Mineta, a longtime Wright ally, was named a deputy and, assuming Coelho had also argued for him, thanked him.

"Help you?" Coelho exclaimed. "The first I've known about it is what you just told me. Do you know who any of the others are?"

Mineta told him that Bonior—*Bonior?!*—was chief deputy whip. Coelho looked stunned for a moment. The appointment was bad enough, but to find out this way? He turned on his heel and stormed away.

Coelho might be the whip, but the whip organization belonged to Wright. Coelho might manage the organization, but only as a delegatee. A final indignity came after the Caucus elected Coelho whip; while members were still applauding, interrupting the applause, killing it, was the announcement of the ten deputy whips. Coelho thought bitterly, *They could at least have waited for the applause to end.*

Lastly, Wright took control of the Democratic Steering and Policy Committee. Members joked that it neither steered nor set policy. But it did make committee assignments (subject to virtually automatic Caucus confirmation) to all the "standing" committees of the House except Rules. Committee assignments could determine members' political future, whether they enjoyed or hated their daily routine, even whether they won reelection. If a member wanted Foreign Affairs because he thought himself a statesman, he went to Steering and Policy. If he wanted Appropriations or Ways and Means because of their power, he went to Steering and Policy. If he wanted Armed Services because of a navy base in his district, he went to Steering and Policy. Thirty-one members sit on Steering and Policy; the Speaker chairs it, and the entire leadership plus the chairmen of the Appropriations, Budget, Rules, and Ways and Means committees automatically have seats. Eight other members are appointed by the Speaker; another twelve are elected by region. A committee assignment requires an absolute majority of sixteen votes no matter how many members attend a meeting.

Steering and Policy was Rostenkowski's natural habitat, as natural for him as the backroom Chicago ward-heeling system he grew up in. Indeed, years earlier he had switched from the Commerce Committee to Ways and Means because, until the 1974 House reforms, Ways and Means gave out committee assignments. When, at the beginning of each Congress, Steering and Policy members rolled up their sleeves, secluded themselves for hours, sent out for sandwiches, Rostenkowski was at home, slipping easily into the undercurrents and intrigues and secret byways that ran through the room. A former leadership aide recalled one fight that continued ballot after ballot, when one candidate's weary sponsor said, "I ask unanimous consent to withdraw my candidate's name"—thus redistributing votes. Rostenkowski shouted, "I object!" O'Neill snapped, "Why the hell do you object? He's not your candidate." Rostenkowski replied, "Never mind why, I just object."

When Wright joined Steering and Policy as majority leader, he seemed lost by contrast. One former O'Neill aide said, "I can't recall him ever being a factor on Steering and Policy." Even at the beginning of the 99th Congress, Wright's last as majority leader, Rostenkowski outmaneuvered him over committee assignments, and hoped to use Steering and Policy as a power base against Wright even after he became Speaker.

Wright made certain he would not. O'Neill had dissipated his control of Steering and Policy by letting factions among House Democrats—

freshmen, blacks, women—choose one of their own to fill several of the eight Speaker-appointed seats. Not Wright. Instead of allowing the freshmen to elect their representative, Wright named a Texan, Jim Chapman, who had actually won a special election eighteen months earlier and was beginning his second term. To the traditional black seat, Wright named Harold Ford, a member of Ways and Means. Wright also named Brian Donnelly, also on Ways and Means. Wright was invading Rostenkowski's own lair, forcing his committee members to split their loyalties. That was not all he did.

Wright asked Jack Brooks, the dean of the Texas delegation, to run for election from his region, knowing he would win and be loyal. And there was Energy and Commerce chairman John Dingell again; bad blood ran between him and both Rostenkowski and O'Neill. Just two years earlier, in O'Neill's last term, Dingell had asked O'Neill to name him to Steering and Policy to give him a strong voice in who was named to his committee. O'Neill refused. Dingell asked Wright for one of the Speaker-appointed seats, promised his support, and guaranteed that the member elected from his region would support Wright as well. "That's two loyal seats instead of one," Dingell said. In return, Dingell would have Wright's support when it came to naming members to Energy and Commerce. It was a deal.

Steering and Policy belonged to Wright.

Wright had other appointments to make—several hundred to boards and commissions and all "select" committees, as opposed to permanent, "standing" legislative committees. The Iran-contra committee, which would investigate the administration's selling of arms to Iran and funneling of profits to Nicaraguan contras, was most important.

To him the Iran-contra escapade represented the Reagan administration's contempt for every element of institutional Washington, including its own State and Defense departments, and the contradictions between its rhetoric and the reality. The administration argued that the law required only "timely" notice to the Senate and House intelligence committees, and claimed that that loophole justified waiting ten months, until after the press revealed the activities, to notify Congress. But Wright regularly invited small groups of four or five national reporters in and quoted from the statute that even if the intelligence committees could not be informed, "prior notice" still had to be given to the bipartisan congressional leadership.

Wright's goal was not to orchestrate attacks on the administration.

He believed the press needed no prodding for that. Instead, Wright wanted to focus the attention of the press on the deeper, constitutional issue. When one reporter observed, "There aren't any sanctions written into the law, there's no enforcement mechanism," Wright replied, "We never felt the need to write penalties into law to require the Executive to carry them out. That's the first responsibility of the President, to faithfully execute the law."

But he wanted also to isolate the investigation, keep it from interfering with what he regarded as more substantive business. He intended to do this with his appointments, which depoliticized the issue as much as possible.

He watched the talk shows one Sunday to decide whom to name as chairman of the Iran-contra committee, and picked Lee Hamilton, based on his reasoned, low-key style, over the gruffer, more earthy Dante Fascell. As members of the committee, he named the chairmen who had jurisdiction over the activities. Foley would represent the leadership. Three of the nine Democrats favored contra aid; all six Republicans certainly would. That meant the committee as a whole favored the White House policy; no one could accuse it of being stacked.

And there were wheels within wheels. Wright was trying to force Republican leader Bob Michel to choose "ranking" Republicans—the GOP counterparts to the chairmen Wright had named. Those particular ranking Republicans did not compare in individual abilities to the Democrats. Michel responded instead to the pressures of his GOP colleagues and chose more junior—and more aggressive, more politically astute—members. The Democrats had an average age of sixty-six; the average age of the Republicans was forty-nine. The Democrats had gravitas and would debate the law; the Republicans were guerrillas and would debate the policy.

Lastly, finally, Wright made appointments to more than one hundred commissions. Each appointment had purpose, advanced his agenda. It was the minutiae of power. Mack had already spent tens of hours, and with Wright the two would spend more hours, going over requests. Not one appointment occurred without thought. Of one plum Wright said, "I don't suppose there's any way I can use this to influence Michel?" Of another: "I want someone on this who will be aggressive and vociferous in looking out for the average American, help him own his own home, send his kids to college, who understands the role of government and the threat of the deficit." And to the Migrating Birds Commission Wright named Dingell, who loved to hunt; it was one more favor to an ally, one more move to solidify his base.

Wright was finally ready to move.

PART II
BLITZKRIEG

A wise prince should rely on what he controls, and not on what he cannot control.

—Machiavelli, *The Prince*

CHAPTER 4

On Tuesday, January 6, 1987, the day the 100th Congress of the United States of America would convene, Wright's senior staff gathered for their daily breakfast meeting in a closed-off section of the Members' Dining Room in the Capitol. The trappings of power were already theirs: before Wright arrived one aide mentioned that a lobbyist was offering them free tickets—scalpers were getting $300 each—and a free trip to New York to see the Washington Redskins play the New York Giants for the NFC championship. Did anyone want to go? Such offers were so routine no one accepted. Wright entered and the talk turned immediately to business. The day before, the administration had delivered its budget to Congress and it included a personal slap at Wright; as an example of "pork-barrel" spending it singled out a $7.5-million project in the depressed "stockyards" area of Fort Worth. That project represented two fundamentally different visions of government: to the administration it was pork, to Wright, investment. He had been pouring federal money into the area for fifteen years and bragged that every one dollar of federal seed money had generated eight dollars of private investment. But beyond the policy difference, the White House was warning that it intended to play rough, and this project would later haunt Wright; his friend and business associate George Mallick had just gotten involved in a major business in the area.

Wright shrugged when an aide mentioned the attack. His concern was substance; his agenda required money, taxes, and he had to convince the press of the need for them. Unlike a President, he had no means of going over the heads of the media, directly to the people; he had to go through them. Reagan's budget included taxes, whatever Reagan called them. "We want to point out every 'user fee' "—his voice dripped with disdain at the phrase—"in this budget, these things the President doesn't call taxes that he's got $6 billion of."

Outside in the hallway an ABC camera crew had encamped, waiting for a shot of him, blocking the passage and collecting a crowd. Members of Congress grow accustomed to anonymity in the Capitol, moving unnoticed through crowds of tourists, and as Wright finished breakfast and left, the camera surprised him, the attention signifying his new position. The hallways were packed. Every two or three steps some-one—a congressman, or a Capitol policeman, or lobbyist, or elevator operator—congratulated him, and he stopped to pump a hand or laugh at some whispered intimacy. Though usually impatient, wrapped as tautly and explosively as a trip wire, he took his time now. He had waited thirty-two long years for this moment and now would savor every element of it.

It was like that all day, like that two hours later when he entered, finally, the House chamber. The chamber too was packed, a maelstrom of colleagues and their families (unlike the Senate, House rules allow members' families on the floor); members clapped one another's backs, greeted one another's children, as if they had not seen each other in years rather than weeks. From above in the galleries, the floor looked like a live thing, some unformed but amoeba-like living creature, stretching here, contracting there, being born into its own identity. *This was the 100th Congress. The 100th!* This day also marked Sam Rayburn's birthday, and Wright had picked it to begin, asking Michel's permission and Michel agreeing, each wanting to get along for both their sakes. While the members milled about, waved to their friends and relatives in the galleries, the Clerk of the House, presiding in the absence of a Speaker, banged the gavel, banged the gavel, banged the gavel, "The House is not in order! The House is not in order!" Slowly, gradually, the House settled into repose one less murmur at a time, ready for its first order of business—to choose its Speaker.

A clerk called—for the only time in the entire Congress—the roll of members and one at a time, as their names were called, every Democrat voted for Wright, every Republican for Michel. Finally the clerk declared, "The Honorable Jim Wright is elected Speaker!" A warm, standing ovation greeted him as he and Michel were escorted to the

Speaker's Rostrum by Tip O'Neill and John Rhodes, the former Republican leader whose son was a freshman member.

Then Michel looked out upon the crowded chamber. It was the only moment he would stand at the rostrum in the entire 100th Congress, and he felt a twinge of frustration and envy; he loved the House, and not so long before had believed that he himself would one day stand there, gavel in hand, the Speaker, but he knew now that moment would not come to pass. Yet his words were gracious: "We intend to work together in a constructive way . . . Our wish that he rule the House with a firm steady hand . . . My high honor to present . . . great state of Texas . . ."

Wright took the gavel amid another standing ovation, and grinned and grinned. He began a speech addressed to his colleagues first, defining himself and them and connecting them to the nation beyond. His voice, arrhythmic and gentle but deep, rolled through the chamber with a message of humility. "We have come here through no intrinsic merit of our own, not like cream rising to the top," he said. "We are ordinary men and women . . . This is the people's House."

Then his tone changed. His voice grew steely, its gentleness disappearing, and the membership sat erect and alert as he warned, "It will be my duty as Speaker to defend and uphold the House in every relationship, at all times and in all places. . . . We present ourselves to the President not as a rival center of power but as partner . . . a full and equal partner. . . . We ask no more. We'll settle for no less."

If Wright had issued a warning, the Republicans quickly responded. The second vote of the 100th Congress was to adopt a set of standing rules. The Democratic package made routine changes—among them, lifting the ban on pronouncing the word "Senate" on the floor (it had always been called "the other body")—from the 99th Congress.

But when Wright, now from the Speaker's Rostrum, recognized Michel to offer the Republican package, Michel yielded the floor to whip Trent Lott and walked out of the chamber. The GOP rules included a provision making out of order—impossible to bring to the floor—the proposal Wright had already made to freeze the top income tax rate.

This was a personal attack on Wright, and more. Voting against the GOP package exposed Democrats in the next election to a thirty-second TV commercial charging, "The first vote your congressman made last year was to raise your income tax!"

Republicans voted for their package 173–0. Democrats voted against 240–2. That quickly the battle was joined.

To win required the ability to manipulate the media, read polls, and play the outside game with the public, and it also required the inside game, the mastery of each detail, each comma on a piece of paper, and a sensitivity subtle enough to read a handshake or a nod. As Wright took charge as Speaker he had that sensitivity and observed, "Did you see Michel walk off the floor after he yielded to Lott? Bob didn't want to associate himself with the attack on me."

This was a moment for subtlety; other times the game would require brute force. The speakership of Jim Wright had begun.

The next day, Wednesday, the House created the select committee to investigate the sale of arms to Iran. On Thursday it passed HR-1, the Clean Water bill, with Democrats voting for it 246–0, Republicans 160–8. (Two weeks later the Senate passed it 93–6.) The Democratic leadership was threatening to ram this bill down Reagan's throat.

Wright laid the foundation for the rest of his agenda too, particularly trade. Already much maneuvering had occurred over the issue. The preceding year the House had passed a bill overwhelmingly; Bob Dole, at White House request, had blocked Senate action. But when trade helped Democrats regain control of the Senate, suddenly the administration wanted a trade bill. Treasury Secretary James Baker told Wright and Byrd that the White House would work with them. With Rostenkowski, who had primary jurisdiction over trade, Baker went further, asking him to abandon the bill the House had passed, to start over from scratch. The two men had cooperated to pass the massive tax reform law in the 99th Congress. Now Baker seemed to be saying, *You and me, Danny, we'll work something out just like we did with tax reform.* The idea appealed to Rostenkowski. Cutting deals with the White House would give him more power and stature and also yield a bill that would become law, that would not be vetoed.

But Wright intended to use trade as another building block of his own power, another warning to his opponents both inside and outside the House. The day before Congress convened he hosted a meeting in his office with half a dozen members, a rump whip task force. The meeting was geared toward action, not discussion. Wright announced that, despite attacks from the White House and the press calling the bill protectionist—and despite the protest of one of the members in the room—the starting point on trade would be to reintroduce the exact bill the House had passed the year before.

Who would sponsor it? Last year Wright had been chief sponsor. But Speakers did not put their names on legislation. This year? Normally chief sponsorship would go to Rostenkowski, the key chairman. But Wright had promised it to Richard Gephardt. Gephardt wasn't in the room but he was running for President. Rostenkowski would be listed second. Wright would call him to tell him the bill would be reintroduced, and he would be listed second.

Co-sponsors? The next day they would have forty-five minutes to work the floor before the bill was introduced. They wanted to maximize the number of co-sponsors as a show of strength, and each took colleagues' names to whip. (They would collect 177 co-sponsors in those minutes; Coelho's whip organization worked well in its trial run.)

Finally, Wright announced that he wanted committees to report their parts of the bill by April 6, before they recessed for Easter. One member worried that the provisions would lie open and exposed over the recess, giving Reagan a target, a chance "to rally the troops in opposition, as he has been known to do." Wright grimaced. The member corrected himself: "Of course, that was in the pre-Wright era."

It was obvious flattery. But Wright liked it. It went with power and he liked it. Already his train had started rolling down the track, relentlessly gathering speed.

Rostenkowski came on board too, in his fashion. *The Wall Street Journal* soon reported, " 'I want to send word to the administration that it had better be ready to modify its posture,' Mr. Rostenkowski said . . . [and] the panel will use as its starting point a bill that the House passed last year despite opposition by the Reagan administration." But if Rostenkowski yielded to Wright on reintroducing the bill, he also told the paper that his committee would move in May. He wasn't used to Jim Wright's speakership. Nor was Wright used to his chairmanship.

Rostenkowski grew up where politics was no game. His father was a Chicago alderman. Once two of his father's precinct captains were found shot dead in a car parked in front of his home. The son resembled nothing so much as Carl Sandburg's poem about his city: *Stormy, husky, brawling . . . the Big Shoulders . . . with lifted head, singing so proud . . . and coarse and strong and cunning. Here is a tall bold slugger . . .*

*fierce as a dog with tongue lapping for action, cunning as a savage pitted
against the wilderness . . . Bragging and laughing . . .*

He liked power, not ideas, and was precisely Foley's opposite: Foley,
the creature of the mind, the abstract, physically awkward; Rostenkowski, who grabbed and felt people, who dug his fingers into people's
arms, who needed tangibles and not abstractions, whose roots sank
deep into Chicago neighborhoods, who left Washington for home almost every Thursday afternoon, not to return until Tuesday morning,
who liked things not to change, who ate dinner so often at the Washington steakhouse Morton's of Chicago that the maître d' kept the same
roomy table empty for "the chairman" no matter how busy. He lived
in the house in which he was born, a house which was also for a while
both the thirty-second ward's Democratic headquarters and a tavern
his parents ran. A few feet away was St. Stanislaus Kostka Church. It
was a neighborhood of hard-working, blue-collar Polish, of triple-
decker houses thick with people and thin of grass and yards, where
people were tough, where kids played ball in the street, where strangers
were eyed. Around his neck hung a four-leaf clover on which was etched
his name, his wife's name, their wedding date, and the names and birth
dates of his four daughters. Two of the four were stewardesses. He was
always attentive to his wife, made sure she was taken care of. Things
had their place; he respected authority and institutions—the Church,
the President, the Speaker.

He was a man's man, loved golf, and measured men simply. Jim
Healey, a longtime aide, said, "As long as he feels a person's honest
with himself and honest with him he can take just about anybody.
Ideology means nothing." As in the old Polish neighborhood, an enemy
was an enemy, a friend a friend, period. George Bush and he served
on Ways and Means together in the 1960s and were friends. The day
after Reagan was shot in 1981, Bush was scheduled to speak at a Rostenkowski fund-raiser in Chicago—remarkable, a Republican Vice
President speaking at a Democrat's fund-raiser. Bush could not appear
in person but still honored the commitment through a telephone
hookup.

Big—one of the biggest men in Congress—a magnificent high school
athlete who won fourteen letters in four sports, Rostenkowski flirted
with a career in professional baseball until his father called him home
to the family business. At twenty-four he was the youngest member of
the Illinois House, at twenty-six the youngest member of the Illinois

Senate, at thirty, anointed by Mayor Richard Daley, in the U.S. House of Representatives. In Washington Rostenkowski remained a machine politician, son of his father, and once a judge reprimanded him for using Democratic Party funds to pay a constituent's parking ticket. He never gave up his job as ward committeeman, a job inherited from his father.

Rostenkowski filled a room with himself, and demanded attentiveness. Lobbyists waited upon "the chairman," entertaining him, inviting him to long golf weekends. The law limited keeping honoraria for a single appearance to $2,000, but Rostenkowski routinely required $10,000—the excess went to charity—as if to say, Look at me! I'm special! (He started demanding more after being on a panel with Democratic power broker Bob Strauss and ABC's Ted Koppel, when Strauss kidded him, "the guy with the vote," for getting just $2,000, while he, Strauss, was getting $10,000 and Koppel was getting $15,000. Rostenkowski fumed; the next time he was invited to appear with Koppel he asked Koppel's fee. "Fifteen thousand," he was told. "Fine," he replied. "I'll take $10,000." The organizer hemmed and hawed: "Mr. Chairman, the law says you can only take $2,000." "Wrong," Rostenkowski replied. "It says I can only *keep* $2,000.")

Few in the House seemed more extroverted, yet those who knew him well called him an introvert, moody, emotional. He sometimes bullied people physically. Once, at a small meeting, Ben Rosenthal, an older, physically slight member, sat in the chair Rostenkowski usually took. Rostenkowski stood over him, his hands on hips, intimidating, and demanded, *Get out of my chair!* It was a schoolyard thing, as if he was going to beat him up. Some people also believed Rostenkowski was anti-Semitic. On another occasion the leadership was discussing Howard Wolpe, who wanted a seat on the Foreign Affairs Committee. Wolpe had a doctorate from MIT and taught international relations before coming to Congress, but Rostenkowski objected. Several men later said (and Rostenkowski denied it) that his objection made others in the room exchange looks. One man recalled, "Danny told us, 'You can't put him there. There are already four kikes on that committee.' I didn't know Wolpe was Jewish. And who the hell keeps count of how many Jews are on a committee?"

Yet for all that, there was something attractive about Rostenkowski in the same way that Sandburg made Chicago attractive. Rostenkowski laid himself out there, let people see all of him. He was like a child in his demand for attention, and children are easily forgiven.

In 1980, Rostenkowski chose the chairmanship of Ways and Means over the whip job. Ways and Means put him in a better position to challenge Wright for the speakership—former chairman Wilbur Mills could have had the speakership for the asking in 1970—and finally let him run his own show. But there was something else, too. Rostenkowski had to prove something to his colleagues, who a decade earlier rebuffed him for reelection as Caucus chairman, and to himself. His colleagues didn't think he had the intelligence to do it. He had to prove he could.

He floundered at first. Gradually his performance improved. First he won firm control of his committee, not through intellectual brilliance or intimate knowledge of the tax code—staff had that—but by taking care of his members. Although he once said, "You might as well kick a guy's brains out if he's not with you," he actually protected the interests of his committee colleagues. Once, over a drink, he told a new member of his committee, "I'll never do anything that hurts you at home."

He also made sure that even his most junior members got what they needed, as long as they asked for it. If a member of the committee fought him, perhaps won committee approval of a provision Rostenkowski opposed, in conference with the Senate Rostenkowski defended it as if it was his own pet. He was the liege lord, responsible for those under him, taking care of them, giving and expecting loyalty. Committee Republicans were treated almost as well. Rostenkowski annually took the entire committee, Republicans and Democrats, on retreats where experts from all sides of the political spectrum had an opportunity to present their cases informally. It paid off for him.

Willis Gradison, a Ways and Means Republican who was respected throughout the House, said, "Danny believes the chairman of Ways and Means has more impact on the future of the Western economies than any other position in the world. He doesn't care at all about substance, but he wants to do good. He wants to be remembered as a statesman."

He liked lobbyists, liked golfing as their guest, but campaign contributions meant nothing to him; he had no idea who gave to his own campaigns and raised relatively little—in 1986 when neither he, Wright, nor Coelho faced serious opposition, he raised only $243,000 compared to Wright's $1,221,000 and Coelho's $736,000. He stopped going to DCCC events, he said, because Coelho presented him to lobbyists with a wink and a nod, hinting that deals could be done. "Hell," Rosten-

kowski complained later, at a time when he had little use for Coelho—
he had helped Coelho get the DCCC chairmanship in 1980, and then
Coelho had turned around and thrown all his weight behind Wright's
campaign for Speaker. "I'm the chairman of Ways and Means. That's
not right."

The chairmanship meant everything to him, the committee meant
everything to him. At the unveiling of his official chairman's portrait,
with planeloads of people flown in from Chicago for the event, people
he had known for decades, with all his family there, with George Bush
and Jim Baker there, Rostenkowski almost broke down, and, his eyes
red, turned to a colleague and said, "You know, my parents worried
I would never amount to anything."

A senior House Democrat said, "Rostenkowski wants power for its
own sake, not to do good with it." Rostenkowski had had only one
definitive legislative triumph in his career. That was tax reform. From
it Rostenkowski emerged as a giant in the 99th Congress. The idea had
not been his. He was still not an innovator, not a leader in the sense
of creating things. But what good were ideas without someone like him
to bring them to fruition? It was still Rostenkowski's triumph.

Wright had opposed tax reform; out of loyalty to O'Neill he had not
worked actively to kill it. But shortly before the House voted, at a
meeting of the Democratic Caucus closed to the public and press, he
had let out all his venom about the bill, excoriating it in a bitter speech.
Danny didn't like that. Danny took that personally.

As it became more and more inevitable that Wright would become
Speaker, Wright's staff and Rostenkowski's staff, who got along well,
had dinner together to discuss minimizing tensions between their principals. Wright had the power to destroy Rostenkowski's chairmanship;
Rostenkowski had the power to make Wright's speakership more than
just difficult. Yet the two men continued to circle each other like two
Indians in a knife fight, tied together by a cord. The only thing preventing real fury between them was the fact that they were not equals.
Wright was Speaker. "I'm a Pole," Rostenkowski had once told a reporter. "The Poles are known to be pretty respectful—disciplined family, Catholic ties." In 1983 he had also said, "I work for the Speaker
and no one else." Back then O'Neill, Rostenkowski's old friend, had
been Speaker. Rostenkowski still believed in institutional loyalty, in a
hierarchy. But . . .

Rostenkowski's hierarchical sensibilities were torn. He was loyal to the Speaker, but also believed that the President, any President, set the agenda for the nation, and that no Speaker approached equality. To Rostenkowski, Wright's ambitions made him a usurper. "The congressional agenda is set by the President in his State of the Union speech," Rostenkowski said. "Nothing anybody else says changes that."

Besides the clash of his and Wright's ambitions and the clash of how each saw the speakership, they also had different views of the legislative process and the conflict between issues and solutions in politics. "The trouble with Danny," Wright said, "is he likes to win too much." By that Wright meant that he believed Rostenkowski would pull back rather than push, would compromise and call it victory, would settle for the smaller rather than attempt the larger.

Rostenkowski *would* rather do something smaller if he was certain it would become law, rather than something large that was likely to be vetoed. Rostenkowski, like most chairmen, saw the world differently from national figures who were trying to lead the nation. Chairmen felt rewarded by watching what they had wrought become law, not by activating the public and leading crusades. Chairmen had only legislative power; they liked to use it.

Legislators—and Rostenkowski was a legislator—wanted solutions. That was far different from being what John Dingell dismissed as "party apparatchiks," who exploited an issue for political gain rather than trying to solve it. Legislators were problem solvers, solution seekers. They did not deal in rhetoric or theory; they had to write real laws which had real effects on real people. If an issue was too large or complex to resolve, legislators, as Dingell said, "oftentimes will deal with a minute part of a problem." If an issue had to be compromised to pass and if principle was not involved, so be it. Half a loaf was better than none—it was a solution. Legislators did not play the same political games as those trying to *lead the nation*.

But for those interested in achieving or keeping power, or in using it to create great sweeping change, legislation could serve a different purpose: it could highlight an issue. The political gamesmen, the ones who tried to move the public, played a different game; they might prefer not compromising, avoiding a solution to an issue, if the issue was useful. They looked for votes, for power; they manipulated issues to win public support.

This, too, created tension between Wright and Rostenkowski. Rostenkowski thought little of the grand political strategists who tried to manipulate Congress to develop an issue. Wright wanted solutions. Yes, he was a legislator; but he had a larger, longer view than Rostenkowski. He was willing to push harder, endure more pain, fight more, and risk more to get what he wanted. Where Rostenkowski saw little point in moving legislation that would be vetoed, or killed in the Senate, Wright believed sometimes that was necessary to build support for the future, or, like a test pilot exploring the limits of a plane, to push the edge of the envelope and find out just what was possible.

And everywhere Wright seemed to be making inroads into Rostenkowski's domain. Rostenkowski got on Ways and Means originally not because of any interest in taxes or economics but because at the time it named members to other committees, which meant power inside the House. Everything about him was geared toward having power inside. But he watched Wright take over Steering and Policy and the whip organization, grudgingly admiring the moves, observing, "Now the whip meetings are a tool for total control. I can't complain. I'd do the same if I was Speaker."

Rostenkowski tried one last maneuver to create a power base for himself, pushing for the creation of a council of committee chairmen. If such a "chairmen's council" were set up, it would immediately become a power center independent of the Speaker, comparable to the assemblage of nobles which forced King John to sign the Magna Carta. Wright would not agree to its creation; he intended to meet with chairmen much more often than had O'Neill, but he would use the chairmen for his purposes. He would not be used by them.

Then Wright made a final inroad into Rostenkowski's domain. Rostenkowski regularly invited the men who ran the cloakroom, or the officers of the House, who were elected by the entire membership, to dinner—the sergeant at arms, the clerk, the postmaster (but not the doorkeeper, who wasn't one of his). It got him little favors that made him feel like a big man—a car picking him up at the airport, special treatment for a visiting constituent. Postmaster Robert Rota joked that he wouldn't tell his successor anything about the special projects he did for Rostenkowski, "so the next guy won't have to be anything but postmaster." Donnald Anderson, who ran the cloakroom, was a converted Catholic, and Rostenkowski was his godfather.

Anderson wanted to become clerk of the House in the 100th Congress, and for that he needed the Speaker's support. He sought that support, got it, then sat down with Rostenkowski in H-208, Rostenkowski's room, the one room that did not belong to Wright in that interminably long winding hallway that snakes around the east front of the Capitol.

Times changed. Rostenkowski, already with twenty-nine years in the House, was fifty-nine when Wright became Speaker. He had had dinner with the same half-dozen members night after night. One by one they had disappeared. Dying, retiring, losing. O'Neill was the last one left, the last real intimate. O'Neill was gone. One by one his closest aides had gone too. Jim Healey and Joe Dowley had worked for him for fifteen years, and Healey's father had sat next to him on the Commerce Committee a quarter century earlier. It took effort to get to know the new members. It took effort to find staff with whom one could be so intimate. He was tired. He didn't want to put out that kind of effort any more.

"What do you think Wright expects?" Rostenkowski asked Anderson.

"Absolute loyalty."

"That's right," Rostenkowski said slowly, enigmatically, drawing the words out, "and he should have it."

Wright was Speaker. Rostenkowski wasn't. *But by God he would run his own committee.*

One adversary Wright had to woo was the press. Once he had called reporters "enemies of government." The tension remained. Shortly before he formally became Speaker, a reporter said, "Mr. Wright, relations between the administration and Congress seem to be getting off on the wrong—" Wright interrupted, put his arm around the reporter, and smiled. But it wasn't friendly. "Well," Wright said, the smile frozen on his face, the killer smile which could intimidate and make one's skin crawl, "I'll tell you that relations between Jim Wright and the press aren't going to get off on the wrong foot and I'm not going to answer that."

Now he began to work at wooing reporters as he had wooed others, believing he could win over almost any enemy. He started inviting select groups of prominent columnists, talk-show regulars, and network reporters to dinners at his home. ABC's Sam Donaldson, *The Washington Post*'s Haynes Johnson, *The New York Times*'s Tom Wicker, *The New Yorker*'s Elizabeth Drew, and commentators Hodding Carter, Martin

Agronsky, David Gergen, and others of their ilk received invitations to his house or to a private lunch.

And despite confiding to a friend, "I'm feeling my way," he began to fill the engine of power he had constructed with himself.

The Clean Water bill was followed by a highway bill which would spend $90 billion, money already collected and sitting in a trust fund, on five years' worth of repairs. The House had passed it overwhelmingly the year before and Jim Howard, the Public Works chairman, had promised Wright to get the identical bill to the floor promptly. This time, though, there was a complication, and the first twist of an arm by Wright.

The highway bill was the kind of issue that, in the years before Wright, had nothing at all to do with partisan politics and induced yawns in the press and public. Geography and region had always dictated how members voted on such issues. But not this time.

Howard supported the fifty-five-mile-per-hour speed limit. It mattered to him; he was absolutely certain it saved lives. But Howard was from New Jersey. Westerners disliked the limit. Dave McCurdy of Oklahoma was leading a rebellion of Democrats who had reached out to the Republican leadership for help in changing it. The Republican leadership gleefully looked forward to cooperating. Anything that split the Democrats, that undercut Wright's authority, helped Republicans.

Such minor insurrections may have been the normal way of doing business under O'Neill, and certainly under Albert and McCormack, but not under Wright. A moderate Democrat, McCurdy was young, attractive, and tough. He had engineered the secret-ballot ouster of eighty-year-old Melvin Price from the Armed Services chairmanship two years earlier. In the closed Caucus, while a dozen members including O'Neill defended Price, only McCurdy spoke against him. But McCurdy did not want to take on the new Speaker. As Norman Mineta said, "Everyone's still trying to figure out how to establish a relationship with Wright. When he gets angry, no matter how close you think you are, he'll just turn on you. And yet the next day he's forgotten it all."

John Mack had already told McCurdy he had "screwed up." Then Wright ran into him in the Rayburn Room, the hall just off the House floor with sofas, chairs, and tables clustered in a dozen intimate meeting places where members huddle with lobbyists.

"Dave," Wright said gently, walking him to the cloakroom door.

"It's just awfully important that we get this bill into conference. We want to demonstrate that we can govern. I want you to focus on the fact it's not an arbitrary action of the chairman. It's exactly the bill the House passed last year after long debate. Jim Howard will be happy to give you some hearings on the speed limit."

The most pressure a Speaker can apply is to ask. It is a lot. Asking forced a member to declare himself. The only pressure more intense was to ask as a personal favor. McCurdy dropped his plan and the effort to change the speed limit disintegrated.

Coelho used the whip organization to maximize the vote for the bill. Some colleagues thought it foolish to press members on a bill certain to pass, but Wright and Coelho wanted to send a message to the White House. In the 99th Congress the House had passed the bill with 345 votes. This time it got 401, with only twenty opposed.

Simultaneously Wright pushed another bill, one in which he created something out of nothing, exercising power in a way not even a President could. The issue was the homeless.

Mitch Snyder, who ran a homeless shelter a few blocks from the Capitol, wanted the bill, too, and had constructed an illegal statue of a homeless family on the grounds of the Capitol. It had to come down. Otherwise every group, from the Klan to the communists, would demonstrate illegally.

But the statue had become a news event, and Snyder understood media power and was willing to take risks. In 1984 he had gone on a hunger strike to force the White House to give him a vacant federal warehouse for a homeless shelter; on the fifty-first day of his fast, two days before the election and with his death a real possibility, the White House had caved in. The Capitol police understood the media, too, and for weeks delayed using force to move the statue. It was January. On camera, Snyder always huddled up as if freezing. The Senate sergeant at arms, Henry Giugni, always appeared coatless, in shirt-sleeves. But the statue had to go.

Scheduled in a few days was a fund-raiser for Snyder featuring the actor Martin Sheen, who had played Snyder in a TV movie. Wright planned to offer a compromise: leave the statue up until after the fund-raiser. He sat down with Snyder one evening and said, "I understand you have a big event planned with Martin Sheen."

"No, sir," Snyder said. "That's just the money machine. The big event is meeting you."

Snyder understood power and wanted Wright's help on legislation. That was easy; Wright supported the bill anyway, and had already scheduled a vote on it for February 11. The statue would come down. Snyder invited Wright to visit his homeless shelter. Wright suggested they go right then.

"I wouldn't like that," Snyder replied. "I'd like to get some press out there."

They agreed to meet at ten-thirty the next morning, a Saturday, with the press. The publicity served everyone's purposes, but the visit moved Wright. The warehoused men and their vacant bitter eyes echoed the Depression, echoed the reasons he had entered politics. He left determined to do something now, right now, to help these people this year, this winter, this month.

Monday morning he called Appropriations chairman Jamie Whitten, and said he wanted money. How could he get it? Whitten, elected to Congress in 1941, found $50 million in an emergency fund. At one-thirty that afternoon, Whitten held an organizing meeting of his committee. At two-thirty he and his thirteen subcommittee chairmen, the so-called College of Cardinals, gathered in Wright's office and Wright asked for their help. Their response was the same as McCurdy's. *Yes.* A few days later, when the committee met to mark up an emergency homeless bill, its ranking Republican, Silvio Conte, sat in the committee room talking heatedly on the phone to the White House, hung up, and said, "The administration is opposed. But I wasn't listening too carefully and I might have got it wrong." With a laugh, he voted for the Democrats' bill. The House passed it 296–79, and once again not a single Democrat voted against Wright.

He was using power, all right. Washington would learn to expect it from him. He did not hesitate; he acted.

Even in the details he acted, understanding that the details, the agglomeration of a near-infinite number of details, determined victory. As the homeless bill began to move, something outside the House he was involved in began to fall apart.

The Council on Competitiveness, a high-level group formed to highlight international trade problems, had asked Wright to host a high-level, bipartisan conference on trade policy. It was to be a major event, scheduled for January 21. Wright had invited Michel, Dole, and Byrd; all had accepted. But the White House wanted to kill the conference because trade—"competitiveness" was the new buzzword—was to be central to Reagan's State of the Union speech six days later. The White House wanted Reagan to take over the issue.

Dole and Michel backed out of their acceptances. The Competitiveness Council withdrew its support unless the event was rescheduled after the State of the Union. One of Wright's aides walked into his office, gingerly reported the collapse of the conference, and recommended taking advantage of it by making it a Democratic event.

"I don't want this to be a Democratic thing," Wright snapped. "I want it to be a congressional thing." *That was part of his agenda, too, to dominate the agenda not just for his party but his institution.* "Does the White House think it can dictate to us when to hold a meeting and what we may discuss? These council people who came up with the idea are getting antsy? Well, they're going to get antsier. If they are now so craven as to run—"

He dialed the number of Alan Magazine, the director of the Competitiveness Council, and his voice turned velvety: "Well, Alan, let's end this confusion about this conference. I need your help . . . Either competitiveness is a serious problem or it isn't. . . . Now I have held out the olive branch, the hand of friendship, the open door to the Republicans . . . Every public utterance I make will say it is bipartisan."

Then Wright made clear the consequences: "It would be deeply, personally embarrassing if a suggestion were made to postpone the date. Once I set upon a course I don't like to be deterred from it . . . Yes, sir, Alan. I thank ye."

The council's sponsorship was back on. Wright had won. A small win, but a win. One week after the conference, *Time* magazine ran a photograph of him and Byrd from the conference, and described the White House as "in an if-you-can't-lick-'em-join-'em mood." Trade remained clearly a congressional initiative.

One element of power required throwing hundreds of Lilliputian lassos around issues and, sometimes, people. Wright had mastered that element.

Already he had begun to tie down his enemies. Three times already House Republicans had been forced to separate themselves from the White House, voting overwhelmingly against it on the Clean Water and highway bills, and splitting evenly on the emergency homeless bill. Private Democratic polls indicated that the public had started moving toward them. Republican polls confirmed those results. It showed. GOP chairman Frank Fahrenkopf and Senate GOP leader Bob Dole emerged from a meeting of the Republican National Committee talking about "compassion."

And already Wright's enemies, personal and political, were stirring.

Wright had two personal confrontations with Ronald Reagan which angered conservatives further. One confrontation occurred on national television, when Wright responded to Reagan's State of the Union address, and one was in private, in the Cabinet Room of the White House.

The morning of the State of the Union, Wright's hair had turned red again, no longer silver. No one at breakfast mentioned it. His press secretary, Charmayne Marsh, reviewed talking points from his speech to be given in advance to Democratic colleagues, so they could echo his theme to their local media. He had written the speech himself, his speech writers functioning more as glorified researchers, and now he went over it again, rehearsing it. In the intimacy of the cereal bowls on this breakfast table, it was powerful. But would it work on television? Much of the day he worked with a media consultant. The broadcast would be from Wright's ceremonial office immediately off the House floor; a new rug was brought in to improve the color scheme. Wright was fidgety at a run-through and complained to the TV crew, "You fellows all say, 'Relax, just talk as if you're sitting in someone's living room.' Then you tell us to sit in the most uncomfortable conceivable position."

The speech was live, in prime time. Wright's people worried that Reagan might make a surprise announcement, requiring a response. The White House had promised an advance copy of the speech to John Mack, but twenty minutes before the speech it had not yet arrived. Mack's nervousness increased. The press had already received advance copies, and a reporter offered one to Mack. Mack refused it, explaining he had made a deal: the White House had promised an advance copy, and they had promised not to seek copies elsewhere.

The only thing you have in politics is your word. Trust was an element of power, too, perhaps the most important element; it created a sense of stability and security.

A moment later the White House delivered the speech. It contained nothing new. Mack hurried onto the floor to give Wright that message while doorkeeper James Molloy announced, "Mr. Speaker! The Vice President of the United States and the gentlemen of the Senate! Mr.

Speaker! The diplomatic corps! Mr. Speaker! The Supreme Court! Mr. Speaker! The cabinet!" When Nancy Reagan took her seat in the gallery (Wright's wife, Betty, had been invited to join her; she had not wanted to accept but felt she had no choice; discovering she was not seated next to Nancy, she would not forget the slight) a standing ovation erupted. Only the packed press gallery remained silent. Then, promptly at nine, Molloy called out, "Mr. Speaker! The President of the United States!" Again, the entire chamber rose in a standing ovation, again except for the packed but silent press gallery.

Reagan soaked up the applause and looked physically well, despite surgery only a few weeks earlier. He began graciously, congratulating members of the 100th Congress and welcoming Wright to the speakership by quoting Eisenhower's welcome to Rayburn: " 'We shall have much to do together; I am sure that we shall get it done—and that we shall do it in harmony and goodwill.' "

But the mood of the chamber was restive. Democrats had listened to him for six years; now they felt new strength in themselves. Wright's aggressiveness had already made them bolder, and so had the Iran-contra scandal. They had little tolerance now for Reagan's rhetoric.

As he recited an agenda of trade, welfare reform, and insurance against catastrophic illness, items which, like Dole's talk of "compassion," reflected the polls' shift toward the Democrats, the members embraced his words. But then Reagan said, "There's more to do. For starters, the federal deficit is outrageous."

Democrats leaped to their feet in another standing ovation, a mocking, contemptuous eruption that confused Reagan, and suddenly Republicans too were on their feet, the chamber rocking back and forth as, like high school boys in an assembly playing out an inside joke, the cheers rolled from the Democratic side of the chamber to the Republican, and back.

The moment lasted, grew longer, Reagan still confused, and when he finally started again he was met by more mock applause. Inside the House, Republicans grew outraged over this lack of courtesy, lack of respect, and they would remember; Democrats grew contemptuous that Reagan, who had quadrupled the deficit, still played demagogue on the issue.

Reagan proceeded: "Now, let's talk about this year's budget. Even though I have submitted it within the Gramm-Rudman-Hollings deficit reduction target"—Democrats snickered; they considered this claim an outright lie—"I have seen suggestions that we might postpone that timetable. Well, I think the American people are tired of hearing the same old excuses. Together, we made a commitment to balance the budget. Now let's keep it. As for those suggestions that the answer is higher taxes, the American people have repeatedly rejected that shopworn advice. They know that we don't have deficits because people are taxed too little. We have deficits because the government spends too much."

Now only one side of the chamber, the Republican side, applauded.

Democrats had hoped that Reagan might make a new opening to work with the Congress. Instead he had closed off communication. His strategy was clear: he would sit back, point his finger at Democrats, and let them stew in his rhetoric.

The cameras followed Reagan as he exited shaking hands right and left. Wright quickly headed for his office for his response, and quickly got to the point: "The American people last November chose Democratic majorities to serve them in both houses of Congress. This doesn't mean that we have to pursue two years of unrelieved conflict. . . . Talk is not enough. What counts is action."

And he cited action—action Congress had already taken on the environment, on roads, on the homeless. He attacked Reagan's "gap between rhetoric and reality," scoring the fact that Reagan talked about education and drugs and international competitiveness, but was proposing a 28 percent spending cut on education, a spending cut on drug enforcement, and had blocked congressional action on trade. And Wright issued a carefully worded call for taxes: "We will be ready right now or at any time to sit down with the President and his top advisers to seek ways to stop piling up deficits by adopting a pay-as-you-go plan. No gimmicks. No selling off assets. No tampering with Social Security. Just get every annual appropriation and every source of revenue right out on the table and see if we can make them match."

Byrd talked of foreign policy bipartisanship and treaded gently past the Iran-contra scandal, then Wright closed. Afterwards, in his office, he watched himself on tape and was not happy; he had hoped to end the criticism of his TV persona. He believed he had failed.

But he did not dwell on it. The speech was important but not that important. Two weeks earlier, Democratic media advisers had tried to convince him to rescind his invitation to Byrd, and do the response himself. He had refused, saying, "It's more important that we have a good relationship with the Senate than that we have good theater."

Then, two days after the State of the Union address, the bipartisan House and Senate leadership went to the White House to see Reagan and his senior cabinet officers. They met in the Cabinet Room, around the large oval table, each chair belonging to a cabinet secretary. Wright sat on Reagan's right. The administration officials began laying out their plans for legislation on welfare reform and trade in so general a way that the Democrats agreed with everything they said. Then the talk shifted to the budget and the pleasantries disappeared. Defense Secretary Caspar Weinberger demanded a $27-billion increase in defense spending.

"Mr. President," Wright said, "I'm not sure you understand the problems we have." He explained that they had to have sixty-one billion dollars' worth of spending cuts or tax increases already, in order to reach the deficit target in the Gramm-Rudman-Hollings law. Reagan two nights before had just demanded they meet that target. Adding $27 billion for defense would mean $88 billion in other adjustments.

"The Russians have outspent us by $500 billion since 1973," Weinberger interjected.

"Cap, that's not what the Defense Intelligence Agency and the CIA say when they testify before the Intelligence Committee. They say Russian military spending has been just about flat," Wright replied. He and Weinberger eyed each other, each unyielding.

Reagan snapped, "Well, I'll give you a chance to save $20 billion tomorrow when I veto the Clean Water bill. That's almost enough for defense right there. Taxes aren't the answer."

"Mr. President, that's a nine-year authorization. That's only $2.25 billion a year." Wright's tone was patronizing; contempt showed in his eyes. The Republicans in the room stiffened. He added, "If you want more military spending, Mr. President, let's pay for it. The longer you refuse to confront reality, Mr. President, the harder it is going to be."

Reagan jerked erect. He was heated, angry. Reagan and O'Neill had had outright shouting matches over the years, but there was something colder and more implacable about Wright. The meeting ended. Wright put his hand on Reagan's shoulder, and said, "Mr. President, we hope that we may advise you with the same candor and frankness that we would if you were of our party. In the sanctity of this room we ought to be able to talk to one another in total candor."

But Wright's comment did not make peace. The entire meeting had played into the hands of conservatives who were urging Reagan to take a confrontational strategy for his final two years in office. They had no interest in working out solutions with the Congress. They wanted issues. Patrick Buchanan, for one, was not even interested in power, at least not in the sense of momentary dominance. He had just left his White House job but was publicly and privately still urging his views upon it. Like Wright, he believed Reagan's last two years could have immense impact on the future, and that what happened in the 100th Congress would resonate for years. Like Wright, he believed the stakes were high. He worried that compromise could eviscerate conservatism, dissipating its energy and focus and condemning it to the wilderness. Veto everything, he argued. All Reagan needed to win then was one-third plus one—the numbers needed to sustain a veto. And he would create a public record which conservatives could campaign on in the future. The hell with Iran-contra. Attack, attack, attack. Bring the government to a halt, if necessary. *Play to the crowd. The conservative crowd. Doing so would make it grow.* That was where the game would ultimately be won. Ignore dirtying one's hands with the legislative process.

The White House listened to that advice. On January 30, Reagan vetoed the Clean Water bill. It had passed the 99th Congress by a combined House-Senate vote of 504–0, and it had passed the 100th Congress, a few days earlier, 499–14. If Wright was willing to confront the White House even when it seemed he could not win, Reagan was willing to confront the Congress even when it seemed he could not win. The media war, the war of rhetoric, had started in December. Now the real war, the grinding, fixed-bayonet, trench warfare of making real policy, had begun as well. This war would prove real indeed.

Wright's speakership was coming into focus. It would be aggressive, and already there was an edge to it. One Republican commented, "Tip could come down off the rostrum and say, 'Lissen, ol' pal, I need you on this one.' It remains to be seen if Wright has the power of persuasion. He's ruling with fear. He used fear with McCurdy. He put his manhood on the line. That's using up your goodwill early. Then what?"

No Speaker in recent history, including Rayburn, had tried to *run* the House. O'Neill had let matters bubble up to him, had stopped well short of even testing the limits of his power. He didn't press on many things; he sensed and smelled the feelings of the membership and spent hours on the floor, just sitting there in one of the front rows, doing business, sifting through the bitching and moaning to sort out the tenor of the moment.

There was something inaccessible, something . . . *distant* about Wright. Compared to O'Neill, Wright rarely appeared on the floor. Already in the first weeks that difference was apparent. When he did appear he quickly grew annoyed at the members who would line up to see him, to invite him to their fund-raiser, to ask for a vacant room down the hall from their office, to ask him to have a word with the Rules Committee about making an amendment in order. He complained, "I'll be talking to one member, and someone else will come and interrupt as if I was just passing time, as if we weren't talking about something important."

And Wright intended to run the House. Unlike O'Neill, he would test his limits, push the edge of the envelope. When a senior colleague advised against embarking upon an uphill, possibly impossible task, Wright replied, "If you don't try, if you concede failure at the beginning, you will not succeed."

That attitude made Wright unpredictable. No one knew what he would do. There are few things solid and stable in politicians' lives; they like to feel they know where their leadership is. They do not like surprises. Trust is crucial to power and trust meant more than just keeping one's word; predictability was part of trust too. In a sense, that was what Reagan had given the country: a sense of stability which made people feel secure. Inside the House, O'Neill had given that to the members. *People wanted to know where Wright was. They wanted to understand him.*

One evening in his office Wright read a *Washington Post* story about Les Aspin, who had just won a fight to retain his chairmanship of Armed Services. Aspin had a Ph.D. in economics from MIT, and had worked on Kennedy's Council of Economic Advisers and as a Pentagon "whiz kid" under Defense Secretary Robert McNamara. He had a knack with the press, understood them, played to their egos, and for years had gotten good publicity by issuing press releases on Thursday or Friday, "embargoed"—meaning reporters could not write about them—until Monday's papers. (That gave reporters plenty of time to write and still take the weekend off, and, since little happened on weekends anyway, the stories got prominent display on Mondays.) Aspin laughed easily and literally clapped people on the back, but was close to no one. One night at dinner he had defined an extrovert as someone who starts a conversation on an airplane, adding, "Don't you hate that?" The *Post* quoted him as saying, "I naturally tend to deal with ideas and concepts and less naturally deal with people. To me, that's always been an acquired trait, a learned trait. Dealing with people is not a natural phenomenon." A colleague had added, "I'm probably one of his best friends and I don't know him that well."

Wright observed with some pain, "That's what they say about me."

It hurt him, this man who had worked so hard for so many years to make friends, this man who had lived in town after town growing up, who had always been the new boy in class. Who had always wanted people to accept him, to *like* him, whose mother had said after he eased up in a boxing match, *He'd rather have a friend than a victim*. At lunch one day in the crowded Members' Dining Room of the Capitol, he sat alone at a large round table waiting for his guests to appear; diners filled other tables but empty space surrounded him, as if an invisible barrier separated others from him. It seemed inconceivable that he, the Speaker, would not be flooded with a train of people paying court. And yet he sat. Alone. He was succeeding at things O'Neill had never thought to try. And yet . . . and yet . . . The clicking of silverware, the bustle of waiters, the business of the House swirled all about him. This was his, this room, this Capitol, all of it his, yet he was at the large empty table, glancing uncomfortably at the doorway, searching for the people meeting him, alone.

It hurt him, and it could hurt his hold on power in this institution.

The weekend after the State of the Union speech, the Democratic Caucus held its annual retreat at the Greenbrier, a resort in White Sulfur Springs, West Virginia. The setting was posh, elegant; the Greenbrier was self-contained, with its own golf course, its own shooting range, its own ice-skating rink, its own masseurs, its own stable. Other guests at the resort wore coats and ties for afternoon tea, semiformal dress for dinner, and children were rare.

But the members' retreat was self-contained even within the Greenbrier, secured by the Capitol police and the House sergeant at arms. Members paid $500 to take their wives and children, to swim with them in midwinter, get to know one another, and listen to political and academic experts. Sixty lobbyists paid $6,000 each as sponsors to go along, to pay for the special train carrying them all, to cozy up to members while they were relaxing. The money did not count as a campaign contribution; it was tax-deductible, and technically went to an educational foundation. Organizers never had any trouble lining up sponsors.

O'Neill had never attended: the retreat was started primarily by the insurgents he had no use for. Wright had always attended. This year he intended to use it to answer members' questions about him.

But on the train ride to the Greenbrier, members had something else to think about. A pay raise. In 1816, Congress raised its own pay from six dollars a day to $1,500 a year, and over half the House lost reelection, including every member from Ohio, Vermont, and Delaware. (The next Congress rescinded the increase.) Voting for a pay raise terrified members. But they wanted one. Since 1969, because Congress regularly exempted itself, senior administration officials, and federal judges from cost-of-living increases given to other federal employees, inflation had cut their real salaries by more than half. Two years earlier, Congress had tried to depoliticize the issue by creating a commission to set their pay. The commission's recommendations went to the President; he accepted or amended them, and the new salaries then automatically took effect unless both houses of Congress voted against them within thirty days. The whole idea was to avoid a vote.

Twenty-five days earlier the commission had recommended a pay increase from $77,400 to $135,000 (the Vice President, Speaker, and Supreme Court Chief Justice would get $175,000). Reagan had slashed the recommendations to $89,500 ($115,000 for the Chief Justice, the Speaker, and the Vice President).

Wright, Michel, Byrd, and Senate GOP leader Bob Dole had agreed to let the thirty-day clock expire, putting the pay raise into effect. It was not an example of Congress at its finest. But the day before House Democrats went to the Greenbrier, the Senate had voted 88–6 for a resolution killing the pay raise. It was pure hypocrisy; senators knew Wright would prevent a House vote. Senator John Glenn, an Ohio Democrat, called the action "an exercise in cowardice. It vexes me when I see what people really want and then see what they do. It was demagoguery—vote no and take the dough."

House members were furious at the Senate. Still, the vote was not a problem—Wright would simply block any similar House action until after the deadline. But later that night New Hampshire Republican senator Gordon Humphrey offered an amendment to the emergency homeless bill disallowing the raise. Senators had to vote for it. This was a problem.

Wright wanted the homeless bill *passed*. And the symbolism was terrible: wrangling over a $12,100 raise for themselves while delaying an emergency bill for the homeless. Political commentators would justifiably devastate them for that. Privately, Wright observed, "If members don't have the courage to vote for it they don't deserve it."

On the train Wright told a reporter that the House would vote on the Senate's version of the homeless bill; if the House wanted a pay raise, members would have to vote for it. As word of Wright's statement spread, members' fury switched from the Senate to him. Real bitterness was developing. One angry member snapped, "The Speaker already got his raise"—$15,000 upon becoming Speaker. Another hissed, "If this doesn't go through Wright's going to be a one-term Speaker!" John Dingell's wife, Debbie, herself independently wealthy, an automotive heiress, started organizing congressional wives to pressure their husbands in case they did have to vote. When one member told his wife to calm down, she exploded, "You calm down! You calm down! You want to keep this job you love so much? The kids will be going to college. We can't go out to a decent restaurant. You calm down, dammit."

At the Greenbrier Foley, Coelho, other members, and Mack filled Wright's posh room and urged him to back down. Finally he did, washing his hands of it and telling Foley, "Anything you do is all right with me, as long as the homeless bill passes promptly."

That was good enough. Suddenly the membership was reassured, and relaxed. The retreat lasted three days. One member's wife, from California, demanded that the hotel change their room from one with twin beds to a king: "I'm not going to see my husband for a month and I'm not spending this weekend in twin beds." Political consultants and economists gave presentations. Mack won the trap-shooting contest.

But bile continued to pour out toward the Senate. The repercussions could destroy the close working relationship necessary to accomplish Wright's goals. Members didn't like the Senate anyway. Senators generally knew less substance, and relied more on staff, than House members. Partly that was because senators had more committee assignments, since a similar workload was divided among 100 instead of 435 people, and partly it was because they had more constituents to deal with. Senators and even their staffs often acted arrogantly toward the House. Foley grew outraged whenever he recalled a Senate aide who tried to prevent Speaker of the House John McCormack from getting on a "Senators Only" elevator. And the House had a dozen contemptuous one-liners representing their feelings: *Any member of the House who leaves for the Senate raises the average intelligence of both bodies . . . The number of prima donnas in each body is the same—one hundred . . . If a presidential election was decided by secret Senate ballot there would be a one-hundred-way tie.*

Now members accused Byrd of breaking his word: he had promised to prevent a vote. Coelho publicly derided the Senate as "a millionaires' club. The Senators are the lords. They have the six-year terms. They are supposed to have the luxury of taking care of the institution. Those of us with the two-year terms end up taking care of the institution." Foley publicly congratulated Wright on his State of the Union response, and added, "I only wish he could have given it alone"—a pointed slap at Byrd and an extraordinary comment for the deliberative Foley to make. To insiders, Foley's rebuke was, if anything, *stronger* than that of a House committee chairman who said, "Assholes. Goddamn fucking cowardly assholes."

The first night at Greenbrier, Friday, at midnight Byrd called Wright to apologize for the Senate vote. Senate rules simply did not allow him to prevent it. Wright replied evenly, "It's done, Bob, it puts us in an untenable position, but you can't undo it. You've given me a problem, but we'll handle it." Byrd called again Saturday night, apologizing again. Wright meanwhile let Coelho know his comments were not helping Democrats.

Sunday at lunch, the last event, Wright exposed himself to his colleagues in a speech. It was unlike any he had given before. It was personal. If members were saying they did not know him, did not know anything about his life, now he told them and tried with words to bridge the gap between him and his colleagues. He wove the personal into a speech about the House, how he loved it, what it meant to him. He told stories of his father, his children, letting colleagues know that he understood how their jobs were tough on their families. "We do try to focus on the quality of life"—getting them home for dinner more, and more regularity in schedules. He tried to build a sense of collegiality and of pride in the House. Then he warned, "I know I speak for all of you when I say we will brook no interference [with] the agenda we have promised the American people. We're not going to be combative. We are going to be firm. We're going to act and we're going to achieve."

Meanwhile, Foley had worked out a plan to delay a vote on the Senate bill including the pay-raise cancellation until Wednesday. That would be one day after the thirty-day clock expired, meaning that the raise would take effect. On Tuesday, the House suddenly moved to adjourn. Connie Mack, a Florida Republican who was running for a Senate seat, tried to block the maneuver and demanded a recorded vote on adjournment—a vote which pay-raise opponents could use as a campaign issue. But the Republican leadership was working with Foley. To force a recorded vote required one-fifth of a quorum, forty-four members. Only sixteen stood. *Bang!* went the gavel. The pay raise took effect. The next day the House by voice vote accepted the Senate version of the emergency homeless bill including the provision killing the pay raise. But the deadline had already expired. The pay raise counted. (Courts subsequently dismissed suits to block it.)

That evening the House parliamentarian brought the bill to Wright at the Kennedy Center, where he was playing a celebrity corpse in a production of *Arsenic and Old Lace*. Wright signed it, formally "enrolling" the bill. The parliamentarian took it straight to the White House.

Earlier that day, House and Senate leadership staffs had met to discuss the agenda of the next meeting between their bosses. Byrd's people asked that the pay raise not be discussed. Wright's people said, "Oh, it will be discussed, all right." They joked about it, but the House staff got their message across. *Understand this. If the Senate sends over a bill calling for a rollback of the pay raise, we're going to attach a limit on honoraria.* (The Senate allowed its members to accept honoraria equal to 40 percent of their pay; the House limited its members to 30 percent.) That would mean that not only would everyone lose the raise, but senators would see their total income cut. *You understand that? Do you? Make sure your smart-ass bosses get that message.* The message took. For the remaining two years of the Congress, despite predictions in the press that moves to roll back the pay raise would come up again and again, the issue disappeared.

The pay-raise issue showed Congress at its worst—afraid of the voters. Members had never been noted for their courage, but this went a step further. It was a small symptom of the new breed of congressmen and women with whom Wright had to deal. Members were in closer touch than ever with their districts, and less inclined than ever to stand up to them. That was particularly true of the class of 1974; seventy-five Democrats entered the House then, in the wake of Watergate. Two-thirds of them won in Republican districts; they had been expected to lose those seats in 1976, but their responsiveness to their districts and their use of campaign technology kept them in office. Rayburn had always said members should not fear their districts. Wright remembered that well. But the bulk of the Caucus had never heard Rayburn.

The issue also showed something else—Wright's willingness to force things on members which they did not want. In this case he had wanted them to vote on a pay raise; in the face of unanimous and intense opposition, he had backed off and left the issue to others. But other issues he would not leave to others.

In the end he got credit. Members got their raise and got to vote no, too. One senior House aide said, "A lot of these guys think that's what the leadership is for, to take care of them. Wright earned himself months of goodwill getting members their pay raise. Months. Don't take that lightly. These guys all have wives and families. And if he hadn't gotten it, he'd have been in trouble."

CHAPTER 5

While the pay-raise issue simmered, the House voted 401–26 to override Reagan's veto of the Clean Water bill. The next day the Senate overrode it 86–14. The Clean Water bill was law.

Simultaneously, other events indicated there would be no cooperation with the White House, only more collision.

After Wright's confrontation with Reagan in the Cabinet Room, White House chief of staff Donald Regan tried the ancient strategy of divide and conquer, tried to maneuver around Wright. Regan invited Byrd and other Senate leaders to the White House to discuss Reagan's trade agenda. Without Wright. Given the pay-raise problem, Byrd would do nothing that might antagonize Wright. He declined. The administration then invited Foley, Rostenkowski, and other House members to a meeting—but not Wright. Rostenkowski called him, asked what was going on, then snorted, "Who the hell do they think they are?"

The incident made Wright both wary and contemptuous of the entire White House operation. He began the slow process of moving his own agenda through the Congress, now in total defiance of it.

Domestic policy came first. The budget deficit frustrated him, was an almost personal enemy, and an implacable one. It was policy yet went beyond policy. Few things, perhaps nothing, mattered more to him than being his own man. It was a question of honor. Owing people prevented that. Owing money prevented that. *Interest meant enslavement. He hated debt.* He repeatedly said in speeches, "We have to stop sending our bills to our grandchildren," and to him it was a moral issue.

Jimmy Carter's highest deficit was $73 billion; Reagan ran repeated deficits over $200 billion. When Reagan took office the national debt was $794 billion and had taken 191 years, from George Washington to Jimmy Carter, to accumulate; in six years under Reagan it rose to $2.3 trillion, and would approach $3 trillion by the time he left office. It was an immense, staggering number. Interest on the debt was the fastest-growing part of the budget, faster than defense, faster than Social Security, faster than Medicare. Over a five-year period, Reagan had cut taxes $660 billion, and raised defense spending roughly that much. He had also slashed domestic spending by $295 billion, but the increase in interest payments alone dwarfed the domestic cuts. The largest tax increase in history, passed in 1982 to recover some of the giveaways of the year before, barely dented the deficit. Another tax increase in 1984 could not even keep up with the deficit's growth. Social Security, Medicare, and interest payments continued to grow, continued to force cuts elsewhere just to stay even, much less bring the deficit down. *Policy had to change.* Wright argued that taxes were "not a question of economics. They're arithmetic."

To some conservative intellectuals, though, the deficit proved useful. They did not actually care about the deficit; they cared about, and wanted to shrink, the size of government, limiting its role to national defense. Trusting the free-market system totally, they wanted to remove the government from the economy almost entirely—the more extreme even wanted to stop the government from controlling the money supply or printing money, preferring a private currency printed by banks. Given a choice between a smaller government with a large deficit, and a larger government with no deficit, these conservatives would choose the small government/big deficit combination. That position provided the intellectual underpinning to the argument that increasing taxes did not cut the deficit, but only allowed government to spend more. Office of Management and Budget director James Miller, a former economics professor, represented that intellectual viewpoint inside the White House, and OMB was the White House agency which wrote the administration budget. Reagan shared this view in an unsophisticated but visceral way, and his comment, in his first Inaugural Address, that "government is the problem" epitomized it.

Wright's view that government should intervene in the economy, creating opportunity through everything from student loans to urban redevelopment, could not have been more different. So much, he believed, needed doing. Nor, like the plains populist he was, did he fully trust the markets. Hadn't unregulated markets led to the Great Depression? Yet the limits imposed by the deficit blocked him at every turn, choked off his initiatives, suffocated him. *There was no money. Not for anything.* With great hoopla, for example, Congress had passed a drug bill warmly embraced by Reagan, but his budget even cut antidrug spending. That was typical of the rest of Reagan's budget.

Beyond the direct impact on government programs, Wright worried that the budget deficit would eviscerate the American economy. If the deficit lacked drama, it did so only because it killed by slow erosion; it was like a man who drank too much—perhaps not enough to destroy his life, just enough to destroy the promise of his life.

Real interest rates—the difference between inflation and the nominal interest rate—under Reagan rose to historic highs, and stayed there. Traditionally, real interest rates in the United States had run 3–4 percent; under Reagan they ran 6–8 percent. Didn't the deficit cause that? And the budget deficit contributed directly to the trade deficit; each stood at roughly $170 billion when Wright became Speaker. Narrowing the trade deficit meant lowering the standard of living for Americans, and also could lead to an increase in inflation.

Had the federal deficit been spent on education, or the infrastructure, or research, it would have constituted investment and likely would have earned returns over time, would have increased economic activity in the future. But the government was in effect borrowing to eat, spending on consumption, on buying airplanes and making "transfer payments," as economists called them, to farmers for price supports, to welfare and Social Security recipients.

The economy was performing well, but it was doing it on borrowed money. Possibly the country could escape a reckoning, but there was no margin for error. Foreign investors were financing the deficit by buying Treasury bills. If they stopped, interest rates would have to rise to attract them back. That jeopardized the entire economy. And the economy carried a debt burden of $11 trillion, proportionate to the debt burden in the 1920s, and paying interest on that debt cost roughly $1 trillion, or one-quarter of the $4-trillion gross national product. For every point that interest rates rose, GNP had to grow .25 percent just to keep pace, to keep interest payments from taking an increasing proportion of the nation's production. It was catch-22: higher rates made growth harder. Americans might someday have to choose between running on a treadmill to pay off creditors, or creating a massive inflation to devalue the debt.

There was no money. The deficit had to come down.

To the Democrats' frustration, Reagan's repeated calls for a balanced-budget amendment, his repeated demands that Congress cut spending and not raise taxes, seemed to protect him from blame for the deficit. There were two reasons: First, there was truth to the "tax and spend" sobriquet he threw at Democrats. Ever since the New Deal, Democrats had been identified with spending programs, Republicans with opposing them. It was difficult for Democrats to convince the public that White House policies had transformed the deficit into a potential nightmare. Second, the economy continued to expand. The damage from the deficit was subtle and long-term.

The budget presented another, specific problem: the Gramm-Rudman-Hollings law, named after Democratic senator Fritz Hollings of South Carolina and Republican senators Warren Rudman of New Hampshire and Phil Gramm of Texas. (Wright despised Gramm; as a House Democrat in 1981, Gramm attended private Democratic strategy sessions, then reported on the meetings to the White House, and later switched parties and went to the Senate.) The law, known as just Gramm-Rudman, was based on the "public choice" theory for which economist James Buchanan won a Nobel Prize in 1986. In essence, the theory stated that government could not make choices which would offend voters, and that neither Congress nor the White House was capable of making specific cuts necessary to lower the deficit. Gramm, a former economics professor, subscribed to the theory, and changed this political equation by using Gramm-Rudman to write into law annual, declining targets for the deficit, which would bring the deficit down to zero in 1991.

If Congress and the President failed to agree on how to reach the target, an axe would fall. This axe was called "sequestration." If the deficit exceeded the targets written into the law, sequestration would automatically make across-the-board cuts to lower the deficit to the target. Exempt were programs for the poor, Social Security, and interest payments, over 40 percent of the budget; the burden of any cuts was split between defense and domestic spending.

Sequestration was a terrible way to cut spending. It set no priorities and did not differentiate between cancer research and a deputy assistant secretary's trip to Paris for a conference. In fact, the idea was that sequestration was so awful that to avoid it, politicians would choose priorities and cut the deficit on their own.

In Wright's first year as Speaker, the deficit target was $108 billion. But the Gramm-Rudman law had made a serious miscalculation. Its targets fell at an annual rate of $36 billion, but its starting point was skewed. The law assumed that the 100th Congress would start with a deficit of $144 billion; cutting $36 billion would yield the target of $108 billion. In reality, the 100th Congress was starting with a deficit of over $170 billion. But the law still required Congress to cut enough to reach $108 billion. Instead of cutting $36 billion, Congress would have to cut between $60 and $65 billion. It could not be done. Not in the real world.

The White House claimed that its budget reached the $108-billion target and insisted that Congress do so. But the White House was, in essence, lying. OMB claimed the deficit was only $150 billion—even though its own internal memos put the deficit near $170 billion—and that its proposals would cut $42 billion from it. But internal OMB memos recognized the fact that the White House budget actually missed the Gramm-Rudman target by $28 billion.

The White House was playing politics. It could afford to because of one final complication: the Supreme Court had ruled that sequestration was unconstitutional. That meant sequestration could not axe defense spending. The only issue, then, was a rhetorical one. The winner would be the one who had the best rhetoric, the one most successful at blaming the other side for irresponsibility. Mondale had tried to blame Reagan and lost forty-nine states. Republicans were already blasting "tax and spend" Democrats, and arguing that the President does not spend one dime, that every penny the government spends is spent by Congress, and therefore Congress must be responsible for the deficit.

The Democrats' rebuttal was to tell the public that the administration's "economic assumptions" were flawed. *Good luck*.

The budget included roughly $300 billion in defense spending, $300 billion in Medicare and Social Security, $150 billion for interest, and $300 billion for everything else—college loans, drug enforcement, AIDS research, farmers, welfare, the space program, the FBI, the weather bureau, job training, air-traffic control. Everything. During

Reagan's administration, the "everything else" had already been slashed by over 20 percent. Taking another 20 percent out of it in one year was impossible. And so Wright wanted to raise taxes.

There was little room left in the budget to play tricks. In fact, previous tricks were haunting this year's budget. The year before, the Pentagon had cut spending by moving one payday from September 30 to October 1, from one fiscal year to the next; that had cut the deficit that year, but increased it now. Hundreds of similar games had played themselves out. At the first caucus of House Budget Committee Democrats, Californian George Miller said, "We've run out of time. This *is* next year."

Congress prepared its own "budget resolution." It was solely a congressional document. The President had no say in it, did not sign it, could not veto it. It was a declaration of congressional policy and signified the power of the congressional leadership. Wright wanted the budget to serve as a political statement, a policy statement almost like a party platform. Republicans did not set policy in a Democratic-controlled House. Congress had been passing budgets only since 1974 but no budget had ever moved through the House in bipartisan fashion.

If Republicans could block the Democrats' budget, they could destroy Wright's efforts to govern through the Congress. Such a failure could mock all his ambitions, break the Democratic Party into factions, and leave those factions squabbling on the House floor.

Success or failure depended on the Budget Committee, a committee whose members represented every constituency of the Democratic Caucus, and included some of the most important junior members of the House. All members of Budget had campaigned for the assignment; it was where the action was, and, to spread that action around, members were limited to six consecutive years on the committee. Most Democrats on it were themselves good inside players, and represented constituencies within the Caucus. They could not be steamrolled inside the committee, but if they could agree on a budget they could bring the rest of the party along with them.

The chairman was William Gray III, a black Baptist minister from Philadelphia. Tall, attractive, slick, he and Wright often would quote line after line from Scripture at each other, and then smile. Gray was elected to Congress in 1978, and during the 1983 budget fight he worked out a deal that allowed both liberals and conservatives to claim victory. One year later he won the committee chairmanship. He talked fast, had a way with words, and like all good chairmen allowed others, on their own, to reach his conclusion.

Razzle-dazzle, showmanship, was his game. In 1986, he broke with tradition and allowed the Republican-controlled Senate to pass its budget first, then put a budget together with more savings. On the floor, only fifteen Democrats voted against it, the best showing ever. Ambitious, an inside player, in 1984 a backer of Walter Mondale, not Jesse Jackson, for President, a man with an audience in search of a larger one, he used the committee to elevate himself to the front rank of party spokesmen on economic issues. He was black but did not threaten "white folk," as Gray put it; he was a black whom whites had plans for, a man Democratic professionals could be comfortable with some day as, say, a vice-presidential candidate or secretary of the Treasury. There was around him a certain sense that somewhere down the road something good would happen to him. But underneath all his ambition, all his laughter, all his joshing with white folks, he knew he was black. Two Sundays a month he went home to preach at his church. He knew his district was black and his congregation was black and that black America did not fare so well as he did in white America. If his edge was beveled, still the edge was there. He almost never revealed this edge to members, but staff and lobbyists often felt it; so did corporate executives, who would find him reasonable, reasonable, then suddenly vicious and bitter.

O'Neill had not gotten personally involved in the budget, except at the last minute to referee disputes, and had left things to the chairman. Wright's approach was different, and the stakes were higher. On February 2, Wright hosted a lunch for Budget Committee Democrats in H-122, the Speaker's Dining Room, a chandelier-heavy room on the first floor of the Capitol, down a corridor with ceiling frescoes illustrating the history of the Capitol building—its burning by the British in 1814, its use as a hospital in 1865. The room was crowded, too small really for this large a group, and staff stood in every corner.

Gray quickly got to the point: "Let me be candid. We need leadership guidance. If there won't be substantial revenues, Mr. Speaker, we need to know now. If you oppose asset sales, we need to know now. There ain't but two choices, raise taxes and cut spending. It ain't fun, folks. Even Reagan called for $21 billion in revenues—he just doesn't call them taxes, or he wants to sell off everything the government owns."

Florida congressman Buddy MacKay, who was key to the votes of moderates, said, "Fifty percent of the American people believe the deficit is our fault. We've got to confront the White House. We've got to set a confrontation in motion so the press will explain things to the American people. This is not the year to let the thing go on. This is the year we force a confrontation."

A member disagreed. The discussion grew heated. One member shouted, another shouted back. Wright had expected this to be difficult, contentious, but not like this. The deficit was doing this, was forcing Democrats to tear at one another. His own initiatives would be jeopardized. This meeting was not moving toward a resolution; it was moving away from one. He could sense the dangers in this issue, for him personally and for the party. Suddenly Wright was red-faced, angry, and the room grew quiet.

"At the Greenbrier," he said, "one member's wife was almost in tears. She said children [at the National Institutes of Health] who are there dying of cancer have always been able to call home to talk to their parents. But NIH cut out those phone calls. Too expensive. For little children dying of cancer to call home! She wanted me to do something about it."

"We don't have real power on this committee," one man said. "We've got to find out what the people with the power want. That's you, Mr. Speaker. We've got to find out what the rules are."

Wright stiffened, then continued. "*Let me tell you something.* I'm convinced the public is ready for Democrats to be Democrats again, and not be Republicans. Don't shy away from taxes."

House Democrats, and Wright, had another agenda besides their economic one. They intended to bring the White House to heel on foreign policy, and particularly in Central America. This continued an institutional shift of power toward the House and away from both the Executive Branch and the Senate. The House traditionally had had little impact on foreign policy. Even during Vietnam, while nationally televised Senate hearings explored every facet of America's involvement in the war, Speaker John McCormack and the conservative Rules Committee blocked liberals for years from getting a vote on any aspect of it. Unlike the Senate, the House had no "advise and consent" role. But in the early 1980s House liberals became intimately involved in both Central America and arms-control issues by limiting uses of appropriated funds. Wright intended to expand the House role.

His involvement began slowly, well within the context of precedent. He had visited Latin America regularly over many years, knew it well, and had even addressed, in Spanish, several Central and South American parliaments. He had also served on the Kissinger Commission, which was created by Reagan in 1982 in an effort to forge a bipartisan policy on Central America.

The issue was Nicaragua. Marxists—the Sandinistas—governed Nicaragua, had suspended the free press, and held political prisoners; they also had supported revolutionaries in other countries. Ostensibly to force democratic reforms in Nicaragua, the administration had created and was supporting a guerrilla force, the contras, and the CIA had mined Nicaraguan harbors. In reaction, Congress passed a series of laws known cumulatively as the Boland Amendment, after Edward Boland, chairman of a key House Appropriations subcommittee, prohibiting any agency of the government involved in intelligence from helping the contras. Led by the National Security Council and White House aide Lieutenant Colonel Oliver North, the administration continued to help the contras anyway, claiming that the NSC was not involved in intelligence, and therefore not covered by the law.

To both liberals and conservatives the issue was a matter of conscience. Liberals saw the contras as murderers conducting an illegal, proxy war which fouled the United States with blood. They had to stop it. And morality aside, they had reasons of state to oppose the contras: they worried that U.S. involvement could escalate into another Vietnam. Once the Sandinistas stopped exporting revolution—the evidence seemed to support their claims that they had—liberals believed the United States should leave them alone.

Conservatives had their own moral justification: freedom mattered more than peace. Freedom was one thing worth fighting, and dying, for. The United States, by sponsoring the contras, had committed itself to them; this time, for once, the United States would stick with its commitment, would not walk away, as conservatives believed America had done from the Bay of Pigs, from Vietnam, from the Kurds. And conservatives worried that Nicaragua would spread revolution throughout Latin America, even north to Mexico.

Congress voted over and over on the issue of sending money to the contras without resolution, for neither the White House nor their congressional opponents would yield. Neither side could win a decisive vote. House Democrats, overwhelmingly, opposed military aid; Republicans overwhelmingly supported it. The issue was important enough that chief deputy whip David Bonior devoted roughly half of all his time to it, an extraordinary amount of time for any member of Congress to spend on a single issue.

It was perhaps the one issue over which a speakership could be lost, the one issue in which some professional politicians, not just extremist activists, would do anything to win. It was a dangerous game. Indeed, it was not a game.

In February, as Congress was overriding Reagan's Clean Water Act veto, the presidents of Honduras, Guatemala, and El Salvador endorsed in principle a peace proposal made by Oscar Arias, president of Costa Rica, a country with the strongest democratic tradition in the region. Arias called for the end of military aid to all guerrillas in Central America from outside sources—including aid to the contras from the United States—in return for total democratization. Nicaraguan officials called the plan "lamentable" because it demanded extreme changes inside their country. The Sandinistas' disapproval was enough to win support for the Arias plan from conservatives in the United States; the Senate passed a resolution endorsing it by 97–1, with even extreme conservative Jesse Helms voting yes. It was the type of purely political resolution that frequently cluttered the Senate floor; events would later show how little the Senate's endorsement meant, even to the Senate.

In the House, Bob Michel suggested delaying any administration request for new military aid to see what came of the Arias plan. Bonior and a handful of colleagues traveled to Central America to discuss the plan with several of the presidents. The administration itself seemed about to embrace the proposal until Nicaraguan president Daniel Ortega agreed to meet at a later, unspecified date with the other four presidents to discuss it.

At the same time, Louis Stokes, chairman of the House Intelligence Committee, came to Wright with some information. Oliver North had intercepted diplomatic communications between the Nicaraguan embassy in Washington and its capital, Managua. One embassy communication had analyzed contra-aid politics and concluded that Wright was the key to ending or continuing contra aid. North had suggested to Robert McFarlane, then national security adviser, that the White House blackmail Wright—threaten to leak the document to the press and imply that Wright was working with the Sandinistas, unless Wright hardened his line. McFarlane had dismissed the idea out of hand. Wright was disgusted and outraged. He told no one of what Stokes had said, but the information strengthened his resolve to reverse the administration's policy.

The first opportunity was coming soon. The year before, Congress had approved $100 million in military aid for the contras, but only $60 million of that money had been spent. Before the last $40 million was delivered, Congress would vote again. The vote was pro forma as far as substance went. To stop that money from flowing, Congress would not only first have to reject sending the aid, it would also have to override a certain Presidential veto. That was impossible. The contras would get the $40 million.

The vote, though, would serve another purpose. It was one move in the chess game to defeat an administration request for more money that would come later this year.

Dave Bonior walked into Wright's office alone and sat down in an armchair, in the small cluster of comfort beside Wright's desk. "I think what we ought to do is go for a vote on a moratorium instead of a straight-up-or-down vote," he announced.

Wright raised his eyebrows. What Bonior proposed violated a law passed less than a year earlier, a law which stipulated that within fifteen days after the President called for the $40 million both houses had to have a straight yes-or-no vote. *It was the law.* Bonior was planning to ignore that law, to evade the yes-or-no vote requirement.

He and a handful of colleagues had worked out a parliamentary maneuver to make the vote on a moratorium, a delay in delivering the money, until all prior funds were accounted for. That took political advantage of all the questions about Swiss bank accounts raised by the Iran-contra scandal. It also made it easier for members to vote against the White House than a straight "no" vote; members could defend themselves more easily against pro-contra activists. Lastly, it created a slope down which members could slide to the fall, when a new military-aid request would be presented. That vote *would* be straight up or down, yes or no. One or two members could decide it, and a "half-no" vote now made it easier for them to vote "no" later. Bonior wanted to exploit every possible edge. He could get away with it because the Constitution gave each house the power to write its own rules; the Rules Committee would simply write a rule for the bill ignoring the law and turning the issue into a moratorium vote. It was the Speaker's call.

"To be honest," Bonior continued, "Foley doesn't want to do it."

Tom Foley was concerned with the GOP reaction. The parliamentary gimmickry would inflame House Republicans; they would scream about abuse of the process, abuse of power. But the White House was ignoring the law too; before delivering more aid, the administration had to certify that diplomacy had no chance to work. The Arias plan was a viable diplomatic effort with a chance to work. The administration was simply pretending it did not exist.

"What kind of numbers do you think we'll get?" Wright asked.

"I think the moratorium will maximize our vote and give our opponents the most difficulty," Bonior said. He had a reputation as a fairly easygoing guy, but that image belied a toughness; he did not hesitate to press and exploit any advantage, or to go for the throat. Wright had wanted someone tough in his job; he had chosen well. Bonior did not want to let his opponents breathe, or have a chance to breathe. He added, "It can build a nice bridge to moderates voting 'no' later."

This was the first decision of Wright's speakership that would reveal the kind of House he intended to lead. Rejecting Bonior's maneuver would mean he would allow the House to work its will. Manipulating procedure meant he would drive his agenda, and that of the Caucus, through the House.

A few weeks earlier, as a joke, Wright had been given a pair of brass balls which he kept on top of the desk. Wright picked them up and held one in each hand, as if weighing them.

"Who's the lead sponsor?" he asked.

"Don't know yet. Maybe Tom if he's willing."

"Make it Tom or yourself."

Foley became lead sponsor of the moratorium proposal he had opposed. *There's only one king,* he had said, *the Speaker.* Even some Democrats objected to the procedure. At a formal meeting of the Democratic Caucus in the House chamber, one member called it "duplicitous." Another complained, "It's a cheap shot."

But it worked. A few days before the vote, the leadership met again.

Bonior was smiling: "We're picking up people we never had. Dyson. Sisisky. The moratorium is turning people up we never saw before. The rule—" which allowed the maneuver, and which would be voted on before the bill—"will be a tough fight though. The President is making calls today. Maybe you can too."

"Let's do it," Wright said, and he picked up the phone.

The morning of the vote the Republican Conference met. Earlier, when the Rules Committee approved the moratorium maneuver, Trent Lott, the GOP whip who also served on Rules, had snapped, "I view this whole process as a sham." *The Democrats were screwing with procedure, screwing them.* Incensed, the Republicans came together; in retaliation they would paint the Democrats as soft on communism. Henry Hyde distributed copies of talking points, later repeated and repeated by GOP colleagues on the floor, accusing the Democrats of "handing Central America over to the Soviet Union." The attack was harsh, harsher than generally heard, and was directed at television—the two million or more people watching House proceedings at a given moment on cable, and network news producers who might use a brief sound bite. And an angry Bill Pitts, Michel's senior aide and an architect of much GOP floor strategy, warned, "If the Democrats want to play it straight, we'll play it straight. If they want to engage us in games, we'll engage them. And we *will* engage them."

On the floor later the battle began when Michel stood and sought recognition from the chair. Then Bonior rose. The floor was almost empty, only a couple of dozen members scattered about, and the two men stood there, Michel staring across the rows of seats at Bonior, Bonior staring back. Tension coursed between them, a tension nonetheless passionate for the constrained language in which it was expressed.

"The chair recognizes the gentleman from Michigan," Wright said calmly. *Bonior. Bonior was the gentleman from Michigan.*

"Mr. Speaker," Bonior said, "by direction of the Committee on Rules I call up House Resolution 116 and ask for its immediate consideration."

"Mr. Speaker," Michel interrupted. "I have a parliamentary inquiry." Only a parliamentary inquiry could block Bonior now.

"The gentleman will state it."

"Mr. Speaker, I was on my feet seeking recognition in order that I might call up a highly privileged motion." Privilege meant that it took precedence over other legislative activity and required an immediate vote; the contra-aid proposal was privileged. "Is the Chair going to recognize a member of the Rules Committee before entertaining my motion, notwithstanding the provisions of law making my resolution a highly privileged one?"

Wright had prepared for this. Before him was the contra-aid law itself and he quoted from it: " 'The procedures were enacted into law, with the full recognition of the constitutional right of the House and the Senate to change their rules at any time. The statute itself [agrees with] clause 4b of [House] Rule XI that 'It shall always be in order to call up for consideration a rule.' " Then he began to cite precedent. "And so, the chair recognizes the gentleman from Michigan."

Michel's words concealed his frustration: "This gentleman knows the rules of the House, too, and one can never appeal the Speaker's power of recognition. I respect the Speaker's ruling in this case."

But his colleagues seethed. *The law said we could vote, dammit. The law said Michel could offer the motion.* Lott now was on his feet, his eyes narrowing, intense, his words tightly constrained by the forced courtesy of the floor. "Mr. Speaker, I rise to a question of the privileges of the House and I offer a resolution."

"As indicated on page 337 of the House manual," Wright replied, "the privileges of the House may not be invoked in any way that infringes [upon the Speaker's] discretionary power of recognition. . . . And therefore the Chair rules that the matter is not a matter of the privileges of the House, and the Chair persists in his recognition of the gentleman from Michigan. The clerk will report the resolution."

The debate over the rule was heated and bitter, its dry formality leaving the Republicans still furious. The vote itself proved anticlimactic. The rule passed 227–198. Wright's telephone calls had made a difference, his power had been felt; the rule had not been a tough fight after all.

In the debate over the moratorium itself, California Republican Jerry Lewis complained that the bill has "literally nothing to do with accounting, but it has a lot to do with cover. It is designed to provide cover." He was exactly right and his words had no impact at all. On final passage, the moratorium passed 230–196.

In the end, the contras did get the $40 million. Reagan did not even have to veto a resolution of disapproval, since the Senate authorized the spending.

But the House vote had sent messages which would have repercussions throughout the year. The vote totals on the rule and on the bill itself were nearly identical, but the votes were not. On the rule, one Republican voted yes; twenty-six Democrats voted no. On the bill itself, seventeen Republicans voted yes; forty Democrats voted no. The discrepancy marked the difference between procedural and substantive votes. The public and the press generally ignored the procedural votes, and Democrats could demonstrate party loyalty on them without hurting themselves politically. *But procedure was substance. It had always been so. Wright was making it so more than ever.*

It was early in the year but already the two parties were moving apart. Wright was the reason. He changed the dynamics, altered the equations of power. He would use the Rules Committee to give himself every advantage and would press his colleagues to the wall for a vote. He *would* exercise power. Unless someone stopped him.

The vote pointed out something else, too: the difference between Foley and Coelho, and what each brought to the leadership. Foley had wanted to give the Republicans what the law called for, a straight-up-or-down vote. Coelho and Bonior—and Wright—had not. It was part of Foley's sense of pace and propriety; he had agreed that the moratorium would help win the issue later, but did not think any advantage gained worth antagonizing Republicans. Their hostility could cost Democrats in many ways.

That analysis was typical of Foley, who usually took the large view, from a distant perspective. Where Wright was driving, explosive, and impatient, Foley resisted impulse and would not be rushed. Even in the hectic madness of a campaign, this sense of pace remained; once when campaign advisers frantically pushed for a decision on running a TV ad, Foley asked when they had to decide. "By eleven o'clock," he was told. "Then we'll meet at ten," he responded calmly. More to the point, when Coelho told people downtown—"downtown" in Washington meant lobbyists—he had no intention of waiting ten years to be Speaker, Foley shrugged and told his staff, "See if he says that next year."

Foley, who seemed disconnected from the physical, even from his own body, who had an elaborate sound system installed in his government-provided car to listen to his Bach, whose office had a spare, uncluttered, abstract feel to it, had had an odd career. There was no obvious press of ambition and yet he was ambitious, no driving passion and yet he had arrived. "I'm a believer in the fates," he said. "I definitely put off long-term personal career planning."

He was aware of contradictions within himself, but saw no need to resolve them. It was not that he believed in or cared about nothing. It was that he believed, or at least tried to understand, everything.

His mother was strong, gritty, dominant, from an Irish immigrant family which settled in one of the dryest, harshest areas of eastern Washington State. Foley took after his father, a judge for over thirty years, a legendary figure in Spokane, a Democrat, and a gentle, thoughtful man.

Growing up, Foley rarely engaged in the kind of physical play his size would have suited him for. Instead, his mind dissected things, taking them apart and putting them together, turning them over and inside out, standing them on their head and shaking out their pockets. He looked and looked and looked, from every angle, curious, cool, analytical, dispassionate. If he had a passion, it was for debate; in debate one explored, analyzed an argument, reacted to pressure not emotionally but coolly. He won the state high school debating championship.

Yet for all his intellect, his abstract view of the world, there was something clearly Celtic about him. A moodiness and depth. A sense of family and loyalty. Committee chairmen were entitled to have their portraits painted; almost all do. But Foley chaired Agriculture and refused. One man close to him said, "I almost think he feels a portrait would freeze his life in some fatalistic way, or capture his soul."

Both his parents were Irish Catholics, and he went to Gonzaga preparatory school and Gonzaga University. Jesuits helped train and discipline his mind. They also exposed him to the random petty tyrannies of life. In college he stayed up late reading, rose late, and arrived in class late. That displeased the Jesuits, who equated lateness with slackness, and they tried to discipline him. Foley neither accepted discipline nor fought it; he was not one to fight when a simpler solution sufficed, and simply transferred to the University of Washington and there finished college, then entered its graduate school to study international relations.

At the same time modernity attracted him—the cool, aloof, abstract lines of what in the early 1950s was considered modern architecture and modern furniture. Foley especially took to the spare, efficient furniture, learned the different styles of chairs and sofas and lighting, knew the names, the designers. He shifted from history to law and back and back again, in no hurry to settle on one, finally resolving on the law, and politics. He loved to analyze systems, loved to find the pressure point through which they could be made to work, and politics stimulated him. What else involved so complex an equation, with every interest in a society involved?

When McCarthyism came to Washington State, when rabid anticommunists attacked faculty at the university, Foley was appalled. He and his roommate talked into the night, but even those discussions were not passionate so much as intellectual. Yet if Foley lacked passion, still he had a firm sense of what he believed was right—and also what was possible. His analytical eye focused ever on the real, the concrete; it kept him in touch with the world, kept him from losing himself in abstractions. Once some graduate-school friends were caught shoplifting at a Safeway, and the store manager offered to drop the charges if they gave him fifty dollars, a lot of money in the 1950s. Foley was outraged by the shakedown, and agreed to represent them informally; he met with regional Safeway executives who promised not to prosecute if he and his friends kept silent about the blackmail.

After law school he became deputy prosecutor in Spokane County, then assistant state attorney general, then moved to Washington, D.C., to work for Senator Henry Jackson. In 1964 Jackson urged him to run for the House. At first Foley thought not. But he ran into a friend at a restaurant who told him if he didn't have the guts to run now he never would. The bluntness shook Foley. Soon he was speeding across the state to file his application papers, arriving only moments before the five o'clock deadline. Helped by having both Lyndon Johnson and Jackson above him on the ticket, and by his family's name and connections—his mother came from a prominent farming family—Foley upset twenty-two-year incumbent Walter Horan by 12,000 votes. The campaign was so gentlemanly that, after it, Horan introduced Foley to colleagues in the cloakroom, and Foley held a reception for Horan.

In the House his intelligence set him apart, and he made himself an expert in agriculture. When in the late 1960s members from Arizona and California wanted their states to get access to water from the Columbia River—few things mattered more than water in his district—Foley repeatedly blocked their efforts. His intellect won that fight: he relentlessly demolished his opponents' arguments, and one newspaper dubbed him "the Perry Mason of the Columbia River."

He developed a reputation as one of the brightest members of Congress, yet he showed no trace of arrogance, no trace of a do-not-suffer-fools-gladly attitude. He would go up to people on the floor and tell them how well they had done in debate, and his comments never seemed insincere. Members talked to him, trusted him, tested ideas out on him. In 1972 he became chairman of the Democratic Study Group, the core organization of House liberals which had been pushing internal reforms for over a decade. After the 1974 election, these reformers ended the seniority system and ousted three chairmen, including Agriculture Committee chairman W. R. Poage. Out of loyalty Foley opposed Poage's ouster, but the Caucus removed him anyway, then reached down into the ranks and with Poage's public support named him—a remarkably junior member, just five terms in the House—chairman. Two years later his colleagues made him chairman of the Democratic Caucus as well.

His career was remarkable for its easy flow. Its only rough spots—and they were rough—were two tough elections. In 1978 he won with only 48 percent of the vote in a three-way race, and got 51.6 percent in 1980. But even then there was never any panic. When advisers worried that his semiformal dress made him seem a bit of a dandy and opponents charged he was out of touch, they pushed him to wear farmer's overalls, or at least jeans, for a commercial. He refused. "There's one vote I want in this election," he said. "My own."

A few weeks after that 1980 election, in which whip John Brademas, another intellectual—a former Rhodes Scholar and later president of New York University—lost, Foley asked O'Neill and Wright for the vacant whip job. He got it.

Two elections later, as Wright began his run for Speaker in earnest and Foley tried to step up to majority leader, colleagues began to wonder about him. He seemed somehow above the fray; he seemed an observer. That was one reason the press liked Foley; he was like them, and his intelligence charmed them—they wanted Foley to like them, to respect them—and he treated them almost as equals, occasionally going off the record in a way that seemed to bring them inside the game. (Wright almost never went off the record.) Members did not feel quite the same about him; even those who strongly supported him wondered about his strength. Publicly they said things like "He may not be partisan enough for a majority leader"—and even that was said anonymously. Privately they said harsher things. Even one admirer observed, "Foley won't fight. You can push him around."

Foley was more complicated than that. Much more. He didn't lack for strength, not exactly. "Just because he doesn't have a one-hundred-miles-per-hour fastball," said Democratic strategist Kirk O'Donnell, "doesn't mean he doesn't throw strikes." But Foley did not push up against members, either pressuring them or demanding of them. Coelho confronted people, sometimes seemed to demand intimacy, but Foley said, "I'm not comfortable with a heart-to-heart, 'Let us bare our souls together,' psychotherapy kind of conversation." Everyone respected his intelligence, and intelligence was an asset, but the majority-leader job demanded toughness, a willingness to fight, challenge, confront, defend the party even when wrong, and *run* the floor, dominate it.

Foley had not shown these qualities. Even his move from chairman to whip argued against it. A chairman was his own boss; the whip was only the number-three man in the leadership. It was not the way most men with ambition rose to power in the Congress. Powerful men took power. A man like John Dingell, chairman of Energy and Commerce, or Rostenkowski of Ways and Means, or certainly Coelho, would not have given up a chairmanship for a third-ranking job. Instead they would have used their chairmanship to build an empire. Foley could have. His committee involved world trade and world politics—relations with Europe, with the Pacific Rim, with the Third World, with China, with the Soviet Union; it involved the financial system and securities through the Farm Credit System and the Farmers Home Administration and commodity futures; it involved rural development and infrastructure. A vast empire could be built on such a base. But Foley did not want to dominate or build empires. He was not a builder at all. He did not set forth an agenda and pursue it. He wanted to *be* engaged, to have the world come to him. He did not root around in the dirt, dig his nails in, and create things.

"I have a sense of disappointment with people who haven't had stressful personal experiences—disappointment's the wrong word but people with easy lives seem often crippled," he said. "Yet my own life has been comfortable. I grew up in the Depression thinking it was a time of prosperity."

Was he crippled somehow? Members wondered about him. His performance as whip had been good in spots, but he had rarely pushed.

He had rarely confronted anyone, had not so much worked to get votes as to count them, had been perhaps too understanding of those who had not wanted to go along.

And some members had problems with his wife, Heather, who ran his office. She worked for nothing; paying her would have violated antinepotism rules. That made her presence stranger; Foley had no money beyond his salary. She was rock-hard, aggressive, very much *there*. They were childless. Sometimes Foley did in fact seem like a disembodied Celtic spirit, morose and keening, she his earthbound connection. It was as if Foley had yielded control over part of his own life to her; while he focused on what he enjoyed, she took over the grit and detail of it, giving it structure and spine, wielding power—arbitrarily and unfairly, according to several people who knew the situation well—among Foley's staff, teaching newcomers who thought they could get to Foley around her that they could not. Foley allowed her free rein.

What disturbed colleagues about Heather was, said one, "She thinks she's a member." There were only two kinds of people in the House: members and clerks. Clerks spoke when spoken to, did the members' bidding, even stood while members sat. Highly intelligent and a skilled lawyer herself, still she was just a clerk, and as a wife both more and less than that. She did not seem to understand or accept her role. Some members defended her. One man, no fan of Foley, observed, "You may not know what Foley thinks—it's always 'on this hand . . . on the other hand . . .' You know what she thinks. She's tough and I like that."

But she seemed to demand attention. Where Foley dressed with formal precision, she often wore jeans and sandals or moccasins. Some colleagues thought it offensive, disrespectful to the institution. House rules required men to wear a coat and tie on the floor. Soon after Foley became whip, at a leadership meeting O'Neill lit up his cigar. She asked him to put it out. O'Neill looked at her with a combination of disdain and wonderment. This was O'Neill's meeting, in his own House, and she, who did not belong there, who was only staff and in a way not even staff, was telling him not to smoke? "You know," O'Neill said slowly, "we only tolerate you in these meetings."

The cigar stayed lit. That same day a hand-written apology went from Tom Foley to O'Neill. Later, when Heather tried to get floor privileges—access to the floor is a jealously guarded privilege for a few leadership aides—O'Neill refused. Once O'Neill invited Foley on a trip to Ireland, but said there was no room for Heather. Foley declined. O'Neill confided to one man that he believed Foley could never become Speaker because of his wife.

Even Foley's ascension to majority leader was not at first certain. Who might oppose him? Members kicked around the names of several chairmen, including Dingell and Rostenkowski, but neither had any interest in being majority leader. Speaker, yes, but leader, no. And Coelho? Coelho, for all his ambition, made it clear he would content himself with the whip job. He knew running against Foley would be overreaching. Gephardt was running for President. Who else? There was no one else.

Meanwhile, Foley campaigned, took nothing for granted, called every Democrat in the House and said he was running. True to his style, at first he asked for no commitments. Not yet. As Wright, in February 1985, was announcing that almost three-fourths of the Democrats had promised their support to him for Speaker, Foley began visiting member after member in *their* offices, a symbolism which escaped no one. He wanted their votes, asked for their views, and listened. Then he handled negotiations with GOP senators—the GOP still controlled the Senate then—over Gramm-Rudman. Some members of the House wanted to fight Gramm-Rudman, just refuse to accept it, but the votes were not there to do that. Foley led the House Democratic team in restructuring the innards of the bill to make it more palatable. The negotiations dragged on and showed Foley at his best, with not only the emotional will and the patience to wait the Senate out, but the intellectual will to take the bill apart and put it back together. In the end, the Republicans could claim credit for having passed the bill, but Foley structured it to protect Democratic priorities, exempting from across-the-board cuts programs for the poorest Americans, and splitting cuts evenly between defense and domestic spending. In the end, no challenger to Foley's rise to majority leader, not even a potential challenger, surfaced.

Foley's sense of pace and enjoyment of the devil's-advocate role could complement Wright's passions and Coelho's aggressive assertiveness—if they could be molded together. But they were still feeling each other out. The system had not been tested. They had not been tested.

CHAPTER 6

White House chief of staff Donald Regan was bleeding badly from wounds inflicted by the Iran-contra scandal. Neither the press nor the rest of the Washington establishment had ever taken to him, and they watched him bleed with satisfaction. He had failed to grasp the subtleties of power, had never massaged reporters' egos to make friends in the press, and he had not compensated by building solid relationships elsewhere. Both the President's ideological and personal supporters considered him disloyal; he had once compared himself to someone walking behind circus elephants with a shovel, implying the President made messes which he cleaned up.

Now, denying responsibility for Iran-contra, he clung to his job. That seemed the ultimate disloyalty: putting his own interests above those of the President he served. Unattributed quotes, and occasionally even attributed ones, appeared in papers demanding that he resign. This was the way things worked in Washington. Rarely did someone go to a powerful man or woman and tell him or her to quit. Instead, the newspapers carried that message to them, and reporters hounded the subject with stories about erosion of power, or shouted questions about resignations.

Nobel Prize–winner Elias Canetti described the phenomenon in his book *Crowds and Power* when he talked about what he called the "baiting crowd," which "is out for killing and it knows whom it wants to kill. It heads for this goal with unique determination and cannot be cheated of it. The proclaiming of the goal . . . is enough to make the crowd form. This concentration on killing is of a special kind and of unsurpassed intensity. Everyone wants to participate, everyone strikes a blow."

On February 26, 1987, the Tower Commission, appointed by Reagan to investigate the Iran-contra scandal, issued its report. The commission—former GOP senator John Tower; former Secretary of State Edmund Muskie, a Democrat; and former National Security Adviser Brent Scowcroft, a Republican—described a rudderless White House and a President who was disengaged from and uninvolved in decision-making, out of touch with even senior aides. The portrait was devastating and shook Washington. Yet the result was to shift power to the White House.

Republicans insisted that the report exonerated Reagan because it did not pin knowledge and responsibility on him. (Evidence at the criminal trial of Oliver North, which occurred after Bush became President, proved that Reagan had participated more actively than either the Tower Commission or later Congressional investigators learned.) Reagan announced he would soon speak to the nation and make his first accounting of the scandal. But the key to the shift of power to the White House was Donald Regan's sudden and ignominious firing—so sudden that he learned of it from news reports on his way to work— and his replacement by Howard Baker, the former GOP Senate majority leader from Tennessee.

The firing acted as a purgative. The fury abated.

The coverage of Regan's departure and Baker's appointment epitomized how the media personalized stories, anthropomorphized policy. Never had anyone of Baker's stature gone to work for *any* President, not even to accept a cabinet post. At dinner parties, Republicans and Democrats alike joked that Baker, beloved by the same establishment which despised Regan, was giving up a possible campaign for President to become President. Story after story praised him, talked of a new beginning for the administration, almost as if Baker *had* become President—and brought a honeymoon with him.

For a moment, perhaps the only moment of the 100th Congress, Wright was dwarfed by events.

He understood the importance of personality, understood that power is contained in personality, and that one individual succeeds where another fails. But underlying policy had not changed; only a handful of individuals had. They were important, yes, but above them and around them remained the same President, and at State, at Defense, at OMB, at Treasury, the same infrastructure of people. Wright trusted Baker personally and welcomed having someone in the White House who respected the Congress. Yet the media coverage disturbed him; he believed it missed the point. He wanted to send a shot across the bow of the new White House team, and perhaps create an opportunity to advance his own agenda. To do so he would use the media.

He called his press staff into his office and told them, "The media is talking about personalities and management style. Baloney. I want to issue a statement"—his first as Speaker on Iran-contra. "It was wrong to deal with Iran while they were making war on their neighbors. It was doubly wrong to do it while professing the opposite to our allies. It was triply wrong to do it in violation of the law, without notifying Congress. The biggest point is the law was broken by the President. His first duty is to faithfully execute the law. I want people to think about that before Reagan makes his speech on Iran."

His staff prepared a formal statement virtually identical to what he had just said. A few hours later, immediately before his daily press conference, he read it to Foley, Coelho, and Bonior. The leadership met like this every day, and brief as the meetings were—anywhere from five to fifteen minutes—they allowed coordination of the message sold to the media. Routinely at these press conferences Wright would either make an announcement or answer questions for ten minutes, then leave to convene the House. Foley, Coelho, and Bonior would remain, usually until reporters had no more questions. Today they planned to have Wright attack Reagan on Iran-contra, then the rest of the leadership would hit him on the budget. The White House was talking about a newly activist, engaged President. They would call its bluff.

Wright signaled an aide to let the reporters in, read his statement, took a few questions, and left. Then Foley and Coelho took over. Foley: "The Baker and Carlucci appointments were very positive but ultimately it is the President who has to make policy." Coelho: "The President has an opportunity to show he's really engaged by engaging on the budget. The future is the budget. This is our next crisis and the President doesn't understand that." Foley again: "The President has to find ways to work with Congress toward solutions to a number of pressing problems, including the budget and arms control."

Wright's comments made the front page of the next day's *Washington Post* and *New York Times,* and the network news shows reported on it. Coelho and Foley expanded on it as planned, and their quotes were featured almost as prominently. The wire services, all the major dailies, the networks all echoed the refrain.

The play was exactly what Wright had hoped for. His statement had been harsh, and perfectly timed, just as Reagan was trying to recover.

The morning the stories ran, Baker paid Wright a courtesy call. Later that night Reagan would make his speech on Iran-contra.

The meeting with Baker was important. Wright wanted to balance his confrontational comment with conciliation, and he wanted also to listen, listen for nuance, listen the way one did when counting votes, listen to see whether anything had really changed. Baker needed to listen closely too. When Baker arrived, Wright played southern gentleman, ushering him to an easy chair and abandoning his desk to join him and a White House aide. The two men bantered, laughed, but the laughter did not reach their eyes; their eyes were neither cool nor warm, just measuring, professional, assessing.

Baker took pains to make clear his role, joking that no matter what the papers said he was not regent, only staff.

Wright silently wondered if that meant nothing substantive would change, then told Baker several things that he hoped the President would say in his speech, "if the President seriously wants to mend fences with Congress."

"I hear you," Baker said. "I'll report that. Anything else?"

"Yes, there is." He reiterated the message in the morning papers, that the best way to banish the image of a disengaged President was to get him involved in the budget deliberations. *That was what mattered. The past was past. That was the future.* But Wright warned, "There's got to be some give in the White House. I want to compromise but if the White House is unrealistic, no."

"I'll probe that." They both knew Wright was talking about taxes. "I'll talk to him. I had that problem when I was majority leader."

Baker gave no indication of compromise. Finally, Wright extended an invitation. O'Neill had always hosted a St. Patrick's Day luncheon, and had always invited Reagan. Wright was continuing the tradition. Would the President like to come? Baker immediately accepted for him, and left.

In a few hours would come Reagan's speech. All three networks had invited Wright to comment afterwards. It would give him an opportunity to pound home the point that Congress and the President should move forward to the budget. The attention span of the press was short; to get a comment in one day's story was one thing, but to influence the thinking of the media or the public usually required relentless repetition. Others would soon start relentlessly repeating to the media an attack on him, an attack which would ultimately have immense impact. But Wright did not want to attack. The shot across the bow was enough for now. And the networks wanted him to attack. With disdain he said, "The press loves a fight, doesn't it?"

What about the network invitations? an aide asked.

Wright refused them.

The next day at his press conference Wright called Reagan's speech "very positive," and quoted to reporters Reagan's promise to seek " 'a new partnership with the Congress' " in foreign policy reflecting " 'the will of the Congress as well as the White House,' " and that the law " 'will be followed, not only in letter but in spirit.' "

In private, too, Wright approved: "The President of the United States should not grovel. You wouldn't respect him if he did. He came pretty close to saying what I wanted him to, what I talked to Baker about, and it will make a difference if he carries it out."

Wright had interpreted Reagan's words as not simply rhetoric directed to the country, but as a message to Congress and to him. That interpretation would loom large in a few months.

Then, suddenly, the furor over the Iran-contra affair disappeared from the headlines. Reagan's approval ratings in the polls, which at their lowest had still been double Jimmy Carter's lowest, started climbing back up. With nothing new to report, the press moved on. It was like a great wave that swept through the city, and returned to the sea.

Wright was helping the press move on. His agenda would not wait. He had already begun a relentless, highly personal effort to maneuver the House into doing his bidding. The budget would be his first real test of leadership.

The first step was to woo colleagues, show them that they were important to him. *Personal acceptance means more to legislative success than ideology:* he had learned that forty years earlier in the Texas legislature. He had entered the speakership without the close friendships which O'Neill had had, or even the feeling of warmth which surrounded O'Neill. But there was a difference between friendships and relationships built on trust and consideration and professionalism; one could have the latter without the former, and they could become just as strong.

Wright set out to build such relationships. Only a few months before becoming Speaker, he had built an extension on his home in McLean, Virginia, so that he could host dinners; three tables of ten each would fit comfortably, more could be squeezed in. He made his guests feel welcome, genuinely welcome, in his home, and most guests were colleagues. "That's smart of him," one member said. "Tip never did that. It's important to be able to say, 'The other night when I was at the Speaker's for dinner . . .' "

Among his first guests were Budget and Ways and Means Democrats. There was no business done at dinner. Wright was wooing them, and they allowed themselves to be wooed.

But almost simultaneously he began exerting pressure on both committees. Indirectly, he let the Budget Committee know how much money he wanted for new initiatives—welfare reform, trade, the homeless, and others. Budget members stiffened when they heard. Those initiatives would cost money, yet the budget deficit had to come *down*. The budget this year would already be the hardest ever. Wright was making it harder still.

Republicans would do nothing to help. Nothing. In the past, Senate Republicans had controlled the Senate and been constructive. Now, able to deny responsibility, they would watch Democrats squirm. House Republicans were even more gleeful. Edward Madigan, a member of the House GOP leadership, told *Congressional Quarterly,* a magazine read closely in Congress, "If I were Republican dictator I would be sitting and staring at the Democrats." And if Democrats passed a tax bill? "I would come down on that like a ton of bricks."

Yet Wright was pushing taxes. Even when Senate Republicans had tried to raise taxes, O'Neill, fearing to expose Democrats to charges of "tax and spend," had refused to go along unless Reagan went first. Now Wright was doing it on his own. Members believe the leadership is supposed to give them cover. O'Neill had done so. Wright was exposing them.

Even in the Democratic whip organization, members resisted. Every Thursday morning the whips met. In the beginning, twenty years earlier, it had been a small, intimate group. Now roughly one-quarter of the Democratic Caucus were whips. Political scientists would call this expansion the politics of inclusion; O'Neill put it more simply when he said, "I'm against any deal I'm not part of." Under O'Neill as Speaker and Foley as whip the meetings had provided two-way communication between the leadership and every ideological and regional interest in the Democratic Caucus, giving the leadership a sense of the mood of the House. "It's the most important half-hour of the week," Foley said.

It was still important under Wright and Coelho, but the tone had changed. The meetings were still held in H-324, now named the Thomas P. O'Neill Room, the townhouse-style two-story room with staircases front and back. High windows opened on the Mall, looking straight down toward the Washington Monument. Half a dozen telephones were scattered along the walls; members did not like to be out of touch. Upstairs some of Wright's staff worked. Downstairs, in the front of the room, the leadership sat, facing rows of members in portable chairs. (The layout of the room was constantly changed.) Other members stood in the back, near the food. Coelho chaired the meetings, and like everything else he did, he organized them tightly and assigned one aide to provide coffee; an assortment of doughnuts; orange, tomato, and grapefruit juice; fresh fruit cup; two kinds of muffins which changed weekly; and a different treat each week for members to carry back to their offices: packages of apricots, pistachios, raisins, prunes, or pears, courtesy of lobbyists for the Western Growers Association. Foley had never provided anything this elaborate; it reflected Coelho's attention to detail, and his recognition that something beyond coffee might bring members in. His staff also took attendance, quietly checking members off as they entered; no one in Foley's operation had ever even considered doing that. Coelho, with Wright's support, wanted to make the whip organization harder-working and more accountable to the leadership. Taking attendance was the first step. (Most members did not realize attendance was taken. Attendance?! Didn't Coelho have it wrong? Didn't Coelho understand that he needed them more than they needed him?) Under the tighter organization the two-way communication dropped off. Members, uncertain about Wright, uncertain about his temper, kept their mouths shut about things they would have complained about to O'Neill. Rostenkowski had started the meetings twenty years earlier as a counterweight to the Speaker. *Now they're a means of total control,* he had observed. *I can't blame Wright. I'd do the same if I was Speaker.*

This Thursday the meeting began routinely, with Foley reading the legislative schedule for the following week. Bill Gray, the Budget chairman, was explaining that Reagan's budget missed the Gramm-Rudman target of $108 billion. "It's impossible. The question is, do we want to use phony asset sales—"

Fifty members simultaneously shouted, "YEEESSSS!"

They were laughing. These whip meetings often had the feel of a fraternity party, with grown men and a few women playing with and to an audience of peers. But Wright smiled tightly, a smile without humor, and said, "Economic policy is just as much where money comes from as where it goes. Ways and Means has to be creative. The question isn't whether we tax, but who. For example, someone suggested to me a tax of one-half percent on buyers and sellers of stocks and bonds. That would raise $17 billion, and England has a tax like that."

A former aide had given him a memo the day before on such a tax. It had appealed to him. But to announce it publicly before discussing it with Rostenkowski? Wright was demonstrating again his willingness to push, to pressure, to demand. He was, for the second time now, not only trying to tell Rostenkowski what to do but how to do it. Publicly. Members in the room who served on Ways and Means were annoyed. *Who did he think he was?*

Wright continued. "We've got to keep the focus on Reagan's taxes. We've got to make the point that he called for $22 billion in revenues. More than half the deficit reduction in his budget is revenues. Most of it is crap like asset sales, but some are real taxes, whatever he calls them. Do we do like Reagan and tax Medicare recipients—"

"NOOOOOOO!"

"Veterans trying to buy a home—"

"NOOOOOOO!"

"Students trying to get a loan?"

"NOOOOOOO!"

"Who do we tax?"

"The Japanese!"

The room rocked with laughter. Wright pretended to like it. He didn't like it. "Look, if we all coordinate this, if we all focus on Reagan's budget, on Reagan's taxes, on the fact that he missed the Gramm-Rudman target, if we all say the same thing, we can make the point."

Then one member complained, "We're talking about taxes here and that's a little ridiculous. Ways and Means never reaches its targets, anyway. It never does what the budget says it should do."

"That's bull!" snorted Marty Russo, a Ways and Means member. "That's just crap!"

Wright pursed his lips. Russo was a Rostenkowski protégé, one of the very few members who had never—never—given Wright his commitment for Speaker. *Ways and Means had the power. It was the most powerful committee in Congress. Let them take a little heat.* Then Jake Pickle rose, seventy-four-year-old Jake Pickle who represented Lyndon Johnson's old district and had been in Congress for twenty-four years. (Pickle was liked, respected, and tough. When Johnson was President, in the days before recorded votes, he sent an aide to sit in the gallery to see how members voted. Once Pickle was voting against Johnson and the man caught his eye; Pickle made an obscene gesture. *Fuck you.*) He served on the Ways and Means Committee, too, and started to defend it, started to say how hard raising taxes was. *Pickle was missing the point, getting away from the issue. Reagan had taxes. If they just all of them pounded that home to the media.* Pressure was building in Wright. He struggled to contain himself. All his plans for his agenda, all his control over the House, seemed to be slipping away. *This has gone far enough.* Suddenly he lost control.

"Jake," he snapped, "maybe if you'd turn up your hearing aid you'd know what I said was we should focus on the fact that Reagan's budget includes taxes and doesn't reach the targets."

The room fell silent. Wright had gone too far. The members had heard about Wright's explosions. Now they had seen one. These men and women were all equals here. In any personal reference, even in small private meetings, they spoke with the carefulness of diplomats. Now Wright had humiliated Pickle publicly.

A moment later Wright apologized, saying that Jake and he had known each other so long, that they kidded each other a lot, said things others might not understand. It was too late. Wright's outburst could come back to haunt him in the long run. If members didn't speak out at the whip meetings, they would do it in small dark corners where it could prove dangerous. Members were sensitive, as sensitive almost to what happened to a colleague as to themselves, because what happened to a colleague could happen to them. *Who did Wright think he was?*

Wright did not relent. Immediately he started scheduling meetings on the budget for the following week: one-on-one talks in his office with first Bill Gray, then Rostenkowski on Tuesday, the day before

Reagan's Iran-contra speech, a session with Budget Democrats Wednesday afternoon, lunch for Ways and Means Democrats Thursday, and immediately after lunch a meeting with committee chairmen.

Before his meeting with Rostenkowski, he sent him, hand-written and hand-delivered the few doors down the hallway from his own office, a memo detailing the securities transaction tax he had raised at the whip meeting. He sent a similar, personal note to each of the twenty-three Democrats on Ways and Means, also hand-written and hand-delivered. Although he said he was not dictating anything—"Please let me know how you feel," he wrote—between the lines came a stronger message: *There will be taxes. Are you with me or not? Are you friend or foe?* O'Neill had never gotten into a committee's business like this. Never.

The notes had just gone out when Bill Gray came in with some aides. Gray explained where the Budget Committee seemed headed. Despite the difficulties, he could see the outline of a solution. As Gray left, Wright said, "The resistance right now isn't coming from most Democrats. It's coming from Ways and Means Democrats. I used to get so tense. I'd go over to the gym and beat the hell out of that punching bag."

He was tense now. Rostenkowski was coming soon. The two men sat down, alone, without staff. Wright said, "We've got to have taxes. Somewhere between $18 and $20 billion. We have to have them."

They talked on. At one point Rostenkowski shouted, "Bullshit!"

Wright's biggest concern had been fighting Rostenkowski inside his own committee. He could not win there, not if Rostenkowski fought to win and had all the Republican votes to start with. But Rostenkowski believed in the hierarchy; in the end, he agreed to go along. Suddenly Wright relaxed, then asked his thoughts on the securities tax.

"I read the memo," Rostenkowski replied, folding his arms.

That night Wright went to a reception. His daily schedule routinely listed half a dozen, but he rarely went to them. Members would invite him and he would say, "Have my secretary put it on my schedule." Then when he did not show up John Mack could say, Jeez, the Speaker was sorry, it was on his schedule but something came up at the last minute. This one he attended, a prince paying court to another prince. Charley Rangel was hosting it. Rangel was a senior member of Ways and Means, and conceivably could be the next chairman. This event was for members and their wives only. Rangel had run for whip against Coelho, and this dinner was to thank his supporters. Rostenkowski was there; so was most of Ways and Means. Rangel, a black man, represented Adam Clayton Powell's old Harlem district; on tax policy he leaned toward Wright. He had black hair slicked back and a fat jocular Santa Claus belly, with a fat jocular easygoing public manner. But his mind worked with intensity and precision; one could almost sense him dividing sentences into phrases, analyzing the meaning of each, putting them back together. This man knew who and what he was, and could step back, see the entire world, know how foolish whatever game consumed him at the moment was, and yet how important it was, too. He knew Rostenkowski had endorsed him for whip but had given him no help, and Rangel remembered that well enough. Wright showed up for Rangel, chatted with Rangel's wife, had a drink and hors d'oeuvres, shared a laugh with Rostenkowski, the two of them relaxed but eyeing each other even as they laughed. And Rangel eyeing both of them. Rangel, on Wright's way out, going to him and saying, "Thanks for coming, Jim." *Thanks for showing the respect.* Afterwards Wright confided, "Rangel's a good ally to have."

He might need him.

Wright pushed Budget as hard as he pushed Ways and Means. On the floor he pressured Gray to move faster, faster. Gray resisted, insisting the committee was moving as fast as it could. Committee members were still seeking alternatives, still searching for an escape from the reality of the numbers. The committee would arrive at the destination. They would have to. But it would take time.

Wright did not want to wait. The same day Howard Baker paid his courtesy call, the same day the leadership tried to force the White House into the budget process by applying media pressure, Wright met with Budget Democrats and told them the budget had to fund new initiatives and cut the deficit by at least as much as the White House had. He concluded, "We need taxes."

Until now, some Budget members had preferred to believe Wright's call for taxes was part of some larger political game, some strategic positioning for the future. Now Wright was telling them flatly he was serious and meant what he said. They listened restlessly, shifting about in their seats. When he finished they pummeled him with questions about the politics, about Mondale's humiliation, about passing taxes on the floor, about the pointlessness of proceeding if the President was going to veto it. The President? Hell! Where was Rostenkowski?

Unlike at the whip meeting, Wright remained cool despite the prodding and said, "I've talked with Danny. Danny's fine. Look, we all agree on the need. You all asked to be on this committee. It's a leadership committee. You are all part of the leadership. When you're in the leadership you do tough things."

The next day Wright hosted a lunch for Ways and Means Democrats, in H-324. The room was used for whip meetings, but now was set up with long, baronial tables. Waiters liveried in tuxedos served steak. Wright was frank and specific. First he made clear that the Budget Committee would call for $18 billion in taxes, then said, "Chairman Rostenkowski and I have talked and we agree that's doable."

Rostenkowski backed him up, but he made two things clear. *First, if we go this route you have to support us. Don't leave us hanging out there—the leadership's responsible for passing this bill. Second, don't inch this $18 billion up to twenty or twenty-two.*

Wright nodded, then reassured them that he wasn't trying to dictate any specific tax. *But* . . . The committee wanted leadership support? Fine, sure. Just give the leadership something the leadership *could* support. Surely they would want, wouldn't they, to preserve Democratic priorities? Surely they would want progressive taxes—the kind Rangel preferred—not regressive ones.

There were other, deeper currents here. Was Wright threatening to mobilize the entire Democratic Caucus behind him, against Ways and Means? Democratic colleagues were jealous of Ways and Means' power, and its special privileges. Who knew? Maybe those special privileges, and all that jurisdiction, could change. But why fight each other? We're all friends here.

Half an hour after the Ways and Means lunch Wright met with committee chairmen. Cuts had to come too. The chairmen made those cuts. He was late and the chairmen were waiting for him in the Speaker's Dining Room, a dozen and a half men sitting at two long mahogany tables facing each other, here, in his domain, under the heavy chandelier, a great gold-framed mirror over a mantel, the corridor outside frescoed with scenes from a glorious history. They could have been barons facing one another a millennium earlier, each chairman with dominion over tens of billions of dollars of wealth and political power and need, assembled to meet the king. At the head of the table sat Wright, flanked by Foley, Coelho, and Gray.

Wright did have power over them. He could block their legislation from the floor, or give them a deadline to report a bill out, or refer bills over which they had jurisdiction to other committees—jurisdiction meant power; chairmen cared about their jurisdiction more than anything—or have Rules allow floor amendments which dismembered piece by piece bills they had crafted for months. But he could not go to war with all of them. His role was to make them face reality, and let the nagging, relentless, unending pressure of the facts bring them to him. Washington always worked like that; once people accepted the same set of facts, options narrowed rapidly. The facts, political and otherwise, squeezed people into narrower and narrower confines. The maneuvering, the deals, took place only at the margins.

Rarely had O'Neill held a committee chairmen's meeting—once a Congress, joked one of his aides—and even then usually the chairman with the most important bill would speak, and they would adjourn. This was already Wright's third meeting to discuss his agenda with chairmen. He was forcing them to face facts early in the process. His schedule demanded it. He called them to order, then let Gray explain:

"We've got three bullets to bite. Defense is first. Freezing defense budget authority saves only $4 billion. In the past it saved $25 billion. Second is revenues. Third, we got Gramm-Rudman—the $108-billion target. Yesterday I had to stop some good Democrats from circulating a letter in the Caucus saying let's stick to $108 billion. I said, 'Fellas, can I sit down with you a minute?' I explained the only way to get a real 108 is do things like freeze Social Security. I mean *freeze* Social Security. Tell people who turn sixty-five this year that they can't collect."

The chairmen disliked the briefing; their frowns and pursed faces and folded arms showed that. Gray outlined what his committee would likely do although it had not yet reached agreement: cut the deficit $36 billion, $18 billion in taxes and $18 billion in spending cuts. Half the cuts would come from domestic programs, half from defense. He concluded, "The budget has to say, 'These are the Democratic Party's priorities. Health—AIDS. Education. New initiatives in trade, welfare reform, catastrophic health insurance.' One way Democrats can distinguish themselves from Republicans is to say this program is worthwhile, we'll pay for it."

Rostenkowski broke in with his piece of reality: "Just raising $18 billion is a task in itself. Forget about passing it on the floor of the House. All these wonderful new initiatives, that's another $6 billion. That doesn't come from nowhere, and it doesn't get piled on top of Ways and Means."

The other chairmen would have to pay for the new programs by cutting existing ones. A bitterness toward the entire budget process spread through the room. More and more it ate into each chairman's dominion, forced real cuts in programs they considered important. In Dingell's Energy and Commerce Committee alone, earlier cuts had forced the National Institutes of Health to fund only 23 percent of its grant applicants and reject Nobel laureates; cuts in the Securities and Exchange Commission had allowed insider trading to explode; Medicare and Medicaid cuts had forced hospitals to shift overhead costs to private insurers, who in turn had to raise premiums 20 percent and 30 percent a year—another kind of tax. Now Gray was demanding more.

The hostility toward Gray was palpable. He was a goddamn junior member anyway. What the hell was he even doing in this meeting? Most of these men had waited twenty, twenty-five years to become a chairman. Now Gray was telling them what to do? They could not take their frustration out on Wright. They took it out on Gray. They attacked.

Dingell was Wright's most important ally outside the leadership. As large a man as Rostenkowski, with a reputation for even greater ferocity and known for taking advantage of every opportunity to expand his reach, he volunteered some cuts his committee might make. *That was strange.* Then he suggested his committee might impose a "slight" oil import fee. That was Rostenkowski's jurisdiction. Dingell added, "If Chairman Rostenkowski does not mind."

"John, you can make all the suggestions you want," Rostenkowski said, eyeing him coolly.

For all Wright's talk of facing reality, colleagues wondered if he wasn't himself denying reality: although Reagan's budget included taxes, he would never agree to those that Wright wanted. What good was courage? Republican senators had shown real political courage in voting for a budget two years earlier which had dramatically lowered the deficit, built upon Social Security cuts. What had it got them? Initially the White House had supported them, but House Republicans had convinced Donald Regan to abandon both the budget and GOP senators. The deficit went up, not down, and Democrats took over the Senate the next year. *And the first requisite of statesmanship is to get elected.*

Many political observers considered Wright's move comparable. Rostenkowski told the press his committee didn't "want to give the President the chance to kick them around and then not accomplish the goal. I think Wright is surprised at some of the resistance he is getting."

The New York Times reported, "Republicans believe that Jim Wright has made a major blunder in calling for a tax increase to help reduce the budget deficit. . . . With undisguised glee, [White House political director Mitchell] Daniels compared the discomfort of the Democrats to 'a worm on a hot brick,' and said they would be allowed to squirm for a while."

The Wall Street Journal's analysis concurred: "Many Democratic lawmakers fear that Rep. Wright's actions are politically foolish." It added that Howard Baker was privately urging Republicans in Congress to drop any calls for tax increases because they would further undermine the presidency. Retaining power took priority over cutting the deficit.

When OMB director James Miller said in a *New York Times* story that "prospects are good" for a future budget summit, Senate GOP leader Bob Dole, who had publicly supported raising taxes in the past, reportedly protested to Reagan, "If you wouldn't work with us when Republicans controlled the Senate, why would you work with Democrats now?"

Tom Wicker, a liberal *New York Times* columnist, wrote about Wright and taxes, too, commenting, "If that's courage, Mr. Wright needs a little less of it."

Maybe it wasn't courage. Maybe it was naivete. Then came a front-page *Washington Post* story headlined "Democrats Find Taxes Treacherous Territory; Wright, Rostenkowski at Odds Over Revenues." The story detailed the difficulties Wright was having, and how even Democratic colleagues were distancing themselves from him. It also quoted Rostenkowski saying, "If you tell me the chemistry is out there on the floor to pass a tax hike, I'll give you a bill tomorrow. . . . But that's not what I hear. Guys keep coming up to me and saying, 'Danny, don't do this to us.' And I tell 'em, don't talk to me, talk to Jim. I want to be a team player, but I also want to put the Democratic Party in a position to win the next election. Jim's sending in signals for a tax hike and I'm saying, 'Jeez, we went over tackle last time and we got killed.' "

Wright attended to the press, worried about it, was sometimes obsessed by it. It was one thing for Republicans to attack. It was another for a Democrat. He said nothing while he read the article at breakfast but the muscles of his jaw tightened. It wasn't the first shot in the press from Rostenkowski. He was getting tired of taking them. And he was beginning to realize he could lose this thing.

The day Wicker's column ran, Wright's driver picked him up at his McLean home at 6:15 A.M. Wright got into the backseat with a brief greeting, and began to work immediately, reading memos and checking the papers. He was tired, but had an early appearance on the *Today* show. *Be sharp*. Every opportunity to communicate counted. Every single one. From there he went to his breakfast staff meeting, from there to a ten o'clock Democratic Caucus meeting. At ten-thirty he was due at the White House for a bipartisan leadership meeting with the President in the Cabinet Room. At eleven-thirty was the daily leadership meeting just before his press conference. *Be sharp*.

There was no time for him to think, no time to breathe. At noon he convened the House and in the next half hour met and had his picture taken with six different small groups, performing for each, charming each, and left for a lunch with the Texas delegation. *There was no space to breathe*. It was already midafternoon, and nonbudgetary issues engulfed him. His staff needed decisions. At two-thirty he was needed on the floor, and had to keep Frank Carlucci, the new national security adviser, waiting. Wright was running out of time. The difference between being majority leader and Speaker was more than he had imagined. It was wearying him. Day after day, minute after minute, people pulled at him.

It was three-thirty now. On the floor colleagues lined up to see him, to ask his help on their own problems. O'Neill had lived there, in his seat up near the front of the chamber while someone else presided, or back in the cloakroom on one of the couches; colleagues could always find him, and knew he would take care of their agendas. *Wright had his own agenda. When could he work on that? Prepare for that?* His colleagues' pressure drove him back to his office. Gray came in to brief him on a development; his staff wanted him. So did other members, who waited outside his office for a chance to catch him. *Just five minutes*, they wanted. *Just five minutes*. At five o'clock General Dynamics, which built F-16 fighters and employed thousands of workers in Fort Worth, held a reception in the Speaker's Dining Room. He had to make an appearance. There were four other receptions on his schedule, fund-raisers for colleagues; if he could appear the lobbyists would make note and the colleagues would appreciate it.

Even at home that night there would be no respite. A *Washington Post* reporter doing a Style-section piece on him and Betty was waiting. *Be sharp.* It was like this every day; twelve, thirteen, fourteen hours after leaving home in the morning, he returned. He had no privacy, no moment of his own.

And what had he done to advance his agenda? Nothing. He felt he had done nothing. The clock was ticking. Time was running out.

O'Neill hadn't worked like that. O'Neill had gotten off to the golf course. Or played poker late into the night with his colleagues. He didn't have to work like Wright. He wasn't advancing an agenda. No Speaker had in decades.

Perhaps that wasn't an accident. Perhaps the institution wasn't meant to be run by any Speaker, but only guided. *The President proposes and Congress disposes.* Wasn't that the way it worked?

Wright had to confront the possibility of losing. Outwardly he was confident. The smile never left him. But the tension showed. One morning at breakfast he commented, "This will be the hardest thing we'll do all year. We could lose this." Another morning he thought out loud, "Maybe we should just let Bill Gray handle it." As if ashamed of his comment, he immediately corrected himself: "But that wouldn't be leadership." The tension showed too in the later and later hour at which he arrived home, sometimes ten o'clock, sometimes eleven, sometimes later. He was working, working, working, as if convinced that force of will and sheer effort could move this enormous burden. By the time he got home he was too tired to talk, to say anything to his wife about what had happened, and he often fell asleep watching television.

What would a loss mean? If he could not even get a budget out of committee, he and the party would become laughingstocks. If the House rejected the budget it would not be much better. The perception of power gave him power. Perceptions were fragile. If he was perceived not to have power he would lose it.

He had sought power. He did not believe he had sought it for its own sake, only to use it. Yet he recognized the mixed motives of men, and understood the weakness of men, and of himself. His father had been an alcoholic, his closest friend and former chief aide Craig Raupe was an alcoholic. Two other former top aides were alcoholics. So were the haunted, tormented writers Larry King and Billy Lee Bramer who had worked for him. Wright knew what it was like to look into the fire. He was not searchingly introspective. But he knew what loneliness was. For whatever reason he had sought power, if he lost it . . . what then?

St. Patrick's Day arrived, and with it the lunch Wright was hosting in the Speaker's Dining Room for both the former and current Irish prime minister, O'Neill, Reagan, Ted Kennedy, and a handful of senators and members of Irish ancestry. Wright arrived early, and sat drinking a Harp beer with Delaware Democratic senator Joe Biden. Bob Dole sat down and traded jokes with Biden about Iowa, the state which held the first presidential caucuses where both were pursuing the presidency. Outside in the corridor the White House press—just a pool—strained against barrier ropes, pushed against police, jostled whoever walked past, pressed cameras to the door each time it opened. Dole turned his head around and glanced at the mob. "Peaceful in here, isn't it?" Then Reagan entered.

The room was suddenly engulfed in a maelstrom as the press pool surged past the rope, took their pictures, and were pushed back by security. It was a scene reminiscent of the riot in *The Day of the Locust,* a scene of hysteria foreign to the Hill where even the most important member or senator—or Speaker—could be found, walking alone down empty corridors, unnoted by history, without advance men handling logistics problems and laying in communications gear, without a soldier carrying Armageddon in a briefcase, unescorted by aides or security, unhaunted by a pack of photographers. As Wright watched the scene his lips froze into a tight smile. Like nothing else, the mob of media, the security and logistical preparation for the President's appearance, demonstrated the institutional advantages the White House had over him. Reagan was at his worst that day, repeating at the table an Irish joke which O'Neill had previously told him was offensive, standing up before this small gathering of the most powerful politicians in America, and *reading jokes* from his famous three-by-five cards. Yet how much easier for a President to get attention! To dominate the agenda! *To do what Wright wished to do.*

* * *

Where were the Republicans on the budget?

At the very beginning of the year Bill Pitts, Michel's top aide, approached his Democratic counterpart John Mack and said they might be able to work something out on $5–6 billion in taxes. (Pitts did it on his own authority, but knew what was possible. As much a creature of the House as any member and the architect of much GOP strategy as the chief Republican floor aide, he sat in a chair Rayburn had once used; he had even gotten married in the House, and his father had held his job before him.) But that did not seem much of a concession; Reagan's budget included over $6 billion in taxes. Mack never got back to him. Then Democrats on the Budget Committee conducted "field hearings" on Reagan's budget in four cities around the country; they were designed to embarrass Republicans by exploring the impact of Reagan's proposals, and to generate media attention. They succeeded. But they also antagonized House Republicans. "If you take the President's budget and beat the hell out of it for a whole month . . ." Bob Michel shook his head angrily. "They want it both ways. Kick the hell out of the President's budget, then bring Republicans in for cover on their own."

Willis Gradison was one Republican who tried to move toward a solution. But he was the only one. A former mayor of Cincinnati, independently wealthy, a Yale undergraduate with a Harvard M.B.A. and doctorate, Gradison was an emerging intellectual force on both Ways and Means and Budget. He believed, "The only way to get the deficit down is through spending cuts and a tax increase. And I voted that way in the past." Fed up with political games, he sent out a "Dear Colleague," a letter distributed by one member throughout the House, saying, "When we passed Gramm-Rudman-Hollings, we thought the 1986 deficit would be $180 billion. We were wrong; at the time the deficit was $233 billion. I do not think it undermines anything to admit that we started in good faith, but with a wrong number." He suggested enforcing "the spirit" of Gramm-Rudman by cutting $36 billion a year from the deficit until the budget was balanced, and ignoring the precise deficit targets which had been thrown way off by the mistaken baseline. Gradison had hoped to generate a bipartisan solution to the problem. He failed. Democrats leaped to embrace his idea; Republicans did not. They believed too much was at stake to let Wright off the hook so easily. They wanted Democrats to hang in the wind for a while. Republicans isolated Gradison. His senior aide Ron Boster observed wryly, "After the 'Dear Colleague' it got pretty cold around here for a while."

By the time Gradison sent his letter, the Republican leadership had already decided to sit back and do absolutely nothing to help Wright, and use his own aggressiveness, his "agenda" against him. They would let Wright push so hard he fell on his face. Without any GOP votes at all, it did not seem possible for Wright to pass anything. They would try to deny him any GOP votes.

The GOP leadership and senior GOP Budget members decided something else too: Republicans would not produce their own budget to show what they stood for. They had always done so before, but not this year. They knew the facts would impel them in the same direction as Democrats—to taxes. If they did that, it would expose them to attack and undermine their attacks on the Democrats. No budget this year from them. Not this year. They would just sit back and vote no.

Long before the budget came out of committee, a key Republican aide predicted what the Democrats would settle on: "There's only one way they can go. We're not stupid. Thirty-six billion off the deficit, $18 billion from taxes, and $18 billion from spending. The budget resolution is irrelevant as far as we're concerned. We're going to focus on reconciliation."

Reconciliation was the name for the bill that enforced much of the budget resolution. Reconciliation included taxes. Then he continued, "We will not give them any cover on this budget. Democrats have to understand that."

Bob Michel had been around, but not quite long enough. Elected thirty years earlier, he had never chaired a committee, never chaired a subcommittee, never served under a Republican Speaker. He had served longer in the minority than any member of the House in history. The only moment in the 100th Congress in which he or any other Republican spoke from the Speaker's Rostrum came on the first day of the Congress, when he introduced Wright as the new Speaker to the House. If not bitter over it, still the frustration gnawed at him. He was not the kind of man to be bitter. Michel loved baseball, the sport which smells of parks and fields and individual achievement and Norman

Rockwell's nation; he came from, represented, and believed in the heartland of America. Thirty years in Washington had also taught him about hardball.

Born in Peoria, Illinois, his father a millwright, his mother a domestic for one of the wealthiest families in town, he had a paper route as a kid, joined the service, and landed in Normandy on D-Day. A war hero, he talked a group of German soldiers into surrendering, and later was wounded. Back home he graduated from Bradley University, then almost inadvertently started working for Congressman Harold Velde, who chaired the House Un-American Activities Committee at the peak of McCarthyism and competed with McCarthy for attention. When Velde retired in 1956, Michel replaced him. Through the sixties Michel attacked "wasteful-government-spending," which he made seem like one word, and was a fervent anticommunist.

He was big-shouldered, attractive if now overweight; his strengths were obvious, his weaknesses hidden. There was something solid about him that went beyond the physical. When he first came to Washington he looked like the Robert Young of *Father Knows Best,* only more solid, deeper, thicker: Young played an insurance salesman; Michel had been just about to start work as an insurance agent when he left for Washington instead. He was a white middle-American: the Kiwanis, the Rotary Club, an honest man who believed in the good of America, who never cursed and used expressions like "goldarn" or "gee whiz" or "golly." His kids grew up in Peoria, three boys and a girl. When they were in college, at one point all three sons at Yale, he would call one or another almost every day.

A man's man who believed a handshake and a man's word were his measure, when Michel counted votes he would look a member in the eye and shake hands and the member almost *could not* lie to him, could not leave him after giving a commitment. There was something about him; even dishonest men were inclined to treat him honestly.

In 1984, when Georgia Republican Newt Gingrich so enraged O'Neill that O'Neill's response forced the chair to reprimand him by "taking down" his words, most Republicans gave Gingrich a standing ovation. Michel kept his seat. One year later the House refused to seat Indiana Republican Richard McIntyre, who had been declared the winner in a disputed election by state Republican officials. A special House committee recounted the ballots and on a straight party-line vote gave the seat to Democrat Frank McCloskey. Republicans denounced this as a flagrant abuse of power, walking out when McCloskey was seated. Michel did walk out, but also walked back in and shook McCloskey's hand. That was the American way, wasn't it? Shake hands and start over.

Michel's reputation and popularity were things Wright longed for. Wright wanted members to think of him as they thought of Michel, and Wright wanted Michel to think well of him. Once in private Wright praised him to the point that Dave Bonior left the room shaking his head, calling it "extraordinary." It was almost as if Wright was the new boy in school who wanted the popular boy to be his friend.

Michel did not view Wright the same way. He had had a special relationship with O'Neill and was close to Rostenkowski, too; in their younger days they had driven the round trip to Illinois together on weekends, and all three loved golf. And Wright? Michel had only a professional relationship with him. Wright had been fairer to him than O'Neill on things like the ratio of Republicans to Democrats on committees, or allowing a vote on a death penalty in a drug bill. But, like most of his colleagues, Michel did not have a sense of the man; after serving with him for thirty years that made him uneasy. Before Wright became Speaker, Michel told a confidant, "He's never broken his word to me but I'm not comfortable when he gives it."

Still, Michel, a legislator, a doer, had never felt comfortable with the confrontational, media-oriented tactics of the extreme right wing of his party, led by Newt Gingrich. He wasn't a grand thinker, concerned with sweeping political forces and strategies. He was here now, in the House now, presented with problems now. He had to deal with them. That was his job, and, by God, he had always done his job. He was interested in tactics which affected legislation here and now. What did all this grand strategy get you? *You're still left sucking the hind tit,* he would say.

His chief flaw: he loved being Republican leader. "The key to leadership is listening," he said. He listened, very closely, to his colleagues. Michel had reason to listen, to look over his shoulder. Twice he had watched GOP colleagues commit regicide and overthrow their leader, once when Joseph Martin, the last GOP Speaker, was defeated for minority leader by Charles Halleck, then again when Halleck was overthrown by Gerald Ford. And Michel, elected leader in 1980, himself took over when John Rhodes voluntarily stepped down as GOP leader to forestall a challenge (Rhodes stayed in the House for one more term).

The GOP restiveness reflected the frustration of being in the minority. As Gingrich grew stronger and stronger within the GOP Conference, as Democratic control of the House tightened, Michel listened more and more. He was not a man who stood out from his constituency at home or from his colleagues in the House. His own tactics changed and hardened, even when they ran counter to his own instincts. One Republican close to him observed, "There are some things you have to do to keep control."

Another Republican said, "Michel's like the old bull in the caribou herd; all the young bulls are going to give him the horn. Trent's the leader. Trent's slick. I want leaders who are slick. Let's say 'skilled.' Michel's not as Machiavellian as Trent or Wright, or Gingrich."

Trent Lott, from Mississippi, tall, dark-haired, with glasses and a TV anchorman's haircut, was the whip, Michel's elected deputy. His relationship with Michel was not that of loyal follower. Lott had his own power base, regularly hosted luncheons to plan leadership strategy without inviting Michel. When the Republicans were making committee assignments for the 100th Congress, Lott organized a coalition of members from small states which deprived Michel of the assignments he wanted for two Illinois protégés, Lynn Martin and Jack Davis. (Michel then asked Wright for a personal favor, to expand the Armed Services Committee for Davis; Wright did.)

Lott was effective. In Reagan's first term, Lott personally kept open lines of communication to moderate and southern Democrats, and he and Michel organized a "buddy system" matching Republicans one on one with them. That helped win major victories. But as the deficits climbed with the enactment of Reagan's policies, the GOP gradually lost the support of these Democrats, and Lott defined issues in more and more partisan fashion. His partisanship paralleled the increased use of the Rules Committee by the Democratic leadership. He sat on Rules and every day confronted the rawest exercise of the Democratic leadership's power. It embittered him.

Lott came to Washington to work for Rules chairman and Mississippi Democrat William Colmer in the late 1960s, when the Speaker had no power over Rules. One lobbyist regularly kidded him, "I knew you when you had real power—when you worked for Colmer." There was truth to the joke. Colmer, and Virginian Howard Smith before him, blocked the liberal agenda of the 1960s from the floor. When Colmer retired in 1972, Lott ran for the seat. He could have run as a Democrat. Instead he switched parties.

The South mattered to him. It was Lott who in 1981 convinced the Reagan administration to seek tax-exempt status for private segregationist academies. It was Lott who in 1984 called for the chair to "take down" Tip O'Neill's vitriolic outburst against Gingrich, and then led the standing ovation for Gingrich. It was Lott who, just before Christmas in 1985, organized the revolt of House Republicans which defeated tax reform, Reagan's top priority, on its first trip to the floor, almost killing it. (The House GOP was incensed that the White House was ignoring them, treating them as if they didn't exist.) One could almost see in Lott a Faulkner character, one who thought, *The bastards deserve it, whatever it is, for everything they have done and everything they ever wanted to do but hadn't even thought of yet; they deserve it all right.*

Like Coelho, Lott raised the intensity level whenever he entered a room, added energy to it, and like Coelho, Lott was well organized. Lott also paid little attention to substance; he attended instead to politics, and the manipulation of an issue—like on the first day of Congress calling for the prohibition on bringing to the floor Wright's proposal to freeze the top income tax rate. Lott's maneuver had been a personal slap at Wright, and also would allow some future GOP candidate to distort the vote on that procedural issue and charge that his Democratic opponent had voted to raise income taxes. It was hardball. And the budget raised the stakes in that hardball.

Lott was bitter. Winners could afford charity; losers could not. At least they could not when they lost day after day, week after week, month after month. When Jim Wright used the Rules Committee to make a Republican victory even more difficult, Republicans, losers in the House for thirty-two years, were becoming without charity.

Michel's focus was legislation. Lott's was tactics and political positioning. Newt Gingrich, a former professor, an intellectual, had something more fundamental in mind: he concentrated on power and theories of achieving power.

Gingrich believed, and worried, that Wright could become a "great"

Speaker, and concluded, "If Wright consolidates his power, he will be a very, very formidable man. We [have] to take him on early to prevent that."

He would take him on through the media.

Serious reporters were attracted to Gingrich by his ideas and his contagious excitement about them, by his political instincts—in early 1985, for example, he correctly predicted, "Drugs are just going to explode as an issue"—his intelligence, his candor, and his willingness to make cold, biting assessments of leaders of his own party. And he manipulated reporters, complimenting them on their questions, introducing those who wrote about his ideas to colleagues as "very serious, very good, one of the best journalists covering this place."

He was in fact passionate about his ideas; those ideas focused on the processes of power, the way to achieve power. There was coldness too, the coldness of raw intellect, of absolute zero. In 1978, trying to recruit volunteers for his campaign, he told a college Republican Club, "One of the great problems we have had in the Republican Party is that we . . . encourage you to be neat, obedient, and loyal and faithful, and all those Boy Scout words which would be great around the campfire but are lousy in politics . . . A number of you are old enough to have been a rifleman in Vietnam. This is the same business. You're fighting a war. It is a war for power . . . Don't try to educate. That is not your job. What is the primary purpose of a political leader? To build a majority . . . If [people] care about parking lots, talk to them about parking lots."

Slightly rumpled with just a hint of an absent-mindedness, Gingrich had the somewhat overweight, soft body of an academic. There had always been something distant in him. The only child of a broken first marriage, born Newton McPherson, stepson of an army officer who moved in when Newt was three, he described himself as "an army brat," and, like Wright, moved from place to place.

His stepfather told *The Washington Post* that raising Newt "really was no problem once I established myself with him. He was really quite tractable. Once he understood there was a man in the family there was no problem."

Gingrich said that his childhood "sobered me," adding that in politics "it's just very hard to have a personal relationship. It probably attracts those who in part get their ego needs from a larger audience because they're too frightened to get it from a smaller audience."

Wright was forced to hide himself by moving constantly to cliquish small towns where he had to work to make friends. Gingrich reacted differently to the rootlessness of army life, to the dominance of his stepfather, toughening himself and exploring the reaches of his own mind, diving inward, seeking a world he could dominate and control. At first he wanted to be a paleontologist, going deep into the past, into another world, into the cold abstractions of ancient bones. But when he was fifteen he visited Verdun, one of the bloodiest battles of World War I, and was terrified and haunted by the ossuary, a memorial of bones of thousands of unidentified men. What was colder than that?

The sight was a concrete manifestation of what power could do and brought home to him the ultimate reality of politics. Within months he wrote a 180-page analysis of world power and announced he would become a Republican congressman. His freshman year in college at Emory University he began dating his high school mathematics teacher, seven years his senior, and soon married her. His vision of himself and his future was so firm as to be electric. Then came graduate school at Tulane University. Always there was his vision. He would not be dominated by anyone ever again. In 1964, before finishing his Ph.D. in European history, he managed a congressional campaign. In 1968 he worked in Nelson Rockefeller's GOP presidential campaign. In 1970 he started teaching at West Georgia College.

Four years later he mounted his first campaign against John Flynt, a conservative Democrat, a racist, a minor symbol of the kind of southern politics that was fast going out of style. In that Watergate year, Gingrich ran as a reformer, lost a very close race, tried again in 1976 and lost another close race. But he never lost sight of his goal and tried once more in 1978. Flynt retired that year, and Gingrich won.

Like Coelho, who had originally planned to become a priest, Gingrich talked of "inner strength that other politicians don't have" and "a calling." A *calling* could be cold too. Although he called Vietnam "the right battlefield at the right time," although he was the stepson of a career soldier, he avoided the service through deferments first as a student, then as a father. He justified his avoiding the draft by saying a "bigger battle" was in Congress, that Congress "decides that people die or are free." One Republican with two decades in the House noted, "He has what the contras would call 'soft hands,' " someone old enough to send others to their deaths while remaining somehow aloof. His passion lay in the abstract; others were pawns with which to play the game. He was insensitive to the personal, rarely factored it into his equations, and played rough. A Republican colleague noted, "Let's just say I wouldn't want to get in Newt's way."

In 1980 his first wife, Jackie, lay in the hospital recovering from cancer surgery. He walked in and, she told *The Washington Post,* surprised her by "want[ing] to discuss the terms of [a] divorce." Speaking of the incident, Gingrich said with some sadness, "My recollection is a little different. What passes between two people . . . it's just very difficult, very painful."

Lee Howell, who was close enough to Gingrich to have asked him to be his best man, told *Mother Jones* writer David Osborne, "[Newt] handled the divorce like he did any other political decision: You've got to be tough in this business, you've got to be hard. Once you make the decision you've got to act on it. Cut your losses and move on."

Gingrich was lonely too. There were moments, isolated in Washington, even in a second marriage, when, he said, he cried. But his "inner strength," his "calling," always sustained him. The calling was power.

Once Gingrich had been moderate: Eisenhower was one of his heroes and he had that experience in Rockefeller's campaigns. But that had been a long time ago. After the 1982 collapse of House GOP dreams of taking control of the House, he became the prime mover behind forming the Conservative Opportunity Society. The COS, made up at first of a half-dozen angry House Republicans, grew out of a debate over how to become the majority party in the House and the nation. COSers scorned the Old Right of the party, the Wall Street pin-striped crowd; they were the New Right, the committed Reaganauts who were swept into Washington in the same tide that carried Reagan.

Reasoning that the GOP had tried cooperation and compromise with Democrats and gotten nowhere, the COS abandoned accommodation, felt no responsibility to govern or to help Democrats pass anything. When Democrats took over the Senate, COSers saw even less reason to compromise and their voice grew stronger within the Republican Conference. Reagan was damaged by the Iran-contra scandal, and the White House staff was headed by moderate Howard Baker. Senate Republicans wanted tax increases to cut the deficit. Only the COS group, the true believers, only they were left. They alone wore Reagan's mantle. There was something almost glorious about it. Lott, though not a COS member, represented them in the leadership.

By the time Wright became Speaker, the COS, once only a handful of members, had grown to 20 percent of House Republicans. Gingrich and they pursued their agenda outside the Congress. Indeed, he used the Congress largely as a prop to frame issues for the media. The doers among Republicans, the legislators, disliked his style; it brought disrepute upon the House.

One media strategy revolved around the live televising of House proceedings over C-SPAN, the Cable Satellite Public Affairs Network. When the 100th Congress convened, C-SPAN reached more than twenty-five million homes, and close to half a million registered voters were watching at any given moment. The audience mattered; one study showed that 93 percent of C-SPAN viewers had voted in the preceding presidential election, compared to 53 percent of the electorate at large. Politicians could understand those numbers.

When the House conducted its legislative business, floor debate had to relate to the bill and each speaker was normally limited to five minutes. So COSers exploited "one-minutes" and "special orders." One-minutes came usually at the beginning of each session when members could speak for one minute on any subject; the one-minutes were aimed at creating sound bites that the networks or local news outlets would pick up. Special orders came after the House had finished its legislative business and members, except for the handful making speeches, had gone home; the speeches could be an hour or more on any subject. Special orders gave the COS an opportunity to orchestrate floor exchanges. Two or three members might simulate a real dialogue, creating action and more interest than a simple speech, coordinating their message, and influencing viewers.

It was a special order which had prompted O'Neill's 1984 outburst. Gingrich had accused several Democrats by name of being "blind to communism," and threatened to "file charges" against ten members, including Wright, who had written a letter to Nicaraguan president Daniel Ortega. (In the letter Wright urged Ortega to hold free elections; he wrote it after the administration asked him to try to influence the Sandinistas.) No one defended the named Democrats. But viewers did not know that the chamber was empty; House rules required the camera to show only the person speaking. The next day, O'Neill, without warning COSers, had also ordered the camera to pan the whole chamber during special orders, revealing COSers gesticulating to an empty hall. That led to Gingrich's exchange on the floor with O'Neill, who called Gingrich's speech "the lowest thing that I've ever seen in my thirty-two years in Congress." Lott then rose and demanded that O'Neill's words be "taken down," erased from the record. It was the first time a Speaker's words were taken down since 1798. Democrats never forgot.

C-SPAN was not Gingrich's only media strategy. He understood its limitations. His goal was "resonance." Resonance *out there*. He knew how to achieve it. Shortly after the exchange with O'Neill, he said in a speech to conservative activists that for months he had been giving "organized, systematic, researched one-hour lectures. Did CBS rush in . . . ? No. But the minute Tip O'Neill attacked me, he and I got ninety seconds at the close of all three network news shows. The number-one fact about the news media is that they love fights. When you give them confrontations you get attention. When you get attention, you can educate."

That lesson had been driven home to him. And Gingrich began to develop a new twist to an old theme, that power corrupts, that thirty-two years in power had corrupted the Democrats. His efforts grew more focused after the 1984 election, after the McIntyre-McCloskey disputed seat, which House Democrats gave to the Democrat. "That was a seminal event," Gingrich said. "That changed the way Republicans thought around here."

It made certain things acceptable that had not been acceptable. "The House really is a collegial institution," Gingrich said, "an intimate place." It had unwritten rules, the violation of which meant ostracism. Ostracism could be very tough in that body. Very tough. But the McIntyre-McCloskey disputes changed the tone among Republicans, brought into question those unwritten laws, sharpened the edge between them and Democrats, refocused the way Republicans viewed Democratic control. Gingrich was focused.

Two years before Wright became Speaker, Gingrich commented, "We are engaged in reshaping a whole nation through the news media." Gingrich, the former professor of modern European history who would soon be comparing Wright to Mussolini, was perhaps familiar with Mussolini's observation, "Another weapon I discovered early was the power of the printed word to sway souls to me. The newspaper was soon my gun."

The target of this gun would be Wright.

While Gingrich waited for the right moment to fire, his colleagues waited too, withholding themselves entirely from the budget process, forcing Democrats to put a budget together themselves. *The Wall Street Journal* analyzed the situation:

> Democrats in both chambers are resisting so large a [military] cut. Some warn that any paring of the military budget could open the Democrats to the old criticism that they are weak on defense, lose them voters, and incite conservative Democrats to ally with Republicans to block a Democratic budget plan. . . .
>
> Liberals resist cuts in social programs. . . . The squabbling is compounded by President Reagan's unwillingness to compromise.
>
> "This is probably a no-win situation all the way around," says Richard Moe, a veteran Democratic adviser.

It was worse than a no-win situation. Budget Democrats listened to a Wright aide specify how much money Wright wanted for welfare reform, AIDS, trade, education—for all his priorities. As soon as the presentation ended, they attacked. Was the Speaker serious? Didn't he understand the problems? Where were they supposed to get the money? They all had their own priorities too. Bill Gray asked members to raise their hands if they supported funding Wright's priorities. There were twenty Democrats. One hand went up.

Gray had been talking continually with Gradison, the Republican most amenable to bipartisanship, to keep the door open for possible GOP involvement. Now, facing disaster, he invited all the Budget Republicans to a private meeting of the committee—practically all business before this had been conducted in a caucus of committee Democrats—and then invited them to participate in writing the budget.

Delbert Latta, the ranking Republican, hesitated, uncertain whether Gray was sincere or offering a trap. Gradison suggested that they buck the decision to their leadership and Latta agreed.

For the Democrats, a nadir had been reached. They had asked for GOP help. The threat of disaster was often the only thing that finally moved policy. Disaster was at hand.

While Gray talked to Republicans, Wright grew even more intense. The vote against his priorities had enraged and humiliated him. It had also shaken him. He was losing this. It was his first test as Speaker, a confrontation he himself had chosen, a definition of all that he cared about in programs, and a definition of his power as well. *It was a test of his power, the first real test, and he was losing it.* Wright was determined he would not lose it.

He found four Budget members sitting together on the floor. One of them, Michael Lowry, who headed the liberal one-hundred-plus–member Democratic Study Group, had a reputation for anger too, and when he got mad he stayed mad for days. But now Wright was not delicate. His fists closed, his voice raised, his jaw muscles tight, his anger flared up, shot across the House chamber. He pounded his fist into his palm. Logic was part of his argument. *Weren't they Democrats? Didn't they understand what they were doing? Didn't they know what was at stake? Didn't they understand they weren't Jim Wright's priorities, they were Democratic priorities? These initiatives reversed the direction of the Reagan years. Already private polling was giving strong support to proceeding with them.* But the convincing came not from the force of his logic. It came from him. The veil had dropped. Suddenly the members could see the fury in him, a cold, intimidating passion not to be crossed. As he launched into them, as other members turned and watched, they could see the stirrings of something deep, of a man who would . . . *what?* Pat Williams did not want to find out: "We saw for the first time a very determined aggressive leader who was bound and determined to do what he believed was correct, come hell or high water."

They bent to him. One at a time he sought out other members of the committee. They bent, too.

And Wright turned his attention again toward the press. Editorials around the country were turning in his favor. He told his staff to see that each favorable editorial was distributed to every Democrat in the House, but warned, "We should not be seen as the ones sending them out. Get the member in whose district the editorial appeared to do it. With a good cover letter." Make it appear that there was a groundswell of support both from the country and the membership.

If editorials favored him, news stories did not. They still talked of the political suicide Democrats were preparing to commit. He believed the press was taking cheap shots. *The Washington Post, The New York Times, The Wall Street Journal* all reported that Democrats were aiming at $36 billion in deficit reduction, but that $36 billion fell $25 billion short of the Gramm-Rudman target. Not one of the stories noted that Reagan's budget did exactly the same thing. Wright had gone over and over the facts with reporters. It hadn't seemed to take. John Mack suggested creating "a tax non-task force" of key members whom the press talked to regularly to put out this line. There weren't more than a dozen members in the House that the national press talked to on any given issue. Privately, make sure those members agreed with Wright— if not, sell them on it—and get everyone echoing the same line. No matter what the question, give the same answer. *Reagan missed the target. Reagan had taxes.* Then reporters would have to print it. But keep it quiet so the press would not realize they were being manipulated. Transfer the pressure from Democrats to Reagan, to the Republicans.

The entire leadership turned more aggressive. The "tax non-task force" turned aggressive. Vic Fazio responded to Reagan's weekly five-minute radio speech and attacked Reagan's budget vigorously enough to make the newspapers—something which rarely happened. Wright himself appeared on *Face the Nation* and did the same. Everyone in the leadership knew what would make front-page quotes.

The offer of cooperation to Republicans was made Thursday. Democrats waited for an answer the rest of Thursday, all day Friday, through the weekend, through Monday. On Monday night, Gradison still believed a deal would be worked out. The GOP leadership was still functioning on O'Neill's timetable of activity Tuesday to Thursday only. Once earlier in the year Michel had tried to hold a leadership meeting on Monday but had to cancel it. No one was around. Now Michel waited, not willing to make such a decision unilaterally. *The key to leadership is listening,* he had said.

Democrats read the delay as an attempt to drag things out, and delay alone could embarrass the Democrats. Now it was Tuesday. Meanwhile, Wright had himself made progress with the committee. And Gray came up with another idea: flush Republicans into the open by holding a public markup session without a chairman's "mark" (a draft proposal). Instead, the committee would work off last year's budget and vote on item after item. Republicans would have to vote to cut programs people wanted, pay for them with taxes, or fail to cut the deficit. *It's not a question of policy,* Wright often said, *it's arithmetic.* That would moot their plan not to offer any alternatives; the GOP votes would inevitably define a GOP position. Tuesday morning at a leadership breakfast with the Senate, Gray discussed his idea. Everyone liked it. And the leadership decided to turn up the heat even more in the press. Technically,

Gray's private offer of cooperation remained open. But it had already closed.

Later in the morning, at the daily press conference, Coelho told reporters that Reagan's budget was filled with "little white lies" and called it "a scam." Wright quipped, "What did the President know about taxes in his budget and when did he know it?"

The words spoken at the press conference spread quickly, carried by reporters seeking GOP reactions. Words mean something to politicians. The word "lie" meant something. Gradison complained, "Coelho didn't have to go for the jugular like that. He's the whip now. He should act more responsibly." Michel even protested on the floor in a "one-minute." Other Republicans were equally angry. And bitterness lingered over the recent vote on contra aid, when Democrats had denied Republicans a straight-up-or-down vote.

By the time the Republicans met to discuss the possibility of cooperating, events had swept past any chance for it. The Republicans knew it, and laid down five conditions for bipartisanship they knew were unacceptable. The first required the Democrats to produce a draft budget—but if they could do that, they did not need the Republicans. The other four conditions dealt with procedures. Procedure meant power. The Republicans were demanding that the Democrats yield power. Jim Wright would compromise on policy. Not on power.

Wright's anger and the threat of disaster had shaken Democrats on Budget loose from their positions and created a state of flux, even if they had not yet settled on a budget. He intended to take advantage of that flux now, to close a deal in principle, if not in detail, now.

That Tuesday afternoon Wright and the rest of the leadership met with the committee chairmen, once again in the Speaker's Dining Room. Almost immediately the group became unruly. The pressure from the numbers was intense. When Gray talked of Gramm-Rudman pressures, one chairman complained, "Don't give us this damn artifical Gramm-Rudman crap. Gramm-Rudman's absurd. It's arbitrary."

"It's the law," Gray said.

"We make the laws," snorted another chairman. "Pass another law."

A third said, "Reagan's budget is phony. The time has come for phony solutions. I'm talking political reality."

"The asset sales we did last year put us $12 billion into the hole when we started this year," Gray countered. "It'll hurt more next year."

"There are politics next year, too," agreed another. "It will be worse. There's nothing in the pot. Nothing. Want to go after veterans' pensions? I can give you $2 billion in cuts but that's where it will be. It'll be a hell of a floor fight."

"Sometimes you just do what's right," Morris Udall said with irony.

"Mr. Speaker, Social Security, that's where the money is." Rostenkowski had been quiet. His comment woke everyone up. He hunched his large body forward, spread his elbows out on the table, took up space. Democrats gained twenty-six House seats in 1982 largely by accusing the GOP of wanting to cut Social Security. For the Democrats, it was as powerful a political tool as GOP charges that Democrats wanted to raise taxes. Ways and Means had jurisdiction over both. But it seemed crazy. How could he take on cutting Social Security, while continuing to resist raising taxes? *He was trying to be responsible, damn it.* "All the studies show the elderly are better off than ever, better off than kids. If we're gonna do anything, it's got to come from there. I know all about the 1982 election but will that go on ad infinitum?"

"Social Security's in surplus," Wright snapped. "That tax is a trust fund."

The meeting broke up. Leaving, Veterans Affairs Committee chairman Sonny Montgomery shook his head and said, "Whew. It's rough in there."

But for all the contentiousness, Wright had accomplished what he needed. He had made the chairmen face reality. They would accept whatever came out of the Budget Committee. It was that or chaos, which would destroy all authority, including theirs. Wright would have to work on some of them, massage them, but they would be all right. He had listened to their complaints. Just sat back and listened. *Sometimes people just want to bitch. Once they've done that they're all right. These guys were all right now.* They had talked themselves out.

Wright's next meeting would produce results directly. It was with Budget. Wright had reversed the 19–1 vote against his initiatives. He had had to. It would have been a terrible precedent to set, had he lost in his first major confrontation. He couldn't let the committee dictate to him. *He was Speaker. Power gave. Power could give things away voluntarily. It could not allow things to be taken from it.* Now the committee would fund them fully, if he wanted them to. But, now, now that he had won, now he could give the committee what it wanted.

Gray recognized that, too. He had asked Wright to come to this meeting to play that game out. It was like the investiture ceremony with Rules Committee members. Now Budget members would explain their problems, and Wright would be reasonable. After thirty minutes of listening, Wright agreed.

"You're saying," Gray summarized, "that you hear us, if we're worried about the out-years take a little off. And if say we give a 2 percent Medicaid increase instead of 4 percent, no problem. As long as we stick to Democratic principles and priorities."

Wright agreed: "Look, so long as we can be honest with ourselves and the American people that we have launched initiatives in trade, welfare reform, catastrophic health care, then Bill, if your judgment and the committee's judgment is that we've done that and you want to cut the amount in them, that's okay."

They had broken through. Wright's backing off gave them enough room to make a deal, to settle on a budget. It would still be difficult, but now everyone knew it would be done. There was a collective release of tension. The whole feel of the room changed, as if it were a submarine breaking from the deep into the sunshine; suddenly the air was filled with grins, members joked. Then Wright looked around the room.

"But that's not all," he continued. "If we do it, agree to it here. I don't want any of our guys abandoning it and giving the Republicans a majority."

They understood. Whatever argument they had inside the room stayed inside the room. Inside the room, they could fight all they wanted. But whatever they agreed to, all of them had to support.

"Take a blood oath," Wright concluded. *"Do it here."*

The next day the Budget Committee formally convened to mark up a budget. Gray planned to vote on one spending program at a time, to flush the Republicans into the open. First was defense. Democrats voted to cut Reagan's request drastically, not even keeping up with inflation. Republicans voted present. Gray adjourned. The next day was a repeat performance.

The whole reason to serve in Congress was to vote. Talk about abdication of responsibility! *The Republican refusal to vote was outrageous.* The press turned on the Republicans. Playing politics was one thing—everyone understood that—but this? Standing for nothing? Refusing to vote? That was something else.

Throughout the Democratic Caucus, members began to rally behind

Wright. Wright had just gotten results from the leadership's own private poll. Results were excellent and that helped, too; the leadership made sure the word got out, quoted results at the whip meeting to demonstrate that the public solidly endorsed Wright's agenda. The public was even beginning to respect the Democrats' ability to cut the deficit. The numbers on that were the best in years and clearly reflected Wright's willingness to talk about a pay-as-you-go approach. If the public didn't like taxes, it liked taking responsibility.

Still, Wright did not let up. He sent a second personal, hand-written note to every Democrat on Ways and Means, enclosing copies of the poll. And he continued to work Budget. The final sticking point was George Miller, a liberal on Budget. A big, powerful, often emotional man, a former college football star, Miller looked like a good man to have a beer with. An odd combination of pragmatist, loose cannon, hard-ass, and conscience, he feared no one and was both a Rostenkowski loyalist and part of what remained of Phil Burton's California machine. His chief concerns were children's programs, which the preceding year the Democratic Caucus had declared a priority. Miller had delivered votes on Wright's initiatives, and as a reward now was seeing his own programs go under the knife. Now he was balking. In a conversation which would haunt Wright's entire speakership, Wright saw him on the floor and soothed him, listened to him and agreed with him, told him they believed in the same things, supported the same programs. They shouldn't be fighting each other. They weren't enemies. They had to work together. "George, I'm for all the things you're for," Wright said. "But we've got to have a budget. Can't you help us?"

Miller agreed to cut another $1.5 billion. Suddenly Marvin Leath, the conservative, was willing to come down on defense spending.

The Democrats were close to agreement. Late in the afternoon Gray stopped in to see Wright. "Latta [the ranking Budget Republican] tells me, 'This refusal-to-vote crap is bullshit but it's what my leadership wants. What can I do?' We've got the Republicans by the balls. I'm meeting my folk"—he glanced up at the clock—"in a few minutes. We'll see if we can work this out tonight."

For the first time in weeks Gray's smile seemed to come from inside him, from joy—not from his sense of the absurd. It still was not easy. For hours, well into the evening, past midnight, Budget Democrats caucused. But the next morning John Mack walked into Wright's breakfast meeting. Wright glanced up at him.

"It looks like we've got a budget," Mack said, "and it's something you can support."

As Democrats were finally settling on a budget, Reagan was coming to the Hill to address the House Republican Conference. Republican members, 150 of them, listened to him say, "We're not going to knock the legs out from under economic growth by draining resources from the private sector into the federal bureaucracy. . . . My answer to the tax hikers—and I hope I can count on you to back me up—is 'No. No! *No!*' "

CHAPTER 7

In the last two weeks before Easter recess, the 100th Congress defined itself. The Congress would in fact set policy, as Democrats had hoped. And Wright would in fact dominate the Congress, as he had intended. The elaborate organization he and Coelho had created would run the House: their attention to detail, their determination to *let not one thing slip* would squeeze every last vote out of the House on issue after issue. His speakership began to resemble a great python trying to wrap itself about a sleeping tiger, preparing to wrap it in a death grip, the tiger just beginning to stir, one eye alert, preparing to lash out. That fight would come in the future. There were more immediate fights. First, Wright would challenge, and vanquish, those whom he perceived to question his authority. He was creating himself with each action, establishing and defining and communicating his very nature with each act. He himself was not sure what to expect. While there was little tentative about him, and when challenged he reared up, still he was not sure of his limits. He would find them.

He liked the budget. It cut the deficit by $36 billion; every dollar was real; it contained no phony devices. Eighteen billion dollars of deficit reduction came from tax hikes and $18 billion from spending cuts—$9 billion from domestic programs and $9 billion from defense—and it did fund new initiatives. But he still had to pass it.

The same day the budget was settled informally in committee, Ronald Reagan vetoed the highway bill, the bill which had passed the House in the first few days of the session. Overriding the veto would be difficult.

Yet Wright's most serious problem, the one which most threatened his authority, was Dan Rostenkowski. No one could win every vote on the floor, but there were always ways to influence policy, even after a loss. One's authority, one's power, was much more fragile than any policy—especially now, with Wright the new boy on the block, with every member of the House, the White House, even the Senate wanting to find out what he had. *Back when Wright was a boy, moving to all those new towns and new schools and new tests, he had taken up fighting.* Each public pronouncement by Rostenkowski seemed a test, and each comment seemed more challenging than the one before. In a speech Rostenkowski said taxes would go to the House floor only if Republicans supported them. Then *The Wall Street Journal* quoted him supporting a gasoline tax increase, the kind of regressive tax Wright specifically opposed. Then *The Washington Post* reported, "Rostenkowski said he had told Wright he would only attempt to raise as much revenue as other committee chairmen agreed to cut. 'I'm not saying [$18 billion] is not doable, but it's an awful load.' "

At breakfast Wright snapped, "I invite him over to sit down and talk about these things and he goes out and says, 'I told the Speaker this and that.' " He fell silent for a moment, then said, "Rostenkowski will damn well do what the Caucus wants him to. You know, he can be removed as chairman of that committee."

Even as a throwaway comment in a moment of anger, the idea of going after Rostenkowski was chilling. His staff tensed, afraid to contradict him, more afraid to agree, and silently looked down at their plates.

A few days later, a Sunday, *The Washington Post* printed more comments by Rostenkowski from a lengthy interview on trade. Wright read it, growing angrier and angrier, circling one paragraph, underlining a sentence, bracketing an entire section. The trade issue had already forced one test of strength between Wright and Rostenkowski, which Wright had won. Now Rostenkowski seemed to be trying to undermine him, seemed to be saying he would ally himself with the administration, and especially with James Baker. They had worked closely together on tax reform the year before. Such a relationship would cut Wright out.

In the *Post* interview, Rostenkowski said, "It's Jim Baker coming up to my office very early this year and saying, 'we can work together, we can work together' "—*and what about the Congress, Rostenkowski's colleagues, what were they supposed to be doing?* "It's Danny Rostenkowski going down to see the President"—*there was Rostenkowski's ego, talking about him and the President, talking about himself in the third person*—"and having Don Regan pull me on the side and say, 'Jim Baker will be the point man and [Commerce Secretary Malcolm] Baldrige and [Trade Representative Clayton] Yeutter will be the workers in the vineyard. . . . ' It's members saying, 'Don't make me vote on Gephardt' "—a provision which toughened U.S. response to unfair trade practices, advocated by Richard Gephardt, who was running for President, and opposed by the White House as protectionist—" 'Jesus, don't make me vote on Gephardt.' " *There was Rostenkowski saying he was representing members' interests, saying Wright, who supported the provision, wasn't.*

There were other comments too, implying that Wright supported the Gephardt provision only because he had caved in to pressure from labor unions, that Wright had said one thing in December, another thing a few weeks later, and another thing now. The theme was clear: that he, Rostenkowski, was in charge; that he, Rostenkowski, had dealt with the White House before and would deal with the White House now in negotiating a bill; that he, Rostenkowski, would take care of members' concerns and Wright was failing them; that he, Rostenkowski, knew what was right.

The interview infuriated Wright. Part of his anger reflected his sense of the institutional prerogatives of the Congress. It wasn't any of the administration's business what Congress passed. Didn't Rostenkowski ever hear of the separation of powers? Congress would pass what it damn well knew was right for the country. If Reagan wanted to veto it, then let him veto it and be damned. The House had passed the trade bill with enough votes to override a veto. The Senate might, too.

But most of Wright's anger was personal.

Rostenkowski was flexing his muscles, was testing—if not outright challenging—him. The Monday *Wall Street Journal* reported on a speech Rostenkowski gave to the Futures Industry Association virtually ruling out Wright's suggested securities transaction tax idea. Rostenkowski had already ruled out Wright's call for freezing the top income tax rate, even though Rostenkowski six months earlier had himself called it the most logical way to raise revenue. Two suggestions by Wright, two rejections by Rostenkowski. Public rejections. *Maybe Danny had forgotten who won the election for Speaker. Maybe Danny forgot he hadn't even run for it. Maybe he needed some reminding.*

At Monday's breakfast meeting Wright, for the second time in a week, snapped, "Rostenkowski can be removed as chairman of that committee."

The earlier comment had not been offhanded after all. Wright had been thinking about this. His staff said nothing, worrying that if Wright started this fight, he might be able to win it. If Rostenkowski could be removed any chairman could be removed, and Wright's power would be enormously enhanced. But what had Rostenkowski actually done? Offend the Speaker by talking to a reporter? Remove a chairman for *that*? No Speaker had attacked a chairman since 1961, when in a grueling, bitter confrontation Rayburn had enlarged the Rules Committee to dilute chairman Howard Smith's power. But that had been different. Smith, a conservative and segregationist, had threatened to block Kennedy's domestic program from getting to the floor. Rayburn had represented the Caucus on a matter of high policy; the Caucus had demanded action. Speakers supported chairmen; they did not go after them. This was dangerous, too dangerous even to contemplate.

Most of the other lords of the House would line up with Rostenkowski. They would have to. Wright would be threatening their own power. Only the most junior members of the Caucus could benefit from dethroning a chairman. The old British concept of "King and Commons," united against the nobility, came to mind, but in this case even the junior members aspired to the nobility. Nor did they trust Wright to use power to advance their interests, as opposed to his own. Wright would have a difficult, difficult fight. It would destroy Wright's speakership if he lost, and could cripple it even if he won.

Immediately after breakfast, consulting with none of his allies, not with Brooks or Dingell, the two chairmen most closely allied with him, not with his leadership, he wrote Rostenkowski a letter and marked it "Personal." It was an extraordinary letter and revealed just how far Wright was willing to go, just how much he was willing to risk, to insure that in his speakership *he* would rule.

A page hand-delivered it to one of Rostenkowski's senior aides, who brought it to Rob Leonard, staff director of Ways and Means. It being Monday, Rostenkowski as usual was in Chicago. Leonard called him and said a letter from the Speaker marked "Personal" had arrived.

Rostenkowski told him to have everyone else leave the room and read it. It said:

Dear Danny,

It was very surprising to me to read the interview with you in yesterday's *Washington Post*. . . . My preference, of course, is to have the cooperation of the White House, unless it must be purchased at the sacrifice of strong and effective legislation. I do not believe we should allow Administration employees to sit in markup sessions [which Rostenkowski allowed throughout the tax reform effort] of any House Committee or dictate the terms of legislation in the drafting process. I do not believe we should give the Administration prior veto rights over provisions we believe to be necessary and effective. . . . The House last year voted overwhelmingly to include the Gephardt provision. Polls indicate the public overwhelmingly supports strong affirmative action of this general type. Dick Gephardt is willing to scale back his provisions. . . . Dick seems willing, in deference to your wishes, to leave it off the Committee bill and offer it as a separate proposition on the floor. To deny him this privilege would be to deny the membership an opportunity to vote for something which they overwhelmingly endorsed less than a year ago. . . . As Chairman of the House Committee on Ways and Means, Danny, you are the designated agent of the Democratic Caucus. . . . As their chosen agents, you and I would serve them poorly if we contrived to deny them the opportunity . . . to vote for a strong, effective trade bill.

As Chairman of the House Committee on Ways and Means, Danny, you are the designated agent of the Democratic Caucus. The threat was clear. Rostenkowski was quiet for a moment, then said sardonically, "We're communicating by letter now? Is this what it's come to?"

A letter? Things had changed, all right. Rostenkowski had become a dinosaur. All his old intimates, the members he had golfed with, played cards with, had dinner with, had disappeared. O'Neill had been the last. Sure, Danny still went out with members, but they were younger now, not contemporaries. It took effort to get to know the new members. He was tired. He didn't want to put out that effort anymore. He didn't even know most junior members' names. And now the chairman of Ways and Means and the Speaker of the House were communicating by letter.

That wasn't the way Rostenkowski would have done it, had he been Speaker. He wasn't Speaker.

But by God he would run his own committee.

Rostenkowski never responded to the letter, never referred to it at all, directly or indirectly. But his tone with the press changed. In a way, the letter marked the real beginning of Wright's speakership. The struggle to override Reagan's veto of the highway bill would mark its first victory.

The highway bill spent $88 billion for road repairs and mass transit over five years. It raised no new taxes, and simply spent money in a trust fund already collected from gasoline taxes. Total spending amounted to less than the congressional budget resolution allowed. When the bill emerged from the House-Senate conference, Coelho pressed the whip organization to turn out the strongest possible vote; the leadership wanted to send a message to Reagan not to veto it, and to test the prospects for cooperation which Howard Baker had talked about. The bill passed the House 407–17, and passed the Senate 79–17. Bob Michel warned Baker that he would vote to override any veto and so would Trent Lott. Several Republican senators met with Reagan personally and tried to dissuade him from a veto.

But the issue was not the highway bill. The issue was who would dominate. Bob Dole, after meeting with Reagan, told reporters, "He needs to demonstrate that he's in charge, that he's effective. One way to do that is to show that you're tough."

Reagan showed that he was tough. He vetoed the bill, complaining that it exceeded his budget request by $10 billion and represented "a failure to exercise the discipline that is required to constrain federal spending, especially pork-barrel spending."

If his veto was sustained, it would demonstrate that Reagan was still in control in Washington, that regardless of the Iran-contra affair, regardless of Democrats retaking the Senate, regardless of Jim Wright's ambitions, he was the boss. He could veto everything, grind the business of government to a halt, compel the Congress to accede to his wishes. Conservatives, led by his former aide Patrick Buchanan, were advising him to do precisely that.

To win, Reagan would need to double the seventeen senators who had voted against the bill. Dole predicted victory for him. Their hopes rested on senators like Robert Stafford, a moderate Republican from Vermont who was one of the chief authors of the bill. Stafford had asked Reagan to sign it, but said he would vote with Reagan if he did veto it: "I think it's critical to his reemergence as an active and powerful President that . . . his veto be sustained."

Wright worried. He respected Reagan's political skills. Only a few weeks earlier, after Reagan's speech about the Iran-contra scandal, Wright had wryly observed, "This old boy, he's clever all right."

If Reagan did win this fight it would encourage him to veto other bills. Wright's hopes for passing significant legislation could disappear. He could be forced to accept what the White House dictated. Publicly he told reporters that Reagan's reasons for the veto were "inadequate. . . . The President should rise above the temptation to pick petty fights and provoke needless confrontation in order to appear tough."

Privately he called Reagan "a foolish and petulant old man." His problem was that the key votes belonged to people who seemed to be beyond his reach—senators, and not just senators but Republican senators. But he would try to extend his reach.

"Obviously I can't preach to Republican senators," he told his leadership colleagues in a strategy meeting, "but support groups"—construction firms, suppliers, unions, city and state governments—"can. If those senators turn their back on them just to pacify a churlish President, they'll incur the wrath of outraged voters. Make sure we get that message communicated. Let's make it hard as hell for Dole. They need to switch seventeen votes. That's hard. We'll make it harder."

There was no doubt as to whether the House would override the veto, but the Democrats needed the largest possible vote to maximize pressure on the Senate. The Democratic Steering and Policy Committee, the group whose chief purpose is making committee assignments, passed a resolution that this vote was Democratic Party policy; that meant the leadership kept track of this vote and considered it when a member asked for a favor. Coelho mobilized a whip task force, the first of the year chaired by Norman Mineta. Coelho was still bitter about his earlier treatment by Wright. When Mineta asked him what his responsibilities were, Coelho snorted, "Beats me." But his competitive juices quickly got him involved.

The biggest problem was North Carolina and Virginia. Members from both states felt the formula dispensing funds treated them unfairly and talked about voting to sustain the veto. At a task force meeting to review the position of every Democrat in the House, one member advised, "There are four Virginians on this list as undecided. Let's deal with them on a higher level. Have Tony, Tom, or the Speaker talk to them in a group."

"In North Carolina they're also taking heat," someone else said. "It's front-page news down there. The Republican governor is putting heat on, and the lieutenant governor's a Democrat who's going to run."

"Triple team these folks."

"The North Carolina chapter of the Associated General Contractors hasn't taken a position. Who'll get the national to come down on them? There are 813,000 jobs involved. It doesn't bust the budget. The trust fund pays for it and people have already paid that money in. It completes the interstate system."

"Who's got Gephardt? He's a no response."

"Have someone from Iowa"—home of the first presidential caucus— "talk to Gephardt."

After the meeting Mineta talked to the governor of Virginia, a Democrat. Public Works chairman Jim Howard called him as well. The governor would help with Virginians. Wright worked, too, talking to North Carolina members, telling them that this wasn't a free vote. They needed everyone, to influence Terry Sanford. Sanford, from North Carolina, was the only Democratic senator who had voted against the bill itself. Wright did not mention tobacco. "I'm not in a position to make threats," he explained. "I don't do that."

But Coelho made it clear: *If North Carolinians voted no, forget about help on tobacco programs. There would be retribution.*

It was the kind of fight Coelho loved. Coelho was the go-getter, the young Turk, the shark. He did not wait for something to happen; he made it happen. His intensity and organization set him apart. Few members—few people—had his intensity. He could look at someone, get up in someone's face, challenging with his intensity. Despite a physical presence, he was not a big man, not overweight; still, a certain softness, not largeness, just softness, around the belly kept him from looking thin. His most dominant physical aspect was his head. It seemed disproportionately large. Dark-skinned, dark-haired, he had dark, probing eyes that gave him a sensual quality. They were also impatient, penetrating but also demanding that their attention be deserved; more than that, they were both probing and set back deep in his face, simultaneously pushing forward and protecting some inner recess. He had a weak chin, thin wrists, a hairy body, and a touch of gray at the temples. Leaning forward, he penetrated the space of whomever he was speaking with. Like Lyndon Johnson, he played the game at close range, challenging by physical proximity, pushing, invading, using the physical discomfort of proximity as a weapon.

He did not hide himself, not even weaknesses. At forty-four, with only four terms in Congress behind him, he won the whip job. Lobbyist friends gave him whips which he mounted on his office wall like crossed swords. His aggressiveness rubbed some people raw.

His comment just after winning election as whip that he didn't intend to sit around and wait ten years to be Speaker had not been forgotten, and his explanation that he had meant simply that he might leave Congress had not satisfied many people.

There was a tension between him and Foley. His approach, his whole operation contributed to it. He hired staff who made things happen, who invaded the domain of the Speaker by talking to the Rules Committee, who invaded the domain of the majority leader by talking about scheduling. *Some people think I have sharks on my staff,* he had said. *I like strong people.* An aide who was a shark echoed him: "He's the only one who won a contested election in ten years. Foley never won one at all."

Still, there was ambivalence in him. Periodically he told intimates he really did sometimes consider leaving the House, and that he had declined a job offer at a *seven*-figure salary. (The offer most likely came from Drexel Burnham Lambert; he had a good relationship with Michael Milken, who invented "junk bonds.") But the ambivalence never paralyzed him; everything he did was at one speed—full speed.

Foley shrugged most things off. But he did not shrug Coelho off. Once Michel and Foley were discussing the schedule for the next week when they both ran out of time; purely routine items were left, and Michel suggested Coelho get together with Lott to finish. Foley refused. "The majority leader sets the schedule," he said. "Not the whip."

Coelho had a cynicism, a sense of realpolitik, almost a bitterness, about him. His strength was in getting things done, doing things better than anyone else, with no illusions. He also had what he called "inner peace"; he had been through the fire and survived. His experiences gave him a rock upon which to stand.

He grew up on a dairy farm in California, the child of Portuguese immigrants. His parents were much older, closer in age to grandparents, and closer to the Old World than the new; more separated them and their son than in most families. His parents believed in devils. As a teenager he seemed to have some demons in him, the way he went at everything with such intensity; he rose early, worked the farm, went to school, and partied. He seemed never to sleep; sleep was the enemy.

Then, at Loyola University in Los Angeles, he began blacking out. At first the blackouts caused few problems. He raised hell at night and was student body president during the day. Never lacking for direction, he planned to become a lawyer; with his intelligence and energy it seemed he could not avoid success even had he wanted to. Then the assassination of John F. Kennedy changed his direction.

"I got infatuated, emotionally attached to a dead man," Coelho said. "JFK was an idol to me. The day he died had a tremendous impact on me. I couldn't drive it out of my mind."

Suddenly the law and the pursuit of money seemed a meaningless, vain way to spend one's life. He decided to become a priest and broke up with a girlfriend of five years.

But the blackouts intensified and when a doctor told him he had epilepsy his world turned black. His Old World parents thought the devil possessed him; the Church said he could not become a priest; the state canceled his driver's license.

Coelho started drinking. He drank as hard as he did everything. He believed that he had nothing to stay sober for, to live for. Even God had abandoned him. He wasn't even good enough to drive. "I had no reason for being," he said.

He turned suicidal. A priest friend, a Jesuit, tried to pull him out of it and got him a job with Bob Hope, just helping out with Hope's family. Hope liked him and, later, said that if he wanted to help people he should get into politics. An uncle got him an interview with Bernie Sisk, a California congressman. Coelho had found his métier.

He saw himself as doing good, as taking his mission to Congress. Quickly he became a force. One man, then an aide to a senator, recalled his first meeting with Coelho and several House members in Sisk's office. He and Coelho were the only staff there, Sisk himself was absent, and Coelho was sitting in Sisk's chair with his feet up on Sisk's desk, telling the members how he thought they should proceed. It was remarkable, absolutely remarkable. When the aide returned to his office, a message from Coelho was waiting. He called back and Coelho said, "You don't know much about this issue, do you? We better have breakfast so I can bring you up to speed."

In 1970 Sisk was talked into running for majority leader against Hale Boggs, who had a drinking problem, by some members who were "friends." But Boggs cleaned up his act and became a sure winner; the members who had gotten Sisk into the race suddenly lined up with

Boggs—Why make the new majority leader mad?—leaving Sisk isolated and humiliated. "That was a good lesson to me," Coelho recalled coldly, seventeen years later. "That taught me a lot. There are a lot of people who use the word 'friend' around here. It doesn't mean much." Coelho also learned from another fight, over parking spaces; Sisk was on House Administration, the insider's insider committee, the committee which controlled the budgets of other committees and members' personal offices, from franking (free mail) privileges to parking. Once a parking slot very close to a garage exit door became free; a senior House member had the very next space to it. The newly free, adjacent space was his by right, but Sisk thought it wasn't worth moving him and gave it to another member. The first member was infuriated. That taught Coelho about turf, the importance of little things, doing things for people; it also taught him how small some members were.

When Sisk retired in 1978, Coelho replaced him, taking 79 percent of the vote in the primary, 60 percent in the election—the lowest total of his career. He entered the House understanding it, and aware of its underside. He won assignments to the committees he wanted, including House Administration.

Rostenkowski took to him, sponsored him, and immediately Coelho became a player, a conduit from the leadership to junior members. He also raised money; though a freshman, he ranked second in the House in selling tickets to the Democratic Congressional Campaign Committee's chief fund-raising event, and he raised $80,000 for Wright's tough 1980 campaign. When the DCCC chairmanship became vacant after the election, Coelho lobbied for the job.

Members from Lyndon Johnson to Tip O'Neill had used the DCCC job as a stepping-stone to real power. Now—given the threat of a Republican takeover of the House in 1982—the job had become crucial. Rostenkowski was Coelho's chief sponsor, and urged O'Neill to bless Coelho's campaign. O'Neill finally agreed to nominate him for the post, which guaranteed his election. But the day before the vote O'Neill reneged without explanation. That, if known, could have started a stampede to his opponent, Tom Harkin. Immediately Coelho told Wright and asked him to nominate him. Wright instantly agreed. The next day only the three principals knew what had happened, and to most members Wright's speech signaled O'Neill's approval. Rostenkowski seconded Coelho's nomination.

At the DCCC Coelho did better than well. He inherited a fund-raising apparatus $300,000 in debt which had raised less than $2 million in the preceding election cycle. His first term as chairman it raised $6 million, his second term $11 million, his third term $15 million. (His GOP counterpart raised $40 million that same campaign.) He went where the money was, to business political action committees with a carrot and stick—simultaneously suggesting that Democrats could work with business and reminding them who controlled the House. He had himself worked for business interests: fighting environmentalists who wanted to impose limits on the amount of subsidized water large farms could use; unsuccessfully pushing legislation which would have allowed major landowners, including Chevron, to get low-interest federal loans; putting together unlikely coalitions, convincing liberal Jews, for example, to support efforts by independent oilmen, who tended to be extreme conservatives, to help their industry, which would lower U.S. dependence on the Middle East. It was legalized extortion; politicians help "friends." Businessmen had to have "access" to get their side across. Money did not buy a vote but it bought access.

He began as well to build an empire, to do what Foley would not do. Inside the House, he demanded and got upgraded status for the DCCC chairman, including a seat on Steering and Policy. Six professionals worked for the DCCC when he took over; seventy worked there when he left, experts not only in fund-raising but in politics, in polling, in media strategy, all at the disposal of colleagues and new candidates. For the men and women running for the House for the first time, a nod from Coelho gave their campaigns credibility, helped immeasurably in their fund-raising efforts. Most PAC money comes not from ideologues supporting a cause but from pragmatists who want to be with a winner. If Coelho pointed to a winner—Coelho was cold; his credibility was on the line, and he did not inflate candidates' prospects—they followed. He confronted contributors who disagreed, called them "idiots," pushed and pushed.

His phone calls for candidates, his visits to their districts, his help when they needed help, his political advice, his interpretations of polling data, were all remembered when the winners arrived in Washington. They owed him. And he did not stop then.

He ministered to them; they were his flock. He remained earthy, like a pragmatic parish priest. In his office was a chair referred to as the "confessional." Members talked to Coelho, told him the most intimate details, about home life and marriage problems, about money problems. He followed up and followed up; if a member asked for something he wrote it down on an index card kept in his suit jacket pocket. Then he did something about it, wrote that down next to the member's name, and filed the information. Nothing fell between the cracks; even if the request went unfulfilled, that, too, got reported back to the member and filed.

He started his own personal political action committee and gave hundreds of thousands of dollars to colleagues, in most cases handing them the check personally—he wanted that direct, personal contact, handing them the check. He learned what member's wife liked to go where for a vacation, and then would find out what company or association was meeting there, and arranged to have the member—and wife, of course—invited, with an honorarium attached. Honoraria were real money, not like campaign contributions; they went straight into members' pockets. Senior members with power bases did not need Coelho's help collecting honoraria—a member of Ways and Means could easily collect the annual limit of 30 percent of a congressman's salary at a few breakfasts, $2,000 (the per-event limit) at a clip—but a freshman or sophomore on Judiciary could not, and Coelho helped. One lobbyist said, "Tom Nides [Coelho's aide] called me with a list of six members he wanted honoraria for." Another lobbyist noted wryly, "When Tony asks for something, we try to accommodate him." If a member's wife or son needed a job, Coelho helped there too. His help was not limited to members. He helped people outside the House, helping them at every level, from getting a job paying $25,000 a year to getting on corporate boards.

All the favors for others meant power. Hundreds, and as it continued year after year, hundreds of hundreds of people, owed him.

What drove him? Everything about him seemed raw and rough-edged. Coelho himself said, "The key to understanding me is epilepsy. That defines me."

His energy and even his desire to become a priest existed before his epilepsy surfaced, but the epilepsy gave his energy a focus, a specific reason to go forward and prove to the world he could achieve. It was where his "inner peace" came from. (Oddly, Gingrich also claimed "inner peace.")

Even his good works had raw muscle to them. He devoted hours to epileptics, both raising money from lobbyists for them—he called Hill & Knowlton, a major public relations firm, for example, and suggested they donate over $100,000 worth of their services to raising money for epilepsy (the company declined)—and counseling young epileptics in one-on-one sessions. What Coelho did on policy was abstract; this was not abstract. He forced those he counseled to focus, to confront themselves in a full-length mirror and say out loud what they liked and disliked about themselves. If they could change it, change it, he told them; if not, then accept it. Similarly, like a football coach reviewing game films, he regularly reviewed events with his staff; he forced everyone, including himself, to face the truth.

In his suite of offices he made one room his sanctum sanctorum. It was tiny, constricted, barely bigger than a closet, and it had no telephone; when he closed the door behind him, his staff could not disturb him. He thought in there, in the quiet. "I know who I am," he said. "I'm not going to change."

Inner peace did not mean simply quiet at the center; to him inner peace meant strength, the strength that comes from the quiet—an inner conviction that allowed him to continue when pressures would rip most men apart, an inner conviction that he was doing the right thing, that he was helping people, that he was trying to make the world better. There was that at the core, combined with the cynicism that, if the world worked a certain way, he would master that way. "The system is corrupt," he said, speaking of fund-raising and PAC money. Rather than wasting energy on a fool's errand, trying to change the system, he would use it. Perhaps he might also have said, *The world is corrupt*, and he would use the world too.

With that same rawness he got into the whip race. Rostenkowski had tried to get him to run for majority leader, which could have shaken the House enough to create an opening for Rostenkowski to run for Speaker. Coelho saw it as a maneuver against Wright, did not believe members would accept him, so junior, as majority leader, and declined. And he came out early in support of Wright. Rostenkowski felt betrayed. *After all he had done for Coelho.* He did not forget.

Coelho ran for whip against Charles Rangel, the black Ways and Means member from New York, and Bill Hefner, a North Carolina moderate. He spent the DCCC's money freely, very freely, on colleagues. He or his supporters contacted every Democratic colleague at least four times, and he personally asked member after member what he could do for them. Nothing put him off, even when one member restated their relationship by making clear, "You can't do anything for me. I can do something for you. I can vote for you." It was a clarity that described the delicate relationship between members and the leadership; the membership had what the leadership wanted—votes.

After the November election, Coelho recontacted every elected Democrat and asked again for a commitment. At the same December Caucus at which Wright and Foley won election by acclaim, Coelho collected 168 votes to seventy-eight for Rangel and fifteen for Hefner, who, rising to congratulate Coelho, joked, "The members have spoken. The bastards."

Coelho had two goals: As the first elected whip he had to convince everyone of his loyalty to Wright. He had given him early backing for Speaker, which helped Wright lock up the race. He could not function in the leadership if anyone doubted his loyalty. Second, Coelho wanted to earn respect for substantive, not just political, advice. At the beginning of the year he planned to keep a low profile, not talk to the press so much. He took to wearing his glasses more often; they toned down his intensity, creating some distance between him and others.

When Carl Albert became whip under Rayburn, his duties were so minimal that his chief aide wanted to quit the leadership job and go back to the district office. He had nothing to do. Coelho found plenty to do.

Now Coelho had his first real challenge overriding the highway veto. He and Public Works members, especially chairman Jim Howard and Mineta, the whip task force chairman, pressed members directly and indirectly, through outside groups—the "special interests." They were important. One leadership aide commented, "If you want to control votes, you have to manage the outside groups."

Coelho and his entire staff knew these groups intimately from fundraising at the DCCC, and he wanted to mobilize them to lobby for bills even if they had only peripheral interest in them, in return for leadership support of legislation they did have an interest in; staying in touch with these groups became the sole job of aide Tom Nides. Wright had also named Pat Williams, a labor Democrat from Montana, as a deputy whip and made him liaison to organized labor. Williams met regularly with representatives of all the individual AFL-CIO unions and AFL-CIO chief lobbyist Robert McGlotten to coordinate efforts on legislation. In the past, union lobbyists had dissipated their strength as each union focused on its own highest priority—one union, say, was most interested in a textile bill, another in workplace safety. Now the unions and Williams agreed to the same list of priorities, and individual unions subordinated their own; this meant that all lobbyists from AFL-CIO member unions would work the same issue at the same time. Shortly after the highway bill veto, Owen Bieber, the president of the United Auto Workers, Tom Donohue, secretary-treasurer of the AFL-CIO, and several union lobbyists visited with Wright to talk about the trade bill. Wright told them he did support their position, then added, "Now let me ask you something. This highway veto, it's a high-stakes roll of the dice. And auto people ought to be interested. The Building Trades. It's very important. The Republicans figure this will create a Reagan resurgence."

The highway bill was not an AFL-CIO priority—at least it had not been—but McGlotten replied, "I'll get right on it."

Meanwhile, Howard, Coelho, and Mineta organized a meeting of almost five hundred lobbyists. Unions were only part of the list. Lobbyists from every conceivable industry and union, from state governments, from city governments, from government unions, from suppliers of materials attended: the National Governors' Association, the American Public Transit Association, the American Road and Transport Builders' Association, individual representatives for each of dozens of cities, the limestone lobbyists, cement lobbyists, gravel lobbyists. The bill was big enough to affect the GNP—$88 billion. The veto could damage the economy.

Both the Democrats on Public Works and the two senior Republicans, John Paul Hammerschmidt and Bud Shuster, sent a clear message to these combined special interests. *If you want this bill, go out and work it. Get your membership back home excited, get them to call the members—and the senators, don't forget the senators. Get the senators.*

Howard knew how to do business. Gruff, plain-spoken, and still a chain-smoker despite a 1978 heart attack, Howard had an open, friendly, earthy quality. Under him, Public Works was the most bipartisan committee in the Congress. He and the most senior committee members of both parties and staff director Dick Sullivan put bills together by giving member after member what they needed for their district. But they kept policy decisions to themselves. They could play hardball; once members who voted against a major bill discovered their names on, literally, a blacklist circulated on the floor as a warning to their colleagues. Another time, Sherwood Boehlert, a Republican on the committee, voted against Gene Snyder, then ranking Republican. For months after that Boehlert could not even get a federal building renamed after a deceased former congressman who had been a friend of Snyder's. Boehlert asked Snyder why. "I don't like the way you vote," Snyder told him. Boehlert gave Snyder an explanation. It made no difference. Finally Boehlert realized Snyder wanted an apology, so he apologized. The next day his bill was reported out of committee. And Snyder wasn't even chairman, wasn't even in the majority. It was that kind of committee. Everyone on the committee knew how to do business. When one lobbyist, a Reagan partisan, called Howard to say he didn't like a tax stuck on his people by Ways and Means—it wasn't even in the highway bill—and he would lobby senators to sustain the veto, Howard warned him he'd never see the inside of his office again. Access is power. Cutting off access would kill him. Then Howard called members of his trade association and said their lobbyist was playing partisan politics instead of representing them. The lobbyist was fired, quickly.

The outside groups, spurred to work and guided by the House leadership, were only one means to reach Republican senators; the leadership had other ways to extend its reach too. One was indirect, to focus the public on the bill with floor speeches. The other two were direct. Very direct.

The Senate had added a provision allowing states to raise the fifty-five-mile-per-hour speed limit to sixty-five miles per hour. Ironically, the first time Wright, as Speaker, had used his power had been to dissuade House Democrats from joining with Republicans to do the same thing. It would have divided the Caucus. Wright hadn't wanted something like that to happen in the first few days of the new Congress. But western senators, mostly Republicans, had demanded it. In conference, Jim Howard had hung tough at first. For all the cigarettes he smoked, for all the horse-trading he did on projects, Howard believed in what he did, saw roads and waterworks as the key to economic growth, and was convinced the fifty-five-mile-per-hour limit saved lives. There weren't many things politicians did that saved lives. He turned down several trades. The speed limit was a question of principle. You didn't compromise principle. But neither did he believe he had the right to thwart the will of the Congress. So he agreed to a separate floor vote on the speed limit. The year before he had won such a vote. This time he lost when some liberal Democrats switched positions. It was a maneuver; they anticipated a veto and knew the speed-limit provision would help override it in the Senate. Now Wright called Byrd: "Tell your western Republicans there will be no damn sixty-five-mile-per-hour speed limit if this veto gets sustained. I kept out of the floor fight before but I won't this time. Tell them you heard from the House there will damn well sure be no sixty-five."

Then, at the regular Thursday whip meeting—the override vote would come the next week—Wright cited polls showing 71–17 percent support from the public for the override of the Clean Water veto earlier; there was every indication that the numbers on this issue were similar. He reiterated what Coelho had been saying: "If you have a Republican senator you're thinking about running against, this could be an opportunity to score some points." They could attack any GOP senator who voted with the White House for sacrificing his state's interests for partisan political reasons. That would strike GOP senators with the fear of God, particularly in the West where constituents wanted to drive as fast as they damn well pleased, not the way those damn easterners thought they should drive. Lastly, the leadership handed out a letter signed by Democrats and Republicans on Public Works, rebutting the charges of pork-barrel spending. Wright turned up the heat: "This override has far-reaching implications. Reagan's trying to exploit this, deliberately trying to pick a fight. Anything you can do or suggest, let us know. This is Armageddon as far as I'm concerned."

Howard swore that if the veto was sustained, the roads would go to hell, jobs would disappear, and angry drivers would blame their congressmen. The leadership sent out a letter signed by Republicans on Public Works to all GOP governors, warning them of the consequences of a sustained veto, suggesting they contact their Senate brethren.

The White House was going at this full speed too; it was its most intensive lobbying effort since the 1981 budget and tax bills. Reagan was speaking personally to GOP senator after GOP senator, individually and in small groups. He needed seventeen more votes. He got twelve, thirteen, fourteen. He was creeping up.

In the House, even after being assured of winning the vote, Coelho never let up. He wanted to prove that the days of the boll-weevil coalition between southerners and Republicans had ended forever. That was important for the future. When an aide asked, "How hard should we push?" Coelho replied, "All the way. I want 100 percent of the

Democratic vote. I want the southerners to know they can vote against the President."

He came close to his goal. The House voted 350–73 to override Reagan's veto, Democrats 248–1, Republicans 102–72. Michel, Lott, and Cheney, the third-ranking Republican, voted to override. Michel and Lott had needs in their districts which the bill met—projects the White House called pork, but which repaired weakened bridges or widened roads which had become major thoroughfares; Cheney, from Wyoming, had the speed-limit issue.

But the time for celebrating had not arrived. The next day the Senate would vote. Wright asked Byrd whom he could use help on. Democrat Terry Sanford of North Carolina, the only Democrat who had voted against the bill earlier, was one. Charles Grassley, an Iowa Republican, was another. Wright talked to Neal Smith, the dean of the Iowa House delegation, and asked who might influence him, then got a former state highway commissioner to call; it didn't work. But Republican Bob Stafford, who had earlier announced that he would support Reagan because of the importance of rebuilding his presidency, was overwhelmed by the lobbying pressure. He would vote to override. Howard sat down with several senators, at Byrd's request, to explain that sustaining the veto meant no bill. Terry Sanford was at the meeting and promised Howard, "I will not be the cause of sustaining the veto."

But Sanford had also promised the lieutenant governor of North Carolina, Robert Jordan III, who was planning to run for governor, not to vote for the bill. The call of party ran head-on into that personal pledge.

In debate, Dole called the issue one which could "determine the strength of the presidency for the next twenty-one months."

Democrat David Boren retorted, "We're not engaged in a childish game of King of the Mountain in some playground."

Then the Senate voted. Reagan had needed to pick up seventeen votes. He got them, all from Republicans. That left it up to Sanford. He stood in the well of the Senate agonizing. Colleagues gathered about him. Alan Simpson of Wyoming, the Republican whip, told Sanford it was a tough vote for him too; his constituents wanted the sixty-five-mile-per-hour limit badly. Simpson asked if he had made a promise. Sanford said yes. "People won't remember the issue," Simpson said, "but they'll remember if you broke your word." Democrats crowded around Sanford too; they told him he couldn't let the party down, he had to vote yes. Sanford was a freshman senator but was sixty-nine years old and not without experience. More than a quarter of a century earlier, in 1961, he had become governor of North Carolina and was considered one of the state's best governors ever; later president of Duke University, he briefly flirted with a run for the presidency in 1976. A distinguished man, a fine man, an intelligent man, not inexperienced with pressure. *But not pressure like this.* Senator after senator waded into the crowd around Sanford. He had promised he would not be the cause of sustaining the veto. Distraught, he voted "Present!"

That left the vote at 66–33. To override a veto required a two-thirds vote of those voting; according to the Senate parliamentarian a "present" vote did not count as a vote. *The veto was overridden.* Democrats started to celebrate. But as Sanford walked off the floor, Lloyd Bentsen approached him.

"You've got to vote, Terry," Bentsen said. *People had elected all of them to make decisions, however unattractive. They had elected them to stand for something. To vote.* "You'll be remembered for this."

Abruptly Sanford turned around. He kept his first pledge, not to support the bill. He voted no.

Suddenly, from a 66–33 victory came a 66–34 defeat—a smashing defeat. Byrd quickly changed his vote to make the final 65–35; that would allow him later to move for reconsideration—only a member of the winning side can ask for another vote.

In the House when members heard of it they were furious. Wright sat in his chair in the ceremonial office, waiting with Foley, Bonior, and his senior staff for his daily press conference to begin; on his face was a look of disgust. Mack said, "It looks like we start from zero again."

"Start from zero is right. It seems sometimes we're always starting from zero." Then he just shook his head. Already White House officials were talking of vetoing two or three other bills if they did not get exactly what they wanted in them. Weariness had set in. He was tired of fighting. "We're running out of time. We're just running out of time."

After a moment, Wright shrugged. "Let 'em in."

The press trooped in, thirty or forty men and women swarming about his desk. "Are you disappointed?"

Wright looked at the questioner coldly for an instant. It was an obvious question, even a stupid one. But it struck a deep chord in him, deeper than the reporter could realize. Everything he had hoped for, his vision for the country—and he had a vision—his personal ambition, his sense of the role of government, everything was involved. Everything seemed slipping away. Finally he responded. "What do you think?"

Coelho missed the daily press conference. He was still working, getting members of the North Carolina House delegation together. If Sanford thought he had felt pressure before, he was wrong. *Now* he would feel pressure.

Sanford told another press conference he voted with the President because he had made a commitment. Watching on CNN in his office, Wright understood. "You give your word, you keep it," he said with resignation, even with approval.

But Coelho was still working and a Democrat sitting outside Wright's office, using the phone, said, "I'll tell you what. If this holds, there will be retribution." Suppose Kika de la Garza, the Agriculture Committee chairman from Texas, simply deleted tobacco from the list of primary commodities and the tobacco program came crashing down? How would Sanford, from North Carolina, like that? John Mack said, "This isn't over yet. It's not over until it's over."

North Carolina Democrat Charlie Rose, who headed the tobacco subcommittee, and the rest of the state delegation went to work on Sanford while their colleague David Price got to the lieutenant governor, the man Sanford had promised his no vote to, warning of retribution and emphasizing the national impact of the vote. *Release Sanford from that commitment, dammit. You're killing us.* He did, saying he did not want the responsibility for such a major party defeat.

It was that simple.

Released from his commitment, Sanford announced he would switch his vote. A euphoric Byrd asked for reconsideration of the vote, and a now-desperate Dole blocked him, until Byrd agreed to delay the vote one day. That would give Reagan time to work on Republicans. Now the thirteen Republican senators who had voted against Reagan would feel the pressure. Reagan needed just one. Any one.

Wright sat alone in his office, at his desk. As always it was cluttered with paper, letters, books, messages. To his left were the sofa and armchairs. Directly in front of him were another sofa and coffee table. Above it, on the wall, was a painting of a country church in Texas, a field of bluebonnets before it, a dark and brooding sky above it. It was the kind of picture that penetrated the soul, that one looked not *at* as much as *into*, that drew one into it, that reminded one of things beyond pettiness and the moment. Wright knew that church, knew that sky.

He did not know how the vote would come out. Maybe Reagan could get one more vote. Maybe not. That didn't matter. What mattered was accomplishing something lasting and permanent. He could do that only if these pointless fights ended.

Neither asking advice of nor informing anyone else, alone, Wright decided to make a private peace offering to the White House. He picked up the phone and called Howard Baker. The call would prove fateful in the months ahead, contributing to Wright's decision to trust and work with the White House on a foreign policy initiative which would begin in cooperation and end in the greatest clash in the twentieth century between a Speaker and a President. Baker got on immediately.

"Howard," Wright began, "we don't know whether the veto will be overridden or sustained but we do know both of us have lost. Our energies and efforts have been wasted fighting each other."

"I couldn't agree with you more, Mr. Speaker."

"Suppose, if we win, we don't gloat publicly. We're gracious. We'll just say, Let's see if we can work together in the future. As a good-faith gesture, I won't let the supplemental on the floor before Easter recess."

It was no idle gesture. Wright was talking about a "supplemental appropriation," which would include arms-control language limiting nuclear testing and requiring the administration to remain within SALT II limits. Secretary of State George Shultz was going to Moscow over Easter—so was Wright—to negotiate a treaty reducing intermediate-range nuclear missiles. A vote was scheduled before Shultz left, and, believing it would hurt his negotiating position, he badly wanted it delayed until after his trip.

But just as badly as Shultz wanted the vote delayed until after his trip, House Democratic arms-control activists wanted it before. The issue had a history.

The preceding year, just as similar language was about to be written into law, Reagan had announced the Reykjavík summit with Gorbachev. In order to give him maximum flexibility in negotiations, Democrats had agreed to drop their efforts to write the language into law in return for what they had believed was a White House pledge to comply voluntarily. Reagan had also promised—giving a pledge to Byrd in writing—to support ratification of a nuclear-test-limitation treaty signed by Nixon and a treaty relating to peaceful use of nuclear explosions signed by Ford. But just after Thanksgiving, the administration launched one new bomber armed with cruise missiles, violating SALT II limits and violating what Democrats had thought was a deal. Nor had the White House yet kept the President's written word to help ratify the old treaties.

The White House action had infuriated House arms-control activists, and the leadership had promised to make the SALT II provisions a priority. They had kept their word. Coelho had helped organize a task force to whip members *inside the Appropriations Committee*. That was unheard of, to whip members inside a committee. When Bill Chappell of Florida, a hawk, chaired a hearing that was tilting against the provisions, Oregon Democrat Les AuCoin excused himself, called John Mack to ask for leadership help, and returned. A moment later, Chappell was handed a note, read it, and whispered to AuCoin, "Will you take the gavel? I've been called to the Speaker's office." Chappell later voted against the provisions but did not otherwise try to block them. AuCoin and others wanted a floor vote. And they wanted it before Shultz went to Moscow.

Now Wright was offering to delay that floor vote as a goodwill gesture to the White House. If the Caucus discovered why, he would have a rebellion on his hands.

"A good-faith gesture won't be the public reason," Wright told Baker. "Whitten tried to rewrite some agricultural provisions in there and it upset de la Garza. For public consumption, that will be the reason given for the delay."

"It's between us, Mr. Speaker. Thank you. I'm sure Shultz will be overjoyed. I'll call him right now. Thank you again." Baker was exultant. Within ten minutes Shultz called Wright to add his thanks.

Wright had planted a seed of cooperation in foreign policy. It would bear poisonous fruit.

The administration and Wright had hardly made peace. A few hours after that phone call, Defense Secretary Caspar Weinberger, a Reagan intimate, had an appointment with him. Weinberger hoped to convince Wright to allow more defense spending. Wright hoped to communicate through him to the President.

The two men epitomized the clash between Democrats and the Reagan administration and strained to stay, for twenty short minutes, within the bounds of courtesy. On one issue after another, dripping unctuous hostility, they clashed, from Reagan's failure to push ratification of the two arms-control treaties, to what Soviets spent on their military—Weinberger contradicted the views of both his own Defense Intelligence Agency and the CIA. When Wright said domestic spending had been cut over 20 percent under Reagan, Weinberger disputed the figures. When Wright warned him that automatic Gramm-Rudman cuts would devastate defense, Weinberger claimed the House budget would be just as bad. When Wright complained that Reagan had picked an unnecessary fight over the highway bill, Weinberger said the bill came in over his budget. Wright snapped, "*His* budget, Cap? It's the country's budget, not his budget, and the bill spends less than the budget calls for, not more. Don't you think the committees of the Congress which spent months working and deliberating have something to say?"

That was the essence of the collision. It was institutional. Who would govern?

One vote. Just one. While Weinberger and Wright sparred, Kentucky GOP senator Mitch McConnell met privately with Dole and Reagan in the Oval Office. He refused to budge. Later that day, Secretary of Agriculture Richard Lyng, with whom McConnell had clashed, visited McConnell and offered to resign from his cabinet post for his vote. McConnell still would not budge. But the White House was trying everything, on each of the thirteen senators. The next morning Reagan went to the Hill to meet with the thirteen Republicans. The Democrats grew nervous. They were certain he would not come to the Hill unless he already had the vote he needed in his pocket.

He did not yet have the vote.

The GOP senators gathered in Dole's office. There Reagan asked each senator to explain his opposition. Then, reportedly, he said, "I beg you for this vote."

The President of the United States. Begging thirteen members of his own party for one vote.

Uncomfortably, the senators refused. Dole asked whether they would all switch if one switched, protecting all of them. No again.

The Senate convened to reconsider the override. Wright had asked Jim Howard to go to the Senate floor, where he stood in the back and said, "All right, you bastards, you'll never get your sixty-five mph again if this goes down." As a last reminder to senators tempted to trade their vote for a special favor, Byrd had Brock Adams preside as the Senate revoted. Adams had defeated GOP senator Slade Gorton of Washington; a key issue had been Gorton's agreement to switch sides and vote to confirm Daniel Manion as a federal judge in return for the appointment of another judge—a liberal judge, ironically. The Senate overrode the veto 67–33. The Democrats had won!

Mack walked into Wright's office grinning from ear to ear. Wright had already heard the news. The two of them bowed to each other, bowed low. Then they shook hands. They had done it.

"It's great!" Mack said. "Turn on the TV! They're kicking hell out of the White House."

"When you pick a fight," Wright answered, "you damn well better win it. They picked one and they lost."

The Democrats were on top. The House Democratic leadership had reached even into the ranks of Republican senators. Coelho had done it. The House had done it. And on top of them all was Jim Wright.

Coelho was on the phone with Byrd: "Big win! Big win! Congratulations." On the phone with Howard: "Congratulations! You can feel free to go on vacation." On the phone to Wright—but with Wright it was back to business; these two did not congratulate each other. "The next step is the budget," Coelho said. "If you can get Murtha"—John Murtha, a prodefense Democrat, key to as many as twenty votes—"under control, it will be easier than we thought. If not, it could be a big problem."

At the regular whip meeting, Coelho congratulated members on the veto override effort, and especially North Carolina's delegation for "educating Mr. Sanford." The mood was jovial. When one member came in late and moved down the aisle, another shouted, "Buddy MacKay! Come on *dooowwwnnnn!*"

But the mood quickly changed to grumbling when the schedule for the following week, the final week before the Easter break, was announced and it did not include the supplemental appropriation with the arms-control provisions. One member demanded, "Why did you do that? What's the strategy behind that?"

Two, three, four members complained. They wanted the vote before Shultz went to Moscow. Coelho moved on, no one in the leadership responding effectively, Coelho changing the subject by asking Gray to brief everyone on the budget the committee had adopted.

"This budget is supported by everyone from Rabbi Schumer of the golden parable to Reverend Leath of the First Baptist Church of Waco," Gray said, referring to Charles Schumer, a New York liberal, and Marvin Leath, the Texas conservative, both on his committee. "We have real cuts of $4 billion more than the President does, and come $200 million under his deficit target under the same economic assumptions. Also, it protects Democratic priorities like education and drug programs—he devastated both."

A member stood up. "I understand there's no leadership position on how we justify the taxes. If I want to say we just close loopholes, that's fine, right?"

"This doesn't direct Ways and Means as to how to reach its goal at all," Gray answered. "It just says $18 billion in revenues."

"What about the rule?" The rule governed what issues would be voted on; if the rule didn't allow a vote on something, there could be none. "I want a chance to vote on the President's budget."

"You'll get it," Foley said.

Gray concluded, "The Republicans don't think we can get a budget. They won't offer one. If we just get 218 votes then the Lord will smile on you."

Wright started to read off some poll numbers to the meeting. Despite the tax issue, the numbers were better than simply good. They were great.

Generally, polls played the greatest role in setting priorities, not in determining how members voted. In defining the agenda, politicians considered two things—their own sense of what was needed, and resonance in the public.

Polls had been crucial to O'Neill's legislative strategy in the preceding Congress. A series of them had convinced him to keep silent on taxes. Then, in the late spring of 1986, DCCC aide Thomas O'Donnell wrote a memo based on polling which led the House Democratic leadership to move legislation on drugs, jobs, and trade.

The strategy seemed to pay off. In November 1984 Republicans had held a ten-point advantage over Democrats on the question "Which party do you think is better at reducing unemployment?" Two years later, Democrats had a twenty-point advantage on that question, gained seats in the House, and regained control of the Senate.

Wright believed in those themes and was continuing them. But on taxes he ignored the polls while paradoxically insisting to colleagues, "The American people are ahead of the politicians on taxes."

His view ran diametrically opposite that of most politicians, who lived by the saying, *There go the people. I must follow for I am their leader.* Wright argued, "We need to be exposed to empirical data, what's on people's minds right now and so forth, yes. But everyone who's ever come out of this White House, [former OMB director David] Stockman, [Reagan intimate and public relations chief Michael] Deaver, whoever, has said it lived and died by the nightly news. What good is that? You should position yourself with a program that is able to lead public opinion. If you don't do that, then you're not making public policy. You're playing a defensive game. You've got to lead public opinion and direct it. Otherwise, you just ride the wave and stay afloat, but have no control over its direction. You simply go where it takes you."

His approach was risky, in some ways arrogant and even foolish, but for now the polls seemed to be proving him right. Although, overwhelmingly, people still said they did not want taxes raised, an NBC/ *Wall Street Journal* poll concluded that Americans approved of a tax increase as part of a budget compromise by a 53–40 margin. A *Time* magazine cover story explored a "new direction" for America, and concluded that on issue after issue after issue, Americans supported the Democratic Party's positions. Wright had copies made of the story and distributed them to every Democrat in the House.

At Coelho's suggestion, the House leadership had just started conducting its own regular polls. The operation did not rival that of the White House, which polled weekly, but it was still useful. Regularity was important to show trend-lines; trend-lines in many ways showed more than the raw numbers. Coelho suggested keeping the polling operation secret; that way they could make results public when they showed good news, and could avoid releasing them when they carried bad news. Wright agreed. They would tell colleagues only that a national poll had been shared with them. Now Wright read the results to the fifty whips to give them courage.

The public was asked whether they would prefer Democrats or Republicans to handle thirteen separate issues. The public chose Democrats on eleven. More important, on the question "Which party do you think is better at controlling government spending?" Republicans in November 1982 had enjoyed a forty-point advantage. That had narrowed to a twenty-point GOP advantage six months before the 1986 election and stayed there—until now. Wright's outspokenness on a "pay-as-you-go" approach had created major movement. Now Democrats had the lead. It made the pain Wright had endured over taxes seem worthwhile. As Wright read off the numbers, the whips listened, nodded their heads in agreement, raised their eyebrows in pleasant surprise.

The leadership began tying up loose ends on the budget. It was going well. Very well. Democrats were falling into line one after another and the budget was ready for the floor.

Even the press had finally come around. A *Washington Post* editorial on the eve of the vote said, "The Democrats have drawn up a balanced proposal—a sensible amount of deficit reduction. The Republicans will denounce it gleefully all day. Their glee would be a little less transparent if it were accompanied by a budget of their own. In a matchless show of courage, principle, and leadership, they have declined to provide one."

On the Wednesday before Easter recess, the rule for the budget passed 241–172. Not a single Republican voted yes and only two Democrats voted no. Passage of the bill itself the next day looked almost that easy. Then a Ways and Means aide who was responsible for protecting Ways and Means turf—especially from Dingell—carefully reviewed the committee report on the budget. "Christ," he said. "Dingell's trying to sneak an oil import tax past us."

The issue was a "user fee" of $700 million to be charged to foreign oil deposited in the Strategic Petroleum Reserve, the Louisiana salt caverns where the government was storing hundreds of millions of barrels of oil as leverage against another oil embargo. Every committee had the right to impose user fees; the Interior Committee, for example, handled admission fees to national parks. But taxes belonged to Ways and Means. And an oil import fee was a tax. It was enough for every member of Ways and Means to vote against the budget.

And an oil-import fee was doubly explosive. It pitted region against region, and split the Democratic Caucus. New England imported almost all its home heating oil and its costs would rise, while the Southwest benefited from higher energy prices.

Technically, the budget only set broad dollar totals for each committee to meet; no matter what it said, it had jurisdiction over how a committee met its target. So the fee was meaningless in a legal sense. But when word first leaked out of the proposal at a whip task force meeting, members who were friends, even housemates, went at each other with hammers.

Disturbed, Coelho went straight to Wright and warned, "We've got a firestorm brewing here."

Dingell and Rostenkowski had no love for each other, and their committees collided continuously over jurisdiction. Physically large, almost as big as Rostenkowski, Dingell was feared and vengeful and could intimidate, could lean his big bear body forward and stare heavily, a withering stare as intimidating as that of any heavyweight champion. Formal, he enunciated each syllable with precision, even with delicacy, including the four-letter words. Like Rostenkowski, he regarded politics as a family business and loved the House. He had been a page as a boy while his father served in Congress—on Ways and Means. His father was small and gentle, but explosive in his own way; once when a chairman tried to gavel him into silence, he grabbed the gavel, flung it against the wall, and warned, "Don't you ever try to gavel me down again!" Decades later, Dingell the son once pounded a gavel so hard the head exploded.

Raised in New Deal politics, his father a sponsor of the Social Security Act, Dingell cared about substance. He knew what he wanted in legislation and, a hunter, he had a hunter's patience, the patience to wait in perfect stillness until the time to strike, almost an animal patience to match the almost-animal violence he sometimes seemed to threaten. He could wait, and wait, and wait, through one session of Congress, through an entire Congress, through another entire Congress.

Dingell knew power, understood it, played rough, and had more than his share of enemies. Once he so berated a fellow chairman a third member walked out of the meeting in embarrassment; another time he pulled a freshman aside on the floor and threatened to make every single day of his entire House career miserable if the freshman didn't stop pushing a particular bill; another time, convinced that committee colleague James Scheuer had lied to him, he abolished a subcommittee Scheuer chaired. Dingell also had fierce defenders; their loyalty was built on respect for his integrity and word, and the knowledge that he remembered his friends and enemies both.

O'Neill and Dingell had collided routinely, both over members' assignments to Energy and Commerce and over the committee's jurisdiction. Dingell always seemed to be poaching on other committees' turf, although he already claimed jurisdiction over 35 percent of the legislation moving through the House. Rayburn, before becoming Speaker, had chaired the Commerce Committee, and he had also reached for, expanded, his power. "Not a day passes in which I do not thank Sam Rayburn for what he did with this committee," Dingell said.

Now Dingell had allied himself with Wright. Rostenkowski, O'Neill's intimate, distrusted, and worried about, that alliance.

Two weeks earlier Wright had sent Rostenkowski that letter. Rostenkowski had not spoken to him since, although he had sent a message by pulling Wright's friend Craig Raupe aside at a dinner party and asking, "What the hell gives with your old boss? Dammit, I'm trying to play team ball. I don't want the Speaker mad at me, and I assume he doesn't want the chairman of Ways and Means mad at him."

But now Rostenkowski was willing to fight. Wright would oblige him. All through Wednesday the fire spread. The leadership desperately looked for a way to put it out. There was none. The rule for the bill had already passed the House, and it offered no opportunity to vote on an amendment to kill the incendiary provision.

The next morning at Wright's breakfast an aide said, "All this will take is a few words from you to Rostenkowski, that jurisdiction over revenue belongs to Ways and Means."

That was what the fight was about, jurisdiction, and it was within the Speaker's power to determine it. But reassuring Rostenkowski could expand Ways and Means' power, and diminish Wright's own. As important as the budget was, and it was very important, it was still only one battle. There were battles every day. He could not win them all. No one could. But Wright would not yield any power; once that was gone it was almost impossible to retrieve. Not now, not in his first four months as Speaker. That could weaken him forever. If he was going to lose any power, it would have to be taken from him.

Wright stared hard at his aide. "The only damn leverage I have over

Rostenkowski is jurisdiction. I'm not going to give that up even if it means losing the budget."

I'm not going to give that up even if it means losing the budget.

It was Thursday, April 9, the last day before Congress recessed for Easter. Wright left breakfast for the 9:00 A.M. whip meeting. Immediately the issue came up. Coelho recognized Barney Frank, from Massachusetts. "I yield to Brian Donnelly," he said.

Frank was a fighter, but he was not as fierce as Donnelly. And, close as Donnelly was to Wright, he also served on Ways and Means and came from Boston. *The only blood oath I ever swore was to my constituents,* he had said. His roots ran deep into his district. It was neighborhood, family. Not just antibusing Irish either. After college he had coached an almost all-black junior high school inner-city football team (he had been drafted by the NFL but didn't try out); he had loved those kids, ached for how hard they worked and how little chance they had. An oil import fee which raised their heating bills made their lives that much harder. There was one last thing.

For half a century, Boston had been represented in the top House leadership. No more. Donnelly had a mean-streets, chip-on-the-shoulder explosive pride, and had to demonstrate that no one could kick New England around just because O'Neill, its protector, had retired. Both the issue and the precedent mattered. Donnelly was an ally of both Wright and Foley. *But his blood oath came first.*

Now he spoke with an intensity that quieted the room: "This is very important to New England. Members from our section didn't know it was in the budget until yesterday. Ways and Means members on Budget didn't know anything about this until yesterday." He was accusing Gray of a fast shuffle. Underneath that was a threat. *Don't fuck with me.* "I talked to the majority leader for two hours yesterday. We're still trying to work this out and the vote's in three hours. Our section wants to work with others. But you can hear Silvio Conte"—a Republican—"in Massachusetts on this without a microphone."

Wright tried to reassure him, promising that any oil-import fee ever enacted while he was Speaker would exempt home heating oil. Then Gray said, "We can deal with this in reconciliation." The "reconciliation" bill changed existing law, including tax law, to conform with the budget.

"I've seen that train coming down the track before. I'd just as soon deal with it now." Donnelly was not budging.

The whip meeting broke up with a feeling of unease. Donnelly talked heatedly and privately to Wright. In three hours was the biggest vote of the year so far, and the centrifugal forces of the House, the thousands of interests and ambitions, were threatening to blow up in their faces.

Meanwhile, as the House convened, Foley sat down with Rostenkowski in H-208, the one room on that side of the House not belonging to Wright, and argued that every chairman had always claimed that the Budget Committee had no authority whatsoever over specific programs. Voting no because of a specific program mentioned in the budget implied that the budget had authority over it; Rostenkowski's position would actually enhance the authority of the budget and the Budget Committee.

Then Foley reported to Wright and Coelho: "Ways and Means is caucusing now. Let's hope the message took." He smiled, steepled his hands, looked up, and prayed.

Coelho said, "It looks good on the floor. The Republicans are down. Murtha's working hard. We're all right if this doesn't blow up."

The House was voting on the budget offered by the White House. Republicans rejected the White House plan by 148–27. Every Democrat voted no. It lost 394–27. The Black Caucus offered a liberal budget; it lost 352–56.

The Republicans had a chance to offer a budget of their own, something defining their position. The "92 Group," a coalition of moderate Republicans who took their name from 1992, the year they hoped to gain control of the House, had prepared their own budget and wanted to offer it. At the last minute, the GOP leadership convinced them not to—it included taxes, so it gave Democrats political cover. Republican William Dannemeyer did offer his personal budget proposal; it lost 369–47.

As the debate proceeded, Trent Lott tried to lure Democrats leery of voting for taxes, arguing in a speech, "You do not ever get in trouble for those budgets which you vote against."

Like the Republicans who were voting against their own President's budget, voting against the Democrats, and not offering their own.

Foley replied contemptuously, "What a motto for statesmanship! What a motto for carrying out the responsibilities and obligations of membership in this body!"

But Ways and Means was still incensed. Foley's argument had had no impact. Standing in the Speaker's Lobby, Donnelly told Foley and

Coelho, "You don't understand. Republicans can beat the hell out of us with that language, whether it has any force or not. They'll damn well point fingers at us. It's very dangerous. But we don't want to blow up the budget. Take the language out in conference."

"The language? Not the $700 million?"

"The language."

"That can be done."

Donnelly left, unhappy but willing to go along. He didn't want losing the budget on his head. Then Foley said, "We don't want any speeches on this. New England isn't fully aware what's going on. The less said the better."

"Everybody's happy."

"I'm not sure Rostenkowski's happy."

"We'll leave it to Donnelly to convince him."

Thirty minutes later, with Wright in the Speaker's chair, the House voted on the Democrats' budget. Every single Republican voted no. But now, with the firestorm handled—not out, but gone underground, burning in the roots—230 Democrats voted yes. Donnelly voted yes. Rostenkowski voted yes. The floor was flush with members. Only nineteen Democrats voted no. *The budget passed 230–192.*

In the chair, with a carefully neutral voice, Wright announced, "The bill is passed and a motion to reconsider is laid upon the table."

Democrats pounded one another on the back. Half a dozen raised a clenched fist of triumph into the air. Trent Lott leaned over a table, stared at the floor for a moment, and clenched his fists too, angrily, as if wanting to hit something. Coelho and Foley shook hands warmly. *We did it!*

As Wright climbed down from the rostrum, joining a sea of congratulations, a wide grin spread across his face, the kind one has no control over, that emanates almost like an infant's from deep inside.

The floor emptied rapidly. Members disappeared. The House recessed for the long Easter break.

Wright was on top, all right, and soon to leave for Moscow to see Gorbachev, who had invited him. But there were disquieting signs even in his moment of triumph. There were currents in the House, unpredictable, chaotic products of a hundred unrelated causes, which no one could control; the near-explosion of the budget demonstrated that. And

Wright was showing signs of hubris. Two days before the vote on the budget, *The New York Times* ran a piece on him which said his "aggressive approach quickly banished the gentler-times decade of O'Neill." The story also quoted him saying—it highlighted the quote in big print—"You don't have to quiver and cower in fear if you think you are right. I am their leader."

I am their leader.

It was a statement that sent ripples of resentment through the House, a statement that O'Neill would never have made, that Michel would never have made, that Foley would never have made, that Coelho would never have made. Even if they had believed it, they would not have made it. His wife, Betty, said, "They elected you Speaker, Jim, not dictator." Raupe, too, winced when he saw it, commenting, "We're all on the knife-edge between confidence and inferiority. And there's a short line between confidence and arrogance."

Over the Easter recess Wright would lead a "CODEL," a congressional delegation, to Moscow. He had something more in mind than a ceremonial visit.

The trip would extend his reach and the reach of the House further into foreign policy, an area in which the Constitution gave the House little role. The President had negotiated treaties for the United States; the Senate ratified treaties; the House had no treaty responsibility. But treaties mattered less and less in foreign policy. The War Powers Act had earlier insinuated Congress into international affairs in a new way, uncomfortable for both Congress and the Executive, and limited the President's authority to put American armed forces in harm's way. But the key to congressional power in foreign policy was appropriations. Money was required to implement policy, and money bills originated in the House. The supplemental appropriation, which Wright had delayed for a few weeks, and which required compliance with the unratified SALT II Treaty, was only the latest effort by the House to exercise power. Wright hoped this trip would add to its influence and advance Soviet-American relations in some way. Many years before, as mayor of Weatherford, he had witnessed an atomic explosion. One did not forget that, ever. This trip would also advance his agenda within the House, and the stature of the speakership. It was a detail. But he was relentless in his attention to detail.

Wright assembled a weighty delegation, including Foley and Coelho and Dick Cheney, the third-ranking member of the GOP leadership who had attended the Vladivostok summit as Gerald Ford's White House chief of staff. Steny Hoyer came—Hoyer, Coelho's ally who had worked so hard to get the chief deputy whip job; he chaired the Helsinki Commission which monitored human rights in the Soviet Union. Also along were Les Aspin, chairman of Armed Services, and Tom Downey, Norm Dicks, Les AuCoin, and Jim Moody, all arms-control activists. (In addition, Downey and Moody served on Ways and Means; after the trip Moody said, "If Jim Wright asked me for something I would find it almost impossible to say no." But one member said, "He invited me because he sees me as being relatively close. I'm not close, but he would see me that way.")

Months in advance of their departure, in his office Wright told Soviet Ambassador Yuri Dubinin, who wore a Texas state pin in his lapel, "It would be very beneficial if we accomplished something concrete which brought together our countries in peace. I don't have any hard-and-fast requirement that something be agreed to, but hope it would be."

An agreement? Between a foreign government and the Speaker of the House? However insignificant any agreement was, it would set a precedent; it was process, and process was power. He proposed to Dubinin that they might agree on any of three possible joint initiatives: to alleviate hunger in the Third World, particularly in Africa; to explore space; to study the Arctic. Alaska and the Soviet Union were so close; perhaps the two countries could demonstrate their engineering prowess and learn something useful to both if they built an ice bridge between the countries. Then, casually, he mentioned what a wonderful signal Gorbachev might send if he dismantled the Berlin Wall. Wright had never thought small. Dubinin promised to take Wright's message personally to Gorbachev.

Wright had an agenda and even in Russia demanded that his colleagues yield to it. He always pursued his agenda. That became clear in Kiev, after the members met with Vladimir Scherbitsky, a member of the Politburo at odds with Gorbachev and head of the Soviet Republic of the Ukraine. Jowly, tough-talking and chain-smoking, Scherbitsky had an air about him of a big-city machine mayor, a Richard Daley of Chicago. He seemed the kind of man who would deal, who had mastered the old ways of power, corrupt ways even, and had built a base so strong that even Gorbachev could not replace him; even in the Soviet Union perhaps some politics were local. Aspin asked him point-blank about Gorbachev's efforts to get rid of him. Afterwards, his colleagues gave him the "Sam Donaldson Award." But Georgi Arbatov, the Soviet Union's expert on America and their escort, complained to Wright.

When the delegation arrived in Moscow, Wright called a members-only meeting. He was angry. Earlier on the trip, in Madrid, he had declared to the European Parliament that "building bridges is the noblest work of mankind." Most listeners had yawned at what seemed boilerplate rhetoric, yet it was a key to understanding him. He believed that he could build a bridge to the Russians, that somehow he could gain leverage on history. Now he told his colleagues he wanted no more questions like Aspin's. This delegation had a purpose, a constructive purpose. They were to look for common ground, something upon which they could build a bridge, build a relationship. Attacking one another would not yield progress.

Hoyer and Cheney objected. They insisted they use every opportunity to confront the Soviets over human rights violations and to pressure them to allow Jewish emigration. To the Soviets, human rights was the single most sensitive issue under discussion; they considered human rights an entirely internal matter.

Wright could not order Hoyer silent. But he could try to control him. Later, in a meeting with Anatoly Dobrynin, Hoyer sought recognition. Wright refused to look on his side of the table, calling on one member, a second, a third, all while Hoyer had his hand raised, until finally he recognized James Scheuer, who was Jewish; Scheuer said, "I yield to Steny Hoyer." Hoyer argued with Dobrynin over human rights issues.

Wright played one more power game—or reacted to one. He was scheduled to meet with Gorbachev privately before Gorbachev received the delegation. Moments before the scheduled meeting, a Soviet official told Wright that Gorbachev would meet with him after seeing the entire delegation rather than before. It was a seemingly inconsequential detail. But Wright understood the way men used details to put others off balance, to control them.

"No," he snapped. "If Gorbachev wants to see me privately he will do it as agreed or not at all."

Gorbachev saw him as agreed.

And Wright's constant, almost relentless willingness to understand made progress. Wright gave Gorbachev a "Letter to Ivan," a copy of a newsletter he had sent constituents twenty years earlier. It was about peace and seeking common ground, and he proposed that both nations cut military spending 5 percent a year for three years. Without any advance discussion, as a total surprise, the Soviets invited Wright to address their nation over television in prime time, unedited. While the American ambassador had sometimes been allowed to offer a brief televised Christmas greeting to the Soviet people, only heads of state had been offered an opportunity such as this. Wright quickly wrote a speech. In it he repeated his message of common interests, even offering to send anyone who wrote him a lapel pin of crossed American and Soviet flags to symbolize friendship. (His office ultimately received seven thousand letters and sent out seven thousand pins.) He voiced not one criticism of Soviet policy, not one note of discord.

But there was discord among his colleagues over the lack of any criticism, even from some Democrats. And Cheney concluded, "Based on this trip we've got a very good professional relationship. He treated me with great courtesy and dignity. But I think he went too far."

Was he always going to go too far?

CHAPTER 8

Newt Gingrich sat in his office in the Rayburn Building mulling over his next step. Instead of pacing as he usually did, he reclined in an armchair, sinking deep into its cushions, undid his tie, and put his feet on the coffee table. He was forty-four years old, an age by which most people have found out whether their lives would fulfill or betray their ambitions. His hair was gray, prematurely so, his belly soft in the way of those who had never done athletic things, as opposed to those whose youthful leanness has been overtaken by age. The former history professor, he still had the air of the academy about him, as if nothing pleased him more than sharp intellectual debate. At the 1984 Republican Convention he had declared, "This is my campus . . . I'm conducting seminars."

The seminars dealt with how to achieve power. He approached the question in the abstract, as if it were purely theoretical, requiring theoretical solutions. The excitement of the analysis attracted him; it was immensely more challenging and had many more levels than a chess game.

Gingrich respected Wright, and had already observed, *If Wright ever consolidates his power, he will be a very, very formidable man. We have to take him on early to prevent that.* But Wright had surpassed even Gingrich's high expectations. Wright had immediately put his stamp on the speakership, confronted and routed the White House with two significant veto overrides, and driven a budget through the House which, if adhered to, would dramatically reorder government priorities.

Polls indicated strong public support for Wright's policies, and his control of the House was firm.

Now, sitting in his office, Gingrich worried. "As far as operational effectiveness inside the House, you'd have to give Wright an A-plus. We're completely disorganized as a result. Even on taxes you now have people out flacking his ideas. Over the last few months Rostenkowski's quotes have changed from 'It would be crazy to bring a tax bill to the floor' to 'I wonder which alternatives we should consider.' That's no small achievement. Wright's just tougher. Trent [Lott] complains about how tough his people are. Bonior on Rules. Coelho's operation. Our leadership has no idea how to handle Wright."

Republicans even lacked the structures of power Democrats had developed. The GOP Conference, including all House Republicans, met more often and was better attended than the Democratic Caucus, but that was too large and clumsy a tool to hammer out a real strategy or exchange of views. The GOP leadership met regularly but had nothing like the daily get-togethers of the Democratic leadership before the House convened. The GOP had nothing comparable to the weekly whip meetings of the Democrats. And only now was Lott organizing whip task forces similar to the Democrats' in a defensive response to the effectiveness of Coelho's operation. *Our leadership has no idea how to handle Wright.*

But Gingrich had an idea how to handle him.

The same day the House passed the budget, the House Committee on Standards of Official Conduct, the formal name for the ethics committee, voted on and then released—during the Easter recess when it would get minimal attention—a 1,451-page report. Wright had nothing to do with producing the report, and not once in the 1,451 pages did it mention his name. But it would prove explosive for him.

It focused on Banking Committee chairman Fernand St Germain of Rhode Island, one of the least popular members of Congress—although he had run unopposed for reelection as chairman, 30 percent of the Democratic Caucus had voted against him. Despite his unpopularity, the committee had hardly conducted a rigorous investigation. For example, St Germain excused many of his actions by claiming to have relied on bad advice from a former ethics committee aide. The aide still worked in the House, but was not interviewed—perhaps out of fear that he might contradict St Germain. Despite the investigation's laxity, the report concluded that St Germain had violated House rules and possibly federal law on his financial disclosure forms, understating holdings by over one million dollars. His staff had pressured regulators to grant favors to a savings and loan in which he was an investor. He had become a multimillionaire through dealings with people who benefited from programs under his jurisdiction, and got sweetheart, million-dollar loans from banks. He violated limits on gifts from lobbyists.

Yet the committee recommended no disciplinary action against him. To let St Germain off without even a slap on the wrist? That was the corruption of power, the arrogance of power, the idea you could get away with anything. Wasn't it? That was a sign of the corruption of the Democrats. Wasn't it?

And Wright was in charge of the House. He was responsible. He could be attacked.

Gingrich had experimented with this theme—the corruption of power—for years. John Rhodes, the former House GOP leader, had voiced it more than ten years earlier in his book *The Futile System*. Gingrich once vowed to drive O'Neill from power, calling him a "thug" and "corrupt." But collegial pressure had restrained him; O'Neill had had many friends. The disputed McIntyre-McCloskey election in the preceding Congress had brought it home in a deeply personal way to House Republicans; Gingrich had called it "Watergate in the House." But that claim fell quickly by the wayside. He had needed a concrete, dramatic example to communicate the corruption theme. St Germain, who had already been the subject of numerous front-page stories in *The Wall Street Journal,* provided the example. And he would try to connect all this to Wright.

In addition, talking about Democrats involved in unethical behavior would counter ethics problems in the administration. Numerous White House officials had been indicted and convicted of everything from insider trading to perjury to racketeering. Most damaging politically was the unindicted attorney general Ed Meese. Gingrich worried, "Ethics will be a big issue in the presidential election. We've got to neutralize that."

Gingrich would go after Wright directly and personally. He assigned his aide Karen Van Brocklin to comb through both national and Texas newspapers, going back more than a decade, for any negative stories about Wright. She particularly sparked his interest with a story about Wright's then-legal, ten-year-old conversion of campaign funds to personal use. What else might be there? A file of such stories began to grow, and, beginning in the spring, he started showing these stories to reporters who interviewed him. Many did. Gingrich, the intellectual leader of the New Right who always gave the press a good quote and who had taken on O'Neill, was an obvious stop for anyone doing a story on Wright or the House. Later in the spring he would begin an outreach program, urging editors and writers across the country to investigate Wright.

If Gingrich could sell reporters the idea that Wright had engaged in questionable past dealings, if he could tie St Germain and Wright together, he could neutralize the harm the ethics issue could do Republicans. He could even take the offensive and charge systemic corruption—a theme of a corrupt House, corrupted by power, by thirty-two years of Democratic rule. He and several COS colleagues began working on a book to be called *A House of Ill Repute*. Democrats ran Congress. Wright ran the Democrats. Any damage inflicted on either had to help House Republicans.

The fact that the ethics committee was the only committee in Congress without a Democratic majority—it had six Democrats and six Republicans—and that the St Germain report had been approved by a 12–0 vote did not deter Gingrich from his theme.

We are engaged in reshaping a whole nation through the news media, Gingrich had also said. *The number-one fact about the news media is that they love fights. When you give them confrontations you get attention. When you get attention, you can educate.*

He would attack Wright, personally and vigorously, and use the confrontations to keep Wright from consolidating his power. His focus would not be only the Washington press. As a leading spokesman of the right, he traveled all over the country and attacked all over the country. He understood that if the press believed that Wright was corrupt, it would go after him forever. He was right. The Washington bureau chief of one of the world's most powerful newspapers confirmed, "If I ever become convinced that someone in public office is corrupt, I will never, ever give him a break, on anything."

Then Wright gave Gingrich's campaign a boost. One step at a time, unknowingly, he slid into the mire and quicksand of the savings and loan industry.

"The savings and loan thing made it possible to create in Jim Wright a symbol of a political machine," Gingrich later said. "The S&L thing also made it current. Currency is important. All the newspaper stories we had were old."

Wright's involvement opened a wound. Gingrich would rip away at it, refuse to let it heal.

The world is a strange place, which each person sees differently. As in the classic movie *Rashomon,* different points of view, different contexts, yield different truths. Nowhere were the truths more different than in Wright's involvement in the savings and loan crisis. The collision of those truths would, ultimately, have explosive impact in Washington.

The problems of the savings and loan industry began in the 1970s, when inflation and interest rates skyrocketed. That caught the savings and loans, often called "thrifts," in two binds. The first came from economic forces: They had made fixed-rate thirty-year mortgage loans at 5 percent, 6 percent, 7 percent, based on low inflation and low interest rates. But inflation meant that they were being paid back in dollars worth much less than those they had loaned out. Simultaneously, regulations imposing interest-rate ceilings on savings accounts and prohibiting paying interest on checking accounts had disadvantaged consumers, but gave S&L's access to cheap money. Deregulation ended all that.

Suddenly S&L's had to pay higher interest to attract deposits than they were collecting from old long-term loans. This arithmetic threatened to put them out of business. Congress came to their rescue in the early 1980s by deregulating their activities further. They had previously been restricted almost exclusively to making home-mortgage loans; now they were allowed to invest in a wide variety of speculative ventures, especially in real estate, even though the government still insured their deposits. Regulators hoped the industry would "grow"—speculate—its way back to health. And the limit on deposit insurance was raised to $100,000 per account. That was big enough to encourage brokers to bundle units of $100,000 deposits, and funnel them to whatever S&L paid the highest interest.

The lack of oversight, the ready source of deposits, and the investment leverage available in real estate attracted a host of high rollers to the industry. Some were simply aggressive; some played close to the legal line in self-dealing; some were outright crooks who devised complex Ponzi-like schemes to siphon off millions of dollars.

Then, in the mid-1980s oil prices collapsed. The Texas economy collapsed with them. Unemployment rose to double digits, and outside of energy itself, the sector hardest hit was real estate. Land and building values had fallen over 8 percent—in some places 20 percent—from their peak of a few years earlier. In a highly leveraged industry, that decline was enough to wipe out 100 percent of owners' equity in many situations. Since S&L's loaned money for real estate and used it as collateral, the real estate collapse devastated the industry's net worth. In many thrifts it turned negative. They and developers struggled to hang on.

Texas and California thrift executives pummeled members of both House and Senate with demands that regulators give them a chance to work through their problems, arguing that when real estate values rose, as seemed inevitable, they would automatically become healthy again. In early September 1986, then–majority leader Wright convened a meeting in his office with several Texas congressmen, both Republicans and Democrats, and Edwin Gray, head of the Federal Home Loan Bank Board (the Federal Savings and Loan Insurance Corporation, FSLIC, which insured deposits, was part of this system) and the chief regulator of the thrift industry. Wright himself knew little about the issue and left after a few minutes, while the others argued.

But he soon became more involved through Craig Hall, one of the largest owners of apartments in the United States and owner of 66,000 apartments throughout the Southwest, most in Texas. In 1986 Hall was stretched thin. He owed a consortium of over twenty lenders $1 billion. If he could not renegotiate the loan's terms, he would go bankrupt. All the lenders agreed to his offer of new terms except one, the Westwood Savings and Loan in California, the single biggest creditor. The S&L was being run by a conservator appointed by Ed Gray.

Hall, a Republican from Dallas, did not know Wright, nor had he ever contributed to Wright's campaign. But he needed political muscle. He hired Bob Strauss's law firm and by late summer had met with several members, but Wright's staff refused him an appointment. Hall went around them, arranging the meeting through the nephew of a man who had been a friend of Wright's for forty years.

In mid-September Hall explained his situation to Wright. He made clear that his bankruptcy would flood the already-depressed Texas real estate market with tens of thousands of condominiums. That would drive real estate values down further and could spark a true depression in Texas. In addition, he presented a study by an accounting firm which claimed his bankruptcy would cost FSLIC $700 million and destroy twenty-nine S&L's, mostly in Texas. Hall emphasized to Wright that every lender but one had agreed to his offer, and the one who had balked was controlled by Gray.

Wright asked Gray for help. He refused. The House was soon to vote the $15 billion capital increase for FSLIC. The majority leader controls the schedule. Wright pulled the bill.

Gray replaced the conservator who was refusing to renegotiate Hall's loan. Wright returned the bill to the schedule five days after pulling it; it promptly passed the House. Wright got some bad press out of his action, but many who understood the industry supported it. James McTeague, a journalist who covered S&L's for the daily newspaper *The American Banker,* said, "If Craig Hall had gone bankrupt, instead of a $100 billion [S&L] problem later on, it would have been a $200 billion problem." M. Danny Wall, the Republican staff director of the Senate Banking Committee who succeeded Ed Gray, later told Wright, "We did have a clown in the Craig Hall thing. He would have brought down the daisy chain [of S&L's in Texas]."

But the Craig Hall incident did not end Wright's involvement. It started it. Gray called Wright to tell him Hall's problem was being worked out, and invited him to call if any new problems arose. Gray's invitation was pure courtesy. Wright took it literally.

And Gray had to listen because the 99th Congress adjourned for the year without recapitalizing FSLIC. The GOP-controlled Senate passed a $3-billion bill including new, controversial provisions just two hours before adjournment. There was no time for compromise. The House, which had passed a clean $15-billion bill, refused to accept it.

Wright's experience with Hall raised questions in his mind about the regulators. He began to learn more.

Gray was a Reagan appointee from the Great Western Savings and Loan, a thrift with close links to Reagan and Attorney General Ed Meese. (Great Western arranged the purchase and almost immediate resale of Meese's California home; the purchaser resold the house at a significant loss.) Gray himself had created a slush fund paid into by the regional banks which he used to pay for a host of questionable expenses, including $9,000 for Reagan's 1985 inauguration. And Ohio Democrats complained bitterly that Gray was playing partisan politics earlier when Ohio's S&L industry and state-run deposit insurance program came tumbling down. "It took him days to return phone calls from [Democratic governor Richard] Celeste," said Representative Mary Rose Oakar, a Democrat on the Banking Committee. Lastly, in addition, after Wright helped Hall, S&L executives all over Texas flooded his office with complaints. They claimed the federal regulators were arbitrarily threatening to put people out of business when problems could be worked out. Wright's encounter with the regulators lent credence to the complaints.

He asked his friend George Mallick, a business partner and Fort Worth developer, to put together a meeting with people in the industry. They expected a lunch with ten or fifteen people. In October one hundred and fifty thrift executives and builders showed up at the Ridgelea Country Club in Fort Worth.

After the meeting, Herman Smith, former president of the National Association of Homebuilders, warned Wright's friend Craig Raupe, "I looked around and saw some good, reliable businessmen. I also saw some crooks." But Raupe did not give Wright that message.

The message Wright and other congressmen—several besides Wright were at Ridgelea—did get in and after the meeting was that the regulators were out of control and wanted to shut people down right and left. Only lack of resources kept the regulators from closing businesses down arbitrarily. (It cost FSLIC money to pay off depositors or subsidize mergers between healthy and insolvent S&Ls.) The $15-billion recapitalization would give them that money, and power. The executives said they were afraid, particularly of H. Joe Selby, a senior Dallas regulator.

Wright also heard accusations that regulators were persecuting Democrats. The charge of partisanship had implications for Tom Gaubert, a thrift executive who was national finance chairman for the DCCC. Gaubert claimed he was being bullied by regulators and called them "Nazis." He believed the industry needed access to politicians to protect it from "Gestapo" tactics, and in 1985 had created a PAC which raised, mostly from other S&L executives, $100,000 and spent it in the special election which sent Texas Democrat Jim Chapman to the House. (The PAC evaded the $5,000 limit in campaign contributions by making "independent expenditures," not coordinated directly with Chapman's campaign.) Chapman's victory had had national impact, and had ended talk of political realignment following Reagan's 1984 landslide victory. Gaubert also raised over $100,000 for Wright in 1985. Two years earlier regulators had taken over his thrift and were running it still. What was left of it, that was. It was hundreds of millions of dollars in the red, and stockholders wanted Gaubert back. He told Wright that attorneys had advised him that regulators had illegally ousted him and then ruined his business. Now he was filing a massive suit against them, and he complained that Gray would not see him.

When Gray called Wright to update him on Craig Hall, Wright asked him to talk to Gaubert. Gray protested that it would be improper, but did. He even hired an outside counsel to investigate Gaubert's allegations. (The conclusion: the agency had treated Gaubert unfairly, though not enough to affect the regulators' final decision.)

But later Wright received confirmation of what he regarded as persecution. Federal investigators were offering to go easy on criminals if they could supply damaging information about anyone on a list with the names of four hundred Texas businessmen. Most were involved in the thrift industry, and many were Democratic contributors. If there had been ten names, fine. Twenty-five names, fine. Maybe even fifty. But *four hundred*!? That could not be a legitimate criminal investigation; it had to be a fishing expedition. In fact, it had to be a witch hunt. Legitimate investigations first found a crime; then they looked for criminals. This investigation seemed to be starting with a list of people, trying to attach a crime to them. It was an outrageous abuse of power.

Wright heard other rumors, too, even more outrageous. Texas S&L executives were saying that Selby, the regulator, was at the center of a ring of homosexuals who were, literally, sadistic, who liked to see men "squirm." Thrift executives spoke of him with real hatred. After he forced owners of one thrift to sign over control, he reportedly laughed in their faces and said, "Now you can call Jim Wright." A seventy-year-old director, who had founded the thrift originally, replied, "Fuck you, you goddamn queer."

John Neible, dean of the University of Houston Law School, supposedly suggested firing him. There were even rumors that Selby was refusing to deal with thrift executives unless they hired homosexual lawyers, who were giving themselves immediate six-figure bonuses. They were bizarre, outrageous charges. They couldn't be true. Could they?

Wright called Gray and relayed some complaints about Selby.

W herever one looked at S&L's one found the rawest mixing of money and power, from the entry into the industry of high rollers and outright crooks, to Ed Gray's slush fund and the Ed Meese connection, to Gaubert's fund-raising. This connection of power and money was about to explode in Wright's face.

Donald Dixon ran Vernon Savings and Loan in Texas. Until the mid-1980s he had given money only to Republicans, but Gaubert connected him to Coelho. The best way to connect oneself to someone in power was to make things *easy* for him. Dixon had an airplane, a jet. He made it available to many a politician of both parties, including Republicans Gerald Ford, California senator Pete Wilson, and Nevada senator Paul Laxalt, Reagan's close friend. Coelho used the plane for fund-raising weekends, when he would hit big contributors over breakfast in one city, have lunch with other contributors in a second city, give a midafternoon speech at a political gathering in a third, and attend a cocktail reception and dinner in a fourth; it was a schedule impossible to keep on commercial flights and on a good weekend he could raise well over $100,000. Wright went often on such DCCC trips, once on Dixon's plane (Dixon wasn't there). Dixon also made his boat, *High Spirits,* which was docked in Washington and was the sister ship to the presidential yacht, *Sequoia,* available to Coelho as a site for fund-raisers, for a nice cruise on the Potomac while people wrote checks. In one four-month period, Coelho used the boat eight times.

Late in 1986, while Wright was sitting in his friend George Mallick's boardroom in Fort Worth, John Mack relayed an urgent Coelho request: could Wright talk to this fellow Don Dixon? Wright did not think he knew Dixon (later he learned he had shaken hands with him at one of Coelho's fund-raisers), and Dixon had never contributed to his campaign. But it was a favor for Coelho, so Wright called him. It was a fateful conversation.

Dixon said regulators were trying to put him out of business *right now.* Today. But if he could get one week, *just one week, maybe less,* he could work out a sale—he had a buyer for the business all lined up, just needed the details worked out.

That sounded like one more arbitrary regulatory action to Wright, like so many other outrageous things he had heard. Immediately he called Gray and said, "Ed, I don't know anything about Vernon Savings and Loan or Don Dixon. I don't know anything about the merits. But he tells me he's got a buyer and needs one week to dispose of his business himself, and he says regulators want to close him down today. I wonder if you could look into it."

Gray told him that closing an S&L required his approval, and he knew nothing about it. So whatever was happening, regulators couldn't be closing the S&L. Dixon would have his week.

Soon after the call to Gray, Wright learned that the regulators had in fact put Dixon out of business that day. Not technically—Vernon S&L stayed open for another four months before regulators closed it. But Dixon had signed away all say in the business, had lost all ownership rights, and a regulator was physically at Vernon all day every day, making all decisions. Dixon was out.

At best, Wright thought, Gray was incompetent and did not know what was happening in his own agency. At worst, Gray had lied to him. *The only thing you have in politics is your word. Without that you have nothing.* Wright was absolutely furious.

He did not even know he had stepped into quicksand.

The regulators saw things differently than Wright—and they knew more than Wright did. Their knowledge made them desperate.

It was true that recapitalizing FSLIC would allow regulators to close sick thrifts down. But allowing them to stay open spread a cancer through the entire industry. Out of Texas's 280 savings and loans, 108 fell short of net worth requirements and were technically insolvent. Sixty-five had negative net worth. To keep operating they needed a constant infusion of funds, and offered high interest rates to attract deposits. Solvent thrifts had to match them, thus raising their costs and jeopardizing their health. In addition, the worst thrifts were continuing Ponzi-like activities.

It was also true that Gray had started out as a partisan, had created and used a slush fund, had even been unresponsive and inept in the Ohio thrift crisis. But he had grown into the job. As the seriousness of the crisis facing him sank in, he had become a better and better public servant. He warred bitterly with White House ideologues demanding deregulation. *And FSLIC had only $2 billion to back up $800 billion in deposits.* Gray was terrified that if the American public learned how bad the situation was, its confidence would disintegrate and a national run on deposits would start. Gray was sitting on top of a volcano, and lava had started to flow. *He had to have more money for the insurance fund.* He would pay almost any price to get it.

With Craig Hall, Gray had felt constrained by a legal conflict of interest. He had not felt it proper to give orders to the conservator he had appointed, and disputed Hall's claim that his bankruptcy would destroy the Texas economy and drown dozens of thrifts. Still, many regulators under him felt relief that Hall's loans were renegotiated.

Gaubert was different. Wright had asked Gray to talk personally to Gaubert, who was complaining about being illegally pressured into giving regulators control of his S&L in 1984, and that regulators had so mismanaged it that two years later it had a negative net worth of $400 million. But Gaubert, clearly a political friend of Wright's, would later be indicted and acquitted for land deals involving an Iowa thrift, which FSLIC subsequently closed. Regulators considered him a shady character. They were disturbed at Wright's requesting anything unusual for him.

More disturbing to Gray was his conversation with Wright about Joe Selby. Selby had once been acting comptroller of the currency, and was extremely well regarded professionally. In fact, Gray and others considered Selby one of the finest professionals in the system. Gray later said that Wright had relayed the accusations that Selby was forcing businessmen to hire homosexual lawyers, and quoted Wright as saying, " 'Isn't there something you can do to get rid of Selby or ask him to leave or something?' " Gray did not fire him.

(Wright said that Gray was a liar, and that he never mentioned anything about Selby's homosexuality to him, and never asked him to fire Selby, although he did relay complaints about him.)

And also disturbing to regulators was Wright's conversation with Gray about Don Dixon. Dixon had milked the Vernon Savings and Loan dry. At the time he asked Wright for help, 96 percent of Vernon's loans, over one billion dollars' worth, were in default. Dixon had paid himself $8.9 million in salary and bonuses over a four-year period, while using company money to buy a $2-million home for himself in California. He spent another $800,000 of company money to maintain it for a little over a year and then sold it, at a loss, to a business partner. Vernon supplied the mortgage. And Dixon had not one airplane but five: two jets, two propeller-driven aircraft, and one helicopter, along with six full-time pilots, all servicing this one "thrift." Dixon had taken over a solvent, respectable business and raped it.

The regulators were stunned that Wright would do anything for someone like Dixon. It frightened them, made them fearful of what price they might have to pay to get their bill passed. And the situation was growing more desperate.

A few months earlier, FSLIC had had a $2-billion dike against a run on the nation's $800 billion in deposits. The regulators' chief litigator William Black said that by spring it had barely $1 billion. Gray and Black were terrified.

Pressure was coming from everywhere, not just Wright. At one point, Republican senator John McCain of Arizona and Democratic senators John Glenn of Ohio, Dennis DeConcini of Arizona, Donald Riegle of Michigan, and Alan Cranston of California together in one meeting pressured regulators on behalf of Charles Keating's Lincoln Savings and Loan in California. Five senators rarely get together in one room for anything except a televised hearing, but Keating had funneled them over $300,000 in campaign contributions. Their very presence, much less their request to reconsider a regulatory decision, had an impact. "They could have just shaken hands and walked away," William Black later said.

But Gray and Black worried most about Wright.

"It seemed like there was nothing we could give him," Black said. "We gave him the conservator's head for Craig Hall. He still comes after you. Gray met with Gaubert. He still comes after you. Then he asks for Selby's head. Gray couldn't look himself in the mirror if he fired Selby. Then he tries to help Dixon. From Gray's perspective, and mine, we were being blackmailed. We paid and the price kept going up."

Meanwhile, Wright was slipping even deeper into the quicksand. He had asked George Mallick to explore the situation, giving him a letter of introduction identifying him as an emissary researching financial industry issues for him. Who was George Mallick? A friend. A millionaire developer back in Fort Worth.

In Fort Worth, Jim Wright was like a god. It was something to watch him at a Spanish festival, crowning a queen, leading a parade, people lining the ways reaching out to wave at him, shake his hand. This was no politician simply courting votes; this was the man who had helped one after another of them; this was the grand seigneur visiting, almost the pope come to the local church; this was the doer, who used power and created change. Change for the better. Change to help his people. Tangible change that one could feel and smell and touch, and made one feel good at having done it. Wright had always been that way; as mayor of Weatherford he had, without any legal authority, forced the gas utility to provide service for the poor sections of town and forced a milk company to change misleading advertising. He had had no authority to do those things, but he had done them. Power was to be used, wasn't it?

Power does funny things to people. It intoxicates. It had intoxicated Wright since he was fifteen years old and addressing rallies for gubernatorial candidate Ernest Thompson, when he had felt the power to move a crowd, make them laugh, make them angry, rally them to his purpose. *That was heady wine. One never gets used to it.* Intoxication blurs judgment.

And people corrupt themselves around power. When former Vice President Walter Mondale was late for an airplane in Minneapolis, after a phone call from a friend, the airplane waited. Once Bob Michel had several stiff drinks at a reception before a speech. His speech rambled; he stumbled from subject to subject. Afterwards he was embarrassed but a lobbyist clapped him on the back and said, "Great speech, Bob! That really was great!" Michel, wanting to believe, gave him a puzzled look and asked, "Do you really think so?" "Absolutely! It was terrific!" People do things for those with power. Make life easy for them.

George Mallick made things easy for Wright. If the campaign needed office space, there it was in Mallick's properties at the cheapest legal rate. If a Xerox machine needed fixing, Mallick would see to it. Phil Duncan, then Wright's Fort Worth office manager, says, "I could call Mallick at 5:00 A.M. and say I needed something and he'd help, no questions asked. He's done a lot for Jim Wright."

Lebanese, a large, beefy, and swarthy man, he dressed with a low-keyed elegance, and had a thin, high-pitched voice which seemed out of place coming from his body. Although he was only somewhat overweight, his flesh seemed to fold about him in layers. He wore his wealth, flashing one large ring and a watch worth thousands; he was not flashy by Texas standards, but neither was he part of any establishment. There was something earthy about him.

He liked the feel of money, actual real dollars going through his fingers, and almost never used a credit card. He liked to control things; the money gave him control. It meant a lot to him to be recognized in a restaurant in New York. He would tip a headwaiter $100 for a table to be able later to hear him say, "Welcome back, Mr. Mallick, so good to see you again."

In his office, too, he liked control, liked people being at his beck and call. During one period he disliked driving, and one girl in the office was assigned to do little more than get cigarettes when he needed them or drive him around.

His home was no different. He was the boss and demanded to be treated as such. At one point he bought each of his four children a condominium as gifts, then sold one of them without telling his son, the owner, and gave him the proceeds. "It's the most patriarchal setup I've ever seen," one man in Fort Worth said. "Being head of the household means more to him than to anyone you ever met in your life."

Mallick needed to be somebody. He did not want from Wright what a lobbyist would want. His needs went deeper than a balance sheet. He wanted Wright's friendship. And that in itself was not enough. He also wanted to push others away.

Wright's daughter Ginger Brown said, "I have to conclude that anyone truly out for Jim Wright's best interests would have to be interested in his family. But George pursued whatever he pursued to the exclusion of Dad's family."

One time Mallick said, "I want to be the person people go through to get to Jim Wright."

More than once he declared, "I want to be the number-one friend— and that includes Craig Raupe."

Raupe had been Wright's real friend since 1950. Wright once inscribed a picture to him, to his "brother." Raupe dismissed Mallick as "a political groupie."

But if Raupe's description of him had an element of truth to it, there was also a depth to Mallick's relationship with Wright.

Mallick's father had been a successful wholesale grocer in Fort Worth. But when he moved to a better neighborhood so that his children could enjoy his financial success, it turned into hell for young George. The segregated all-white school had to accept him—technically. But his desk was separated from his classmates, put over in a corner, and his teacher talked publicly, to the class, of the neighborhood going down. His high-pitched voice lent itself to being mocked. It was. Kids made fun of him—"rug merchant," they called him, "sand nigger." Everyone in school thought they were better than he was. "My father moved to that neighborhood to help us," Mallick recalled. "It was the worst thing he could have done to us."

He was an outsider. The establishment refused to accept him. He became a developer, building small shopping centers, apartments, and, in 1967, when just thirty-two years old, Mallick Tower, the first office building in years put up in downtown Fort Worth. That tower which he put his name on, in the middle of downtown, forced the city establishment to acknowledge him. The Jaycees virtually had to, and did, name him Outstanding Young Man of the Year. But he was still rejected for membership in the country club. And he still could not get financing for his projects in Fort Worth. In 1968 he tried to get involved with Hubert Humphrey's presidential campaign; those running it locally, the Fort Worth power structure, shut him out.

He and Wright met in 1963, when Wright dedicated a shopping center Mallick had just built. After the ceremony they had a cup of coffee together and hit it off. Mallick built things. Wright belonged to the Texas populist tradition and distrusted big business (with the emphasis on "big"), but he had never shared the antidevelopment, antibusiness attitude of eastern liberals. Wright's chief hobby was gardening. He got satisfaction in digging his fingers in the dirt and watching something come from it. *What do you have after two hours of golf? When I spend two hours in a garden I see things grow.* His beliefs fitted into America's tradition of boosterism; he wanted to see things flourish, expand, saw himself as a builder, too, a builder of people through government spending on education and a builder of business through government spending on infrastructure in bridges, roads, and waterways. He could identify with Mallick, who had taken a chance trying to make downtown Fort Worth bloom again. Something more personal passed between them, too. Mallick longed for acceptance. And Wright accepted Mallick. He was an outsider, all right, and felt an outsider's pain. Wright, who had spent his growing-up moving from town to town, always the new boy in school, had worked for acceptance all his life too. Mallick said, "I am an outsider. Jim Wright's an outsider too."

Within a year after first meeting they made a joint investment. When Mallick Tower was finished, Wright dedicated that, too, this time with pomp, landing on its roof in a helicopter. They grew closer.

Both of them went through personal difficulties at the same time, in the late 1960s and early 1970s. Three years after finishing his tower, Mallick was all but bankrupt, owed $6 million, was being sued and investigated by the FBI. (No charges were ever filed, and the *Fort Worth Star-Telegram* quoted the plaintiff in the lawsuit as saying Mallick was a "victim.") When he had to sell the office building named for him, the establishment laughed at him. Wright could empathize with that all right, too. They grew closer still.

As Mallick faced his troubles, Wright's personal finances and life were hitting a nadir. His finances had never recovered from his use of personal funds, and borrowed money, to pay off the $70,000 campaign debt from the 1961 Senate race. In 1966 he had hoped to run for the Senate again, had sought a mass of $10 contributions to fund his campaign. He had pictured himself the people's champion. But the people did not respond, and he had not run. The rebuff had turned him inward. Checks he wrote would have bounced, except that they were written on a House checking account and the House sergeant at arms does not bounce checks written by members. (Wright always made them good.) Trying to make back the money he had used to pay the campaign debt, he took chances in investments that ended in disaster; especially disastrous was a Pontiac dealership in Leesburg, Virginia, which cost him tens of thousands of dollars.

And his marriage had deteriorated, ending in divorce. A loner anyway, a failure at least by his own standards of ambition when he did not reach the Senate in two attempts, he now faced financial failures too. He had entered Congress almost a rich man, accepting an 80 percent cut in pay, from roughly $70,000 a year to the $12,500 a congressman then made. It had not bothered him. He cared about the power to make history, not money. But now all he had was debts.

Through most of this period Craig Raupe was in Miami, vice president of Eastern Airlines. Mallick was in Fort Worth. He would have Wright over for dinner. Their mutual troubles only reinforced the friendship.

After divorcing Mab in 1972, he gave her what money he had along with alimony and child support, and married Betty Hay. (Years later Mab said, "He did give me what he could. He still does. Honestly, I don't think Betty knows about it.")

Wright's friends had all liked Mab. They were cool to Betty at first. All except George and Marlene Mallick. Betty and Marlene got along famously, did many things together. When the Wrights were in Fort Worth, the two couples saw each other often. Mallick moved even closer.

Wright loved Betty. Really loved her. "He used to carry pictures of her around with him and bore people with them," said one person who had known both since their marriage. "I'm not talking about pictures in a wallet. I'm talking about an album, a goddamn photo album.''

He knew how hard her life had been and wanted to take care of her. She liked nice things. Not outrageous, not extravagant, but nice. She could see what Marlene Mallick had. So could Wright. Marlene had money to spend. But Wright's finances continued to sink. His net worth fell to $68,000 in 1976, barely one-fourth (after inflation) what it had been when he entered Congress.

And Wright wondered about his children. Shouldn't he leave something to them, whenever his time came? Rayburn had died penniless but also childless and wifeless. *Men feel like a failure, too,* Betty once said, recalling when they got married.

She would fight for him, help him secure his flanks, keep watch for enemies. If he was sensitive to criticism, she was supersensitive, fierce in her loyalty to him. Didn't she deserve comfort? he wondered. Didn't his kids deserve something? Didn't he at least deserve to get this terrible weight off his back?

After being elected majority leader, he had made that comment: "When I started out as a young man I was a real purist. I took no contribution of more than $100 and nothing from people affected by legislation. But, hell, after a while you see everyone is affected one way or another. You can't raise any money like that. My position now is if the law says it's all right, I'll take the money. I've complied with the law."

He held that fund-raiser, justifying it as paying himself back for the personal funds he had used fifteen years earlier to pay his Senate campaign debt, and converted $98,000 (half went to taxes) to pay off personal debts. He was out of debt. Finally.

But then the press had come after him. It went after Betty too. She was still on the payroll of the Public Works Committee, making $24,000 a year. House rules prohibited members from employing their spouses, but Betty was grandfathered because she had started work seven years before their marriage. In fact, to avoid the appearance of impropriety, she had forgone merit raises after marrying Wright. The press still wrote damning stories. She quit, and for the first time since she was fifteen years old did not work. They still needed money.

Reenter Mallick. Wright had risen to majority leader; Mallick had risen too. He had started new projects, and when the Fort Worth establishment refused to loan him money he had reached out of state, to New York, to the West, for money. By the 1980s, financing for his projects was coming from such places as the Grand Cayman branch of the Union Bank of Bavaria.

By 1986 Mallick could tell the *Fort Worth Star-Telegram,* "I'm not a billionaire. I'm a modest millionaire. I'm never going to be a Rockefeller. I know how much is enough."

Enough meant a Park Avenue apartment, an opulent home in Fort Worth, the $100 tips to headwaiters to get a table. To celebrate Wright's twenty-fifth anniversary in Congress he hosted a lavish party, lavish even in Texas, his message to the Fort Worth establishment.

In the mid-1970s, Wright began turning more and more to Mallick for financial advice. They had been making joint investments for years. Now, under Mallick's guidance, and helped by unrelated investments that benefited from skyrocketing oil prices, Wright's net worth suddenly jumped from $68,000 in 1976 to, five years later, over $500,000.

One day in the late 1970s, Wright and Betty were having dinner with Mallick and his wife, Marlene. Wright was laughing about the car dealership he had lost so much money in. Betty said, "I wish I had been married to him then. I'd have taken care of that."

"Oh?" Mallick said. "You're a businesswoman?"

Early in 1979, Betty started working for Mallick, primarily looking at real estate investments. It was another opportunity for him to move closer to Wright, and Betty was intelligent and effective. It was part time, and her salary was $18,000. Mallick provided free housing to several employees; he liked having them close, at beck and call, liked to feel himself their patron. It was personal to him. It was the patriarch in him. Mallick told the Internal Revenue Service that their occupancy of apartments was a condition of employment. That meant the free rent was not compensation, and therefore was tax-free; his lawyer, bookkeeper, and other employees lived in his apartments. With Betty on the payroll, he gave the Wrights a rent-free and tax-free apartment too, although they stayed there only half a dozen or so days a month. Mallick was making things easy for Wright, really wanted him to live there. He knew better than to consider himself a patriarch of Jim Wright, but having Wright live in something Mallick owned—that was special. It was a sweet deal. But the IRS itself had approved the arrangement. *My position now is if the law says it's all right, I'll take the money.*

Soon the Mallicks and the Wrights combined their two family names and formed Mallightco. In February 1980, Wright put in $58,000 in stocks; Mallick put in $58,000 in cash. For Wright, the company was serious business; for Mallick it was a toy. "My average deal is five to ten million dollars," he said. "Mallightco deals in the thousands. It's more like an investment club." Still, *Mallick had merged into Wright. Mallightco! What was closer than that?*

The company doubled its value the first year to almost $250,000. Mallick's accountants advised him to create some deductions for it, so Betty, who was vice president, in January 1981 switched payrolls from Mallick's own company to Mallightco. She looked for more investments and followed regional stocks. She enjoyed dealing with her own money, and liked to learn from scratch about investments they considered. She was willing to take a chance, but was not a high-flyer. Preservation of capital came first.

The company became a cash cow, paying dividends as well as Betty's $18,000 salary, and loaning the Wrights almost $120,000. Mallick did well also, collecting the same dividends, borrowing $48,000 from the company, and selling it his wife's one-and-a-half-year-old Cadillac for $10,000 while she often continued to use it, until Betty took it to Washington three years later, still technically a company car. It was the kind of thing small businessmen did all over America.

Wright's daughter Ginger worried, "Mallick was playing in an arena he knew nothing about, trying to mix his type of investment schemes with the political world, and they just won't mix. He was not sensitive to the fact that he had partners who would be held up to the light and judged by the world, based on what he did."

Wright let him do it. In the late 1970s he was sometimes ambivalent about and frustrated in Congress. In many ways he had less power as majority leader than he would have had as chairman of Public Works. There was no reason to believe he would be Speaker anytime soon. *I've seldom felt quite so despondent about this job. I seriously—truly more seriously than ever before—contemplate retiring from this well-nigh impossible task,* he had written in his journal back in 1979, as he was forming his partnership with Mallick.

Raupe said, "There would be periods when Jim just felt like the world was moving past him and that he had nothing. Nothing to leave his kids, nothing compared to what he had had when he entered Congress, nothing compared to what other people had. He periodically feels, 'I worked so hard, for so long, and I don't have anything.' He winds up doing something not wise."

The free apartment was not wise. And as the Texas economy collapsed along with oil prices, the company's profits disappeared. Betty left the payroll in January 1985. She had another job at precisely twice the salary, but Mallick still wanted them living in his demesne.

Mallick rented them the apartment for $21.67 a day (pro-rating a monthly rent), charging only for the days they were in Fort Worth. The local paper inquired into the arrangement. Mallick explained that the apartment would have stayed vacant if Wright didn't use it. That was true: he owned other apartments as investments and kept them vacant to avoid wear and tear. The reporter asked the counsel of the House ethics committee if the arrangement was all right. The counsel said it seemed to be. Three years later, Wright had an independent appraisal made of the condo and bought it.

For Mallick, the friendship meant more than anything; it meant more than acceptance by the establishment. He and Wright were the establishment. Where were those who had excluded him before? On their knees to Wright. More than once he hissed, "They're not going to kick George Mallick around anymore."

He didn't care about money, not where Jim Wright was concerned, and had always avoided involvement in anything with federal dollars attached so no one could accuse him of benefiting from his relationship. Then, in August 1986, Billy Bob Barnett came to him. Barnett was a giant of a man with a glass eye who had played basketball and football at Texas A&M and in the NFL; his basketball teammates used to overload one side of the court on fast breaks so he could see them to pass the ball. He ran Billy Bob's, a huge honky-tonk, big enough to contain half a dozen different bars and a rodeo ring where cowboys rode real bulls inside the bar.

Billy Bob's was in financial trouble, and it was the single largest business in the depressed stockyards area of Fort Worth. That was the same area into which Wright had been pouring millions of dollars of federal redevelopment aid since 1974; more money for the stockyards, involving infrastructure through flood-control funds, was moving at the time. If Billy Bob's closed, it would be a political embarrassment; Republicans had attacked as wasteful much of the spending in the neighborhood. If it closed before the election it could become an issue. News of Mallick's likely involvement temporarily relieved financial pressure on Billy Bob's, and the threat of its closing dissipated. In December 1986, Mallick and Barnett finally reached an agreement: if Mallick could find $27 million in financing, he would get 17 percent of Billy Bob's company. Mallick talked to Drexel Burnham Lambert and others but could not generate any capital. In February, Barnett kicked him out of the project; later Billy Bob's closed.

But a few weeks after Wright became Speaker—and a few weeks before Mallick left the project—the Fort Worth paper reported Mallick's involvement. It was one more thing that didn't look good—Wright's business partner getting into something that benefited, even if indirectly, from federal dollars. Already, as Wright approached the speakership, his business ties to Mallick had worried his political friends, including Bob Strauss, who tried to end them. His law firm had done some business for Mallick, but the two men did not have a relationship. Strauss invited Mallick to his Washington law office, and, he later recalled, said, "I don't know you, Mr. Mallick, but I know you're a good friend of Jim Wright. I'm not sure you're aware of the intensity of scrutiny he will be under as Speaker, or that you may come under because of your friendship. Please keep in mind that anything you do will reflect on him if it appears on the front page of *The Washington Post*."

Then Strauss, using his gift of framing an issue in a way which makes people rethink it, told Wright: "Your relationship with Mallick is very personal and I don't presume to comment on it. But you should realize you create more problems for him than he does for you. He may be forced to pass up profitable opportunities for fear of embarrassing you."

The comment seemed to register. But it did not affect the Wright-Mallick relationship. And the savings and loans? Wright had asked Mallick to look into the savings and loan thing for him, had given him that letter of introduction in effect identifying Mallick as his agent. Mallick's extensive real estate holdings gave him at least the appearance of a conflict of interest, but that appearance did not deter Wright.

"That letter was a sop to Mallick's ego," another man close to Wright said. "He waved that letter all over the Southwest and in New York. It caused some problems with Bob Strauss."

"Jim's the hardest man to help I know of," Strauss sighed.

The letter showed that Mallick had become, in writing, the number-one friend.

By the time Mallick handed in his S&L report in February it had become irrelevant. Wright did not read it, although his staff did. (It accused regulators of arbitrarily adding to industry problems by suddenly imposing tighter regulation, and made no mention of the widespread wrongdoing by industry executives—ranging from highly leveraged, high-risk investments to self-dealing and outright fraud.)

Wright had already decided to oppose the $15-billion FSLIC recapitalization which he had voted for only weeks earlier, and to support a $5-billion package backed by the industry's biggest trade association, the U.S. League of Savings Institutions. Wright also supported a proposal of Texas GOP congressman Steve Bartlett requiring "forbearance" by the regulators. The House Banking Committee chairman was St Germain; he, too, had supported the $15-billion bill just weeks earlier, but switched positions to accommodate Wright.

The regulators were desperate for more. Roy Green of the Dallas Federal Home Loan Bank decided to present his case directly to Wright, and asked Bob Strauss to get him an appointment. On February 10, at three-thirty in the afternoon, Green, William Black, Joe Selby, and another regulator walked into Wright's Washington office, hoping to convince him to support a larger bailout bill.

The meeting would ultimately have an impact far beyond the savings and loan industry; it would play a key role in Gingrich's effort to destroy Jim Wright.

Wright sat behind his desk, flanked by staff, Mallick, and Mallick's son Michael. The four regulators sat facing him. Mallick's presence disturbed them; they had come prepared to show Wright confidential information about Don Dixon, the man Wright had called Gray about, the man who had told Wright he needed just one week to finalize a sale of his Vernon Savings and Loan, even though 96 percent of its loans were in default. That information was confidential; the regulators could not share it with Mallick present.

Instead, Green began his presentation with charm, and explained that the "sickest" S&L's had to be closed to save the healthy ones, adding that only a handful had to be closed. He made no accusations of wrongdoing. Green did most of the talking for half an hour. Then Selby said, "We just want to show you we don't have horns."

Wright eyed him, wondering whether Selby's comment was unintended irony or a deliberate provocation, then suggested that when real estate values rose again, the balance sheets of these S&L's would improve. So why not give them forbearance? "Isn't there some way to do that in a general way?"

"We are giving forbearance," Green replied.

"People are afraid," Wright continued, looking at Selby. "Solid businessmen are frightened of you. They tell me you've been punitive. They say, 'If Joe Selby heard me say this, I'd be out of business.' "

"Joe does so much," Green said. "People don't know."

"They worry that if FSLIC gets $15 billion they'll put people out of business willy-nilly. Seems to me that's what you were doing."

"Let's talk about Vernon, if that's what you're raising," Green said. "We didn't know anyone was interested in buying it."

"It's funny Dixon communicated that to me, whom he didn't even know, and didn't tell you. I wouldn't know Dixon if he walked in that door. But what about all those other guys out there? Do they get the same treatment? I was a boy in the Depression. I saw the effects of a terrible economy in stark terms."

Green explained that there must have been a misunderstanding between him and Gray, that there were differences between signing a consent to merge, having a conservator appointed, and actually closing the savings and loan entirely.

Wright snapped, "They didn't want any of those things. They wanted a week. Dixon said he had a buyer and needed a week. Mr. Gray told me there was no way he would not have that opportunity. You're talking semantics now, you're talking words."

As Wright continued, William Black grew angry. He thought all this was a sham, that Wright had been helping one of the sleaziest S&L operators in America because he was a political buddy. *That's who he was going to bat for?* Black thought. *Wow!* In his mind's eye he pictured Wright on the floor, using and manipulating words. Suddenly, virtually calling Wright a liar, he snorted, "I'm not from Washington. I'm not talking 'words.' "

The muscles of Wright's face jerked for an instant, then he continued. "It *is* words. Mr. Gray told me this person could not be put out of business for a week—"

Suddenly Black interrupted again, saying that Gray had spoken the truth. Wright started again and Black disputed him again. Suddenly Wright leaned forward, furious, his words spat out in a tight, hissing, controlled rage. *"Now you wait just a goddamn minute. I waited patiently for you. Now you just wait."*

The room fell silent, tense. Only seconds passed but they were heavy, heavy seconds. Finally, awkwardly, Green apologized for any miscommunication between Gray and Wright and brought the discussion back to policy, to the consequences if the Federal Deposit Insurance Corporation, a separate agency which insured bank deposits, took over S&L oversight. He ignored Black, seemed to dismiss him, and Black sat fuming silently.

As they left, Green invited Wright to call any time with any problem—"If you want a week for someone, we'll give a week. If you want a month, we'll give a month. Whatever. Just call."

Green was offering to protect any political friends Wright wanted protected, as a price for getting the $15-billion bill. It was part of the swirl of power.

"I don't want to do that," Wright said, shaking his head. "I don't *ever* want to call you."

The meeting ended, and Wright forgot about his exchange with Black.

Black didn't forget. Black had become his enemy, an enemy determined to hurt him. He was a full-bearded man in a city where beards were a badge of nonconformity, a leftover from the sixties; his job was to find fraudulent S&L operators. He had demanded to be present at this meeting, and later bragged that Wright had not intimidated *him*. Wright had angered him. And Ed Gray, who had once done public relations for one of the country's biggest S&Ls, knew the industry media intimately, was an enemy too.

They had to be. The situation kept getting worse. When FSLIC's $2-billion dike against a run on $800 billion in deposits declined to barely $1 billion, Gray and Federal Reserve chairman Paul Volcker made plans to protect the U.S. financial system if the worst case, a national run on S&L's, happened.

Black and Gray thought Wright was blackmailing them. They fought back, hard. They had to. Black later said, "The only area we could compete was the press. We felt we had the better side of the argument. We talked to everyone who would listen to us."

Their media campaign began slowly.

Word of Wright's intervention for Dixon, and Dixon's excesses, began to leak to the press. Gray talked with an underling of Jack Anderson, and Anderson wrote a column—as many as eight hundred publications ran some of his columns—in mid-March accusing Wright of pressuring regulators to go easy on a sleazy operator. "Yes, I called Ed Gray," Wright said with a cool anger when he read it. "I would have done it for anyone in the same situation. I never met Dixon in my life." The story bothered him mostly because it impugned his reputation.

The stories would get worse.

And it was a major story in Texas. Texas reporters had written about the whole S&L issue over and over. The *Dallas Morning News,* the *Fort Worth Star-Telegram,* the *Austin American,* the *Houston Chronicle,* the *Dallas Times-Herald* began to focus on Wright and S&L's. From a policy perspective, few Texas papers supported his position. Black was making the rounds of Texas papers, saying things about Wright that raised questions at best of propriety, at worst of corruption. Black gave reporters his home phone, urged them to call him anytime they wanted to talk about Wright, wrote them personal notes, visited different papers' editorial boards, leaked to individual reporters. One Texas reporter said, "Black was obsessed by Wright."

Black seemed convinced that Wright and Don Dixon were cohorts, that Wright had known exactly whom he was helping, and implied a political payoff. As proof, he told one writer that Wright must have known about Don Dixon before the meeting with regulators because "we'd sent him the information, back door through [Georgia congressman] Doug Barnard. Barnard was given a memo to get to the Speaker." But Black sent the memo on February 27. The meeting was February 10. And Black actually sent it to Barnard's aide Richard Peterson, who said, "We were dealing in policy. Not specific institutions. Barnard never saw the memo."

Black told reporters that after Wright's phone call, Dixon's S&L was allowed to make several hundred million dollars in bad loans for four more months before finally being closed. But Wright's phone call had had no impact. Regulators had taken over Vernon. Technically, Dixon remained on the board, but neither he nor the board had any authority over a Texas state regulator named Earl Hall, who became the de facto chief executive officer and made all decisions.

Black spread more innuendo. Jim Pierebon of the *Houston Chronicle* said, "I'd talked to Black in the past and sometimes he'd call me back, sometimes he wouldn't. But now Black became 'available.' You'd call and it was, 'Come see me.' You'd walk into his office and it was as though he had nothing in the world he'd rather do than talk about Jim Wright. . . . He had plenty of numbers to back up his allegations. We carried his assertions. But when I tried to flesh them out, I couldn't. I became quite skeptical of his accuracy."

Bartlett Naylor, then chief investigator for the Senate Banking Committee who shared information with Black, said, "I have a lot of respect for him. He was trying to catch crooks and do the Lord's work and people were trying to stop him. . . . But Bill's self-righteous. He prides himself on standing up to powerful people. He sees evil conspiracies everywhere. He goes well beyond the normal role for a counsel. He said very negative things about Wright personally. He's hyperbolic."

And a national reporter who covered the industry said, "If you think it was all Bill Black, you're underestimating Ed Gray. He had it in for Wright. He's the one who really knew the press. He was the one who had been the public relations executive."

Inside the House Wright was having problems on the issue too. He wanted a $5-billion package. Strong sentiment existed on the Banking Committee for the $15-billion package. The industry was in shambles, and the sooner it was cleaned up, the less expensive it would be in the long run. If things got worse, taxpayers might have to pick up the tab. It might already be too late to save taxpayers' money. Mallick had estimated the cost at $50 billion, but estimates kept rising.

Wright and his Texas colleague Mike Andrews testified before a closed caucus of Banking Committee Democrats about their concerns about the regulators, and their fears of giving them too much power. A subcommittee still approved the $15-billion plan, although it included language requiring forbearance. The vote stung Wright. That night Wright gave Jack Brooks a ride to a dinner. They talked about it. "Wasn't it a shame," Wright said, "that Ed Gray would go to the newspapers and lie about him and then win?" Brooks had heard all the complaints from thrift executives too. The next day the full committee was going to vote on the bill. At breakfast, one Wright aide said, "I think I can turn the vote around. Should I?"

"No!" Wright said firmly. This had already become stickier than he wanted. "Stay out of it. The forbearance language is all I care about and it's in there."

Wright and his staff did nothing. But Brooks worked the committee hard. So did Andrews: "I talked to everybody I could get my hands on. Probably fifteen. I went to younger members I knew well. I think I did some good." The full committee voted 25–24 to reverse the subcommittee.

That only sparked more bad newspaper stories about Wright's involvement. *We talked to anyone who would listen,* Black had said. He was a fighter, and was fighting for his life. He continued, "We make no bones about it. We had the Speaker of the House and the U.S. League [of Savings Institutions] against us. They could bring in five hundred executives on a blitz in a minute. All we had was the two of us, Ed Gray and me. We generated very favorable editorial comment."

It was an understatement. Wright grew sick of S&L's, sick of everything about the issue. He was angry at the press criticism. The S&L issue wasn't even important to his agenda. But it was affecting his agenda, was beginning to leak into the Washington press corps; Washington reporters were a particularly receptive audience because criminal excesses of the Old Court Savings and Loan in Maryland had virtually destroyed the state-insured S&L system. Its operator, Jeffrey Levitt, who with his wife went to jail, had gorged himself on millions of dollars and his story became a long-running soap opera in *The Washington Post.* And tens of thousands of innocent depositors in Maryland's Washington suburbs had their funds frozen for months. The Washington press corps was definitely receptive to stories of S&L abuses.

Clearly this thing could have an impact on the larger game. When an aide asked what the next step was, Wright snapped, "Just get this thing out of my face!"

Then, the last weekend in April, in Texas, he got a call from Treasury Secretary Jim Baker, who flew down the next day to talk in person while attending the same event. Baker told him Ed Gray was being replaced, then made a personal plea for Wright's support of a $15-billion package. Wright asked if Baker would agree to some language constraining the regulators. Baker said fine. They had a deal. Back in Washington, St Germain again reversed his position to be on the same side as Wright.

Wright was happy to get out of this thing.

He wasn't out. Three days after Baker talked to him, regulators filed suit against Don Dixon to recover $350 million. It looked as though Wright had switched positions because of that, and generated a host of new stories. When one Wright aide announced he was preparing a point-by-point rebuttal of Black's insinuations, another snorted, "About fucking time."

Meanwhile, the House was preparing to vote on the recapitalization bill. In a corridor outside the House chamber, Wright ran into the U.S. League of Savings Institutions lobbyist and the association president. They thanked him for his help, then said, "We've got to do something about that reevaluation of property values. Let me give you these figures."

"I can't talk about it now," Wright said.

They insisted. Suddenly Wright exploded: "Listen! My back got tired of carrying all you people! When those bastards were writing all those stories about me, I was alone. Where were you then? This is a two-way street. That's the way things work up here. You come and tell me your problems but you don't tell the press. You don't do a damn thing to support yourselves or me. You left it to me to do it all."

Just before the vote on May 5, Wright made a rare floor speech to make clear he did support the $15-billion figure Jim Baker wanted, which was opposed by the industry. But that was only his personal position; it wasn't a leadership position. Coelho was working against the $15 billion. Coelho had to lie low publicly—he had asked Wright to speak with Dixon because his fund-raising role made him sensitive to any public contact with regulators—but he could work the floor. (He later told a reporter his name never appeared on the phone logs of regulators.) And in every district in America, local S&L executives had gotten the word to work their congressmen hard. The House rejected by a massive 258 to 153 the position which Wright, the White House, and the committee chairman all supported. Republicans, including Gingrich, voted against Wright and the White House, and for the industry, 98–72. The S&L's hadn't needed Wright at all.

But still it wasn't over. Even after the House voted, Black continued his private campaign, seeking out reporters. Then he, a liberal Democrat, called Karen Van Brocklin, who by now was working actively for Gingrich to undermine, even destroy, Wright. That was what Black wanted too. "It was my birthday and I wanted to go home," Van Brocklin recalled. "He just started unloading these things on me."

*   *   *

And Black was talking now to the major national media. In June, more than a month after the House passed the bill, *Newsweek* ran a major story entitled "The Wright Man to See." Although the story stipulated that "not even Wright's sharpest critics accuse him of doing anything illegal," it accused him of "parochial meddling" and explored Gaubert's fund-raising and Coelho's use of Dixon's yacht and airplanes. When the story came out, Wright said calmly, but coldly, so coldly, "I must say, I do not feel I have been well served by my staff in this matter. You have allowed press innuendo to besmirch my reputation."

The next day it got worse, with a *New York Times* editorial that read, "Does Jim Wright want to be known as the Speaker of the House or defender of some Texas banking hustlers? Parochialism is the most charitable explanation for his campaign to prevent regulators from closing bankrupt savings and loans in his home state. . . . The thrift issue may thus help to determine whom Jim Wright wishes to speak for— politically connected Texans or the House and all American taxpayers."

Wright sat in his ceremonial office, his anger running deep. Parochialism! How dare they charge him with parochialism? Without him, the federal loan guarantee that prevented New York City from going bankrupt would never have passed Congress. Was that parochial? Now his own section of the country needed assistance. Should he do less? He and his aide Marshall Lynam ran down the names of people who could respond to the *Times* and settled on Felix Rohatyn, the investment banker and Democrat who had run New York City's financial rescue operation. Lynam called him. Would he send a letter defending Wright to the *Times?* Of course he would. Wright got on the phone and thanked him. That afternoon Lynam drafted a letter and sent it to Rohaytn, to use or rewrite as he chose. (The letter never appeared.)

Then, to try to head off further damage, Lynam and Duncan talked with *Washington Post* editorial writers to explain Wright's actions, hoping to convince them not to write an editorial; they failed. They did the same at *The Wall Street Journal* and failed. Five days later Jack Anderson went after Wright again. Would this thing ever end?

And Newt Gingrich sat, like Madame Defarge, knitting together his file of press clippings. Coolly, patiently, repeating the same things over and over to reporters and in speeches, planting seeds. In one speech Gingrich summarized what he was telling reporters, what he was saying in other speeches all over the country in addition to talking about the savings and loan issue:

"The House is a corrupt institution. Let me give you the facts. . . .

"Fact: In the mid-1970s [Wright] converted $100,000 from his campaign fund to his personal use.

"Fact: In the late 1970s he handed [Egyptian President Anwar] Sadat—during the Camp David Peace Accords—he handed the President of Egypt, in a meeting he had as the number-two man in the House, a personal letter on behalf of a Texas oil millionaire who allowed Wright to buy into several proven oil wells. The letter asked Egypt to give this guy the Sinai concessions [to produce oil].

"Third fact: He pressed the Carter administration to lower the price to an oil company for national forest leases at a time he was being allowed to buy into the company's gas wells. . . .

"Fact: He forced the Appropriations Committee to give $11.8 million in an unmatched, unrequested grant to the city of Fort Worth, which has never asked for it, for a project in the stockyards [an area being redeveloped in Fort Worth] which primarily benefits people who are Jim Wright's personal business partners."

Gingrich's audiences reacted with outrage to this standard speech. And reporters listened too, especially since the charges were backed up by story clips.

Some of Gingrich's charges were half-truths; some were flat falsehoods. Wright had rebuttals. If anyone asked.

Yet even without Gingrich's added distortions, some of the things Wright had done needed explaining. They created an impression of someone who played close to the line. Craig Raupe later told a reporter, "I don't understand how Jim Wright can be so politically in tune and then be almost totally blind to appearances."

The reason was simple. Wright looked at the things he did and saw nothing wrong with them. Nothing. *If they think they do not like me it is because they do not know me.* So Wright had written in the affirmation he carried around, the affirmation in which he urged himself to keep his own passions contained. It reflected an insecurity. In his private journal he once wrote, "Is it an insatiable thirst for approval which drives me?" Why should he care if anyone liked him? He was Speaker of the United States House of Representatives! *And he was worrying about whether people liked him?*

It reflected hubris, too, and arrogance—putting the burden on others to understand him. And it was naive, incredibly naive: why would cynics, like journalists, or political enemies assume the best when they examined his actions? Wouldn't they more likely assume the worst?

Meanwhile, Gingrich was creating resonance. *If I ever become convinced that someone in public office is corrupt, I will never, ever give him a break, on anything,* one prominent journalist had said. Reporters who wrote nothing about the charges were affected by hearing them. Then came that *Newsweek* story about savings and loan lobbying, "The Wright Man to See."

The savings and loan thing made it possible to create in Jim Wright a symbol of a political machine, Gingrich had said. *All the newspaper stories we had were old. It also made it current. That was important.*

The press was playing things exactly as he had hoped. In June after *Newsweek*'s story, Gingrich decided that when the time was ripe, "I will demand an ethics committee investigation of Jim Wright."

He planned to manipulate the media to make the time ripe. The fact that he had voted the way savings and loan lobbyists wanted and that Wright had in the end opposed the industry did not disturb him.

You're fighting a war. It is a war for power, he had said. *We are engaged in reshaping a whole nation through the news media.*

The press is always this great *thing* out there in politics. Its impact is felt on dozens of levels in making policy and exercising power.

In the narrowest, inside-the-Beltway sense, the area in which Gingrich had no interest, the press was used to communicate between factions of policymakers inside Washington. In this role, the three most important newspapers, *The Washington Post, The New York Times,* and *The Wall Street Journal,* are almost a messenger service. This is the world of nuance and interpretation. Any story, or for that matter any unattributed quote, in any of the three main papers is attended to and analyzed by others concerned about a given issue. Print lasts. One gets it on one's fingers; one has to wash it off. Print has feel, color, smell. It is tangible, there, a thing to mark up, copy, pass around and read and reread and file and look up a year later and think about and consider and grow angry over or happy over. Policymakers use the three dailies to stake out positions, declare themselves, feel out others for responses and force them to define their positions. (Television rarely gets into this part of the game. The daily struggle over the detail of governing, and subtlety, escapes it.)

Gingrich ignored that narrow function of the press as he ignored policy. His interest lay in the power the press has to set the agenda and to define reality by describing, whether it describes the real or not. His interest lay in the power of perception, a power which the press dominates. It always has. Two centuries ago Edmund Burke observed, "There are three estates in Parliament, but in the reporters' gallery yonder, there sits a fourth estate more important by far than them all."

The fourth estate. It is heavy, ponderous, powerful, and potentially dangerous, and its relationship with those in power is a complex one: simultaneously symbiotic, parasitic, and adversarial. In theory it stands outside, the object observing the subject. In fact, like the Heisenberg effect in physics, observation alters the state of being. Reporting something can change it. Beyond that, the seeming "subject" often reverses roles and manipulates the press. And the press affects itself and influences itself. Depending on mood and individuals, the media can be as cold and relentless as a glacier carving out a gorge, or as intimate as college roommates exchanging stories about their sexual experiences, or as vicious as dogs ripping at one small piece of exposed flesh.

There are two chief paradoxes in the relationship between journalists and the powerful:

First, despite the media's generally adversarial tone and its aggressiveness, it is almost entirely reactive in choosing what stories to cover. This reactiveness amounts almost to passivity, and leaves the media open to manipulation and exploitation. The press affects issues and people it covers, and is affected itself by them.

Second, the intense competitiveness of the media yields a sameness. And, as in many competitive professions, its members have large egos and large insecurities, and want simultaneously to stand out from the pack and to be confirmed by it.

The most obvious aspect of the relationship between journalists and those they cover is the adversarial tone reporters take. The press sees itself as the judge of politicians, the monitor of the state. This institutional sense of separateness, of sitting in judgment, is not simply an abstract concept; it shows itself each year at the President's State of the Union speech. Out of simple courtesy everyone in the House chamber—members of both parties in House and Senate, justices of the Supreme Court, members of the diplomatic community, everyone in the galleries looking on—applauds the President when he is introduced. Except, that is, for one silent pocket, one dead hole of silence in the chamber; journalists in the press gallery, directly above and behind the dais, sit silently, making no motion of approval or disapproval. It is easy to see how a member might sneer, *Objective? Ha! Hypocrites is more like it.*

Yet for all its adversarial nature, the media's agenda is imposed upon it. Rarely do reporters actually generate stories. They react, they receive. The line between subject and object becomes blurred. Stories come from events: a floor vote, a press conference, a terrorist bombing, a leak. The Pentagon routinely comes under media attack over procurement scandals after congressional committees either leak or hold public hearings following investigations. Investigative journalists rarely break such stories with digging.

Even when investigative reporters do expose new information, they rarely are true "enterprise" stories, i.e., stories generated entirely by a reporter. Most investigative pieces start with a leak, and leaks serve the purpose of the leaker; they represent an effort to manipulate the media.

Charles Babcock, an investigative reporter for *The Washington Post,* did break stories about Reagan's attorney general Ed Meese, and would break a major story about Wright. Speaking of his own uncovering of Meese's scandals, he said, "It was all public information. Nobody believed that. Even my own editors thought it was leaked to me." Even his own editors believed someone had handed him the information.

In the first weeks of Bush's administration, stories suddenly appeared about Secretary of State Jim Baker's ownership of several million dollars' worth of Chemical Bank stock while Treasury secretary, when he made daily decisions about Third World loans that greatly increased the stock's value. Yet Baker had listed his ownership on financial disclosure forms. No reporter bothered to review those forms for four years, until he became secretary of State, and, even then, the story was leaked to reporters by White House counsel Boyden Gray. (He later admitted mentioning Baker to reporters.) Gray was using the leak to divert press attention from his own conflict-of-interest problem. Brooks Jackson, a *Wall Street Journal* investigative reporter who would later hit Wright hard, said, "That's a black mark on all of us [journalists], that we didn't uncover that Baker stuff."

The media's generally adversarial tone masks its passivity, masks the fact that it has had its agenda imposed upon it. Former White House press secretary Larry Speakes expressed the tension between the manipulators and the manipulated when he told reporters, "Don't tell me how to manage the news and I won't tell you how to report it."

How the media does report stories is a function of the interplay between reporters' and editors' sense of responsibility and fairness, their egos, and their and their publications' (or broadcasts') competitiveness. This creates the second paradox: ego and competitiveness result in sameness, rather than independent thought.

Policymakers manipulate reporters' egos to influence stories. If a cabinet secretary invites a reporter to breakfast, the following day's paper will frequently contain precisely the story the cabinet secretary wanted printed. Former network anchor Eric Sevareid observes, "The press can be bought by leaks because of ego."

Often, individual reporters, particularly those from the major national media, have immense egos. Once Wright returned a phone call in the evening to ABC's Sam Donaldson; the ABC switchboard patched Wright through to Donaldson's home where the operator told him Wright was calling him back—but didn't say Wright was actually on the line. "I'm at home now," Donaldson said, evidently annoyed that Wright presumed to disturb him there. "If he wants to talk to me he can call in the morning."

It is not only network superstars who have large egos. Reporters' egos, and the institutional egoism of the press, operate at every level. William Choyke was newly assigned to the Washington bureau of the *Fort Worth Star-Telegram* in 1977. At the time he was twenty-seven years old, barely half Wright's age, and inexperienced in Washington. Wright, with twenty-two years in Congress, had just become majority leader of the House of Representatives. Recalling the time, Choyke said, "Here I was, fresh to Washington. Here he was, just elected majority leader. It was sort of like we were coming up together."

Edmund Burke, a member of Parliament, may have been manipulating reporters himself when he called them "more important" than the members. In more recent history, no one played reporters' egos better than James Baker. One reporter recalled, "I was writing something for a third-tier publication. Most people in Washington never heard of it. He gave me an interview. When I sat down he was on the phone, got off, apologized, and said, 'We won't be interrupted again for twenty minutes.' What he was really saying to me was, '*You're very important.*' You don't think I wasn't flattered?"

One of Baker's first acts after being named secretary of State, even before meeting with career foreign-service officials, was to host a reception for diplomatic reporters. When the stories finally broke about his conflict of interest he escaped serious damage. When he was finally forced by public pressure to sell his stock, a subheadline in *The Washington Post* read, "Action Said to Go 'Well Beyond' Ethics Rules." Soon the story died. On a TV talk show, veteran journalist Jack Germond marveled at how gentle reporters had been and concluded, "Only Jim Baker could walk away from this thing."

Reporters need strong egos; to do their job properly they must not be intimidated by the powerful. And they need strong egos to survive the competitive pressures. But a strength is often a weakness.

Except for professional athletes, journalists may compete more than people in any other profession. *The Wall Street Journal, The New York Times,* and *The Washington Post* compete incessantly. An outer circle of major papers tries to break through into this inner circle, including the *Los Angeles Times,* the *Baltimore Sun, The Boston Globe,* the *Christian Science Monitor,* and even the *Washington Times,* which, run by the Reverend Moon's Unification Church, became important because of its access to conservative Reagan administration officials. Similarly, *Time* and *Newsweek* compete, while *U.S. News & World Report* tries to penetrate into the top tier. And each network newscast rating point translates into millions of dollars. Not only do publications compete, reporters compete—within their own organizations for time on a broadcast, for a front-page story instead of a page-fifteen story. And they dramatize the facts to get there; sometimes they cross the line and distort the facts. This eagerness to dramatize distorts the truth more than any ideological bias. Although conservatives have often complained about liberal bias in the media, the Reagan administration, by far the most conservative of recent presidencies, was much better treated than those of Carter, Ford, Nixon, or Johnson. Halfway through Reagan's presidency, then–Vice President Bush agreed that "the media has treated the administration pretty well."

What reporters care most about are "good" stories—what *Washington Post* editor Ben Bradlee called "Holy shit! stories," stories that wake people up, that get people's attention. Those are "good" stories.

Sevareid calls journalists "dramatists at heart"; political writer David Broder calls them "fight promoters." They are always looking for a way to get attention to their stories. The pressure to dramatize, or hyperbolize, a story is not the only problem generated by competitiveness. The most serious is that competitiveness combines with the ego of reporters—and their insecurities, since their names are attached to their stories—to yield the opposite of what one might expect. Instead of dozens of independent and different assessments of the truth, the media moves toward a consensus view.

That consensus view begins with reporters, who are covering the same story, sitting next to each other on campaign planes, or sharing facilities in the House and Senate press galleries, or finding themselves compressed even closer together in the rabbit-warren press area of the White House. Reporters compare one another's notes of what someone said, which improves accuracy, but sometimes conversations move to the next stage, as one reporter will say, or another ask, what he or she thinks the story lead is. A sameness develops, a lack of independent thought. And, more important, reporters read one another's stories.

According to a *Wall Street Journal* study, every day 89 percent of Washington reporters read the *Post,* 73 percent read the *Times,* and 51 percent read the *Journal;* the second-tier publications are widely read as well. Nine percent of Washington reporters, for example, read the *Christian Science Monitor* regularly. The first day's stories of an event often differ widely, as each writer pursues his or her own interpretation. But then the sameness begins to appear. At worst, inaccuracies start to ripple through stories; reporters rarely check a "fact" which they see in another story and therefore, unknowingly, repeat inaccuracies. Falsehoods become almost impossible to correct; they become what Norman Mailer called a "factoid." A consensus view on major stories forms by the third or fourth day, partly because more is known but also because reporters, having read competitors' stories, adjust their own stories, pull themselves back into the crowd. Any reporter who takes a different line must justify himself or herself to editors. James Doyle, former chief political correspondent for *Newsweek,* observes, "Your editor sees the AP lead, the *Washington Post* lead, the *New York Times* lead. You have to have great will power and self-assurance to go in a different direction."

Or to write a different story. Editors press. Weeks after the House had finished with the savings and loan issue, a national reporter walked into Wright's office and asked about his involvement. Wright's aides were puzzled. Why now? "My editor saw the *Newsweek* piece and said, 'I've got to have that story,' " the reporter replied.

Editors send reporters "rockets," which *Washington Post* reporter

Thomas Kenworthy defines as "a phone call late at night that somebody else has a story we don't have. And you better get on it."

Reporters want to be first but want others to follow. They want to stand out but be confirmed in their judgment. Jerry ter Horst, once President Gerald Ford's press secretary and a former *Detroit News* bureau chief, said, "When I had an exclusive, I never wanted it to be exclusive very long. I'd call friends in the wires to push it."

The cluster of reporters hounding after one story resembles what Nobel Prize–winner Canetti described as a "pack" in *Crowds and Power:* "In the changing constellation of the pack, in its dances and expeditions, [a member of a pack] will again and again find himself at its edge. He may be at the center, and then, immediately afterwards, at the edge again. . . . They are not a multitude and have to make up in intensity what they lack in actual numbers. . . . I am here deliberately opposing all the usual concepts of tribe, sib, clan. . . . Those well-known sociological concepts . . . stand for something static. The pack, in contrast, is a unit for *action.* . . . The truest and most natural pack is that from which our word derives, the hunting pack."

The press as a whole can also resemble Canetti's "crowd," as editorial writers and columnists begin to echo the primary reporters on a story, and editors take reporters off other beats and assign them to the hot story. The crowd becomes denser, more crowdlike both in numbers and in interpretation as each journalist's story becomes influenced by his colleagues' and all the stories become more and more alike.

Canetti wrote, "The most important occurrence within a crowd is . . . the moment when all who belong to the crowd get rid of their differences and feel equal. . . . Before this the crowd does not exist. The crowd needs a direction. . . . Its constant fear of disintegration means that it will accept any goal."

The press is a force, all right, but it has no direction of its own, no goal. It takes its direction from the outside. The crowd, and the press, follows. Jimmy Carter observed in 1989, "When a President is running high and has favorable reaction in the public opinion polls, he's also treated with kid gloves and deference by the press. If he starts going down, though, then he's condemned by the press."

A direction can be imposed upon the press in several ways. It can be turned, abruptly, through an overarching dominant event—a breakthrough in international peace, or an explosive new policy, or a scandal. It can also be steered, more gradually, like an ocean liner being guided into a berth. Or a general tone, like a continued economic recession or period of growth, can dictate its direction. In those cases, the press reflects fundamental realities outside itself, in the same way a stock's price will ultimately reflect the underlying value of a company. But the press can also depart from realities, just as the stock market may indulge in speculative or fearful frenzies about the future of a stock. The difference between the political press and the market is that the press has a greater ability to create a self-fulfilling prophecy. *Power is perception. One who is believed to have power has power.*

Direction can also come from what Canetti called "crowd crystals," "the small, rigid groups of men, strictly delimited and of great constancy, which serve to precipitate crowds. Their structure is such that they can be comprehended and taken in at a glance. Their unity is more important than their size. Their role must be familiar; people must know what they are there for. . . . The crowd crystal is *constant;* it never changes its size. Its members are trained in both action and faith. . . . The clarity, isolation, and constancy of the crystal form an uncanny contrast with the excited flux of the surrounding crowd. . . . The return of the moment when they are needed is as certain as the appearance of new crowds. Individual crowd crystals precipitate crowds."

The press obsessed Wright, but in a more personal way than it obsessed Gingrich, and Wright lacked Gingrich's sophisticated understanding of it. At one point, after some negative stories appeared soon after he became majority leader, he stopped giving Fort Worth reporter Choyke interviews. Choyke caught him in the Speaker's Lobby and said, "Congressman, you're just not used to the scrutiny you'll get as majority leader." Wright replied, "Son, you're not trying to scrutinize me. You're trying to screw me."

Unimpressed with the ability and intelligence of most reporters who covered the House, Wright patronized them, and sounded sanctimonious, disingenuous. He would take precious minutes to try to make reporters understand something, and then grow frustrated when they did not see things his way. He would interrupt a reporter's questions to say tensely, as if trying to dictate the story, his voice with that gentle, intimidating rumble, "You're not writing down what I'm telling you."

The press frustrated him. He failed to recognize the line Larry Speakes had drawn between managing the news and reporting it, and his sensitivity to criticism prevented him from skillfully manipulating the media. In 1979, to reporters in his office he accused the press of being "enemies of government." In a speech to newspaper editors he used slightly more diplomatic language but said the same thing. On another occasion he said, "I wish [the press] would try to be part of the solution."

The press responded with hostility. One national reporter who covered Wright said, "Reporters don't like Wright. It's amazing the things they say about him. Some of it is anti-Texas bias. They assume he is a wheeler-dealer. They're suspicious of him. They like Foley. They like Coelho. He seems to like talking to the press."

For all Wright's problems with the press, he recognized its power. He started those press luncheons, invited reporters to his home for dinner. He believed that they, like everything else, would fall to his will. But Coelho could stand in the hall and put his hand on one reporter's shoulder, punch another playfully on the arm, laugh with them. He did not need to invite them to lunch. Wright had to build on the foundation O'Neill left.

After the 1980 election, with Reagan in the White House and Republicans controlling the Senate, O'Neill became the unquestioned symbol of the Democratic Party. With celebrity status virtually thrust upon him, the daily press conferences, which had in the past focused almost exclusively on that day's floor business, became events, and O'Neill's statements were designed to make news.

In the 99th Congress, Democrats also began to respond in organized fashion to Republicans' exploitation of C-SPAN's televised House proceedings. Then–chief deputy whip Bill Alexander of Arkansas tried to get his colleagues involved in coordinating their "one-minutes," and made some progress. California Democrat Don Edwards chaired an ad hoc group on media strategy which called producers of talk shows to suggest guests, and called editors of major papers if they felt their side had been treated unfairly.

As the 100th Congress began, the leadership took charge of a new media effort. A working group planned to meet weekly under Foley's chairmanship to define a message-of-the-week. They intended to then use one-minutes and special orders, as well as interviews, to get that message out. If they could get the relatively few Democrats whom the national press sought out to say the same thing, they could create resonance. Wright himself, in addition to the media lunches and dinners he hosted and his frequent appearances on TV interview shows, started looking for a public relations expert to elevate the stature of the speakership and launch an outreach effort to editors outside Washington. He put one man on the payroll temporarily, then offered a job to another, finally hired a third, all in addition to his regular press staff.

Still, compared to the White House, the Democratic leadership's press resources were primitive in the extreme. The media tends to personalize issues; it would much prefer to cover a President than 535 members of Congress. Even if a single member of Congress could, on a particular issue, personalize a story in the way a President does, no member of Congress could rival the White House's ability to dictate pictures—and thus story—to television networks. Congress was geared toward moving legislation; the entire structure of the leadership was geared toward the most prosaic, least visually attractive, most internal elements of policy making. However much members of the Democratic leadership talked of the press, their lack of pictorial resources made it impossible to compete with the White House in terms of television.

As the year proceeded, even the meetings to plan a message-of-the-week ceased. Foley didn't have time, especially after the Iran-contra hearings started. The meetings never started up again. The one-minutes and special orders were exploited an issue at a time, not with any long-term strategic planning. Democrats had no strategy, and no insistent theme.

Gingrich had a theme. He understood the media well, and played reporters' egos too. He introduced more than one journalist to other congressmen by calling them, "One of the most serious, intelligent, and solid reporters there is covering Congress."

He understood what made a "good" story, too, and how he could use the media's desire for drama. *The number-one fact about the news media is that they love fights*, Gingrich had said. *When you give them confrontations you get attention.*

Gingrich had a strategy. And every single message he sent out either directly or indirectly reflected it. He would become his own crowd crystal.

The crowd needs a direction. Its constant fear of disintegration means that it will accept any goal.

CHAPTER 9

Wright waited. He had to wait, for the Senate to pass its budget, and then for House and Senate to reconcile their different versions. Congress had already missed the April 15 deadline for finishing the budget, undercutting the claim that Democrats could govern. And, although he was in control in the House—no one doubted that—the floor was growing restive. One could feel it.

Rayburn used to say that if one could not smell the mood of the House, if one could not walk on the floor and feel it, then one did not belong there. Under Wright, the floor mattered less and less; the leadership, the Rules Committee, and the whip task forces restricted its role. More and more, the floor simply ratified policy. But the floor still mattered.

Normally the House convened—activating the floor—at noon on Mondays and Tuesdays, either noon or 2:00 P.M. on Wednesdays, and 10:00 A.M. on Thursdays. Committee hearings were held in the mornings, so as not to conflict with floor activity. Mondays, when many members were still home in their districts, were usually given to bills considered under "suspension of the rules." They were noncontroversial, did not go through the Rules Committee, and required a two-thirds vote to pass. The only members on the floor would be those directly involved in the bill, to put the debate into the record. Some of the bills passed by voice vote (all it took was one member saying "Aye!" if no one said "No!" and if no quorum was demanded); recorded votes were routinely "rolled" to Tuesday afternoon. Notice of votes and the schedule was important; missed votes could become an election issue. And some members viewed their vote as sacred. Through the 100th Congress, William Natcher, first elected to the House in 1952, had never missed either a vote or a quorum call. Scheduling required cooperation with the Republican leadership, to avoid a surprise demand for a quorum call and a recorded vote.

Tuesday mornings members straggled back to Washington, and Tuesday afternoon usually had the "rolled" record votes from the "suspension calendar"; debate on legislation usually took up Wednesday and Thursday. Thursday the House always convened early so it could finish business in time for members to take early evening flights home. Friday was usually a brief pro forma session.

In midweek, with the House in session, usually no more than thirty members could be found on the floor. Wright would open the House, stay for twenty minutes, then hand the gavel to a Speaker pro tem. A dozen members giving one-minute speeches would wait their turn, then leave. Legislative business would begin and the House usually became, formally, "the Committee of the Whole" and whoever held the gavel—never the Speaker—would be addressed as "Mr. Chairman" instead of "Mr. Speaker." Someone from each party's leadership would stay on the floor, as would the bill's floor manager, usually a chairman or subcommittee chairman, and his "ranking" GOP counterpart. If the rule for the bill called for two hours of debate, the floor manager for and against each controlled one hour of time. They doled it out to colleagues who supported them in intervals generally no longer than five minutes. "I yield three minutes to the distinguished gentlewoman from Connecticut," the manager would say, or, "I yield to my friend the gentleman from Louisiána such time as he may consume."

The floor had a casual feel then. The few members lounged about, sitting together in small clumps in the rows of comfortable tan leather seats, each wider than those in a first-class airplane cabin; perhaps one had his feet up on the row in front of him. Two or three members would be standing in the back, their feet massaged by the plush blue rug, near the door to the cloakroom, smoking cigars, leaning against the brass rail behind the last row of seats.

But in every congressman's office TV sets monitored the floor. If something happened, if the bells went off or the circle of small lights which surround every wall clock in the Capitol lit up indicating a vote, members would suddenly interrupt appointments and flock to the floor. It only took seconds to actually vote, to slip a plastic card the size of a driver's license into a slot and push a button. But few members just voted and left. The floor was like a marketplace; members used the floor to do business, to look up someone with whom they needed to talk. They voted, lingered, listened, got a soda or a sandwich from the hot-dog stand in the cloakroom and talked, before returning to offices. Whipping was done on the floor—it was more efficient to find a colleague on the floor than place a phone call to him or her. So activity ebbed and flowed; the floor swelled, reaching its peak between fifteen and twenty minutes after a vote started as members flooded it, then contracted as most left. The rhythm of the floor was real and tangible to those sensitive to it; it emanated from the exchanges among members.

One could read those exchanges. There are 448 seats in the chamber. Though none are assigned (unlike the Senate, where each senator has a desk, fixing him in place), certain groups gravitated toward certain seats. Was there someone with one group who did not belong there? If so, what was he doing there? What was Norm Dicks doing with that guy? They hated each other. What were they talking about? It couldn't be arms control, not with them. It had to be the Price-Anderson Act. Yes! Dicks seemed to be making progress with them. How many votes did that mean? Four? And over there, those members listening to Stenholm, what were their expressions? Did they seem to be agreeing? Noncommittal? Over there, that guttural laugh coming from Murtha— that wasn't the way he laughed at a joke, it meant something else. He was going to stick it to somebody.

When the House reconvened after Easter a discontent pervaded it. Instead of being refreshed members seemed worn out and irritable. They came to the floor and left it impatiently. Their jokes had a harsher edge and there was less communication between groups, more atomization. There were undercurrents on the floor, and they were flowing not so much against as simply away from the leadership, away from Wright. One *could* feel it.

Wright had accomplished almost everything he had hoped for at this point of his speakership. Yet policy moves so incrementally in Washington that no single success or even group of successes matters much. Almost everything happens at the margin, an inch at a time, and opportunities always arise to undermine a victory or mitigate a defeat. Only victory after victory after victory has true impact, sinks in, shifts direction. What Wright had so far achieved could be washed away in one vote.

Wright recognized this, and recognized also that he could not let up on his concentration. Analyzing his own style he had said, *It's like simultaneously playing chess and Ping-Pong. A lot of what I do isn't calculated in some arcane sense, but a lot of what I say to a member is calculated in ways in which I have only a vague sense myself. I don't think consciously of this strategy or that tactic. Things are too fluid for that. I have goals in mind and pursue those goals.*

Calculation had become so ingrained in him as to no longer be conscious. *I never knew if something upset him because his reaction was always to laugh,* his first wife had said. His mind processed many things, worked on so many things simultaneously, employed that horizontal aspect of his intelligence. The horizontal is surface; penetrating it was difficult. Calculation was hardly unique to Wright. He often quoted Lincoln, the great lonely and stoic figure, who had said that the best way to destroy an enemy was to make him a friend.

Wright was not making friends now. He had already extended his reach far enough to rub up against limits members expected him to respect. What would happen if he bunched his fist and tried to punch a hole in those limits? No one knew. But the first rumblings were there.

He drove so hard. One potential problem was created by his use of the Rules Committee. Through it, Wright was dictating what happened on the floor of the House. The committee could send bills to the floor under an "open rule," a "closed rule," or a "modified closed rule." Open rules let the House work its will: members could offer any germane amendment. (The Senate has no germaneness requirement; with some exceptions, any amendment can be offered to any legislation.) A closed rule allowed no amendments whatsoever. A modified closed rule allowed a specific few. There had for years been a trend toward more restrictive rules, many of which just made the House more orderly, but Wright accelerated that trend and limited Republicans' options. Rules staff reviewed almost every rule with John Mack. Rules Committee Democrats were getting restive; they were all inside players and had sought their assignments because Rules gave them power within the House, made them players on all major legislation. Only members of Congress could even testify before them. Wright had driven home the need for loyalty and they understood that, but they resented simply rubber-stamping Wright's decisions.

Democrats were restive. They welcomed their victories but wondered about the style. The minimum needed to win had satisfied O'Neill; Wright and Coelho seemed interested in the score. So far that had paid off, particularly in overriding Reagan's veto of the highway bill. But members did not like being pushed for votes. The more Wright and Coelho pushed, the more members were likely to say sooner or later, *Leave me alone for once. Is every goddamn bill a leadership initiative?* Marty Russo of Ways and Means observed, "If there's a problem with this leadership, it's that they want to win too much."

The first Thursday after Easter the floor handed Wright his first defeat. It was minor, but it was a warning. The issue was the supplemental appropriation.

The "supplemental" appropriates money for unanticipated needs, not included in the thirteen individual appropriations bills (for transportation, defense, agriculture, etc., each produced by a different Appropriations subcommittee) enacted each year. Supplementals do not necessarily exceed budget limits; the committee routinely keeps its regular funding bills under budget to leave room for a supplemental. But Appropriations chairman Jamie Whitten and his committee reported out a bill spending $11.3 billion, $2 billion more than the budget allowed. That violated the budget law—*the law,* passed by Congress and signed by the President—which prohibited voting on any bill exceeding the budget. Whitten didn't care. The dean of the House, first elected in 1941, he came from rural Mississippi. Like Wright, he saw the government as a builder and saw his committee as investing in the country; both on the floor and in private meetings he decried the concern over "paper wealth" as opposed to "real wealth"—land, roads, schools. Although he had cooperated in writing the 1974 law which created the budget process, he had come to despise the constraints it placed on him.

Wright was not happy with the supplemental. It was terrible politics and violated everything he had said all year about fiscal responsibility and pay-as-you-go policies. But he had to balance national politics with internal management of the House. He did not want to take Whitten head-on. Whitten had cooperated all year, until now. Wright needed his future cooperation, too, to get all thirteen appropriations bills through the House before the next fiscal year began. Power politics would likely dictate sending all of them to Reagan in one giant package, but Wright still wanted them through the House individually and on schedule. Reluctantly, to accommodate Whitten, Wright had the Rules Committee waive the budget law. When reporters asked about the supplemental exceeding the budget, he replied that by the time it became law it would comply with the budget. He would rely on the Senate to bring Whitten into line rather than do it himself.

Buddy MacKay had other ideas.

MacKay, from central Florida, had a simplicity about him, an honest plainness which was penetrating and strong. He looked like the kind of guy everyone *would* call "Buddy." Like a kid, sort of. Still boyish-looking in his mid-fifties, he was a nice guy and most of all he seemed earnest. He laughed easily enough and yet was deadly serious, like a bulldog who would not let go of a thing. He scorned political posturing and played the game with colleagues and the press the same way— straight up; he wanted to sit down and simply solve the damn problem. He was so earnest.

But he was not a fool. Unlike Jimmy Stewart's character in *Mr. Smith Goes to Washington,* MacKay understood power. He had political scientist friends and constantly analyzed the internal workings of the House, the fault lines which divided it, so as to better exercise power. Junior despite his age (his fiftieth birthday came a few weeks after entering the House in 1982), half a generation older than many of his classmates, he did not have the time or patience to wait for power to come to him. He wasn't the go-along-to-get-along type anyway. In a dozen years in the Florida senate (in seven of those years the Florida press named him "Most Valuable Legislator"), he had belonged to a group nicknamed "doghouse Democrats" because they bucked the leadership so often. He quickly recognized that the House was immensely more complex than the state senate. Ways and Means, for example, alone had more members than the entire state senate, along with its own traditions, its own internal rhythms, its own enemies. The swirl of factions and forces, of regions, generations, ideologies, and parties, could sweep across the House floor in great surges.

MacKay saw that as an opportunity. An entrepreneur, he carved out a power base among the powerless, among those who otherwise would have been carried impotently along by those surges. The political classic *Plunkitt of Tammany Hall* advised those who wanted power to ignore grand theories and tell a precinct captain, *I got one vote, mine, and if you do what I want I'm with you.* It advised that it was even better to go with a friend and say, *I got two votes, mine and his.* That's what MacKay did. When he found himself cut out of the loop his first year in the House, he and classmate Tim Penny, from Minnesota, organized a budget study group of others not in the loop. They kept their ego out of things, did not use the group as a justification for self-promotion, and therefore won the allegiance of colleagues. The group met regularly to exchange information and listen to speakers, sometimes other members, sometimes economists. More important, they often voted together. They began to get attention. In 1984, he and twenty-two colleagues, mostly moderates and southerners, voted as a bloc and defeated a major appropriations bill. Suddenly they demanded attention. From outside the House, people like Federal Reserve chairman Paul Volcker came to talk to them; from inside, Rostenkowski and Wright and Foley all began to woo them. Jim Slattery of Kansas was one activist, Charlie Stenholm from Texas was another, Tom Carper of Delaware a third, but MacKay was their leader, the most respected member of the group. The next year he and Slattery were put on the Budget Committee.

MacKay was determined and had his own views but was also practical, had a knack for putting coalitions together, was trusted, and was willing to compromise. But he would not simply take orders. That made MacKay a dangerous man. There was another thing about MacKay. He was tough. Early in the year Wright spoke to him briefly on the floor.

"I like team players," Wright said.

"I like to play on a team," MacKay answered, "as long as I'm in the huddle when the play is called."

MacKay had an agenda and would take risks—and in some cases would even put the country at risk—in pursuit of it. The first item on that agenda was cutting the deficit. He considered it outrageous policy and stupid politics to allow an over-budget supplemental on the floor immediately after having passed a budget which included taxes.

If Wright wasn't going to do anything about the supplemental, he would. If the leadership enjoyed playing whatever cozy games with Whitten they were playing, he would try to bring them up short in a hurry. On the morning of the vote on the supplemental, he and several members of his budget group decided that, together, they would confront the leadership at that day's regular whip meeting.

At 9:15, Coelho called the meeting to order and quickly warned, "The Republicans have elevated the supplemental to a party position. They had three whip calls yesterday to get Republicans to understand that. They want to give the President a win."

MacKay, in the back of the room, stood up. "I just want to say I think it's a mistake to bring this bill up. It's over budget. I'm on the team. I voted for the budget. I thought the leadership was committed to the budget."

Coelho dismissed him peremptorily, not even deigning to respond himself, calling on a member of Appropriations who lectured him that Reagan's request exceeded the budget too. As far as MacKay was concerned, that was irrelevant. He looked around for support, for his colleagues who had promised to back him up. No one said a word.

Fuming, he left the meeting and looked up Republican whip Trent Lott. Rules had made an amendment in order to impose across-the-board cuts in the bill to bring the supplemental under the budget. The prerogative of offering the amendment belonged to the Republicans. MacKay wanted to offer it. Lott's chief interest was stopping Wright's juggernaut any way he could. Having MacKay offer the amendment could win Democratic support from people who would vote against something offered by a Republican. Lott quickly agreed.

MacKay and other Democrats in his budget group met immediately. There were no recriminations about their failing to back him in the whip meeting. That was the past. The vote was the future. The first lesson of Congress is that the most important thing is the next vote. Quickly they ran down a list of Democrats who would decide the issue, mostly moderates and a few individuals with a history of antagonism toward Appropriations. Coelho was running whip task forces to hold the same Democrats; MacKay was running meetings to rip them loose. Each group met several times during the day, narrowing the list, going over the names, zeroing in on people.

On the floor colleagues were attacking the bill relentlessly. A conservative Republican moved to eliminate all foreign aid, including $300 million for Central America which both the White House and Wright badly wanted. Wright voted against the amendment, a symbolic act to show how much it mattered to him. It was the first time all year he had cast a vote—Speakers can vote but traditionally do not except to break ties. He lost anyway. Then a liberal moved to cut $432 million from a farm program, and won a $90-million cut. One region was attacking another, one interest attacking another. The leadership was losing control of the floor.

Members were getting angrier as evening came. *Thursday* evening. Already they had missed flights back to their districts, back home to see their wives and kids. They were stuck here and getting angry. They went out to dinner and grew more angry. With each vote on each amendment, the mood worsened. It was moving toward midnight. Some members went out for a drink, came back to vote, went out again, came back half-lit and bristling with annoyance. Claudine Schneider, a moderate Republican from Rhode Island, stayed in her office, alone, coming to the floor only to vote: "The vibes around this place are too negative."

The leadership worried about the mood, worried that MacKay's across-the-board cut would pass. Coelho and MacKay talked, MacKay saying, "You guys have a vested interest in this too. Who's running this place? You or Jamie Whitten?"

Coelho asked, what if MacKay exempted the homeless from any cuts? Several liberals had suggested the idea. If MacKay did that, Foley and Coelho would vote for his amendment, guaranteeing passage. MacKay was in a corner. He had already told Lott nothing would be exempted. He couldn't go back on his word. Member after member asked him. He couldn't do it. Then Wright sat down next to him and said, "Democrats stand for something. Not just dollar signs. Packaged with the homeless exemption it's a good amendment. Can you do that?"

MacKay shifted uncomfortably. How could he spurn the Speaker when the Speaker was coming 90 percent his way? He couldn't. Rising, he crossed the aisle to the GOP side to tell Lott the homeless would be exempted.

Lott stared at him. *That wasn't the deal we made.* Lott had expected to win this, the first win for Republicans of any consequence all year. Now it was slipping away. They were losing both the political issue— if Democrats voted with MacKay they could not be accused of breaking the budget—and a victory over Wright.

"You're peeing on my leg, aren't you?" Lott said bitterly.

"But I'm looking you in the eye while I'm doing it."

When MacKay's amendment came up Lott and Michel voted against it, arguing that homeless funds should be cut too. But 121 Republicans voted with MacKay. So did 142 Democrats. MacKay won 263–123.

Wright had prevented a major embarrassment but he was not content.

He wanted to erase the one blemish of the day. It was approaching 2:00 A.M. The vote eliminating foreign aid had been taken in the Committee of the Whole, the parliamentary fiction in which the House conducted most of its business. Final passage of legislation occurred when the Committee of the Whole "rose" to become the full House, at which time it could reconsider amendments which had passed (but not those which had lost) in "committee." The House was doing that now on a Jack Brooks amendment which could help Texas win the multibillion-dollar super-collider research project. Brooks had tried to slip it past the House and had won approval by voice vote, with the floor all but empty; members had discovered the ploy and were now rejecting it 288–97. Wright wanted to vote again on foreign aid. He worked it hard, and nine members promised him they would not let their vote beat it. It was close and those nine were enough to win. Wright voted for it again. The nine members sat unmoving, watching the vote totals shift on the electronic scoreboard. Each waited for another to go first. If one went, the others would follow. Wright would win. For a moment the vote seemed to be moving away from Wright. One member decided Wright could not win even with his vote, and voted against him, and the others broke against him, too.

Wright had his first defeat. It wasn't major. In the end, in the conference, the money for Central America was restored. But the floor, and MacKay and his group in particular, had sent him and Coelho a message, if they chose to read it.

In 1980 the United States exported $50 billion of goods and services more than it imported. By the mid-1980s, it was importing $150 billion more than it sold. The single biggest reason for the reversal was the budget deficit. International currency flows were why.

The budget deficit at its peak equaled almost 75 percent of the net saving in the U.S. economy. The only way to finance both it and other credit needs of the economy was with foreign capital. To attract it, real interest rates reached historic highs. Reagan's tax cuts also attracted foreigners. They poured their money into American investments.

But to make U.S. investments, foreigners first had to convert their money into dollars. They had to buy dollars. The increased demand sent the price of the dollar up; it took more Japanese yen or German marks to buy a dollar than it had. Speculators got into the game too; just as they traded commodities like oil or wheat, now they were trading dollars. They believed the dollar would go up so they bought it. The dollar rose more.

The increase in the dollar's international value had a dramatic impact on trade: American products were priced in dollars. A rising dollar raised the price of U.S. goods to foreigners, hurting exports; simultaneously, it lowered the price of foreign goods to Americans, spurring imports.

Historically, currencies had been traded internationally to service trade in real products, and a currency's value reflected that country's trade balance; if a country bought more products than it sold, it generally indicated a weak economy and the country's currency fell. That raised the price of goods it imported, lowered the price of its exports, and helped correct the trade balance automatically. Now, suddenly, international capital flows—decided by financial traders looking at a computer screen in London, New York, and Tokyo—dwarfed the amount of money changing hands over real products. The automatic corrective mechanism broke down. The United States could have both a huge trade deficit and a high dollar.

Compounding the impact of currency flows were other factors: poor quality, gas-guzzling American automobiles; the freest major market in the world; protected markets in many countries which exported massive quantities to the United States; enormous U.S. demand for consumption, also related to the budget deficit.

By 1984, the trade deficit was $123 billion a year and still rising. In the summer of 1985 the trade issue demonstrated its political potency in a special election for the House held in East Texas.

After Reagan's landslide victory the year before, Republicans hoped to bring about a political realignment comparable to that following the New Deal. A Republican victory in this "yellow dog Democrat" district (a phrase which meant voters would choose a yellow dog before they'd vote for a Republican) would mark that realignment. It would also add immense impetus to a Republican campaign to convince Democratic state office holders throughout the South to switch parties. The national Republican Party poured resources and expertise into the campaign. So did Democrats, especially Wright and Coelho. "One issue in this race is whether Jim Wright is going to be Speaker of the House," one Democrat declared.

The GOP candidate, the favorite, was Edd Hargett, an attractive rancher, engineer, and former star quarterback at Texas A&M. He raised almost $1.2 million for the race, including over $235,000 from PACs. It was a huge war chest for a House race, especially in an area with inexpensive media markets, whose biggest city, Texarkana, had a population of 31,000.

The Democrat was Jim Chapman. He raised $580,000, only $32,000 from PACs. It wasn't enough. Coelho and Wright turned to Tom Gaubert, who raised another $100,000 from Texas savings and loan executives and spent it himself to help elect Chapman.

A Democratic primary opponent of Chapman had run a hell of an ad: he had held an American-made baseball bat, which Japan excluded from its markets, while standing near a Toyota. People watching kept waiting for him to swing the bat at the car; he didn't, just as, according to Democrats, American trade policy did not hit back. The ad made the trade issue jump in the polls. Chapman used it to put Hargett on the defensive because of Reagan's inaction on the issue. At one point Hargett said, "I don't know what trade policies have to do with bringing jobs to East Texas." Chapman pointed to layoffs at steel plants in the district.

He won with just 51 percent of the vote and promptly became a Wright favorite. The talk of realignment died, and so did the GOP effort to get Democrats to switch parties. And national politicians discovered an issue.

Within a few months the administration reversed its position on the dollar. Reagan and former Treasury Secretary Donald Regan had interpreted the high dollar as a vote of confidence by foreigners, something to brag about. They refused to intervene in the markets. But now James Baker, a master at defusing political problems, was Treasury secretary; six weeks after Chapman's election, Baker announced an international agreement to lower the dollar. It had begun falling anyway, as international currency traders had finally started worrying about underlying economic fundamentals. The budget deficit could not continue forever without harming the economy. And the United States had been transformed from the largest creditor nation in history early in Reagan's first term into the largest debtor nation in history five years later. After Baker's agreement, the dollar's fall accelerated. The administration argued that the trade figures would improve dramatically within a few months.

Wright, then majority leader, had turned to the task of overseeing an omnibus trade bill. It wasn't just politics to him. He worried that the trade deficit would eviscerate the American economy. Although he recognized the impact of macroeconomic forces, he also believed a thousand policy details could make a difference, details such as encouraging research and development, changing patent law, retraining displaced workers, increasing support for high school science teachers, not to mention forcing foreign countries to abandon unfair trade practices. He did not trust the markets to solve the problem. Weren't the markets represented by the smug arrogance of American automobile manufacturers? impersonal international currency traders? stock market takeover games which forced American corporations to neglect long-term solutions and focus on quarterly earnings? Why should he trust the markets? The markets went through great swings, like a river which flooded and ran dry. He believed the role of government was to channel and dam the river, to minimize the damage of excesses and exploit its natural force. Even an administration-appointed commission headed by Hewlett-Packard chief executive John Young had concluded that aggressive action on trade was needed. The White House had ignored this report, but Wright had not. At every opportunity he insisted that "the trade deficit will not cure itself."

In the 99th Congress, Senate Republicans, at White House request, had blocked the House-passed trade bill. The trade deficit had only worsened since then, setting a record in 1986 (and heading for another record in 1987). Private Democratic polls revealed that a remarkably high number of respondents personally knew people who had lost their jobs because of imports. Trade was no longer an abstract policy debate; it had become real to the average voter. That got the attention of politicians.

Republicans took polls too. The White House wanted a seat on the train.

The maneuvering had started early. Late in 1986, Wright, Byrd, Rostenkowski, and Bentsen had met and agreed to make a trade bill the chief legislative priority of the 100th Congress. But Jim Baker had also been talking to Rostenkowski. They had just finished working closely together on tax reform, against Wright. It did not escape either of them that an alliance between them could be useful to both—to Baker, because it affected the substance of legislation and could undercut Wright, to Rostenkowski because Baker's support guaranteed a bill would be signed, not vetoed, and because an alliance with the White House strengthened his hand against Wright. At issue was not only substance but power.

So Rostenkowski had wanted to junk the preceding year's bill and start from scratch. Wright had overruled him, and had seen to it that the bill the House had just passed was reintroduced as a starting point. That had clearly claimed the issue as a congressional initiative.

In January, in a meeting with committee chairmen, Wright explained his plan: the bill would involve almost every committee in the Congress, and would be a massive piece of legislation, with the biggest single piece belonging to Ways and Means. By April 6 all the committees would report their bills out. During Easter recess staff would work to meld the bills together, leaving issues which only members could resolve for the week of April 22, when the Rules Committee would meet. The following week, the House would vote. While he spoke he watched the chairmen. Most nodded enthusiastically. Rostenkowski sat silently with his legs crossed, his arms folded, his face scrunched in disapproval.

While Wright was laying out his schedule, Hill GOP leaders met with Reagan and White House officials. Michel advised Reagan to focus on a narrow bill, warning that any comprehensive package would contain much he would not like. But Jim Baker wanted a comprehensive bill. In the wake of Iran-contra, the White House and Reagan personally needed to be seen as taking charge.

Michel shrugged. It was the administration's call. But administration factions fought over the bill. Two weeks later, instead of comprehensive proposals all they offered was more rhetoric and an antitrust reform bill from Commerce Secretary Malcolm Baldrige. Michel told them it would never emerge from the Judiciary Committee. Even Wright couldn't get things he wanted past Judiciary chairman Peter Rodino. Privately, Michel was contemptuous, snorting, "We waited for *that*?"

Wright wasn't waiting for anything. At a White House meeting, he warned Reagan that if the administration wanted input they had to prepare their proposals quickly. In trade, unlike foreign policy, Congress had absolute constitutional authority, and Wright was prepared to assert it. Without specific congressional authorization, for example, the White House could not even send a representative to negotiate a new round of the General Agreements on Tariffs and Trade, the GATT.

But the administration remained confused. Howard Baker, soon after moving into the White House, told Michel to deal with Jim Baker on trade. Less than an hour later an angry Clayton Yeutter, the U.S. trade representative who had cabinet rank, called Michel and contradicted Baker's statement. Later, Yeutter testified before Ways and Means and said, "I hope the Wright timetable is subject to change so that the congressional leadership can give full consideration to the President's proposals."

The administration had had four years to develop such proposals. They still had not. Wright wasn't waiting any longer.

Michel sat in his office in the grand, old part of the Capitol; it was much grander than Wright's and had belonged to the Republican leader ever since Rayburn, after retaking the speakership from his friend Joe Martin in 1955, had declined to force him to move. Solid, even stolid, Michel pondered how to win White House input and decided to play on Wright's promise of bipartisanship. He wrote Wright a letter proposing that the leadership staffs get together with White House officials to produce a bill with near-unanimous support. It was a shrewd move. Any such plan would increase the leverage of both House Republicans and the White House. Their voices would be louder negotiating inside a room than they would be on the floor of the House.

Wright recognized the ploy. "No!" he snapped, after reading the letter. The Caucus would not be dictated to. "That's what the committees are for. We're not going to have any triumvirate doing this."

The legislative process began. This was what Wright had wanted power for, what he had waited for all those years. Not to hold power, but to exercise it.

Trade was a complicated issue politically. Polls showed support for an aggressive effort to force open foreign markets, which reflected an innate American belief in fair play. But polls also showed disapproval of protectionism, which reflected the visceral American belief in competition. "Fairness" worked politically. "Protection" did not.

Wright tried to avoid the protectionist label, constantly reiterating in public that the bill's goal was to open foreign markets rather than close America's, and repeatedly warning committees to keep any product-specific or industry-specific language out of their sections of the bill.

The big issue was Richard Gephardt's amendment which stipulated that if a country had a large trade surplus with the United States and also engaged in unfair trade practices, the administration had to negotiate an end to those practices. If the negotiations failed, and intermediate sanctions failed, the President had to impose tariffs and quotas to lower the offending country's trade surplus with the United States by 10 percent a year. There was an escape hatch for the White House: the President could avoid taking action by stipulating it would not be in the national interest.

No one claimed that the proposal would solve the trade deficit. Gephardt himself stated that no more than 15 percent of the trade deficit could be blamed on unfair trade practices. Still, the idea that foreigners were stealing jobs from American workers was a powerful one. Gephardt hoped to ride it all the way to the White House. Wright liked the proposal. It wasn't an ambiguous policy; it required tangible, measurable, concrete action. Wright liked legislation that left marks, like the highways and ports he had built; he could get his hands around it and feel it and feel that it accomplished something. *Congress* was forcing the President to respond. It shifted power from the White House to Capitol Hill.

Rostenkowski opposed it. He had co-sponsored an even stronger version of the amendment the year before, but now was being a statesman, opposing it, he was allying himself with the White House against Wright. Ways and Means Republican Bill Frenzel, who also opposed Gephardt, told *The Washington Post* that he was "one of the most surprised folks around. . . . I think with the spirit of the subcommittee . . . there exists a good chance for a trade bill. . . . We've made monumental strides."

Rostenkowski's comments to the *Post* on Wright's role in the trade bill and his preference for dropping Gephardt's idea without even voting on it had prompted Wright to send that letter in which he had in effect threatened a war to remove him from his chairmanship. *Danny, you and I are the designated agents of the Democratic Caucus,* it had read. After that letter Rostenkowski curbed his tongue, but still planned to take Wright on on the floor.

For a solid year, the White House and editorial writers had argued that the amendment was protectionist, that it echoed the Smoot-Hawley tariff, the high point of protectionism, which had exacerbated the Depression. Gephardt had rewritten and toned down the amendment, but whatever the merits of the case, it had become a virtual symbol of protectionism.

Washington State Democrat Don Bonker had chaired the Caucus task force on trade in the 99th Congress, and had voted for the tougher version of the Gephardt amendment earlier. Now he wanted it out and complained, "We're sacrificing our legislation on the altar of his Presidential candidacy."

A lot of Democrats agreed.

All through February and March, country after country sent officials to try to convince Wright that the Gephardt provision threatened the world trading system. They became routine, an ambassador or trade minister settling into the sofa to the left of Wright's desk, Wright moving to the armchair beside him, an aide bringing coffee. Routinely a foreign official would call the provision "retaliatory," and Wright would counter with "reciprocal."

To complaints from the Australian ambassador and trade minister, Wright replied, "I just don't comprehend this. You have a trade deficit with the U.S. of two to one. This doesn't hit you at all, and yet the administration has got you singing their song. You have domestic import controls, do you not? And you come here and tell me this?"

Korea would be hit by the amendment, and the Korean trade minister told Wright, "I came here on a buying mission. This trip will transfer $500 million to the U.S. We are interested in switching our sources of supply from Japan to the United States. We're running a deficit with Japan." With no pretense of subtlety he added, "We will switch electronics purchases from Japan to Texas Instruments, and buy petrochemicals in Houston."

Japanese ambassador H. E. Nobuo Matsunaga visited too. In formal tones he congratulated Wright on his election as Speaker, and agreed that Japan had to increase imports of American goods. But he also complained about congressional resolutions condemning Japan for violating a semiconductor agreement: "This of course is not a matter for Congress. On this I will talk with the government."

Wright's eyes narrowed. It sounded as if Matsunaga did not even understand the American political system, as if he did not understand Congress was the government too, as if he considered it a parliamentary system in which Wright headed an opposition party out of power. Could that be possible? Could he be that arrogant? Could he so misunderstand America?

Matsunaga continued: "Another thing—on the prime minister's visit to the United States. It has not yet formally been decided but very probably will be at the end of April. The main objective is to talk to

President Reagan and high officials of the government. But I presume he would like to come to Congress and meet with people here also."

Wright remained silent for a moment, controlling his annoyance. Then, in a tight controlled voice, he replied, "Mr. Ambassador, on April 28 and that week, we'll have trade legislation on the floor. The administration knows this. It will not be protectionist, though some will call it that. It will not name Japan. But in my judgment it will contain something similar to the Gephardt amendment. The members of the House leadership will be very busy, preoccupied with this legislation. You must understand the administration may want to use the prime minister for their own purposes politically. I'm sure that is not his desire. I don't know if the prime minister wants to be here at this time."

Wright rose, ending the audience, adding, "Please extend my personal greetings to the prime minister."

As Wright had declared three months earlier, the vote would occur the week of April 28. Members rarely concentrated on an issue until they had to. If it wasn't a major issue, if the whole debate had occurred in another committee and beyond the reach of the front pages, they often knew little of either the merits or the politics.

They could learn both in a hurry, however, if they wanted. If the leadership was involved in the issue, the whip task forces both counted votes and educated colleagues, giving arguments for and against. Issues were argued on the merits and on the politics.

Good lobbyists were even more careful. They never oversold, just laid the facts out there and let members decide for themselves. "I want the facts, without a twist to them," Coelho explained.

The best lobbyists always protected members. Once Gary Hymel, O'Neill's former floor aide, took his client to visit a member and won his support. But from the tone of the conversation Hymel realized the member did not recall that he had voted the other way on the same issue a few years before. Flip-flopping was politically dangerous. Later, Hymel called back to warn the member and give him a reason to justify switching. Members trusted Hymel and those lobbyists like him not to expose them to political risks. That trust gave lobbyists power; some members let lobbyists they trusted go so far as to write legislative language for them to insert. Lobbyists who were trusted became almost adjunct staff. Campaign contributions and honoraria mattered plenty; they guaranteed that a member would take the time to hear someone's argument. With a few members, especially on issues that did not touch their districts, money had more influence than that. But anyone could write a check; money was transient and impersonal. Trust was something earned, personal and permanent—and also fragile. Coelho said, "If a lobbyist lies to me just once, I won't open his mail, I won't return his phone calls, and I won't see him. And I'll tell his clients they're not getting good representation."

When voting on issues that had not hit the headlines, as members interrupted a meeting to go to the floor, they often did not know what they were voting on. There were hundreds of votes; they could not know the subtleties of each. The Capitol police kept open a clear pathway to the doors of the chamber, but on both sides of the pathway a gauntlet of lobbyists held their thumbs up or down. *If he's for it I'm against it,* members might decide; or *If he's for it, I'm for it.* Or they might stop for a moment of conversation with a lobbyist they trusted. Just inside the chamber, members "worked the doors" doing the same thing. Working the doors required a knack: a member had to sum up a position in one convincing sentence that did not mislead. Trust was everything.

But the Gephardt amendment was politicized. The Ways and Means bill would not include the provision. The floor would vote on adding it. It was pure politics. In March, Coelho was already organizing task forces, and coordinating efforts with lobbyists for unions and companies supporting Gephardt. The AFL-CIO had already tested its alliance with the leadership on the highway bill override. The Gephardt amendment was part of both its and Wright's agenda, and it used its muscle now. AFL-CIO lobbyist Bob McGlotten had created labor councils of local union leaders who met regularly with their congressmen in forty-five districts; he had chosen places where members were receptive, and voted the AFL-CIO's way roughly 60 percent of the time. It was more efficient to try to raise their voting percentage to 75 percent support or higher than to try to raise someone with a 20 percent support score to 35 or 40 percent. Grass-roots pressure carried weight. McGlotten himself carried weight. Unlike most business lobbyists, he had the authority to make a deal without checking with anyone above him. Members could run a compromise by him and he could put the entire political infrastructure of the AFL-CIO behind three words: "I'm with you."

Coelho coordinated his whipping efforts with McGlotten and others. Internal whip counts were very sensitive; what a member told another member was confidential, and no one in the whip organization would share a member's name with a lobbyist. But they would tell McGlotten, "You might check Indiana again. That's a little soft." Evy Dubrow, with the International Ladies Garment Workers Union, later said, "Tony twisted my arm every day for two weeks. He knew he had me. He just wanted to make sure I was out working." Coelho did the same with business lobbyists supporting Gephardt.

Chief among them were Chrysler lobbyists, working at Chairman Lee Iacocca's instructions. In Detroit, Iacocca hosted a dinner for six hundred Chrysler suppliers, businessmen scattered all over the country. At each table were telegram blanks; the suppliers were invited to fill them in and address them to their congressmen. Chrysler would send them. Then Iacocca came to Washington, met with whip task force members, and worked the bill personally. He was effective and commanded a member's attention; lobbyists could not treat a member as an equal. Iacocca could.

Rostenkowski was not sitting back. Most business lobbies opposed the Gephardt amendment, even if they supported a trade bill, and they were fighting hard too. The U.S. Chamber of Commerce targeted 125 members for grass-roots lobbying efforts. And Ways and Means staff started putting together a lobbying coalition against Gephardt. Retailers took the lead; if import prices went up, sales went down. But the coalition was run naively. At one meeting, with seventy lobbyists in the room and a senior administration trade official urging them on, William Danes of the American Retail Federation said, "Keep these meetings quiet. John Mack and Jim Wright don't know about them." No meeting with seventy lobbyists representing fifty different organizations, with fifty different interests, could keep anything quiet. Within an hour after the meeting's close, Wright's office knew every significant word spoken in it. But the next day members of the coalition met with Rostenkowski in the Capitol. The fight was intensifying.

The first day back after the Easter recess Rostenkowski gave a speech to the American Council for Capital Formation, a group of capital-intensive companies organized by Charls E. Walker, a deputy Treasury secretary under Nixon who lobbied tax issues. Rostenkowski spoke plainly: "Some of my colleagues are not interested in changing our trade laws. They are interested in establishing an issue. I want to elect a Democratic President in 1988 as much as anyone in the House. But faced with a choice between good legislation now and the uncertain promise of bigger victories in two years, I come down on the side of acting now. I will tell my colleagues we should pass a bill the President can sign. We can accomplish much if we focus on what is possible. If we fail, if we spend two years jockeying for position, we'll find out how much political blame there is to go around. And there will be a lot."

In late April the full Caucus met in the House chamber. Gephardt, Rostenkowski, and Wright all spoke. Gephardt was hardly ever in Washington anymore; his time went to Iowa and New Hampshire. But he was in town to work this. Members congratulated him after his speech, telling him it was the best one they had ever heard him make, he should take it on the road, his presidential candidacy was coming around. Then Wright reassured colleagues who wanted to produce a law, not a vetoed bill, that he would appoint "reasonable" conferees; in other words, he was willing to compromise with the Senate, not insist on the Gephardt provision. That statement carried another message between the lines, a message of power: *Wright would appoint conferees.* The Speaker had the power to appoint all members of conference committees with the Senate. But, with rare exceptions, past Speakers had automatically appointed whomever the committee chairmen named. That practice had become so routine that sometimes the committee chairman had simply handed a list of names to whoever happened to be occupying the Speaker's Rostrum at the moment. Not anymore. *Wright would appoint conferees.* Then Rostenkowski spoke with a rough eloquence.

Members listened uncomfortably. Afterwards, walking across the Speaker's Lobby to check the Associated Press wire, one worried, "This makes me nervous as hell. If Danny wins, what's that mean for the Speaker? If the Speaker wins, we still need Danny for everything else this year—welfare reform, catastrophic health, taxes, that's all his committee. I don't like this at all."

Rostenkowski didn't like it either. It was bad for him, bad for everybody. A week before the vote, as Coelho geared up the whip organization, Rostenkowski called him and demanded, "Do I understand the leadership is determined to come in against Ways and Means?"

Coelho yielded not an inch. "That's not true. We support Ways and Means' product, along with a few amendments. It's not Gephardt and the leadership coming in against the committee. It's you coming in against what you knew was the leadership position."

Rostenkowski thought about that, thought about it hard, thought about his entire relationship with Wright. Despite everything Wright had said and done, until recently Rostenkowski had not really believed that Wright was going to go against him in an organized fashion on the floor. The whole leadership operation was supposed to support chairmen, not oppose them. Wasn't it? Now Wright was using the whip operation against the carefully considered product of a committee of the House. Rostenkowski believed in loyalty and believed in authority—the Church, the presidency, even the speakership. *If Wright wanted it that much* . . . As the vote neared, Rostenkowski began to back off. There were other ways to win besides winning.

Mack reported the change to Wright: "From what I can make out, Danny's not after a confrontation. He said the other day, if Gephardt passes the House he'd support it in conference. The members don't want a confrontation either. They're getting nervous."

Then Rostenkowski sent a clear message. He called Mike Andrews, the Texan on Ways and Means whom he had tried unsuccessfully to keep off his committee. "Mike," Rostenkowski said, "I think you ought to vote with the Speaker on this. It means a lot to him."

That was a signal to Wright that he intended no arm-twisting; he would fight, but on the merits of the issue only. But he also sent another message then, telling Wright that even if he was not going to go all out to win, he wasn't afraid of him either. He circulated a "Dear Colleague" letter to every member of the House, arguing against Gephardt. Usually members tried to get as many colleagues as possible to sign such letters. Rostenkowski could easily have gotten cosigners. He signed it alone.

One week before the vote, the whip count listed 160 Democratic members as undecided or not responding. Marty Russo, the Rostenkowski protégé from Chicago who served on Ways and Means, told a task force, "Look, that's too many for us to handle. We're the guys who zero in on people. Do another whip call to clear up the rest. Let's just do the members leaning yes or no. I'll take Ways and Means and Illinois. This is real sensitive on Ways and Means."

Meanwhile, the Republican leadership sat down in Wright's office to discuss the rule. They complained they were getting steamrolled. Bill Frenzel said, "This was bipartisan until two weeks ago. Is it or isn't it?"

"What do you want?" Wright replied. Frenzel and Michel ran down a list of things. Wright gave them everything they asked for. The rule was settled. The structure of the votes and the bill were settled.

It was like shaking hands before the kickoff. The only thing left was the vote itself. Suddenly the pressure intensified. The White House exploded into action, with Reagan personally calling members, using the press to castigate Gephardt's proposal. Republicans began to believe they could win this, win something significant finally. The press was on their side. It seemed every newspaper, *The Washington Post, The Wall Street Journal, The New York Times,* the *L.A. Times,* the *Christian Science Monitor,* opposed the amendment editorially, every story about it included quotes from economists damning it, on every talk show someone from the White House or an economist was blasting the idea.

Joe Kennedy, the freshman son of Robert, caught Gephardt in the hall and joked, "Say, you don't really care what happens to this, do you?"

"Just vote the good of the country," Gephardt said, laughing.

"You don't really want us to do that, do you?"

"Hell no."

Listen to everything. Everything, even jokes, means something here. Kennedy later became the only member from Massachusetts, Democrat or Republican, to vote against Gephardt.

When the amendment came up, 420 members sat in the chamber to listen to the final arguments. It was a rarity and a compliment. Michel argued, "The road to hell is paved with good intentions." But members had not come for Michel's speech. They were restless. Wright sat, picking at his teeth, in the front row, not at the Speaker's Rostrum but on the floor where he could work members who needed working. Several times Michel was interrupted by the gavel. "The House is not in order! The House is not in order! Will the members in the aisles please take a seat or retire to the cloakrooms!"

Then Gephardt spoke: "This may be the most important vote we take this year. You've been lobbied by groups and groups and groups. What I want you to do now is forget about all the lobbying. Think about the interests of the people in your district. Organized labor wasn't elected to Congress. Neither was business. You were." His voice varied in tone, rose and fell, found a theme of populism and strength and sounded it. He looked solid, confident. His amendment required fair play. Other proposals talked about it. "There are two paths. One is the status quo, standing pat, saying that words are enough. The other way is tougher."

In the press gallery reporters commented that they had never heard Gephardt so articulate. His stock for the presidential race had just gone up. If his amendment passed.

Rostenkowski spoke well, too, arguing the substance, too, defending the committee's version of the amendment, which required a dollar-for-dollar action for any lost export opportunities. And Rostenkowski also spoke to his colleagues. He announced, "I for one am not going to hold any grudges against people who vote against my position."

Vote your conscience, Rostenkowski was saying, as both a peace offering to Wright and a sign of his strength. Now members, from deep in their throats, started yelling, *"VOOOOOTTTE!"* interrupting the speech. *"VOOOOTTTTTE!"* The time for talk had ended.

"VVVOOOOOOOTTTTTE!"

"All in favor?" Wright, back in the chair, called out.

"AYYYEE!"

"Opposed?"

"NOOOOO!"

"In the opinion of the chair, the nos have it."

"Mr. Speaker!" demanded Gephardt, on his feet. "On this I ask a recorded vote!"

The vote began. With most members in the chamber it went quickly—the rules require a minimum of fifteen minutes for a vote, to give members time to arrive from their office buildings, but the vote would stay open as long as the person in the chair chose to keep it open. Within the first minute, over one hundred members voted. Within five minutes, over two hundred. Ten minutes, 350 members. And the vote read 177 for Gephardt, 178 against. Foley voted no, everyone knew Foley would vote no, Foley had to vote no, had to vote his district, most of the West Coast opposed Gephardt on this, but Foley made no effort to beat it and his staff rooted for it. Members and leadership staff clustered around the computers, two on each party's side, which could break down votes by party, class, committee, or state. If a name flashed on the screen with a vote different than expected, Coelho or Bonior or one of the whips jerked erect, searching the floor for that member, stopping him before he left the chamber, massaging him, trying to bring him back in the fold. With four minutes left it was 182 yes, 188 no, then 189 to 190, 191 to 191, 197 to 196, 205 to 202 with forty seconds left, 205 to 205 with thirty-five seconds, 206 to 207 with twenty-eight seconds, 209 to 209 with time expired. Then the slow, last votes, *Come on, come on, we need this, you said if we needed it we could have it. Well, we need it.* Two minutes after time expired it was 212 to 210, 213 to 210, 216 to 211, that was it! That was the win! Two seventeen to 212. *Then Wright voted, for the second time all year, to make it 218.* Cheers broke out, wild clapping; 218 was the magic number, more than half the 435 members of the House. The final count was 218 to 214. Wright had won.

In the hallway afterwards, Gephardt was laughing, grinning, smiling, members congratulated him, yes, yes, thanks, his staff grinning, patting people on the back. Now for certain he was, had become, would be, a contender for the presidency. He was no longer a pretender.

And Rostenkowski? Democrats on Ways and Means voted against him 17–6, Democrats from Illinois voted against him 9–3. His own protégé, Marty Russo, who said, "I'm as close to the chairman almost as if he's my father," had worked hard for Gephardt. But that did not show Rostenkowski's weakness. It showed his strength. He had needed to switch only two votes to win. Could he have switched two votes? He had worked hard, worked his butt off, stayed on the floor for the vote working, working, working. But he had argued the merits only. He hadn't leaned on anyone. Could he have switched two votes if he had made it personal? Had gone out and put himself on the line asking for the vote? There was a difference between a colleague saying, "This is good policy. You should support it because of X, Y, and Z," and laying himself naked, open, saying, "I really need you on this. I'm asking for your help. Can you help me?" Members did not like asking for votes like that. That was special. That meant declaring friendship or enmity. No threats or promises were needed. Everyone understood. To have Rostenkowski's big shoulders, big square face, big hands, right in front of one, to have him say, *I need your help. I'm asking for your help. Can you help me?* That was something else again. Could he have switched two votes?

On final passage of the entire nine-hundred-page bill, Wright made the closing argument. He tried to provide a bridge for Republicans to cross back on to support the bill. It passed with 290 voting yes, enough to override a veto. Only six Democrats voted no. Only one Republican amendment—an insignificant, anticommunist rhetorical one—had passed. The bill was a major victory for Wright. But the Gephardt vote had again left a lingering bad taste among some Republicans. Wright had voted. To an outsider that seemed of no consequence. But those most intimate with the House, with the institution, took note, believing it betrayed the special nature of the speakership: yes, the Speaker led the majority party, but he also represented the entire House. "I don't like it," complained one Republican. "The Speaker shouldn't vote. He didn't have to. It's a partisan act and a bad omen."

Wright promptly sent hand-written notes to several members for whom Gephardt had been a tough vote. Later he would send more notes to more members who had helped, but the ones who had really made a tough vote would get a note that day. "No matter who you are," he explained, "you like to be stroked once in a while." He planned to conciliate Republicans with a gracious statement in his press conference. And in the next whip meeting, the regular Thursday morning gathering of fifty members, Foley said, "Whatever position you took, let's congratulate Dick Gephardt. It was a great speech. Dan Rostenkowski made a great speech also. I think it was a great moment in the history of the House. We'd have been proud if it had been on national television."

Then Gephardt said, "I want to thank all of you. I know it was divisive for the Caucus. I want to thank my chairman for not working hard to defeat it."

The whips cheered. Rostenkowski sat there, in one of the back rows, his arms stretched out over the backs of chairs beside him as if they were draped around the shoulders of comrades, silent, silent, impassive, yielding nothing, looking at Wright.

CHAPTER 10

The House itself was trying to work its will even as Wright tried to impose his upon it. The supplemental appropriation had been a warning. So was the Gephardt amendment, which even with all the new aggressiveness of Coelho's whip operation shrank from a 139-vote victory margin one year earlier to a four-vote margin. On the floor Mickey Leland, a black from Houston, was saying, "Mr. Speaker, I ask for the immediate consideration of a resolution commemorating"—he started laughing, one hand covering his mouth, the other covering the microphone, then steadied himself and proceeded—"commemorating the fiftieth anniversary of Ducks Unlimited."

At a whip meeting came the report that the House might be getting a new telephone system—a contract worth tens of millions of dollars—because of outrage over the fact that several years earlier AT&T had given the Justice Department telephone records for several members of Congress in response to a subpoena. And not only had the company turned over the records, it had never notified Congress. "That is just absolutely intolerable," one member said. Members didn't like the Executive Branch looking into their business, and they claimed constitutional justification.

Then Foley announced at another whip meeting that the following week's schedule included a "labor" bill—an AFL-CIO priority prohibiting unionized construction firms from operating nonunion subsidiaries. Wright owed the union this for its help on everything else. Members erupted. They hated labor bills because no matter how they voted they made enemies. A vote that made enemies was a tough vote.

(Politicians dislike offending anyone. Supposedly an aide once read old-time South Carolina senator Olin Johnston a press release denouncing communists for their perfidy and Godlessness and evil. Johnston approved it, then had a second thought and asked, "How many them communists you reckon we got voting back home?") Foley earlier had told one member, "Labor raised money for you, set up phone banks for you, gave you volunteers, did everything they could to elect you, and now you don't want to vote on this bill?"

"Right," his colleague had responded.

One member jumped to his feet and angrily complained, "I don't know about your state but let me tell you about my state. My two senators go into the AFL-CIO convention and get a standing ovation. Then they walk across the street to the Chamber of Commerce convention and get a standing ovation. *And the reason they can do this is that the Senate is smart enough not to schedule any damn labor bills for a vote!* Why are we scheduling one for a vote?"

Why? Because of the deal the leadership had made with labor: co-operation for cooperation.

"The House has already passed this bill twice," Foley said. "You've already gotten it on your records. We thought this would be the easiest vote. The Senate will vote this year. Labor knows we're not scheduling any more labor bills unless the Senate passes them."

"What?!" one member hissed from the back of the room. *"Did he say there were going to be more labor bills?"*

Wright was bumping into another limit, one which had dangerous connotations. The members lacked courage. They did not want to stand up to someone who had power over their reelection and who wanted something. It was politics at its worst; it was cover-your-ass politics. Members did not like making enemies of either organized labor or the business community. *Those people would raise money against you. Hell, they'd even run someone against you.*

Everywhere Wright turned now he bumped into limits, pushed against them, stretching them out further. Against the advice of his own staff, he tried to push the Agriculture Committee to rewrite the farm bill, which was supposed to cover four years and had been passed barely a year earlier. Wright considered it an election promise; Democrats had just campaigned on the farm issue, and he believed they now owed it to farmers to do something. To pressure the Agriculture Committee, a DCCC aide put together a meeting in H-324, the same room used for whip meetings, with dozens of interest groups who claimed to represent altogether over 100 million people. It was a bizarre coalition. Even the Union of American Hebrew Congregations sent a representative; he explained his presence by saying, "We see the potential for a social explosion, an outburst of anti-Semitism in the Midwest if the economy doesn't improve." They all wanted action. Complained one farm group president, "We took part in the system as you folks advised us to do, we turned the Senate over, and now people are saying so what?"

Facing the group, in a semicircle of chairs where the leadership sat in whip sessions, were half a dozen Agriculture Committee members, who carefully tried to sound receptive while promising nothing. But Wright continued to press, continued to press, and slowly the committee began to see that perhaps they might do *some*thing, and decided to move a farm credit bill to help family farmers. One insider noted, "They would not have budged without the Speaker. Jim Wright's will made that happen."

Everywhere Wright was pressing, pushing, and he was doing it to a body that had not been pressed or pushed before. His agenda demanded all his time, all his energy, all his focus.

And as much as he pushed others, he also was pushed. His schedule had not improved since earlier in the year. It seemed endless. On Thursday, May 7, it began with a seven-thirty breakfast with Dwayne Andreas, the chief executive of Archer-Daniels-Midland: Andreas dealt directly with Gorbachev, and had both administered Hubert Humphrey's blind trust during his vice presidency and contributed $25,000 in cash to Richard Nixon's 1972 campaign which had ended up in the hands of the Watergate burglars. They talked about the Soviets, even discussing Gorbachev's taking down the Berlin Wall. Then came the 9:00 A.M. whip meeting, then one of a Speaker's petty responsibilities which ate up precious time—getting his picture taken with the day's guest chaplain—then his press conference, opening the House, three separate luncheons to shake hands at, a handful of brief midafternoon meetings with members on their personal business, a member of the Japanese Diet, and three late afternoon–early evening receptions each of which required his presence—they were hosted by ABC's *Good Morning America* show, former members of Congress, and editorial cartoonists. He would not get home until nine. Little of that day advanced his agenda directly; such days frustrated him.

The next morning, Friday, at six-thirty, he arrived for makeup at the ABC studio for an appearance on *Good Morning America;* then came the staff breakfast, morning meetings, a lunch with national reporters to talk about the budget. In midafternoon he flew by private jet to Corpus Christi for a colleague's fund-raiser that night, then Saturday morning flew to Laredo for another colleague to tour a plant, meet with local businessmen, speak at a lunch for his colleague's business supporters, then attend a larger meeting for him, then fly home that night. He needed to do those things; his colleagues appreciated it. They did advance his agenda. But not directly.

And his formal schedule understated the demands on his time. It listed only appointments, not conversations on the floor that took time, or phone calls that took time, or an aide's interruptions that took time. Sometimes Wright wanted simply to escape; his personal office had a door which opened directly to the hallway. Only he used it. Sometimes he left his aides sitting in his outer office while he slipped out the back. He felt relief, a weight lifted from him, like a child unexpectedly getting out of school.

He would go home at night, late at night, say nothing to his wife, and fall asleep watching television. The schedule—his agenda—was draining him. He could feel it draining him. His wife, Betty, and he had no time together. He had worked and worked and worked as majority leader but this was something else again. There was no respite, never, ever, never a respite.

Wright had started the year spending nowhere near the time on the floor O'Neill had; on the floor a crowd of members always descended on him asking favors. Wright needed that time to make phone calls, think, talk to people about his own agenda. But he knew not being on the floor weakened him.

"I want to spend more time on the floor," he said. "I should. But it's hard to schedule that." *Schedule time for the floor?* O'Neill had lived in his seat in the front of the chamber, or in the cloakroom; he hadn't liked it either and once complained, "I'm tired of kissing all the members' rings." But all that time on the floor meant he had always known the pulse of the House. Wright risked misreading it. It wasn't anything that would hurt him immediately. The danger would come over time, the danger that he would grow away from it. And it from him.

Also on May 7 the Senate finally passed its budget—a month after the House. The budget was on Wright's agenda.

He was still tightening his control. Earlier he had indicated that he would not view appointments to House-Senate conferences, as his predecessors usually had, as a ministerial function, a simple ratification of a chairman's choice. Such appointments were the prerogative of the Speaker, and he intended to exercise all of the Speaker's prerogatives. But he had been too subtle. Budget chairman Bill Gray handed parliamentarian Bill Brown a list of his choices for budget conferees. Brown handed the list to the member occupying the chair. *Bang!* Down went the gavel and the conferees were appointed. When Wright found out he lashed out at Brown, who would not do that again. But it had happened this time.

Wright had intended to talk to the conferees before appointing them and reach an understanding that in return for serving on the conference they promised to be flexible and listen to the leadership. A couple of the conferees, George Miller and Marty Russo, worried him. Now that understanding had not been reached. It was too late. Briefly Wright considered withdrawing the list, but that would embarrass and infuriate Gray, Miller, and Russo. He would have to let it go. And the budget conference was beginning to look like trouble.

The Senate budget, which passed with every Democratic senator and three moderate New England Republicans voting yes, included several items House Democrats disliked. One was a "two-tier" defense-spending figure. If Reagan signed an $18-billion tax bill, defense budget "authority"—which authorized the Department of Defense to sign contracts for future spending—would be $301.5 billion. If he did not sign the tax bill, that would drop to $295 billion. But the House had allowed only a flat $289 billion for defense authority. In addition, the Senate wanted to count $7 billion from the early repayment of Rural Electrification Administration loans as budget savings. It was an accounting gimmick. The early repayment was no different than a homeowner taking out a new mortgage at a lower interest rate and paying off the old one, but the Senate wanted to claim the repayment as revenue even though over time it actually lost money (without the refinancing, the government would have taken in more money in total). Worse, the Senate was simultaneously counting the money from REA to offset spending in the supplemental appropriation; it was counting twice what should not have been counted once. Its budget reflected one thing: a decision to get something, anything, into conference.

The conferees met May 12 and 13 to make speeches. Then they recessed. The entire negotiating process would occur in private, between Bill Gray and Lawton Chiles, the Senate Budget Committee chairman from Florida. Both Chiles and Gray said publicly and privately that they expected a fast, easy conference. Democrats could certainly work with Democrats, they said. But Chiles and Gray soon were at each other's throats.

After three weeks of negotiating, Chiles and Gray had made no progress. The Republicans were starting to laugh. Now the leadership had to get involved. Intimately.

This budget wasn't just up to the Budget Committee; this budget was to be a statement of the party's priorities and policies. The leadership didn't get involved to negotiate. Leadership got involved either to bless an agreement or to exert enough pressure to shake issues loose so that others could settle it quickly. Three weeks of stalemate was long enough. House and Senate Democratic leaders sat down for breakfast with the two Budget chairmen in the Speaker's Dining Room.

Wright had worked out his own proposal and offered it. It was not simply a ploy; at this stage one stopped playing games. He thought it went far enough toward the Senate position that it could conceivably be accepted without any significant changes. Yet Byrd said nothing after he proposed it and Chiles balked, saying that Wright's offer certainly was progress, yes, but the Senate needed still more for defense and more cuts in domestic spending.

"Gee, Lawton, I'm disappointed." Wright's voice was calm, but he was seething. "If you don't like this, give us a variation. But let's show movement of some kind."

"It's not what I want," Chiles replied. "It's what will pass the Senate. If we lose [Georgia senator and Armed Services chairman] Sam Nunn because of the defense number, we lose four or five votes with him." *But there was no counterproposal.*

"Look," Byrd said, "I'm for anything that will get fifty-one votes. I'll support anything you come up with."

Byrd was refusing to intervene. The meeting broke up. Afterwards, a House aide said contemptuously, " 'I'll support anything you come up with.' That's leadership?"

* * *

As day after day passed, Republicans became more and more gleeful. They had lapel buttons printed up with the logo "Where's the Budget?" and began a string of one-minute floor speeches packaged for television saying much the same thing. Democrats had bragged for months they would govern. This was how they were doing it?

The House leadership called senators, including former House members, to check Chiles's claim that a lower defense number would cost them votes, maybe enough to lose the budget. They found out he was telling the truth. It wasn't the dollar figure but the principle; senators demanded zero real growth on defense—spending that kept pace with inflation. That was why they could not yield. There was a big symbolic difference between maintaining spending and cutting it. More days passed. Each hour became more painful.

With Wright's assent, Gray caved in.

Gray agreed to the "two-tier" defense number, one if the President signed a tax bill, a lower one if he did not. But the issue was less the numbers than the appearance of fairness, and the appearance that the House had yielded to the Senate. The defense number would be $300 billion in budget authority; this was $12 billion under Reagan's request, but only $1.5 billion under the Senate figure—and $12 billion above the House figure. In defense "outlays" (the amount of money actually spent in a given year) the agreement called for $289.6 billion, $1 billion less than the Senate figure, $8.6 billion above the House figure. Taxes were $19 billion. If Reagan vetoed the tax bill, defense spending would fall close to the House numbers. And the budget credited the entire $7 billion from REA as revenue.

When Gray reported the deal to his colleagues at a regular whip meeting, he put the best face on it, announcing, "The House got its way on domestic spending and economic assumptions. Taxes went up a little. There's zero real growth in defense outlays, and if the President doesn't sign the tax bill defense only gets $283 billion."

Gray made it sound good to members who did not know the budget, but Budget Committee members quickly objected. Barbara Boxer stood up and said, "I just want you to know, this zero real growth figure is $8 billion more than the House voted for."

Then Charles Schumer, also on Budget, complained, "This REA sale is crazy. It puts us more in the box than ever next year. We not only have no way to replace the revenue we're counting this year, but we lose income from the interest. And the Agriculture Committee wanted to use the money to pay for a farm credit bill. We should kill this deal."

Schumer, George Miller, and Marty Russo, who all served on Budget, shared a house with Leon Panetta, who had been forced to rotate off the Budget Committee but was already expected to become its next chairman. Their group was called "Animal House," and Boxer was close to them. "Animal House-plus" referred to the four and her. All were Rostenkowski intimates, and none of the housemates had pledged their support to Wright for Speaker. Miller, who had already had a run-in with Wright over the budget, was from California and went further: "I came here [in 1974] as a Phil Burton man. I inherited a whole set of friends and enemies. Wright was the enemy."

Wright tried to quiet the membership, arguing, "We'll all be subject to severe criticism if we don't produce a bill."

But the meeting broke up with members in a sour mood. Immediately afterwards Rostenkowski called Wright, demanding to know, "What the hell is this about a higher tax number?"

Wright didn't like the budget either. Like the liberals, he considered the numbers skewed too far toward defense. Like them he recognized the numbers would ultimately have impact in the real world. But he wanted to move forward, move to the rest of his agenda. He had other battles to fight, and he could not control the Senate. All his intelligence confirmed Chiles's vote count. There was no choice. You do what you have to do. Now he had to bull this budget through the House. A Steering and Policy meeting the first of next week would pass a resolution making the budget official party policy. That would warn members the leadership would consider this vote whenever a member wanted a favor.

But a revolt, a full-scale revolt, was brewing. Three Democrats on the conference committee, South Carolina's Butler Derrick, Russo, and Miller, did not want to sign the conference report—which, since no Republican would sign, meant a majority of the House conferees opposed the agreement. Without the signatures of at least two of those three, there would *be* no budget agreement. Miller told a reporter, "If the Republican Senate had brought us this proposal we'd have kicked their ass all over Washington."

Miller and Russo. Both were big, physical men and strong liberals. Miller was tall, weighed a good 250 pounds, and had been a college football lineman. Russo stood six five, built like a basketball power forward. Miller had passion. He could explode and would fight. He also had influence; he knew substance and colleagues did not consider him a "show horse," a maneuverer.

Russo, one of the ten deputy whips, was not viewed as a substance person the way Miller was. From Chicago, he had an almost father-son relationship with Rostenkowski, and people thought of him as a hothead. Once he reversed Ohio congressman Ron Mottl's vote in a committee by grabbing him in a headlock and saying, "What are you trying to do? Screw the chairman?" Mottl was a friend he could fool around with but still . . . Another time Danny Akaka had promised him his vote but sat in a phone booth in the cloakroom as time was about to expire. *That was bullshit, to promise your vote, then say, "Gee, sorry, I didn't mean to let time run out."* Russo kicked open the door and carried Akaka onto the floor. Russo had badly wanted Bonior's job as chief deputy whip, telling Wright that by picking him Wright would also get all his housemates. No one worked harder whipping than he did; he loved that stuff, loved working his colleagues. But he was thought of as someone who added inside muscle to someone else's idea or strategy. Colleagues did not see him as influential in his own right.

Miller, Russo, and Derrick were not the only angry Budget Committee members. This whole thing had been strictly a Chiles-Gray private deal, with leadership input. Committee members who had sweated for tens of hours to produce the House budget had been cut out. Worse, Gray had caucused with them to ask their views on the two-tier defense gimmick and the REA sale. They told him to reject both. He accepted both. *I'm against any deal I'm not a part of.* The conferees had met almost a month earlier, and not once since. Now the conferees were supposed to sign on to this lousy package? *The hell with you.* Miller, Russo, and Derrick refused to sign the conference report, and their committee colleagues backed them.

Byrd knew the deal would pass the Senate. He wanted to vote. But the House could not go forward. Wright told Byrd on the phone, "I don't think either Miller or Russo are susceptible to the argument that this looks bad for all Democrats. Let me ask you, any give over there?"

The answer was no. When he hung up he shook his head. "I don't believe they think we're serious over here. They think we're bluffing. But it is serious."

Wright's will had finally exceeded his power.

* * *

He was so damned tired of this. Privately he railed at the mistake made in appointing conferees. If he had talked to Miller and Russo first and gotten an understanding, this problem would not have occurred. The budget would have come out of conference, and he was convinced that, given the alternative of failure, the House would have passed it. Wearily he started one last round of massaging, wooing, and cajoling, beginning with a personal letter to Budget Democrats. "Democrats were looking great for the first five months of this year," it said. "Now we are starting to get panned." Then he went individually to one member of the committee after another. He assured Dick Durbin, from a farm district in Illinois, that they'd pass a farm credit bill this year and fund it somehow. *That was a commitment.* To Mike Lowry, the Washington State liberal who headed the Democratic Study Group, the DSG, he said, "What do you think we could do to put together a budget?" To Pat Williams, a labor Democrat, he said, "You know we've got to act."

He talked to Butler Derrick. *Derrick served on Rules. He was a team player.* Derrick still didn't like it but would sign the conference report. But Russo and Miller still refused. Finally Wright asked Miller, "Is there anything that could be done that you could support in good conscience?"

Miller, with the rest of the committee, tried again. The committee in effect took itself over, steamrolled Gray, and came up with a new proposal with defense numbers higher than their earlier offer, not dependent on tax increases. The Senate had promised not to comment on it, but within an hour Chiles issued a press release saying the idea widened rather than narrowed the differences. House members were angrier than ever.

As the week drew to an end—without an agreement—Wright decided to act unilaterally. He had that power. At the Thursday whip meeting he explained, "I've informed the Senate that the House simply will not accept what they say is their bottom line on defense."

The meeting erupted in applause and cheers, loud ones, led by Russo.

"I wouldn't applaud," Wright snapped. "This makes us look bad, very bad, all of us." Then he announced his plan. It was a power play, and the victim was the Senate: "The House may move a resolution next week saying that for the purposes of appropriation bills the House budget will be in force. We did that in 1985 when the budget was late.

When Republicans controlled the Senate." He looked out the window for a moment, angry. "We'll do it. One way or another we'll do it. If we do it without a budget we'll still do it. I'm not going to let this thing destroy our capacity to perform."

The law said that appropriations bills could not reach the floor until after passage of a budget resolution, but the Rules Committee could override that law and allow the House to move forward. The Senate could not move; its rules required sixty votes, an impossible target without GOP agreement, to approve budget waivers. If the House proceeded, it would isolate the Senate, make it look incapable of action. The press would soon enough target it for criticism, hold it responsible, create an election issue for every senator on the ballot. Within moments after Wright's announcement, word arrived in the Senate. Wright left the whip meeting and went directly to H-210 for his regular press conference. A phone call from Byrd was already waiting. While the press waited to be admitted, Wright talked to him.

"Well, Bob," Wright said. "I just look foolish if I keep making happy talk in light of what's happened. . . . All right, all right. . . . I won't say anything publicly until we meet. Three o'clock is okay. How about in H-201? That's the room just barely on the House side."

Moments later, to the press, Wright revealed nothing of his plans. But Coelho broke an unwritten rule—*Never question a colleague's motive, much less a colleague of your own party*—saying, "One man may be more interested in becoming the Democratic Party's presidential nominee than in compromising for a Democratic initiative."

It was a calculated move to bring pressure on Sam Nunn. Then, at the meeting in H-201, Byrd started taking the lead, leaving Chiles in the background. Gray was not even there; he was too busy trying to calm his committee. Wright argued that Reagan would never sign a tax bill, so real defense spending would end up lower than the House offer. But the Senate did not care about that reality. The issue was politics, not substance. Image, not reality. It didn't matter to Senate Democrats what the number really was. They simply would not put themselves in a position to be blamed for cuts. Byrd offered to drop defense outlays, actual spending, $1 billion—the deficit was measured in outlays, although the press usually focused on authority because it was a higher number. Wright rejected it. But it was the first movement out of the Senate in days.

The next morning *The Washington Post* ran an editorial attacking

"The Flubbocrats," and ridiculed Byrd and Wright for saying they would show that they "knew how to govern. What they're well on their way to proving instead is that they cannot even produce the budget resolution, which is a plan to govern."

Wright seethed.

The next week began with a prime-time speech by Ronald Reagan, attacking Democrats again on their inability to produce a budget, calling for process reforms, and once again promising to veto a tax bill. It was the first major shot in what was about to become an artillery barrage launched by Republicans.

But that attack, which the press was already beginning to echo, and Wright's threat to have the House proceed unilaterally put even more intense pressure on the Senate. Senate Democrats began to crack.

The House and Senate leadership met yet again. But this time it was members only. Every time Chiles had come close to agreeing before, his aide Richard Brandon had slipped a note to him; he had read it, and raised a new objection. House members and staff were fed up with Brandon, and with Chiles, for paying attention to him. This time no staff was permitted. Inside the room, Byrd complained that if the House moved forward unilaterally, "It would reflect failure."

"Well, Bob, we haven't succeeded," Wright responded.

He promised to delay his plan one more day. It was an easy concession to make: he had not planned to move until the next day anyway. From that meeting Wright went directly to see the Budget Democrats, one more time in the Speaker's Dining Room. It was hot, the middle of June in Washington, with members cramped into a room too small for them all. They were angry. Wright, Foley, and Gray all soothed the committee. Foley explained, "The trouble is, without any Republicans, Democrats in both bodies exhausted their political resources to get something through each body. We tell them we've come halfway, more than halfway, and they tell us that's not the point. They talk about votes. If Nunn doesn't vote for it, he takes five senators with him and they can't pass it. It doesn't matter if defense is $1 billion short of inflation or five dollars short. The symbolism is elsewhere."

Then Gray said he had run into Nunn that morning on the *Today* show, asked what was wrong with the last offer, and it was clear Chiles had not relayed it accurately to Nunn, adding, "We may have less of a problem than we thought."

One member exploded, "That son of a bitch Chiles! We don't have an honest broker here."

Wright's voice rumbled, *"We've got to show we can govern."*

The meeting broke for a floor vote. One Wright loyalist pulled him aside and asked, "Why don't you just say you want it done today?"

"I thought that was what I was saying," Wright replied.

When they reconvened after the vote, the members were still hot, still angry. But they knew Wright was correct. One could sense that while the anger and frustration remained, positions had changed. The facts, and Wright, had worn them down. They would accept the two-tier defense figure and the REA money.

Wright and Byrd held one more members-only meeting. Wright said nothing of the progress he had just made. The Senate had been going through the same process, agreeing on concessions. Everyone was worn out, frustrated, and disgusted. It was at such moments that one man who knew what he wanted, who continued to push, could prevail. It was time to strike. The House leadership was willing to yield, but hid its willingness and pressed hard. Now. After all this time. The Senate gave in too.

The last House offer had been $295.1 billion for defense, whether Reagan signed a tax bill or not. Now the Senate agreed on $296 billion with new taxes, but only $290 billion if new taxes did not become law. Even the higher figure was well below zero real growth.

Wright still had to get one more signature on the conference report, and then pass it.

On the floor he sat down with Miller, who still argued the defense number was too high and domestic spending was too low. He refused to sign. Wright pressed him: "You trust me, don't you? If Reagan doesn't sign a tax bill, he won't get one more penny for defense than the lower figure."

But Miller would not budge. Wright, barely controlling his anger, abruptly stood up. Gray meanwhile had talked to Russo. Russo forced him to lop $700 million off Ways and Means' responsibility. But he would sign. They didn't need Miller. At four Byrd called Wright to report, "If we want to make the news tonight, we have to have a press conference by five. Can you come over?"

Wright talked to Gray, who replied, "I have to talk to Russo one more time."

"God damn it," Wright steamed. "How many times does someone have to say he's with you before he is?" A few minutes later, Wright, Foley, Coelho, Russo, and half a dozen staff walked into H-210, the Speaker's ceremonial office, and closed the door. Rostenkowski was in Poland. It was four-thirty. Russo had all the responsibility for the committee on his shoulders; he called Ways and Means staff to check one more thing while the members stood around. It was four-forty-five.

"Let's go," Wright demanded.

Russo tensed, then said, "I want to talk to the Speaker alone."

The room emptied. Russo, tall, much taller than Wright, towered over him. Wright was tight, coiled. Both of them were ready to explode, both contained themselves. Wright needed his signature and had no choice. Now Russo was saying he had the same problems with the budget that Miller had.

"Marty, if Reagan doesn't sign the tax bill he's not going to get another penny in defense spending. He's not going to sign it. Just the other night he promised to veto it again."

Russo inhaled deeply, then put his arm around Wright's shoulders. "Jim, I'll do this for you. That's the only reason. I'll do it for you."

Russo was making this personal, saying he was compromising principle for the Speaker. Nothing was a higher sacrifice. Wright would owe him. Wright didn't want his signature on this basis. But he had to accept it. He thanked him in clipped tones.

They opened the door. Outside waited Foley, Coelho, Gray, a dozen aides. The press conference was on the Senate side in a few minutes. The whole group—with Russo's elbow held by Mack, who did not want him to escape—hurried down the corridor from H-210, the single room on the House side farthest from the Senate, toward Byrd's office. It was a long walk and everyone was on edge. Gray was fuming, muttering, "Byrd couldn't wait thirty fucking minutes so I could tell my committee about the deal. I've got my caucus bouncing off the walls." When they finally arrived, Russo saw Chiles with a piece of paper in his hand. The numbers on it were not the ones he had been told.

"Hold on," Russo complained. "This thing says Ways and Means has another $100 million to do in 1989, $200 million in 1990."

"The budget can't break up over $100 million in the outyears," Wright snapped. "Don't quibble over that."

"I don't like being treated like a child!" Russo retorted. And he stormed out.

Thirty minutes after the press conference Wright was apologizing to him, soothing him, telling him he was right, walking him down a corridor, patting his shoulder. Russo put his arm around him. The deal was done. But feelings on both sides were hard.

Only the floor vote remained. There were two problems: George Miller and Charlie Stenholm, the party's liberal and conservative extremes. If either one deserted, passage would be jeopardized. Word came back that Miller himself would vote no but would not work to kill it. That left Stenholm. He had supported the original House version because it included $36 billion in real deficit reduction. The conference agreement claimed $36 billion in deficit reduction, but $7 billion came from the REA money. Stenholm was not happy.

"Stenholm's not the only one with that problem," one member said as the whip task force gathered to plan their moves. "There's no question there are phony savings in here. It's the only thing the Senate would accept."

"Send Marvin Leath to talk to Stenholm."

"Don't send Marvin," warned Buddy MacKay. "He'll tell him the truth."

They were crowded into a small first-floor room in the Capitol in Coelho's domain. Nine members sat around a table; another dozen sat on couches. Staff stood in the corners. Suddenly Tim Penny, who with MacKay cochaired the budget group, got up and walked out of the room. It was a fact not lost on those remaining. Penny was quitting the task force. He might even work against passage.

The room grew tense.

Coelho turned to one member and demanded, "You're listed as a 'no response.' Are you with us?"

"Hell, he's sitting right here," said a colleague. "Of course he's for it."

"You've got to ask a direct question," Coelho snapped. *That was the only way to count. Anything other than a definite yes was not a commitment.* "You can't let him laugh it off. Are you okay?"

"I'm a yes."

They ran down the list of members to talk to, each member at the table taking some. There would be three more recorded votes that day, so they could whip their colleagues when they came to the floor. The meeting broke up and Coelho started to leave. Five members sat unmoving at the table. Coelho turned back and asked, "Why aren't you out working?"

"We're trying to figure out what to tell 'em. When the truth's precluded, what other arguments do we have?"

Stenholm got a deal. Butler Derrick and Martin Frost, both of them members of Rules, promised him a chance to cut $7 billion in real spending by guaranteeing that he could offer amendments to cut each of the thirteen appropriations bills. They even promised to vote with him on some of them. Stenholm agreed. With him came the conservatives. The bill was ready, the whip count showed a comfortable victory, and floor debate started. And the budget almost exploded one last time. *Wright felt like Sisyphus.*

Rostenkowski, back from Poland, was informed by his staff that $300 million in savings that Dingell's committee was supposed to make might come from an oil-import fee. The same problem had almost blown up the budget when it passed the House, and was supposed to have been eliminated in conference.

Rostenkowski caucused with his committee. They were angry, fed up, ready to destroy the budget. If an oil-import fee was in the budget, they would vote no. With his committee behind him, Rostenkowski stormed down the hall from H-208, the one office that did not belong to the Speaker in that long, long hallway that wrapped around the east front of the Capitol, to H-210, the Speaker's ceremonial office. Wright came in from the floor and sent for Dingell.

The rule for the budget was about to be debated. Word came out from H-210 to delay things, slow things down. "I move to strike the last word," said the Democrat handling the debate. It was a parliamentary maneuver, formally a motion to change the last word in the legislation under consideration, which guaranteed an additional five minutes' time.

Dingell strode through the Speaker's Lobby and said, "We'll do anything we can to help the Speaker, but we don't want to be left out in the cold without support, not knowing who our friends are."

He and Rostenkowski agreed on that anyway. The door closed. Inside, the cold anger between the two men filled the room. All year long these two bulls of the House, Dingell and Rostenkowski, had been heading for this confrontation. Now they had it. Later Coelho said, "When that happens you just want to get out of the way."

Rostenkowski saw not a friend anywhere. Not Wright. Not Coelho, his one-time protégé who had turned against him and backed Wright. Not Foley, that intellectual who seemed aloof from everything, and who was loyal to the Speaker. Not Dingell, sure as hell not Dingell. Tall and straight with that precise elocution and eyeglasses which belied his ferocity, Dingell intimidated those who could be intimidated and would yield nothing: *Not a single day passes in which I do not thank Sam Rayburn for what he did for the committee.* Rayburn as chairman had increased the committee's power by simply taking power.

Alone or not, Rostenkowski was not backing off. This was about power and power meant the future. He owed this fight to Ways and Means, to his committee and its future. This was the time to find out just what the alliance between Dingell and Wright meant. He would fight here. Now. Before he grew weaker. Now, when the votes of his committee could bring Wright down.

Rostenkowski and Dingell stood side by side, towering and angry and not looking at each other, the two of them standing beneath the great tinkling chandelier crafted by Paul Revere, appealing to Wright who sat behind his leather-topped desk, barren of paper. It was to Wright the judge they came. That was part of the role of Speaker, to judge disputes. Ten years earlier the element of leadership-as-judge had helped Wright beat Burton for majority leader. *Some members had wondered that if Burton was in the chair, "Is that bastard gonna rule fairly, or is some kind of deal involved?"* Now Rostenkowski and Dingell wanted to find out.

They did not shout at each other. They did not even address each other. Instead, each made his case to Wright, referring to each other by title only, with cold, deadly formality. Their words were as tense as the atmosphere. The issue was jurisdiction. Jurisdiction meant power. And Wright controlled it. Wright was the one who said which committee was allowed to do what.

"Danny," Wright said, trying to calm him. "I'm not telling you where to get your $19 billion in taxes. I'm not telling John where to get his money."

"I just want to know where the hell Chairman Dingell *intends* to get that money."

"I want to know where the hell the Ways and Means chairman thinks I'll get it."

"The New England people are convinced there's a deal cut to get an oil-import fee."

"There's no deal cut. But I'm not prepared to cut a deal excluding it."

The leadership had already proposed the easiest solution: transferring the $300 million to Ways and Means. That solved the jurisdiction problem. But Rostenkowski had rejected it. What else was there?

Hell. The budget had lost its purity when they included $7 billion in phony savings. Wright already had a sour taste. What was another $300 million? It was cheap if it could prevent an internecine war.

"Suppose," Wright suggested, "we just said that John doesn't have to do the $300 million. He can fall short of his target. How's that sound?"

"Well, Mr. Speaker, I'm amenable to it," Dingell said, "but I don't know whether Chairman Rostenkowski is."

Rostenkowski pushed his lips forward, twisted his face, but was satisfied. "It's all right with me."

Ten minutes later Rostenkowski was giving a speech on the floor in support of the conference agreement. That left no doubt where he and his committee stood.

The budget passed 215–201. Three Republicans voted yes. The Senate passed it 53–46, on a similar party-line vote. But the numbers had meant nothing. They had destroyed the budget to pass it.

CHAPTER 11

Wright was exhausted. The entire House was exhausted. Yet at breakfast the next morning Wright prepared to move on. Normally there was a sense of power in his simple daily breakfast ritual, he and half a dozen aides sitting at a round table, he surrounded by staff, his good humor becoming their good humor, his silence becoming their silence. Now there was a sense of power frustrated. He sat silently, pouring skim milk, which he disliked, over cereal, which he disliked, to control his weight, the only sound that of the clicking of silverware. Finally an aide broke the silence, relaying a member's request to use a large, empty closet down the hall from his office to put in three laser printers; he needed them to print two million newsletters, ten to every household in the district. Newsletters helped win reelection. "Some day on some vote in some Congress I may need him," Wright said. "I'll tell him personally he can have it."

Maybe the vote Wright needed would come this year, on taxes. It would still be a fight, even though members had voted for them in the budget. His will was relentless; he would not let up, not allow the House time to breathe. Another aide handed him a poll reporting that by a 66–26 margin the public preferred freezing the top income tax rate, instead of letting it drop further, to taxing cigarettes and beer. *See to it that everyone on Ways and Means gets that poll. But make sure it doesn't come from the Speaker's office.*

He was not going to let up. He was going to guarantee that the legislation that implemented the budget would conform to his priorities. He was going to push, to force Ways and Means to mark up a tax bill that raised money from the rich, not from excise taxes. Excise taxes were regressive. He sounded almost desperate as he declared, "We've got just a few weeks to convince Ways and Means to write a Democratic tax bill."

Almost while Wright spoke, Rostenkowski was addressing Buddy MacKay's group in 210 Cannon, the Budget Committee's large, airy hearing room. It was in the oldest House office building, named after Joe Cannon, the Speaker who had simultaneously served as Speaker and chaired Rules, personally appointed the members and chairmen of every committee, and so abused power that a 1910 revolution had stripped him and his successors of it, leaving them naked to the mercy of chairmen. Now, three-quarters of a century later, a new Speaker was still trying to recapture the power Cannon had lost.

It was only June and early in the morning and air-conditioned but already a stickiness dampened shirts. Rostenkowski sat at a long witness table surrounded by members and looked out at an audience of more members, thirty-five or so, and another thirty-five staff. He saw few friends but many potential allies. He attacked.

"The train is on schedule but we're packing it with dynamite," he warned. It was a reference to Wright's determination that the House function on time, on schedule, promptly, with a tax bill. "When they blow that train up, it will be the Democratic Party which suffers. . . . Right now Reagan's making us look like fools. The Republicans just sent out a [direct-mail fund-raising letter] blaming Democrats on taxes. You judge what a letter does by whether there's a second mailing. They did a second one. Now they're considering a third. The polls say the same thing. You want to freeze the [income tax] rates? Fine!" His fist slammed into the table. "Freeze the rates. Just give me the votes. Not one Republican finger will be lifted to help on that, and it's a certain veto."

Every word he spoke would find its way to Wright. Rostenkowski knew that and counted on it. "I think members want the cover of a closed rule, so they can say they had no alternative. I'll be goddamned if I sit there as chairman of Ways and Means and put a package out there on the floor that's dismembered by Democrats." *Don't let the Rules Committee allow a bunch of amendments to rip the bill apart*, he was saying. Then his fist slammed the table again, demanding of his audience, "And when it does get out there, don't run for the high country!"

Ways and Means almost always got a closed rule—allowing no amendments at all—on tax bills. The theory was that taxes could have so many unintended consequences that nothing should become law unless the committee first examined it carefully. But Ways and Means was the only committee in the House which routinely enjoyed a closed rule, and members resented it. There were rumors Wright might allow amendments if the bill was not to his liking. Rostenkowski was warning Wright against that. And he was telling all the Caucus members that if they voted for the budget, with the taxes in it, they had damn well better vote for the tax bill when it came up.

Then he reported on his dinner the night before with Howard Baker, who had said that Reagan seemed adamant against taxes, but worried about military spending. Rostenkowski concluded, "I would suggest we're following a course which gives too much wiggle room to Ronald Reagan. We need to present him with something which cuts the head off the military. Then Baker and Weinberger will tell him he has to sign the bill."

That last message was one of alliance between him and those in the room, and against the leadership. The issue was technical, involving the arcana of extending the limit on the national debt and amending Gramm-Rudman, two inextricably intertwined bills. But like so much procedure, at stake was power. At stake was whether Democrats could force the White House to accept their agenda. That fight would come later.

S till Wright did not let up. He seemed to feel he could change the very nature of the House with his own will, as if he could make it an extension of himself, to extend his control even into members' personal lives through his control of the schedule. He wanted the House to work, to perform. He was trying to make the House as relentless as he, as hard-working as he. Members had resisted this incursion into their own time. But Wright did not relent.

The coming of summer always reminded those who had come to Washington that they had come to a southern city, in some ways still more southern than the Atlanta or Charlotte of the New South. The black waitresses who had worked for years in the Members' Dining

Room and who knew everyone and were familiar with everyone seemed darker in summer, anachronistic. The Rayburn Building had been built on a swamp. Heat was heavy in the air. Crowds of tourists flocked to the Capitol, choked its corridors. The young sharks of staff members wore the paper-thin seersucker suits one associated with old southern senators, and still sweat soaked through the backs of their shirts.

With summer the Capitol Building itself seemed to change. It turned whiter, bleached white in the sun. From below, from Pennsylvania and Independence and Constitution avenues, it dominated the landscape, did not sit atop Jenkins Hill so much as become it, layered and multileveled, with cornices and balconies, and terraces, and great sweeping stairs, and recessed cavities like some great ancient fortress built into a cliff. In summer, as the heat made the Capitol seem to shimmy, it had the feel of a man swinging in a hammock.

The House was not resting easy. Wright was driving the institution, driving it. It needed a rest. One could walk through the halls and feel it. Coelho was driving it, too, with Wright's imprimatur, trying to create a structure which forced members who wanted to play a role to do so under leadership auspices. The leadership did not run everything. But it ran more things than O'Neill had ever contemplated running. It ran too much.

Members kept telling the leadership not to schedule any votes for three days after the July Fourth recess. If votes were scheduled they would have to be in Washington. They couldn't miss a vote. No votes would give them an extra week off, time to go camping with the kids, to hit the beach, to relax. Wright refused. Members grew angry. Members were even angrier when they came back after July 4 and found nothing significant on the floor, no real reason to be in session. The mood in the House was foul and dangerous. One leadership aide said, "We won't bring people back next July Fourth, I'll tell you that."

But Wright kept pushing.

He did not like to lose. The thirteen appropriations bills were moving through the House. In return for Stenholm's support of the budget, Martin Frost and Butler Derrick had promised he could offer amendments making across-the-board cuts in each of them, vote with him on some. The appropriations bills were Stenholm's chance to get back his $7 billion—to transform the phony savings in the budget into real savings.

Stenholm won an almost $700-million cut in the appropriations for the Treasury and independent agencies. The vote was 218–203 and looked decisive, but the leadership decided to reverse it. They worked it hard. John Mack talked to one member loudly, very loudly, for the benefit of three freshmen standing a few feet away. The three freshmen switched. Coelho and an Appropriations member promised Brian Donnelly support for a project in his district if he'd switch. He switched. Another member switched, then another. The leadership could win this thing. Finally Coelho approached Frost and Derrick; both considered themselves members of the leadership. They switched. Stenholm's allies lacked the muscle to fight back. Tim Penny tried to hold Donnelly, telling him, "We've got to make a stand." Donnelly replied, "What's this 'we' stuff? You make your statement. I've got what I want. I'm leaving you." It was months before Penny, whose office was next to Donnelly's, talked to him again. Stenholm worked the floor, tried to hold his votes, watched the floor swing against him, all the time silently thinking, *I thought the leadership wasn't going to call out the dogs on this. I thought we had a deal.* He lost, 207–210. After the vote Stenholm walked over to Coelho, shook his hand, and said, "You beat me fair and square." But he would remember.

Still Wright kept pushing.

He angered Dingell and Rostenkowski, who became sudden allies against him, by promising Claude Pepper, chairman of the Rules Committee, to allow him to offer a bill for long-term health care. Pepper, first elected to the Senate in 1936, was defeated in 1950 by George Smathers, who had called him "Red" Pepper and accused him of "practicing celibacy" before his marriage; he was elected to the House in 1962. Eighty-seven years old, he had pounded a table with his fist and said, "Please, Mr. Speaker, let me bring this bill to the floor." He had waited forty years for the chance. Wright had agreed. Rostenkowski and Dingell were outraged. The Rules Committee had enough power dictating procedure; it was not supposed to produce substance, especially substance in their jurisdictions. Dingell and Rostenkowski talked about refusing to offer the catastrophic illness insurance bill unless Pepper agreed to drop his demand. They aimed the blow at Pepper but when Wright heard the news he exploded, "Goddammit! Not while I'm Speaker. We can't have committee chairmen thinking they have the right of scheduling. That's a blow to the Speaker's power and I'm not going to have it." The message was carried to Dingell and Rostenkowski. They yielded; in July the catastrophic insurance bill passed the House 302–127.

It was not Wright's only incursion into health policy. He stretched his power one more time and brought together Otis Bowen, secretary of Health and Human Services; Dingell; his health subcommittee chairman, Henry Waxman; and Appropriations subcommittee chairman William Natcher to plan a program against AIDS. Wright was plunging deep inside the administration, directly, ignoring the White House, to decide administration policy. Bowen was willing to cooperate; it was he, a physician, who had forced the White House to come forward with a catastrophic health insurance plan. A former governor of Indiana, Bowen understood power and recognized that the meeting could serve his purposes well.

"What do you want?" Bowen asked. "A recommendation on how to spend $400 million more than the White House asked for?"

"Yes," Dingell said, adding, "and don't clear it through OMB."

"Could you write me a letter asking for this?" Bowen had to protect himself.

"Certainly," William Natcher, the relevant Appropriations subcommittee chairman, assured him. "I'll send it today."

"Will I have to take the money from elsewhere in HHS?"

Natcher shook his head. "Not if the legislation is drafted correctly."

Bowen smiled. The members smiled. They all understood one another.

The day Stenholm saw his victory reversed, there was other action on the floor too. Newt Gingrich tried to strike money for the Fort Worth stockyards project, seeking to generate bad publicity for Wright. For now, Gingrich was just a gnat buzzing around Wright's ear. He knew his amendment would lose—in fact, Democrats used procedure to prevent him from offering it, to take from him the opportunity to highlight the issue. But the floor activity, the C-SPAN viewers who watched, the one or two reporters who paid attention, those who would read the next day's *Congressional Record,* all fitted into the web he was spinning.

Liberals were angry over substance, too. Lieutenant Colonel Oliver North was turning the Iran-contra hearings into a showcase for himself.

The two chairmen of the joint investigation, Senator Daniel Inouye and Congressman Lee Hamilton, lost control. Polls showed movement in favor of the contras—from 71 percent opposed to contra aid, 22 percent in favor, to 65 percent opposed, 35 percent in favor. The trend lines were disturbing. Chief deputy whip David Bonior kept a running vote count on the issue, and they had lost a few votes already. He worried, "I've been getting calls about the hearings from activists all over the country saying, 'What the hell is going on?' The idea was, if we stuck to process questions and constitutional questions, they were so important it would be easy to carry the day for us. We didn't want to debate the policy itself. I'm not sure that was right. The House Republicans are all arguing the policy."

There was a feeling among liberals that the leadership should do something, develop some strategy to turn things around. Hamilton did not seem to be getting at the facts. On the committee itself, Democrats were in an uproar over concessions Hamilton had made to North. The members wanted action from Wright and, for a change, he was not acting.

By midyear, it had become clear to those who tracked the passages of power in Washington that a new force had emerged. *Wright.* If the House did not rest easy, if undercurrents were stirring, still he was well on his way to defining the agenda, and he was well on his way to creating a new role for the Speaker. Special circumstances had helped him, yes. The White House was weakened by the Iran-contra scandal, yes. Democrats had taken over the Senate, yes. Wright benefited from the honeymoon and goodwill which any new leader receives, yes. But that had only helped create an opportunity for him. He had exploited it, and in so doing had surprised even his colleagues.

The congressman who had said, shortly before Wright became Speaker, "I think his strength is at the level of getting new rugs in members' offices, and maybe he can translate that into legislative victories," now confessed, "I'm in awe of what he has done." Even Stenholm, who conceded, "Strains between the Speaker and myself have been very great," added, "Winning. That's why I've worked hard to be a part of the team. The Republicans forfeited leadership on budget matters. They have nothing that they can come to me and work a deal on."

The Republicans had not understood Wright when he took power, and did not understand him yet. They had no allies on the Democratic side; now even Stenholm was with Wright. Occasionally in the past Republicans had won some victories by simply working harder than O'Neill and Foley's whip organization. But Republicans could not outwork Wright or Coelho's whip organization. Jerry Lewis, a California member who was rising in the GOP leadership, complained, "We have not been successful in working with anyone on the other side of the aisle. Wright's control of Rules—we have not developed an effective strategy to counter that at all. It has caused a lot more unity in the Republican Conference, but that unity doesn't count for much. As for influencing what happens inside the House, we have just enough votes to be irresponsible."

Wright had eclipsed Bob Byrd as well. Byrd had hung back, hung back, hung back, on several of Wright's initiatives. And he had tied the Senate up for weeks trying to end a filibuster against a campaign-finance reform bill; that delay had forced the budget and appropriations process behind schedule. The press had sensed, finally, the shift in power, and through the press Wright's presence began to be increasingly sensed. More reporters were turning up at his daily press conferences. To illustrate a story on the Senate, *The New York Times* ran one photograph—of Wright. *Congressional Quarterly,* in its assessment of Wright's first six months, declared, "[Wright] wants to be known as a policy maker, not just a master of procedure. Indeed, he sometimes seems to view his office as on a par with the presidency."

Reagan tried to regain the initiative by confronting the Congress. His controversial nomination of Robert Bork to the Supreme Court was one move. So was a call for an "economic bill of rights" on July 4, which included more attacks on domestic spending, another call for a constitutional amendment to balance the budget, and a new demand that a "super majority" in Congress be required to raise taxes. *The Washington Post* ran a page-one story, echoed by other papers, headlined "Reagan's Mood Is Uncompromising . . . Efforts on Bork, Economic Agenda Reflect a Rightward Turn."

Reagan's new campaign worried Foley. Foley measured men carefully, analytically, and understood that compromises did not simply happen; people had to make them happen, and doing so required enormous effort. He told Wright, "I don't think Reagan has the physical and psychological energy necessary to work out any compromises."

Wright shrugged. "I believe Ronald Reagan is like a cornered animal.

He's lashing out. He doesn't want to work with Congress, doesn't trust many people, but is upset that people don't trust him. He began an offensive against Congress to try to deflect attention from Iran. It hasn't worked."

It hadn't worked. In a major televised speech, Reagan appealed to people watching to contact their congressmen. Members compared notes. "How many calls did you get?" "None. How about you?" "I got two, both against Reagan." It was a far, far cry from the days when his appeals generated a flood of public support. Private Democratic polls showed tremendous overall movement on economic issues toward Democrats. So did a *Washington Post*–ABC poll.

Wright had not become a star, a media favorite. Yet the debate over policy was his debate; the issues argued over were his issues; the institution setting the agenda was his institution.

He was not simply occupying the great, high-backed Speaker's chair, the chair which sat atop the three-tiered marble rostrum, a rostrum more grand than anything else in the American government. Much of what he had done in his first half-year as Speaker had been designed to gather power to his office. He had power. Now, more than ever before, he was about to exercise it.

He had mastered the inside game. That inside game translated rhetoric into reality, but it did not soar, did not inspire. Outside, the game outside, that was where Wright was about to step, about to wrestle directly, in full view, with the President.

PART III
THE
GAUNTLET

A prince should choose wise men for his government and allow them to speak the truth to him . . . then he should make up his own mind, by himself. He should put the policy agreed to in effect straight away. . . . With that impetuous move of his, Julius achieved what no other pontiff, with the utmost human prudence, would have achieved. It is better to be impetuous than circumspect; because fortune is a woman and if she is to be submissive it is necessary to beat and coerce her.

—Machiavelli, *The Prince*

CHAPTER 12

On July 22 at three-thirty in the afternoon, Tom Loeffler, a former Republican congressman from Texas, walked into Jim Wright's office. Ten days earlier the White House had asked Loeffler to help them pass military aid for the contras. Wright believed it was a courtesy call. It was more than that.

Loeffler had a knack for working the Hill. He was a doer interested in results, enthusiastic and baby-cheeked and big-shouldered, his conversation laced with phrases learned playing football at the University of Texas. *Make something happen! Raht now! Do it raht now!* He combined can-do bursts of energy with persistence to get things done— he was the kind of man who would wait on the phone for long, long minutes on hold, *Dammit, let's get this thing settled now,* rather than leave a number and wait for a return call. He did make things happen.

He had worked for Gerald Ford's administration, then, in 1978, won a House seat and quickly established relationships across the aisle with Democrats, particularly with his classmate and fellow Texan Stenholm. In the Reagan administration's early legislative victories, Loeffler had played a critical role, and at thirty-nine he became the House Republican chief deputy whip. But life in the House frustrates all junior members, especially the minority, and Loeffler had too much impatience, too much energy, to sit tight. He ran for governor of Texas, but lost in the GOP primary. Since then Loeffler had gone back and forth from a law practice in San Antonio to his ranch and to Washington.

Then the administration asked for his help. It badly needed credibility in Congress. Admiral John Poindexter, the national security adviser, and North were gone, but Assistant Secretary of State Elliott Abrams remained. Abrams had repeatedly "misled" Congress about administration policy in Central America, and had just explained to the Iran-contra investigative committee he had not been "authorized" to tell Congress the truth. In Congress one's word mattered, and Abrams had demonstrated that his was worthless. Both Republicans and Democrats who backed the contras told the White House that Abrams's presence on the Hill would cost them votes. The White House hired Loeffler.

Immediately he began talking to former colleagues on both sides. One of his first conversations was with Coelho. He went straight to the point, asking, "What price is your vote on this?"

Coelho laughed at the directness. He liked doing business that way. But he replied, "There isn't any price."

"Come on. There must be something."

"Not on this."

Loeffler nodded. He hadn't really expected a different answer. But he was curious about one thing. When he had left Washington, Wright had been reasonably close to agreement with administration Central American policy and had supported the White House on El Salvador—at considerable political risk inside the House. "How did the White House screw up its relations with the Speaker?" Loeffler asked.

"By not treating him as a leader. You lost an opportunity to have some bipartisanship."

"Do you think it's too late?"

"It's never too late. But you can't pull anything off on this."

Maybe. Then Loeffler learned something else from several pro-contra members about a plan of Bernard Aronson. Aronson was a Democrat who had had a senior post in the Mondale campaign. But he worried that weak-on-defense charges could cripple his party, and he had helped the administration develop strategies to pass contra aid in the past. Early in the year, during a brainstorming session in Republican congressman Henry Hyde's office with Democrat Ike Skelton, Republican Mickey Edwards, and others, Aronson had come up with an idea: a bipartisan peace plan. "It would end once and for all the crap about a negotiated settlement," Aronson told the group. Neither he nor anyone else in the room believed the Sandinistas would seriously negotiate a move toward democracy, but a bipartisan peace plan would force the Sandinistas to reveal their antipathy for it. Then contra aid would pass. To avoid tainting his plan with GOP fingerprints, Aronson would work with Democratic senators, but briefed Frank Carlucci, the national security adviser, on the idea, even giving him a draft peace proposal. Carlucci liked the sound of it.

As Loeffler gathered this intelligence, as he put together a rough vote count, he became convinced that military aid to the contras could not pass the House. Not without some deus ex machina.

Loeffler began to wonder. Publicly Wright had always opposed aid to the contras, but he was no friend to the Sandinistas. They had lied to him personally and to the Organization of American States in 1979 when they had promised to maintain democratic freedoms and hold free elections. Richard Pena, who had worked for Wright on the issue, had not hid his pro-contra views and, unknown to Wright, had even tried to sell weapons to the contras. GOP congressman and presidential candidate Jack Kemp, who had discussed Nicaragua at length with Wright, said, "I wouldn't say this publicly—I wouldn't want to get him in trouble with his liberals—but I think Wright leans toward the contras." And Henry Hyde, the GOP conservative who held up the pro-contra side at the Iran hearings, added, "The White House is stupid when they try to antagonize him. They should be stroking him at every opportunity. He's someone they could work with."

Now, on a muggy July day, sandwiched in midafternoon between a meeting with the Future Homemakers of America from Weatherford, Texas, and a discussion with Coelho, Byrd, and Democratic pollster Peter Hart, Loeffler visited Wright. Wright liked Loeffler; he had always played it straight even when they had fought over votes from the same southern Democrats. They exchanged pleasantries and talked Texas politics, then slid into Central America.

Loeffler wanted to establish his credibility and warned Wright that although the White House budget called for only $105 million in military aid for the contras, in September the administration would ask for $200 million, possibly more. Unsaid but understood was that such a high figure might allow the White House to negotiate a compromise on military aid. Then Loeffler added, "I've talked with the President about this at length. He's really serious now about a diplomatic solution."

"That's good," Wright said, reviewing the prospects of the peace plan put forward by Costa Rican president Oscar Arias six months earlier. In two weeks the presidents of Costa Rica, El Salvador, Guatemala, Honduras, and Nicaragua would meet to discuss it.

"They need support," Loeffler said. "I've been wondering, would you be willing to make a joint statement with the President in pursuit of a diplomatic solution?"

Loeffler had not walked into Wright's office intending to make that suggestion, nor had it been discussed specifically in the White House. But the entire history of contra aid, of Bernard Aronson's talk of a bipartisan plan, of Wright's past dealings with the White House on Central America, made it logical. Before Wright could answer Loeffler was already trying to sell him on the idea. Loeffler remembered listening to Wright talk of Rayburn, and knew that he had wondered about greatness. He had offered Coelho a deal; he offered Wright a place in history: "It would be precedent-setting, enormously important—it would involve the Speaker of the House in foreign policy in a new way. What significance for the speakership! The importance to our allies, to the Soviets, to the world, of seeing the United States united in foreign policy—it would be just tremendous! It would call the bluff of the Sandinistas. I could explore it with the President tonight if you're interested."

The significance of the proposal did not escape Wright. Nor did the dangers. If he took part in anything that turned out to be a ploy—the White House had employed many in the past on contra aid—the Caucus would explode. That explosion could destroy him. He thought for a long moment. Finally he said, "Frankly, some members on my side would view that with great suspicion."

Loeffler repeated that he had the chance to set an historic precedent. "This would happen in total confidence. If you give me the okay to explore it, I would talk only to Will Ball, Ken Duberstein"—Ball headed Reagan's congressional relations and Duberstein was deputy chief of staff; they were among the very few people in the administration whom Wright trusted—"Howard Baker, and the President. Absolutely no one else."

How would it look, Wright wondered, if it came out—as he believed it certainly would—that the administration had approached him about a peace initiative and he had refused even to talk about it?

"All right," Wright said.

Loeffler jumped up, enthused. "I'll come back tomorrow to report."

Wright did not share his enthusiasm. Partly he saw the dangers, the ramifications. Partly his mind was already engaged; he was working, thinking, planning, anticipating. *It's like simultaneously playing chess and Ping-Pong.*

Loeffler walked out of Wright's office into the reception area, picked up the nearest phone, and dialed; he could not even wait to return to the White House. "Get me Will Ball," he said. "Tell him I need him when I get back—alone."

Wright had a sense that rules did not apply to him. The power of the speakership did not give him that sense. But that sense was there. It showed itself in an occasional wild flash in his eyes, and it came from a faith that he could succeed where others failed. It made him willing to put everything he had on the line. Thirty-two years in the House had taught him about boundaries, about the limits of power, but he was willing to try to create new boundaries. There was an innocence, if not naivete, in that. Innocence has nothing to do with the past, with what someone has experienced; one is innocent to the extent one ignores the past and exposes oneself to the present. There was an existential element to him. Gingrich understood this and observed, "He creates himself when he acts."

Wright did create himself by acting. Sometimes he acted carelessly or impulsively, as with the savings and loan intervention. He had misjudged that issue on both substance and its political importance, and had allowed distrust of the regulators to color his judgment on the problem. Central America was different. There was no doubt of its importance. And he had knowledge.

A few months earlier he had sat next to Sergio Ramirez, the Nicaraguan vice president, at a dinner honoring Jimmy Carter and asked what it would take for the Sandinistas to democratize their government. Ramirez had insisted it would take only an end to the war. Wright believed Ramirez to be an honest man, but also one who was used as a front man by the Sandinistas and who had little power in Nicaragua. Still, the conversation had been interesting and had started him thinking about some kind of initiative. If there really was a chance for peace he had to pursue it.

So much was at stake both politically and personally. Politically, Democrats needed a policy to be *for*. If the worst case happened, if Democrats ended contra aid and the extreme left of the Sandinista junta took command and started a wave of executions, Republicans could smear Democrats for a generation. Wright had lived through the McCarthy days, the accusations of "Who lost China?," the accusations that Democrats were at best unpatriotic dupes of communists.

What was at stake for him personally? No issue generated the intense emotions which contra aid did, and the Caucus overwhelmingly opposed it. *Overwhelmingly*. Liberals equated it with murder. Suppose he and Reagan did produce a joint statement? Suppose it failed? Reagan would promptly demand several hundred million dollars of military aid. It would pass. If that happened, Wright's power would disappear.

His power did not emanate from force, from coercion. One could not coerce a colleague, a fellow prince. "Threats don't get you any-where," Wright observed. "They don't work and they make enemies." Power worked more subtly. O'Neill believed, "Power is perception. If people think you're powerful, you are powerful." Power in Washington is almost evanescent. Dingell called power "a very ephemeral thing. It depends upon the trust of your colleagues. Their trust allows you to lead. Members will follow you. That gives you immense power, but it is also very fragile. It can be destroyed in an instant."

If Wright went forward and failed, if it looked as if the White House had made a fool of him, the trust of his colleagues would evaporate. He would become irrelevant. For a while, he could continue to sit in the chair—maybe—but he would be irrelevant. The liberals who dom-inated the Caucus would despise him, would feel they owed him noth-ing, less than nothing. When he asked for their vote they would laugh at him. *How could he trust the White House?*

The White House had no credibility on contra aid. Publicly, it pursued a "two-track" policy of military pressure and diplomacy to get the Sandinistas to democratize their country. But whenever diplomatic ini-tiatives seemed to be making progress, the administration abandoned them. Before the 1984 presidential election, United States negotiators sat down with Sandinistas in Mexico. After Reagan's reelection the United States canceled another scheduled negotiating session. Those talks never resumed. In 1985, before a key contra-aid vote, the White House again promised a diplomatic initiative, and convinced Demo-cratic moderate David McCurdy of Oklahoma of administration sin-cerity. McCurdy endorsed its plan and sold it to moderate colleagues. Contra aid passed. Suddenly the diplomatic initiative failed to materialize.

And how trustworthy was a State Department featuring Elliott Abrams, who had confessed he had not been "authorized" to tell a closed, secret session of the Senate Intelligence Committee the truth. Then there was the White House memo in which Poindexter, then national security adviser, proposed continually negotiating with Nicaragua to blunt congressional criticism, but never agreeing to a treaty. Poindexter was gone but Abrams had been part of all that, and was still the dominant administration force in Central American policy making.

It seemed clear that privately those running Central American policy would settle for nothing less than the removal of Sandinistas from power. They saw the security of the United States threatened by Nicaragua, indirectly, because leftist revolution could spread to other Latin American nations, including Mexico, and directly, through the establishment of Soviet bases on the American continent—indeed, the Sandinistas in 1987 were building a runway long enough to accommodate threatening military aircraft.

How could Wright trust the administration? If he did, maybe he really was a fool.

Suppose Loeffler could be trusted and was telling the truth. Weren't there others in the administration who would cut Loeffler's throat just as quickly as Wright's? Didn't the administration show a dozen times a week that it was at its own throat? Even if Loeffler deserved trust, even if Howard Baker did, even if Reagan himself truly wanted a diplomatic settlement, wouldn't others in the administration sabotage it?

Then again, maybe Wright's gesture of preventing a floor vote on arms control until after Shultz went to Moscow had made a difference. *Peace. Blessed be the peacemakers.* There was just the possibility that the White House was being straight with him.

The next day David Bonior sat in Wright's office reviewing a memo on contra aid, then said, "We've lost a few votes, but there are other members who are reachable."

Wright listened quietly, quiet enough to put Bonior on edge, then casually mentioned Loeffler's suggestion.

Bonior stiffened. He had devoted several years of his life to stopping contra aid. Wright had named him chief deputy whip because of it, and his appointment had reassured Caucus liberals of Wright's position. Instantly he saw the ramifications of Wright's joining with Reagan.

"Why now?" he asked. His voice was tense. "Why five legislative weeks before asking for more military aid? They've lied to us so often. My instinct is this is a setup."

As he left Wright's office, Bonior ran into Loeffler coming in. They eyed each other for a moment, each wary of the other, standing in Wright's doorway. Bonior had played football, too, Big Ten football. While Loeffler had been the Republicans' link to southern Democrats, Bonior was the Democrats' link to a handful of moderate Republicans. Despite Bonior's reputation for being easygoing and laid back, he was tough, tougher than most people knew, and played to win. *A lot of people around this place are naive about power,* he once said. Now, his voice perfectly even, he said, "Hello, Tom."

"Hello, Dave."

They did not shake hands. Loeffler closed Wright's door behind him. Bonior watched, watched as the door closed, then pressed his lips together, wondered about betrayal, and left.

Loeffler told Wright that Baker, Duberstein, and National Security Adviser Frank Carlucci were ready to come see him *now, tonight.* Then he again appealed to Wright's goals for the speakership: "Howard picked up on the significance immediately. He said how important it would be for the Speaker and for the future."

Wright said sharply, "I have no interest in this unless it could go somewhere."

Loeffler reassured him of Reagan's sincerity, and added that he would be Speaker, and the Democrats would run the House, for a long time.

"The Democrats might," Wright interrupted. "But if I do this I might not."

He explained that he could not meet that evening, and the next day, Friday, he was flying to Puerto Rico. Monday was the Speaker's Club golf tournament, for those who gave $5,000 to the DCCC. Tuesday. They could not meet before Tuesday. Loeffler left.

Wright had not put him off because of his schedule. Time was critical; anything that was going to happen he wanted to happen prior to the meeting of the five Central American presidents. But before seeing Baker and Carlucci he needed to pursue his own sources. And he had to think. Yes, the significance of making a joint foreign policy proposal with a President appealed to him. He wanted to go forward. Everything in his personality drove him forward. But Loeffler's effort to manipulate him by appealing to his ego would not decide him. If he was going to risk his speakership, he would do so only if the reward justified it. Only one thing justified the risk: the possibility of success, of peace.

The next day he flew to Puerto Rico with his grandson; they jet-skied together, swam, and Wright attended some formal functions. His family gave him a rootedness, just as a place in history would. But he did not simply relax. The brother of Costa Rican president Oscar Arias—it was Arias who had advanced the peace plan his fellow presidents would discuss—was also in Puerto Rico to attend the same events Wright had come for, and served as his brother's presidential chief of staff. Wright pulled him aside, explained what was happening, and asked about the chances for a peace agreement at the meeting of the Central American presidents and about the impact a Reagan-Wright joint statement might have. Wright also talked with other Central Americans and arranged a phone call with Arias. More phone calls went out to other parts of Central America, and other sources of information were tapped.

Wright's intelligence-gathering convinced him that an opening for a negotiated peace settlement did exist. Back in Washington on Monday, he called Bob Strauss, one of the few Democrats Wright trusted who also had access to the White House, briefed him, and said, "I'm going to run some traps before I talk to the White House. Could you check this out for me too?"

But the key was the Sandinistas themselves. Wright needed a better feel for them. He called Carlos Tunnermann, the Nicaraguan ambassador. Wright began graciously, exchanging pleasantries in Spanish, then switched to English. This was serious business; he wanted to be certain he was saying precisely what he meant at all times.

"Mr. Ambassador," he asked. "I wonder if you could come up here at some time convenient for you? Perhaps ten o'clock tomorrow morning? Good."

Wright hung up, put on slacks and a knitted shirt, and left his office for the golf tournament to collect checks for the Democratic Party.

Tuesday morning, July 28, Wright called Bob Michel and invited him to join him and Tunnermann. There were two chief reasons to ask Michel; Wright was still trying to build a good relationship with him, and including Michel also would prevent right-wing Republicans from attacking him. They met in room H-201, down the hall from his personal office, the last office on the House side, a few feet from where, on the other side of a heavy bronze door, tourists passed through metal detectors at the entrance to the Rotunda. Outside, the great steps leading up to the Capitol were already filled with a zigzag line of tourists, already uncomfortable in the morning's summer sun.

The room was filled with memorabilia. One wall was covered with old campaign buttons of colleagues and pictures of Texas congressional delegations. Mounted on another wall were the wide, sweeping horns of a Texas longhorn steer, beside a plaque that read, "Don't tell me it can't be done. Show me how it can." The opposite wall was covered with a collage of photographs of friends, of his wife, of him. A photo of him boxing. In his Army Air Corps uniform. Being sworn in as Speaker. The boxing gloves of Sugar Ray Leonard hung there. A giant-screen TV sat in the corner. Chairs lined the sides of the room, and one large table sat in the middle of it, covered by a maroon tablecloth. Plates of fresh fruit and memo pads and pencils were at each seat. Off to the side were coffee and pitchers of iced tea.

Three Nicaraguans, Michel, and Wright shook hands and exchanged introductions. Wright invited them to sit down. The Nicaraguans did, uncomfortably, and here, now, one could understand how easily a man could be intoxicated with power. Tunnermann had brought William Vigil, deputy foreign minister, and translator Sophia Clark, the niece of Foreign Minister Miguel D'Escoto. This woman and the two men seemed inconsequential: Tunnermann, in his mid-fifties, short, dumpy, serious, nervous, mopping sweat from his face; Vigil, much younger, in his twenties, thin, with a scraggly goatee and sharp eyes; the woman attractive, blond and blue-eyed. They seemed insubstantial somehow, like the small country they represented. The average American was larger, stronger, thicker than Tunnermann or Vigil. Representing the power of the United States, facing representatives of this nation, which was literally a banana state, once virtually ruled by the United Fruit Company through the U.S. Marines, were Wright and Michel. Here, in the Capitol of the United States of America, with thick columns and great halls and powerful men all about them, representing the vast, rich strength of America, it would be easy to find oneself intoxicated, to believe that one could reach across the table and crush these people, that these people were in one's power. The Nicaraguans seemed to sense that also; perhaps that accounted for Tunnermann's nervousness, for Vigil's surliness—there was nothing overt, just a glint in his eye, as if to say that if an American had the arrogance of power on his side, the young Sandinista had the arrogance of history, of Vietnam, on his.

Immediately Wright tried to dispel reminders of arrogance. As a waiter hurried over to pour his coffee, he protested. "Oh, no. Please. Our guests first."

Beneath Wright's velvet graciousness lay power, the delicate dance of power, and he and Michel, two shrewd, strong men, knew it well. Wright began with a stern message phrased diplomatically: he had lived through the who-lost-China attacks on his party and the McCarthy period which followed; he was not about to see that happen again in Central America. And even Democrats who opposed aid to the contras wanted democratization in Nicaragua. The Sandinistas had promised democracy in 1979 to the Organization of American States and personally to him. And Oliver North had changed the dynamics. "Perhaps military aid to the contras will be extended," Wright warned ominously, "but that gives us a small window of opportunity here."

Then Michel spoke. He also began graciously, saying that members of his family had married Hispanics, and he echoed Wright's words, adding, "I've been criticized by militants in my party for seeking a two-track policy of military aid on one hand, and diplomatic initiatives on the other. This Speaker, unlike the last Speaker, has pressures on him too. Texas is not like Massachusetts politically." He, too, talked of a window for a negotiated settlement, but warned that if negotiations were to start they would have to make rapid progress: "The Speaker and I have both been involved in negotiations long enough to see when they're dilatory, when nothing's going on."

Tunnermann replied in English: "I believe this is the most important conversation I have had in my three years in Washington."

He reviewed the overtures his government had made to the Reagan administration. "We never got an official response to any of these proposals. We never got any kind of response. Bilateral talks were called off when we actually had a date set for the next meeting in early 1985. After your election you seemed to lose interest. What do we ask from the United States? The right to be, to exist, to carry out our revolution, but not to threaten the security of the United States."

Then he switched to Spanish, more confident of the translator's ability to capture precise nuances of meaning. They spoke for thirty minutes. Wright listed three primary concerns which any agreement would have to resolve: first, Soviet and Cuban military advisers would have to leave Nicaragua, and the dispute would have to be settled about the long runway being built; second, Nicaraguan aggression against its neighbors, or the supply of guerrillas elsewhere, would not be tolerated; third, human rights and democracy within Nicaragua had to be assured.

Tunnermann nodded and said, "My country is suffering." Five percent of the population had been killed or wounded in the war, 50 percent of the budget went to the war. "We have only a survival economy." He promised that if a peace settlement were reached, his government would remove Soviet and Cuban advisers, while simultaneously recognizing the historic presence of the United States in the region. He admitted that the Sandinistas had supplied guerrillas earlier, but insisted that such supply efforts had ended. He offered to allow verification. The runway and any other points could be negotiated, again recognizing that the United States required ongoing verification of any agreement. On human rights he said, "You suspended the Constitution in World War II, in the Civil War. Just as Vice President Ramirez told you, if you take away the cause, you take away the effect."

Michel commented, "When we get down to the bottom line, when we look to the south of us we hope to see a free people. We can't get around basic fundamental freedoms of press, worship, movement."

"That's why our people rebelled against Somoza."

"Cubans rebelled against Batista too. Castro has not been an improvement."

Then Wright made his point. "Do you think it is possible this is one moment in history where we might explore an agreement? Do you feel if there's a good-faith effort made by the U.S. we could reach one?"

"Yes," Tunnermann instantly replied.

Wright rose. As they shook hands, Tunnermann concluded, "It may surprise you, but in my three years here I have never had the opportunity of a conversation like this with any member of the United States government. I have never spoken with Ambassador Habib"—Philip Habib, who was the State Department's Central American special envoy. "I have had the pleasure of meeting Assistant Secretary Abrams, but that was not a dialogue. It was a monologue."

The meeting was over. Wright had liked what he heard.

Later that afternoon Wright and Michel sat down with Foley and Dante Fascell, the pro-contra Democrat who chaired the Foreign Affairs Committee; William Broomfield, the committee's ranking Republican; and Howard Baker, Loeffler, and Carlucci. The three White House officials insisted Reagan sincerely wanted a peace agreement. Foley emphasized, "There can be absolutely no linkage between this and contra aid. No connection! No implication that if this fails, the Speaker is expected to support contra aid."

The Republicans agreed. But Foley was worried. He knew that was not enough. If Wright went forward and failed, contra aid would surely pass. The group broke for a vote and, walking down the hall, Foley shook his head and warned, "We've got a situation here where if it's not handled right, we'll have a revolution in the House."

No issue mattered more than contra aid. Seventy-five members—30 percent of the Caucus—belonged to the anti-contra-aid task force; although the next vote was months away, fifty-three had attended the last meeting. Nothing mattered to the Caucus more than contra aid. Nothing. Already a revolution was brewing. Bonior did not know if he could support Wright in this. He had to try to stop it, and called Coelho and said they had to get together. Coelho said he was busy now. "This is serious," Bonior said. Coelho came.

The next morning Strauss confirmed the sincerity of Howard Baker. Wright read a draft treaty the Sandinistas had offered the United States to get a sense of their negotiating posture. And he got back on the phone to Central America. Every piece of information indicated a fluid, volatile situation. A joint Wright-Reagan peace proposal might serve as a catalyst to solidify an agreement.

Then Arias and Wright talked on the phone for twenty minutes. Mack listened with his eyes, his eyes absorbing everything, the slightest change of expression in Wright's face, the way he sat, the way he moved. Wright asked details about each country's position, about possible difficulties, about Arias's own plans. When Arias said the five presidents were considering waiting to see what happened in Congress on contra aid, Wright snapped, "*Don't wait for us.* That would destroy the window. As soon as the House votes, either you'll have all-out war in Nicaragua if aid passes, or the Sandinistas will be able to do whatever they want if it fails." He closed, saying, "I thank you. You've been very helpful. Blessed are the peacemakers. You're high on the list."

Wright had decided. He would proceed. He gathered his staff to plan the logistics of an announcement. Not one of them believed he should do this thing—one worried, "He'll have his head handed to him"—but not one of them advised against it. His staff didn't play that role. Their function was to execute his wishes. Once one aide had advised point-blank not to do something, and Wright had told him, *I didn't ask you in here for your counsel.*

Stopping Wright was up to Foley, Coelho, and Bonior, and maybe

Mack. They had to stop him. Quickly they put together a meeting of half a dozen key members with him, expecting those members to condemn any joint peace plan and pull Wright up short. The group included liberals George Miller; Mel Levine; and Matthew McHugh; Wayne Owens, who represented junior members; and David McCurdy, a key to moderate swing voters. McCurdy had sponsored the bipartisan proposal in 1985 only, he believed, to be betrayed by the White House; he now opposed contra aid.

Wright understood the purpose of the meeting. He knew also he could not get too far in front of the Caucus. He gave no indication that he had largely decided to proceed, telling them, "My antenna went up, that they're just trying to use me. I wanted to run it by you fellows. I am thinking we might do well if we offer a plan. The presidents are meeting next week. It would have to be quick."

His colleagues peppered him with questions. Wright knew El Salvador president Napoleón Duarte well. What did Duarte think? If he could accept the deal, would the Sandinistas? Duarte and Ortega hated each other. Was the White House sincere? If it was, why did it need Wright at all? Then they turned blunt.

"Of course, the administration sees this as an automatic lever to pull to get more contra aid," McCurdy said.

"Loeffler gave them a vote counter they didn't have before," Coelho added. "They know now they can't win in the House. Therefore, they want someone to pull their chestnuts out of the fire. You would be spectacular. The symbolism of the Speaker would be spectacular for them. If the Sandinistas turn the plan down, then Reagan's on TV pushing contra aid and we're trapped. There's enormous risk. For six and a half years the administration has cared about absolutely nothing except public relations. Nothing for the future. Just the immediate present, how to make Reagan look good."

But Owens wanted Wright to try it. Then Miller surprised Wright, surprised everyone. Wright, still angry over his budget impasse with Miller and anticipating his opposition, had not even wanted him at the meeting. Now Miller said almost sadly, "The White House has lied so much. Will they really hold hands with the Speaker? And the Sandinistas—a lot of things, even if not intentional, can lead us into a trap."

Miller stood up, this huge man who could be fierce and unpredictable and yet had a gentleness about him. He walked around the table, stood in front of the TV screen tuned to the floor, stared at it, stared at the floor as if envisioning all the passions this issue loosed, but understanding that beyond the floor was life and death. Finally he said, "But if there's a chance for peace, to stop the killing, you have to take the risk."

The meeting had not gone the way Foley, Coelho, Bonior, and Mack had wanted. There would be more meetings to dissuade Wright. Owens would not be invited to the next meeting—that was no accident. And Miller immediately changed his mind, becoming convinced it was a trap. But Wright had already seized on his endorsement. He informed Byrd and Senate Republican leader Bob Dole of what was happening. He was going ahead.

Wright was alone that week. His wife, Betty, was out of town and the house was being painted. Fumes made it almost uninhabitable. When he got home he invited Loeffler and Richard Pena, the Texas Hispanic with jet-black hair, expensive suits, and ardent anticommunism who had done his staff work on the Kissinger Commission, for dinner. Pena was important for another reason: extremely fluent in Spanish, he could listen on the phone when Wright spoke to Central Americans and pick up nuances Wright might miss. The three ordered a Domino's pizza and sat outside waiting for it on the deck, then eating it outside in the July evening, trading the smell of paint for the heavy languid smell of a gardenia bush which Wright had tended. Loeffler had brought some paper—the proposals written by Bernard Aronson months earlier. Wright and Pena looked at them, and Wright began to dictate his own thoughts. A peace plan began to take shape.

Even while Wright worked on a peace plan with the White House, new fronts were opening in his war with it on domestic policy. At issue were two completely separate, yet politically connected, proposals. Both involved procedure. Both involved power. They would determine whether Democrats could force the White House to accept their agenda.

The first issue was raising the limit on the national debt—the total debt the government owed. Congress set the "debt limit," and Treasury could issue bonds only so long as the national debt did not exceed it. With a budget deficit adding new debt each year, with the compounding effects of interest on the old debt, the national debt kept rising, and periodically Congress had to pass a law to raise the limit.

Passage was always difficult, even though the debt was an effect of policy, not a cause. Raising it simply allowed Treasury to borrow money to pay the government's obligations: to pay interest to bond-holders, or bills due to defense contractors, or Social Security checks to retirees. Still, the debt limit symbolized the deficit.

Earlier in the year, both Howard Baker and Jim Baker had met with the bipartisan House leadership in Wright's office and asked for help in passing a new debt limit that would be high enough to carry into the next administration. Wright had agreed—if Michel and the White House would get a majority of Republicans to vote for it.

Jim Baker had protested, "The majority party has a responsibility to govern."

Implicit in his comment was the assertion that the minority party should be allowed to be irresponsible. House Republicans had always overwhelmingly voted no on raising the debt limit.

With the GOP voting no, Democrats, particularly those with GOP members in neighboring districts, balked at voting yes. Wright had asked Baker about exerting pressure on Republicans by getting small-town bankers to call them. Baker had replied, "Educating the bankers would take too long. They like high interest rates."

Still, the limit *had* to be raised. In the past, reaching the debt limit had meant a worst case of government checks being delayed. But two years earlier Treasury had used gimmickry to temporarily evade the limit while it waited for Congress to act. To prevent any such evasion from recurring, Congress had stipulated that if the debt limit expired, a new lower limit would be in force.

Lowering the limit created an economic doomsday machine. It meant that if the debt limit was not raised, Treasury would not be able to issue new bonds to pay interest to bond-holders. The United States of America, for the first time in its history, would default.

Financial markets were already nervous, and a default could conceivably destroy the confidence of international investors in American government securities. That could send interest rates shooting upward, spark a market crash, and precipitate a worldwide depression. At the meeting with the two Bakers, Michel, and Lott, Foley had joked, "We shouldn't call the bill a debt extension. We should rename it the vote on worldwide recession, higher interest rates, unemployment, and collapse of the financial markets."

"That would be a close vote," Lott had deadpanned.

But it was serious business. The debt limit *had* to pass.

That transformed the debt limit into a hostage. Both Phil Gramm in the Senate and Buddy MacKay in the House seized it. "It's the only leverage I've got," MacKay said. "I'm not letting go of it."

The original Gramm-Rudman bill had been attached to an earlier debt limit. But the Supreme Court had ruled unconstitutional Gramm-Rudman's enforcement mechanism, the trigger of "sequestration," of automatic across-the-board spending cuts. MacKay and Gramm wanted to attach a new, constitutional Gramm-Rudman trigger to the debt limit. The White House and Wright both wanted a clean debt-limit extension without any amendments, but they lacked the votes to pass it.

The MacKay group was serious. Elsewhere, though, the hypocrisy level was climbing. The White House worried that fixing Gramm-Rudman could force it to choose between real, automatic cuts in defense spending or signing a tax bill. Despite all the administration rhetoric about cutting the deficit, it did not want Gramm-Rudman repaired. The House Republican leadership was looking for an escape hatch for them, and proposed limiting any automatic cuts to $18 billion. The deficit target written into the law required over $60 billion in cuts.

On July 29, as the conference on the Gramm-Rudman trigger and the debt limit was about to start, MacKay hosted the most intense meeting yet of his budget group. Foley and Rostenkowski had different ideas on how to proceed, and they presented their arguments in front of forty members.

Foley began, "Assume the Senate will act responsibly—"

"Why?" a member snorted. "Waiting for the Senate to help is like being on the *Titanic* and hearing the *Lusitania* is coming to rescue you."

His colleagues laughed; there was a sardonic, bitter quality to the laughter.

Foley went on, explaining how his idea on how to fix the Gramm-Rudman trigger trapped the White House in a box politically. The old trigger had been nullified by the Supreme Court because it called for a congressional agency, the General Accounting Office, to order the Executive Branch to implement the across-the-board spending cuts of "sequestration." That violated the separation-of-powers clause of the Constitution. Foley suggested rewriting the law to require the President to sign any order from GAO. That made the President the one who actually issued the order to the Executive Branch, thus eliminating the constitutional problems.

Suppose, he argued, that Congress passed a bill including both tax increases and spending cuts. If the bill became law, it would cut the deficit. Then there would be no automatic spending cuts, no sequestration.

But suppose the President vetoed it because of taxes. Almost immediately he would be given the sequestration order. If the President signed sequestration, the public would recognize he was responsible for cutting programs they liked. He would take the blame. And the public might be educated to the need for taxes. If the President rejected sequestration to avoid cutting defense spending, responsibility for the deficit would fall squarely and dramatically on his shoulders, exposing the emptiness of his rhetoric.

The other plan to make the Gramm-Rudman trigger constitutional—favored by Rostenkowski and MacKay—was to make OMB, a White House agency, pull the trigger. Foley argued that while that solved the constitutional problem it did not solve the political one: "Then the President can blame a Democratic Congress for sequestration. You will give Ronald Reagan the triumph of across-the-board cuts and no taxes. He can always cry national security and demand a supplemental [appropriation] for defense later."

Rostenkowski disagreed and shook his head vigorously. He believed that an automatic, unavoidable trigger which guaranteed cuts in defense spending would force Reagan to sign a tax bill. "I don't want to make a political statement," he said. "The bottom line is doing something about the deficit. If we give either the President or Congress the option of doing nothing that's what we'll get. Bring Reagan to the table! The only way to do that is to threaten to chop off the head of defense. I want to legislate in the hope the President will sign the bill. All I'm trying to do is make raising revenues as easy as possible. They weren't my idea. Tom and I talked. I want my proposal on the floor. Let the members vote."

Later, MacKay warned Coelho privately that if the Foley trigger came out of the debt-limit conference he would vote no. Even if it meant forcing a default by the United States government, even if it risked plunging the markets into chaos, he would vote no. And they had better act fast. The August recess was scheduled in nine days, for August 7. If the leadership asked for another short-term extension to carry into September, he would vote no. *Settle this thing now.* Or, he warned, "I'll gather all the votes I have and fight. We'll just grab ahold and see who wins."

The next day Foley's prediction that the Senate would act responsibly fell flat. With strong White House support, the Senate passed an amendment sponsored by Gramm. It fixed sequestration, but pushed the deficit problem onto the next President by setting the deficit targets so low that the first one could conceivably be met by cutting as little as $8–$10 billion. The early repayment of REA loans—a bookkeeping transaction rather than a real deficit cut—could account for $7 billion of that. But the next President would have to cut at least $45 billion a year.

While the Senate voted, Thursday, July 30, Rostenkowski visited Wright in his office and said the Gramm-Rudman conference—Rostenkowski would chair it—would lower the deficit target, and that he could raise $12 billion in taxes without a problem. Was that okay with Wright? Wright thought for a moment. The peace plan was consuming him. Passing a tax bill would be difficult. Very difficult. Democratic senator Fritz Hollings, the lost name on Gramm-Rudman-Hollings, had already suggested to Wright the same $12-billion tax figure, just before Wright left the Hill to have pizza with Loeffler and Pena. Wright told Rostenkowski it was all right. Then they laughed: they might let the Senate euchre them into that number in return for concessions elsewhere.

Rostenkowski walked out of Wright's office wearing a broad smile. He would chair the debt-limit conference and could breathe freely again. No one was looking over his shoulder anymore. Wright's power had limits. Wright had a new preoccupation.

After Rostenkowski left, Wright hosted lunch in H-201 for Foley, Michel, Howard Baker, Loeffler, and George Shultz. Though the secretary of State, Shultz had not been included before, and he was leery of any foreign-policy initiative that came out of the White House—especially one which involved Congress. He looked askance at Loeffler, whom he did not know well and whom he considered a politician lacking substantive knowledge of the issue. Such a combination could be dangerous in foreign policy. Wright and Foley at least knew the issue. But he listened.

Wright repeated that any peace proposal had to stand alone, independent of contra aid. No "two-track policy of subsidizing war while talking peace." For the first time, the United States would advance a peace proposal that existed "on its own, without a club in the closet."

Wright worried that the pride of the Central Americans alone could force rejection if the plan were accompanied by a threat.

Shultz disagreed, arguing that the only reason the Sandinistas were willing to negotiate was military pressure from the contras. Negotiations were fine, as long as military pressure did not let up.

Shultz's statement worried Foley. He repeated, "There is no linkage between this initiative and contra aid. *Absolutely none.* Failure of the initiative does not imply our support for contra aid."

Baker and Loeffler jumped in, reassuring, reassuring, trying to sink the hook into Wright, promising that Reagan would not propose military aid until late September at the earliest, giving a peace proposal time to show progress. Then Foley demanded to know why they had come to Wright anyway. Why did they need him at all?

"The President doesn't have any credibility," Loeffler explained. "If the President made the proposal it would be dismissed as empty rhetoric."

The comment made sense to Wright. And a decision had to be made, *now.* If he did not act soon there would be no point in acting at all. The Central American foreign ministers would get together in four days. The presidents would meet in one week. Any initiative had to occur before then. He was determined to proceed.

But he was alone. Not a single member or aide close to him agreed with him. That afternoon Coelho, Bonior, and Mack sat down in H-210, Wright's office off the floor. Nothing any of them had learned had altered their conviction that this joint peace proposal was a trap, a terrible trap which would end up with the passage of military aid to the contras and which could destroy Wright's speakership. They decided to meet for breakfast with Wright the next morning and confront him. No Tommy Loeffler leading the cheers. No outsiders who might act as a wild card. No one except Wright, Foley, Coelho, Bonior, and senior staff.

Wright meanwhile kept looking for support. He found little. That evening a close friend pulled him aside at a fund-raiser for Jim Howard. While lobbyists watched from a distance, afraid to intrude, the friend, intense and worried, asked, "Have you set up any objective milestones to measure Baker's or Loeffler's word by?"

"I am relying primarily on the word of Baker," Wright replied.

"Isn't that a thin reed for something like this? Mr. Speaker, please don't let your vision for the speakership interfere with your judgment."

Wright's eyes flashed and he smiled his tight dangerous smile. He was angry and unmoved, and left the fund-raiser for dinner with Craig Raupe at Germaine's, a Eurasian restaurant in Georgetown and Raupe's favorite. Raupe also was leery. After dinner, Wright, with his wife out of town, went to see Byrd, who lived less than a mile from him in McLean, Virginia. Byrd was the first person to react positively. Wright went home late, and stayed awake much of the night.

In the morning came the breakfast.

The House was not in session. It was a summer Friday, July 31. Coelho showed up in jeans. So did Mack. Immediately after breakfast they would leave with their families for Bethany Beach, three hours away on the Atlantic. They needed to relax. The Capitol was still, deserted, empty even of tourists. It was early. The corridor by Wright's office dark, the Rayburn Room dark.

Inside H-201, a lone black waiter silently served cheese omelets, bacon, biscuits, juice, and coffee. No one wanted to start the discussion. By coincidence, Lee Hamilton, chairman of the Iran-contra Committee, had written an op-ed piece in that day's *New York Times* and an aide had distributed copies of it. He called for a diplomatic initiative founded on a cease-fire, no contra aid, and improvements inside Nicaragua. Reading it gave people an excuse not to talk. This was tense, difficult, for them all. Wright sat at one end of the table, the same table at which he had sat with the Nicaraguan ambassador. Foley sat to his right, Coelho and Bonior to his left, the few aides at the far end.

"To be blunt," Coelho finally began, "Tommy Loeffler's a paid lobbyist. I'm very skeptical. You're such a valuable commodity, Mr. Speaker. I'm afraid. I just don't trust them. They've been playing the same game for six and a half years."

"My position is this," Wright said. "I remember executions in Cuba, in China. David, you said the other day there was no indication there'd be a bloodbath, but I think some Sandinistas are capable of it. Where are we as a party if we beat contra aid and those terrible things happen? If there's any real chance for peace, we have to take that chance. We're always talking about consultations with the administration. Now they're consulting seriously. Are we supposed to say we didn't mean it?"

They went back and forth, back and forth, over the same ground. For thirty minutes, Bonior said nothing, only stared, silently, at the plate before him. Now he spoke. "Correct me if I'm wrong. Shultz had no give yesterday. No sign of any change. He was still talking about military pressure as well as negotiations. They still plan to ask for contra aid in September. What Lee Hamilton is doing, that's what we ought to be doing."

"Write articles?" Wright asked disdainfully. "Is that what we ought to be doing? Talk about peace instead of doing something about it?" Glaring at Bonior, he continued, "People who are interested in peace do something about it."

Bonior, a Vietnam-era veteran and antiwar activist ever since, looked coldly back at Wright. Even more coldly he replied, "Mr. Speaker, I've spent most of my political life working for peace. I don't need someone telling me I have no interest in it. I don't think if you go forward it means peace, Mr. Speaker. I think the initiative will fail and they'll be able to say, 'Look, we tried the Speaker's plan, it went nowhere, now give us the aid,' and they'll have the votes. I think the initiative will mean war, Mr. Speaker—three hundred million dollars' worth of war."

The table was still.

"I didn't mean to be combative, Dave," Wright said finally, softly. "It comes down to trust."

"Has anyone seen the *Washington Times* story?" asked Foley's aide George Kundanis. The *Washington Times* was owned by the Reverend Moon's Unification Church, the "Moonies" who sold flowers in airports; it was ultraconservative and few Democrats read it. They were reluctant to give Moon twenty-five cents. No one but Kundanis had read it. He sent for a copy. A page quickly brought it. Foley read aloud a front-page story based on an interview with National Security Adviser Carlucci: Reagan would call for $300 million in aid, " 'after Congress adjourns the first week in August.' "

"When we're scattered and helpless," Coelho interjected.

Foley continued: " 'We need a bipartisan foreign policy and I think things are now moving,' Mr. Carlucci said . . . But President Reagan intends to take his case to Congress, use his veto powers during the recess, and 'press his own foreign policy forcefully.' "

As Wright listened, his face first sagged with disappointment, then tightened with anger. *Veto? Press his own foreign policy forcefully? $300 million in contra aid in September?*

"Get Carlucci," Wright snapped to Mack.

Mack dialed the White House, asked for him, and nodded. Wright picked up the phone, waited on hold while Carlucci's secretary played a petty power game, then said, "Frank, how are you? I'm meeting with Byrd this afternoon. Could Baker come by? Good. Now there's this story in the *Washington Times* . . . Their 'interpretation'? . . . Oh . . . Misquote? . . . Uh-huh." As the conversation continued, people around the table smiled; they could hear the peace plan disintegrating. The room grew lighter with the release of tension, the bursting forth of smiles.

Wright hung up. He was more disappointed than angry. "At the end he started talking about negotiations with contra aid too, just in case. These people are playing too many tracks. They want a *Good Housekeeping* Seal of Approval on bootleg whiskey."

Foley and Coelho attacked the administration's double-dealing. A bitterness, even a sudden hatred, for the administration coursed through the room like a wave, then dissipated. Political games were one thing; setting up the Speaker of the House was another. Foley added that nothing happened quickly in Central America and no one was speculating about any progress to be made when the presidents met in six days. If an agreement were close, speculation would be in the press. The administration would drag this thing out, drag it out, then say they needed more contra aid. The Speaker would be left holding the bag. Through all this Wright sat silently, his thoughts his own, private.

Breakfast had lasted over two hours. Coelho and Mack got up to go to the beach. Looking at the way they were dressed, Foley kidded them. Some of the staff stopped for a moment in the dark Rayburn Room, sat on a sofa in the coolness. It had the feel of a museum almost, cool, dark, a deserted museum. And of history. Coelho saw them and came over for a moment.

"Saved by the *Washington Times*. The irony. They don't think anyone on the Democratic side reads it."

"They don't. Except for George."

"People think the Speaker doesn't listen to anyone," Coelho added. "He does listen. This proved that. Bonior will be all right. He's been called every name in the book. He doesn't take kindly to having his sincerity questioned, but he'll be all right."

The Speaker's joint initiative with the President seemed over. Dead.

The next day Wright was leaving for Texas. They all could relax now. But Wright wasn't relaxing. He was thinking.

The peace initiative had died with the phone call to Carlucci. An hour later Costa Rican ambassador Guido Fernandez breathed it back to life. Just before noon he walked into Wright's office for a final conversation before returning home to prepare for the Central American summit. They talked for forty-five minutes, and Wright showed him a one-page memo that outlined the basic aspects of his proposal. Fernandez was enthusiastic and said if Wright and Reagan jointly endorsed such a plan, it could well spur the Central Americans to an agreement. *If the five countries reached a peace agreement,* Wright thought, *what difference did Carlucci's dissembling make?*

But if the five countries did not agree, he would be isolated from his Caucus, and possibly even from Foley, Coelho, and Bonior. Years earlier he had played a small, serendipitous role in Egyptian president Anwar Sadat's historic first trip to Israel, which had led to peace. He had been in Egypt and become convinced of Sadat's sincerity, then traveled to Israel and carried that message. When Sadat arrived, security forces emptied the King David Hotel of all except the Sadat and Wright parties. The memory of Sadat's enormous gesture had riveted itself in Wright's mind. Sadat had brought peace between Israel and Egypt, and had been killed for it. If Wright went forward and failed, more than half of the Democratic Caucus would become his permanent enemy. *So what?* What risk was that compared to Sadat's?

He could minimize that risk. He had been willing to rely on Baker's word. That had been naive. Carlucci had made him leery. Before proceeding further, he would demand evidence of White House good faith. National Security Council staff had asked him to give the Sandinistas a deadline of September 30 to respond to an initiative to prevent their dragging out negotiations, keeping Congress from voting contra aid, and starving the contras out. That had made sense and he had agreed. He could demand that the White House honor the same deadline—the White House would not call for contra aid until after September 30, nor make rhetorical attacks on the Sandinistas.

It was midafternoon. He left his office alone, followed at a discreet distance by a Capitol policeman, walked down the silent corridor past

H-201 toward the Senate, entered the Rotunda. The great frescoed iron dome soared above him; a burst of light and activity surrounded him. Tourists stared as he walked past; he smiled back, shook a hand of someone who said he was from Fort Worth, and then reentered the cool quiet of closed-off corridors on his way to Byrd's office, where he briefed Byrd, Dole, and Sam Nunn.

They were receptive, but he remained uneasy and returned to his office. It was a strange mood for him; optimistic, a doer, he believed he controlled his own fate. This was beyond his control. He could not make peace happen; at best he could create a structure which allowed it to happen. For the moment, he went back into himself.

People called him a loner. Perhaps he was. But this wasn't something one asked others about. He had to search his heart. *His* heart, not others' advice. At the center of him his ambition and his values and his loneliness came together. Somewhere in the center of him lay the answer.

He wanted to be around the few people he could be himself with, who he knew cared about him and not his power. His wife was still away. He called his sister Mary Connell and invited her to dinner. She, the poet who had once dreamed of the Nobel Prize for herself, had published three books of poetry but now wrote fund-raising letters for the DCCC. They both still had their dreams; only Wright's were far closer to realization. They ate at the Four Seasons Hotel in Georgetown; the restaurant was elegant, and empty. It was summer in Washington. Mary laughed, thankful that at least no one would come up to them complaining about a Social Security check. Wright told her everything that had happened and mentioned Cardinal Miguel Obando y Bravo as someone who might end up serving as a mediator between the contras and Sandinistas. She was a natural rebel against all authority and complained, "He's a conservative."

Suddenly Wright exploded at her, his face reddening, his words lashing her. She was stunned. This angry, powerful man of the world was not the brother she knew. Suddenly she realized how much pressure he was under, how isolated he felt, how uncertain he was, how much he needed support. She had never seen him under such pressure. *For God's sake, wouldn't someone tell him he was right?*

It was ten days since Loeffler had first walked into Wright's office. Lord, oh, Lord, he was tired. And yet, under it all, despite the pressure and the fear and the risk, lay something untouched and serene in him. He had decided.

Over the weekend Wright reviewed the peace proposal word by word and Pena carried to him White House requests. On Monday morning his draft was distributed at a ten-thirty meeting he called in the Speaker's Dining Room. It included administration officials, the bipartisan House leadership, the Senate Democratic leadership, and key chairmen and ranking House Republicans. Wright had expected several Republican senators, but only Bob Dole attended. The administration had done the inviting of GOP senators and, in order to exclude Jesse Helms, the conservative ranking member of Foreign Relations who might blow up any tentative agreement, had asked only Dole.

Wright got to the point quickly and his language was uncharacteristically blunt: "Our apprehension has been that if we went forward, some in the administration would not be in earnest. One week after we launch an initiative, the President would go on TV and say how bad the Sandinistas are and we need $300 million to fight them. If that happened I'd be screwed. All of us who said we'd work with you would be screwed. It would be like me saying, 'Come, let us reason together' while I kick you in the balls. Certainly the Sandinistas would reject a peace overture then. Tom Foley and I have repeated over and over that there must be absolutely no linkage between this proposal and contra aid. The White House wants us to join in a bipartisan initiative. I would like to. If I do, it's not two tracks. Not diplomacy and military pressure. It's one track. Diplomacy. If you want me to embrace you, support us. We've got a September 30 deadline for the Sandinistas. I'd like a commitment from the White House you won't go on a rhetorical binge between now and September 30. If we go forward together, then we just talk peace—*peace*—until then. Now that's my speech."

There was silence. After a moment Shultz and then Michel responded; both talked of the need for military leverage against the Sandinistas.

Wright disagreed. "I would rather have our heart and soul and effort put into a peace plan than have us mobilized against each other, lining up opposing armies in the Congress, and approve or reject contra aid by six, eight, ten votes, with no consensus. If for once we can unite, speak for the United States, it could have an electric effect on Central America. But that effect would be obliterated if the President or other people make speeches condemning one another or talking contra aid. It would cast doubt on our good faith. The President is key to that."

Dick Cheney objected, but Shultz read aloud the last sentence of Wright's draft which stipulated that if the deadlines were not met "the parties . . . would be free to pursue such actions as they deem necessary to protect their national interest." He was satisfied that that meant the threat of contra aid still hung over the Sandinistas.

Foley interrupted. "We're on the verge of a very dangerous misunderstanding. If the assumption is, in the absence of Nicaragua's agreement, then Democrats will support aid, that's a mistake. We must reiterate as we have from the start: this is a peace plan. It has nothing to do with whether contra aid passes or not. The separation is absolute and antiseptic."

Henry Hyde countered, "I'll just make the point that if your enthusiasm for no aid goes, say, from ten to seven, that will be very useful."

It was a telling point. That was precisely the fear the Democrats had. If the plan failed, swing Democrats would vote for aid. Coelho pursed his lips unhappily.

Then Lott complained, "This entails risk for us too. We're not without risk if it entails pulling our punches. The trap will have trapped us."

The trap will have trapped us. Bonior and Foley exchanged a glance. Wright did not like it either and said, "We need to be real candid with one another. All I'm saying is, let's give this our best effort and try to make it work. If it doesn't, I'll follow the processes of the law and schedule a vote on contra aid."

Shultz said he would meet with the President that afternoon. But he added, "It is time to decide."

Wright closed the meeting with one request: "It would be better not to say anything to the press."

Nothing had leaked yet in Washington, but that morning newspapers reported that Nicaragua was proceeding with plans to acquire Soviet MIGs. The Sandinista junta included a war faction. Wright believed the war faction had let that story out to kill the chance for a peace initiative by arousing U.S. conservatives. He called Nicaraguan vice president Sergio Ramirez to complain. Pena talked with Central Americans involved in preparations for the presidents' meeting; despite the MIG story, they were hopeful.

Wright's leadership colleagues, accepting the inevitability of his pro-

336 · JOHN M. BARRY

ceeding, grudgingly signed on. Both to protect him and minimize the damage of failure, Coelho beseeched him to allow them to orchestrate the agreement. Foley would take the lead in negotiating for him with the White House. "Tom's got more questions than they have answers," Coelho said. Foley wanted to do it. It would raise his profile and consolidate his own position inside the House, insulate Wright, and force the White House to give the best possible terms. Wright agreed.

At six-fifteen that night Shultz and Howard Baker sat back down with the bipartisan House leadership in H-201. No commitments had been made yet, no deal finalized, but they were going forward. Shultz and House Republicans picked over Wright's draft.

"On your point number one regarding the security interests of the U.S., can we add 'threat to the region'?"

"Yes," Wright said.

"This doesn't mention naval bases," complained Cheney.

"Why not change 'landing facilities' to 'facilities'?" Wright suggested.

"Do we imply by this that before a cease-fire the contras and Sandinistas must meet?"

"Not necessarily face-to-face. They could use a go-between."

They came to a sticking point over language demanding free elections. Republicans wanted to specify a presidential election. "The heart of the whole issue is whether Sandinistas will yield power peacefully," Cheney said.

"You want to tell them to amend their constitution," Wright argued. "I want them to live up to it."

Coelho seconded him: "Dick, we're sitting here as if these people are our subjects. This is a marketing tool. We're trying to get them to the table."

They compromised on language calling for "an electoral commission [to] be established to assure regular elections open to free participation by all."

After two hours Shultz said, "It's settled. Numbers two and three we'll leave the way the Speaker wrote them. As for some of the ambiguities in here, that's not necessarily bad."

That was it. The Democrats were nervous, nervous as hell.

Bonior: "I think it must be made clear that the Speaker is taking an incredible risk. You've got to quiet things down. Your own troops are out there running vicious anti-Sandinista ads. They should disappear."

Foley: "Before everyone signs off, I suggest a day to think about this."

Coelho: "There are people on our side we have to talk to. We can't spring this on them."

Lott objected. "I thought from this morning you wanted to do this."

Loeffler: "I don't want to cut off debate but I recommend the bank be closed. The clock is ticking."

Baker: "We should do it as quickly as possible. I think the plan ought to be announced up here, by whomever you designate, and have the President come up here."

"The Speaker is symbolic and you know it," Coelho countered. "That's why you're here. Before we do any of this, the two symbolic leaders should have a face-to-face and see what each means by this, not what the Secretary of State and chief of staff mean."

"All right," Baker said. "Also, I have enough of the senator left in me to say we can't leave the Senate out of this entirely."

Wright agreed. "Howard's got a point." *I'm against any deal I'm not a part of.* "People will be supportive if they are consulted in advance."

They worried about the press, but so far only one reporter had noticed Shultz's car and asked a cop who the Secretary of State was meeting.

It was late. The meeting broke up. Every Democrat was desperately concerned. "This is crazy," said one. "I don't want to undercut him but it's crazy."

Wright walked outside into the dark heavy August night and glanced back at the Capitol. It was ablaze with light, the white marble almost luminescent. The immensity of the building struck him, an immensity that went deeper than its size. Its secret narrow stairways, walled with blocks of rough stone as cool as a dungeon, spiraled into the root of the earth, and its simple strong lines, the thick, straight Corinthian columns, reached backward into history. It was the grandest building in the nation, white and shining, and for all its grandeur was unintimidating. Its cavities and openings and hidden private places welcomed. It was more than a building. The night was quiet and still. A jogger was running through the plaza, now empty of parked cars. Wright's driver was waiting for him. They drove home.

*   *   *

The plan agreed upon Monday evening, August 3, began:

A PEACE PLAN

Recognizing that the Central American presidents are soon to meet to discuss the issues involved in achieving peace in Central America, the United States desires to make known its views on certain of the basic elements that need to be included in a peace plan.

With respect to Nicaragua, the United States has three legitimate concerns for the well-being of the hemisphere:

1. That there be no Soviet, Cuban or Communist block [*sic*] base established in Nicaragua . . .

2. That Nicaragua pose no military threat to its neighbor countries . . .

3. That the Nicaraguan government respect the basic human rights of its people including political rights guaranteed in the Nicaraguan constitution . . . free speech, free press, religious liberty, and a regularly established system of free, orderly elections.

Beyond this, the United States has no right to influence or determine the identity of the political leaders of Nicaragua nor the social and economic system of the country. . . .

The plan called for an immediate cease-fire in place, the establishment of a reconciliation commission, sanctions against both the contras and the Nicaraguan government if either tried to stall past the September 30 deadline, and the involvement of the United States in "bilateral discussions with the governments of the region, including the government of Nicaragua, concerning security issues." The word "bilateral" would later become key.

Tuesday, August 4, began with the biweekly breakfast with the Senate Democratic leadership, this time in the Lyndon Johnson Room just off the Senate chamber. Summer recess was scheduled for Friday. Virtually all of official Washington would empty; members, staff, lobbyists, Hill reporters, all would disappear. They were all restless for recess. Everyone was.

Byrd wondered about keeping Congress in session until the debt-limit Gramm-Rudman conference was settled. "If that happened," Foley said, "it would take every cop on the Hill to protect the Speaker from the members."

They all laughed. Wright said he would see Reagan that afternoon and invited Byrd to join him. Byrd noted that it was the Senate's turn to make the five-minute response to Reagan's weekly radio talk. He offered it to Wright, to talk about his peace plan.

"That's gracious of you," Wright replied, "but it would be better if it were broader than just a Wright initiative. It would be better if you"— Wright inclined his head toward California senator Alan Cranston— "or Alan did it."

With all his southern courtliness Byrd declined. Cranston said nothing.

Wright was isolated, all right. They were willing to let him hang in the wind. Wright pressed his lips together, then thanked Byrd for the time.

Coelho sat silent, sullen, his arms crossed. Bonior, too, was silent. There seemed no way to stop this. By coincidence, the contra leaders were in town to begin the push for more aid. A House aide whispered, "Maybe the contras will blow this up for us."

Immediately after breakfast Wright left to brief the task force against contra aid in H-324. He did not expect to win their support. He had to win their tolerance. If they attacked him publicly, made him obviously isolated, it would undermine the plan. Long tables took the place of the rows of chairs laid out for the whip meeting. Twenty-five members listened intently to his presentation.

He finished. A member asked, "Has the President signed on?"

"I'll see him this afternoon."

"The White House is signed on but the President doesn't know anything about it yet," one member snorted.

"I'll say one thing, you've got guts," another member said. Another: "I appreciate that you're motivated by a desire to stop the killing."

But then the criticism, ominous criticism, poured on him. This was the heart of the Caucus, the most active members, the most respected, the hardest working, here, in this room, and they tore into him. Perhaps five supported him, and another three or four had yet to make up their minds. The rest attacked. He stayed longer than scheduled, much longer, listening, listening, listening, answering, his voice never losing its patient, gentle tone. Finally he had to leave to brief senators. The task force broke up, many of the members steaming.

Wright was forty-five minutes late getting to Byrd's office where key senators of both parties sat. Senators did not like waiting, for anyone.

By the time he arrived, Shultz had already gone over the plan—and made a crucial change which Wright found out about later. Wright and the senators talked for an hour. Then he returned to his office.

Waiting back in H-201 was the Nicaraguan ambassador. The Sandinistas had earlier been given a draft of the plan. What was their response? If this thing wasn't going to work, he could still back off. A waiter served lunch while Wright's impatience conflicted with the gracious formalities of diplomacy. Tunnermann said his government believed the plan had "positive aspects."

Wright had put his ass on the line for that? For "positive aspects"?

After the lunch he walked onto the floor. Members clustered around him, ten, fifteen, twenty, talking to him, asking him questions. A few rows away liberals from the earlier meeting were also clustered, their hands speaking, pointing fingers at one another, a fist pounding. It was midafternoon. Suddenly Wright had other problems.

His planned meeting with Reagan was postponed. Reagan had a doctor's appointment. *A doctor's appointment? Interfering with something of this magnitude? Bullshit!* Something was going on.

And the press had gotten into the story.

For two weeks Wright had been involved in this issue. Not a word had gotten into the press. Gradually, more and more members of the House had learned of it, and they, too, had kept quiet. Every day the leadership and their staff had expected to open the paper and see everything they were doing on the front page, but it had not happened. Then Shultz had briefed a handful of senators. Within minutes after that meeting, the information leaked—supposedly from Connecticut Democratic senator Chris Dodd—and within an hour of the meeting the wires were moving stories about a peace initiative.

And the stories were wrong. Or if they weren't wrong, then Wright was in trouble.

Wright retreated from the floor to his office, sat down with his staff, and was slapped with stories off the wires. UPI's Helen Thomas was quoting a White House source that Reagan would announce a peace plan soon, and that it was designed to make contra aid more palatable to the Hill. Marlin Fitzwater, the official White House spokesman, said the peace plan "is tied to the [contra aid] request. Peace and funding are all tied together."

"If that newspaper story gets to any of those countries the plan's in trouble," Pena worried. "It's just devastating for that story to run. No one I talked to at the White House ever said one word about linkage."

Wright called Will Ball, who explained that Fitzwater had been kept in the dark about developments and had been asked the question before being briefed on the new line. It would be corrected. "Well, Will," Wright said, "I think I know how John the Baptist felt when they served his head on a platter."

Another aide walked in with a tape from ABC News of Sam Donaldson interviewing Shultz. Shultz was saying, "In the meantime . . . the contras will give a good account of themselves." Then Donaldson concluded, "This probably means more aid but not necessarily peace."

Wright watched it in silence, then hissed, "These guys aren't playing straight. *Get me Baker.*"

For the first time all year while still working, Wright poured himself a drink. Then he had a second.

Howard Baker, Loeffler, and Ball said they were trying to put out the same fires that Wright was. Just hang on. But it was a rough ride. The flow of accurate information had not kept up with events.

Reporters were calling sources. But this plan had been so tightly held few knew about it. Defense Secretary Caspar Weinberger learned of it only from the first press reports; he had exploded, and demanded that the President see him before Wright. (That was why Wright's trip to the White House had been postponed.) The few administration officials who had been dealing with Wright were at the highest levels, so high that the media believed that they were only spouting an official version of events, and that the story lay elsewhere. Fitzwater's confusion seemed to confirm that.

Most of the media's usual administration sources did not know what was happening but would not admit ignorance; one reason they talked to the press was to feel important, and ignorance of something this significant undercut their own importance. These sources confirmed this was part of a grand strategy to win contra aid. Others who did know the details purposely said the same thing; they were manipulating the media to destroy the chance that Nicaragua might take the initiative seriously. If Nicaragua rejected the plan, the worst fears of the liberals would materialize: Bonior had said, *I think the initiative will fail and*

they'll be able to say, "Look, we tried the Speaker's plan, it went nowhere, now give us the aid," and they'll have the votes.

That night Wright's sister Mary called him to say, "I'm glad the President finally got you to go along on a peace proposal."

The pressure had destroyed his sense of humor. "Thanks a lot," he snapped, slamming the phone down. She called back and said soothing words to the answering machine, knowing he was listening, until he picked up.

At breakfast the next morning, Wednesday, August 5, his staff released their tension by trading Texas political stories. One quoted Gib Lewis, speaker of the Texas House, as advising one young state senator to go to funeral homes every day and sign the register. "It's great public relations," Lewis supposedly told him. "The folks read it and say, 'I didn't know Daddy knew the senator. Isn't it nice that he stopped by?' Dead men tell no tales." Another story involved another state legislator, just elevated from the state house to the state senate, who told a caucus of his new colleagues, "I know you've heard I'd introduce a bill for anyone for $50. I understand that I'm in the senate now. The decorum here is different. I promise I won't do it for less than $500."

Wright did not seem to be listening. There was no eagerness in him. This thing had hold of him now; it was pulling him along wherever it went. He was caught in the momentum like everyone else. He was no longer in control of it. The flood of newspaper stories seemed to be saying that. It was too late to stop it.

The foreign ministers were meeting in Guatemala now; soon the presidents would arrive. His aide Wilson Morris reported, "The word from Guatemala is fairly positive."

Wright nodded absently.

"Will Ball just called," Mack said. "They're having an awful time with Weinberger."

"What about this Gingrich thing?" Wright asked. Gingrich had just accused Wright of improperly interfering with savings and loan regulators. Everyone shrugged it off. Gingrich also wanted a vote to force the ethics committee to reopen an investigation of Fernand St Germain. New allegations of serious wrongdoing by him had surfaced, and the committee had already found that St Germain had violated House rules, misreporting by a million dollars and seeking special favors for banks

he had invested in, and federal law had recommended taking no disciplinary action. Ethics chairman Julian Dixon wanted to fight Gingrich's move on the floor; he had the votes. Wright said fine and rose. He was on his way to see the President.

"I care about Shultz's word and Baker's word," he said as he left. "I don't trust Reagan. Even if he means something when he says it, who knows if he'll remember. I don't know if I'd feel any better if he swears an oath."

The House Republican Conference was meeting at that same moment Wednesday morning. Loeffler was there, along with Elliott Abrams and NSC aide José Sorzano. The Wright-Reagan plan committed the administration to accepting the Sandinista government if they respected democratic liberties. That acceptance of a Marxist state on the continent incited the conservatives, some of whom believed that Ollie North had turned around the vote on contra aid, to accuse the White House of a sellout. The day before, while the administration and Wright were talking, the contra leaders had been in both Michel's office and the White House. No one had informed them of the peace plan. That was outrageous! Loeffler briefed his former colleagues, and Abrams said, "If you're for democracy, this plan will bring it—but only as a contract, not as a negotiating position." After fifteen minutes Michel and Loeffler left to join Wright at the White House. As Loeffler walked by, Jack Kemp called him a communist. Kemp was joking. Barely. Abrams stayed for forty minutes more, going over details. Not one House Republican voiced support for the plan.

In the Oval Office Reagan, Wright, Shultz, Baker, Foley, Michel, Byrd, and Dole—the most senior members of the United States government—gathered. Wright was handed a copy of a twenty-one-point memorandum prepared by the White House at Weinberger's insistence. Reagan said, "This is our interpretation of what the agreement means."

"It doesn't need any interpretation," Wright replied, barely glancing at it. "It speaks for itself."

They began to discuss just what they were agreeing to do. Reagan still wanted contra aid of some kind, even if peace was reached. "You can't expect them to go out and get a job," he said. It was a legitimate point, but they agreed once again that the Democrats had made no commitment, of any kind, to support contra aid, of any kind. And

Reagan agreed with Wright's demand not to criticize the Sandinistas or to ask for contra aid until after September 30. Wright promised not to use the Rules Committee to block or manipulate a vote on his request.

They disagreed over when the Sandinistas would have to hold elections, but Reagan suggested, "A little confusion over that isn't bad."

The meeting ended. Outside the White House, the press surrounded people as they exited. Wright, for a change, liked what he was hearing. The day before, Michel had talked of Reagan's desire to "eradicate" the Sandinistas. Today Michel said, "Let's give it a chance."

But riding back to the Capitol Wright read the twenty-one points. Most had never been raised in any discussion with him. Worse were the points that had been discussed. One point said that the administration assumed Ortega would not be allowed to finish his term in office, implying new presidential elections. Yet Shultz and Baker had specifically agreed to avoid any reference to that in the plan. Wright's jaw tightened as he read further. Point number nineteen contradicted the President's promise of moments earlier: it stipulated that he could publicly condemn the Sandinistas and call for contra aid if they had not accepted the plan within two weeks, instead of two months. From his car phone Wright called Baker, didn't reach him, arrived at the Capitol, and stormed up the stairs to his ceremonial office—which was closer than his personal office—and called again. His voice was calm. And cold. "If that's your interpretation, all bets are off. I will feel betrayed. I have said repeatedly in meetings that the White House had to cool its rhetoric. I have made a big point of it and thought it had been accepted. Then I see this thing written on a piece of paper I haven't ever seen before, never heard referred to before."

Baker told him the White House needed it, they had to have it, or their right wing would do everything possible to sabotage the deal: "Kemp called me three times, cussed me out, said, 'You sold them out, you sold them out!' " They needed this twenty-one-point thing to reassure the right wing and stop that kind of talk. Baker swore it would not leak. No one was saying Wright had agreed to it anyway, and no one would say that.

Foley walked in. He was upset about the twenty-one points, too, pointing out that it interpreted a "communist" base as a Sandinista one. "I'm afraid if they start circulating this thing to their hard right,

the right will come back and say, 'You promised this. Now do it.' "
He shook his head. "I guess now it's a test of their sincerity."

Wright hung up. Baker was offering him precious little to cling to.
For an instant he thought, *It isn't too late to blow the whole thing up*.

But it was. He turned on the television. CNN was going live to the
White House for an announcement by the President. Wryly he wondered what had happened to Baker's earlier suggestion to have the
Speaker make the announcement, to have the President come up to
the Hill for it.

"The plan's out there now," Wright said. "It's got a life of its own."
Maybe they had trapped him after all. He turned to an aide. "We need
a strategy to handle the press."

Reagan and Shultz were on CNN now. Coelho walked into the room.
Reagan made a statement, took no questions, and handed the microphone to Shultz, who hailed the "great leadership from the Speaker."
Asked about skepticism among Democrats who thought the administration was only maneuvering for more aid, Shultz said, "There is
skepticism among people with varying shades of opinion. This is not a
ploy. The President believes in it, and the Speaker believes in it. What
we need now is to do everything we can to bring about peace."

CHAPTER 13

It was still Wednesday, August 5. Soon after Wright returned from the White House, Mike Lowry, chairman of the liberal Democratic Study Group, the DSG, and known for his temper, grabbed him as they walked onto the floor and laid into him. *This thing was playing out exactly the way everyone had warned Wright it would. What was he going to do about it?* Les AuCoin, an Oregon liberal, exploded and would not calm down. Jim Moody and Chuck Schumer, two mainstream, activist members, were disgusted: the White House was making a fool of Wright.

Wright understood his isolation and the distrust he had engendered. He would devote the entire day to meetings, one after another after another after another, each with a discrete element of the Caucus, to stroke and massage and reassure colleagues. The first meeting, in H-201 where so much of the negotiating over the plan had occurred, mattered the most: it was a small core group of the anti-contra task force. Just before entering he pulled Foley aside and said gently, "Tom, will you explain things to them? They see you as having the same concerns that they do. I'm not sure how they see me."

Foley nodded. They sat down and he began, "I want to make it clear that we considered whether this might be a sham."

He explained exactly what the Speaker and the President had agreed to, then asked for support: "It's certain that we can't fight among ourselves."

"Did the President indicate any change in his attitude?"

"No," Foley replied.

"What do you think?"

"We'll find out."

"We can say we did everything on our part to move peace," Wright said. "That's our position."

Russo banged one fist into his palm. "We need a core group of four or five guys to go on the floor right now and spread out. We've got to say, 'Jim Wright took an enormous risk, he did it on behalf of the country, and at issue is Reagan's credibility.' "

Foley agreed: "Play it 'The Speaker took a risk for peace. What's the President going to do?' "

Use the press. If everyone said the same thing, if every Democrat in the House made the same point, they had leverage.

"One-minutes," Bonior said. "We need to make one-minutes today, repeating and repeating, 'Ronald Reagan's credibility is on the line.' "

If that message went out, the burden would fall on the White House to demonstrate its good faith. Develop a groundswell of cynicism. *Force* the White House to act in good faith. Intensify the scrutiny.

But resistance and anger remained. One man complained, "If we end up getting snookered and our only defense is that they didn't negotiate properly, that will kill us when we vote."

"I agreed with you yesterday," another member interrupted, "but that debate is over."

"There's a major piece on the floor right now," Russo said. Gingrich's call for a new ethics investigation of St Germain was being voted on. Some members were listening to the debate, and all of them would soon arrive to vote. "We ought to get out there."

The meeting broke up with the members heading for the floor. Wright retreated to his office. A call was waiting from Fernandez, the Costa Rican ambassador, in Guatemala. It was a brief but crucial conversation. Fernandez asked Wright to send down a representative. Wright would send his former aide Pena. Then Fernandez asked if the Central Americans had to accept the entire Wright-Reagan plan. "Certainly not," Wright replied. "We wouldn't presume to dictate the terms of a settlement between your countries. Those judgments are yours to make. I don't care whose plan it's called. In fact it's preferable if it's President Arias's plan."

Wright hung up and headed for a DSG meeting. In the Rayburn Building 150 members waited for him. St Germain had just won his vote: the ethics committee would not reopen the investigation and he was off the hook. Wright stood to the side while Bonior preached the line decided upon: "The plan tracks Arias, which we have been touting for two or three months. Many are skeptical, but it was felt by the Speaker and others that we had to give peace a chance. The Speaker's taking an incredible risk. If there's a message that goes out from this Caucus, it's that the President's credibility is on the line."

When Wright started to speak, the members broke into spontaneous applause. It went on and on and was genuine—but it was for his courage, not his position. He started to speak. A sudden high-pitched chirping, like an onslaught of locusts, sounded as 150 beepers went off at once, all announcing, "This is the House Democratic Cloakroom . . . Members have fifteen minutes to record their vote." The room erupted in laughter. Wright smiled and said, "I think they'll hold the vote open." He talked on, concluding, "There is a chance for peace. We're acting in good faith. I believe the Democrats are now clearly for peace, that we have a plan."

Immediately following, Wright went to the Cannon Caucus Room, the largest room in the House outside of the chamber itself, for a press conference. Before going in he huddled with Pena, who had no time to go home for clothes for Guatemala, barely had time to get to the airport for a three-twenty flight. Pena asked for Wright's instructions. Wright replied, "Tell my friends, Duarte and Arias, that we are not dictating anything to them. We want to offer all the support we can. Tell them I will abide by any outcome they reach." Pena was on his way. Wright walked in and met the press.

Bonior and Coelho had gathered up a dozen leading liberals, including George Miller and Lowry, to stand by Wright's side before the reporters to help kill stories of dissension. Quickly one reporter made that point, asking, "What's Bonior think of this?"

Bonior stepped forward. "I'm at his right hand."

By the end of the day Wright had talked with virtually every member of the Democratic Caucus. The liberals still didn't like it. But he had won their tolerance. No House liberals were attacking him, not even anonymously, in the press, although Ted Kennedy on the Senate floor was calling the peace plan "a sham."

Meanwhile, Wright juggled TV interview requests, saying, "There are two critical points. My time and who."

MacNeil/Lehrer. Of course. *Good Morning America.* Yes. What about this weekend? *Meet the Press* offered eighteen minutes; Brinkley offered only nine but had higher ratings. They chose the longer time—print reporters would watch whatever show he was on and they were more important on this. The important audience for the moment was inside the Beltway.

"Those meetings with the members were good," Wright commented. "John's always trying to get me to talk to those fellows and I ask him why. It's good."

"It inoculates you," an aide said.

"Yes." He laughed. "And I may need that soon."

At seven o'clock the next morning, while Wright was about to appear on *Good Morning America,* Loeffler called John Mack to apologize for the stories in the press and explain they were having some difficulties getting everyone in line. Mack hung up nervously and got the papers. *They're screwing us,* he thought.

The whole point of the peace plan was to develop a bipartisan policy that had credibility, that did not seem a ploy. If a different message went to Guatemala . . .

The stories with potentially the most serious consequences ran in *The New York Times.* The *Times!* The most respected and the most powerful paper in the country. Its reputation as "the old gray lady" gave it solidity, gave it tremendous authority. Readers believed it. Readers around the world believed it.

The first story the *Times* had run, in Wednesday's paper based on Tuesday's events, had been written by Linda Greenhouse, its chief congressional reporter. It had been among the most accurate stories written about the peace initiative. But *Times* editors took the coverage away from her. "I guess they just decided it was a White House story," she said.

Thursday's paper, based on Wednesday's events, had several stories, none written by Greenhouse: a page-one news story by Steven Roberts and a news analysis written by Joel Brinkley, both White House reporters, and a report from Guatemala by James Lemoyne. Lemoyne's story, given the smallest play of the three, reported that all five Central American countries welcomed the Wright-Reagan initiative warmly. Roberts and Brinkley played the story differently. They reported it exactly as contra supporters, who wanted to manipulate the *Times* and other media outlets to influence events, had hoped.

Contra supporters wanted the Sandinistas to reject the peace overture. That would bring to life Bonior's nightmare: *We tried the Speaker's plan, it went nowhere, now give us the aid, and they'll have the votes.* The best way to force rejection was to convince the Sandinistas the plan was an insincere ploy designed to get more contra aid.

What gave this plan credibility in Central America was Wright's involvement. Leaders trusted him. And the significance and the symbolism of the Speaker of the House of one party joining with the President of the United States of another had an electric effect in the region. (It also had potential future ramifications for American foreign policy. State Department historian William Slaney, House historian Raymond Smock, and Senate historian Richard Baker all agreed: the last member of Congress to become so prominently and intimately involved in foreign policy had been Henry Clay, before the War of 1812.)

Those in the administration who wanted the peace plan to fail therefore tried to downplay Wright's role. They found a ready audience in the press, and particularly in the *Times*.

In Joel Brinkley's "news analysis," Wright's name did not appear. The story did not even refer to him. Nor was there a single reference to the meeting of the five Central American presidents—the meeting Wright had hoped so much to influence—which was occurring that same day. Brinkley concluded that the plan was strictly a ploy. The story's first sentence read, "As it has before, the Reagan administration offered a Central American peace plan today in the full expectation that Nicaragua would reject it, several Administration officials said. . . . The Central American states also were caught unaware, State Department officials said."

In Steven Roberts's twenty-nine-paragraph-long, page-one news story, Wright's name appeared first in paragraph twenty-three. The first sentence of the story announced the agreement. The second sentence read, "But many Democrats expressed concern that they were being deceived and that the plan, discussed with congressional leaders on Tuesday, was primarily a public relations tactic." That was the discussion in which Shultz briefed senators because Wright arrived forty-five minutes late. The third sentence of the story read, "Some administration officials said the plan was offered in the full expectation that Nicaragua would reject it. The reasoning, they said, was that such a rejection would assure approval of renewed aid to the contras later this year by demonstrating the insincerity of the Sandinistas."

Roberts's story was all true, but only part of the truth. Brinkley's story was naively narrow and badly flawed. Both stories reflected several institutional problems of the White House press corps. One is that for reporters, as for a President, the White House represents the pinnacle of their profession. White House reporters dominate the front pages of newspapers and the nightly news. They lose perspective, overemphasize the importance of happenings in the White House, and underemphasize anything that occurs elsewhere. And White House reporters must cover whatever issue the White House chooses to emphasize on a given day, even though they may have no background in the issue. What they do know is politics, so they tend to focus on who's-on-top stories. Their—unavoidable—substantive ignorance also makes them easier to manipulate. In a speech to political scientists, Roberts himself observed, "At the White House, the odds favor the sources of news, not the reporters. The power of officials to dole out or withhold information is sizable; returning or not returning phone calls is the ultimate leverage. But on Capitol Hill, the advantage shifts to the journalist. Sources are everywhere. The people who try to dissemble or prevaricate lose their credibility and get left behind."

The tendency to emphasize political gamesmanship in coverage, rather than substance, was fed by sources trying to manipulate the *Times*. One senior White House official insisted, "There is no question that the most senior three people—Baker, Shultz, and the President—were sincere. Hell, in 1984 Shultz himself cut Weinberger, [CIA director William] Casey, and the NSC out of the loop and met with [Nicaraguan president Daniel] Ortega to explore a negotiated settlement. They wanted this thing to work. They were not setting Wright up. But I think [Elliott] Abrams's people at State and the NSC people were trying to kill the peace plan, particularly José Sorzano."

Sorzano, a violently anticommunist Cuban refugee, would not return telephone calls from reporters who knew Central America well, like *Newsday*'s Roy Gutman, author of a book on the region. Gutman might ask too many questions. But Sorzano reportedly talked to the White House press corps. Anonymously. The press has to be willing to grant anonymity to get information. Anonymous sources are especially important—but also especially manipulative—when contradicting a public position. The anonymous attacks were a way of exercising power. They threatened the chances for peace. The *Times* reporters were used. The power of the *Times* magnified the impact.

Also angry about the stories was Howard Baker. He told a White House senior staff meeting that morning, "This is the drill. We talk peace. We work peace. We don't say this thing will fall apart. Understand?"

His rebuke came too late. The stories put intense, new pressure on Wright. Early that Thursday morning he had appeared on ABC's *Good Morning America,* and was in his H-210 office before 8:00 A.M. watching a tape of his performance on the preceding evening's *MacNeil/Lehrer.* The tension in him showed. He had an odd, disconnected calm, as if trying to block everything out. Everything. While events swirled around him, he had gone into the center of himself again, looking for quiet, for judgment, for strength. A man asked if he was going down to breakfast for some coffee and he replied offhandedly, "Yes. Yes. That sounds good."

They walked out of H-210, into the Speaker's Lobby, and down the marble stairwell that spirals down from the House floor almost directly to the room Rayburn had used for the Board of Education, where the most powerful members of Congress met each evening for a drink, where Harry Truman learned he was President, the room Wright had taken possession of when he became Speaker. Halfway down Wright stopped. The balusters were sculpted cast iron. He stared at one section and said, "Isn't this statuary beautiful? The deer, the cherubim."

The art was permanent; its beauty had been here before him and would be here after him. He ran his hand over one piece, the iron cold to his touch, yet his caress so gentle it made the iron seem somehow soft, malleable.

"Stopping to smell the roses, huh?"

He straightened and smiled. "Yes. Sometimes it's the only way to keep your sanity."

"Dingell says this iron came from British cannon captured at the Battle of New Orleans. The architect's office said it had no record of that but I wouldn't dispute Dingell."

He smiled. "Certainly not to his face."

They proceeded downstairs to his usual private table in the Members' Dining Room. A couple of aides were there. He seemed still out of focus but sat down and poured a cup of coffee. Then, gently, he said, "I think today I should be with my colleagues."

Directly across the hall was a regular Thursday prayer breakfast, for members only. No staff, no special guests. Absolutely private. Sonny

Montgomery of Mississippi had started the breakfasts years before. He was a tough opponent on the floor, and much of his strength evolved from these breakfasts. But the breakfasts were sincere. A member would relate something very personal and what it had meant to him. Wright had occasionally gone over the years. Once he had talked of the death of his infant child, and a Republican who heard him later said, "I hadn't believed he had the kind of depth he showed." Wright had not attended a prayer breakfast all year. But today he wanted to withdraw with his colleagues and his God.

As the prayer breakfast ended, Mary Rose Oakar complained to him about a resolution condemning the World War I genocide Turkey committed against Armenians. Supporters of the resolution considered it important; Turkey denied that the genocide had occurred. It was scheduled for a vote that day. Oakar relayed a warning she had just received: passage of the resolution could bring down the pro-U.S. government of Turkey. Could he do something? She pressed him as they rode the elevator to the third floor and walked down the corridor to the Thursday whip meeting. All right, he said. If it could actually topple a friendly government, he would keep it off the floor at least long enough to look into her concerns.

Wright was abstracted as he made his way through the members crowded around the table of fresh fruit, coffee, doughnuts, muffins, and juices supplied by Coelho's lobbyists. He took his seat at the front of the room next to Foley. Coelho called the meeting to order. As he said, "The majority leader will read the schedule"—the routine with which every whip meeting began—Wright was whispering to Foley, telling him the Armenian resolution would not go to the floor. Foley made the announcement.

Both Bonior and Coelho looked surprised. By coincidence, both their districts had heavy concentrations of Armenians. Unrelated to their leadership posts, both had gotten personally involved in passing this resolution. As the announcement sank in, they both grew angry.

Bonior began to seethe. Wright's peace initiative had hurt him. For three years he had been the point man for House Democrats on the issue. Suddenly Wright had flown off on his own without asking his advice at all. That had been humiliating and hurtful. Yet he had responded with utter loyalty, had perhaps even compromised his principles. Wright thought *he* had been under pressure? It was Bonior whom all the liberals in the Caucus had been complaining to, putting pressure on. It was Bonior whom all the peace activists around the country were calling and calling and calling and calling. It was Bonior whom everyone was asking, *How could you? How could you?* Now that loyalty was rewarded by Wright's pulling this bill without asking his advice—hell, without telling him. Bonior grew more and more furious, felt more and more humiliated. Foley was speaking. Abruptly Bonior stood up and started down the aisle. He wanted to get out before he did something he'd regret. He had to get out. His clipboard, packed with leadership information, fell out of his hand. He bent down, picked it up. Then he stopped. Why did he need a clipboard filled with leadership information? *I quit,* he thought. He flung the clipboard to the floor, and stormed out.

The air was thick, heavy, the members nervously silent. As Coelho did every week, he asked Wright to say something. Today, worried, Wright said simply, "I have no announcements to make."

"WHEW!" said one member.

The entire room erupted in laughter, laughter swelled in one part of the room and rolled across to another, then rolled back, laughter spoke to the tension in the room, the tension in everyone. But it did not break it.

An hour later Wright met in his ceremonial office with Coelho, Bonior, Oakar, and William Ford, the chairman of the committee which reported out the Armenian resolution. They were hot, all of them hot. The State Department opposed the resolution, Ford said, but even they weren't claiming it would bring down the Turkish government. Then he started to attack Oakar. Wright intervened: "Don't yell at her. I'm the one who made the decision." Ford stopped, then threatened to resign his chairmanship if the resolution wasn't rescheduled. Bonior too demanded it be put back on the schedule. Wright agreed. Bonior stayed chief deputy whip. Later that day it was voted on, and the rule was defeated. (Heavy lobbying by Gary Hymel, the former O'Neill aide, and an investment of close to $1 million by Turkey did it.) But Ford, Bonior, and Coelho were content: what had infuriated them was procedure, Wright's arbitrary action, not substance.

And suddenly things began to look better. Peace activists in Guatemala were on the phone to people like George Miller, reporting that reaction in Central America was positive. Very positive. Wright had credibility there, and if there was true bipartisanship it could have an impact. Nicaragua had publicly welcomed the plan and called for immediate discussions with the United States. Reporters asked the administration to respond. An Associated Press story quoted Fitzwater that talks would occur only " 'in a regional context involving the other Central American states,' " and saying that Shultz "spurned" Ortega's offer, quoting Shultz: " 'I think it's critical to establish that there is no way in which the United States would want to sit down with Nicaragua to decide what is right for Central America.' "

Wright's aide Wilson Morris brought him a printout of the AP story. He sat at his desk, read it, bunched his fists, and said nothing for a moment. Regional talks were necessary, but the peace plan also specifically called for "bilateral discussions." That meant the United States talking to Nicaragua. Wright called Shultz. Shultz said the wire story was inaccurate and the quote was out of context. He had not spurned talks with Nicaragua. He had only tried to put it in a regional context. *Dammit*, Wright thought, *when will this administration get its story straight.*

He got off the phone with Shultz and called Baker, who explained that the United States didn't want to seem the "colossus of the North," that the whole idea was to let the Central Americans know the United States would not try to impose its will on them.

"That's fine," Wright said, "but when you give a guy X days to respond and he says the next day let's talk, and you say no, then that's a problem." Baker promised to have the President call. Soon the phone rang.

"Hello, Mr. President," Wright said. "How are you? . . . That's very good . . . I heard that from a man down there too, that the response from the presidents of the four democracies was very favorable . . . I understand the position taken by Secretary Shultz, not wanting to engage in bilateral discussions because it makes us appear as if we're dictating something. But at the same time, I hate to be in a position to say we want an answer, they say, fine, here are some points we want to discuss, and we say, no, we won't discuss them . . . I understand. We've got to let countries in Central America take the lead . . . I think you're absolutely right about that."

Wright hung up, shook his head, and said, "Boy, talking to him is like punching a pillow."

Downstairs in the Capitol, liberals were meeting. They were rallying behind Wright now and wanted him to appoint some of them as observers to the peace talks during recess, which began the next afternoon. They wanted to see Wright the next morning about that—Wright, as Speaker, had the sole power to authorize official trips, which the government paid for. Mack asked when he wanted to see them.

"*No!* I'm tired of meetings." He was tired. Looked tired. Was finally wearing down. *It's not what you've done but what you have to do,* he thought. He could see the road ahead; God, there was so much to do. He inhaled deeply. He wanted to withdraw, shrink away from the exposure. But he was not too tired to protect his prerogatives. Disdainfully he said, "These are self-appointed observers."

Mack disagreed. "They want you to appoint them. These guys are supportive. They're skeptical but rallying. They want to cover the talks during recess so they can call you if they need to."

"Give them my phone number but tell them not to call."

Both of them laughed. Wright shook his head. *Lord, he was tired.*

But there was no escape. As the afternoon wore on, events seemed cascading out of control; happening so fast in so many different places that there was no opportunity to, no possibility of, controlling them.

Pena called from Guatemala and said the Nicaraguan foreign minister was refusing to allow the Wright-Reagan plan to be discussed in the five-nation peace conference. Wright was livid and told Pena that if the Sandinistas were creating difficulties then he should return to Washington. *That would put pressure on the bastards.* The Costa Ricans convinced Pena to stay. Ted Kennedy was attacking the plan again on the Senate floor. And Wright got another phone call, from the Sandinistas, saying that two documents were circulating. The one Wright's office had sent—and was distributing to the press in Washington—said "bilateral." The one from the administration, which it was giving to the press, did not. Which was it? It was a crucial point. The word "bilateral" bound the administration to negotiate with the Sandinistas. Wright said the agreement included the word "bilateral." And a man told Wright, "*The Washington Post* has that twenty-one-point memorandum."

Wright exploded. "I'll denounce them! Baker swore up and down that would not get out. I'll denounce them!"

He was out of control himself, the tension breaking through. The man who told him of the leak backtracked, saying he could be mistaken, tried to calm him. Then Loeffler arrived, tried to calm him, too, and begged for patience.

The President fully understood his agreement, Loeffler insisted. Wright would even be allowed to review and edit the major speech Reagan would give on Central America, scheduled for the following week. The senior people, the people who counted, were all in agreement. The lower echelons were the problem. He conceded, "It is taking a while to get some of these people in the administration in line, but last night when Kennedy said it was a sham and Jack Kemp called it a surrender I thought we must have a good deal. Getting people like Chris Dodd and Henry Hyde supportive, which they are, that's the only way to break the back of this Marxist-Leninist state."

Wright narrowed his stare. *That wasn't the deal.* "I don't trust Danny Ortega, but I'm not out to break him. As long as there are free elections and free speech, if Ortega's elected that's fine with me. I talked to Shultz today. He said he wanted a regional solution. I agree. The Central American countries must be able to work out a plan. The first hill to overcome is figure out how to get the contras and Sandinistas into agreeing on the cease-fire. The Sandinistas say they won't talk to the contras directly. Ortega said he wanted to talk to the owner of the circus, not the clowns. Us. We say we won't talk to the Sandinistas. Who's the go-between? The Church? They seem the most obvious. Maybe someone else. If we delay, it'll be the end of the month and no one will have gotten off the dime. The clock's ticking."

Then Wright leaned forward. He was sitting behind his desk, Loeffler in front of him, and Wright suddenly seemed to take on great weight. If he publicly accused the White House of bad faith, a war would erupt between the administration and Congress unlike anything even the previous six years had seen. His voice was dangerously calm and he said, "There's another thing. Our document has 'bilateral discussions' in it. So does the original. The document distributed at the White House does not."

Loeffler explained, "That happened in the Senate"—the meeting which Wright arrived late at. "It's an honest mistake." Dodd, the Connecticut Democrat, had suggested taking "bilateral" out because it sounded limiting. To make Dodd happy Shultz had agreed.

"Frankly, that's outrageous," Wilson Morris interjected. "The deal was between the Speaker and the President. How can you rewrite the Speaker's document, unilaterally change crucial wording, without his consent or even knowledge? Reporters are picking on the 'bilateral' thing. Steve Roberts is asking, 'Doesn't that mean there's an unbridgeable gap?' Andrea Mitchell [of NBC] is going to go with the story in thirty minutes."

Loeffler looked at the clock. It was six. "We've got to get you and Shultz talking. I'll make that happen. Hook 'em."

Hook 'em. It was a University of Texas football saying, short for "Hook 'em, Longhorns." It meant Loeffler was going to get this done. He stepped into Wright's outer office and dialed a number. "I need to talk to Ed Fox"—the assistant secretary of State for congressional affairs—"and I need him *right now.*" He waited on hold. Five minutes. Ten minutes. Fox came on the line and Loeffler said, "Look, this thing is going on the news at six-thirty. We'll have a major controversy and we can avoid it. Let's get this thing done."

Wright's press secretary, Charmayne Marsh, called Andrea Mitchell and asked her to wait. By now it was six-twenty-four. The phone rang on the desk of Wright's personal secretary. "That's probably Shultz right now," Loeffler said.

Shultz and Wright agreed it was a nonissue. It was six-twenty-eight. Morris got on the phone to Mitchell. "The Speaker and the Secretary have talked. They agree there is no dispute. It's a 'nonissue' that arose accidentally."

That story did not run.

Loeffler started to leave, then turned around and said, "The next time I'm here, if I talk about anything but hunting and fishing throw me out. Not football. Football's too controversial in Texas."

At four-thirty the next morning, Wright's telephone rang. Groggily he picked it up. It was the Costa Rican ambassador Fernandez. Wright quickly focused. Fernandez explained that President Arias had asked him to call, that the president was certain he would not mind being awakened for this news. President Arias wanted to thank him for his support and to tell him that without the stimulus provided by the initiative Wright had co-sponsored with Reagan, the agreement would not have been possible. Wright jerked awake. The five Central American presidents had settled their differences and, God willing, would sign a peace agreement later that day. *They had reached a peace agreement.*

Wright closed his eyes and said a short prayer. A calm spread through him, a deep joy, as deep as anything he had ever known. *Blessed be the peacemakers.*

Later in the morning Pena called from the airport in Guatemala. He had waited to see if the agreement would collapse. It hadn't, and now he confirmed it. He had been down there for two days, in the tropical heat, had gone down only with the clothes he had been wearing, had been up all night. He was a mess. But if tired he was also exhilarated and offered more details on the agreement.

Wright's daily press conference began at nine-forty. It was Friday, August 7, eighteen days after Loeffler had walked into Wright's office, the last day before Congress recessed until mid-September. Before Wright said anything, a reporter asked, "Mr. Speaker, do you have a time for the debt-ceiling vote?"

"I will let Tom Foley tell you about what is going on there. Let me give you a little bit of news that I think is very good news. I got a phone call at four-thirty this morning . . . You probably need to refine this but . . . Ambassador Fernandez said the five countries have accepted the Arias plan for peace in Central America with certain modifications and variations embracing some of the things that we had recommended." He outlined the agreement, then added, "As I say, you probably need to keep your fingers crossed, and just hope that it doesn't come unglued."

"Mr. Speaker, how is that going to affect the decision on holding off requests of aid for the contras by the administration?"

"Well, I think yesterday Secretary Shultz said that it was not timely to sit down in a bilateral way with the government of Nicaragua and arrange the fate of Central America, that that was the business of Central America. I think he tacitly made a commitment to live up to whatever the Central Americans themselves would agree to. I cannot conceive of the United States . . . trying to do anything but rejoice and cooperate with it."

Wright was smiling. He knew the settlement was a fragile thing, and feared the pressures the administration could apply. He was jumping to embrace the agreement, hoping it would force the administration to delay any disapproval, to give the agreement time to jell. Still, all the administration's talk of "a regional context" the day before, all its insistence that the United States could not sit down and dictate to the Central Americans a peace settlement, had now backed it into a corner.

Conservatives were, he thought, cornered by another fact: when Arias first proposed his peace plan months earlier, the Senate had passed a resolution endorsing it 97–1.

Reporters rushed out of the press conference and called the State Department. State denied that an agreement had been reached. Then a State Department official called Morris to tell him the same thing. Where did the Speaker get these ideas?

For years State had bullied Central Americans to support the contras. They resented it. Earlier, Arias had been infuriated at what he regarded as slights during a visit to Washington. As a result, State Department intelligence was poor. Wright had estimated the chances of an agreement as reasonable; thereafter he had taken a great risk to increase those chances. State had been stunned by the agreement. And this would not be the last time the administration found itself out of the loop.

Word spread quickly through the House. Exhilaration flooded through the Caucus. *Peace. Did you hear? Peace!* An hour and a half later, the State Department said an agreement had been reached but no accord was signed. Wright's meeting with the liberals who wanted to observe the peace talks came late in the morning. They gathered in H-201. Waiters had laid out coffee, sodas, iced tea, and cookies in a corner of the room. A positive force of joy flooded the room, a pure, deep satisfaction and joy.

But there was another note, too, a private note of discord. Just before the meeting Coelho asked for a few moments alone with Wright. Wright invited him into his office. While their colleagues waited down the hall, Coelho told Wright he didn't think he was being treated properly. The Armenian resolution was only the latest instance, the tip of the iceberg. Coelho was the whip, had been elected whip by the Caucus, and expected not to be treated like the odd man out of the leadership. Coelho's complaint registered. Wright apologized. He meant it. For a moment his eyes watered. The two felt suddenly close. But it was a reminder that each had his own agenda and his own ambition.

They left Wright's office together, walked down the hall together, and walked into H-201 where twenty members suddenly burst into applause—loud, long clapping, some members pounding the table. *"Mr. Speaker! Mr. Speaker!"*

Finally Wright, blushing, embarrassed, stopped them, started the discussion about protecting the peace agreement from conservatives who might try to kill it. It had not even been signed yet.

George Miller warned, "There are dozens of pressure points. Arias has a brother with a loan from OPIC"—the Overseas Private Insurance Corporation, a government agency—"for $375,000. Duarte's generals can be influenced by the U.S. We have to make clear to the Central Americans they can talk to *you*. You're the counterpoint. The civilians have to know they can deal with you. You'll be here long after this administration disappears. You can give [Honduran president José] Azcona backbone to stand up to his generals. You already have."

Miller was suggesting establishing a virtual State Department in the Speaker's Rooms. He distrusted the administration that much. He wanted to create a permanent, new base of power within the Congress. Wright frowned; for the moment he would wait and see what the administration did.

Later that afternoon Wright taped the Democrats' response to Reagan's weekly five-minute radio address. He spoke of the peace agreement and of bipartisanship and closed: "May we all ask the blessings of God on their endeavor."

Just then Wilson Morris walked in with a wire story out of Guatemala. The five presidents had signed the agreement.

"By God," Wright said. "That's great."

It was August. Hot. Congress was exhausted. Already members were filtering out of Washington, off, finally with their families. But Gramm-Rudman and the extension of the debt limit still held up recess.

Buddy MacKay had sworn he would fight any extension, even one that just carried through the summer recess. *We'll just grab ahold and see who wins,* he had said.

Thursday night at nine Rostenkowski, Foley, and Vic Fazio had met with Domenici, Chiles, and Bentsen to see if they could settle it. At 10:00 A.M. Friday the House sent an offer. The Senate sent a counteroffer back. The House went into recess until three. The Capitol was empty, deserted. The halls had an eerie echoing feel to them. At three-twenty-five leadership staff wanted to know if a deal was done. At four-thirty the House suddenly convened. There was no deal—they'd settle it in September. MacKay heard of it almost inadvertently and hurried out of his office, heading for the floor to force a vote. The visitors' galleries were empty. The press gallery empty. Four or five members were in the great echoing chamber. Foley and Rostenkowski were there, with Trent Lott guarding the floor for the Republicans.

Rostenkowski offered a motion to approve a debt-limit extension to carry until mid-September.

All in favor?

One member said, "Aye."

Opposed?

Silence.

The ayes have it.

Bang!

MacKay arrived breathless in the Capitol. He had practically run the last yards and in the August heat he was sweating. Had he arrived in time, he could have forced a vote by simply saying, "Mr. Speaker, I object to the vote on the grounds that a quorum is not present." A recorded vote would have followed. But he arrived too late. Now he was furious, believing that the leadership had pulled a fast one, had acted dishonorably in not giving proper notice of floor activity.

Foley soothed him, swore that the mistake had been an honest one, and had had nothing to do with the leadership.

"If it were anyone but Foley I'd have called him a liar," MacKay said a few hours later, still fuming, fuming, determined more than ever to, next time, *fight*.

For now, at recess, even Newt Gingrich was weary, worn out. "There's a sort of biological feeling you get around this place sometimes, that you're not going to get any more work out of us no matter what," he said. "You're just exhausted."

He was on his way back to his office, where he took off his jacket, unbuttoned his collar, poured himself a Scotch, and began ruminating about the peace initiative. "That's a real leadership thing Wright did. We may be about to lock horns savagely over ethics, but that was real gutsy."

The year so far had not gone well for his party. That did not concern him. Indeed, he believed Wright's dominance was playing into his hands by driving Republican colleagues into his camp. He was right.

House Republicans had first responded with scorn to Wright's claim that congressional Democrats would govern. But Wright had governed. Shortly before recess, the GOP leadership changed. Presidential candidate Jack Kemp resigned his third-ranking leadership post and was replaced by Dick Cheney of Wyoming. Jerry Lewis stepped into Cheney's fourth-ranking post. The new leadership was more cohesive, more geared to the House. They decided to become more aggressive. No more sitting back and voting no on everything. That hadn't worked. They would prepare party alternatives to major Democratic initiatives. Michel appointed task forces for a GOP version of catastrophic health insurance and of welfare reform. They also decided to set up a task force on congressional reforms, and attack the way Wright ran the House through the Rules Committee. "We're not going to sit here and just take it," said a Republican aide.

That echoed—and borrowed from—Gingrich's own themes, which by now had matured into a sophisticated, carefully planned, long-term campaign against Wright.

The campaign began in an abstraction. Indeed, Gingrich seemed to abstract everything. In 1985 he had sat eating lunch, grabbed a napkin, and drew a triangle on it, labeling the sides of the triangle "reality," "personal lives," and "people's values," and explained, "All successful politicians have to be inside the triangle. Democrats grew outside of it with things like gay rights."

It was a capsule analysis of what would become a driving theme of his in the future, a theme which George Bush's 1988 presidential campaign would echo, an effort to define Democrats as permanently outside the triangle and outside the mainstream of American values and symbols to drive a wedge between Democrats and voters. He wanted to define them out of existence.

Another of his abstractions was a construct of "all human activities." He believed they occur at four levels, arranged in a hierarchy. "Vision is at the top of that. What is your vision of what you're doing? Then once you have a vision, what is your strategy? . . . What are the projects that you've assigned to do that? . . . The bottom level after vision, strategies, and projects is tactics. . . . One of the major problems of the Republican Party is that we focus on tactics. The result is that the vision and strategy level of the left kills you."

Vision. Strategy. Projects. Tactics.

Gingrich's vision included both the achievement of power and, he said, the reification of his Conservative Opportunity Society. The two were inextricably intertwined. It was power which had fascinated him ever since his visit, at fifteen, to the World War I battlefield of Verdun, when the power of nations had been burned into him, made tangible in the mass of unidentified bones. It was power about which he had written a 180-page study a few months later. And nothing drove home the ramifications of power, and its abstract ruthlessness, like the modern European history which he had gone on to study and teach. One Republican had said of him, *The contras would say he has "soft hands."* He seemed more the kind of person who pulled strings than who crawled through the jungle and killed with a knife. Wright by contrast was filled with passion, explosive passion. *He creates himself when he acts,* Gingrich had observed. Gingrich was pure analysis; he looked for weakness, for something to exploit, and when he found it he went after it coldly and methodically. The realpolitik of history mocked those who did less.

The other aspect of his vision, his new conservative society, superficially resembled Reagan's view of the world. But Gingrich was not a raw, inflexible ideologue. Reagan had essentially preached the same clearly defined vision for over twenty years. He achieved power when the nation finally came to him.

Gingrich's vision was not nearly so well defined as Reagan's, and it lacked both Gingrich's usual intellectual rigor and the emotional pull of Reagan's strong, simple themes. Indeed, Gingrich's society seemed as much a pragmatic political vehicle to gain power as a vision to be reified. The essence of this society was the entrepreneur, and its devil was the "statist" government which had developed in the preceding half century. In this, Gingrich borrowed from the antiestablishment, pro–little guy, libertarian streak that ran deep in American life.

Yet Gingrich blurred his ideological message—and sounded much like his generational counterparts among Democrats—by also wanting an activist government. He just did not want a big government. He disagreed strongly with Reagan's statement that "government is the problem," and explained, "There's a big difference between a big, bureaucratic government, neutrality, and privatization"—using the government to get the private sector to advance social goals. "We created airlines by subsidizing airmail. We created the microchip industry through the Pentagon. These were conscious strategies."

Even in the area of values, pragmatic politics blurred his ideological message. He said, "Anticommunism is a bedrock, core value of the Republican Party," and anticommunism was basic to the COS. He talked, too, of family and other social values. Yet he understood that the wing of the GOP most interested in values, the antiabortionists, the Moral Majority supporters, the people who campaigned against the

Equal Rights Amendment, were threatening to the postwar baby-boom generation, which was his market. Beginning in 1988 and extending well into the future, baby-boomers would make up more than 60 percent of the electorate. It was the generation that was most exposed to technological change, the generation of the sexual revolution, the generation which had matured during Vietnam and Watergate and tended to distrust all big institutions, but especially the government. It was the generation of the "Me Decade" too. He warned, "The party that wins the baby-boomers will win in the future. If we allow the fundamentalists to dictate party policy, we doom ourselves to being a permanent minority."

What is the primary purpose of a political leader? he once said. *To build a majority . . . If people care about parking lots, then talk about parking lots . . . You're fighting a war, a war for power.*

Reagan's and Kemp's visions came from a center within each of them; it expressed their visceral selves. Gingrich's Conservative Opportunity Society was a marketing device to achieve power. He talked of inner peace, but that peace came from intellectual self-confidence—not from pure faith but from a faith in the correctness of his analysis, from a confidence that that analysis had launched him in the proper direction— the direction of power.

His strategy in pursuit of power did not include advancing his objectives legislatively. He was no legislator, nor did he service his constituents particularly well. There were 435 congressional districts in America, and 404 of them got more federal dollars than his. *We are engaged in reshaping a whole nation through the news media,* he had said. His strategy was to use the House floor and his position as a congressman to influence the media and, through it, the world outside Congress; then the world outside would in turn influence colleagues.

It was a destructive, not constructive, force which he hoped to generate. Kemp had also ignored internal House dynamics and tried to generate and exploit external political forces. But he had moved issues forward: he brought respectability to "supply side" economic thinking, converted Ronald Reagan and the bulk of the Republican Party to it, and transformed it into legislation. Kemp did not serve on Ways and Means, but through the 1980s he had more impact on tax policy than Rostenkowski or any member of the House or Senate.

Gingrich devoted his efforts to destroying Democrats, not to advancing issues. *He would not be dominated. Not ever again.* When the year began he decided that Wright had to be confronted. How—Gingrich's "projects"—came into focus only gradually; Gingrich would attack him both personally and by the House attacking. He and his close allies were already at work on a book titled *The House of Ill Repute.* "The Democrats have run the House for more than thirty years," he said. "They've gotten sloppy. The House is a corrupt institution, corrupt in the Lord Acton sense."

But that was too abstract to make the front pages. More than three months earlier, the ethics committee whitewash of St Germain had given Gingrich a concrete, communicable issue to exploit. Soon thereafter, he assigned an aide virtually full-time to track negative newspaper stories about Wright, going back to his first entry into public life, then started giving reporters packets of those negative stories. Simultaneously, he became convinced that ethics could become a major issue. "The cover of *Time* deals with ethics," Gingrich said. "Tammy Faye and Jim Bakker [TV evangelists who were exposed as con artists and possibly sexual deviants], all these things are ethical issues."

One reason ethics had become a theme was the emergence of the so-called sleaze factor—a reference to all the administration officials who had ethics problems, or had even gone to prison, and to the expectation that the issue could be important in the next presidential election. Attorney General Edwin Meese was the GOP's biggest problem. Meese had intervened to help get defense contracts for the Wedtech company, while Wedtech was paying his close friend, who had bragged about his ability to deliver Meese, several hundred thousand dollars. Wedtech executives and politicians went to jail for bribery and fraud. Though no charges were ever filed against Meese, one of his own assistant attorneys general resigned, saying that he would have sought an indictment against him, and a special prosecutor later said Meese had "probably violated the law." Other GOP embarrassments included former White House aide and Reagan confidant Michael Deaver, who had been convicted of perjury, and former White House political director Lyn Nofziger, convicted of illegal lobbying. (In 1989 an appeals court dismissed Nofziger's conviction.) There were dozens of others.

Republicans were desperate to find Democrats with problems to neutralize this sleaze factor. Gingrich believed he could do more than simply dispel it. He had used the ethics issue before to communicate with the media, in losing congressional campaigns in 1974 and 1976. Elected to an open seat in 1978, in his first term in the House he had pushed for the expulsion of Charles Diggs, a Detroit Democrat convicted of financial misdeeds who ultimately resigned. He recognized the potency of ethics as an issue.

"The media values its liberal bias less than it values honesty in government," he said. Or perhaps it valued nothing more than a good headline. He intended to attack and attack and put Democrats on the defensive. *The number-one fact about the news media is that they love fights,* he had said. *When you give them confrontations you get attention.* Attention allowed him to make his case.

His instinct about the importance of the ethics issue had been confirmed one week earlier when he heard data gathered from focus groups, conducted by the Roosevelt Center for American Policy Studies, a nonpartisan think tank. Gingrich explained, "Republicans have an advantage on family values, belief in right and wrong, that kind of thing. The guy who briefed the COS on the focus groups said, 'I'm a lifelong Democrat and I'm terrified.' Swing votes could create a landslide for the GOP. The number-one thing people want is integrity."

More than a month earlier he had decided to demand, at some future time, an investigation of Wright. But even then Gingrich's campaign against him had been somewhat inchoate. Now it was intensifying, and he knew exactly what he would do and how he would go about it. A few years before, he had suggested making radical changes in the Social Security system. They had been provocative ideas, basically nonpartisan, but Democrats had oversimplified his proposal and capitalized politically on it. It had taught him a lesson: "I got ahead of myself. I was proposing a solution before the public understood there was a problem."

He would not make that mistake again. His goal was to build public perception of questionable behavior, and then strike.

His tactic was to create stories. Just the day before he had forced a vote on reopening the ethics investigation into Banking chairman Fernand St Germain.

In advance, trying to generate what he called "resonance" in the media which would maximize his impact, he had written on July 1, then again on July 21 to Fred Wertheimer, president of the nonpartisan good-government lobby group Common Cause. Common Cause had credibility with the press which Gingrich lacked. His letter included long, detailed accusations against St Germain and other Democrats (no Republicans), including Wright and Coelho. Gingrich asked Wertheimer to help, to demand action from the ethics committee. Eight days after Gingrich's second letter, Wertheimer did write the committee, demanding that the committee act against several of the members Gingrich had named—but not against Wright and Coelho—and charging that the committee "has abdicated its responsibility to vigorously and effectively enforce the ethics rules and standards that apply to Members of the House of Representatives."

Gingrich promptly staged a special order for his C-SPAN audience, citing Common Cause's letter about ethical improprieties committed by Democrats. It was a little piece of resonance.

Then Gingrich forced his vote on St Germain. It was all part of building his case. And if it got little press play, that was only because the Wright-Reagan Central American peace proposal dominated the news.

He hadn't really expected Wertheimer and Common Cause to call for an investigation of Wright—not yet anyway. That had been a long shot, comparable to winning the World Series. Common Cause's respectability would almost force an investigation. If getting Common Cause's Wertheimer to act against Wright took time, Gingrich had time. The reward, over time, was power. Just this August 7 morning, a political ally had sent him a memo saying, "The vote . . . strikes a rich vein that can be mined for Party advantage in regaining Congressional numbers and influence."

In a few weeks, he would try for grand-slam home runs—getting Ted Koppel's *Nightline* show and *60 Minutes* and others in the major media to raise the issue of corruption in Congress and specifically of Jim Wright. He would also begin in methodical fashion to build resonance, to make a record of charges in the print media in cities all over the country, like a baseball player working his way up through the minors. Or like a gardener, planting seeds.

Whenever he visited a city—and as the leading intellectual light of the New Right he traveled often to make speeches, in Miami, Seattle, Boston, Atlanta, elsewhere—he would seek out local political reporters, local investigative reporters, local editorial writers, and plant seeds with them. He also began offering reporters powerful attributed quotes. Few people in Washington would publicly attack anyone, much less the Speaker of the House. But he would.

Ten days earlier the *Washington Times* quoted him for the first time saying, "Wright's the least ethical Speaker of the twentieth century."

Two days earlier *The Wall Street Journal* quoted him saying the identical thing. It was a quote which would "get attention," as Gingrich knew. It would draw reporters writing about Wright to Gingrich, and to quote him. Over time, if the quotes appeared in enough places, it would create his resonance.

He had time. He was not impatient. Now, sitting in his office, his jacket off, sipping a Scotch, hours after Wright's gamble seemed to pay off with the five Central American presidents' signing of a peace agreement, Gingrich said, "Look, I don't think Jim Wright's a Mafia don."

But Wright was the symbol, a means to an end. Years before he had vowed to drive O'Neill from office and called him "corrupt." O'Neill had had some questionable financial dealings headlined in *The New York Times,* and had even been investigated by the ethics committee over Koreagate. But collegial pressure and media disinterest had forced Gingrich to abandon that campaign. Wright had neither the personal relationships with colleagues O'Neill had had, nor was he the media's darling. If Gingrich could destroy Wright, destroy the symbol, Republicans might succeed in gaining large numbers of House seats. Democrats had gained forty-nine in the election a few months after Nixon's resignation. Gingrich continued, "Wright's a useful keystone to a much bigger structure. I'll just keep pounding and pounding on his ethics. There comes a point where it comes together and the media takes off on it, or it dies."

He was keeping Michel, Lott, and Cheney informed. Later, an expression of disdain passing across his face, of knowing that for a change he had been used, that perhaps someone else's soft hands were involved, he recalled, "They were quite willing for *me* to do this. No one asked me to stop."

For a moment he switched subjects, and marveled at the courage and ability to assess a situation and strike which Wright had just shown with his peace initiative. Gingrich raised his glass, stared into it for a moment, and added, "If he survives this ethics thing, he may become the greatest Speaker since Henry Clay."

Still, Wright was riding high. The Central American peace agreement had finally created a core group of members who believed in him and his leadership. Perhaps Wright would never become popular in the way O'Neill had been popular, but he had given House Democrats a new sense of authority, of governing, of ruling. Even before the Wright-

Reagan plan, House Democrats had come to respect his ability to run the House. Now that respect went deeper. Democratic members were *glad* he was Speaker. Bonior, who had come so close to quitting the leadership, would soon start talking about Wright running for President. Many thought what Barney Frank, a leading liberal, told him bluntly: "Quite frankly, you're doing a better job than I thought you could do." A *U.S. News & World Report* profile of Wright said in a tone of surprise, "Democrats are downright boastful of their Speaker—who, finally, has given them something to be *for* instead of against."

Earlier Wright had confided, "I'm feeling my way." Yet even feeling his way he had gone forward, had spent the first half-year of his speakership trying to set a new direction for policy. He had largely succeeded. And he needed to feel his way no more. The peace initiative made Wright stronger, more sure of himself, stronger within the Caucus. It also made him more dangerous.

Power was a zero-sum game: Wright had gained; others had lost. The presidency had lost. Struggles between Congress and the Executive over foreign policy had almost always been over efforts to limit the Executive Branch's freedom to act. The War Powers Act epitomized that conflict; it required the President to remove American armed forces from areas of hostilities within sixty days unless Congress authorized their remaining. Wright had done something different; he had initiated a policy, outside the White House. The Senate's foreign policy role, too, had been eclipsed.

How had Wright succeeded?

Chess and Ping-Pong. A lot of what I do isn't calculated in some arcane sense, but is in a way in which I have only a vague sense myself. I have goals in mind and pursue those goals.

He explained, "I knew the blind spots of one faction or another would keep them from seeing the opportunity that did exist. After talking with people in Costa Rica, El Salvador, and Nicaragua I became convinced a possibility existed for making peace. I had not seen those possibilities coalesce before. I did rush to embrace the Guatemala accords. I didn't want to give the administration time to react. That threw them into a position of ambivalence for a few days. When they finally said they still supported the Wright-Reagan plan it had no standing."

Administration officials had seen none of those openings, largely because their rigid adherence to contra aid had dried up their sources of information. Wright listened to every faction. The administration did not.

He had seen an opening in a fluid situation, gone for it, and hoped for the best.

Conservative critics inside and outside the administration attacked the Guatemala accords as falling short of the Wright-Reagan plan in addressing U.S. national security concerns. There were three chief differences:

First, Wright-Reagan gave the Sandinistas sixty days to reach a cease-fire. The Guatemala agreement gave them ninety days.

Second, Wright-Reagan required a cutoff of Soviet-bloc military aid to Nicaragua. The Guatemala agreement called for a resumption of the Mexican-sponsored Contadora talks on the subject. In those talks Nicaragua had already agreed to give up such aid. Tunnermann, the Nicaraguan ambassador, had also promised Wright and Michel that his government would expel Soviet and Cuban advisers. Bilateral negotiations could resolve this.

The third and most important difference was that Wright-Reagan allowed the United States to continue humanitarian aid to the contras and maintain them as a viable force until a final settlement was reached. The Guatemala accords allowed only aid for resettlement.

The administration had said it wanted the five Central American countries to reach a regional agreement by themselves. Now there was a regional agreement. The administration had to decide whether to work within the agreement to improve parts it disliked, or try to kill it.

Reagan vacillated, first saying that the United States would be "as helpful as possible." A few days later in a nationally televised speech, he said, "We welcome this agreement . . . [but] we have never been willing to abandon those who are fighting for democracy and freedom." But the next day, the White House was telling reporters that the Wright-Reagan plan "is still the operative agreement," ignoring the peace agreement. One day later, Fitzwater said, "Both plans are operative. . . . We don't favor one over the other."

The Guatemala accords forced into the open what Dick Cheney called "confusion over our objectives in Nicaragua. If the objective is to replace the government in Nicaragua, then you pursue a different policy than if you want a diplomatic settlement."

The main administration proponent of diplomacy was Philip Habib, the President's special envoy to Central America. He sought approval for a trip to the region to protect U.S. interests within the framework of the peace accords. The White House refused to let him go. He resigned. That left the field inside the administration to those who wanted to destroy the Sandinistas, period, led by Elliott Abrams.

Contra supporters now focused their attacks on Wright. *The New Republic* complained of "the failure of Loeffler, Shultz, and Baker to wring a commitment from Wright to stick with the [Wright-Reagan] plan until its expiration date, September 30." A *Wall Street Journal* editorial said, "Nicaragua was lost once and for all to the communist empire." Former United Nations ambassador Jeane Kirkpatrick— whom Wright considered a friend—wrote a *Washington Post* column attacking him as well.

Ten days after the agreement, the State Department briefed its ambassadors in the region, and advised them that the United States had national security interests which transcended the accord.

In mid-August the Sandinistas broke up a demonstration and arrested two leading critics. The administration pointed to the action as evidence that the Sandinistas would never allow free speech or democracy. Carlucci said the White House might propose contra aid in September. Howard Baker immediately contradicted him.

Honduras was a problem too. Contras operated from Honduran bases near Nicaragua. The peace agreement required closure of those bases. But of all the Central American countries, Honduras was most susceptible to U.S. pressure. Two years earlier the White House had bought civilian support for the contras in return for an additional $25 million in economic aid. And it was barely a democracy; President José Azcona had to keep the military content. The military received its aid from the United States directly—it was not channeled through the civilian government. Honduras also would need U.S. help to deal with the thousands of armed contras on its territory if the war ended.

Worried about administration pressures on Honduras, the House leadership applied its own. On August 25 the leadership arranged a lunch with the five Central American ambassadors and the Reverend Timothy Healey, president of Georgetown University. The lunch had a purpose: to lean on Honduras and Nicaragua.

Half an hour before the lunch, Wright and Arias talked on the phone;

Arias detailed several ways in which the Hondurans were dragging their feet. Coelho would sit next to Roberto Martinez, the Honduran ambassador. "Work on him," Wright said.

They ate in the Speaker's Dining Room; this lunch was elegant, with fine china and white-gloved waiters moving with a silent crispness. In the formal setting each word carried extra weight. Coelho told Martinez, "This is a golden opportunity to develop a long-lasting relationship between Central America and the United States. The Speaker wants to make this a focus of his speakership. The administration will be in office seventeen more months. The Speaker will serve ten years."

The implications of the comment were obvious: it was a threat as well as an invitation. The Honduran Martinez proposed a toast to Wright: "To you, sir. The words of Representative Coelho are music to my ears."

Through the smiles the tension increased. The pressure increased. Coelho complained about delays. Finally Martinez said, "I will be very candid. No doubt the five governments want peace. Yet because of the old Chinese obstacle of saving face, three of them have tremendous difficulty talking with insurgents. It will require some third party approaching both sides to reach a cease-fire. Some outside force. Perhaps from outside the region."

"Are you talking about the Pope?" Coelho asked.

"You can't deliver the Pope," Healey said.

"Very few Jesuits can," Coelho laughed.

Wright made a note of Martinez's comment. *Some outside force. Perhaps from outside the region.* Then the pressure shifted to Tunnermann, the Nicaraguan ambassador. Coelho warned that delays in the process could lead to more contra aid. Each member of the leadership complained bluntly about the Sandinistas' interference ten days earlier with the protest demonstration, and the arrest of two protesters.

"How did this happen?" Wright asked.

Tunnermann pressed his lips tightly together and said, "It will not happen again."

A week after the lunch—and after Wright publicly accused Honduras of dragging its feet at the request of the White House—Honduras announced that it would comply fully with the peace accords, including the closure of the contra bases. Three days later the Sandinistas allowed a large protest rally to proceed without interference, and released those arrested at the earlier demonstration. Ortega also wrote to the contra leadership about implementing the peace accords; it was the first official contact ever between the Sandinistas and the contras. The contra directorate met with Reagan and then, in the Dallas–Fort Worth airport, with Wright, and suggested passing a new aid package which held military aid in escrow pending Sandinista compliance with the treaty. Wright rejected the idea, then raised another issue: intermediaries were needed to negotiate a cease-fire. The Red Cross was one possibility. The Church, and particularly Cardinal Miguel Obando y Bravo, a determined critic and a powerful figure in Nicaragua, was another. The contras quickly endorsed Obando. Wright would feel the Sandinistas out on him. Progress seemed tortuously slow. Still, there *was* progress.

But hostility between the White House and Wright over Central America was about to break into the open. Arias, and his moral authority, remained the key to peace. Already Wright had publicly suggested that he receive the Nobel Peace Prize, which would intensify the pressure on all sides to comply with the peace accords. Wright also wanted to increase Arias's stature by inviting him to address a joint session of Congress. Joint sessions are called by the President. Initially Howard Baker welcomed the proposal, but Carlucci and Abrams objected. So Wright invited Arias to address the Democratic Caucus in mid-September. To hell with the White House. The Caucus would formally invite House Republicans and the Senate to attend. If the Republicans boycotted it, they would look as if they were trying to sabotage the peace process.

The conflict over Arias's visit was a symptom of tensions. Ever since Wright had endorsed the Guatemala accords, conservatives had argued that Wright had violated his deal with the President by abandoning their joint proposal. Conservatives insisted that left the administration free to move for contra aid.

On September 9, in a cramped conference room in the Rayburn Building, Carlucci and Under Secretary of State Michael Armacost delivered a message to the Democratic leadership and Bob Michel. The forty-day-old experiment in bipartisanship in Central American policy ended.

Carlucci and Armacost were annoyed to start with. They had followed Wright to the Rayburn Building and waited in the conference room while he met privately with Rodrigo Madrigal, the Costa Rican foreign minister, who then briefed seventy-five Democrats. It was another reminder that Wright was operating independently of the administration in Central American policy. By the time Wright, joined by Michel, walked into the makeshift meeting room, Carlucci was angry.

Wright was angry too. Michel had just told him Republicans might not accept his invitation to attend the Caucus address by Arias. Out of Michel's earshot, he told an aide, "I'd take that as a personal affront." Michel would learn of his displeasure.

When the Democratic leadership finally crowded into the room, Carlucci announced that the next morning Shultz would tell the Senate Foreign Relations Committee that on October 1 the administration would call for $270 million in contra aid.

It was startling news. There were still two months until the November 5 cease-fire deadline. Four days earlier, thirteen Latin American countries had asked the administration not to ask for aid. Now Carlucci was quoting a figure higher than any the administration had ever bandied about before.

Wright responded with controlled anger. "Frankly, I'm disappointed. My understanding was you would pursue peace."

"In the absence of a clear signal of support, the contras will dissolve," Armacost said.

Carlucci turned to Wright. "What you told them in Texas, that they wouldn't get more money, demoralized them. They're deserting."

"When there's peace," Wright snorted, "people leave the army."

"I was disappointed to read your statement in the paper that Honduras was dragging their feet because of the administration," Carlucci continued. "You're asking 15,000 people to put their lives in the hands of the Sandinistas."

"If you'd like a vote in early October we can give you one," Foley said. "You'll certainly lose. What kind of message would that be to send the contras?"

"Maybe vote after November 5," Michel agreed. "Not now."

Wright stepped out of the room and Coelho leaned forward, toward Carlucci. His voice was very cold, almost a hiss, and it raked over Carlucci, threatening him: "If you try to blame the Speaker for the 'demoralization' of the contras, we'll come after you. We'll get you."

Flustered, Carlucci replied, "If you don't blame us for destroying the contras we won't blame you for blowing up the peace plan."

He had gotten backwards what he wanted to say and sat red-faced. The next morning Shultz backed off only slightly, declaring that the administration would ask for $270 million in contra aid at an "appropriate" date. Meanwhile, the Democratic Caucus met—with one member in the chair and two on the floor—and by voice vote decided to invite Republicans to their Caucus for Arias. Immediately afterwards, Wright walked into the cloakroom, called Michel, and told him the Caucus had just "unanimously" voted to invite Republicans. Now Michel's reaction was, "Oh? They voted?" Boxed in, with Wright waiting for an answer, he accepted the invitation.

That weekend, in a coordinated communication barrage, the administration attacked the Arias plan. In an interview in *U.S. News & World Report,* Reagan was asked if the plan was "fatally flawed." "Yes, yes," he replied. Shultz, on the September 13 *Face the Nation,* talked about the old "two-track policy" of diplomacy combined with military pressure. On *Meet the Press,* Howard Baker said the same thing.

The deal with Wright was dead. Each side was convinced the other had violated it.

Meanwhile, Foley, Coelho, and Bonior were talking with Alfredo Cesar, a member of the contra directorate. A Stanford graduate, Cesar was articulate, attractive, and winning; he insisted the contras wanted the peace process to work. Coelho said, "You seem more willing to move peace along than the administration."

"Your perception is absolutely correct," Cesar replied. "The plan addresses 60 percent of our concerns, and none of the administration's geopolitical worries."

Less than a week later, *The New York Times* and other papers ran a dramatic photograph—huge rolls of newsprint being delivered at *La Prensa,* the anti-Sandinista newspaper closed by the Nicaraguan police in June 1986. The paper was reopening, two months earlier than the peace accords required. It was either brilliant public relations by the Sandinistas or a sign of their sincerity. The accompanying story quoted Enrique Bolanos, who headed the Nicaraguan business federation and was "among the most uncompromising Sandinista opponents . . . Mr. Bolanos hailed the accord as 'the successful culmination of our struggle.' "

The struggle was not over. It was just beginning. And also begun was a new conflict both personal and institutional, a new bitterness, between Jim Wright and Ronald Reagan, between the Speaker of the House and the President of the United States.

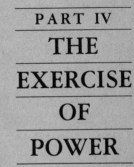

PART IV
THE
EXERCISE
OF
POWER

If there had come a time when it was necessary for him to act with circumspection he would have come to grief: he would never have acted other than in character. . . . Fortune is changeable whereas men are obstinate in their ways.

—Machiavelli, *The Prince*

CHAPTER 14

Hardly anyone in Washington noticed, and the national press did not report, the passing of the first deadline in the Gramm-Rudman law. That law required that the Office of Management and Budget in the White House and the Congressional Budget Office issue their initial "sequestration" reports, identifying the deficit reduction needed to bring the deficit down to the $108-billion target by August 17.

CBO estimated the fiscal deficit at $183 billion. OMB estimated it at $161 billion. (Foley said, "Thank God for OMB.") According to *Congressional Quarterly,* to meet the $108-billion target without raising taxes, sequestration—the automatic, across-the-board spending cuts— would have to slash 19 percent of the unprotected defense budget and 13 percent of the domestic budget. *Nineteen percent?! Thirteen percent?!* It would affect every person in America. OMB and CBO also lowered their estimates for economic growth, and raised estimates for interest rates, which meant that both predicted that the deficit would increase in future years unless policy changed. Both had been predicting a future decrease in the deficit, even without policy changes.

Only a few months earlier, both the President and OMB director James Miller had loudly demanded that Congress meet the $108-billion target, and do so without tax increases. Now the administration was silent. Gramm-Rudman called for the immediate convening of a special joint House-Senate committee to enact legislation reducing the deficit. Congress did nothing. The administration did nothing.

The markets around the world reacted nervously, with sudden steep drops and tentative climbs back up.

On September 9, the House reconvened. It was a Wednesday, after more than a month off. Members were unfocused, like students back for the first day of school. No one seemed ready to work. A sizable number of members would not even return for another week.

At 10:00 A.M. that morning the leadership met in Wright's office to review the legislative schedule for the rest of the year. By now, more than halfway through Wright's first year as Speaker, with the intensity of the Central America initiative behind them, the leadership team had settled into their roles.

Wright had every reason for confidence, basking as he was in praise from his colleagues. His suite of offices had been changed, too, made his. Rugs had been taken out, new ones brought in, his ceremonial office repainted in the burnt orange of the University of Texas—Jonathan Fuerbringer of *The New York Times* put on his sunglasses the first time he saw it. Wright's personal office had been rearranged, the refurbishing of his staff's offices planned, according to his wife's directions. She had wanted to do much more; Newt Gingrich's presence on the subcommittee that funded the renovation stopped her.

No longer were the Speaker's Rooms those of Tip O'Neill, simply occupied by Jim Wright. They were now Jim Wright's. Final changes would come over the Christmas recess, but now the physical stamp of his speakership had finally been imprinted on the Capitol. Wright was rooting himself. It was as though he had finally come home; this was it, this *House,* this was where he would be. He was rooting himself not only here, physically, but in time and place and history as well. He had launched an effort to trace his family back in County Tyrone in Northern Ireland. These things mattered to him. Time and place, defining himself, rooting himself, mattered. He had lived in enough towns when he was a boy. Moved enough back then. Now he was here to stay.

Foley and Coelho had also come into their own. Foley's performance so far as majority leader had engendered new respect among his colleagues. *Foley won't fight.* Even a Foley admirer had conceded early in the year. But Foley had shown force in the peace initiative, and his stature in the Caucus had risen. He had engaged Republicans on the floor, too, publicly in debate and privately in maneuvering. Once when a Republican amendment to create a bipartisan commission to close military bases was about to pass, he explained to members how that was a back-door way to increase the power of Republicans. "Who runs this place?" he had asked, switching enough votes to win.

He was also wary of Coelho, protective of his prerogatives too. Even Republicans had noticed an edge between him and Coelho, when scheduling was discussed. Foley worried that Coelho's constant pushing to maximize votes could backfire someday.

Coelho recognized the tension between himself and Foley. He didn't think Foley pushed hard enough. Back during the winter he and several colleagues had slept on a heating grate to dramatize the plight of the homeless. Coelho had heard a rumor that Foley had mocked him for that, had belittled it as a stunt, to reporters. It didn't sound like Foley, but Coelho believed it. It was true his staff was aggressive. He had hired self-starters; his floor aide Steven Champlin once told a member the leadership wanted him to vote a certain way, and the member had stared at him, then had said slowly, drawing the words out, "Who the fuck are you?" Coelho himself took Foley's aide George Kundanis to lunch and asked him what the hell the trouble was. And he had confronted Wright on that last day before recess, hours after the Central American peace agreement was announced, complaining that he was not being treated properly. Still, even Coelho was satisfied. He had never expected an easy transition, and Wright had promised to be more sensitive to him.

Coelho was comfortable by now in his offices, Wright's old offices, and when he was not comfortable he retreated into that one small room not much bigger than a closet, without a telephone, the door of which his staff did not open. And he was building an empire, a base independent of Wright. Lobbyists were paying for little things that helped members, such as seminars on making their offices more efficient. The whip task force meetings, the gatherings of ten to twenty-five members which focused on passing a given bill, were supplied with coffee, iced tea, soda, and fancy cookies. After members joked about calories, they were replaced with the California touch of broccoli, carrots, strawberries, cauliflower, and dip. A generational change. He also was continuing what he had done at the DCCC, funneling honoraria from lobbyists to members too junior to collect them on their own, helping their wives get jobs, their children get jobs. Coelho had gotten the architect of the Capitol to spruce up the House office buildings which, compared to the Senate's, had always been neglected. Suddenly painters and plasterers

382 · JOHN M. BARRY

flooded the House office buildings and the House side of the Capitol; the House was sparkling. Members liked that. Empires were built on little services like that. And he hadn't lost a vote which the task forces had worked.

Bonior had moved into a Capitol office, too, a small suite with an inside passageway connecting it to Foley's. His own room had a couch and a small, round conference table, more like a dinner table, and no desk. More than anyone else's in the leadership, his loyalty had been tested. He had managed to walk a fine line between that loyalty and principle, and his standing with both members and leadership colleagues had risen, his toughness proven.

More important, members of the leadership complemented one another: Wright made decisions, Foley played devil's advocate, Coelho executed, and Bonior helped. Perhaps a little tension only made each of them sharper. They had accomplished much of what they had set out to do. They had redirected the government's priorities; trade, transportation infrastructure, clean water, catastrophic illness insurance, farm credit, and homeless bills had all either moved through the House or would very soon. Most had been opposed by the White House, but some had already become law. The rest likely would. Wright had worked members hard, much harder than O'Neill had. But all along he had held out the carrot of an early recess for the year. If the House had to wait around, formally in session (neither House nor Senate could recess for more than three days without the other's consent) until the Senate acted on crucial legislation, maybe they could meet pro forma and give the members a week off here and there. Byrd wouldn't like that—it would make the Senate look bad, the House having finished its work, just twiddling thumbs waiting for senators to get to business— but House members would like it. Michel and the Republicans would like it just as much as Democrats.

Foley joked that he had sworn a blood oath to the members that there would be "backbreaking, tough votes" this first week after recess to get the members back in town, "but I forgot about the committee chairmen. They weren't too willing. Do you still want to tell committee chairmen that any legislation they want passed this year has to be reported out of committee by October 15?"

"Yes," Wright replied. "But they shouldn't stop working. We'll need legislation for the floor in January."

They talked briefly of the contras. Carlucci had written Wright a letter asking for $400,000 a month to help them, most of it to keep a CIA presence in Nicaragua. Foley observed, "That's a political issue, not a money one. We should do it. Otherwise, if the peace process collapses, they'll point the finger at us and say we crippled it."

All agreed to that. The only legislative business left for the year was implementing the budget. But Congress could not move until it knew precisely how much it had to cut from the deficit; that figure would be settled in the conference on Gramm-Rudman and the debt limit. So Congress had to wait: the schedule had to be pushed back. In three weeks the fiscal year would begin. They would need a short-term "continuing resolution" to appropriate money to run the government. This short-term continuing resolution would run until November 10.

Then the real war with the White House would begin, over full-year appropriations and the "reconciliation" bill. Before recessing for the summer, the House had passed nine of the thirteen bills and had finished committee work on two others. (The Senate had passed none, had not even finished committee work on any.) Appropriations covered "discretionary" spending, such as buying an aircraft carrier or hiring more FBI agents or subsidizing scientific research.

Continuing resolutions originally had served as temporary, stop-gap bills, whenever Congress failed to finish action before a new fiscal year began. Routinely they had continued funding at existing levels for a few days or weeks, usually for only one or two government departments, until new bills with new spending levels passed. But they had evolved into instruments of power.

Packaging all thirteen appropriations bills in one giant full-year continuing resolution, with new funding levels reflecting new policies, transformed a "C.R." into such an instrument. It meant that for the President to get the defense funding he wanted, he had to accept domestic appropriations he did not want. It also meant that a veto would close the entire government down and raise the stakes. Even though Wright wanted the House to pass each appropriation bill individually, from the first he had intended to wrap them together in one bill when he sent them to Reagan.

It was a congressional power play, not a Democratic one. The 99th Congress, with its Democratic House and Republican Senate, had put all thirteen bills in one continuing resolution the year before, but that had been the first time in history.

Other spending was mandated by law. For example, everyone eligible for Social Security benefits was "entitled" to receive them. Hence the name "entitlements." To cut entitlement spending, Congress had to change either eligibility requirements or benefits, and that meant Congress had to change, or "reconcile," existing law to meet budget requirements. All changes in law were combined in one "reconciliation" bill. Most committees had some reconciliation requirements. Ways and Means had the most. It had jurisdiction over the largest entitlement programs, Social Security and Medicare. And taxes involved rewriting law. The reconciliation bill included taxes.

Appropriations bills and reconciliation were the final step in the annual budget process. In a way, the budget Wright had struggled so hard to pass meant nothing. It was only rhetoric. The budget resolution is solely a congressional document: the President has no opportunity to veto it, and it has force only inside the Congress. Appropriations and reconciliation implemented the budget, made real spending decisions and raised real taxes. Reagan could veto implementation. Passing the budget was a battle. Implementing it was the war.

When the conference on the debt ceiling and Gramm-Rudman reconvened, it suddenly seemed that the White House was boxed in. Rostenkowski had wanted the leverage which automatic spending cuts, sequestration, would give him. Automatic sequestration would force the White House to choose between signing a tax bill and cutting defense spending.

His strategy seemed to be working. The White House, working through several Republican senators in the conference, tried to kill the provision for automatic cuts. Rostenkowski insisted on keeping it, and so did Democratic senators—and one GOP senator, Phil Gramm, who had pride of authorship. Democrats and Wright despised Gramm. Democrats joked that the most dangerous place in Washington was between Gramm and a TV camera, but their bitterness went back to that time in 1981 when Gramm, then a House Democrat, had sat in on Democratic strategy meetings and informed the White House of Democratic plans. But now House Democrats and Gramm agreed: the White House be damned.

The administration tried to buy off Rostenkowski with promises. Jim Baker called him and said he did not have the authority to talk about taxes but thought he could sell something to the President. Rostenkowski replied, "I'm tired of that game. Get the President into it first."

Then OMB director James Miller talked to Rostenkowski and Lloyd Bentsen, the Senate Finance chairman, about taxes. "You don't know what this means," Miller said.

"It means you're cooperating with us," Rostenkowski told him. Miller asked what revenues Rostenkowski wanted, and Rostenkowski said, "Look at Treasury I and II [the two administration tax reform proposals of 1985]. The President supported them. You tell me what you want."

Rostenkowski was almost gleeful. The automatic cuts weren't even in place yet and just the threat of cutting defense was working. *The Wall Street Journal* reported on his and Bentsen's meetings with Miller, and added, "Financial market jitters have increased the pressure on the White House to show some signs of progress in reducing the deficit."

Rostenkowski was not about to let the White House out of the box. With him and Bentsen working with Gramm, the conference reached agreement in mid-September: automatic sequestration was part of the agreement, and the constitutional issue was solved by making OMB initiate the sequestration order. The rest of the agreement: The debt limit itself would be raised to $2.8 trillion, high enough to last six months into the next President's administration. The deficit target would be $144 billion instead of $108 billion, and it would decline gradually to a balanced budget in 1993. Taxes weren't specifically part of the law, but it was understood, at least by Democrats, they would be $12 billion.

At 8:00 A.M. the morning after the agreement was reached, Rostenkowski briefed Buddy MacKay's group, explaining that he had gone over the plan in advance with Wright and Foley and they had agreed on all the details. "So I'm not out of step. For a change."

The group laughed, its mood jubilant. MacKay had been an ally on this issue. The fight had not ended, but this group's ideas seemed to be working. A member asked, "Where's the White House been?"

"Claude Rains," Rostenkowski said. The Invisible Man. He related his conversations with Baker and Miller about taxes and summed up, "Eight weeks ago a 'high administration official' was saying sequestration. Now the same one is saying, 'Let's make a deal.' The Republicans are in a very embarrassing position."

The entire political edifice of House Republicans was built around opposition to taxes. That had been the reason they had refused to offer any budget at all. Recognizing that a budget could not be put together without taxes, and not wanting to compromise their rhetoric by advocating them, they had simply declined to offer a proposal and voted against every other alternative. Now, if the White House accepted taxes, their entire edifice would crumble. Those in the room could smell a major political triumph.

Then Barbara Boxer, a liberal close to George Miller and Marty Russo, spoke. "You have my admiration—"

"But not your support?"

She laughed and continued. "What about the two-tier defense figure and taxes?"

It was a question with significance. This agreement made moot the budget Congress had passed earlier; now taxes would be $12 billion instead of $19.3 billion. And the official budget had included two different defense figures. If Reagan accepted $19 billion in taxes, defense would get one number. If he did not, defense would get much less. *What did the new tax number mean for defense? Did defense get the lower figure, the higher figure, something in between?* It was important, very important.

Bill Gray, who often monitored MacKay's meetings to sense the mood, interrupted—the overall budget was his area, not Rostenkowski's—and said flatly, "Unless there's $19 billion in taxes, it's the lower defense figure."

Boxer and other liberals nodded in satisfaction. *Good. That was the way we understood the deal.* Russo and Miller were pleased.

The debt limit and Gramm-Rudman bill passed and included the provision for automatic spending cuts; it was uncertain whether Reagan would sign it. Congress passed the short-term continuing resolution. And the House passed a farm credit bill, which, except for implementing the budget and passing welfare reform, completed virtually all Wright's agenda for the entire 100th Congress.

He even succeeded in feeding stories to the press exactly the way he wanted them. One vehicle he used was a "Sperling breakfast." Godfrey Sperling of the *Christian Science Monitor* had started them decades earlier and they had become a Washington institution, held in the Sheraton Carlton not far from the White House. Once the breakfasts had involved a handful of reporters in intimate conversation with a policy maker; now they were quasi–press conferences, sometimes with as many as thirty or forty reporters. Stories which said, "At a breakfast meeting with reporters" usually came from a Sperling breakfast. Wright did not like them much. He thought the breakfasts were geared toward generating a controversial headline rather than understanding a policy.

But that fitted perfectly what he now had in mind. Day after day, he had endured White House attacks over Central American policy and had not replied with a personal attack. Not anymore. At the breakfast he said Reagan "hasn't the faintest idea of the contents of legislation or the application of real facts to real problems. . . . [He] has the ability to psych himself up to reject factual data if it doesn't conform to his preconceived notions. . . . He's ignorant of the facts a President ought to know, and willfully so."

The fact that the Speaker of the House said such things of the President of the United States was in itself news. Stories the next day carried Wright's words, and they let the White House know he could play rough, too. *Before you pick a fight, you ought to make sure you can win it,* he had told them once before. He had ratcheted up the intensity another notch.

In late September, Costa Rican president Oscar Arias arrived, and triumphed. A short, self-confident, and self-contained man, bred of wealth and an intellectual, he was given a warm hero's welcome by Wright. The press did not even seem aware that technically Arias was addressing a Democratic Caucus, rather than a formal joint session of Congress. In his speech he called military aid to the contras "the main excuse for the Sandinistas to do all they have done in the past, to abolish individual freedoms, to abolish pluralism, to make of Nicaragua a more dictatorial country."

Later, in a private question-and-answer session with members, Arias argued that moral force and international isolation would cripple the Sandinistas if they failed to comply with the peace accords. Afterwards, Gingrich climbed the steps of the Speaker's Rostrum and told Wright, "I congratulate you. Arias is a serious man. Frankly, he won me over."

Wright seemed in absolute control of the House, about to challenge the President for supremacy.

Then Gingrich's campaign in the press began to flower. And other rumblings, inside and outside the House, began to reverberate.

The whole point of the Gramm-Rudman fix was to force Reagan to choose between defense cuts and taxes. But Bill Gray had assured thirty members that with the new lower tax figure, $12 billion instead of $19 billion, defense would get only the low-tier number from the now-outdated budget resolution.

That low-tier number was $283.2 billion in outlays, actual money spent. Sequestration would cut defense by only another $2.9 billion. For that little, Reagan would have little reason to accept taxes. Democrats had to offer him more than that as, in effect, a bribe. An aide told Wright the Senate was asking whether the defense number was flexible, given $12 billion in taxes.

"Presumably," Wright answered, "if we get two-thirds the taxes we were looking for, we might go halfway between the two tiers of the defense number. That will be solved in the appropriations process."

Wright had just defined the policy of the House. But Gray's words had already spread among liberals who cared most about the issue. It meant trouble. Serious trouble.

September 17 was the two hundredth anniversary of the Constitution of the United States. Dozens of members had asked Wright to reserve that day for House consideration of their bills. Wright gave it to Norman Mineta and Robert Matsui, two Japanese-American members, for a bill which apologized and provided some compensation to Japanese-Americans interned during World War II. At the whip meeting the morning of the vote, Matsui spoke of his own imprisonment as a six-month-old infant. Then Mineta rose from his seat near the front of the room. Intense, intently serious, he said, "You can be objective, unemotional about this. It's different for me." Like Matsui, he talked of the personal meaning of this bill. The whips grew uncustomarily still, then erupted into applause. A week earlier members had doubted the bill would pass at all, and Mineta was given the option of delaying it until the count improved; he chose to proceed. The personal appeal had impact. The bill passed with 243 votes.

Republicans had their own ideas on how to use Constitution Day. As part of their new confrontational style, they staged a media event: nailing a scroll filled with complaints about the way the House was run to the door of Wright's ceremonial office, H-210, the office at one end of the Speaker's Lobby. The office door was less than six feet away from the elevator the press used to go to their third-floor facilities. The scroll accused Democrats of "disenfranchising" the 92 million Americans represented by Republicans, and protested what they called abuses of power in the form of committee ratios which underrepresented Republicans, Rules Committee limitations on amendments, and "whitewashing" ethics investigations. The Republicans hoped for a crowd and a photo opportunity. They got neither. Their media event got not a single line in any major newspaper.

A week later, asked his response to the nailing of the scroll on the door—and the complaints it cited—Wright said, "What are you talking about?" No one had even bothered to mention it to him. When it was explained, he quipped, "Were there ninety-five theses?"

The fact that no one took them seriously only made the Republicans more frustrated, more angry. And more dangerous. Despite the lack of impact, they had committed themselves to pursuing the line of argument which echoed the corruption-of-power theme of Gingrich. They would keep working it, working it, hoping it would erode Wright's base of power.

Wright accommodated Michel on the short-term continuing resolution, which would appropriate money to run the government from the beginning of the new fiscal year, October 1, until November 10. Wright agreed to Michel's request to include $3.5 million in humanitarian aid for the contras for those six weeks even though the CIA said that the contras had enough money to last into January. The move would also protect Democrats from charges that they had abandoned the contras or "lost" Nicaragua if the talks broke down.

At breakfast Wright explained, "I want to make things easier for Michel. He's got a thorn in his side."

"I just don't want the thorn in your side," John Mack warned.

The money for the contras sent angry ripples through the Democratic Caucus. To prevent the floor from erupting, Wright put the money in a "self-executing" rule governing debate of the continuing resolution. Passage of the rule would mean that contra aid would be "deemed to have passed." There would be no separate vote on contra aid.

He was exercising power through his control of procedure, hiding substance in a procedural vote. It was precisely the kind of abuse the Republicans had just complained about in their scroll. But they did not complain about this. Democrats did. Dick Cheney walked into Coelho's office and promised to defend the Democratic leadership on the floor. "I trust Cheney," Coelho said.

The Sandinistas told Wright's staff they understood the political necessity of the contra aid, and would not complain even though the peace plan forbade it. Simultaneously, Ortega announced the uncensored reopening of the radio station run by the Catholic Church.

Wright told his daily press conference that this would be the last money the contras would get. He would go to war over it next time.

The biggest thorn remained Gingrich. *U.S. News & World Report* ran a major story on Wright. It was laudatory but included Gingrich's comment, the same comment he was repeating to reporters over and over, that "Wright is the least ethical Speaker in this century." And even though the story focused on Central America, it referred to Wright's intervention with the Federal Home Loan Bank Board for Texas savings and loans, concluding, "The incident has left Wright, at the very least, with an unsightly political scar."

Every time Wright thought he was shut of that damned issue, it came back to haunt him. The savings and loan thing would not go away. *Newsweek* had done that story. *The New York Times* had done it. *Business Week* was doing it. The Texas papers, the *Houston Chronicle, Dallas Morning News, Austin American-Statesman, Dallas Times-Herald* had all done it over and over. In late September, a writer asked him what disappointments he had suffered. Wright did not mention any policy. Instead he talked of the press coverage of his involvement in the S&L issue.

"That was a failure," he said. "I haven't quite figured out why. I am chagrined that I apparently have not been able to get a serious writer to focus on a serious problem, to get the press to understand that the entire industry in Texas is strained and the Texas economy is at risk, and that that is why I stepped in. Perhaps it was my impatience, my unwillingness to explain to every reporter who asked all the details of the situation."

Those words masked an anger at the press, an anger at what he considered strictly a public relations problem. He was not yet willing to admit that he had made even a policy mistake in trying to restrict the regulators. And even if he had made a policy mistake, it infuriated him that the press implied ethical wrongdoing.

There was another story coming soon, a very bad story about him. And he knew it was coming. In a moment of quiet, he began ruminating about how the House had changed since his arrival more than thirty years before. The sense of collegiality, which he had hoped to restore, had eroded. The world had changed.

"Sportsmanship," he said. "That's changed around here. It's changed in boxing too. I recall when I was boxing there was a light heavyweight in the Olympic trials named Egan. Never heard of him before or since. His scheduled opponent had a cut and a doctor was going to make him forfeit. Egan told him if he wanted to box to put a white patch over the cut and it would still be white when the match was over. He wouldn't hit it. These days if you have a cut, a weakness, they go after it, beat on it, pound it, try to exploit it, until they kill you."

On Thursday, September 24, *The Washington Post* ran a front-page story whose impact would ultimately shake the House, shake all of Washington. It was written by investigative reporter Charles Babcock.

Babcock started working on his story partly because he believed that any Speaker should be scrutinized. But he also had gotten particularly interested in Wright because of his conversion ten years earlier of campaign funds to personal use. It had been perfectly legal at the time, but Babcock went to his editor Bob Woodward and suggested a close examination of Wright might prove fruitful. Earlier, Babcock had broken many of the stories that created problems for both Attorney General Ed Meese and former Democratic vice-presidential nominee Geraldine Ferraro. Babcock started researching the story even before Wright became Speaker, worked on it off and on for months, and put the story together in four intensive weeks.

He examined Wright's involvement with savings and loan executives and decided nothing there was worth reporting; it didn't seem Wright had acted improperly. He looked at Wright's business partner George Mallick, who had gotten involved in a depressed area of Fort Worth for which Wright was getting federal money. Mallick's involvement there had lasted only four months. That didn't seem to be anything. But in reviewing Wright's financial disclosure forms he had noticed a similarity between two names, Madison Printing, which did campaign work, and Madison Publishing, from which Wright received royalties for his book *Reflections of a Public Man*. When Babcock asked detailed questions about it of Wright's staff, they seemed tense and refused to let him interview Wright, requiring him to submit written questions. That made him more suspicious. And he discovered that Carlos Moore headed both the printing and publishing companies. Wright's staff let him see the book contract. And his story became explosive.

"House Speaker Jim Wright (D-Tex.)," the lead paragraph went, "has received almost $55,000 over the past two years as royalties on a book he wrote that was published by a longtime friend whose printing company was paid $265,000 for services to Wright's campaign committee last year."

Wright received a 55 percent royalty for the book, compared to usual royalties of 15 percent. Further, Moore had gone to prison in 1975 for income tax evasion on $90,000 he had taken from a Teamsters union political fund. Moore, at the time a Teamsters lobbyist, had insisted he had used the money for possibly illegal contributions to politicians. He chose prison over naming them.

On the surface, the book looked like a scheme to launder campaign contributions.

(It wasn't, as a later, thorough investigation proved. Moore himself had suggested that Wright write the book, and despite the high royalty had made a substantial profit on it.)

That day and the next a firestorm of phone calls from reporters hit Wright's office. The immediate repercussions of the Babcock story were less damaging than expected. Congress had just recessed for Rosh Hashanah and no members were around. Over time, though, the book would become corrosive. Ironically, the *Post* ombudsman distributed an internal memo criticizing Babcock for making much of little. But more would ultimately develop.

Bob Strauss, Coelho, and others had urged Wright to set up a blind trust and sever all but social ties to George Mallick. A blind trust killed stories. It gave the press nothing to bite into, eliminated any appearance of conflict of interest. With a blind trust, the cuts Wright had suffered would heal. He began to set one up.

But the pack was forming. Now every major newspaper and magazine wanted to send its own investigative reporter out to see what he could dig up. *Newsweek* was already poking around. So was the Texas press. A month earlier Brooks Jackson, *The Wall Street Journal*'s expert on politics and money, had written a major investigative piece about Wright and had failed to uncover anything new. Another writer kidded Jackson that Babcock had outdone him. Jackson, a competitor, reacted angrily. He would write more stories about Wright.

A few days after Babcock's story appeared, when David Montgomery, the bureau chief of the *Fort Worth Star-Telegram*, asked for an interview to talk about his finances, Wright exploded. *Damn this thing*.

Damn it to hell. Now if you have a cut, a weakness, they go after it, beat on it, pound it, try to exploit it, until they kill you.

Wright still saw the whole issue as a problem of press relations, not of substance. *If they think they do not like me it is because they do not know me,* he had written on that affirmation he had carried with him for so long. He believed that if people would only listen to his explanation, they would understand that he had done absolutely nothing wrong. He refused to admit that even if all his explanations were true, even if the press accepted them, many things he had gotten into looked like conflicts of interest. He had ignored those appearances, and shown not so much bad judgment as no judgment.

"The book was just lagniappe," Gingrich said later, using a New Orleans expression for a serendipitous something extra. "I was going to proceed regardless, but it certainly helped."

Wright's a useful keystone to a much bigger structure, Gingrich had said. He did not want to let any wounds heal. *I'll just keep pounding and pounding on Wright's ethics. There comes a point where it comes together and the media takes off on it, or it dies.*

The criticism did not make Wright pull back from his agenda. If anything, he plunged more deeply into it. He found escape in it. That was what mattered. That was what he cared about and where he would leave a mark, where he would root himself in time and place. That was worth fighting for.

His own agenda, his own power and his own policies, drew all his energies. He needed power to carry out his plans. Each new committee assignment fell into his web. When a seat on Appropriations opened up, he said, "I can't afford to have any more members on these key committees who aren't leadership people." In his ceremonial office just off the floor, he discussed the opening with his staff. Half a dozen people wanted the seat. Of one colleague, he commented, "I'm not sure his district would allow him to support the leadership."

"I'm from his district," an aide said. "He can support you."

Wright smiled coldly. "I know that. I'd rather say that I don't trust his district than that I don't trust him."

He would examine each candidate's record on fourteen "leadership votes" so far that year, talk to whomever he intended to support—his support was tantamount to election—and insure that that member understood the responsibilities a seat on Appropriations carried.

Another element of power was money. Lyndon Johnson first rose to power through the DCCC, funneling campaign money to colleagues. O'Neill had once chaired it, and had called money "the mother's milk of politics." Coelho used it as a stepping-stone. Wright viewed DCCC fund-raising as crucial to his job. By late September he had taken almost twenty trips for the DCCC to raise money for colleagues. The weekend Babcock's story about Wright's book ran in the *Post,* Wright was exhausted, worn out, and physically ill. He needed rest. But he had scheduled a trip with DCCC chairman Beryl Anthony and he kept his commitment.

They started Friday night in Memphis, then Saturday hit Tuscaloosa in mid-morning, Birmingham for a $5,000-a-plate lunch, and Atlanta for a $500 afternoon picnic—where people could shoot baskets with Dominique Wilkins, the basketball star—and a $1,000 evening cocktail party, and on Sunday went to Hilton Head before returning to Washington, all in the Philip Morris corporate jet. That was better than a campaign contribution for Philip Morris. It made things easy for those in power. Federal Election Commission rules governed payment; all passengers paid first-class fare plus one dollar; that was much cheaper than chartering the jet. The trip was important and had a theme: bringing the South back home, back to the Democratic Party. In each city Wright would sign up new members of the Speaker's Club, which cost $5,000 to join, and appear at less expensive events also. The same weekend, Foley was raising money in North Carolina and Armed Services chairman Les Aspin was raising money for the DCCC from defense contractors in California.

The first event was a $1,000-a-plate catfish fry in Memphis on the roof of the Peabody Hotel, one of the grand old hotels of the South. From the roof one could look out at the sunset and feel all of southern history rolling down the Mississippi River, a few blocks away. Blocks of warehouses built for cotton merchants lined the river, heavy with the Old South. But Memphis had joined the New South. What better symbol of the service economy than Federal Express, headquartered in Memphis? The rooftop swarmed with Federal Express executives. Indeed, the roof swarmed with businessmen from all over the South. "These people live and die by the tax code," said a DCCC aide.

Wright told them in his gentle rolling tones, as alluvial almost as the river itself, "People are coming home to the Democratic Party, there is a link between the Democratic Party and the South. The party is coming back together." Then he made other points—how the South, just as in former times, now dominated the Congress—in the Senate, Stennis of Mississippi, Johnston of Louisiana, Bentsen of Texas, Nunn of Georgia, Chiles of Florida, all chairing critical committees, and in the House Whitten of Mississippi, Chappell of Florida, Bevill of Alabama ran Appropriations. It was a recitation which could not fail to impress businessmen interested in getting access to people who could get things done, in giving money to those people.

The next morning, sitting in a limousine riding to the airport, Anthony and Wright talked about businessmen and politics. Anthony recalled 1981, when his business supporters attacked him for opposing Reagan's budget and tax bills. Wright nodded and said, "Yes, it hurts you deep inside when these people you've done so many things for over the years turn against you." *When people you thought were your friends turn against you.* This was cold business.

Then in Tuscaloosa the business turned hot. Wright addressed a state party gathering at a Holiday Inn. The air-conditioning was overwhelmed by the crush; with all the seats taken, all aisles crowded with party people, black people, union people, it could have been a revival meeting with folks waving hand-held fans in front of their faces, and Wright spoke of a different kind of power, of "our party," of poor folks and working for change. It was old-time politics and Wright warmed to it like old-time religion.

Then back to money: the $5,000-a-plate Birmingham lunch, the $500 mid-afternoon Atlanta picnic, then the cocktail party at the Commerce Club where Wright told executives from Coca-Cola and elsewhere, "Votes don't cross district lines but money does. Politics is not a spectator sport."

The weekend would raise $350,000 for the DCCC, putting it at $3.5 million for the year, $1 million ahead of the pace for the preceding nonelection year. He was making a difference.

But after one event a reporter asked him about his book. Wright brushed past him, saying only, "At least I wrote it."

Wright needed all his power for the tax bill. He had never stopped applying pressure on Ways and Means and now the bill was moving. Ironically, relations between him and Rostenkowski had improved. They had fought a dozen serious battles already this year. At times Rostenkowski had privately raged, "That *jerk!* That *jerk!*" But Wright had been fair in choosing conferees for the trade bill. It was complex legislation, over a thousand pages, and balancing his policy desires and jurisdictional fairness was not simple. He had not given Dingell more representation than he deserved. Rostenkowski would chair the conference and had told Wright he appreciated it.

But taxes put them at war again. Wright's pushing had begun the day the Caucus nominated him for Speaker and never abated. He had generated pressure on the committee through other members too, all designed to force the committee to produce a "Democratic" bill, which taxed upper-income people—and avoided the excise taxes Rostenkowski wanted. Shortly before summer recess Rostenkowski had requested that the full Democratic Caucus meet to discuss taxes; he and Wright had each tried to orchestrate the discussion by getting members who agreed with them to speak. Wright's symphony proved more successful, as colleague after colleague said similar things: "To write anything but a purely populist bill is crazy." "We've got to be strong, be resolute, and hit Reagan at his weakness. Tax the rich." "Since when is it irresponsible to tax the rich?" At the end, the only audience was Ways and Means staff taking notes. "That's okay," a Wright supporter had observed. "They're the ones who count."

Now in September Wright pushed harder. The liberal Democratic Study Group, the DSG, agreed with him and opposed excise taxes. On the DCCC fund-raising trip, Beryl Anthony, an Arkansas member on Ways and Means, asked Wright in a moment alone with him, "Would you really give the DSG an amendment on the tax bill?"

The question had weight. If Ways and Means levied regressive taxes, the DSG would seek an amendment to propose a liberal alternative. That would pit much of the Caucus against Ways and Means Democrats. Rostenkowski had enough problems without that. Tradition was involved, too. Tax bills almost always come to the floor under a "closed" rule which allowed no amendments to be offered, just a Republican substitute. It was one of the historic prerogatives of Ways and Means not enjoyed by other committees. If Wright told Rules to give DSG an amendment, that could set a precedent for the future. Months earlier Rostenkowski had told MacKay's budget group, *I'll be goddamned if I sit there as chairman of Ways and Means and put a package out there on the floor that's dismembered by Democrats.* He didn't want any amendments.

Deliberately, believing that his answer would get back to the committee, Wright replied, "If Ways and Means doesn't come up with a good Democratic bill, Beryl, I'm afraid I'd have to give them an amendment."

And Wright was preparing if necessary to fight for that amendment on the floor. Pat Williams, the deputy whip who served as liaison to organized labor, brought AFL-CIO chief lobbyist Robert McGlotten to see him about scheduling more labor bills. Wright said he supported those bills and would see to it that they reached the floor. Then he asked, "How interested is the labor movement in taxation? We fight like the devil over where the money goes, but it's just as important where the money comes from. If we made a battle for a Democratic tax bill, not to tax poor folks, how enthusiastic would labor be?"

"We've been behind you from early on," McGlotten replied. "But we can't even get anyone to raise the question of freezing the top rate on Ways and Means."

"That's just one committee of the House. The House can't let it write a Republican bill. We've got to find a way to get a Democratic bill. Maybe we'll revisit that."

McGlotten, unlike most lobbyists, had the authority to make a commitment on the spot. Behind his word stood all the AFL-CIO. He gave it: "You let us know and we'll help."

After McGlotten left, Wright turned to Mack. "Are they getting the message on Ways and Means? Everyone I talk to I give it."

Rostenkowski was getting it.

Rostenkowski would give Wright a bill. But it would be Wright's job to pass it.

Ironically, Rostenkowski's conversations with Jim Baker and OMB head Jim Miller had convinced him that taxes would become law. Sequestration had changed the game. Other members of Ways and Means shared that view. Mike Andrews, a Ways and Means member, said, "There's a feeling on the committee that if we don't hit income tax rates, gouge on excise taxes, if we do base-broadening and loophole-closing stuff, the President will sign the bill."

That sense on Ways and Means, that Jim Wright's power would pull a tax bill through the House and that the President would sign it, would have repercussions which would change Wright's speakership forever.

To Tom Downey, who chaired the Ways and Means subcommittee that handled welfare reform, reconciliation was beginning to look like a vehicle instead of a death trap. Ambitious and arrogant, Downey had been elected from Long Island in 1974 when he was twenty-six years old. Baby-faced, he could still pass for twenty-six. His colleagues had a mixed view of him: his arrogance rubbed many the wrong way, but his intelligence, his hard work, and the fact that he kept his word made up for it. He also had a core group of supportive colleagues built around constant basketball games in the House gym. Only a few months earlier the chairmanship had dropped into his lap—Caucus rules had required the former chairman to resign his post—and welfare reform, as big an issue as anyone could care to handle, was his first test as a chairman.

Momentum behind welfare reform had been building for years. States from Massachusetts to California had developed ballyhooed programs to get people off welfare. The National Governors' Association, under Arkansas Democratic governor Bill Clinton, had recently proposed a major welfare overhaul. Even Reagan in his State of the Union message had called for it. All the reform proposals emphasized work. As Clinton said, even liberals now recognized that not only did society have a responsibility for individuals, but the individual had "a responsibility to society."

Moving welfare recipients into the work force would save money over time but cost money in the short term. The government would have to subsidize people while they trained and continue medical coverage in entry-level jobs without benefits. The bill put together primarily by Downey and Education and Labor Committee chairman Gus Hawkins cost an extra $6 billion over five years, compared to a GOP bill developed by Colorado's Hank Brown, the ranking subcommittee member, which added a little over $1 billion. Members supported welfare reform, but not Downey's price tag.

Downey wanted his version of the bill to pass the House untouched but knew it would have difficulty. It would need strong—very strong—leadership support. It would need the kind of intense, back-to-the-wall pressure which the leadership would exert to pass the tax bill, formally called "reconciliation" since it also cut entitlements and reconciled current law to the budget. Downey wondered, why not attach welfare reform to reconciliation? Reconciliation had a specific legislative function and welfare reform had no business being included. But if it was included, the leadership pressure to pass the tax bill could carry Downey's bill through the House. And who knew? Maybe it could carry it all the way into law. Downey asked Rostenkowski to include welfare reform with taxes.

There was a deep irony here, perhaps more than irony. All year Rostenkowski had talked about how difficult it would be to pass a tax bill—difficult to get it out of Ways and Means, more difficult to get it through the House, more difficult still to get one out of the Senate, and most difficult to get the President to sign it. Welfare reform would add to that burden.

But Rostenkowski was loyal to members of his committee and tried to help all of them when he could. He especially liked to help subcommittee chairmen, especially when they came to him and asked for help. Like a feudal system, power worked in both directions: the liege lord had a responsibility to his vassals in return for their support.

Perhaps there was another factor, too. Rostenkowski had already made clear he considered it the leadership's job to pass the tax bill once Ways and Means reported it. Perhaps, somewhere in his mind, just under the surface, voiced to no one, perhaps not quite even to himself, was the thought, *All right, Mr. Speaker. You wanted a tax bill. Here's a tax bill. Incidentally, it's got $6 billion in new spending in there too. Now show me what you can do. Now show me what a powerful Speaker you are. Now pass it.*

Rostenkowski agreed to include welfare reform in reconciliation.

He informed one of Wright's aides of his plans, but did not tell Wright personally. That was not like him. He did not use staff in that way, and believed if a member had something to say, the member should say it. But it allowed him to say Wright was informed without informing him. *He was the chairman of Ways and Means. By God, he would run his own committee.* The next day he told his committee Democrats in caucus. In addition, he announced Ways and Means would report the tax bill out October 15.

As Ways and Means was caucusing, so were Budget Democrats, who were reviewing reconciliation. Frank Guarini, a New Jersey Democrat who served on both committees, arrived at Budget as the caucus was breaking up and repeated Rostenkowski's announcement. Californian Vic Fazio grabbed Guarini at the door and said, "Wait a second. Welfare? How much will *that* cost?" *Six billion?!* Fazio was incredulous and furious. Even if it could pass the House—the politics were awful, a tax bill packaged together with a major new initiative practically screamed "tax and spend, tax and spend"—it gave the President new excuses to veto the bill.

It was evening now, and the House was quieter even than on weekends. Not even tourists moved down the corridors. But a spark of activity burned in H-209, where Mack's desk sat amid others in a medium-size room. A handful of leadership staff was working. So were some of the parliamentarians. They weren't happy about Rostenkowski's declaration of his plans. If that declaration stood, it meant a fight, a serious fight, and they were not looking forward to it.

The following Tuesday the bill raising the debt limit and changing Gramm-Rudman—changes designed to force a choice between taxes and defense cuts—became law. Reagan signed it while denouncing it: "To those who say we must weaken America's defense, they're nuts. To those who say we must raise the tax burden on the American people, they're nuts."

Words have meaning and resonance and undertones to politicians. Reagan's comment sounded like a declaration of war, and an insult.

Barely an hour after the White House bill signing, Wright sat down with committee chairmen around that long baronial table in the Speaker's Dining Room to talk about reconciliation. The delays over the Gramm-Rudman changes had destroyed the schedule Wright had already set—committees were supposed to report their bills out by September 29. This *was* September 29. Wright announced the new schedule. It was Rostenkowski's. Wright would give him that. By October 15 committees would finish their work. The bill would be on the floor either the following week or the week after that.

Rostenkowski told his chairmen colleagues that Reagan had just denounced the debt-limit bill. He shook his head with disappointment. "Jesus, every Republican leader in Congress voted for that bill." That was true: every single member of the GOP leadership in the House and Senate had voted for it. Even Gingrich had. Reagan was insisting that he get his way, and everyone else be damned. Rostenkowski added, "When Reagan signed it he quoted the general at Bastogne. He said 'nuts' to us."

"He said that, huh?" Wright bridled. All the chairmen stiffened. Most were World War II veterans. Then Wright told Rostenkowski: "If he's determined to veto the tax bill anyway, don't let him be saving the poor folks. Don't let him play populist, and make us out as elitists."

"As I understand it, only four people knew he was going to sign the bill until he made the announcement," Rostenkowski replied. "They couldn't tell Weinberger. He'd have jumped out of the Pentagon. Playing with Reagan's like playing with ghosts. We're just going to have to govern."

"That's exactly right," Wright said. "We're just going to have to govern." A look of satisfaction flashed across his face. Finally Rostenkowski was ready to work with him. *It was about time.*

They weren't going to fight over taxes anymore. Rostenkowski would write a "Democratic" bill. But the news about welfare reform was sending ripples of outrage through the House.

Bill Pitts, Michel's senior aide, complained to Mack, "You want the President to sign reconciliation or not? Why is welfare reform in there? He won't sign that. It's got no business being in the bill. That bill's for deficit reduction. Why do you want to protect Downey?"

"If we take it out, will the minority leader enthusiastically support reconciliation?"

Pitts did not answer. That was the way the game was played: *if you get something you want in—or out—of the package, you are obligated to support the package.* If Michel wasn't going to support it anyway, who was he to say what was in it?

Still, Michel wrote Wright a letter formally protesting the inclusion of welfare. The letter was delivered to the press galleries six hours before being delivered to Wright's office.

Democrats were unhappy about putting welfare reform in reconciliation too. Wright did not like it either. Rostenkowski had not discussed it with him before making the decision. Now the two men talked and decided to do a whip count. If the package could pass, welfare reform would stay in the bill. But if it looked shaky, they would strip it out.

On October 1 Ways and Means met. Rostenkowski planned to raise the $12 billion in pieces. He first put on the table an $8 billion package. Reagan himself had called for three billion dollars' worth of these taxes. Another three billion dollars' worth had been introduced earlier in legislation cosponsored by Rostenkowski and ranking Republican John Duncan.

But Duncan and Bill Frenzel, an influential Republican on the committee, said they preferred sequestration. Let the axe fall and the hell with it. When Rostenkowski called for the first vote, on a tax Reagan himself had requested, Ways and Means Republicans voted present as Budget Committee Republicans had done a few months earlier. William Archer, a Texas Republican, declared, "I don't think we'll vote for anything."

Rostenkowski hadn't expected that. He had always treated the Republicans well, gave them everything he could, and prided himself on his committee's bipartisanship. "We don't consider Ways and Means Republicans to be like other Republicans in the House," one Democrat on the committee said. "They're different." A GOP aide echoed that thought in a complaint: "Republicans on Ways and Means think they're special. The leadership can't tell them anything."

But now Ways and Means Republicans were playing partisan games. Rostenkowski was furious. *The hell with them.* A committee Republican suggested a deal. Maybe they could support the $8 billion, and if Democrats wanted more they could have a separate floor vote for the extra $4 billion.

"Have Michel talk to Wright," Rostenkowski replied. "That's not my area."

Republicans believed—rightly—that Democrats wanted to use GOP votes on the noncontroversial taxes to claim bipartisan support for tax increases, and then ram through the rest with just their own votes. Republicans would not do that. They had refrained from participating in any element of the budget process all year. But they would consider some deal. At least Michel would.

All year House Republicans had advocated nothing and opposed everything, opposed both their own President's budget and the Democrats'. Yet Michel recognized the need for revenue. He was also appalled by the automatic across-the-board cuts of sequestration. Sequestration marked a breakdown of government. To avoid sequestration the deficit had to come down $23 billion. He believed if Republicans supported $8 billion in taxes and $15 billion in spending cuts— roughly a two-to-one ratio of cuts to taxes—they could act responsibly and reclaim the upper hand in the politics of the deficit. He had already told both Jim Baker and Howard Baker that he wanted to try to work something out with Democrats on taxes. They warned him Reagan was opposed but told him to see what he could do. Now it was time for Michel and Wright to get together.

But it was late. Months before, Gray had sent serious feelers out inviting Republicans to cooperate in forging a truly bipartisan budget.

Republican distrust of the Democrats had delayed their response. *Yes,* they had thought, *maybe we'll help, but first we'll make sure the invitation isn't a ploy on your part. Then we'll let you swing in the wind for a while. Then we'll rescue you. Maybe.* The window had slammed shut long before any of that had happened. Long before.

Since then the parties had moved far apart within the House. Bitterness had steadily increased. Republicans resented Wright's having maneuvered them into a position just a few days earlier where they had had to attend Arias's speech despite the White House opposition to his peace plan. The parties were far apart. So far apart. Michel was sitting down with Wright to try to work things out, but it was hard to see one conversation bridging that gap.

Michel had expected the meeting to be candid, blunt, and private with just him and Wright and their aides Pitts and Mack. But when he walked in he saw Foley and a half-dozen aides. Michel was a careful man. He said as little as possible in public. And this many people was public.

Wright sat behind his desk, with Michel in an armchair to his left next to Foley. Pitts sat on the couch directly in front of Wright. A secretary brought some coffee and they started out talking about safe subjects—golf—and moved to the schedule. Michel suggested, since the House had nearly finished its legislative business while the Senate was way behind, that maybe they could let the members go home for a week here and there, returning when they needed to. Foley said they had been thinking of the same thing. Members liked it, and it put a spur in the Senate.

Then they eased into harder subjects. What about Energy and Commerce? They owed $300 million, which Wright had said—back when he needed to pass the budget conference report—they could ignore.

"You're right," Wright said. "We'll try to make that up some other way."

The deficit reduction was supposed to be $23 billion. Could it come from $18 billion in spending cuts, $5 billion in taxes?

Wright laughed. "Come on. It's half and half. Plus, if we don't get the tax bill, more comes out of the military. You wouldn't want that, would you?"

"Try to think of the guy downtown," Michel said, referring to the President.

"We're borrowing three trillion dollars. We can't raise $12 billion in taxes? Send the bill to our kids, Bob? And our grandkids?"

"Where do you want to get that $12 billion?"

"The majority party in Congress has something to say through the tax code," Wright declared. It would use the tax bill to define itself, define its priorities. "Ways and Means will take some of the President's proposals. Everyone will give a little."

Then Pitts spoke up. Except to provide technical information, it was unusual for an aide to jump in with any member, much less with the Speaker. But Pitts, whose father had had his job before him and who had gotten married in Michel's office, was unique. Sensing that Michel wanted him to handle this, he did.

"Maybe my math isn't all that good," Pitts said. "The cuts used to be $18 billion. Now they're $11 billion. They used to be $9 billion domestic, $9 billion defense. Now they're $2 billion in domestic, but still $9 billion cut from defense."

"We've cut domestic spending 34 percent since 1981 on a current services basis."

"We're here to work out what's possible. Your bill may not pass."

"That may be," Wright said. "I'm getting tired of this. I proposed the simplest thing. No more tax cuts for people making $200,000 a year. Was that considered on its merits? No. Your party acted like demagogues. I proposed that we pay for what we use up, instead of borrowing the money. Was that treated responsibly? No. You sat back and did not give one bit of help this year. Not one damn bit. And that's damn irresponsible. If you want to do it again, fine, but we'll surely point out what you're doing. You come in here, having given us no help all year, and now you're dictating to us conditions for your help? Your bottom line is no revenue?"

He was angry. His gaze narrowed, grew fierce, his voice rumbling. He was almost, for an instant, out of control, a thin line away from crossing into rage. Then he pulled back within himself.

"No, no," Michel said, conciliatory for a moment. "We can maybe weasel out a little revenue."

But the conciliation lasted only for that moment. Pitts complained that welfare reform didn't belong in reconciliation.

"Fine," Wright replied. "If that's what's needed for Republican votes. But the first thing, Republicans on Ways and Means have to participate. If that's the sticking point, we can talk about that."

Foley added, "But we can't concede that for Republican votes, then not get any."

"It's only one sticking point," Pitts replied.

Wright pressed his lips together tightly. He was not about to surrender issue after issue in return for a few scattered GOP votes. Pitts suggested that Republicans would support $8 billion in taxes with two floor amendments. Democrats would have one raising another $4 billion in taxes; Republicans would have one cutting an additional $4 billion.

"We already agreed it would be half taxes, half spending cuts," replied Mack. If Pitts was going to talk, so would he.

"*We* never agreed to that."

"That's precedent," Wright declared. The meeting was over. "I want you to have options in voting with which you're comfortable. Ways and Means usually has a closed rule but we can explore that."

Michel rose to leave. Wright also stood, saying, "We're crippling America's capacity to grow with these policies. I think you're selling your people short. Business people, your supporters, recognize it. They tell me that taxes are the way to go."

Michel snorted. Those same business people were also urging a cut in the capital gains tax. Wright and Michel shook their heads over that. It was the first thing they agreed on that day.

The next day the papers reported that Michel had offered to cooperate on $8 billion and that Wright had rejected it. Members began to ready themselves for the final collision.

The tax bill started moving through Ways and Means as the committee, with no Republicans voting yes, approved $6.3 billion in taxes. A day later, in the Senate Finance Committee, Republicans copied their House counterparts and refused to participate.

Back in the House, Rostenkowski met one-on-one with each of his Democrats. *What did they need?* he wanted to know. What special transition rule worth millions of dollars to a hospital, or a campaign contributor, did they need to vote for the tax bill? They told him and slowly the package came together. It hit the wealthy through higher taxes on publicly traded limited partnerships. It also raised several billion dollars with a 50 percent, nondeductible tax on profits made from "greenmail," which would discourage some hostile corporate takeover activity, and by eliminating tax subsidies of highly leveraged corporate buy-outs. The committee passed the bill on a party line, 23–13 vote.

Suddenly they had done it. Suddenly Ways and Means Democrats were smug. Sitting in the committee offices, a Rostenkowski aide was reviewing the bill. He was proud. *They had done it.* "The Republicans were unhappily surprised. We raised $12 billion without hitting the lower or middle class. We try to squeeze as much policy as we can out of anything we do."

The aide was ready to move on. The phone rang. It was a member, calling about a little favor to be stuck in the technical corrections bill. "Whose list is it on?" the aide asked. "Who did you give it to? All right, I'll find it and take care of it."

In a week or so, the House would vote on the tax bill. After that would come the continuing resolution, the "C.R.," which would combine in one package all discretionary spending, all thirteen individual appropriations bills for the next year.

Everything, the entire year's work, was coming down to two bills, reconciliation—taxes, entitlement cuts, and welfare reform—and the continuing resolution—appropriations. The fight over those two bills would determine who controlled domestic policy; it would determine from whom the government got money and where that money went. They would be the last battles of the year, the fiercest, and the most important. That was where Wright would exercise his power.

CHAPTER 15

The entire Washington establishment seemed to be shifting toward Wright. His colleagues had come around on taxes and so had the press. Rostenkowski responded to Reagan's Saturday radio talk, and, remarkable for him, launched a personal attack on the President. The Senate Finance Committee voted for an $11.7-billion bill by a strong 13–7 margin, with all eleven Democrats and two of the nine Republicans voting aye. Ranking Republican Robert Packwood, though voting against the bill, called on Reagan to abandon confrontation and negotiate a deficit-reduction package with Congress. Even so, a collision between Jim Wright's agenda and Ronald Reagan's seemed more and more certain. Whoever won, Wright was defining the battlefield.

Congressional Quarterly ran a cover story entitled "Reaganism, A Spent Force?" and answered in the affirmative, although adding that an arms-control agreement would salvage some luster. A *Washington Post* editorial accused Hill Republicans of "playing a shabby game on taxes. There is no group that bewails the deficit more loudly than they. . . . [But] it was only the deficit reduction [they were] for, not the means of achieving it." *The New York Times* wrote a story describing a White House and congressional Republicans in retreat, outmaneuvered by Wright in Central America and unable to win Senate confirmation of Supreme Court appointee Robert Bork. A *Post* front-page story concluded, "The Democratic-controlled Congress and the White House yesterday began hurtling toward a collision over the federal budget. . . . In a defiant statement, Reagan called the tax plans proposed by House and Senate committees 'an exercise in fiscal irre-

sponsibility.' He vowed to veto the proposals if they are passed by
Congress. . . . Sen. J. James Exon (D-Neb.) [predicted] 'the greatest
series of confrontations that anyone living today has ever seen between
the executive and legislative branch.' "

There was another front-page *Post* story that day, about a disturbing
decline in the financial markets: "Treasury Secretary James Baker said
. . . the recent burst of higher interest rates contributing to the decline
in stock and bond prices was not justified by the outlook for inflation.
As Baker met with the president, Chemical Bank, the fourth largest
bank in the nation, announced an increase in its prime rate from 9.25
percent to 9.75 percent . . . the sixth increase this year."

Yet as the press finally started to turn in Wright's direction, signs of
restiveness in the House began to surface. The schedule had been
destroyed, for one thing. In early October House and Senate Democratic leaders met in the Lyndon Johnson Room near the Senate floor
for their biweekly breakfast. When the defense appropriation came up,
Hawaii senator Daniel Inouye, a senior member of Appropriations,
observed dryly, "I think it will be a long session."

Walking back toward the House, Wright muttered, "The Senate just
voted 98–0 to condemn China over human rights in Tibet. If a mad
dog in Portland, Oregon, bites someone, the Senate passes a resolution.
They'll pass that crap, tie up the floor, but won't move real legislation."

Foley agreed: "The Senate really is bad. And it's getting worse. It's
not Byrd's fault, or Dole's either. Every individual senator has the
baton of the marshal of France, the ability to stop everything."

House members shared that bitterness, but took it out on Wright.
He was the one who had worked them hard all year, brought them
back the week of July 4. They had contained their bitching because of
his promise to end the session and recess early, possibly even before
Thanksgiving. Now that wasn't going to happen. They had worked so
hard they were now actually running out of legislation to put on the
floor. *But they were still here.*

Members were tired of being pushed. There was an undercurrent.
But Wright kept pushing.

Charlie Stenholm, the conservative Texas Democrat who had anchored the "boll weevils," the southern Democrats who had voted with
Republicans in the early 1980s, had collected 235 co-sponsors to a bill
calling for a balanced-budget constitutional amendment. When Wright

first heard of the bill he exploded, hissing, "Son of a bitch! How many Democrats? Sixty? Those chickenshit bastards!" He refused to allow a floor vote even though Stenholm was well short of the two-thirds needed to amend the Constitution. Stenholm responded with a "discharge petition." If 218 members, an absolute majority of the House, signed it, the bill would go to the floor. Discharge petitions were held at the desk below the Speaker's Rostrum. To sign it, a member had to walk onto the floor and up to the rostrum with the House in session. The press could not go on the floor, could not find out who co-sponsored the bill but had not signed. The leadership told Democrats to go ahead and co-sponsor the bill if they had to, "but don't sign the discharge petition."

Coelho advised a whip task force, organized to block Democrats from signing, to keep it private, intimate, personal: "Make this member to member, not staff to staff." Still, the pressure would be intense. Instead of just one whip talking to undecideds, three or four would talk to them. *That would show how serious they were.* One member insisted, "We've got to make clear there's retribution here. With all respect to O'Neill, he never punished anyone. Someone's got to start doing it."

But another warned, "Some of these guys are getting mad. They're talking about voting against us on other stuff if the leadership doesn't let up."

They're talking about voting against us on other stuff if the leadership doesn't let up. Bearing down harder would not control that sentiment. Only letting up would. The leadership didn't let up.

The House passed the labor bill which Wright had discussed with the AFL-CIO's Bob McGlotten before asking for help on taxes. It was another exercise of leadership power. Buddy MacKay was as willing to make tough votes as any member of Congress; to cut the deficit, he had done the unthinkable and voted for both tax increases and Social Security cuts. Even he complained, "Why do we have to keep voting on these things that have no chance of becoming law? Reagan is certain to veto it, even if the Senate ever got off its ass and voted on it. Members are grumbling. Very few have the guts to confront the leadership, but there's resentment out there on the floor."

Usually the leadership left openings for members to balance their voting records. But this leadership was squeezing so many things it was closing off the outlets. The resentment was growing. And now reconciliation was coming.

Wright, too, was complaining, but about other things: "I am upset over the loss of time. I always feel I should be doing something more productive. Whenever I go on the floor for fifteen minutes, one colleague after another comes up to me. I write these things down that they want. That's a whole day's work getting those things done. If I weren't there, they'd go to John, or Foley, or Coelho. The things would get done. I want to be in my office on the phone, calling people, getting them to do things to get important issues moving. I want to control the agenda, not be reacting so much."

His comment reflected the frustration of every Speaker; even O'Neill, famous for attending to everyone's concerns, had said, "I'm tired of kissing all the members' rings." But O'Neill had kept doing it. O'Neill could always be found in the front rows of the floor or in the cloakroom. Power is isolating; it naturally grows apart. O'Neill, who had no aggressive agenda, concentrated on staying in touch. Wright stayed in his office. *Trying to get important issues moving.* John Mack rarely came to the breakfast staff meetings anymore; his own time was too precious to waste listening to some of the things discussed, and he liked keeping his business private. But one morning he showed up with business he considered important, sat with a plate of pancakes and sausage, and reviewed a dozen different skirmishes between allies which Wright had to adjudicate. Dealing with such collisions was the Speaker's job, but twice Wright, his daily penance of raisin bran and skim milk before him, said, "Don't bring these people around to see me."

Mack did bring those people around, and Wright's colleagues were satisfied. Wright understood the importance of leadership-as-service-institution. A few weeks earlier he, personally, had given that member the extra closet he had asked for, commenting, *Some day in some Congress on some vote I'll need him.* Wright knew that that helped build power. *But he was weary of that truth.* That impatience in him, that sense of running out of time, wearied him of it, almost as if he feared that if something did not happen *right now* it would never happen, that his time in history would have flashed by. Republican Jerry Lewis, a member of the GOP leadership, complained, "If he wants to be Rayburn, why's he have to be Rayburn in one year?" Rayburn was Speaker for seventeen years.

Wright was less interested in smelling the floor, servicing it, than he was in using it, molding it, even forcing it. Oh, he remained firmly in control, all right. Even the contra-aid hawks among the Democrats, like John Murtha, backed him up on Central America. Murtha had often helped the White House on contra aid, but when Carlucci asked him for help again, Murtha called Richard Pena and asked if Carlucci was trying to undercut the Speaker. "Yes," Pena said. "Fuck 'em then," Murtha snorted.

But members were tired of bending their knee to him. And reconciliation was coming. And reconciliation had tax increases and welfare spending increases in the same bill. *Tax and spend! Tax and spend!* The politics were devastating.

Tom Downey did not make things easier when he defended his bill at a MacKay group meeting—an extraordinary meeting since usually only Democrats were allowed but Hank Brown, the Republican, had been invited to explain his welfare bill. A southern Democrat complained to Downey, "Your bill makes it look too easy to stay on welfare. At least that's the way the average guy in my district perceives it."

"With all due respect," Downey retorted, "if we designed the bill for the mentality of the average man, we'd have the Republican bill."

It was an incredible statement, one that would reverberate through the House. One of the moderates laughed, then turned to Brown and said, "Take it away, Hank."

If members of the Democratic Caucus were restive, Republicans were resentful and bitter. They released a study showing that through the middle of September only 57 percent of the bills sent to the floor were debated under "open" rules, meaning that any germane amendment was allowed. By contrast, 64 percent of the bills in the 99th Congress and 88 percent in the 95th Congress, ten years earlier, had had open rules. Wright had even more dramatically expanded the use of "self-executing" rules, meaning that the rule for a bill included substance. The most recent example was the inclusion of $3.5 million in contra aid in the rule governing the short-term continuing resolution. Republicans had welcomed that particular move, but still argued that Wright was beating them by structuring votes unfairly. A few months before Wright became Speaker Gingrich had said, "You don't mind losing if you've got a clean vote. If he gives us that, he'll take a lot of the poison out of this place."

Instead, Wright had structured votes to Democratic advantage. Procedure was honor codified. Justice Felix Frankfurter wrote, "The history of liberty has largely been the history of procedural safeguards."

And on reconciliation?

Welfare reform would be included in a self-executing rule. It would be "deemed to have passed" the House if the rule for reconciliation passed. That meant that the House would not have a direct vote on, much less a chance to amend, a major, $6-billion-plus initiative. It was a power play by Rostenkowski, not by Wright. But Wright was going along with it. *Welfare reform had no business being in the bill in the first place. But as part of a self-executing rule? That was outrageous!*

Republicans resented as well Wright's Central American involvement. Many felt he had betrayed the President by abandoning the Wright-Reagan initiative so quickly. The GOP hostility revealed itself after the Democratic leadership pulled a bill off the schedule reauthorizing an independent prosecutor for Executive Branch officials accused of wrongdoing. One member at a GOP leadership meeting snorted, "They've got the votes to pass it. They just want to wait until after Wright announces he's setting up a blind trust."

The Republicans chortled. A blind trust was rumored. Ethics was on all their lips. There was a meanness to the comment; usually colleagues viewed another's troubles with understanding. Members lived by the rule "Those in glass houses don't throw stones." But the Republicans had a growing *get him* attitude toward Wright.

That growing enmity cost Wright votes. In the past, Democrats had often gotten votes on economic issues from a cluster of moderate Republicans. Not many, but even a handful made a difference. The year before, seventeen Republicans had voted for the Democratic budget. This year not one Republican had voted for the Democratic budget. It was the price of Wright's aggressiveness, his having so directly confronted the White House. But it also reflected his use of procedure, and his lack of personal friends in the GOP. Wright had to win with Democrats. He had done extraordinarily well all year. Incredibly well. So well that his opponents doubted their ability to block his juggernaut. *The perception of power is power. Demoralized opponents do not fight so hard.* Stenholm said, "It kills me, but I think reconciliation will pass. There's tremendous leadership pressure on it."

That was why Downey had wanted his welfare reform bill included.

But if Wright lost a vote here because of substance . . . a vote there because of personal revenge . . . a vote here because a member wanted to send a message of discontent . . . a vote there because of a single

district's concerns . . . if his sensitivity to the House slipped just a little
. . . if the whip system did not operate perfectly . . .

Wright could be beaten, all right.

And the higher he made the stakes, the more important a defeat
would be. All year long everything he had done had pointed to the
reconciliation bill, the tax bill. He had forced the budget through the
House. He had forced Rostenkowski to bow to his will. He had confronted the President, and he had elevated the reconciliation bill to the
highest level. He was using it to declare once and for all his dominance
in policy.

The train's on schedule but it's loaded with dynamite, Rostenkowski
had said. Rostenkowski had loaded it with dynamite. He wanted it to
pass; it was still his bill. But passing it was Wright's job. *You wanted
a tax bill, Mr. Speaker? Here it is. Now pass it.*

Wright had distractions. Ever since the *Post* story about his book, it
seemed that every day another reporter from another publication asked
about his finances. *The Wall Street Journal*'s Brooks Jackson was working on a second story. So was *Newsweek*. They seemed less interested
in the book than in everything else. The savings and loan thing. His
involvement in the stockyards in the North Side area of Fort Worth.
His business dealings with Mallick.

In his office late one October evening he sat back and looked for a
moment at the painting on the wall of the small country Texas church
beneath the brooding sky. One could lose oneself in that painting, in
the field of bluebonnets, or inside the church, or waiting for the heavy
raindrops to pelt down and wash everything clean. He knew that church,
had prayed in it. Now he longed for its peace.

"I'm just so tired," he said. "It seems someone's always coming up
here constantly asking about my finances. I resent the insinuations. I've
been helping the North Side for fifteen years, long before Billy Bob
Barnett was involved. Tomorrow I'm going to announce a blind trust,
put everything I have in that. Now no one will be able to say anything."

Wright was discovering that power was not only used but tested,
intimately examined. He recoiled, drew even more inward, more concentrated on his goal. It was as if he believed he was running out of
time. And what was his goal? History. He was desperate to leave his
mark on history. Something in him demanded expression. He was an
artist. He had kept that journal. He still regularly poured out his

thoughts on oral history tapes. And yet, all that he expressed was superficial. He did not let his true thoughts show, much less his heart. He hid himself from himself. Rayburn, Wright's great hero, once wrote, "You wouldn't think it but a fellow gets lonesomer here, I think, than anyplace almost . . . Everybody trying for fame." And Wright drew even more inward.

His wife, Betty, said, "I see him in a different light than I did before. I may have felt at one time that I had influence over him, but not now. He's going to do what he's going to do." She smiled sadly, and continued, "This has not been my best year, or the best year of our marriage. If we have one night a week alone, that's a lot. When I see him at the end of the day, he's tired. Something will have disappointed him. I don't see the highs, working out of problems. I haven't shared that. If I ask him a serious question, he turns it into something silly. He doesn't show a lot of ebullience. He's always going on to the next thing. He doesn't savor or enjoy any accomplishment or victory because once it's happened he's on to something else."

Now that the blind trust was being set up, Wright's aide Marshall Lynam called Bob Strauss's office to ask him to try to kill the *Newsweek* story. Strauss's assistant refused even to relay the request. The world didn't work that way anymore; people didn't go around killing stories at major national publications, and it made one look foolish to try. Having failed to kill the story, Lynam and other aides, but not Wright, spent three hours with *Newsweek*'s bureau chief and two reporters going over everything. Everything. Gingrich's aide Van Brocklin had been feeding them information.

Wright invited reporters from four Texas papers and the wire services to lunch to explain the blind trust: $187,317 in assets were going into it, everything except his house and some family-owned land worth less than $15,000. He gave the reporters a statement which said, "The assets in my estate are considerably less than those usually involved in blind-trust arrangements. I am not an individual of large personal wealth and never have been. In relative terms, my net worth probably was greater when I was elected to Congress at age thirty-one than it is today."

It was a true statement but irrelevant to the question of propriety. Indeed, even appearances of impropriety could destroy public confidence. The lunch lasted for two hours as Wright went over and over details of his finances. The questioning was not hostile, but it was persistent. Wright was intense, serious, as if he realized for the first time that his personal financial dealings could bring him down, could destroy him.

There was that train ride to Chicago so many years ago, to that meeting with the salesmen of his and his father's company. He had gotten on that train a young man, only twenty-five years old, knowing that while he was away the filing deadline for the election of mayor of Weatherford would pass. Getting on that train had punctuated his decision to stay out of politics, out for good. But riding north, preparing for the sales meeting, for the making of money, listening to the rhythm of the rails, he had wondered, *Is this really what I want to do the rest of my life?* He had answered no, and had left that train.

For a moment he seemed about to become emotional—his voice cracking—but he regained control of himself. "I don't care about money," he told the reporters, insistent, haunted, almost pleading. "I never cared about money."

He cared about his speakership.

Ultimately, economic policy depends upon three discrete worlds: those of the financial markets, concentrated in New York; the world of politics, concentrated in Washington; and, subsuming both, the world *out there,* the "real" world, of real people who make and sell real things, where men and women live their lives, raise their families. In the end, the real world and economic fundamentals dominate. But that end can take a long time coming. Normally, each of the three worlds goes around in its own orbit, only vaguely aware of the other two. But occasionally those orbits intersect, and shake one another.

Money and power are cold things; the two are related, but are not interchangeable. The one becomes the other only through a string of mutations. In the markets money is pursued almost in the abstract. Power matters only to the extent that it furthers the accumulation of money. In Washington power is pursued almost in the abstract. Money matters only to the extent that it furthers the accumulation of power.

If fear and greed drive the markets, then survival and ambition drive Washington: the fear of losing an election makes politicians cautious; the desire to climb higher drives them forward.

The markets have a major impact on Washington. When the stock markets rise, people back home are happy. When they fall, they are not. Interest rates provide an even more direct link between the markets and politicians. In September both the stock market and interest rates began to get members' attention as stocks started to slide. Interest rates had started rising earlier, and continued rising.

One reason was that foreign investors seemed to be tiring of financing the U.S. budget and trade deficits. Their money had transformed the United States from the biggest creditor nation in history, which it was even through most of Reagan's first term, to the biggest debtor nation in history by 1987. But foreigners were growing unhappy about those deficits. There seemed no end to them; the government seemed to be doing nothing to bring them down. As a result, foreigners became less willing to put their money in dollars, and the internationally traded value of the dollar fell.

Yet the United States still needed foreign financing. There simply was not enough money available domestically to take care of credit needs. To attract foreign investors, interest rates had to rise. Those higher interest rates would in turn weaken the economy.

Democrats had bored the public with talk of the budget deficit. Mondale had lost forty-nine states talking about it. The deficit had not hit home economically. But if interest rates rose, or if inflation started up—a likely result of a lower dollar—the deficit would have a profound impact on people's daily lives. Their boredom would end in a hurry.

Now interest rates were rising. Investors had been nervous earlier, even when the stock markets were still going up. Now the markets had started down. The week ending October 9 saw the largest weekly decline in the Dow Jones average in history. On Monday, October 12, the market was flat. On Tuesday, ironically the day Ways and Means Democrats approved the bulk of the tax bill, including antimerger provisions, the market rose. On Wednesday it fell. On Thursday, October 15, the prime rate rose—the sixth increase of the year and the second in ten days.

That same Thursday morning, new trade deficit figures showed a sudden, significant increase. That meant the dollar might fall still further, and drive interest rates up still higher. Investors had expected the trade deficit figures to fall, and calm the markets; instead the trade figures added to its nervousness.

Ways and Means formally voted out its tax bill. Reagan's reaction offered more evidence that the White House would not compromise, would not work out a solution to the deficit: "If Congress should actually pass a tax hike, my answer will be simply this: veto."

Treasury Secretary James Baker suggested to reporters that the

United States might let the dollar slide still further to punish West Germany for raising interest rates. In effect, Baker was threatening an international economic war.

There are thin lines in the markets between nervousness, fear, and panic. Baker's and Reagan's comments were communicated instantly to the markets. The prospect of economic warfare between the United States, Germany, and Japan, and of political warfare between the White House and Congress sent investors across the line from nervousness to fear. October 15 saw huge trading volume, the fourth heaviest day ever, and the Dow Jones average set an all-time record for the biggest point loss in a single day by dropping ninety-five points.

The record did not last long.

On Friday, the Dow Jones average dropped 108 points. Volume topped 338 million shares—the most shares ever traded in a single day. The dollar continued to slide. The Dow Jones average set a record for the biggest weekly loss; it was the second record weekly loss in a row.

Saturday did nothing to calm fears. Baker publicly attacked the Germans again for raising interest rates, saying, "They should not expect us to simply sit back here and accept [it]." His statements made sense if his only concern was getting West Germany to reverse course. But after two successive days of record-breaking losses in the markets—indeed, two successive weeks of record losses—the markets wanted reassurance and stability. Baker offered more instability. On Sunday, Baker appeared on *Meet the Press* and repeated that statement. He also blamed the market's fall on the Democrats' tax bill. That comment suggested that Baker was more interested in playing politics than in sitting down with Congress and cutting the deficit.

Sunday night—New York time—foreign markets opened and investors started selling heavily. (Nicholas Brady was then an investment banker [a close friend of George Bush, he later became Treasury secretary under both Reagan and Bush] who would soon head the administration-appointed commission to investigate what would become the market crash. His commission's report officially blamed the budget deficit. But according to *The Wall Street Journal,* he privately told a group of select investors that the crash was precipitated by a sudden, huge sale of dollars by Japanese traders disturbed by James Baker's comments. That sale came early Monday morning.) The London markets, which opened six hours before American ones, collapsed. When the New York Stock Exchange opened, it followed suit. Eleven of the thirty stocks that made up the Dow Jones average did not open on time because a flood of sell orders overwhelmed the few buy orders.

By the time of Wright's daily, late-morning press conference, the Dow Jones average was down 125 points. The leadership discussed how to answer the inevitable question about the market.

"Be careful," Foley warned. "Don't say anything that could affect it further."

Wright decided that if asked he would comment blandly about interest rates and the budget and trade deficits. Through the day the market surged and retreated, each move more violent than the preceding one. Down one hundred points, down two hundred points, back up to regain half that loss—*then suddenly down 250 points.* Volume was immense, overwhelming communication of price information on stocks. Bargain hunters withdrew from the market because they would not buy a stock without knowing the price they would pay. Sellers did not withdraw; they dumped shares to protect what was left of profits or to cut losses, and because of automatic, preprogrammed decisions, or in simple terror. The market hovered for a while—like Canetti's crowd, waiting for a direction, waiting for some spark to send buyers flooding back looking for bargains, or for sheer, pure panic to take over. For whatever reason, at three in the afternoon, the market imploded. Down three hundred points, down four hundred points, down *508 points.* Volume marked the terror—over 600 million shares traded, almost twice the volume record set only the Friday before, and another 60 million shares' worth of orders were never executed. In percentage terms, the loss almost doubled that of October 1929.

The panic was cold and gripping.

What now? *What was going to happen now?* Would the markets collapse further and drag the world into another Great Depression? If the budget deficit was the problem, the markets would not stabilize unless they had confidence that the government had a rational policy to bring the deficit down, that politicians would address the problem and not just blame one another. Gramm-Rudman was no policy. It was an excuse not to have a policy. Roger Boothe, chief economist at Lloyd's Merchant Bank in London, told *The Washington Post,* "I think the essence of the problem is a lack of confidence about American economic policy and a worry that U.S. interest rates are going higher."

What was the policy? Who was in charge?

* * *

Reagan's first public comment as the markets imploded: "The leading indicators are sending a message—steady as she goes." Later in the day he said, "Everyone is a little puzzled. . . . There is nothing wrong with the economy. Everything is fundamentally sound. I don't think anyone should panic because all the economic indicators are good. . . . How about how many people must have sold out in order to get a profit?"

Reagan's statement eerily echoed Herbert Hoover, who in 1929 said that "the fundamental business of the country . . . is on a sound and prosperous basis."

Fitzwater said there were no crisis meetings anywhere in the administration, no emergency situation, and commented, "One day a market does not make." The administration was likely to accept sequestration rather than agree to tax increases. As to a summit with Congress: "We think there are better ways to deal with the deficit. . . . Our position on a summit has been for a long time that it is not the most productive way to reach agreement on the budget. . . . It gives a platform to those who want to raise taxes."

Jim Miller went further, again blaming the Democratic tax bill for the crash and saying deficit reduction "is up to Congress."

Jim Baker, away on an already-scheduled trip to Europe, issued a joint statement with the West German finance minister declaring that the Germans and Americans were in agreement on interest rates and the dollar. He left Germany for his next stop in Stockholm. The market continued its dive. His plane turned around, back to the United States, back home.

Pressures were pushing both Wright and the White House toward a budget summit. Byrd and Bentsen had already called for one—as had Buddy MacKay all year. But neither Wright nor the White House wanted to meet.

Wright had been involved once with the White House in a budget summit. It hadn't gone well. O'Neill had delegated to him the task of working out a compromise with the administration years before, and Wright had spent hour after hour with Jim Baker. But Baker had lacked the authority to cut a deal, frustrating Wright. Then Reagan had made untrue public statements about the negotiations. Furious, Wright had responded on the floor and barely stopped short of applying the word "liar" to the President—but he came close enough to outrage Republicans. Wright did not relish more such negotiations. Monday night, prominent, desperate Wall Street investment bankers flew down for a DCCC Speaker's Club dinner. While the Washington Redskins and Dallas Cowboys collided on a television screen, the Wall Street people huddled with Wright. They urged a summit. He replied, "Talk to the White House. They're the ones who don't want to compromise."

Tuesday morning before his daily press conference, Wright, Foley, and Coelho discussed strategy. The House was already scheduled to vote the following week on reconciliation; the bill would raise taxes and cut entitlements. Should the bill go forward?

The leadership's chief concern was obvious: to keep the market panic from spreading to the real economy. Market expectations were translated to the economy chiefly through interest rates and psychology. Washington had only indirect control over either at best, and even that indirect control was only at the margins. But policy makers were the only players in the economic equation who made a conscious effort to affect events. Every other economic player simply assessed the likely direction of events and reacted accordingly. If policy makers seemed in control of the deficit, if the deficit seemed headed downward, the psychology of the markets could improve and interest rates stabilize.

The markets wanted action. Reconciliation was action. It cut the deficit, instead of talking about cutting the deficit. Abandoning it could be interpreted as a lack of political will to make difficult choices. Proceeding with it might demonstrate that will.

On policy issues—where government money would come from and go to—the bill would clearly strengthen House Democrats. If there was a budget summit, sitting down with an already-passed bill meant that they would control the discussions. And Foley pointed out that if they pulled the bill from the schedule, the advantage on policy shifted to the Republicans. The White House could hold fast in a summit, and the House Democratic leadership could not reschedule the bill without being accused of torpedoing a compromise. Republicans would suddenly have the stronger hand.

There were reasons to pull reconciliation from the schedule. The markets and the public wanted bipartisanship. Proceeding was a unilateral action, not a bipartisan one. Partisanship had already surfaced. Republicans were blaming the crash on anti-merger provisions in the tax bill, even though the market had been collapsing for weeks, and the one day the market rose had been the day Ways and Means had marked up those provisions. (Rostenkowski had already said he would drop them in conference.) Proceeding with reconciliation could be seen as more partisanship, and disturb the markets.

Still, if they waited for real bipartisanship from the White House it might never come. Wright, Foley, and Coelho unanimously agreed. Reconciliation would go forward.

They would try to talk their way to bipartisanship. Wright would make a conciliatory, prepared statement at the press conference, then repeat it from the well of the House so the nightly news could use it. He would make the same points at a lunch he would host for national reporters. In addition, Democratic attacks on Republicans in one-minute speeches would be canceled. And Coelho would throw out hundreds of lapel buttons he had been about to distribute which read, "GOP-AWOL—Absent Without Leadership."

"The press will ask about a summit," Foley advised Wright. "You'll have to say the hand of cooperation is out."

An aide reported that Reagan was just then meeting with the six Republican 1988 presidential candidates. "That's perfect," Coelho said. "The world's falling apart and he's playing politics."

They let the reporters in. Wright read his statement: "This is a day to set aside partisan posturing. . . . The crash [stemmed from] a growing recognition of the fragility of the bubble of borrowing which has boosted our economy in the 1980s. Congress stands ready to act. We earnestly invite the active participation and cooperation of the President as we seek solutions. Next week the House will pass a reconciliation bill as one first real step toward deficit reduction. Failing to take this minimum action could be interpreted as a signal that the United States is incapable of making hard decisions. This, however, is not enough. Far more needs to be done. As soon as we pass reconciliation, I invite the President to join with the bipartisan leadership of Congress in convening an Economic Summit. I do not refer to a staged event or an empty public relations show. Rather, the President and the Congress must be willing to sit down together to work out a new real approach."

At the press lunch the reporters wanted to hear about war between the White House and Wright, not cooperation. One reporter told Wright that the OMB's Miller was already shooting down the summit idea, and Jonathan Fuerbringer of *The New York Times* asked what Wright would do if Reagan vetoed reconciliation.

"You're missing the point," Wright said. "I'm trying to appeal to the President to sign reconciliation. It's a modest step. Then we go on from there. We have to act. I lived through the Depression. Santayana was right when he said if we don't remember the past we are doomed to repeat it."

The reporters did not buy Wright's conciliatory tone. As the lunch broke up, Jeffrey Birnbaum of *The Wall Street Journal* turned to a colleague and said, "This compromise stuff is such an incredibly thin veneer. You wonder how long it will be before he drops it."

While Wright was offering cooperation, Bob Michel was trying to sell the White House on a budget summit and taxes. He was rebuffed. But the markets spoke up again.

Tuesday the Dow Jones average of thirty large companies rose a record 102 points, but most stocks actually declined—a bizarre and dangerous discrepancy. More important was what occurred away from the market floor, as market players tried to settle their trades. To do so they had to borrow money, usually a routine short-term transaction. But lenders did not want to lend.

Their reluctance grew out of a breakdown in the flow of information. The day before, the immense trading volume—over 600 million shares, almost twice the previous record—had overwhelmed communication of price information and orders. Now that same tidal wave of information chaos was swamping lenders, who could not judge which borrowers were financially sound but simply lacked cash at the moment, and those who had been wiped out. Just as buying had dried up the day before, now lending did. Without credit, market players could not pay their debts. Large-scale defaults, especially given the mood of panic, could ripple through the entire financial system of the United States and turn it into a vast series of crashing dominoes. In late morning the financial system began to quiver and shake. Federal Reserve chairman Alan Greenspan acted immediately, flooding Wall Street and Chicago with funds and announcing the Fed would do whatever was necessary to solve the liquidity problems. The disaster never occurred, and remained unknown to the general public. But the crisis was nonetheless real, and more dangerous than the market crash.

Word of it quickly penetrated the White House. The threat was not lost on Howard Baker, Jim Baker, and others. *The White House had to do something.* The White House—the President—had to appear to be in command.

At 3:45 P.M. the two Bakers, Greenspan, and Beryl Sprinkel, chairman of the Council of Economic Advisers, walked into Reagan's private quarters. The Bakers wanted no dissent when they approached the President. OMB head Jim Miller, who opposed a budget summit and new taxes—Miller, like Phil Gramm a former Texas A&M economics professor, shared the public-choice economic theories which had led to the Gramm-Rudman bill—was purposely not informed of the meeting and excluded. In a forty-minute discussion, the Bakers, Greenspan, and Sprinkel told the President he had no alternative but to agree to a summit with Congress, even though that meant with Jim Wright, whom he by now despised. And a summit meant a tax increase.

That morning White House aides were shooting down the idea of a summit with Congress to the press, and rebuffing Michel's suggestion. At five Reagan walked onto the White House lawn where a helicopter would take him to see his wife, Nancy, who was recuperating from surgery, and announced, "I am directing that discussions be undertaken with the bipartisan leadership of the Congress. . . . I am willing to look at whatever proposal they have."

That fell short of calling for a summit, but it moved in that direction and opened the door to taxes. Yet a moment later Reagan sounded less than conciliatory when he added, "I have never gotten a budget that I have asked for, and the Congress is responsible for the deficits."

That evening Wright, the leadership, Rostenkowski, and Gray met to talk once again about reconciliation. The issue was whether to include welfare reform. Rostenkowski pointed out he had included "shadow" taxes hard to identify to pay for it. Taking welfare reform out meant it would have to go to the floor later naked, as a straight spending bill. But including it, as part of a self-executing rule, made passage much more difficult. Foley said, "The only reason to take it out is to pass the rule. We need to find out."

There was a whip task force meeting the next day; the whips would run a count and get a feel. Foley did not want to push; he just wanted to count. It was a crucial difference, a voice of caution that set loose undercurrents in the room.

Rostenkowski glanced from Wright to Foley to Coelho. The leadership supported welfare reform. It was one of Wright's initiatives. So what if Rostenkowski had stuck it in reconciliation, even though it didn't really belong there. The whips had pushed on everything all year. They would sure as hell push on reconciliation. Why was welfare different? *Maybe the leadership couldn't be trusted. Maybe they were trying to stick it to Rostenkowski.*

A page interrupted to announce that Reagan had just called for discussions with Congress. They fell silent for a moment, the tension between Rostenkowski and the leadership put aside.

"Fine," Wright said. "After we pass reconciliation."

"I don't know," Foley warned. "There's a chess game going on here. If he calls a summit in the next few days, you have to go."

"We'll go through the whip effort anyway. Make sure the members know this is a leadership vote. This goes on their permanent escutcheon."

"If we lose this it's a disaster," Foley agreed.

"Another thing," suggested Coelho. "Let's change the name of the reconciliation bill. No one knows what that means. Let's call it the 'Guaranteed Deficit Reduction' bill."

They agreed. Foley said wryly, "This is megapolitics."

By the next morning "clarifications" of Reagan's statement indicated that he was not yet talking about a summit. He was talking about sending aides to talk to people on the Hill. Wright recalled the negotiations a few years earlier which had failed, he believed, because White House negotiators had lacked authority to deal. This seemed a repeat. He was angry. At his daily press conference he said a summit would occur only when Reagan "sits down and tells us, 'Okay, I'm ready to face reality.'"

This had gotten personal. All year the White House had attacked Wright for pushing taxes, and even many of those who agreed with him on substance had called him a fool politically to push them. Now the markets seemed to be saying he had been right substantively and politically. Now he wanted the satisfaction of seeing Reagan admit he was wrong.

Without the President's involvement, Wright told reporters, there would be "plateaus," not a summit. His voice laced with sarcasm, he snorted that if Reagan sent up Jim Miller, Miller could talk to Bill Gray; George Bush could talk to Tom Foley.

His comment infuriated Republicans in both the House and the White House. One GOP member said, "Who the hell does he think he is, equating himself with the President?"

That day, Wednesday, the Dow Jones average jumped 179 points. The White House contradicted itself. While Fitzwater told assembled reporters that everything but Social Security would be on the table in talks with Congress, Jim Miller told the Associated Press that Reagan would not accept a tax increase. Reagan seemed to support Miller, reiterating his claim, "Tax increases result in reduced revenues, and reduced tax rates result in increased revenues." He added that the market crisis "would appear to be [over]. . . . We've got a crisis brought on by [Democrats] over the last fifty years."

The news wires made communication almost instantaneous. An angry Wright called Howard Baker. Was there going to be a summit or not? Baker calmed him down and said there was, and that he, Jim Baker, and Jim Miller wanted to come up later in the day to discuss it. Wright asked if they could leave Miller out of it.

"You and I disagree about a lot," Baker replied, "but we don't disagree about that. Unfortunately, I have to bring him."

The press that morning had revealed that Baker had excluded Miller from the meeting where Reagan was convinced to seek a compromise. Miller and the right wing were up in arms. Baker could not exclude him from now on.

At two in the afternoon Wright's office was crowded. Howard Baker, Jim Baker, Jim Miller, and Will Ball sat down with Wright, Foley, Gray, and their aides. The Bakers sat in chairs, Wright behind his desk, Miller on a sofa directly opposite him. Everyone smiled, but the smiles hid nothing. Despite the number of people there, the meeting was brief, almost pro forma. They knew what had to be done. Wright was gracious, even more gracious than usual. Was everyone comfortable? Would you like coffee? But the steel lay visible underneath.

Howard Baker began, saying, "The President instructed us to come up here and explore a bipartisan package. The President stated 'no preconditions.' Nothing is on or off the table."

"We're all here," Wright replied. "We've got people here who know the budget. Let's do it."

The administration officials were taken aback. Right now? Wright reviewed his unhappy experience in budget negotiations a few years before. Baker did not respond, only shrugged and said, "We're a long, long way from where we were yesterday."

Wright pushed harder. "We've been handicapped all year by Republicans following White House instructions and not showing up, offering no votes at all. The guidelines have been and should be fifty-fifty taxes and cuts, and fifty-fifty in cuts from domestic and defense."

Jim Baker agreed. "That's common ground."

Howard Baker seconded it. "Mr. Speaker, there's no disagreement on that."

Wright nodded with satisfaction. *He had won.* "If we can start from that premise we can pursue this thing."

But he had to have a commitment to accept taxes from the President. He explained that wire-service stories claimed that the President and Miller would not accept taxes. Glancing coolly at Miller, he concluded, "We've got a bill ready and we're serious about it, even though it's only a drop in the bucket compared to the deficit. I'm willing to sit down with the President before or after reconciliation. I'd go see him right now. But he's got to be involved. I'll see him anytime if he's serious."

Tomorrow. They would see Reagan tomorrow. Foley mentioned reconciliation again. It would reach the floor in a week. Pulling it would make them vulnerable, he explained, to charges of bad faith if the talks foundered and they later tried to reschedule it.

"I don't know why you should stop on it," said Jim Baker, "but don't expect us to say anything nice about it."

They talked further. Jim Baker summarized their agreement. It would be fifty-fifty, spending cuts and revenue increases. They would say nothing to the press. Social Security was off the table. The principals—Reagan, Wright, and Byrd—would not get involved in the daily negotiations.

Then Jim Baker added, "It has to be self-executing—everything happens at once."

Baker was suggesting that some special procedure be developed so that tax hikes and spending cuts occurred simultaneously. His comment reflected administration fears that Reagan would sign a tax bill but Congress would not make agreed-upon cuts. Such a deal implied that the budget summit would actually write legislation, rather than have it go through normal committee processes. It would violate the very nature of the Congress, and infringe on its independence of the Executive Branch. Anger flickered in Wright's expression.

"No," Wright said. "There's no way to do that."

Miller complained that the Appropriations Committee wasn't counting expenditures properly, that according to OMB's accounting, the appropriations bills exceeded the budget.

Wright reddened. It was Reagan's OMB, headed by David Stockman, which had invented nonexistent savings and later admitted to having produced phony figures. It was Reagan's OMB, headed by Miller, which used absurd economic assumptions—while its own internal memos showed it knew the truth—to claim it cut the deficit to $108 billion and put pressure on Congress. Now Miller was telling him how the House should count? Now the administration was telling Congress, which constitutionally was responsible for appropriating the money, how to count? Wright suddenly exploded at Miller, excoriated him, lashed him, humiliated him.

The room fell silent after Wright's outburst. Silent. One man coughed. *Cabinet officers were not talked to that way. Hell, no one was talked to that way.* Even Wright seemed stunned by his outburst for a moment. Then he spoke up again, as if nothing had happened, saying he would talk to Byrd and get back to them. He and Byrd would see the President tomorrow.

Later, Wright and Byrd issued a joint statement reaffirming that Reagan's "personal involvement in the process is essential without any preconditions"— in other words, taxes would be included.

Then Wright and Foley briefed Rostenkowski, Whitten, Coelho, and Bonior. Foley talked about the two Bakers' cooperativeness, saying, "I was frankly startled."

The Wall Street Journal and other papers had blamed the crash on Jim Baker's comments about the West Germans and the dollar. Wright added, "They must be hurting up there in the White House, and know it."

"What do you expect from us?" Rostenkowski asked Wright.

"Number one, to pass that guaranteed deficit reduction bill."

That morning MacKay had hosted another of his budget groups. They had become an independent power center. Without these group meetings, individual members inclined to oppose Wright would have had to confront the leadership's arguments, the whipping, alone, without any sounding board. In MacKay's meetings they discovered colleagues who felt as they did and learned that they were not isolated, not out of step; they became more willing to resist the leadership. And they knew that if they voted together they could affect the outcome. The leadership knew it, too.

One of the chief arguments for reconciliation was that the only alternative was sequestration. That morning Leon Panetta explained how terrible that was: *AIDS research slashed. The military slashed, its worst hit in the post-Vietnam era. Agriculture slashed. FBI slashed.* His voice droned on and on and on, the relentless monotone itself driving home the relentless impact of sequestration. *Members would each lose $36,000 for their own staff. Committees would lose $4 million. Antidrug efforts slashed. Education: one million students cut off from Pell grants.*

Panetta argued that the public didn't understand what sequestration meant; once they did they would hold Congress responsible. *Reconciliation had to pass.*

The members at first seemed supportive. They all agreed they had to help stabilize the markets, reassure them. They wanted the tax bill linked to the appropriations bill so that the press and the public could see that Congress was cutting spending even while raising taxes.

Charlie Stenholm even talked of Social Security cuts. That's where the money was. Nervous chuckles met his suggestion. He stiffened. "I've got no problem with revenues as long as we cut spending. It's the best politics, and the best thing for the country."

Others disagreed, became uncomfortable with the politics. The talk switched to welfare reform. Sparks suddenly flew. They resented the way it was being rammed down their throats in the rule. The politics were terrible. The message it sent the markets was terrible. Member after member agreed. *Welfare reform in a tax bill was crazy. Crazy politics, crazy for the markets.* They grew angry, and directed the anger at the leadership. One member asked, "Does the leadership have a strategy?"

"I'm prepared to vote for the tax bill," said another. "What I can't and won't do is vote for a bill that combines taxing and spending. Welfare reform! Christ! I think it's a terrible mistake and waters down the message we're sending to the country."

The hostility grew and grew. They weren't going to vote for it.

Later that day a member who had been there, a leadership loyalist, grabbed Coelho in a hallway and told him, "That MacKay group today, it was unbelievable. These guys were going crazy over welfare."

"If you tell Danny to take welfare out of reconciliation," Coelho replied, "he'll tell you to go to hell."

"Who's running this place? You guys or Rostenkowski? When did I ever jump ship? I'm not saying, 'These guys are saying this.' I'm saying *me. I'm* saying it. You've got a problem."

But the leadership was in a confrontational mood. The next morning began with a House-Senate Democratic leadership breakfast. One member spoke derisively about the Republicans' unwillingness all year to talk about a budget compromise, but now, suddenly, they called for statesmanship. With a bitter irony, Byrd said, "We politicians understand the importance of demonstrating statesmanship."

They all laughed. Wright said he would demand a commitment from Reagan to support the product of a summit. "I don't want to spend three weeks in this thing and find out he doesn't mean it. A few years ago we did that and it was the most unproductive exercise I've ever been through. Then he got on TV and lied about it. 'Lied' is the right word. I'm not going to go through that again."

"Do you have an audience with His Excellency today, Jim?" a senator asked.

"No. He wants the press conference today to be his show."

"I hope they stick the pipe to him," snorted Rostenkowski.

Immediately following the breakfast was the weekly whip meeting. The subject was reconciliation.

"The most important vote will be the rule," Butler Derrick said. "It's very, very important."

Did the rule include welfare or not?

"The rule allows it, along with a GOP substitute," Coelho said. It hadn't actually been decided yet whether welfare was in or out, but any show of uncertainty would increase the pressure to drop it. So Coelho sounded certain, did not give an inch.

"Party vote, right?" asked Charles Rangel, the black Ways and Means member who had run against Coelho for whip. "Party vote" meant it would be remembered by the leadership for a long time.

Coelho nodded firmly. "Party vote. A big one."

CHAPTER 16

Late in the evening Charlie Stenholm sat outside Wright's office—not in the more private waiting area, the room where Wright's personal secretary reigned, but in the receptionists' area outside that. It symbolized the distance between the two men. Though their districts bordered on each other's, and Weatherford itself was now in Stenholm's district, the two had never gotten along. In 1978 Wright had supported Stenholm's primary opponent. Members didn't forget things like that. Tall and straight, Stenholm had done the grunt work in the early Reagan years that had kept the boll weevils organized. Time after time in those days Wright had sat next to him on the floor and asked for his help and time after time he had shaken his head no and said, "I can't, Jim. No, sir." In 1984 Stenholm had even talked about running for Speaker against O'Neill as a gesture of discontent. Stenholm had paid for his distance, too, in petty little signs of contempt from some colleagues. When he spoke at one Texas function in Washington, only one Texas Democratic colleague bothered to show up.

Now he sat fidgeting, nervous, outside Wright's office. When he finally talked to Wright he arranged a meeting between him and a group of members the next morning.

Wright expected half a dozen. Stenholm arrived with twenty-five. One after another they trooped into Wright's office, southerners and moderates and even some liberals, too many to fit, jamming the office, filling the chairs and couches and standing, crowding in on the Speaker. A leadership aide stood in the back of the room and took down names. They had the leadership's attention, all right.

Stenholm spoke first. He applauded Wright's statement that $23 billion was only a start in deficit-cutting, then suggested dropping welfare reform from reconciliation, keeping the taxes, and making it two dollars in spending cuts for every dollar in taxes. Freezing everything, including Social Security cost-of-living adjustments, would just about do that. That would be a dramatic package, with real impact in the out-years. Stenholm wanted to be allowed to offer this package in an amendment.

"That's difficult," Wright replied. "The DSG has a substitute they want to offer. I can't say yes to one, no to another."

"So what?" said another member. "Why not let Charlie and the DSG both offer amendments?"

Let the House work its will. Why should Wright control everything through the Rules Committee? It was a warning that Wright had squeezed hard all year and they were tired of being squeezed.

"Give us votes," Stenholm urged. "Give us alternatives. Otherwise we all will do what we have to do."

"What's important," said a third colleague, "is welfare reform. If it comes out, I'll vote for the bill and work for it. I can't vote for it if it's in there."

Half a dozen others joined in. Wright urged them to vote for reconciliation regardless. It was crucial politically and for the country, he argued.

The meeting ended without resolution. Stenholm stood up and said, "If welfare's in there, reconciliation will lose."

Later that day the whip task force on reconciliation met, chaired by Marty Russo—the same Russo who had given Wright such trouble over the budget, who shared "animal house" with George Miller, Charles Schumer, and Leon Panetta, and who was a deputy whip and on Ways and Means. The leadership had picked him to chair the welfare reform task force, and when welfare was folded into reconciliation he continued as chairman. No one worked harder whipping than he did; he loved it and was one of those members who seemed totally of the House, totally an insider. His word was his bond. He took care of colleagues, spoke up for them to the leadership when they did not want to speak up for themselves. Though he pushed hard—it was he who had once kicked open a phone booth in the cloakroom and dragged Danny Akaka onto the floor for a vote—he also protected members from pressure, saying when appropriate, "Leave him alone on this. It's not a good vote for him." But if colleagues valued his willingness to work hard, they paid less attention to his opinions. His three housemates had influence; each was seen as an intellectual heavyweight, or standing on principle. Russo was seen as a sergeant: useful, necessary even, but not a prime mover. He was sensitive and touchy about his reputation; he longed to be taken seriously.

Twenty members showed up at the task force meeting and the first thing anyone said was, "Is welfare in or out?"

Russo replied, "The chairman's right here. Ask him."

That meant Rostenkowski, who was standing off to the side. He rarely attended such meetings—his presence marked its importance—and the members turned toward him for his answer. He smiled, a smile the Cheshire cat in *Alice's Adventures in Wonderland* would have envied, and said, "That's a leadership call."

The members chuckled at his pretended deference. One called out to Coelho, "Tony! The chairman's looking for direction!"

The two men measured each other with their eyes, laughing but cold, and it seemed as if in an instant all their personal history passed between them: Rostenkowski's sponsorship of Coelho's bid to chair the DCCC, which had gotten Coelho started; Coelho's early support for Wright's campaign for Speaker that Rostenkowski considered a betrayal; rumors that Rostenkowski kept talking about taxes on wine, an industry close to Coelho in California, to avenge himself ("Danny wants to fuck wine to fuck Coelho," one man believed). Then Coelho laughed, hard and deep. They were on the same side now. But there were other tensions. One member close to Wright and Coelho made a suggestion and Russo, Rostenkowski's protégé, worried that something was going on he didn't know about; he interrupted and snapped, "I'm chairing this task force." A moment later he apologized but the feel of the room was not good.

They started counting the rule for the bill, not the bill itself. Usually a rule was easier to pass because Democrats could support their party's procedural control of the House and still vote against a bill. Not this time. This rule passed welfare reform. This time procedure had too much to do with politics.

A majority of the House was 218. They would not get a single Republican vote on the rule. Only 155 members were listed as yes. And some of those were shaky. They went down the list, name by name, and the whips reported. "No." "Undecided." "No." "No." With each report the tension mounted. "Undecided." "Undecided." "No." "Undecided."

The vote wasn't for a week. On most bills, a count with those numbers would guarantee easy passage. Sometimes members didn't decide how they would vote until they walked onto the floor, past the phalanx of lobbyists who lined the corridor into the chamber with their thumbs up or down—if they trusted a lobbyist to protect their political interests, they might follow his or her advice—past the members working the doors who tried in one quick sentence to convince them to vote one way. But that casual approach applied to legislation which was of little national import, when members knew little about it, and it had no effect on their districts. This bill was of national import, and everyone already knew the arguments for and against. The number 155 was not a good count.

A member who had gone with Stenholm to Wright's office stood up and said, "The undecideds aren't going to move until they know what's what."

Then he walked out. With welfare in he was a no.

Coelho's eyes followed him out. The pressure built inside the room. Coelho read off a long list of members who had already said yes. "I want them checked again."

This was serious, for both the whip organization—if some whips weren't counting accurately—and for the bill. A commitment was a commitment. Wasn't it?

Thursday, October 22, was the day of Reagan's second press conference of the year, the first in five months. The day before, the Dow Jones average had shot up 179 points; Reagan had said the market crisis "appeared to be" over, and an unnamed White House official told reporters, "No one's told me there's been any change on taxes." It seemed a budget deal was off. But Thursday the Dow Jones collapsed again, down seventy points. That ended any talk about market recovery, and put a budget agreement back on track. Reagan opened his press conference that night with a strong statement, reaffirming his commitment to "meet with the bipartisan leaders of the Congress." There would be no preconditions, and everything except Social Security would be on the table.

The press laid into him. There was a hostile tone about the questions, a personal tone. The press seemed less interested in getting information than in getting Reagan, in making him eat his words. They had been kept at bay throughout the Iran-contra mess, had been forced to shout questions at him while he got on his helicopter and pretended not to hear—although he answered those he wanted to.

Question: *Walter Mondale said, "Mr. Reagan and I will both raise taxes," but the difference, he said, was that you wouldn't tell anybody. Now, aren't you going against your own campaign pledge if you're about to negotiate for new taxes?*

Question: *Today you are ready to meet with Congress. What has caused this transformation after months of refusing a budget summit?*

Question: *Let me ask you, sir, why did you change your tune on tax increases from "over my dead body" to "keeping any increase as low as possible"?*

If Reagan started strong, he began to writhe, to hedge, to brag almost that his budget had "$22 billion of additional revenues in it." He referred to this fact repeatedly to escape tax question after tax question. And he repeatedly blamed Congress for the deficit.

The next morning's papers quoted Chiles and Coelho as welcoming Reagan's statements, while Byrd said Reagan showed "considerable courage and statesmanship. . . . By his answers tonight, the President indicated to me that he is flexible and he sincerely wants to negotiate and achieve a package we can all support."

Wright had not made himself available to reporters the preceding evening. He was already angry over Central America: tension with the administration was continuing over the peace process. Just the day before he had met with José Azcona, the president of Honduras, and was now convinced that the White House was trying to destroy, not advance, the peace process. Trust was in short supply. Now, at breakfast, angry, he reviewed a transcript of Reagan's remarks and underlined inaccuracies while his staff sat around the table in silence. Others, even Coelho, dismissed Reagan's factual errors as sloppiness; Wright viewed them as lies.

Reagan had said, "I submitted a budget program early in the year, and as they've done every year I've been here, [Congress this year] simply put it on the shelf and refused even to consider it." *A lie.* It had gone to the floor of the House and Senate; out of a total of 535 potential votes, it got forty-five. It was rejected 490–45.

Reagan had said, "For more than half a century that was dominated entirely by Congress, both houses of the Congress by one party, they have followed . . . deficit spending. And some of us said year after year that this would keep on to the point that it would get out of control. And it has, just as we said it would." *Bullshit!* Reagan tripled— *tripled!*—the national debt, accumulated over the preceding two centuries, in six years.

Reagan had said, "The President of the United States cannot spend a nickel. Only Congress can authorize the spending of money. And for six years now I have repeatedly asked the Congress for less money and they have turned around and given more. . . . We haven't had a . . . budget since I've been here." *More bullshit! More lies!* Congress actually had appropriated less than Reagan asked for.

Wright wanted to beat Reagan, beat him into the ground. When he first became Speaker he had wanted to work with him. That day when Congress overrode the veto of the highway bill, while the result was still in doubt, Wright had called Howard Baker and told him that whoever won, they should stop fighting and cooperate in the future. Then he had made that gesture of friendship, delaying the vote on arms-control provisions until after George Shultz returned from Moscow. The Caucus had been angry at the delay, and would have erupted had the members known the reason for it.

But Wright no longer trusted the administration.

The idea of confrontation seemed to drive him now. The anger was deep and running in him, through him, deeper than something that could be released in an outburst. He wanted to host a press lunch to contradict and correct Reagan's inaccuracies, and said, "I'm trying to get the public to understand this son of a bitch is a liar. Byrd, Chiles, even Tony didn't prove that."

They disagreed. "Then your confrontation with Reagan becomes the story."

"So what? You don't think I owe it to the Congress—I am after all the constitutional officer of the Congress—do I not have a responsibility to defend the Congress? Byrd, Bentsen, and Chiles won't do it. [*Washington Post* columnist] Mary McGrory is writing that Congress is fawning on the President. I'm not. She doesn't know that I'm not."

His staff calmed him, cooled him. They convinced him simply to issue a statement and attach a Budget Committee document to it, citing the factual errors. Maybe it wouldn't reach millions of people. But it wouldn't explode anything either.

Later that day things did not cool down. Reagan sat on a Labor Department panel about job creation and commented, "Those who have to make a decision about investing in the future of our economy see some very disturbing signs on Capitol Hill. . . . We see a Congress that is unable to get control of deficit spending. It backed away from its Gramm-Rudman-Hollings deficit reduction promises, and there are many who, while refusing to cut spending, insist on increasing taxes."

Wright saw the quote on a wire-service printout. He crumpled it angrily in his hand, more determined than ever to dominate. To win.

He did not calm over the weekend. On Monday, before seeing the President and formally agreeing to a budget summit, he shifted back and forth from minutiae to serious business: *How are we coming on the Christmas card photos? . . . For the* Newsweek *story*—the magazine was still investigating him—*get a map of Tarrant County and mark all the places where I've put money into the district, show them it's not just the North Side. . . . Get me a list of those user fees Reagan proposed. . . . I need a breakdown of this budget freeze.*

Just before going to the White House, he met with the leadership and his budget experts. Coelho had talked to Wall Street people about what the markets needed: $23 billion in deficit reduction, which Gramm-Rudman required, would be enough to stabilize the markets, so long as there was discipline in the out-years. Wright nodded, and said, "I don't want a one-year patch-up. I don't want to have this problem every year. We want to get a glide path down for the deficit."

Then he told them he was willing to cut Social Security cost-of-living increases. Democrats had won twenty-six House seats in the 1982 election, and White House threats to cut Social Security had been a significant factor. A GOP vote to cut Social Security had also played a role in the Democrats' recapture of the Senate the preceding year. Republicans were wary, suspicious and wary, of Democratic traps on Social Security. It was the one item Reagan had said was off the table. It was also the only way to cut the deficit significantly. Suggesting cuts there impressed everyone in the room that Wright was serious about this thing, and Gray was already packaging the words to sell: " 'Entitlement reform.' That's good."

Twenty minutes later Wright was in the Oval Office.

It was one week after the crash. The earth was shifting underfoot again; markets were terrified again. The Hong Kong stock market had reopened after being closed for four days; it fell 30 percent—30 percent in one day! The Tokyo market was down 5 percent. The New York Stock Exchange, as they met, opened down; it would drop 156 points, the biggest loss ever except for the crash itself. In some ways this day was more frightening than the week before; it seemed to confirm terror. There was the panic of no boundaries, of a man out wading who was knocked over by a wave and, coughing up water, turned around, reached his foot down to regain balance and touch bottom and there was no bottom, and he felt the cold gripping his belly.

Pressure was intense. Reagan made a special effort to be gracious. Byrd responded in kind, smiling, saying, "Let's forget the past."

They all feared the markets' reaction to disagreement. But Wright had no patience for delicacy just now. The markets gave him an advantage, and he wanted to press it. He raised the issue of the reconciliation bill several times, saying it was just the first step in a major multiyear solution to the deficit. Jim Baker warned, "We've got to be careful. If we talk of more than $23 billion and don't achieve it, the markets could go to hell."

Michel wanted Wright to pull the bill from the schedule—earlier he had sent Wright a letter complaining that it flew "in the face of" bipartisanship—but no one backed Michel up. Wright took silence for assent. *Go ahead with the bill.*

Wright pushed again, bringing up the split of fifty-fifty between taxes and cuts. But only he was willing to risk walking out of the room with nothing to talk of except an impasse, and, as if by common consent, the subject shifted away from him toward the makeup of the group. Byrd proposed three Democrats and three Republicans from each body. Wright had wanted three Democrats and two Republicans but Byrd had undercut him. He had to agree. Appropriations chairman Jamie Whitten, Rostenkowski, and Gray would represent House Democrats. But Byrd did give him an opening; he had not intended to appoint Foley, preferring the three aggressors. *All of them would fight. They were all fighters. They could make a deal but they could fight too.* He named Foley to attend as an "observer"; no one could object to such a slight numerical edge. The two Bakers would represent the White House, although Miller and Carlucci would often be in the room. Michel, Trent Lott, and Silvio Conte, the ranking member of Appropriations, represented House Republicans. Senior senators would represent relevant Senate committees. Nothing firm was agreed upon, except to refrain from attacking one another in the press. Howard Baker ended the meeting saying, "Let's not talk about $23 billion so much that we're locked into that and no more."

Now, on the White House lawn after the meeting, Wright tried to use the press to box the White House in by declaring—after all, no one had contradicted him when he raised these points—that they had agreed on "real deficit reduction" ("real" was a code word for no asset sales); "more than $23 billion if possible—we'll do over half of that this week in our guaranteed deficit reduction bill"; and "a long-term solution."

If those ideas made it into enough stories, the White House would have to go along with them. On the drive back to the Capitol his attention turned back to reconciliation. It would provide a skeleton that could structure the entire negotiations. The House would vote in three days. It had become more important than ever. He wanted to take no chances. It had to pass, with the strongest possible vote.

After the brief White House press conference Wright returned to the Capitol. In a hurry, he did not even take the time to go to his personal office, instead heading for his closer ceremonial one, and called Tom Downey. *Now Tom, you know I support your bill. But to pass reconciliation, it might become necessary to drop welfare reform. If that happens I'll schedule it promptly, just as soon as you want. But if welfare does have to come out, Tom, will you support reconciliation?*

Wright hung up. "Downey's on board if we take welfare out."

He was ready to take it out and made more phone calls looking for votes. So many years before, in 1948, thirty-eight votes had cost him reelection to the Texas legislature, and almost ended his political career. After that campaign, people came up to him apologizing, saying if they had only known he needed their help, if he had only asked, they'd have voted for him. "Until then I had figured people would vote for me because I was so wonderful," he snorted, contemptuous of his own ego. "I thought it was self-evident. After that I realized that people want to be asked."

Now he was asking. While he made calls, Foley met with lobbyists from over forty organizations in H-324 and pressed them to lobby for reconciliation. Sequestration would devastate everything from farmers to defense, he warned. It would devastate *them*. They left fired up, eager to work. Coelho had already scheduled another meeting with more lobbyists.

All day the market slid lower and lower. In 1929, after the initial crash a series of smaller quakes had sent the market down far lower still. Was this happening now? Gerald Ford called Reagan, Wright, Bush, Dole, and Byrd from New York with the same message: the markets needed an agreement quickly, and it had to include taxes.

John Mack worked on language to link reconciliation with the appropriations bill, the long-term continuing resolution which would be voted on the following week and include $7 billion in spending cuts. Several members had asked for that linkage, so they could tell constituents that they had to vote for the tax increase to get the spending cuts. The language went in the rule. Self-executing. The rule also fixed a problem over agriculture which would have cost two votes, and settled other disputes. Self-executing.

Wright was looking for votes everywhere. He said, "If Stenholm's plan includes Social Security cuts, which he emphatically says it does, we'll let him offer it and beat it on the floor."

In return for getting a vote on his plan, Stenholm had to agree to vote for the rule, against the GOP substitute, and for final passage of reconciliation. It was dangerous. If Stenholm dropped Social Security cuts from his proposal it could pass. "We don't want to tell him you can't offer it because we might not be able to beat you," one member worried. But they needed his vote. Stenholm said he was considering the deal and would get back.

Tuesday pressure intensified. The budget summit itself was beginning and the AP quoted Fitzwater that no one had agreed to a fifty-fifty split between revenues and spending cuts. Wright hissed, "I'm damn tired of this. I had an agreement with Baker and Baker. Are they trustworthy or not? Fitzwater may not think they've agreed, but that fifty-fifty is what they're going to get."

Yet in the daily press conference, for the first time all year, a gap— small but significant—opened between Wright and Foley. The media defined expectations, which defined success or failure, and Wright and Foley emphasized different things. Wright tried to use the media to lock the White House into the fifty-fifty split between taxes and cuts. Foley was silent. But when Wright left to open the House, Foley advanced his own message: "I personally am not committed to raising one single dollar more than $23 billion. . . . Success is $23 billion. That's the goal. We don't want you coming up to us and asking, 'Mr. Congressman, why is it that you haven't reached your targets and why shouldn't the market go down Monday?' "

Thirty minutes later, Wright hosted lunch for his negotiators in H-201, before the first budget summit meeting that afternoon. Much had happened in this room already this year. Now he gave his appointees his instructions: "We want to do $23 billion *first,* and we want to stand tough on our [reconciliation] bill. Then whatever happens, happens. But I want the conferees to stand tough."

Although Byrd and the White House wanted a quick resolution, possibly even this week, Rostenkowski agreed with Wright and said, "I'm going to stonewall until we pass reconciliation. We're doing a lousy P.R. job—I'm not blaming anybody, but our message isn't getting out. Sunday on TV Sam Donaldson asked me what specifically I was going to do. He didn't even know we had a bill. I was flabbergasted. That's a White House reporter asking a White House question." Then he shook his head, like a lion shaking its mane, and declared, "I'd like to talk to the membership."

Staff walked out into the corridor. They had their own troubles. One lit a cigarette. "The Senate can't pass their bill anyway. They're stalling, waiting for us to pull their ass out of the fire."

"The Agriculture Committee came up with savings about as real as the carpet we're standing on." They were standing on marble. "You know who led the fight for that phony bullshit? Stenholm."

Inside the room Rostenkowski argued against allowing any amendments at all to reconciliation. Not Stenholm's. Not anyone's. He didn't like the precedent it would set of allowing amendments to tax bills, and worried that a well-designed amendment might pass. And welfare reform should stay in. He believed outside political forces made passage inevitable. "Jim, these members can't vote against the bill," he insisted. "They've got to vote for it no matter what they say. Put them on the spot and see if they'll vote against it. They can't."

"This bill has got to pass," Wright countered. He saw no need to ram welfare reform down the members' throats. He, not Rostenkowski, was hearing all the complaints. "And we've got to maximize the votes for it."

It was odd, a reversal of their roles. Rostenkowski, despite his image as a muscle man, had his committee's loyalty because he took care of his members and protected them politically. There was ego in that.

One committee member said, "He gives you what you need but he wants you to beg. It's the power he likes." It was the feudal relationship. One asks; the other gives. But still he took care of his members. Otherwise his power would dissipate. Wright had the reputation for ramrodding things through. Now Rostenkowski was the one who wanted to use the raw power of the leadership to get his way, even though it would expose members to political attack.

All year Wright had pushed Rostenkowski. Rostenkowski had done what he wanted. Now he was pushing Wright. They were still defining their relationship. Wright's power was not arbitrary. He owed Rostenkowski. There was the future to think of. Rostenkowski had done his job, done it all year, could have blocked Wright a dozen times and never did. He gave him a tax bill, and one like he wanted. *Now was Wright going to screw Ways and Means or was he going to pass the bill? Ways and Means gave you your bill, Mr. Speaker. Now pass it.*

Freshmen Democrats were worried. Most had won tough races and the first reelection campaign was always the most difficult. Most were listed as undecided on the whip count. Now almost the entire freshman class, twenty members, was gathered in a room in Coelho's domain to hear from the Speaker, the majority leader, the whip, and the key subcommittee chairman.

When Wright entered, the freshmen rose. It was odd, this show of respect, members of Congress—princes in their own right—standing for him. More-senior members would never have done it. He smiled in appreciation, and began to talk softly, so softly they leaned forward to hear, speaking not of politics, or of favors, but simply of the merits of the bill, the reasons why the economy needed the tax bill—*You understand how hard cutting spending is. You've been confronted with it. You understand how much damage the deficit will do if it's not cut. You understand why we need some taxes.* Welfare reform, too, was a good bill, even the President had called for welfare reform in his State of the Union speech. And so it would be included as part of the rule for reconciliation. "You can nitpick any bill to death. You can always find an excuse to vote no. But Felix Rohatyn, Gerald Ford, half a dozen other people have been talking to me about the need for taxes as part of the package. None of them has mentioned welfare. Tax and spend is better than borrow and spend, borrow and spend, borrow and spend.

It's the constitutional responsibility of the House to move a tax bill first. That is our institutional responsibility. And if we can't vote for this tax bill, what can we vote for? It's a good bill."

His voice was still soft, soft but insistent, soft but piercing, soft but dogged, dogged, dogged. Then he stiffened, bunched his fists, and his voice, though still soft, tightened. "If we pass this, then we're strong. If not, then we have no position. The markets will read that as a terrible message, and they will be right. This is the most important vote of the year." He closed simply, saying, "Do this if you can."

He left. Foley took over and made it simple, an issue of power. He talked about the rule, and procedure: "It's a question of who's running this House."

Then Coelho. Coelho leaned hard, harder than Foley, harder than Wright. He was closer to the freshmen, had as DCCC chairman given each advice, helped each raise money, helped each win. "You came here to govern," he told them. "Nobody said it was easy. I know what you really want. You want to vote no and have the bill pass. *Look me in the eye and say that's not true.* You look me in the eye and tell me that."

Even in this group of twenty, Coelho's intensity had a physical feel, like a man pushing his face forward, making others withdraw. He did not let them escape. *Look me in the eye and say that's not true.* He pushed, pushed, took names. Are you with us? The pressure seemed to pay off. Only three of the twenty freshmen said they would vote no, and one of those three said he would vote yes on the rule.

But the pressure, the pressure was on. It wasn't the best way to count. Counting votes resembles gathering intelligence; it should be done coolly, without pressure. Whipping is delicate, trying to convince while simultaneously trying to get an accurate feel. Members were saying yes when they wanted to say no. Coelho had always counted so accurately. In his own election as whip he had asked his own campaign manager point-blank for his commitment. But how solid was a commitment given at the point of a gun?

"You can't bully people," Jack Brooks, one of the toughest members of the House, once observed. "Every now and then, you might tell a member, 'That'll hurt you at home.' You never want to ask someone to do something they're really against, or that hurts them in their district. They're the sole judge. The test is not whether someone votes with you but whether they tell the truth about it. If you say straight out you're not for it, well, I can't fault you. I know where you are. That's your business. Flexing muscle is foolishness. Nobody does that, the Speaker least of all. Even Lyndon Johnson as President said you have to be careful not to unintentionally hurt someone. If you expect a little charity, it behooves you to be thoughtful."

At least one freshman had been unintentionally hurt, insulted by Coelho's lecture. The member signed on, but the more he thought of it later, the angrier he became: "Who the hell does Tony think he is? 'You came here to govern,' he says? That's pretty goddamn patronizing."

It was a tough vote. At the next whip task force meeting, even task force members raised objections. Why take a tough vote on this? they asked. Why not just wait for the budget summit to settle things?

"With the climate in the country we can't afford not to pass it," Coelho argued. "If there's a summit deal, we can stick it in in conference. But we can't afford to wait. We've got to be responsible, go through this process so Reagan can veto it." *And get all the blame for the deficit.* Then he turned hard-line again. "If we have the votes on the rule there's no reason to allow any more votes"—no amendments.

But Coelho didn't have the votes. Only 173 members had said yes— almost all the improvement since the preceding count came from freshmen—with twenty a firm no. If the leadership lost twenty more Democrats out of the sixty-five leaners and undecideds, they would lose.

MacKay had gone to Coelho and said with welfare out the rule and the bill would pass easily. He suggested the whips do another count, asking if members would support the bill if welfare came out.

Coelho never did it. Why not?

Asking MacKay's question would have spread rumors through the Caucus, created a backlash, showed weakness. Coelho believed some liberals would vote no if welfare reform came out. And he thought members were using welfare reform as an excuse, that their real objection was taxes and taking welfare out would make little difference.

There were deeper reasons, too—Coelho's view of the House, and his relationships with Rostenkowski and Foley. *If we have the votes on the rule there's no reason to allow any more votes,* he had just said. But many members viewed the House as a deliberative body, a town meeting, and the floor as the place for deliberations. The more limitations, dictated by Rules and the leadership, placed on the floor, the more members were cut out of policy-making on issues that did not pass through their own committees. To Coelho the floor was a place to ratify or reject policy, not to make it. Wright and Foley saw the floor halfway between the others' view and Coelho's.

The Caucus was willing to accept some manipulation of procedure for reasons of convenience—it allowed them to get home at a reasonable hour, and it protected them from tough votes—and power; it allowed Wright to exercise power as its surrogate. But it wanted Wright to recognize limits. That wasn't because of sympathy for Republicans. On the few occasions Republicans had controlled procedure in 1981, they had pioneered exactly the things they later decried as abuses of power when Democrats did them. On the very first procedural vote of this year, Republicans had taken what even Dick Cheney conceded was "a political cheap shot at the Democrats," and even tried to infringe on the constitutional right of free speech by making it out of order to discuss raising income taxes on the floor. But members, especially those who had worked so hard in the sixties and early seventies to democratize the House, wanted the leadership to recognize limits.

But perhaps Coelho's own agenda had gotten involved. Here was a man who had gone to Wright the very day of Wright's greatest triumph, when the Central American peace agreement was signed, and confronted him, complained to him that he was not being treated properly. Here was a man who felt sometimes like the odd man out in the leadership, whose own deputies had been picked by Wright without consultation. His reputation as a tactician without deep convictions, as someone clever but not deep, pained him. "One of our big goals this year," said a Coelho aide, "is to erase the idea that Tony isn't substantive."

Maybe this vote could help Coelho do that, and also establish himself as a dominant force in the House. The whip had never been that important before. Coelho had made himself important. Demonstrating convictions would add to the respect with which he was viewed. Conceivably, it could make him more of a force even than Foley. Foley had everyone's trust, had the reputation for depth and substantive knowledge, but there were doubts about him. A prominent Democrat complained, "Tom looks very handsome and he speaks very well but I never know what side he's really on. He stands at the gate and urges you to vote to approve the [previous day's] journal. He never says, 'Hell no, you son of a bitch, we can't do that.' It's always, 'Well, we could but . . .' " No one ever said that about Coelho.

There was one last reason to keep welfare in, part of the inside game: Coelho did not want to give Rostenkowski ammunition to use against the leadership, to be able to say the leadership could not deliver on a tough vote, that it was unreliable.

Whatever the reasons, Coelho pushed and kept pushing. In the afternoon, outside Wright's office, Coelho and Mack ran into each other. Coelho insisted that the Black Caucus would walk if welfare came out of the bill. Mack wanted names, reached for a list in Coelho's hand, and Coelho pulled it away. They were joking, and the two had long been friends—real friends, not friends the way people in Washington used the word. But there was no doubt where Mack's loyalties lay. It was Mack who had suggested Bonior as chief deputy whip, instead of Coelho's intimate. This was business. *What are the names?* Coelho wouldn't give them. Later Mack asked Bill Gray, a black, if the Black Caucus had a problem if welfare came out. Gray looked puzzled and said, "Not that I know of."

That evening Wright sat down with Mack in H-210, the ceremonial office. "Ceremonial" was the right word. It had a sterile formality. The light came from the huge chandelier, too big for the room, crafted by Paul Revere; it had hung in the White House until its tinkling in air drafts annoyed Teddy Roosevelt, and he had ordered it removed. On the walls hung portraits of nineteenth-century Speakers. The oak desk was bare, its top barren, its drawers empty. Though Wright used the room often enough, it had no lived-in feel. Now, with the night black outside it took on a surreal quality. The door was closed. In his personal office aides might open a closed door, but no one would open this door, with him in with Mack. They reviewed the names of members who had a problem with the bill. Hughes? Visclosky? Cooper? Wright looked at name after name.

"These are good people," he said. "We can't lose these people and win."

"Those freshmen aren't so sure either, when you ask them one-on-one, out of the group."

What difference did it make if welfare was in this bill? We put our guys through the wringer and the Senate's not going to do it anyway, not in reconciliation. Wright pointed at one name.

"You'll never get him. Fear. You can see it in his eyes," said Mack.

"That's the trouble with this place," Wright snapped. "Too many people here who shouldn't be in Congress. No guts. That's what leadership is. If you don't have it, you shouldn't be in government." He looked over the count. "We're at the point we should be picking up votes. We're not. I'm uneasy. This is too big a vote to be uneasy on."

Wright had decided. Welfare was almost certainly coming out. He picked up the phone and called Stenholm.

"Charlie, how are you?" The massaging began. The leaning began. *Pressure? What's pressure? There's nothing higher than the Speaker asking for your help. There's nothing higher than that.*

"Charlie, I had planned to have you offer your substitute. . . . They're not with you on that?" Stenholm couldn't get enough people to support both raising taxes and cutting Social Security to make it worth putting on the floor. So he didn't want to offer it. It would only show how weak his position was, which would undermine any chance of the budget summit doing something big. Wright continued.

"Charlie, I value your information. If we took welfare out, do you think it would pass? . . . I think you're real important, Charlie, I think you're key. . . . Could I have your help? . . .

"I know the White House, Charlie. The only thing they understand is strength. This matters for the institution, too, for the House. It certainly matters for me."

Wright listened for a moment, then said, "I never put it to you quite this way before, Charlie."

All those times back in the early 1980s, Wright would sit down next to Stenholm on the floor, argue for a vote, and Stenholm would shake his head and say, "Jim, I just can't do it." Wright had taken it personally, had wondered about his own ability if he could not even convince a junior colleague from his own state, but he had never asked on a personal basis. Now he would. That was the one thing higher than the Speaker asking for help. Asking on a personal basis. Wright was saying please help him. Wright dropped all pretense and made himself vulnerable, in a way naked. Members did not expose themselves like that.

"If this doesn't pass, my name is mud. I said we're going to do it. My name would be mud, my reputation zero. They'd say, 'Hell, he can't even deliver the House' . . . Appropriations? You better believe it, buddy. That language is in there. . . . I want $23 billion just for starters. I'm committed to doing more. . . . Not your vote, Charlie. I want your help." *He had it.* "Thanks! Thanks a lot, buddy!"

They hadn't made a deal. Stenholm's support remained contingent upon welfare coming out of the bill, and Wright had not promised to remove it. He had kept the "if" in his request. Still, Wright had all but announced it would come out. Stenholm expected it out, and, with it out, he had agreed to work for the bill. Stenholm *was* key. *Not your vote, Charlie. I want your help.* With Stenholm working actively for the bill passage became certain. There was something else. Wright had made it personal. Stenholm had said yes. It was personal to Stenholm now, too.

That could become a bridge to Stenholm for the future, a healing of old wounds on both sides. They had their resentments. A healing would begin out of mutual self-interest but it might build upon that, into trust and respect and a positive desire to work together wherever possible. If that happened, Wright's base within the Caucus would become more solid than O'Neill's had ever been, and in many ways—in useful ways, in ways which allowed things to get done—more solid than Rayburn's. Rayburn was Wright's standard for a great Speaker, and he constantly, privately, measured himself against him. Rayburn. Lonely Rayburn. At that moment, as Wright hung up after talking with Stenholm, Wright's speakership seemed capable of achieving the greatness and permanence he had dreamed of.

CHAPTER 17

Members packed the Budget Committee's hearing room the morning after Wright's conversation with Stenholm. It was as big a turnout as Buddy MacKay had ever had. His colleagues filled the seats at the long witness table where the guest speaker sat, overflowed into the rows of seats where staff usually sat, overflowed onto the long double-decker dais where members sat during formal hearings. They had come to hear former Federal Reserve chairman Paul Volcker's thoughts on the market collapse. While he spoke, word spread: Stenholm had talked to the Speaker and welfare reform was out of the bill. Stenholm was going to support both the rule and the bill. One member asked Volcker how he thought the markets would react to the tax increase in reconciliation.

"I don't think that would be bad," he replied. His main concern was that any deal reached in the budget summit would be long-term and serious.

And welfare reform?

"I have no idea of the specifics of the bill, but it would be preferable not to send a mixed message"—a mixed message of tax and spend.

These members respected Volcker. He was saying exactly what they had been saying. They were surer than ever they were right.

An hour and a half later, Wright sat down with Coelho and Foley in H-210 to discuss whether welfare would be in reconciliation. The floor vote would come the next day, but the Rules Committee would soon meet and needed to know what to do. It had to report the rule for the bill today; House rules demanded a one-day layover between committee action and legislation reaching the floor. Even the Rules Committee could not void that requirement; only a two-thirds vote on the floor to suspend the rules could do that. Wright did not have to decide this instant, but soon.

The count was up to 187. *That was all.* And they were still counting the rule. Who the hell knew how many were willing to bend to the pressure on the rule but vote against the bill? Wright wanted welfare out.

Coelho fought the decision. "We need twenty-eight more to pass the rule, counting absences. I see thirty-four, without even using the big gun—you."

"Wait a second, Tony," Wright replied. "There are guys on here saying no, who we don't lose often. We've got a chance of losing this bill. Stenholm and Leath will try to help, if we take welfare out."

"I don't believe that. People are 'no' because of taxes. They're using welfare as an excuse. Stenholm's a 'no' on taxes."

"Stenholm's problem isn't taxes. The same with others. The count hasn't moved in twenty-four hours. That makes me nervous."

"It's too early to decide. There's something more important here. Leadership. You've said this is the package. You'll be sending Baker a message that you can't deliver."

"I'll tell you what's important—passing the bill is important."

"I talked to a group of fifteen members this morning on scheduling," Foley said. "This came up. They said the bill would take off like an airplane if welfare came out."

Coelho countered, "The Black Caucus is saying if welfare comes out they're 'no.' You lose as many as you gain."

That was a major factor. A very major factor. Wright and Foley were unhappily silent for a moment, absorbing the information.

Then Foley suggested, "Is it an impossible alternative that, if we lose the rule, we simply go back for another one?"

If the first rule with welfare in it lost, the Rules Committee could excise welfare and leave just reconciliation. It would mean keeping the House in Friday, because of the layover requirement, but it made sense.

They would run one more whip count, then decide. The House convened at noon; they would call for a vote on approving the journal of the previous day. That would bring all the members to the floor where they could be contacted quickly and efficiently. Foley and Coelho left. Wright picked up the phone and started making phone calls in alphabetical order. The first one was to Les AuCoin. He had a long way to go.

When the House convened, Wright himself worked the floor while members voted on the journal (Republicans, as always, voted against its approval 97–65). Foley talked with Agriculture chairman Kika de la Garza to iron out a jurisdictional problem between him and Rostenkowski. Wright talked to Jim Cooper, a Rhodes Scholar, son of a Tennessee governor, and then Dingell, chairman of the committee Cooper was the most junior member of, talked to him. *Sure would like your help.* Everyone on the whip task force combed the floor. Suddenly the chamber broke into spontaneous applause when Buddy Roemer entered. Roemer had been a heavy underdog in the Louisiana gubernatorial race. He won. Down-home, one of the best poker players in the House, redneck-seeming but Harvard-educated, he left little doubt that his ultimate goal was the White House. Members crowded about him, shaking his hand, hugging him, and he gave an impromptu speech—"Thank you for all your heart and all your love and all your concern. . . . I already miss this place. . . . I'll tell you how I won it. I laid it all out on the line."

That was the way Wright was playing it, laying it all on the line.

At twelve-thirty the leadership met again. The count looked better—up to 213. In addition, five members had said they would help if absolutely necessary: they swore that their vote would not defeat Wright. But Volcker's impact was being felt. Virtually the entire MacKay group looked like "no" votes if welfare stayed in the bill, and MacKay would actively work against it.

"What about final passage?" Foley asked. "People who say yes on the rule, no on the bill? We can lose the rule, and that's not a disaster. Losing final passage is a disaster."

"We should get seven to ten Republicans on final passage," Coelho predicted. They returned to the list of swing votes. Coelho picked out a name. "It's taxes with him."

Foley and Wright both disagreed. "Tony, he told both of us with welfare out, he'd vote for it and work for it. He can't back up on that."

They had ten more votes if welfare came out. But Coelho warned again that the Black Caucus would walk then, costing more votes. "I don't like welfare in the bill," Wright grumbled. "It shouldn't have been in there in the first place. A damn power play by Rostenkowski."

"If we get 218," Foley said, "let's go for it." *That wasn't like Foley, playing tough. Was he competing with Coelho?* Wright had to make a decision. In or out?

What was the decision? Wright looked straight at Coelho. It was Coelho's job to count. Wright thought back to the day just before summer recess when Coelho walked into his office and said that Wright wasn't treating him properly, that he was not being respected. Now Coelho was saying they had the votes, and that taking welfare out would lose votes in the Black Caucus. If Wright overruled him, it would be the ultimate statement of no confidence.

Wright wanted to take it out of the bill. This was the most important vote of the year. It was his decision. *Stick a $6-billion program, a major program affecting all of American society, in a self-executing rule, to be rammed through the House without even a separate vote, much less a chance to amend it? What was his decision?* Not Foley's. Not Coelho's. Not Rostenkowski's. What was his? He looked at Coelho.

Welfare reform was in.

Outside, in the Speaker's Lobby, standing on the carpet thick with history, with the stiff, antique furniture—some of it original with the Capitol itself—to the side, the racks of newspapers from around the country, the Associated Press wire, the winding staircase with the iron-work which Dingell insisted came from British cannon captured at the Battle of New Orleans behind him, the staircase going down to the Board of Education, Rayburn's room, Mack worried. "I've done a thousand vote counts in the last eight years. Winning ones and losing ones. I always knew where we were. I don't know on this one." He looked through the swinging doors to the House floor, looked at it as if it were a strange and dangerous jungle, and fell silent, then added, "There's a different feeling out there."

The floor of the House, the members leaning against the brass railings in the back of the chamber, or lounging in the couches in the cloakroom where they, smoking cigars, could make themselves inaccessible, was the inside game. Wright worked it.

While he worked it the outside game intruded upon him. Earlier Jesse Jackson had walked into his office. The visit set into relief the role Wright had, the way in which he was now exercising power. He and Jackson got along well and, at least on many economic issues, believed in many of the same things. Yet they were a study in contrasts, of opposite kinds of political forces. Jackson saw himself as a messenger and a vehicle and spoke of a new world; now one could see for all of Jackson's ego a humility. There was the sense, which would increase during the campaign, that for all his ego, his campaign humbled him, too. People poured their hopes into him as if he were a vessel; he carried something larger than himself. Jackson was a visionary.

Wright had a vision but was no visionary. He rooted about in the dirt of policy, got the grime of compromise under his fingernails, had learned so many years ago that *personal acceptance meant more to legislative success than ideology.* There was little elegiac about his role. He was a doer. To Jackson, details were insignificant; to Wright, details defined the world. He had not so much sought that role as it had fallen to him. He envied the other. *Recalling his first time speaking, at age fifteen, before a political crowd to help elect Ernest Thompson governor of Texas, Wright had said, "That's heady wine. One never gets tired of it."* He commented that at a recent Michigan state party dinner he had said the same thing Jackson said later, "but the Speaker of the House does not get the attention a presidential candidate does. That's a fact of life."

But it wasn't the position that demanded that attention. It was the man. Their different roles became clear as they talked and Jackson mentioned in passing one of his campaign proposals to use public pension funds to rebuild the nation's physical infrastructure. It was an idea about which Jackson knew so little that a few weeks later when at a group interview half a dozen tough, national reporters asked him about it, he stumbled, then turned to an aide and asked plaintively, "How am I doing?" It was the same with other specific proposals he had made, and the reporters grew embarrassed at his ignorance and did not pursue him, left unasked planned follow-up questions. Wright knew his own proposals intimately, knew not only the details but the logic behind them. As he and Jackson continued and Wright referred to the various pieces of legislation the House had moved, one got a sense of how in Wright's mind he was knitting these individual bills together to form a policy. He was building something with all that rooting about in the earth; if no one else could see it, he could. *Digging up the mud, molding it into blocks, baking it. This was where Wright's soul went, where he created things.* Jackson had no aptitude for that, no interest in it; he inspired others, moved others, to put those blocks together. The two men were opposites yet each was totally, absolutely, wholly political; their roles complemented each other.

But this was not a courtesy call. Jackson came to ask Wright to be ready to intercede privately in the presidential campaign if one candidate started taking uncalled-for shots at another. Jackson saw himself as the most likely target. "The Democratic Party needs someone who can call folks up and say, 'This doesn't make any sense, don't do this,'" Jackson said.

Wright agreed. Jackson also told Wright his life had been threatened but James Baker was refusing to provide Secret Service protection—protection which would start anyway in ten weeks. Could Wright help? He agreed to call. After Jackson's visit Wright talked of his respect for courage—"political courage, moral courage, physical courage."

The courageous made history. History beckoned Wright. Ambition was justified by good works. Protestants have always been particularly good at confusing the two.

The Rules Committee was meeting on the third floor of the Capitol, across the hallway from the press gallery, marking up the rule. Downstairs on the first floor the whip task force, at long last finished counting the rule, was working on final passage of the bill. Both would be voted on the next day. Wright rarely attended a task force meeting. He walked in. Marty Russo, the chairman, said, "The rule's up to 217 now, from 187 yesterday. Your presence was felt, Mr. Speaker. Thank you."

Wright nodded but he was still uneasy, and huddled with Beryl Anthony, from Arkansas. Then Anthony picked up the phone to call Bill Clinton, the governor of Arkansas who headed a bipartisan National Governors' Association welfare reform group. Could Clinton make some phone calls to Arkansas members? And could they send telegrams to everyone else? Yes.

Russo read off a name. One whip reported, "The stuff the Republicans are throwing out about the bill cost us his vote."

"It was the *Wall Street Journal* story this morning, about all the goodies in the bill for some people," said someone.

Ways and Means Republicans had leaked a list of tax breaks Rostenkowski had used to buy votes. The *Journal* had trumpeted them. Wright venomously spat, "People wrap the garbage in newspapers."

Things weren't supposed to go this way. Losing votes at this stage. Now was when votes started flocking to you if you had any momentum. On his way to the meeting he had said, "My instinct was to pull welfare. I don't feel right about this. I should have followed my instinct." Now he announced, "If we lose the rule we're going to come right back with another one, with welfare out."

Russo winced. Wright's words might make some members think they had a free vote, that they could kill welfare and still pass the tax bill. "Mr. Speaker. Do you want that strategy to get out?"

"No," Wright said, shaking his head.

But there were forty people in the room.

The task force broke up. Outside in the corridor, David Bonior snorted, "There's so much shit in this bill. A hundred million for big chicken farmers like Perdue. Rostenkowski's in this pissing contest with Harold Washington"—the black mayor of Chicago, at war with the white political powers—"over some municipal thing. If we do win the rule, final passage is not at all assured."

Another Wright ally commented, "This is all a fuck-up. Foley didn't want to be the one to say take it out. Maybe it was his reputation for not being a tough guy. We're way behind where we should be. The whip organization needs a kick in the ass. To do all this just to keep Ways and Means happy—bullshit! It's bullshit!"

Then word spread across the floor about the money the Appropriations defense subcommittee had given the Pentagon. The original budget resolution had included those two different defense figures: if $19 billion in taxes became law, defense would get a high number; if Reagan vetoed taxes, defense would get less. Now the tax bill had dropped from $19 billion to $12 billion. Wright had told Appropriations to split the difference on defense spending between the low and high numbers. Russo heard of it and was furious. When he had agreed to sign the budget conference report, Wright had said defense would not get one penny more than the low number unless the $19 billion tax bill became law. Wright believed he had been speaking figuratively; Russo didn't see it that way. *Wright gave me his word.*

Stenholm was angry now too, angry with a deep personal anger. Wright had asked him for help on a personal basis. He had said yes on a personal basis, assuming welfare came out. He had told colleagues welfare was out. Wright's call had been almost . . . embarrassing. He had forced an intimacy, bonded them. That intimacy meant they must move closer or hate each other. He had thought after Wright's call that maybe they could work together in the future, maybe there was a softening of the hardness between them. He had hung up with a good feeling. *But welfare was in the bill.* Stenholm hadn't found out until he walked on the floor. Wright had made a fool of him. *Wright hadn't needed his vote or his help so he had spurned him. Asked him on a personal basis and then didn't even have the courtesy to tell him no deal. Wright had made it personal and then decided he hadn't needed him and spurned him.* They had screwed with him on the budget, screwed with him on cutting appropriations, and now this? *Well, it was personal now, all right.*

Calmly, hiding his anger, Stenholm walked over to Wright on the floor and asked what had happened. Wright explained that liberals like Gus Hawkins, the black chairman of the Education and Labor Committee, and the rest of the Black Caucus would vote no if welfare came out. Stenholm walked over to Hawkins and congratulated him: "Well, Gus, you got them to keep it in."

Hawkins replied, "I did not. I don't care if welfare's in the bill or not."

Stenholm did not wonder what was going on. He knew only that people were screwing around with him. He would put everything he had into beating Wright.

You wanted a tax bill, Mr. Speaker? Here it is. Now pass it.

Thursday morning, the morning of the vote, the vote count looked all right on paper. But the House was seething. The weekly whip meeting in H-324 was seething. The Caucus, for the first time all year, began to splinter. There were so many agendas, so many ambitions, so many beliefs. There had been so much pressure all year. But the exercise of power was foreign to the nature of this body. These were colleagues. They each felt responsible for half a million people. *The only blood oath I ever swore was to my constituents,* Brian Donnelly had said. They each had a vote. They were each equal.

Liberals complained over the defense appropriations, then exploded, all but calling Gray a liar, when Gray quoted figures that seemed to play it down. And defense spending wasn't even in the bill about to be voted on. It had nothing to do with the bill. As members shouted at one another, Wright tried to regain control.

"That's next week's problem. You have a commitment from us for savings on that. Please. Please, let's talk about this week's game."

"We'll turn this into a task force," Coelho announced. "Final passage. If you're in the whip organization you're supposed to work."

It was another assault on their dignity. *"You're supposed to work"?! The hell with you.* Most of the whips walked out.

An hour later a new problem surfaced. Members started asking about a pay raise—what the hell was this pay raise in the bill that they had just begun hearing about?

"That's a bullshit, phony issue, and we can take care of it in the C.R.," Coelho told a final task force meeting. All federal employees were scheduled to get an automatic cost-of-living raise of 4.5 percent. To save money, reconciliation cut that raise by one-third. But that meant members of Congress, as federal employees, got $2,700, and it was too late to take it out of this bill. It could be fixed soon, but not as soon as Republicans could distribute the information to their news outlets. Paul Harvey, the syndicated conservative radio commentator, was on the air with it. The AP had sent the same story over the wire. Members' offices started getting angry phone calls. *Raising our taxes to pay for your raise? When you bastards already got a $12,000 raise this year?* It was a potent issue.

The task force broke up. Coelho and the leadership staff stayed behind to run down a handful of names. How about this guy?

"He's okay. I had his biggest fund-raiser call him last night."

"No he's not. He's wrong on the rule, right on final passage. That's Stenholm. Stenholm's working hard."

"He told me yes."

"That was before Stenholm talked to him."

"Christ. If Stenholm's making ground up we don't even know about . . ."

The vote on the rule would come at noon. The task force broke up at eleven. Members flooded the floor for a quorum call at eleven-thirty; both sides' organizations worked the members hard. GOP whip Trent Lott complained in a floor speech, "In this case [the rule] contains ten amendments, nine of which you will never get to vote on separately. That's because they are automatically adopted if you accept this rule. This is what is called a self-executing rule. . . . The amendments strike all of the Education and Labor and Ways and Means welfare provisions and then insert a whole, new 148-page compromise which no one on the Rules Committee had seen when we reported this rule. . . . The only thing in this rule that is allowed separate consideration is the Republican substitute. All the Democratic amendments are self-executing, but we have to make our amendments the old-fashioned way, by earning them with separate debates and votes."

But if Democrats were exercising power, Republicans were playing politics. GOP members were unwilling to desert their political mantra of no taxes, wearing buttons that said "Kill taxes." Michel had yielded to their sentiment. The GOP substitute did not include his own proposal for $8 billion in taxes; instead it called for a spending freeze.

That sounded good in floor speeches, and allowed Republicans to claim purity in their opposition to taxes. But spending cuts were easier to talk about than make. The deficit had to be cut at least $23 billion. The GOP proposal cut the deficit only $15 billion and left an $8-billion hole where Michel's tax plan would have been. Despite the market crash, despite the outside demands for at the very least cutting the deficit by $23 billion, given a choice between calling for taxes and falling short of the target, Republicans chose to fall short—*35 percent short*. They didn't come close.

All year partisanship had fed on itself, frustrated each side, driven each side apart. *We have just enough votes to be irresponsible,* Jerry Lewis, a member of the GOP leadership, had ruefully observed. Faced with the irresponsibility of the minority, the majority grew contemptuous of it, more determined to govern in spite of it, and more arbitrary; faced with the increasing arbitrariness of the majority, the minority grew more irresponsible, and more destructive of the institution.

While the debate proceeded, members worked the floor. Dingell talked to Buddy Roemer in one part of the chamber while Stenholm hung back. When Dingell moved away, Stenholm moved in. Then Stenholm with Leath. Then Stenholm with another member, and another, Stenholm ally Tim Penny with his list of names, working Roemer, shaking his hand—they got him!—Rangel and Coelho looking over their list. Of all the House, less than a dozen would decide the issue, all of them Democrats. Two members and Foley's aide George Kundanis talked to Les AuCoin. Wright talked to AuCoin. Got him!

Now Wright stood in the well of the House, the pit of the amphitheater. The chamber was full as he closed debate: "This bill contains $12 billion in real revenues. I do not think I have heard anybody say they are not real. It also commands some $11 billion in additional deficit reduction through savings. You can quarrel whether all of that is absolutely real, but most of it is. This bill is not perfect, but it is a start. It is something. It is deeds instead of words. . . . We can say, oh, I would have voted for it if they had packaged it a little differently, or if only they had scheduled it on some other day. We can hypothecate any number of theoretical choices. Those are not the choices that we have."

As he spoke, shouts of "VOOOTTTE!" rang out in the hall. "VOOOTTTE!" The time for talking was over. "VVVOOOTTTE!"

Wright continued. "We have been marching up this hill all year, knowing we had to face this choice sooner or later. . . . That Constitution which we have been at pains to honor this year very plainly and un-equivocally says that all revenue measures must originate in the House."

VVVVOOOOTTTTE! "If we perform our duty today, we can bring something real to the bargaining table with the President and with the Senate. . . . If you are serious about deficit reduction, this is your chance. Vote aye on the resolution, aye on the rule, aye on the bill."

The vote on the rule started. The leadership fell behind almost im-mediately by ten votes, then fifteen. The quick spurt came from op-ponents who consciously tried to create a surge of momentum on their side; in close votes, with members undecided to the last, such psycho-logical ploys sometimes influence one vote, two votes. That could make the difference. Slowly the Democratic leadership climbed back up, down twelve, down eight, down four, down two. But the mood of the House was running against them. The leadership fell back. No Repub-licans voted with them. Thirty-five Democrats voted no. Thirty-seven. Forty. *Forty-one!* A loud cheer went up from Republicans! *Forty-one Democrats, combined with all the Republicans, meant an absolute ma-jority*. Then forty-three, forty-four, forty-five. Democrats who had promised to support the leadership if their votes would make the difference had started voting no. Ultimately, forty-eight Democrats voted no.

The final result: 203 in favor, 217 opposed.

On the biggest vote of the year Wright had been beaten! The Demo-cratic juggernaut had been stopped!

The chamber was strangely still and Michel rose and addressed the chair. "Mr. Speaker, under somewhat otherwise normal conditions, noting our unanimous vote on this side, we would be elated with this victory. Mr. Speaker, we do not look upon it that way. . . . It has been my feeling that men of goodwill might bring their divergent thoughts together. . . . Members have attempted to express their desire to give their bipartisan negotiating team a chance. . . . I for one am grateful for the vote defeating the rule, but we are not gloating over it. . . . I would hope that it would signal our intention . . . to work together, hand in glove, in a bipartisan way to come to a final resolution."

Wright, on the floor, rose to respond. "I appreciate what my friend the gentleman from Illinois has suggested. He has been consistent, suggesting all along that we delay, and see if we can get some signal as to what the President will accept before we try to pass anything. If we do that, it puts the total initiative in the hands of the Executive Branch of government over something that the Constitution declared was the primary business of the House of Representatives. I bow to the majority. The majority quite obviously did not want this particular rule . . . [with] a welfare reform bill. . . . Therefore, the Rules Committee will meet at twelve-forty-five and we will be seeking another rule."

Lott rose. "What does this now mean? This matter cannot be brought up again today. . . . Are we going to be in session tomorrow to continue this effort?"

Foley answered him: "As I understand what the gentleman has just told me, it is most unlikely we will be given authority to proceed with a rule filed on the same day. Under those circumstances, it is my duty to inform the House that not only will there be roll calls this afternoon, but the House will come in at ten tomorrow and will stay in session until we finish the reconciliation bill."

Newt Gingrich rose, while hostile Democrats shouted, "Regular order!" *Don't let him speak.* "Regular order!" Lott yielded to him and Gingrich said, "I just want to make a point to every member of this House to watch the next few hours. The leadership brought a rule to the floor that a significant number of Democrats told them was unacceptable. . . . The country will not profit from the next three days being focused on this particular bill and a partisan fight in this particular House when the country is asking for a bipartisan effort and a bipartisan vote won today."

Democrats were furious. *Gingrich. Gingrich the most partisan member of the House complaining about partisanship. Gingrich gloating. God . . . damn . . . him.* Buddy MacKay jumped to his feet and Foley yielded to him. MacKay was burning, raging, his words a hiss: "I just wanted to say on behalf of a number of Democrats who have been trying to proceed in a bipartisan manner that the speech made by the gentleman from Georgia"—all of twenty seconds long—"is one of the most destructive things that could have happened today."

The chamber emptied. Members headed back to their offices. In the Speaker's Lobby, MacKay pushed his way through a flock of reporters and grabbed Wright's arm. "Mr. Speaker, I'm voting with you and I'm going to help you all I can."

This fight had only begun.

The leadership moved across the hallway to H-210. For Wright it was as if all the detritus had been cleared away, all the excuses, all the complications. What was left was pure action. It was what he loved.

"Okay. What did we lose by?"

"Fourteen. We need a change of eight."

Wright named one member. "He said he was with us on the rule and voted no. Get him in here. There are fifteen members who told me personally they would vote for the bill if welfare came out. Put together a meeting of all the moderates we can get, down in 201." He turned to Martin Frost, who asked what he wanted in the new rule, and ordered, "I want it clean."

Foley, Coelho, and Mack each picked up one of the telephones scattered around the room. Wright went over names. They were going to win this thing dammit. They were going forward and would win it. Rostenkowski walked in: "You've got to get hold of Gus Hawkins. You're affecting his legislation."

A few minutes later, Wright returned to his personal office and called him. No, Hawkins, a black, didn't care if welfare came out of the bill now. He hadn't cared if it was in in the first place. Wright's jaw tightened. *That wasn't the information he had been getting.* Bill Gray reaffirmed what he had earlier told Mack: the Black Caucus didn't care. Later Charles Rangel, a black, said it was news to him that the Black Caucus had threatened to vote no if welfare came out.

Then Mack suggested something. A few years earlier O'Neill had lost a rule. It had been a minor fight, and he had formally adjourned the House and then convened it again immediately. That had created, for parliamentary purposes, a new legislative day. The parliamentarian had ruled the action permissible. Then he had brought a new rule onto the floor.

Wright could do the same thing. They did not have to wait until tomorrow. They could bring the rule back this afternoon. There were two reasons to do so. First was convenience; members had made plans to be home tonight and in their districts tomorrow. Now they would have to cancel their appearances and stay in Washington. Second was politics. Overnight the GOP might gain momentum; the next day's papers would trumpet Wright's defeat. That would weaken him and their position in the budget negotiations. But if they voted today and won, the story would be his victory. The defeat would be erased and forgotten.

There was one reason not to do what Mack suggested. The rules prohibited considering a rule the same day the committee acted upon it. Adjournment, followed by convening again, would satisfy the technical parliamentary requirement but would clearly violate the spirit of the rules.

Did Wright want to go forward?

It was a defining moment. Everything, all year, had pointed to this bill. But that was policy. Honorable men could disagree on policy. Wright prided himself on fairness, talked of his love for the institution and his responsibility to protect and represent it. *Procedure was honor codified.* Wright wanted this bill passed. This was his responsibility too. The Constitution required that tax bills begin in the House. To do anything else, even to enter these budget talks, without a bill was to compromise the integrity of the House. *Or was it just ego? Just willfulness? Just wanting to win?* Wright was determined to act. He was caught up in his passions and his nature. *Damn everything else.*

They would do what Mack suggested.

Everything for the rest of the 100th Congress, for as long as Jim Wright would remain Speaker of the House, would flow from Wright's decision.

The decision was not totally arbitrary. If Republicans agreed, for the sake of scheduling convenience, there was no problem. Foley went to check with Michel. Their conversation was brief. Foley later said, "If Michel had objected, we might have reconsidered. He didn't. He just sort of grunted."

Now Wright sat in his office making calls, looking for votes. An aide suggested he call Stenholm.

He erupted. "He lied to me. I somewhat prostrated myself before him and he pissed in my face."

Wright was incorrect. Stenholm had made no commitment unless welfare came out; it was Wright who had abused Stenholm. *You have to be careful not to unintentionally hurt someone.* Wright had created an enemy out there on the floor, an enemy who worked hard, a dangerous enemy.

But everything else was moving on schedule—the phone calls, the meetings, the strategy. In H-201 twenty moderates waited for him. They had all voted no. He briefed them: "This is where we are. We're getting a rule that takes welfare out. The loss was a bad signal for the market. Before we leave tonight we're going to try to reverse it." He explained that they would formally adjourn, then immediately reconvene, creating a parliamentary fiction of a second legislative day. That would allow them all to have Friday free to return to their districts as planned. In the back of the room a member shook his head in admiration and muttered, "Who digs these things up for him?"

Then they moved on. MacKay said, "Mr. Speaker, we've had a very agonizing week. I was one of those who signed a 'Dear Colleague' urging a no vote. But you might be right as well as I. I see this not as a partisan shot but as an opening in a bipartisan debate. I'm with you."

Other members echoed him. They got to their feet, clustered around Coelho, told him yes or no. Most were yes.

Half an hour later, in the same room, liberals, Ways and Means members, and blacks came in. Wright explained the situation. George Miller, who like his housemate Russo had given Wright such a hard time on the budget agreement—except unlike Russo he had never agreed to that budget—complained about the extra $3 billion Appropriations had given to defense spending which would be voted on the following week. Wright offered to give him an amendment to strike it.

"Mr. Speaker," he said, "I don't say this as a threat. I'm not going to let you down. But I don't want an amendment. It would lose. I want you to cut the $3 billion."

"I can't give you that commitment right now. But maybe you have a point."

Then Rostenkowski spoke angrily. "The trouble is with the group that was in here before—the whip count. Twenty gave us commitments but ten lied to us."

Already there were hard feelings in the Caucus. They would get harder, and more people would lie.

*   *   *

It was midafternoon. Wright had done what there was to be done for the moment. He went to lunch in the Members' Dining Room and sat there, calm and certain. Action calmed him. The fight calmed him. His favorite poem, which he learned as a small child and knew by heart, was Kipling's "If." *If you can keep your head when all about you/Are losing theirs and blaming it on you./If you can trust yourself when all men doubt you./But make allowance for their doubting too.* He loved that poem. Action itself was his element. And he was acting. It was inaction which frustrated him, inaction which made him explode. But speaking of why he had left welfare reform in the rule, why he had overruled his own instincts, a hard edge came into his voice.

"I did it because I trusted my vote counters. I trusted people who told me things that weren't true. Maybe I won't trust them so much anymore. We ought not to flimflam ourselves."

Coelho was his chief vote counter. He never raised the issue with him, observing, "You have to work with people as they are, not as you wish them to be." A few days later Wright invited Coelho to join him on a trip to Costa Rica over Thanksgiving and to the Holy Land for Christmas. But Wright would not forget.

Then it was time to go back to the floor.

While Wright was eating lunch, the reconciliation task force met. Marty Russo wasn't there. Russo considered himself chairman of the welfare reform task force; welfare was gone now. So was he.

He was angry, too, over the $3 billion extra that defense had gotten. That afternoon he played basketball in the House gym. As he went for rebounds his elbows whipped through the air, sharp elbows flying; playing defense he put his body on people, and with the ball he dared others to get in his way. When anyone said anything—anything—to him he flared up. A colleague thought, *What the hell's wrong with Russo?*

It was twenty minutes to three. Foley took the floor and moved that "pursuant to clause four of rule sixteen, that when the House adjourns today it adjourn to meet at three-fifteen today."

Rumbling spread across the floor, waves of hostility coming from Republicans. What kind of new outrage was this? Lott rose angrily and demanded a roll-call vote on the motion. The vote was a question of procedural control of the House; Democrats voted yes, Republicans no. Even Stenholm voted with his party, and Foley's motion carried 243–166.

Ed Madigan, the chief deputy GOP whip from Illinois, his words masking his rage, asked, "Do I understand the purpose of our having two legislative days in one calendar day is so that the House avoids the necessity of having a two-thirds majority to be able to consider this? . . . So what we are doing is just to further diminish whatever role the minority is entitled to play in the deliberations of the assembly, is that correct?"

Foley tried to calm the Republicans, saying it was strictly a convenience to allow members to keep appointments in the district for Friday. But there *was* no calming the Republicans. This was a power play, a raw power play, and they knew it. The floor hissed and sizzled with emotion, wrapped within the tight formal constraints of decorum.

Conservative Republican Robert Walker said, "I wonder if the gentleman understands why we would be a little upset. . . . I would say to the gentleman from Washington, I mean we are being terribly abused and this is an outrage in the way the House is being conducted." Democrats on the floor interrupted with sarcastic groans. "Well, you can all moan but I will tell you this is a terrible injustice. For a party that says it stands for fairness and justice you all are abandoning any pretenses of it on the floor today."

Foley repeated, "This is nothing more than an attempt to complete the legislative program without the necessity of an unscheduled Friday session."

William Dannemeyer, another conservative Republican, said, "Genesis tells us that the Lord created the world in seven days. We are now witnessing the creation of an eighth day. I just ask the gentleman, does he have a name for this new creation?"

"Yes," replied Foley. "It is called the Guaranteed Deficit Reduction Act."

The House adjourned at 3:05.

At three-fifteen it reconvened, with all the accoutrements of a new session including a new prayer by the chaplain, and the announcement by Wright with which he opened every session, that "the chair has examined the journal of the last day's proceedings and announces to the House his approval thereof."

Angry Republicans demanded a vote on approving the journal. This was no device to bring members to the floor; this was raw anger. Walker rose again. "Parliamentary inquiry, Mr. Speaker? We are about to cast a vote. Is the journal available for inspection by the members?"

"The journal is indeed available," Wright said evenly.

"Yes," snorted a Democrat. "In shorthand."

The vote was party line again. As soon as the floor had emptied after the vote, a Republican moved to adjourn. Members returned to vote once again. But, inexorably, the Democratic machine marched forward. At four-forty-five in the afternoon, the House approved the second rule, once again on a party-line vote, once again voting on control of the House, once again even Stenholm voting with his party.

Now it was on to the issue at hand. The tax bill. At least things had reduced themselves to the simplest point. *You wanted a tax bill? Here it is. Now pass it.*

The pay-raise issue was growing, spreading. It may have been a phony issue—it would be eliminated in next week's appropriations bill—but it was a big issue. Hometown newspapers were calling members' offices. Walker was on the floor bringing it up, bringing it up: there had been an automatic cost-of-living raise in January, in February the $12,000 raise, now this cost-of-living raise of $2,700: "If the members believe that deficit reduction means raising our own salaries, then vote for this bill. . . . It is plain to the voters that you will have voted to raise their taxes so that you could raise your pay."

It had looked easy, looked assured, with MacKay's help and other moderates. And the members assumed Wright had the votes. But no one knew for sure. Several of the moderates who had told Wright they were with him told Coelho, "I don't want you all to misunderstand— I'm with you on the rule, not the bill."

The debate went forward on the floor while Wright, in his ceremonial office, worked the phone, worked one member after another. "Who the hell am I calling?" he asked at one point an instant before saying, "Hey, how are you?" while an aide wrote down the name and shoved it in front of him. It was an Oklahoma member. Wright told him his colleagues in two adjoining districts were now voting yes, protecting him, and asked, "Do you have any specific personal problem?" But the man had made a campaign pledge to vote against taxes; no favor Wright could do could outweigh that.

Wright got a report that Bill Richardson of New Mexico wanted something personal, all right: to chair the platform committee at the Democratic National Convention. Wright, the convention chairman, would have much to say about appointments but fumed, "I'm not giving that away. A fellow has to understand you don't vote against something like this and get that."

Another man in the room suggested, "You don't have to promise. Just tell him Paul Kirk will see him next week. You don't have to say it. Have Mack say it. A staffer. That's no commitment."

Wright shook his head no. He wouldn't mislead him like that. But he could go at it another way: "Tell him you heard a member say that that SOB can't ask for something like that if he votes no here."

The leadership tried a new ploy: asking members who were going to vote no to not vote at all. It might be an easier sell than a yes vote, and members could protect themselves by pointing to a no vote on the first rule. But it was also the most delicate of all requests. The whole purpose of a member of Congress is to vote, to represent his constituents. Asking members not to was like asking them to violate their most solemn personal and institutional responsibility. Wright didn't want to ask that. But members got asked that.

On the floor, the debate moved forward. Off the floor there was a reception for the Minnesota Twins, who had just won the World Series. Days earlier Wright had said he would attend. Now he had other priorities. So did Stenholm, who haunted the chamber throughout the afternoon, with dogged, dogged persistence wearing colleagues down, showing them information on fact sheets, making one argument after another. Republicans could not whip Democrats, nor could Democrats whip Republicans. But Stenholm could whip Democrats. He was doing it.

At 7:05 in the evening, the time allotted to debate ran out. It was time to vote on Michel's substitute. Democrats defeated it 229–182, while Wright went from member to member, checking most closely with those who had told him they would not let the bill lose—they would vote with him if they had to. He pulled Jim Chapman aside, the man who had won the special election in Texas two years earlier largely because of Wright's personal involvement, the man whom Wright had taken care of since, naming him to Steering and Policy as the representative of the freshman class even though he had served in Congress for eighteen months before that class's election. Wright had helped him repeatedly, had just a few weeks earlier blocked an airport bill handled by another ally, Norm Mineta, from the floor until Chapman's personal concerns were taken care of. What Chapman was in the House, he owed to Wright. Chapman assured him that his would not be the vote to beat the bill.

Then came the vote on final passage. Wright took the chair. "The question is on the passage of the bill," he announced.

The first vote was by voice and pro forma—no one would accept its result—yet both sides shouted loudly.

"In the opinion of the chair," Wright announced, "the ayes have it."

"Mr. Speaker! On that I demand the yeas and nays!"

As with every roll-call vote, the panels behind the press gallery, above and behind the Speaker's Rostrum, receded and the wall became a gigantic tote board, with each member's name lit up; a red light beside it would indicate a no vote, green yes. On either side of the chamber a clock began counting from fifteen minutes down to zero while also noting the vote totals. The leadership clustered around the computer terminals—each side had two, one in the front of the chamber, one in the rear—on the floor which would show vote breakdowns by party, region, state, by almost any way of dividing the membership. Already almost the entire membership was in the chamber, eager to finish business and leave for the weekend. Quickly the count rose, and remained close throughout. The Republicans started ahead, Democrats pulled even at 158 each, then fell behind 158–162, then pulled ahead 172–168. Wright seemed in control. Nick Rahall from West Virginia, who disliked what the bill did to coal—eliminating tariffs on certain imported coal, something Rostenkowski stuck in to make Floridians Sam Gibbons and Claude Pepper happy—was surrounded by Coelho, Mary Rose Oakar, Jim Scheuer, and others, and three members literally had their arm on him. *All right, goddammit.* He voted yes. George Hochbrueckner wanted to get on the Committee on Science and Technology; he voted yes. So did Paul Kanjorski; he voted yes. Roy Rowland, the only physician in the House, wanted to get on Energy and Commerce where he could deal with health issues; he voted yes. Tim Valentine wanted to get on Armed Services; he voted yes. All of them had had discussions earlier with Coelho: no promises—a committee assignment wasn't Coelho's to give—but enough. (A week later Steering and Policy created temporary assignments on Science and Technology for Kanjorski and

Hochbrueckner; the other committee seats had to wait for the next Congress.)

Coelho squeezed. He had been responsible for naming Tim Penny an at-large whip. Now Coelho told Penny he might have to reconsider Penny's role in the whip organization if he voted no. But Penny was a prince too. He voted no. Buddy MacKay, a close friend of Penny who supported Wright now, thought it was a stupid threat: "What do you need this whip thing for? To put on your résumé? They need us, we don't need them."

Suddenly a red light went up by Chapman's name. *Chapman had voted no.* Members surrounded him now—what was going on? What was wrong? Wright talked to him. Nothing was wrong, Chapman said, it was just that it looked like they wouldn't need his vote after all, things were looking pretty good, so he had voted no. If they needed him, he'd switch. But Chapman had made himself high-profile. Half a dozen other members—Hochbrueckner, Roy Dyson, Wes Watkins, had said the same thing, but they would simply vote late if needed, not attract attention by switching.

Meanwhile, George Miller and Pete Stark, two California liberals, walked into the men's room off the Speaker's Lobby. *Stark who five years earlier had on the floor called Wright a "cocksucker." Colleagues had pulled Wright away from him, Wright threatening to knock him down, Stark humiliated, having to apologize.* Stark chaired a Ways and Means subcommittee. Members of committees, certainly Ways and Means subcommittee chairmen, supported their committee's product.

Miller was tense, volatile, an emotional man. He had ridden over in the subway thinking he would vote yes. But that $3 billion in extra defense spending gnawed at him. That afternoon he had told Wright, "I'm not going to let you down." But he remembered back when he and Russo had balked at signing the budget conference agreement and Wright had said unless Reagan signed a tax bill raising $19 billion, defense would get not one penny more. Maybe Wright hadn't meant it literally, but Miller and Russo had taken it literally, had taken it as a deal—even though Miller never signed the budget. Well, now defense had $3 billion more, and taxes would at most be $12 billion. Gray had given his word too. Suddenly Miller thought, *What am I? A horse's ass?* Wright was making a fool of him. He stiffened. Rage flooded through him. Wrought up, tense, almost in tears, he walked onto the floor, shoved his voting card into the slot, and punched the button for no.

Across the chamber, John Mack saw him come in, looked up at the board, saw the red light next to his name. "*George!*" Mack shouted.

Miller waved his arm in dismissal and disgust and stormed out. Mack shouted, "Mr. Foley! Miller just voted no!" Foley ran after him, racing against the elevator, racing to catch Miller before the elevator arrived, caught him, and said, "We're going to lose this thing."

"Tom, I'm just so goddamn mad, just stay away from me."

Foley was taken aback. "I just thought your vote was a mistake."

"I can't help you."

The elevator came. Maybe Coelho would have confronted him, demanded that he explain, gotten him back into the chamber where colleagues would have surrounded him. Or maybe Miller would have shoved him away. Foley watched him step onto the elevator. A moment later, Mack looked up at Stark's name. *Stark had voted no.*

On the other side of the chamber, Russo came in. He blamed the defeat of the rule on Wright himself, on Wright's comment in the task force that he would get a second rule if the first one lost. He was furious over the defense spending too. From Chicago and on Ways and Means, he had almost a father-and-son relationship with Rostenkowski. This was Rostenkowski's bill. Russo walked in, voted, walked out, and went straight to the airport. It was seven-thirty now. There was an eight o'clock flight to Chicago. He could make it easily. A Wright ally checked the board—*Russo voted no*—then ran up to Rostenkowski and jammed his finger into Rostenkowski's chest. "Your man fucked us!" he shouted. "Your man!"

Rostenkowski, dumbfounded, looked up at the red light by Russo's name.

Brian Donnelly rushed to the rostrum and told Wright, "If you're going to win this thing, you better get out of the chair and down on the floor."

Wright hurried down, hurried over to Rostenkowski. The leadership had computer printouts of votes, knew who had said yes but hadn't voted yes. But the printouts told you who but they didn't say where. There were 435 members of the House, and almost all of them were now swirling, wondering—or hiding. *Try to find someone on the floor who doesn't want to be found.* Wright started looking for those who had said they'd help if needed. His votes were in the back row. From the other side of the chamber Bob Michel saw the commotion, looked up at the board and saw Russo's vote, and thought, *We're going to win this thing*.

The clock counting down the remaining time stood at 0:00. Where the hell was Chapman? The vote stood 201 for the bill, 202 opposed, then 201 to 204.

The time on the clock didn't matter really. The rules said a minimum of fifteen minutes was required, but the vote stayed open at the discretion of the Speaker. The vote could stay open forever. If it was a tie, the Speaker could vote. *Where was Chapman?* Now it was 202 to 204, 203 to 204, as those members who had promised not to let Wright lose voted yes; 204 to 204. *Thank God! The Speaker could save the bill!* But suddenly the other side came up with two votes: 204 to 206. Then it was 205 to 206, 205 to 206, 205 to 206. *Where the hell was Chapman? Was he on the floor? Why wasn't he on the floor?*

"Chapman's in the cloakroom!"

Coelho ran in after him. At first he could not find him. The two cloakrooms, one Democratic, one Republican, fold around the outside of the chamber. Along one wall was a line of telephone booths; in the corner, in the middle of the cloakroom, was a hot-dog stand. Chapman was in neither area. Then Coelho looked around the corner. In the far end, on a couch, in an area where the overhead light bulb had been removed so it was darker than the rest of the room so members could lie on a couch and sleep, was Chapman. Coelho said they needed him. Chapman shook his head. He wasn't coming out.

Outside in the chamber the vote remained 205 to 206. The Republicans were exuberant, the chamber raucous. Abruptly a shout rang out from the GOP: "Regular order!" It quickly became a refrain. "OR-DER!" "REGULAR ORDER!" *Make the vote final.* But a leadership aide ran up to the chair and told Wright that Russo had made a mistake, was on his way back from the airport, hold the vote for Russo. Bonior, as if to confirm it, held up one finger and shouted, "ONE MORE!" It was a routine announcement, telling the chair to hold the vote open for someone hurrying from his office across the street. Bonior was playing for time. Jim Moody echoed, "ONE MORE!"

Coelho and Chapman argued, then Coelho came out and found Mack. "He's not coming out!" Coelho hissed. "He gave the commitment to the Speaker, not to me. You go in after him."

The chorus of Republicans in the chamber grew louder and louder. Wright announced, his voice absolutely calm, "We are proceeding under regular order. The chair has been advised that there are members on the way who desire to vote. The chair will accommodate their wishes."

The floor fell into a strange hush, a wild stillness. Trent Lott now ran across the chamber, up the aisle on the Democratic side, out into the corridor, stood outside and looked into the night, down the great stairway that leads to the plaza, then returned and shouted to the chamber at large, not to the chair, "There is no one out there, no one in sight!"

Regular order! Regular order! REGULAR ORDER!

The clock ticked. Wright started to speak. Mike Lowry ran to the front of the chamber, playing for time. "Mr. Speaker, how am I recorded?"

Bonior echoed him. "Mr. Speaker, how am I recorded?" Then Martin Frost. Then Bill Ford.

The parliamentarian advised Wright that, ever since the electronic voting system began, such requests were considered dilatory. Mack was in the cloakroom, leaning on Chapman, leaning on him, leaning on him, not with threats but with *You owe it to him. You can't let this happen to him. Everything he's done for you, you've got to do this for him.* Wright announced, "The chair will announce that there is no procedure for members to ask how they are recorded. They may look and see. The chair has been advised that there were other members en route to the chamber."

He stood above the floor, alone atop the rostrum, alone, speaking into that hushed wildness. With each passing second his reputation for integrity grew more damaged. Evidently Russo wasn't returning. He grew embarrassed, felt the eyes of the entire chamber, felt the pointlessness of further delay. Finally he announced, "If there are no other members who desire to vote or to change their vote, all time has expired."

The Republicans cheered! *They had broken the machine!* This victory! This massive victory! *They had broken the machine!* Bonior yelled— just to delay—he wanted to change his vote from yes to no and asked for the red card which members used to do so. But bursting down the aisle from the back door, desperate, charging—*Hold the vote!*—came John Mack! Behind him was Chapman! Coming down the aisle. Wright saw them, leaned forward to Bonior, and said, "Take back that damn red card."

Bonior looked up. Chapman asked for a green card, to change his vote from no to yes. The House was in an uproar.

As Chapman switched his vote, Wright's voice rang out—never varying throughout the count in inflection, always even—"If there are no other members in the chamber who desire to vote"—*BOOOO! BOOOO!* rang out in the hall, an extraordinary outburst for the House of Representatives, shouts of *BUSH LEAGUE! BUSH LEAGUE!*, a raw, almost murderous anger unleashed, Trent Lott so furious he slammed his fist against the solid wood lectern before him and shattered it—"or if there are no other members who desire to change their vote, on this vote the yeas are 206—"

"Mr. Speaker, I have a parliamentary inquiry!" shouted Gingrich. It was the only way to stop the announcement of the result. Now it was he who played for time. Madigan, a member of the GOP leadership, had assumed Wright would win and had skipped the vote to keep previous plans to go to the Kennedy Center. Was he on the way back? How long until he arrived? Or had they not yet contacted him? But they needed two votes, since one would create a tie which Wright would break. Only one Republican, Jim Jeffords, who was running for a Senate seat in Vermont, had voted with the Democrats. *Where was he?*

"The gentleman will state it."

"Mr. Speaker, I would inquire of the parliamentarian and the chair, once the Speaker has said the vote is closed and all time has expired, and we have that on the tape, on the videotape, once that has been done how can that be reopened?"

"The chair will state that it always has been the disposition of the chair and of every occupant of which the present occupant is aware to permit any member who is in the chamber to vote or change his vote so long as he desires to do so. The chair had been advised that there were other members en route and therefore the chair was holding open, and still holds open, if members wish to change their votes or other members wish to vote. . . . If no other members desire to vote or to change their vote, the yeas are 206, the nays are 205."

Mickey Edwards was on his feet—every member was on his feet— "Mr. Speaker! I have a parliamentary inquiry!"

"The gentleman will state his parliamentary inquiry. If it is a parliamentary inquiry the chair will entertain it."

"I do have a parliamentary inquiry. I would say the Speaker did not answer the last one. After the chair has said, 'All time has expired,' which the chair did, can you then reopen the vote?"

Under the rules of the House, Wright's having said "All time has expired" meant nothing; what made the result final was saying "The bill is passed" or "The bill is defeated."

"The chair will respond. On more than one occasion, the present occupant of the chair and in the chair's observation other occupants have permitted members to vote so long as these members are in the chamber and obviously desiring to cast a vote."

"Further parliamentary inquiry!" Edwards said.

"The chair will ask"—Wright now ignored Edwards—"if any member desires to vote or to change his vote? And if not, all time has expired. The yeas are 206, the nays are 205. The bill is passed." *The bill is passed.* "Without objection, a motion to reconsider is laid upon the table."

BUSH LEAGUE! BOOOO! BUSH LEAGUE! BOOO! BUSH LEAGUE!

Bill Gray rose for a routine, always-granted, entirely nonpartisan request: "I ask unanimous consent that all members may have five legislative days to revise and extend their remarks and include extraneous material on the bill just passed."

"Without objection, so ordered. The chair lays before the House—"

"*I OBJECT, MR. SPEAKER!*" shouted Walker.

"Let the chair understand. The request was that members have five legislative days in which to revise and extend their remarks. Was that request objected to?"

"Yes!" Walker demanded, his voice filled with hate. "I objected, Mr. Speaker!"

"Objection is heard."

Now Brian Donnelly was at the podium. *This was ugly. Get Wright out of there, out of the chair.* Donnelly took the gavel and let Wright disappear.

Edwards was on his feet again. "Mr. Speaker, I have a parliamentary inquiry. I am not asking a policy inquiry. I want to know the rules of the House of Representatives. After you have announced that all time has expired, may additional votes be cast or votes be changed?"

The parliamentarian provided the answer and Donnelly said, "The chair will state that the rules of the House state that the roll call will be open for a minimum of fifteen minutes, and that beyond that it is at the discretion of the chair."

Wright had acted within the rules. At eight-twenty-five the House adjourned.

While members poured out of the chamber, Wright stood in the Speaker's Lobby in the middle of a crowd of reporters saying softly, "It's not much of a mandate, that's for sure." Chapman came down the corridor, alone, contemplating the heat he had exposed himself to, and unknown by the press—moments earlier they were shouting, "What happened? Did someone switch? Who switched? Who's Chapman?"— punched the button for the elevator.

Peering into the mob scene, waiting for the elevator, Chapman asked, "Who's that in there?"

"The Speaker."

Chapman stared for a moment, then turned away. The elevator came. He headed home.

Finally Wright broke free of the press. Pat Williams tried to comfort him. Wright shook him off. "It's marginally better than a loss, I guess." After a moment he headed down the hall, down away from the floor, to his back office. At times during the year he had been tired. Even weary. But that tiredness had always been physical. He was sixty-four years old but vital, with a well of energy; a few weeks earlier, kidding a younger member, he had jumped down on the floor and done some stretching which a twenty-five-year-old athlete would have had trouble doing. Now he seemed old. Like old men one sees on the street whose bodies have shrunk, whose clothes hang limply, who have become less than they once were. It was as if he had been beaten, worse than beaten, as if the fight had gone out of him and the pride and force with which he naturally carried himself had disappeared and so his clothes hung limply now, his whole body sagging. In his office, he smiled weakly, tried to joke. "I don't feel so good now, that's true. I was holding the vote open for Russo. Someone told me he was coming back. I was holding it for Russo. Not Chapman. . . . It didn't help my reputation. To have people impugn my integrity"—he shook his head sadly—"to have Republicans shouting like that." He shook his head again. Then he fell silent.

He was a man who had dreamed of greatness and largeness for himself and greatness and largeness for his institution. A House like Rayburn's House, a House where colleagues respected one another, where Rayburn and Republican leader Joe Martin had loved each other—yes, loved each other—where when Martin was defeated for reelection as Republican leader by Charles Halleck, the man to whom Martin fled was Rayburn, his old dear friend Rayburn.

All year Wright had talked of Rayburn in private, at home, had thought of him constantly. Rayburn was the standard. This vote had destroyed Wright's vision of the House, reduced it and him now to partisanship, narrowness, divisiveness. It wasn't what he had wanted. It was the opposite of what he had wanted. Deep within him was an ache. A friend offered comfort by talking of Rayburn's similar moment in the chair shortly before World War II, when, while votes shifted back and forth, he had abruptly declared the vote final and preserved the draft by a one-vote margin. He too had been bitterly attacked.

Wright shrugged, lethargic, then sat alone with himself and his thoughts. At home that night, for one of the very, very few times that year, he talked with his wife about the vote. "Why did I do that?" he wondered. "Why?" Although he said also, "If I had to, I'd do it again."

The House was empty. It was nine-thirty. Bob Michel was standing in the corridor outside his office, an office Rayburn had once occupied. His quarters were so much better than Wright's; they were in the old part of the Capitol, elegant marble and tile on the floors, Oriental splendor in the ceiling frescoes, the old marble fireplace from the days before central heating, and space, much more space in Michel's own office than in Wright's. It had been the Speaker's office, but Rayburn and Joe Martin had alternated between Speaker and minority leader, and the last time Democrats took control, in Wright's freshman term and two years before Michel's election, Rayburn had suggested to Martin that they just stay where they were instead of moving. The minority leader had kept those rooms ever since.

Now Michel was standing there telling a reporter Wright's action was "outrageous." The reporter left and Michel turned to another man. He seemed more saddened than angry and said, "Here's something that shows the way this place really operates. The Democrats are all in .

traces. It's been that way all year. My fellows tell me I ought to be outraged." His voice sounded bitter. Then he sighed, and it seemed as if the air went out of his anger. He wasn't outraged. Standing there with his hands stuck in his pockets, he seemed like what he was, a grown-up version of an all-American boy who got excited over baseball, to whom expressions like "Aw, shucks" and "dadgum" came naturally. Wright's ambition was to make history, to change things. Wright had courage, and will, and led, but his will had become a brutal, divisive force. Michel wasn't that kind of leader. *The key to leadership is to listen,* he had said. Listening, he had compromised his own beliefs that afternoon: he recognized that taxes were necessary, had proposed them to Wright, but had excluded them from the GOP substitute which therefore did not meet the deficit target. He had made no effort to stop some political games his GOP colleagues played, which he believed were wrong. "There are some things you have to do to keep control," one man close to him said, justifying him. He had also failed to anticipate his colleagues' anger, and had not protested when Foley told him of the second legislative day. Michel would not and could not get the results Wright did, would not and could not take the entire Washington policy-making establishment, shake it, and redistribute power within it. Wright had done that.

Yet Michel still seemed to have something so solid about him, solid through and through even with his flaws. Like the institution itself. Tonight the institution had been damaged. If Wright was in pain, so was Michel. Michel had the same vision as Wright, of a House warm with collegiality and bipartisanship. Republicans like Gingrich had consciously tried to destroy that comity because they believed it had led to accommodations which had kept Republicans out of power for all of Michel's thirty-two years in the House. Michel had the forces of politics and personal ambitions to contend with, keeping them in line. Even without Wright, the frustrations of Gingrich and his allies would have strained the institution as never before. With Wright's agenda that stress grew by an order of magnitude. Would the institution tear itself apart?

Thinking of the future, the long-term future, Michel said, "Oh, these hard feelings will wear off. But he just doesn't have any give. He just doesn't have any give."

What if the hard feelings did not wear off? *The key to leadership is listening.* For a moment he hardened too.

*   *   *

The leadership staff was sitting in H-210 having a beer. They called the clerk's office to get a videotape of the vote. The Republicans had asked for a copy too. "Screw 'em, we want it now. Let them have it at eleven tomorrow morning." The tape arrived and they watched it.

"Look at that! Look at that!" They marveled at Wright's calmness in the chair as Republicans were demanding explanations. "God, he was great."

The parliamentarian reported that this year alone eleven votes had been held open longer than this one.

On the tape, the boos started, the shouts of "Bush league!" and "Steamroller!"

"God, that's ugly," said one man, stunned.

They had never, never seen the House like that. Never. Then they started going over a printout of Democrats who voted no. Seven guys had lied to them. Seven. Five more had told them they would vote yes, then took a walk, did not vote at all.

Coelho and his aides believed the result confirmed what they had said all along, that complaints about welfare reform were only a smoke-screen, that the real problem had always been taxes. Stenholm's problem wasn't taxes, though, and Stenholm had worked his butt off trying to beat Wright.

And the market? How did the market react? How closely did the market monitor the tax bill? By the time the House started voting on the first rule—when observers assumed Wright would win—the market was already up fifty points. After Wright's initial defeat, it rose more and closed up ninety-two points. But that could not have been because of Wright's defeat; the next day, after the bill had passed, the market went up fifty-five points more. The market couldn't have cared less.

At one o'clock in the morning, now Friday, Rostenkowski was on the phone to Miller, raging at him not for the vote—every member's entitled to vote how he wants—but for the lack of warning. If he had told someone they could have planned for it. "You don't want to wake up out of a sound sleep with him on the other end of the phone," Miller later said. "He was livid."

Then Rostenkowski called Russo in Chicago, and raged at him. Russo loved the House, really loved it, loved working with his colleagues, loved being part of the leadership. Now where would he be? What kind of future did he have in the House? What had he done to himself? At two-thirty in the morning, upset, distraught, maybe he had had one or two, he called Coelho.

There was another phone call too. Early Saturday morning George Miller lay asleep at home in California. The phone rang and his wife woke him. It was the Speaker. Wright was calling to say he would take out the extra $3 billion in defense spending. Of Miller's vote Wright said only, "It's all behind us. Let's work together."

Miller thanked him and hung up, more puzzled than ever about the kind of man Wright was. *After what I did to him, he's doing this for me?* It didn't make sense. It didn't make any sense. Suddenly he thought that Wright was a larger man than he had believed, a larger man than he had shown.

Perhaps Wright had had to do it. On Friday several members representing the Democratic Study Group asked him to take it out. Perhaps Wright was manipulating Miller, getting mileage out of what he would do anyway. Or was he? Why call Miller, who had just hurt him so badly? *Why?* There was a mystery to Wright. Miller sat in bed, thinking, laughing, *No one's scoped Wright out yet. He's wild. Ha! Wild! And, yes, maybe he could be a great Speaker.*

CHAPTER 18

In the early morning light, the Capitol seemed like some sixteenth-century Italian cathedral: complex, articulated in detail, uplifting. Outside, the great columns reached backward into the origins of democracy. Inside, as if contained within the high dome, the morning sun silhouetted bronze and marble statues of past American statesmen and heightened the colors of the tiled floors and the frescoed walls and ceilings. In the bowels of the building, immune to the world of power above them, workers prepared food and repaired furniture.

The Capitol continued as it always had, but Wright's speakership had changed. The vote on reconciliation—what irony, that name—had changed relationships among members, changed the way the Republicans acted, changed the House itself. In the days after the vote the depth of the change sank in.

Wright had stripped power bare and exposed truths, uncomfortable truths. Members shied away from that nakedness. They wanted to avert their eyes, like people who did not want to see cripples, or dwarfs, or amputees, or those who bore terrible scars, in the hope that not looking would make them disappear. The truth was that the leadership would strong-arm people, and that some members were cowards.

Wright had called Bill Richardson three times the day of the vote. Richardson, who had wanted to trade his vote for the platform committee chairmanship, never called back. The next week he told Wright, "I'd have voted with you if I had just known how much you cared about it." Later he used another excuse: "I was going to vote yes anyway when Coelho started telling me I had to. I just got so mad at him, Jim, I voted no just to spite him. I'm sorry."

Wright smiled that smile of iron teeth and said, "Well, I'm disappointed in you."

The leadership made no apologies. Bonior said, "A lot of people around this place are naive about the use of power. We're not playing a game. For everyone who thought it was a Pyrrhic victory, two people thought it was good. They liked it. It proved we could be tough when we had to be."

Coelho, when asked about Republican reactions, said, "My only response is, what difference does it make what the Republicans think? The only significant question is whether it hurt Wright and the leadership in the Caucus and the answer is no."

But Coelho was wrong on both counts. The action had ripped open wounds that would have difficulty healing, even within the Caucus. True, some Democrats liked what Wright had done. Howard Berman, a California liberal, said, "Maybe Wright was heavy-handed. That's leadership. I'm glad he did it. He had to win." Liberals were more upset with Miller, Russo, and Stark. A close friend of Miller's said, "George's vote was a tantrum which was inexcusable on something serious. . . . If Wright had lost, that would have been very significant. He had to win. He played hardball to win. So what? I'm interested in the future, not history. So are most people around here."

Others were not so sure. Buddy MacKay did not lack for courage and had voted with Wright, but the whole experience bothered him: "Reconciliation undid a lot of what Wright's done this year. It's like we're dealing with a 'catch-dog.' You turn him loose when you've got something cornered but you don't know what it is. The problem with a catch-dog is, he'll catch something and won't turn it loose even if you don't want it. That's what Wright seems like . . . The leadership is not listening. After a while you feel, 'The hell with 'em. Maybe they'll pay attention to my vote.' "

Tensions surfaced in a meeting in H-201 over the $3 billion in defense spending. When a liberal laughed—at an entirely unrelated joke—a conservative hissed, "Goddammit! Is this a joke to you?"

"Don't lecture me," the liberal snapped. "I voted for the bill."

Wright interrupted to try to redirect the bitterness. "Ronald Reagan will never fulfill his part of a bargain unless you force him to. I tell you, he won't. He's a self-centered son of a bitch. I've dealt with him for seven years. He has contempt for Congress. That's why we had to go forward with reconciliation. Already the sons of bitches are not bargaining in good faith. I want leverage with him."

That leverage would come from a low defense number and some arms-control language. The liberal asked the conservative, "Are you with us?"

"I'm not with *you,* but I heard the Speaker. I know what has to be done."

It wasn't the best way to hold the Caucus together, and Wright knew it. It would get worse.

At the first regular whip meeting after the reconciliation vote, Coelho was out of character, seemed so low-key, appealing quietly to members to give them accurate information on whip counts. But another member jumped up and said, "Last week was not that tough a vote. We may have some tough ones coming up. I hope we have more guts."

Members straightened, angry at being called cowards. Some shouted back. There were hard feelings.

Contra aid was dividing members, too. Another short-term continuing resolution was needed to run the government until mid-December. It included $3.2 million for the contras, and was the second C.R. to include contra aid. Privately, Coelho warned Wright, "Many of us won't be able to vote for the C.R."

Wright caught the inflection. *His own whip was saying he'd vote no? But members of the leadership had a responsibility to keep the government running. Did Coelho have his own agenda? Was that what welfare reform had been about?*

"Oh, Tony," Wright said. "Say 'Some of them,' not 'Many of us.' "

A few days later fifty House liberals got together and let Wright know they would not again vote for one penny of contra aid, not even in a short-term C.R. The Caucus was being torn apart.

Wright was not the first Speaker to exercise power. Republican Thomas Reed, one of the great Speakers in history, earned the epithet "Czar"—a cry of hatred—for his use of the rules toward the turn of the century. "Gentlemen," Reed told Democrats, "I am about to perpetrate the following outrage," and, "The right of a minority is to draw its salaries, and its function is to make a quorum." Dick Cheney, the heir-apparent to Michel (Trent Lott, fed up with the House, had decided to run for the Senate), had written a book in which he had praised Reed, and Wright quoted it to reporters.

But Cheney's views had changed, and so had his relationship with Wright. And Cheney was the bellwether. He was a conservative, but had always distanced himself from Gingrich and believed that the minority had a responsibility to participate in the legislative process rather than use it to create political issues. He was solid, respected, trustworthy, a westerner, from Wyoming. Not unlike Michel, if sharperedged, he was one of the few House Republicans who could compete with Gingrich on an intellectual level and was wholly comfortable with ideas. Reasonable, White House chief of staff under Ford, he had more breadth and more depth than most politicians and was not naive about power. There was also something unyielding about him, something hard and unreachable. On the Easter trip to the Soviet Union with Wright, members had played one of those psychoanalytical games; according to his score, one profession he was suited for was a funeral director. His colleagues and their wives had laughed and he had flushed. But Wright had pierced deep into him.

Earlier, he had been pleased by Wright's fairness in handling such issues as the Iran-contra investigation, and had said he had "a good professional relationship" with Wright. Now he told a *National Journal* reporter, "[Reconciliation] was the most arrogant, heavy-handed abuse of power I've ever seen in the ten years that I've been here. You have a Speaker who's perceived by Republicans and Democrats alike as a guy who can run the place, not because he's respected but because he's a heavy-handed son of a bitch and he doesn't know any other way of operating, and he will do anything he can to win at any price, including ignoring the rules, bending rules, writing rules, denying the House the opportunity to work its will. It brings disrespect to the House itself. There's no sense of comity left. Why should you, if you are a Republican, and given the way Republicans are treated, think of a Democrat as a colleague? They aren't colleagues."

It was as if he and his GOP colleagues suddenly realized Wright was an entirely different man from anyone they had dealt with before. The rules had changed. Bill Gradison, the sole Republican in the House who had ignored politics months earlier to offer Democrats help on the budget, a week after the vote said, "It takes a lot to politicize me. Wright's done it. I'm partisan as hell now."

The House had worked its will on the first rule. Republicans had won. Wright had bent the House's will to his. O'Neill had always let the House work its will. The feeling among Republicans was, *Do anything. Get him.* If opportunities did not arise, they would create some. Gingrich would create some.

Republicans had a theme now and it was Gingrich's theme: the corruption of power, highlighted by a personal attack on Wright. The Republican Policy Committee distributed a statement accusing Democrats of having delayed reauthorizing special prosecutors against Executive Branch officials to give Wright a chance to set up a blind trust "and avoid the appearance of any potential conflict of interest." It was one thing to make snide remarks like that in private; it was another to put it down in a policy document—not even a campaign document. *If they want to engage us, we'll engage them,* a senior Republican aide had said. *And we will engage them.*

Gingrich had been attacking Wright personally for months. Now Lott and others picked it up. And if Wright could bend the rules for his own purposes, why couldn't others break unwritten rules for their purposes? Wright would deserve anything he got. Gingrich had preached direct confrontation for years. Members who had ignored him, disdained him even, now paid attention. One week after the reconciliation vote, Cheney stood on the portico just outside the House chamber and expressed his colleagues' deep, lingering fury: "Wright told us Republican votes don't count as much as Democratic votes." In a grudging and unhappy acknowledgment of fact, he added, "It's made Gingrich a big man in the Republican Conference."

The morning after the reconciliation vote Wright returned to the Capitol. It was Friday and as usual few members were around. The events of the night before haunted him. He told himself he had done the right thing. Yet he had self-doubt. And he worried that his actions had poisoned his relations with Republicans, had poisoned the floor. Those taunts, those shouts, those boos echoed painfully in his mind. Every time he walked past the chamber he heard them. In his thirty-three years in the House, never had the floor erupted like that. He knew he should let the House settle. Just settle back into its own rhythms. But the world did not stop for him. Events did not wait. Only his will could move things in the direction he wanted. He could not pull back or everything he had worked for would collapse. Only his will maintained that edifice. He had no choice.

And so he learned about power and about himself. The use of power requires ruthlessness. It is the nature of power. Power can be used quietly and with subtlety; its use can be disguised. But it cannot be used gently. Gingrich understood this better than Wright. Power is abstract, and has its own truths. Wright had it confused with other things, from collegiality to issues. He had to learn its truths, and learn of his own ruthlessness. Passion, not ruthlessness, had driven him on reconciliation; he learned ruthlessness lay in him too.

He wanted to pull back, to let the House rest. He could not. Over the next few weeks he would come to dominate Washington. The next few weeks would determine budget priorities and whether there was peace or war in Nicaragua. Neither was abstract. The two issues moved independently of each other. Except for Wright. Wright wove them together. Wright drove both of them. He believed his role was forced upon him. But he did not back away from it.

When he first arrived in his office he did little things to retain control, writing personal notes in longhand to fifteen Democrats who had made a tough vote for him. Their names went high on the friends list. An aide gave him a list of Democrats who had walked away from their commitments, those who had promised to vote yes and had voted no, or had not voted at all. That marked another change from O'Neill. When O'Neill once lost a vote under similar circumstances, an aide handed him a list of members who had broken their commitments; O'Neill refused to look at it, saying, "I don't want their names. I'll need those guys tomorrow." Wright wanted to know; those guys might need him tomorrow too.

Then, if there had been any doubt about whether he would release the House from his will, Rostenkowski called and said he had to see him *right now*. A few minutes later he ushered James Baker into Wright's office. Wright invited them to sit in the armchairs at the side of his desk, and joined them there. Baker, always so slick and confident, had the look of privilege, the smooth self-assurance of one who had inherited wealth and position and had later confirmed with achievement society's earlier endorsement of him. His eyes were both distant and alive, as if they saw the world as a place that existed for his amusement. Like Wright, he always had an agenda, and everything he did was in pursuit of it. But unlike Wright, he was not an independent operator, at least not on budget issues, and the agenda was not his own. Rostenkowski was different from either of them; his agenda was simply to play the game successfully, rather than to reify any particular policy view. He had worked well with Baker on tax reform; Baker had played to his ego—*It's you and me, Danny, deciding the fate of the economy.* But then Baker had had the authority to make decisions.

Now Rostenkowski saw Baker's other side. In the budget talks he was backing away from his earlier statement that the fifty-fifty split between revenues and spending cuts was "common ground," saying that he had defined asset sales as revenues. Asset sales? Asset sales were phony savings. Selling loans the government had made to students, for example, brought money in immediately, but sacrificed future interest and principal payments. It helped in this year's bookkeeping but hurt in future years. Even if the government could get a fair price in the markets, asset sales were at best a break-even proposition. The one common theme coming out of Wall Street was that any cuts had to be real. But Baker repeated his call for asset sales now.

Wright grew angry. Rostenkowski was angry, too. This was getting nowhere. Baker rose to leave, then turned back. Suddenly, for a moment, his self-contained manner cracked, and he tried to explain: "There are people in the White House who think I'm deserting the President just by coming up here and talking to members of Congress." He hesitated, then continued, "I've got about six more months left here. You two will be here for longer than that, perhaps a long time. In a way I'll be glad to get out of it. That man in the White House just makes it hell."

Wright suddenly understood the enormous pressure Baker was under. But it did little to lessen his anger.

Lunch made him angrier still. He and his wife, Betty, joined Dwayne Andreas, the chairman of Archer-Daniels-Midland. Andreas, a secretive man—when he took over ADM he eliminated the company's public relations division—played politics through money, which gave him access to American politicians at the highest levels, including Reagan. This was the man who had helped Hubert Humphrey, gave Nixon a $25,000 cash contribution which ended up in the hands of the Watergate burglars, and more recently helped Bob Dole buy a condominium. Andreas could deal with people in power as peers, which distinguished him from lobbyists who arranged golf junkets and honoraria. Andreas also had access to the Russians.

At lunch Andreas updated him on the results of a discussion they had had earlier in the year, when Wright had said that if Gorbachev wanted to make a symbolic gesture to improve U.S.-Soviet relations, he should tear down the Berlin Wall. Wright had said the same thing to the Soviet ambassador, while Andreas had pursued it with Gorbachev. Gorbachev had seemed interested, Andreas now reported, adding that he had conveyed that interest to Reagan. Reagan, a few weeks after Andreas had told him, traveled to the Berlin Wall and called on the Russians to tear it down.

Wright's face hardened. Reagan's declaration had destroyed any chance of the wall coming down, since Gorbachev could not appear to bow to him. Wright fumed, "It just makes me have utter contempt for Reagan. He spoiled the chance for a dramatic breakthrough in relations between our two countries. It bespeaks his pettiness and self-centeredness. He just couldn't bear Gorbachev doing it of his own volition."

The afternoon made Wright no calmer. Byrd called and said, "I'm worried that the budget talks might collapse. Let's you and I go down there and not let that happen."

The negotiators were at an impasse. They sat in S-211, the grand, high-ceilinged, chandeliered Lyndon Johnson Room a few doors from the Senate chamber, amid a faint odor of paint from recent refurbishing. OMB chief Jim Miller had offered a proposal which froze total appropriations by raising defense and cutting domestic programs; he was also insisting on no more than $4 billion in new taxes, less than the White House had included in its budget.

Wright and Byrd walked in, providing a new audience to explain things to. Republican senator Pete Domenici started talking about a "2 percent solution," holding both appropriations and cost-of-living increases for Social Security and other retirees to a 2 percent increase for two years. A package like that would produce dramatic deficit cuts, something that would not simply allow them to escape the political pressures of the moment but would bring the deficit under control. It would also yield enough flexibility to rearrange the priorities of government just as Wright wished. Would Democrats accept Social Security cuts? Wright indicated interest, and the group turned to taxes. The Senate Republicans were receptive to a fifty-fifty ratio of spending cuts to taxes. Baker looked uncomfortable and said, "I'm laboring under some restraints."

The men in the room turned to him. What the hell did he mean, "restraints"?

Baker seemed to withdraw into himself and evaded their questions. The others pushed him. *Come on, Jim, what restraints?*

"The revenue figure has to include asset sales," he finally said.

In addition to everything else that was wrong with asset sales, Gramm-Rudman prohibited counting them as deficit reduction.

"We can amend the law," Baker said.

The hell they would. *Anything else we don't know?*

Baker hesitated again, then started to confess his limitations. He could only accept revenues that matched domestic spending cuts dollar for dollar. Defense spending cuts would not count. And no matter how much domestic spending was cut, he could not accept more than $8 billion in tax increases, including several billion dollars in user fees. The figure was an absolute, inviolable limit, not a negotiating position.

It was as if a sudden chill had entered the room. This was not good faith. The White House was not bargaining in good faith. Wright was convinced he had done the right thing in pushing reconciliation; he would not hesitate to apply his will again. Byrd too had had enough. Furious and coldly formal, he said, "We just cannot operate in this fashion, Mr. Secretary. We can't fault you, but this places great limitations on our capacity to reach an agreement. I'm going to ask you to go back down to the White House and tell the President that all of us up here find that that is a limitation we cannot live with, and plead with him to understand the importance of what happens if these talks break up, and the importance of allowing you more freedom. And, Mr. Secretary, if you cannot get him to do it, I should like the privilege of the Speaker and myself and the Republican leadership seeing him to explain the importance of facing reality. If he then refuses to do it, then I think I should have to tell the public why these talks have broken down."

Byrd's threat had the desired effect. The following week Jim Baker assured the group that his restraints had been lifted. There need be no public confrontation with the President. But there was still no progress.

At a House-Senate Democratic leadership breakfast, Wright, impatient, pressed the senators to pass their reconciliation bill. Then Congress could bypass the summit, and force Reagan to choose—with the markets staring at him—whether to sign or veto a bill. Coelho seconded the idea, arguing, "Losing's better than doing nothing. If it loses, at least we'll show it's from Republican votes." But Byrd would not move on reconciliation, although he did suggest passing some appropriations bills. Later one of the House Democratic negotiators told the MacKay group, "Our problem is largely the cowardice of the Senate."

It was not only Democrats who wanted to move. Michel was more a legislator than a politician. He invited Wright to a lunch, just the two of them, and mentioned that the White House had asked him not to negotiate with the Speaker. But here he was, wanting to move forward. Wright later told his negotiators that Michel had proposed a spending freeze and some nonspecified savings from Social Security. "I told him," Wright went on, "if we froze COLAs at 2 percent we should put a 2 percent income-tax surcharge on the wealthy. He didn't say anything to that." But with Michel silence did not mean assent.

Social Security was a problem. Publicly it was "off the table." But it cost roughly $230 billion a year, and was growing at almost a geometric rate as COLA increases acted like compound interest, and demographics kept adding beneficiaries. Leaving it off the table made a large deficit-reduction package impossible.

Senate Republicans were calling for Social Security savings. House Democratic leaders were willing to go along. As Foley observed, "In this room, I'm for capping COLAs too. . . . It's absurd to cut COLAs for people who are working and pay them to people who are not. But I'll be damned if I say so if there's no motion from [House] Republicans." Foley and his colleagues demanded only symmetry; as Wright had told Michel, if the elderly sacrificed, so should the wealthy.

But this wasn't the first time Social Security was at issue. Once before the White House had called for Social Security cuts, and the proposal became a major election issue in 1982. House Republicans had lost twenty-six seats, destroying both the working majority they had forged with conservative Democrats and their dreams of winning control of the House in the near future.

Now the budget summit would certainly force House Republicans to swallow tax increases, which meant abandoning the political rock upon which many of them had stood for years. Asking them to accept Social Security cuts went too far; it required them to trust Democrats not to attack them over the issue. Trust was in short supply. Edward Madigan, the respected chief deputy GOP whip, someone regarded as a responsible legislator, rarely used the press to send messages but he used it now, warning that if the budget summit cut Social Security, "I don't think there would be fifteen Republicans who would vote for that. . . . It [would be] 1982 all over again."

For the first time in the 100th Congress, House Republicans had power—the power to say no. And despite Michel's delicate exploration of the issue, they were saying no.

Wright had another worry—a *Newsweek* story. Its reporters had been working on the story for several months now and had dug into every corner of his financial dealings, had met with Wright's lawyer and staff— and with Gingrich's staff. This story, too, was a sign of his power. Now reporter Mark Miller finally sat down with him and asked question after question about Fort Worth and his personal finances. None of the magazine's research had revealed anything potentially illegal, nor any indication of Wright's benefiting from any of the millions of federal dollars he had poured into Fort Worth—"If we had found any evidence of wrongdoing we'd have printed it," Miller later said. "We didn't." And yet . . . and yet . . . Wright seemed so *intertwined* in things. Weren't the appearances bad? Didn't he think it seemed like a conflict of interest? Then the reporter asked more personal questions, kept pressing.

Suddenly Wright told him to turn off the tape recorder. He did. Then Wright began to talk of his grandchildren and his father, about how he was trying to teach his grandchildren the importance of both charity and savings. He wanted them to avoid the problems he had had. *He had spent his adult life in debt and he hated debt.* He wanted them to learn to handle money. *The money problems that were haunting him, the petty-ass chickenshit bullshit money problems that were dogging his speaker-ship, that his enemies were trying to use to hurt him.* Suddenly he choked up. *Was this thing never going to leave him? For God's sake, his net worth was $187,000. He had had twice that when he had entered Congress, if you figured in inflation. What had he done? Even this reporter admitted there were only bad "appearances." Could that destroy him?* His eyes watered. He stopped speaking, blinking the tears away, cleared his throat. The reporter looked silently at the floor, embarrassed.

Wright had been sleeping fitfully, waking up at three in the morning, at five if he was lucky. He wished for a respite. He tried to create one, to create peace with Republicans. A Republican amendment on minor legislation was ahead by one vote. Wright's vote would defeat it. He refrained from voting, and then waded into the crowd of members on the Republican side of the chamber—though the mirror image of the Democratic side it was territory where Wright almost never went—and told the sponsor he had purposely let it pass. It was a humbling thing for him to do, an admission of error, an apology. But Republicans derided his gesture; among them he seemed a modern-day Richard III, abandoned and desolate and surrounded by enemies.

There was no respite, or time or opportunity to wait for one, not unless Wright was willing to let go, to let his agenda die.

Wright would not let that happen. Foley chaired the budget talks. Foley was loyal. But Foley's agenda was not Wright's agenda. Foley's style was not Wright's style, and their styles differed enough that the substance differed too. Foley's strategy was to avoid failure, not seek bold success. He feared failure. Wright did not. Wright made things happen. Foley allowed things to come together. He had a brooding Celtic tendency to see the dark side, the worst case. Foley feared that failure to reach an agreement or have it pass and signed into law might trigger a second market panic and in turn a worldwide depression.

Fear of failure was a weapon used by those who did not fear it. Wright worried the White House could use it against Foley, and against Democratic priorities. Foley had his own weapon with which to fight back: patience. But it was not a weapon Wright understood or was comfortable with. Tension developed between the two men; it was never expressed but always there.

While Wright grew impatient, Foley waited. No votes were taken on anything in the summit and so proposals continually resurfaced. Only raising income taxes on the rich was dismissed flatly, after Jim Baker told Foley, "The President will agree to that sometime between his impeachment in the House and his trial in the Senate."

So, day after day the negotiators met without progress, usually in S-211, occasionally on the House side in an Appropriations room. Issues, particularly Social Security, would come up, be put aside without a vote, then come up again. The first time it was mentioned, Silvio Conte, the ranking Republican on House Appropriations—he personally supported Social Security cuts since it took pressure off his committee—told a joke. An Englishman, a Frenchman, and an Italian were captured by cannibals and told they would be eaten and their skin used to make a canoe. The Englishman slit his wrists, the Frenchman stabbed himself in the heart, and the Italian stabbed himself all over. The cannibals looked at him, puzzled, and asked what he was doing. *I'm screwing up your canoe,* the Italian told them. Conte would repeat the punch line over and over and over whenever a politically dangerous proposal arose: "We're just screwing up the canoe."

Sometimes the mood swung from levity to hostility in seconds. Once Baker said to Bill Gray, "Yeah, we be bad." Gray stiffened; his surface charm disappeared at any hint of racism and he was capable of exploding. Gray's aide whispered to him that Baker was kidding, he really was, *let it go,* and Gray sat silent but furious. Later Baker apologized.

Still Foley waited. The clock ticked and the deadline of November 20, when sequestration took effect, neared, and Jim Miller won battles on "scoring" issues which structured the result. For example, programs which improved the collection of bad debts had always been counted as savings. Miller insisted they count as revenues and won. And after a House Appropriations aide several times contradicted Miller's facts, Miller demanded that staff be excluded.

"Fine," Rostenkowski snapped, staring at Miller and Baker. "Everyone who's not an elected official out."

Rostenkowski did not want to sit in a room and cut detailed legislative deals with them; their presence infringed on congressional prerogatives on the legislative process. But Miller stayed and Hill staff left.

Meanwhile Foley waited—for the debate to wear everyone down, for weariness itself to become a coalescing force, for the facts to impel others, exhausted, in the direction he wished. If ever Michel and Lott indicated support for Social Security savings, that would be the time to lock it in. But Michel remained absolutely silent when it was discussed, and Lott opposed it. After one more meeting with no progress, Rostenkowski pointed to Foley and said, "There's the most patient son of a bitch in the world."

Wright grew frustrated. His way to control was to act; action was creative. *He creates himself when he acts,* Gingrich had observed. Only action would bring order to a chaotic or hostile world. Knowing only one way to go—forward—Wright gathered his negotiators into his office ten days into the talks and said, "Keep this in this room, but we're probably not going to get an agreement. Ultimately we've got to be seen as responsibly moving forward."

It was a warning to Foley to act. But for all Foley's loyalty, his strategy was ingrained in his nature. Progress did not come.

Wright put together a plan for Congress to take control, and the next day hosted a lunch for House and Senate leaders in the Speaker's Dining Room, where so many budget battles had been fought earlier. His plan called for real deficit cuts of almost $30 billion, and it did not touch Social Security. Fifty-five percent of the deficit reduction would come from spending cuts, 45 percent from taxes. But Republicans would have to swallow a Democratic tax bill and Democratic spending priorities. Wright waited for a response.

Mark Hatfield, a Republican senator, said politely, "That's a great idea."

But he didn't endorse it. Neither did anyone else. Worse, no one made a counteroffer. No one else proposed anything. Afterwards, climbing the stairs to his office, Wright turned to John Mack and snorted, "What did you think of that lunch? It was the most disappointing damn thing. This is the most frustrating day. Nothing has gotten done. I can't identify any forward movement."

"You got a taste of the meetings. These guys won't do it."

"Then we've got the wrong guys in the meetings."

Wright's decision to create the second legislative day had been made in passion. He was about to act without passion. Here was Foley, loyal Foley. Wright would cut him off if he had to. There was no passion in this, only a cold will, a calculating will, a will which taught Wright something not only about power but about himself. There was nothing abstract about the budget to him; it was as tangible as digging a trench. He remembered in the Depression the poor bastards who never got a chance. He believed government gave the poor bastards a chance, and that Reagan wanted to give the rich bastards more. All year he had fought to change that. He would have his way.

Power was disconnected, without give, isolating, abstract and impersonal, a cutting loose. Wright confronted the coldness of power in a way he had not yet done in his speakership and turned cold. He would cut Foley off. He would accept what power required of him.

He decided to name Pat Williams and Leon Panetta as "alternates" in the budget talks. Panetta would replace Gray as Budget chairman in the next Congress (Gray had to rotate off the committee). He knew numbers and details and had good links to the MacKay group, most of whom were now wary of Gray. Panetta was a link to Caucus moderates. Williams, the liaison to organized labor, came from Montana. The men who worked the copper mines sent him to Congress. Once he told a DCCC board meeting, "All this money we're raising from business, that's great. But they're not with us. They'll leave us in a second. Don't ever forget, there's a fundamental difference between the two parties." Maybe most members of the Caucus, junior ones anyway, were managers now, not ideologues. Williams wasn't so far removed from when striking miners faced machine guns.

Wright called Williams and told him of his appointment. Williams called Panetta to tell him. Panetta replied, "What the hell is an 'alternate'?"

They could figure it out. Wright would use them to manipulate the outcome of the talks, and even manipulate Foley. As House Democratic negotiators gathered in Wright's office, Wright pulled Williams aside and said, "Pat, I know if you can buy it I can buy it."

Williams carried Wright's banner and trust. Not Foley. Williams. Any deal had to make Williams happy. He spoke for Wright.

At the same time Wright was sending Williams and Panetta into the budget talks, he applied his will to the Central American peace process. He was sensitive to constitutional issues, but this fight revolved around contra aid. The Constitution made the House preeminent over appropriations. And the White House had invited him into the peace process. The White House seemed determined to sabotage that process. He intended to make it work, to will it to work.

November 5 was the original deadline for a cease-fire. There was none. That day a tense and unhappy Wright had breakfast in H-201 with Victor Tinoco, Nicaragua's deputy foreign minister. It was only the latest of a series of meetings on Central America.

For weeks House Democrats had been trying to advance the process. Earlier, the vice president of Honduras had talked with Foley, Coelho, and Bonior in Foley's office. The Honduran military had helped create the contras, and under White House pressure its government allowed them to operate from its territory. But the vice president had seemed to invite help when he said bluntly, "Even though we are a democracy, we are not a full democracy. Our military has a lot to say about what happens. You negotiate military assistance directly with our military, you don't go through the civilian government. You may have more influence on our military than we do."

The next day Wright had run into several Honduran military officers in the Rayburn Room; he delicately but firmly had insisted that the peace process go forward. A week later, Honduran president José Azcona had come to Wright's office and argued that to show good faith the Sandinistas had to release political prisoners. A reopened newspaper could easily be reclosed; it would not be so easy to rearrest freed prisoners. Wright had nodded, then warned, "Democrats have been in power since 1954. The members of the Appropriations Committee are amenable to helping you. We would look with very great disfavor on anything that slowed the peace process."

The warning registered. Azcona soon joined Arias and Salvadoran president José Napoleón Duarte in asking the White House to delay any request for contra aid. The three presidents also demanded that the Sandinistas negotiate directly with the contras, although if necessary through a go-between. Then Arias won the Nobel Peace Prize. Its prestige was a powerful weapon that muted White House criticism and increased pressure on both the contras and Sandinistas. But the peace talks did not move.

Wright tried to move them. The sticking point was a Sandinista demand to talk directly to the Reagan administration, not to the contras. The administration refused and had its own demand: that the Sandinistas sit down face-to-face with the contras.

Wright wanted both sets of talks to proceed, but recognized the Sandinistas would speak to the contras only through an intermediary. In August he had proposed to the contras that Cardinal Miguel Obando, a Sandinista critic, serve in that role. They had immediately agreed.

In mid-October, congressional leaders sat down with Reagan, Shultz, Howard Baker, and Carlucci. Reagan complained, "The contras are entitled to meet directly with the Sandinistas."

"Mr. President," Wright replied, "we can go on all year with the contras saying they'll only speak to the Sandinistas and the Sandinistas saying they'll only speak to you. Obando seems acceptable. Why don't we go for that?"

Reagan finally agreed, although he rejected talks between the administration and the Sandinistas. Wright had another inch of progress. He returned to his office, called Nicaraguan vice president Sergio Ramirez, and urged that the Sandinistas accept Obando. But on October 29—the same day the House voted on reconciliation—the Sandinistas rejected him. Ramirez announced, "The only dialogue we have considered useful is with the government of the United States. This is an invariable position of the national government."

Now it was a week later and Wright sat across from Tinoco. Wright suggested Obando again. Tinoco replied, "He is unacceptable."

There was always an edge to Wright. Almost never did he truly relax. It was that edge in him, the careful internal balance he maintained, that made others uneasy around him. Now the pressures on him were the most intense he had ever experienced. Everything he had worked for, dreamed of, risked for seemed slipping away. Suddenly he exploded, lashing the Sandinistas. All the venom stored up in him over the preceding week poured out less in words than in tone, in the dark flush of his face.

Tinoco shrank back and quickly said, "No! You misunderstand!" Good news! They would soon release a thousand political prisoners (estimates of how many they held ranged from 2,500 to 10,000), satisfying the demand of Azcona and others. And they would negotiate with the contras through an intermediary, just not Obando. "I am authorized to ask you to serve as the intermediary."

Wright was embarrassed by his outburst. He cleared his throat, then formally, graciously—suddenly diplomatic—refused.

There were a dozen reasons to decline. The most important was that the administration was sensitive about his activity. "The State Department resents my involvement already," he said. "We don't need any more hostility from there."

He ran through several names with Tinoco, and later on the phone with Miguel D'Escoto, Tinoco's superior. Philip Habib, formerly Reagan's special envoy to Central America. Jimmy Carter. Gerald Ford. Argentina's president Raúl Alfonsín. D'Escoto asked Wright to accept the task in name and designate one as his agent. Wright laughed. One does not designate someone of that stature as one's representative.

That day Ortega announced that the Nicaraguan government would negotiate with the contras through an intermediary, that 981 political prisoners would be freed, and that a full amnesty would take effect once compliance by other Central American nations was verified—once Honduras stopped allowing the contras to operate from its territory.

The next day Wright talked to Carter, called him "the champion peace-maker I know," but did not ask him outright if he would serve. Carter did not volunteer. The Sandinistas had no choice. Ortega announced that his government was asking Cardinal Obando to mediate between them and the contras.

Obando did not accept the invitation. He was considering it.

Nicaraguan president Daniel Ortega would be in Washington the next week to address the Organization of American States. And Obando wanted to see Wright before accepting. The Sandinistas asked Wright if he would see them both. Wright agreed.

Friday, November 6, Republican budget negotiators visited Reagan and asked for his guidance. Reagan slammed his fist on the table and blasted the Democrats for pushing taxes on him. But he offered no positive suggestion or proposal. Domenici began to push his own plan, which included a Social Security COLA cut. Would that be acceptable as a last resort? Reagan said he had to look at the whole package first, but perhaps "as a last resort," yes.

Then Michel offered a proposal. Spending had already been frozen for seventy-four days—the two short-term continuing resolutions had done that. Another 104 days would be a six-month freeze. That was $5 billion. What about that, and $8 billion in hard taxes and "user fees," $5 billion in entitlement cuts—other than Social Security—and $4.9 billion in defense cuts. Would the President accept that?

It wasn't great. He didn't like it. But, yes, that was acceptable.

That afternoon Michel offered his plan to the group. For the first time, the Democrats saw defense cuts they could accept and a tax figure they could work with, and his plan had White House approval. Michel had broken the ice. They could begin to move toward a deal.

On Monday morning, House Democrats put together a response. They gathered in Wright's office and Foley ran down the details. It included $12 billion in taxes and totaled $28.4 billion in real deficit cuts, considerably more than Michel's plan.

Wright liked it and turned to Rostenkowski. "What do you think, Danny?"

Rostenkowski endorsed it. Wright nodded, then asked the group, "Can we sell this?"

"I think we can, Mr. Speaker," Panetta answered.

"Let's treat this plan the way Michel did," Wright said. *Leak it.*

After they got some media credit, they could move toward bipartisanship. They could begin to move toward a deal.

Tuesday night heavy snow blanketed Washington. John Kennedy once joked that the city combined the grace and charm of the North with the smooth efficiency of the South. Washington remained a southern city in its response to snow. Wednesday, Armistice Day, November 11, the city stopped dead. Nothing moved anywhere, except in the Capitol.

Reporters encamped outside S-211 where the budget negotiators met. Most arrived dressed informally, with Jim Baker in jeans and cowboy boots. It was tedious for the reporters; they were like men and women on jury duty, bored, doing their duty, eager for any crack in the tedium, swarming over anyone who emerged from the room. For staff, who were routinely expelled from discussions, it was no better. But inside the room, for a change, the negotiators started to make real progress.

On the other side of the Capitol, down winding turns of corridors, unknown to the bored reporters, Danny Ortega walked into Wright's office.

Ortega seemed more like a pudgy adolescent than a head of state. Average-sized with a thick mustache and black black hair, he wore a coat and tie but his clothes did not hang right; unlike so many of those who entered Wright's office, impeccably dressed in their dark suits of power, Ortega looked like one of those people who, no matter how hard they tried, would never look quite proper—as if his natural state was one of dishevelment, but who had made a special effort to be neat. It was difficult to reconcile his appearance with his history: he had robbed banks as a teenager to fund the revolution, survived prison and torture, killed men in close combat, trained as a guerrilla in Cuba. He was courteous, deferential even, his manner both casual and intense, like a scientist intent on his work and careless about all else. But underneath the deference and seeming eagerness to please Wright was a man of toughness and Machiavellian abilities. After the revolution he became the only ex-guerrilla in the junta running the provisional government; gradually he came to dominate that junta, expelled moderate elements, and became first among equals in a directorate in turmoil. The only clue to that ability was his intensity, his focus. He spoke solely in Spanish through an interpreter, and joked that he had never been in a snowstorm before.

Wright laughed, offered coffee, apologized for the disorder of his office and desk, and quoted Franklin Roosevelt's saying that an empty desk meant an empty mind. Perhaps it was Wright's way of identifying with Ortega's seeming disorganization, to make him welcome, as he always tried to identify with some aspect of others. They shared something else: although Ortega was first among equals, he could not make unilateral decisions and had to placate factions within the directorate. Wright could identify with that well enough.

The two fenced for a moment. There were nine people in the room but Wright and Ortega seemed to fill it; their intensity made the others shrink. Ortega had lied to Wright once before about holding free elections. Now Wright's words were heavy with messages; he praised Tunnermann, the ambassador, but that very praise reminded Ortega that Wright had been told the Sandinistas would expel Soviet and Cuban advisers, forswear aggressive designs on their neighbors, and restore democratic processes, all if the United States ceased financing the contras.

Ortega did not answer directly—putting Wright on guard—saying instead that he believed the peace agreement was viable. He added that Cardinal Obando, who had not yet agreed to serve as an intermediary, wanted to see Wright and the papal nuncio in Washington. Perhaps they could all meet at the nuncio's residence on Friday? Ortega said he would offer a peace proposal, adding that, if Obando did mediate, "We think the cardinal should have the help of Congress."

Ortega hoped he would anyway. Sandinistas considered Obando an enemy forced upon them. They feared that he would impose terms on them which went well beyond the peace accords; if they refused, he might blame them for destroying the peace process. A congressional presence might limit him, or if the talks failed at least provide another assessment of why.

"What does the cardinal think?" Wright asked warily.

"I met with him. He thought it was a good idea that we meet with you so he could be supported by Congress. The U.S. is key to quick action. Unless the administration's attitude changes it is hard to implement the agreement. It affects Honduras and the internal dialogue in Nicaragua."

"If the cardinal agrees, I agree," Wright said.

Ortega asked to return the next day to describe the cease-fire proposal he would give Obando Friday.

*   *   *

That same day the budget negotiators came within $700 million of closing a deal. Republicans held open that small gap as an excuse to give them a chance to check with Reagan. They had agreed on $10 billion in hard taxes, and $4.9 billion in defense cuts. The next day's newspapers reflected the optimism. Trent Lott, the most embittered man in the room who one day earlier had called Democratic proposals "totally unacceptable," now said they were "very close." Even Foley, who had spent so much effort trying to keep the press from speculating that agreement was near, said they had made "substantial progress . . . moving toward a bipartisan agreement."

So ended Armistice Day.

Early the next morning GOP senators went to see the President without their House counterparts. As he left his office for the negotiations at 10:00 A.M., he commented, "I think we'll wrap this up today."

But GOP senators and White House officials began to pick apart what had already been agreed upon. James Baker had earlier said tax figures should be "gross," not net. That meant that Rostenkowski and Bentsen could not raise $12 billion, give $2 billion away to buy votes, and produce a "net" of $10 billion. Miller suddenly demanded accounting changes which would require an additional $2.5 billion in domestic cuts. Carlucci, who had just been named secretary of Defense, said, "We can't go for more than $4.4 billion in defense cuts."

It was a major step backward. As the morning session ended, an angry Michel complained to the reporters staking out the room, "It's like the whole damn fleet is going to sink and the whole air force is going to drop out of the sky because they can't get that last half-billion dollars."

House Democratic negotiators briefed Wright in his office. Panetta suggested delaying COLAs three months, which would save $2.5 billion. They would use it as a counteroffer when Domenici called for COLA cuts again. Wright and Williams talked about a legislative and press strategy in case the negotiations failed. Then Wright, his eyes on Foley, bitterly castigated the White House. It was a show as much as anything. *No agreement for the sake of agreement.* After they left Wright turned to an aide. "Do you think they got the message?"

"Gray, Panetta, and Williams did. I don't know about Foley."

Thursday, while the budget negotiators were arguing, Wright met with Ortega, then Shultz, then the contra directorate. Not long before,

State had called a meeting of four of the five foreign ministers whose presidents had signed the peace agreement, not inviting Nicaragua. In protest at State's excluding Nicaragua, other ministers boycotted the meeting. State had in effect excluded itself, cut itself out of the loop. But each of the five nations and the contras sent representatives to Wright. He was indeed running Central American policy, and he intended to force both the Sandinistas and contras toward peace.

Ortega arrived in mid-morning and he and Wright exchanged congratulations—it was Ortega's birthday and Wright's wedding anniversary. D'Escoto, the foreign minister, read the cease-fire proposal. Ortega added, "What is important is this little word here, 'proposes.' This is not an ultimatum. This is an open proposal."

Wright welcomed the statement. The time for posturing was over. He, his aide Wilson Morris, and an aide to Byrd made several suggestions to increase the chances for acceptance of their plan: drop inflammatory language about "sabotage by the intransigence of the United States and irregular leaders," add guarantees that after a cease-fire the emergency laws in Nicaragua would be rescinded, and clarify procedures to keep armed clashes during a cease-fire from escalating into threats to the process. They would talk with Obando the next day.

Two hours later, Shultz walked into Wright's office to ask for more money for the State Department. Wright shrugged; he was unreceptive to administration officials opposing taxes while asking for more appropriations in their areas. He replied, "For everything we should do, there is a domestic call we can't meet. The problem is, we've doubled military spending and cut revenues."

Then Wright informed Shultz of his meeting with Ortega, adding, "They want me to have people to assist them in the negotiations, probably oversee them. I thought somebody like Loeffler might be good, to represent the President's point of view."

"His expertise is Congress, not negotiating a cease-fire," Shultz replied tersely.

"In the next day or so I expect to see Obando and Ortega."

Shultz listened stoically, expressionless, worried about turf. He did not want anyone outside of State involved at all. Not Loeffler or Wright or anyone. He did not want State involved either. He said, "The cardinal should play a role, but in the end the Sandinistas and contras must talk directly. If he wants help, the Central Americans should provide it. We would hope you would make the same point. I would decline if I were you."

Wright disagreed. "They asked to talk. My instinct is I'm doing the right thing. I believe Ortega is ready to deal."

"Nicaragua hasn't even come close to complying."

There was no point in arguing. Shultz had offered his opinion: stay away. But the administration had invited him into this, and Wright did not work for Shultz. *If the administration stood in the way of this peace process, then by God someone had to push it forward.*

Late that same afternoon, five members of the contra directorate sat down with Wright. Wright intended to convince them that they had no option but peace. They talked for an hour, about cease-fire technicalities—defensible boundaries, resupply routes. Then the contras talked of good faith. What if the Sandinistas were not serious?

"Then they will become isolated in the world," Wright replied.

"Castro has lived isolated for many years," Adolfo Calero observed. "We need more than moral condemnation."

"You mean," Wright said gravely, driving his message home, "when will the Sandinistas become so unpalatable that we will resume military aid? My opinion is there will not be support again for military aid."

The room grew cold and still. The United States had started this war, had created this movement; though many contras were tainted by corruption and connections with Somoza, the dictator whom the Sandinistas overthrew, others were democrats truly fighting for freedom. Thousands had died: proportionately, more Nicaraguans had died than Americans in Vietnam and World War II combined. Now Wright was cutting them loose. Wright was presenting them an ice wall.

A few days earlier he had shown Foley how cold he could be. Now he was showing the contras the true coldness of power. Power was white, blank; a great white slick surface, abstract, ungiving, impersonal, objective. It was the absence of heat, passion; it was pure will, isolated. *Negotiate the best deal you can,* Wright was saying, *because that is all you will get.*

Soon he would turn the same ice front to the Sandinistas.

At six o'clock Assistant Secretary of State Edward Fox called Wright's adviser Richard Pena. Fox was furious. They had just heard from reporters that Wright was seeing Obando at ten-thirty the next morning.

Wright hadn't told Shultz that. This was a hell of way to find out. Outrageous! Pena told Fox he was crazy. True, Wright hadn't told Shultz he was seeing Obando at ten-thirty. But the specific time had not been arranged then. Wright had said he expected to see him "in the next day or so." (State Department notes included the phrase.) So how could Shultz claim he had no notice?

It was a sign of the tension. Venting rage on the small thing allowed Shultz to escape his own responsibility for the large thing—his loss of control over a chief administration priority.

Late that evening Wright got a phone call from a lobbyist. Papal nuncio Pio Laghi, he reported, had been warned that if Obando saw Wright, Obando could not see Shultz.

"How do you know?" Wright asked.

"Laghi's standing right here."

"Put him on."

Laghi expressed concern that the cardinal was being used as a propaganda tool. Wright said, "I don't want to see the cardinal unless he wants to see me. Do you want me to come?"

"Yes. You're the catalyst."

"That threat about Shultz. Was it Elliott Abrams who made it?"

"Yes."

Wright hung up and called Shultz, who denied having given an ultimatum but confirmed that he would not see Obando. He repeated his view that it wasn't good for Americans to get involved in this process.

Two weeks earlier, *Congressional Quarterly* had run a lengthy story entitled "New Contra Politics: Wright the Dominant Force." Central America was one of the administration's two main foreign policy priorities—the other being arms control—yet Jim Wright, a congressman, dominated it. That marked a major shift of institutional power. Wright justified his role on the grounds that the White House had asked him to help push a diplomatic solution. That was ironic. According to Ed Fox, State Department officials had supported the August Wright-Reagan plan because they viewed it as "a domestic political deal which would free" them to act. To those officials, the agreement among Wright, Reagan, and Shultz on a policy meant that Wright would leave State alone to execute it. They had expected Congress and Wright in particular to step back from day-to-day maneuverings. They had expected the Wright-Reagan plan to cage Wright. But, convinced of administration bad faith, he had not stayed in the cage. Now he was rampaging, and they had no control over him at all. He had taken control.

Superior information allowed him to dominate policy. The administration would not talk in any depth to the Sandinistas; it also dictated, rather than listened, to those to whom it did talk. Wright's attitude, by contrast: "I treat them with respect and listen to them. I understand their pride."

Now Shultz was saying Wright should step back. Should he?

Even now, the administration claimed it supported the peace process—the countries in the region certainly did—and Shultz was telling him to leave it to Central Americans. But the Central Americans had come to Wright. Perhaps Shultz sincerely wanted a diplomatic solution. But Elliott Abrams and others who ran policy day to day, it seemed clear, did not. If Wright withdrew, peace would be in the hands of those who seemed determined to sabotage it.

This was a large thing, for Wright to proceed. Shultz had said no American should get involved. Wright was involved. The administration had gotten him involved. The delicacy of his position, of the Speaker of the House dominating one of the two chief foreign policy priorities of the White House, did not escape him. Neither did it stop him. If he proceeded, it would be a great reach of power that violated the institutional integrity of the State Department and the White House. Yet if he did not proceed, he would be leaving peace in the hands of those whom, he was certain, did not want peace. He did not trust the White House. He did not trust Elliott Abrams. Neither did the Central Americans.

Shultz had given his opinion. Wright did not share that opinion. He was going to see this thing through. Obando had not yet accepted the role of intermediary. He would see Obando.

Friday, the thirteenth of November, the budget negotiations moved close once again to agreement. Domenici, Packwood, Hatfield, Chiles, and Conte were still pushing for Social Security savings, and Panetta offered his idea of simply delaying COLAs for three months. There seemed a consensus. At the end of the day several negotiators waited for Foley to close the deal, a deal including Social Security cuts. But he delayed. The memory of Madigan's comment haunted him. *Cutting Social Security won't get fifteen Republican votes.* Lott was absent, and sure to raise hell. Foley decided to leave Social Security savings hanging out there over the weekend. If the idea could survive on its own for a few days, without an avalanche of criticism, maybe it was safe enough to include. But it would have to live on its own. The budget summit broke up for the weekend, close to a deal but without one.

Wright was scheduled to fly this day to Fort Worth on a chartered jetliner nicknamed "The Cowtown Clipper." It would carry several hundred lobbyists to Texas for Wright's biannual $1,000-a-plate fund-raiser that night. Weeks earlier, a Wright aide had invited several lobbyists to cruise the Potomac for dinner on a private yacht, saying to each, "I'm inviting you on the most expensive boat ride you ever went on." Wright did not attend, but each person on the boat had been asked to raise $50,000. Over the past few days the money had poured in, one aide handing another an envelope full of checks from the most recent mail. "There's eighty-five in there." Eighty-five thousand dollars. Money was being transmuted into power. Most of the money would go through Wright's PAC to other candidates. It was the system, the way the world worked, and another sign of his power.

Now Wright had his mind on substance, not process. He, his aide Wilson Morris, Bonior, and Paul Warnke, Carter's arms-control negotiator, went to see Pio Laghi on Massachusetts Avenue's Embassy Row. Wright brought Warnke because the Sandinistas had said Obando wanted an American to serve as liaison to him. He did not trust the Sandinistas in that regard, but if Obando actually requested such a liaison Warnke would be available.

Waiting were Ortega, D'Escoto, Tunnermann, and Obando. Obando was bull-like, lacking in the diplomatic skills one might expect from a Prince of the Church; he had been raised to cardinal not because of his skills but to make him a more formidable opponent of the Sandinistas. Ortega greeted the group with a wry smile, saying, "The peace efforts have been gathering force."

Wright shook hands warmly, then turned to Obando and reassured him, "Your accepting this role is the indispensable linchpin which makes possible the dialogue between the government and the resistance. I am eager and anxious to be of any assistance *you* desire. We will not attempt to impose any help on you."

Obando asked questions. The most important one: Was he supposed to be a message carrier or act more as a chairman, who might push both sides toward his ideas? As for a liaison with the Congress, "I appreciate the competence of the men here, but I would like to name my own team. If feasible, I would like the talks to take place in Nicaragua."

Ortega disagreed: "The position of the government is that this is an intermediate step in the short term for a cease-fire, leading to full political integration and participation. The role you would play is as an intermediary, bringing proposals. In practice your function would go beyond that."

Then Ortega explained again how useful it would be for Wright to have some involvement, some liaison to the cardinal. And he insisted that the talks be in Washington, arguing that there both sides would be under pressure from Congress and the administration, forcing both parties to work seriously.

Ortega was appealing to Wright. The Sandinistas had earlier told him that Obando was "unacceptable" as an intermediary. Yet they had accepted him because of Wright's insistence. Wasn't that enough?

Wright spoke. His voice was gentle but the message was cold once again, cold as it had been to Foley, cold as it had been to the contras, yielding nothing, rebuffing Ortega on point after point: "The cardinal is the single most qualified person and commands respect. He must have more moral authority than just a messenger. Where? I have no opinion. It should be wherever the cardinal wishes. As for my help, we are at the cardinal's disposal. He is free to choose anyone."

It would be whatever the cardinal wanted. Wright would stay out of the negotiations unless Obando personally, specifically asked him in. He was delivering the Sandinistas into the hands of one they considered their enemy. Ortega's face tightened. He accepted what he had to accept. Outside the building, they all met the press announcing that Obando would act as an intermediary in cease-fire talks between the contras and the Sandinistas. Wright wore that eerie, intimidating, iron smile he flashed so often. Television cameras rolled, reporters asked questions, and the evening news was made. More so than Wright knew.

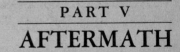

PART V
AFTERMATH

When trouble is sensed well in advance it can easily be remedied; if you wait for it to show itself any medicine will be too late. . . . If you cannot be both feared and loved, it is better to be feared.

—Machiavelli, *The Prince*

CHAPTER 19

Reporters peppered the White House and State Department for a response to Wright's meeting with Ortega and Obando. They got one. The administration attacked angrily. Reagan himself was infuriated. So was Shultz. White House spokesman Marlin Fitzwater castigated Wright's conducting "personal negotiations." State Department spokesman Charles Redman added his official rebuke: "We don't think it's desirable for the United States to inject itself directly" into the talks. Unattributed quotes were harsher. Wright was an "egomaniac"; he was "interfering in the foreign policy of the United States"; he was "in over his head and didn't understand what was going on."

By the time Wright landed in Forth Worth, his morning meeting had become news. Big news. All three networks wanted him on their evening news shows. The story was not the substance of the meeting; it was power—his perceived grab for it, and the administration's effort to slap him down. Wright did not back down. When NBC's Tom Brokaw asked, didn't he think it was improper for him to deal in this way against the wishes of the administration, Wright replied, "Tom, I don't need the permission of the administration. I represent the American people too."

Even Michel was outraged. Privately he stormed at Wright, stormed at his infringement on executive prerogatives. Publicly, on *Meet the Press*, he called Wright's move "absolutely wrong."

The contras had become symbolic, symbolic of honor—would the United States again send out people to fight and abandon them?— symbolic of loyalty to the President, who had been so damaged by the

Iran-contra scandal, symbolic of freedom. And symbolic of Wright's activism. Republicans still believed he had betrayed the President by immediately abandoning his and Reagan's joint peace plan and embracing the Central American peace agreement. Now they grunted with disdain at the "Wright-Ortega" plan. Gingrich said, "You cannot overestimate the importance of anticommunism in the Republican Party. The symbolism of Wright meeting with Ortega on Armistice Day, Veterans Day, just shook people over here. I think it bothered Cheney more than reconciliation."

Cheney, a former White House chief of staff, believed in the prerogatives of the Executive Branch. Reconciliation had outraged House Republicans, made them sensitive to any further slight, any further reach for power. Now came this giant step by Wright. "Jim Wright has radicalized House Republicans," Cheney said.

They set up a task force chaired by Cheney to develop responses to Wright's aggressiveness. There was the feeling, spreading among House Republicans and conservatives outside the House, that Wright had to be stopped.

In Fort Worth the Friday night fund-raising dinner was going well. It was at the Tarrant County Convention Center, at the edge of downtown. Some of the old Texas and Washington political hands winced at the memories: near there John Kennedy, on the last day of his life, had attended a huge breakfast hosted by Wright before leaving for Dallas. The dinner raised close to $1.5 million. Everywhere in Fort Worth this weekend Wright was the hero, the people's hero, returned triumphant. Saturday afternoon a five-dollar barbecue at the Will Rogers Memorial Coliseum, a vast building whose floor was designed for livestock more than for people, drew seven thousand. Several dozen House colleagues flew down, and one after another they took the stage to praise Wright while the crowd ignored them. They quieted only for Wright himself.

Long, long ago, he had discovered he could control a crowd with words, move them, make them laugh. Now he played with this crowd. His voice did as much as his words; it had an intensity to it that made people lean forward; it was soft, too, so they strained to hear it; yet it soothed and washed over them. He remembered who married whom and whose grandson was at what college, he knew his district block by block, and he began to speak to his people of great events, of what he had told Gorbachev, of what he had told the President. Great things touched the crowd through him. His message was of peace, world peace and peace in Central America, and for a moment, bathed in his soothing voice, one could feel peace, the restfulness and glory and wonder of peace. Two days earlier he had gone to a play based on *All the King's Men*. Now, wading in lobbyists' money, sought by the national media, at war with the President, and surrounded by his own people, Wright was Willie Stark. A Speaker of the House is closer to the people than any other national politician in perhaps any country. Wright drew strength from his contact, his intimacy with these people; like Antaeus, his contact with the earth gave him strength. It was a far cry from Washington, all right. This was where the power came from.

Then the moment passed and he gave up the microphone. The noise of the crowd rose back up; their attention drifted again.

Sunday morning the *Times* and the *Post* both had front-page stories on Wright. Steve Roberts of the *Times* wrote about the poor relationship between him and Reagan: "The latest evidence of the feud appeared Friday when the Speaker virtually ignored the White House while consulting with . . . Ortega. . . . The White House, trying to control its irritation, said it was concerned about 'any outside influence' disrupting the peacemaking process. In Mr. Reagan's view, according to White House aides, the Speaker is an egotistical and untrustworthy congressional leader who see himself as a coequal of the President. For instance, they note, Mr. Wright refused to participate directly in the budget talks . . . saying he and Mr. Reagan would review the proposed compromise when their deputies had completed their deliberations. Mr. Wright in turn . . . described Mr. Reagan as 'a person with whom you can't seriously discuss serious issues.' "

Wright read the *Times* story in Fort Worth. It disturbed him. Neither he nor the country benefited if it seemed personal animosity interfered with running the government. Then Wilson Morris, who had accompanied him to Fort Worth and then returned to Washington, called and read him the *Post* story. It infuriated him. In it, reporter John Goshko quoted an unnamed administration official "involved in" foreign policy—almost certainly Elliott Abrams—who accused Wright of an "exercise in guerrilla theater" that had dealt "a serious setback to the peace process."

Outraged, Wright called Howard Baker, demanded a meeting with the President, and said, "If you people have got something to say to me, say it to my face."

The meeting would occur Monday morning. Commentators on the Sunday interview shows had attacked him too. Then Monday, on his way to defend himself on *Good Morning America*, Wright read a *Post* editorial accusing him of an "intervention into the day-to-day running of foreign policy that was breathtaking in its scope and whose like is hard to recall. . . . He overreaches recklessly. . . . Our misgivings do not center now on the substance but on the procedure. Mr. Wright appears to have gone way over the line that separates opposition from interference."

He felt isolated. It seemed everywhere he turned he came under attack. At ten o'clock he sat down in the Cabinet Room across the table from the President, the Secretary of State, the Secretary of Defense, the National Security Adviser, the White House chief of staff. The titles gave the men weight. Wright was on their ground, alone facing all of them, with the press, too, against him.

He opened with a peace offering, saying they had to kill stories like the one in the *Times*, which implied that personal animosity prevented their doing the business of government.

Reagan agreed, then said, "Ortega's a liar. You can't believe anything he says. We started with the Wright-Reagan plan. Now we've got the Wright-Ortega plan."

Wright stiffened angrily and replied, "That's not right, Mr. President."

Reagan left, turning the meeting over to Shultz. Shultz attacked him again. "I told you I didn't think an American should be involved in it."

Wright began to get angry once more. They might have waited to hear what had gone on in the meeting with Obando before attacking him. And what had he done? *Tried to bring peace.* Accusing him of dealing "a serious setback to the peace process" was a lot of posturing crap from an administration that had done nothing but try to block it. He told them what had transpired with Obando, then it was his turn to attack, telling Shultz, "I know damn well who said that chickenshit 'guerrilla theater' crap. It was Abrams. If someone on my staff was so craven as to leak a vicious story about you as was done to me, I'd fire his ass."

Powell and Carlucci shifted the subject to policy. Ortega was a lying son of a bitch, they said. He wouldn't do anything that wasn't forced down his throat. Then they said the contras needed $30 million of military aid. Could Wright help?

Wright was incredulous. To attack him, and then ask for help? He replied evenly, "I suspect if I were to try actively to pass that, it would lose. The votes aren't there."

The meeting ended with nothing resolved. At his daily press conference and at a lunch with White House and diplomatic reporters he defended himself again. He repeated and repeated that the White House had invited him into this, he was only trying to make the thing work. That evening on *MacNeil/Lehrer* he added, "I must uphold the Legislative Branch as coequal with the Executive. . . . The people who wrote the Constitution never intended the Congress to be subservient. . . . My job is to work with whomever is President and I shall do that. But also my job is to represent the people of the United States as expressed by their elected representatives."

His colleagues had elected him Speaker. Those chosen by the people, professionals who knew their business, who were not fooled by images, who knew reality, had chosen him. The members of the House had elected him. *He was the Speaker of the House*. That was a powerful mandate. Only now were people, including his colleagues— and including himself—beginning to understand how powerful he considered it.

The Sunday interview shows had talked about Social Security as well as Nicaragua. Budget negotiators used the shows to hint at cutting the program to test the response. Even Lott had observed that if a broad deficit-reduction program hit every area, then "something could be looked at" in Social Security.

Monday morning the reaction hit. The National Committee to Preserve Social Security and Medicare had already contacted its 4.5 million members and flooded Capitol Hill with telegrams; it geared up again. Chiles's likely Senate opponent, Republican House member Connie Mack III, attacked him hard on it. In New Hampshire, the state with the first presidential primary, Jack Kemp lambasted Dole for his willingness to accept a tax increase.

The negotiators were shaken by the reaction. Then Rules chairman Claude Pepper, born in 1900 and the champion of the elderly, held a press conference jointly with the American Association of Retired Persons to attack Social Security cuts. News of Pepper's press conference seemed to suddenly suck all the air from the room. People were silent. COLA cuts were dead. Foley said, "Let's move back to other areas."

But there were no other areas. And tempers were fraying. Conte repeated his punch line about "screwing up the canoe" and people eyed him testily. After Foley called once again for no leaks, a Republican said, "I'm getting tired of his whining."

The next day Wright hosted another breakfast in H-201 with the two Bakers, Jim Miller, Dole, Michel, Byrd, and Foley, hoping to put together a large package. No one mentioned the foreign policy confrontation. They had enough to argue about. Jim Baker demanded again that the $10-billion tax figure be "gross." Wright insisted the White House had no business telling Congress what to put in a bill. Baker replied, "Now you sound like Danny. There's no way we do business unless it's gross."

Baker would win that argument—the Democrats' position was not defensible in the press. Wright complained about the White House insistence on $2.5 billion more in entitlement savings. There was no way to do that without Social Security. Byrd asked about a gasoline tax. Baker said no. Byrd, looking again for fairness, asked about delaying the COLAs and matching it with a delay in lowering the tax rates. Baker said no again, but asked about a luxury tax. Now Dole objected: "Every jeweler in America will rise up." Howard Baker had to leave: "How shall I report to the President on COLAs?" They were where they were yesterday. Nowhere.

An hour after the breakfast ended, Bob Strauss called Wright. Shultz had just invited him to lunch. There was only one thing that could be about: the meeting with Ortega and Obando. Wright gave him his side. His voice sounding like a boy forced into a fight at risk of being branded a coward, he added, "Tell them I'm not hurt at home or in the House. . . . If they take me on, inflict pain, every time I'm attacked I'll attack them and I'll still be standing afterwards. . . . If I backed off I would have no self-respect, you see. . . . They think they have a right to excoriate people to bring them into line. Well, they've got a different animal now. If they want a truce, okay, but I'm not afraid of the bastard. . . . This is latter-day McCarthyism. If they refer to a Wright-Ortega plan again, they'll have a fight."

Perhaps he could win it. Maybe the press would turn. That day's

New York Times lead editorial read, "There's such a hollow ring to [administration] complaints about free-lance diplomacy by Speaker of the House Jim Wright. . . . Objections to trespassing into foreign policy would carry greater weight if, even now, there were a sensible policy to trespass on. In his Saturday radio talk, Mr. Reagan continued to suggest that the United States had no role in [the] Nicaraguan conflict . . . which is worse than nonsense, it's insulting nonsense." It was accompanied by a front-page story that included Wright's view, quoting him as saying, "Some people in the administration are scared to death peace will break out."

Perhaps the *Times* editorial had registered on Shultz too. At one-thirty in the afternoon, Strauss called Wright from the State Department, then Shultz and Wright talked. They quickly worked out a six-point agreement. Half an hour later, Strauss and Shultz came to see Wright. Before their arrival, one of Wright's aides said Shultz planned to put out a statement after their meeting. Wright snapped, "If there's a statement, it will be a joint statement."

There was. The three men talked briefly in Wright's office, then went to the press gallery where Shultz read the first three points of the agreement. Wright read the last three.

"Mr. Speaker! Have you agreed not to meet with Central Americans involved in working out a peace settlement?"

"No." His answer was firm and unequivocal and uncontradicted by Shultz.

Elsewhere in the Capitol the deficit-cutting package was getting smaller and smaller. While Wright and Shultz talked to reporters, White House negotiators presented their first proposal in weeks. It called for $250 million more in defense spending than had been agreed to, and no COLA cuts—but it still called for the $2.5 billion in domestic cuts the COLA cuts would generate. Foley shook his head. This was not progress.

Jim Baker said that without those domestic cuts, the White House would not go for $10 billion in hard taxes. Taxes would have to drop to $9 billion, plus user fees and tougher IRS enforcement.

Bill Gray checked with Michel's aide Bill Pitts on how many Republicans would vote for delaying COLAs and $10 billion in taxes. "Less than 30 percent," Pitts told him.

The next morning, Wednesday, Gray reported that to Wright, who replied, "That's not enough. Our guys in the South would be surrounded by Republicans voting the other way. It wouldn't pass."

Gray described the package as it seemed to be taking shape. "I call this the 'wimp-out' package. The media will eat us alive."

Foley and Williams suggested preparing three packages—one with $24.8 billion in hard, real deficit reduction, one with $28 billion, and one with $37 billion—and presenting all three to the President, explaining they needed his active support to pass either of the larger ones. Then they would let him choose, and share in any blame. Democratic Senator Bennett Johnston also had a large, last-gasp package including COLA cuts.

That morning, the House Democratic Caucus heard the "wimp-out" package described. Gray tried to put the best face on it: "Ronald Reagan said he wouldn't do two things—raise taxes or sign off on defense cuts. He's doing both. This is not what Bill Gray might have written on his own, but I hope you will support it."

Simultaneously, Jim Baker was briefing the House Republican Conference. There the plan's outlines were put to a vote. Only two Republicans voted yes. The proposal got eight votes from Senate Republicans. When Baker walked back into the negotiating room he pulled open his coat wide and quipped, "See the blood?"

No one liked the plan. Yet it moved inexorably forward. Whenever anything else surfaced, someone shot it down. Wednesday night Wright walked into the negotiations and asked, "What about a VAT?"

A value-added tax was an excise tax on the value added to a product at each stage of production. Virtually every European country had one; in effect, it was a federal sales tax, although an invisible one. It could raise huge amounts of revenue, but was also controversial and complicated. It was not the kind of thing that could be thrown together in a few days or even weeks; it would require long, detailed examination. Wright's suggestion went nowhere, but the fact that he made it indicated that they had run out of options. No one liked the package. But there was nothing else.

They had only one more day to reach a deal. The deadline for sequestration was Friday, November 20.

On Thursday morning, as members crowded around the muffins, fruit, and coffee before the regular whip meeting, Pat Williams was exasperated and concerned—but impotent. He huddled with Wright and reported that the idea of giving Reagan three plans had died. House

Democrats could not do it alone and no one else would cooperate. Bennett Johnston's plan was also dead. The negotiators stalemated over every new suggestion that would yield a big package. And they had to do something. "Personally, I don't give a damn about Wall Street," Williams said. "They passed the '81 tax bill that got us into this mess. But we do have to do something for the world, so Baker can go to Germany and Japan and say, 'We did this, what are you going to do?' "

A few minutes later the whip meeting began. Wright declared, "This package is not heroic. It's not painless either. Danny had to swallow a number of bitter pills. We're in the position of damage control now. We may not look real good doing this, but we avoid looking real bad. I hope you swallow hard and support it because the alternative, sequestration, is worse."

But later, in private, he showed his disgust: "Grown men have sat around in that room for eighteen days. That's too goddamn long."

The White House raised one more demand, that it approve each individual tax increase and appropriations cut, a demand which grew out of conservatives' distrust of Congress's willingness to keep its commitments. (Reagan complained bitterly that Congress had reneged five years earlier on an agreement to cut spending $284 billion, in return for his support of a $98 billion tax increase. Actually, $108 billion of the $284 billion in savings was supposed to come from lower interest rates, which never materialized; OMB was supposed to make $47 billion in unspecified "management savings," which also never materialized; more than half the remaining savings were to come from the military, which Reagan himself blocked. In the nondefense area, Congress did enact most of the savings.) Neither the House Democrats nor the White House negotiators would yield. And they were still arguing over "gross" or "net" tax numbers.

Wright waited restlessly for the issues to be resolved. They weren't. At midday he finally walked into the negotiations and demanded, "You've got to do this thing tonight."

The men stiffened. *If it was so damned easy, they'd have done it already.* Jim Baker said, "I was just talking to Danny about not raising fourteen billion to get nine."

"I'll take all the crap out," Rostenkowski replied. "Just give me ten billion, gross."

Baker shot back, "I'll tell you what. You and I sit down and we'll work out something." It was an offer to put the tax giveaways Rostenkowski wanted to use to buy votes in another piece of legislation in return for giving Baker input into tax policy. "You take two dollars for Democrats, give me one dollar for Republicans."

But now Rostenkowski did not want to sit down with Baker and work something out, and allow the White House to insinuate itself into the legislative process.

"No! That's out. Out! The trouble with you, Baker, is you want to scrap our bill and start all over."

"That's the way it ought to work."

"Hell, no! We're going to conference with our bill."

Angry, everyone angry, Rostenkowski stood up, unfolding, stretching, leaning threateningly over the table, making his large body, his physical presence and anger, suddenly a factor. There was a moment of tension. *This whole deal could blow up yet.* He snorted, then turned to Foley. "Tom, you've got my proxy. I won't agree to any covert deal. I've got to listen to my members."

Rostenkowski was sick of it, and out of it. Wright left a moment afterwards. Pushing then could have destroyed everything. Two hours later, late that afternoon, the talks recessed, to reconvene at seven. There was a reception that evening, also at seven: the unveiling of a portrait of Jack Brooks, chairman of Government Operations. Wright, on his way to it, ran into Rostenkowski in the hallway outside the House chamber. Wright said he was going back to the talks.

"Jim, go down there if you want. I won't tell you what to do. But I don't think you should. If you lay something hard on them it'll blow up and they will blame you."

Wright hesitated for a moment, then agreed. It had taken all year but now the two of them thought exactly alike. They shared the same frustration, the same anger. For a moment they seemed two giants of the Congress for whom nothing was impossible. But the moment passed. Rostenkowski headed one way, Wright the other. Then, in the Rayburn Building, he ran into Panetta coming from the reception.

"Leon, Danny's position is he'll accept nine billion gross, but in return they don't try to tell him how to write the bill. I want this finished tonight."

"I'll pull Baker aside. If he agrees, it's a deal."

It was almost 8:00 P.M. now, an hour after the talks were supposed to reconvene. The negotiators had gathered but Foley did not bring the session to order. Instead he moved around the table, taking a few minutes with each man, talking privately about whichever details were most important to that individual while others talked in clusters of two or three. It took him almost an hour to work his way around the table while the others were engaged in a general discussion. At nine—*bang!*— he gaveled the group together.

"We're very close," he said. "We've made a lot of progress. We'll reconvene tomorrow subject to the call of the chair on one hour's notice."

Bang!

Outside, the press stood stunned at the adjournment, grabbing negotiator after negotiator. What happened? What happened? No deal? Disaster?

But the deal was done, done with a whimper rather than a bang. Foley had pulled one last maneuver, adjourning without formal agreement to avoid having conservatives learn details in the morning papers, thus giving them an opportunity to convince the President to balk. The strategy worked: The next day's *Wall Street Journal* story read, "Budget negotiators abruptly adjourned last night without an agreement. . . . Negotiators asserted the talks hadn't broken down. . . . Mr. Baker and Treasury Secretary James Baker left the Capitol quickly after adjournment. Democratic participants went to a private meeting in the office of House majority leader Thomas Foley."

Williams, Gray, Panetta, and key staff sprawled about Foley's living room of an office, not so much celebrating as unwinding. No one was ecstatic but they were in good humor. Relief mixed with exhaustion. They reviewed language of a statement of principles Baker wanted. Two points infringed on congressional authority.

"The Speaker wouldn't like that," Foley observed. The two points disappeared. "The rest is okay."

The budget talks disappointed. There was no long-term solution. Why?

The negotiators were bargaining over a federal budget of $1.055 trillion. After adjusting for inflation, that was a 19 percent spending increase since Reagan took office.

A total of $151 billion went to pay interest on the debt and was immune to cuts. Although nominal interest rates had fallen in half since Reagan took office, the debt had increased so much that interest was the fastest-growing part of the budget, up 66 percent after inflation.

Under Reagan, defense spending rose 42 percent after inflation; it doubled in absolute dollars and accounted for $287 billion.

Social Security, other pensions, and Medicare increased 25 percent after inflation, to $355 billion. Almost two-thirds of that was Social Security, which escaped any cuts or other kinds of savings.

Under Reagan, other entitlements increased 3 percent to $142 billion, although items such as food stamps dropped while farm subsidies more than doubled.

Discretionary domestic spending—education, housing, mass transit—fell 22 percent in the Reagan years after inflation adjustments, to $175 billion. Democrats, particularly House Democrats, did not want to give any more.

Wright in particular did not want to give any more. He saw the programs which he believed in, programs he saw as investments in the nation, eviscerated. He wanted to reverse the White House's priorities and reexpand government investment. The White House wanted to enshrine its priorities and to shrink further the government's role.

That was the grand collision, the collision of visions. It led to the chief stalemate. But there was also pure, vote-grabbing politics involved, particularly on taxes and Social Security.

Taxes had long-term deficit-cutting impact, since they grew with the economy. But the White House and many House Republicans—not Senate Republicans—had made resistance to taxes *their* issue. Limiting taxes, of course, was also a means of limiting government activism. The White House and House GOP had begun by resisting income tax increases, but gradually, almost inadvertently, broadened their rhetoric into opposing all tax increases. That rhetoric trapped them, to the point that the White House in the negotiations initially opposed tax increases it had itself proposed in its budget.

Democrats and Senate Republicans were willing to cut Social Security, which also would have generated large future savings. But House Republicans were embittered by the memory of Democrats demagoguing the issue in 1982. Influential GOP congresswoman Lynn Martin had warned Foley, "An elephant remembers five years." The reconciliation bill did not make House Republicans want to trust Democrats.

The bigger political factor was the public. Although it rated the deficit as the number-one national problem, it opposed taxes, opposed Social Security cuts—by 84 percent to 14 percent, according to one private

Democratic poll—and opposed cuts in domestic spending. It only supported modest defense cuts. Until the polls indicated the public understood the problem better, understood that, yes, difficult choices had to be made, few politicians wanted to make them. The only way would be if they had political cover.

The President could have provided such cover. But the President offered no proposals, other than cuts earlier proposed in his budget— a budget which had gotten only forty-five votes out of a potential 535 when voted on in the spring.

Other cover could have come from Claude Pepper, on Social Security cuts. Pepper was eighty-seven years old, but his mind was sharp. He was tough enough to pound his fragile fist on a table for things he believed in when arguing with Rostenkowski and Wright, and he was also a team player. In 1983 he had actively supported, and made the difference in passage of, Social Security cuts. Wright had treated him very well all year. Had Pepper actively supported a deal which hit Social Security, he would have protected politicians from attack. But neither Foley nor anyone else tried to bring him into the process, and Pepper ultimately killed Social Security cuts with a press conference denouncing them. "Foley's very, very smart," said one negotiator. "But if there was a flaw in the summit, it was that we did not bring Pepper in early to provide cover for a cut in COLA increases."

Panetta said, "I don't think Tom ever thought we had the votes to touch Social Security. He saw two danger signals—Michel just sat silent whenever they came up, and Lott kept saying no, no, it wasn't doable."

At several points in the talks, Foley could as chairman have closed a deal including Social Security cuts and achieving substantial deficit reduction. He purposely let those opportunities slip away. He did not want to take the risk of reaching an agreement and having the House vote it down.

His was a calculated, reasoned stance. The stakes were immense— a potential market collapse which could drag the world into recession or worse. Foley took the safe route. One base at a time. Don't make mistakes. Let things happen. But then, when one waits for something to happen, sometimes it does not.

"There was an assumption," said a leading House Democrat, "that the governing bodies in the Congress were House Democrats and Senate Republicans. That was the case when Republicans controlled the Senate. It's still the case, even though Democrats took nominal control over there. We see each other as the responsible parties, the ones who must take charge, the ones with whom each of us must deal. If we and Senate Republicans can reach an accommodation, the issue is settled. That was the way we looked at each other in these negotiations."

But that assumption was wrong. *We have just enough votes to be irresponsible,* Jerry Lewis had said. House Republicans, neglected so long and so often by everyone—by Wright, by Senate Republicans, by the White House—exercised power by saying no.

In the end the deal covered two years. It cut the deficit by $25.2 billion (plus $5 billion in asset sales, so headlines would proclaim that they cut $30 billion) the first year and $42.4 billion (plus another $3.5 billion in asset sales) the second year. The first year taxes totaled $9 billion in hard taxes, $2 billion more in user fees, $17.3 billion the second.

The numbers, the priorities, represented a Democratic victory. Wright did not feel victorious.

Pat Williams joined Wright at breakfast the morning after the deal was informally reached and reviewed the details of the agreement. Wright snapped, "This is abject surrender."

Williams chuckled. "This thing does sort of make the Budget Committee unnecessary. The whole process was flawed. That became apparent the first few days. We made Jim Miller a legislator. People talk about a parliamentary system. We just went through one. I don't like it. But this language lets Danny do what he wants. Reagan agreed to significant defense cuts. We protected our program priorities. The President's budget next year has to comply with these numbers too."

"I don't give a damn about the President's budget."

Wright stared at his cereal. Raisin bran with skim milk, as usual. He hated eating cereal with skim milk, as usual. Disgusted, he left abruptly, leaving the cereal untouched in his bowl, leaving his staff and Williams uncertain of his intentions.

Half an hour later the House negotiators gathered upstairs in his office. The mood was sour, as if they were picking up something dirty. And one last glitch had appeared. Jim Baker had given Byrd new language he wanted in the agreement. One paragraph implied distrust of Rostenkowski's word. Furious, Rostenkowski jabbed his finger in the air. "Sons of bitches! Baker knows me better than that!"

Other language stipulated that Reagan had to approve specific taxes raised. Wright thought that issue had been settled, dropped. It was an unprecedented intrusion of the Executive into the Legislative Branch. People had complained that Wright had usurped Shultz's role? That was nothing compared to this demand. Maybe the media couldn't understand the significance of it, but, by God, it directly contravened the separation-of-powers clause.

Wright finished reading the list of demands, crumpled it in his hand, and threw it on the floor. Baker had gone too far. If he wanted a fight, he had one. Wright sputtered, "How could we be so craven to accept this? What would future constitutional historians think of us?"

He sat down and wrote language which was the precise reverse of Baker's demand: "The ingredients composing these figures will be determined through the regular legislative process and conference agreement, subject to the President's signature or veto."

"If Baker won't accept that," Wright declared, "there's no deal."

His colleagues agreed. Wright got on the phone to Byrd and explained his position. "I hope you'll stick by me on this." He hung up. "Danny, in the Oval Office, you, Jim Baker, and Reagan will go off to the side, look at the language, and agree. Then we'll say we're with Rosty."

One after another, the members complained about their Democratic colleagues in the Senate. "I'd as soon have a Republican as Chiles," Wright said.

When Republicans had controlled the Senate, Domenici had chaired the Budget Committee. Democrats had worked better with him.

For a few minutes they talked details unhappily, with gaps of silence. No one liked the deal. Foley tried to soothe his colleagues: "You know, the Republicans have a problem on the numbers. We won on the numbers. We've got to let the liberals know we took their shirts on defense. But we can't brag about it. It's hard enough handling Michel anyway."

Rostenkowski left to inform his committee caucus of the details, down the hall in H-208. He promised to take care of them: "Russell Long [the near-legendary former chairman of the Senate Finance Committee] never in his best days got a bill through the Senate without amendments as sweeteners. We'll see what Bentsen can do. If the Senate adds anything, anything at all, I'll be damned if I leave my committee out in the cold."

At three o'clock the leadership saw Reagan to make the agreement official. It was a pro forma meeting; earlier, Jim Baker had immediately yielded to Wright's demand. Reagan congratulated everyone on reaching agreement. Wright and Michel told him he would have to work to pass it. Then they went out to meet the White House press corps. It was a short walk, barely more than a dozen yards, from the Oval Office.

The press room, converted from the small swimming pool John Kennedy had used, was cramped. In the rear, a beehive of partitions separated reporters' organizations. Rows of chairs as in a miniature lecture hall were laid out before a small stage set in front of the White House backdrop familiar to news watchers.

The press corps had waited with some excitement for this meeting. Despite Wright's unhappiness with the budget agreement, reporters interpreted it as a congressional triumph—even Wright's personal triumph—over the President. All year Reagan had said no to taxes, no to defense cuts, had sworn they would be implemented only "over my dead body." All year Wright had insisted on both. Now Reagan was agreeing to both.

It marked Wright's second major triumph over the administration in seventy-two hours—just three days earlier Shultz had gone to the Hill. This shift in the balance of power gave the room an uncomfortable, volatile feel. Even without that uncertainty the room would have been tense. Power is always accompanied by tension; even when it seems to lie quiet, that quiet comes from a dynamic equilibrium, like the stillness of the rope in a tug of war. The whole setting—the White House backdrop, the President playing host, in control—was designed to communicate power. Presidential power.

Now the Speaker of the House and the President of the United States were climbing onto the stage and stood side by side. Their personal animosity added to the volatility. Before them bristled the steel thistles of a briar patch of microphones and cameras, technicians and reporters; other men accustomed to attention and power, Byrd, Dole, Foley, and Michel, stood aside, seved as props. Reporters pushed against one another, wrestling for position; they were unruly, not quite sure of what this meant, eager to get at the President.

Reagan spoke, then offered the microphone to "Jim" for a brief comment, followed by Byrd, then Foley. Reporters began asking questions. To reassure the markets that the government was not paralyzed by personal animosity, Reagan pretended to cordiality with Wright. After he answered a few questions, he turned to Wright and, for the second time calling him by his first name, said, "Jim, would you like to take a question?"

Wright stepped up to the microphones so casually that he suddenly seemed in charge, totally in charge and even at home. *This was what he had waited for all these years. This command.* He spoke with a relaxed precision and casual expertise that communicated strength and command. His eyes glinted with a wildness that separated him from other politicians. He did not appear to be a man a reporter wanted to take on and seemed . . . *heavy* somehow. While Reagan shuffled about the stage uncertain where to stand, Wright even when admitting failure was authoritative, strong. Asked about raising income tax rates, Wright responded, "I think it would be unrealistic for me to expect to pass any rate increases." *"I think," "for me," "to pass." It was as if he were the prime mover, as if everything were up to him.* Reagan was ill at ease—and stepped back.

The shift in control seemed physical. Watching on Capitol Hill, a senior GOP aide exploded in outrage, "Goddammit! Did you see Wright push the President away from the microphone?"

Wright had not pushed Reagan away. Reagan had yielded to him in a gesture of body language, in an ironic echo of Reagan's own rise to power almost eight years earlier, when he had seized control of the microphone in a New Hampshire primary debate and established himself as the dominant political force in America.

Wright had become his rival.

In this past one week, from his meeting with Ortega and Obando, to his fund-raiser which raised almost $1.5 million, to Shultz's trip to the Hill to make peace, to this seeming triumph in economic policy, Wright had forced those who followed the dance of power to take note.

It was this week which, to the Washington press corps, marked his rise to the pinnacle of power in Washington, as virtual coequal to the President. *This was what he had waited for, had worked to achieve.*

Soon after, Coelho gave him a memo marked "personal and confidential" on a "year-end communication strategy." It argued for pressing home their advantage, pointing out, "Our chances to regain the White House will be enhanced by our ability to control the Washington story line this year." Virtually every media outlet would do an end-of-the-year wrap-up story, and those stories would make excellent vehicles for their message—that Congress had "been setting the nation's agenda since the start of the 100th Congress." *That Congress governed.* Coelho had prepared talking points on issues: Central America—polls had indicated that the administration had blundered in attacking Wright over it—the general noninvolvement of the President, fiscal responsibility, lending "a helping hand to working people."

Wright called a leadership meeting in H-201 to discuss it, and Coelho's plan was adopted enthusiastically. The best way to control the press was to feed it constantly, to so gorge it with one message that it had no room for any other. The leadership would get this message to members and staff whom reporters interviewed regularly, trying as always to get everyone to repeat the same theme so that the media inevitably echoed it.

Wright had his own way of reaching out. After the media strategy meeting he invited everyone to his office. Coelho collected all the copies of his memo and burned them in Wright's fireplace—the media would have found a good story in an effort to manipulate it. An aide put on a videotape of Wright's coming appearance on the Reverend Robert Schuller's Sunday morning television service. Wright, standing next to Schuller, filled the screen. He talked of his own preaching experience in a singsong evangelical voice, his face flushed and wearing the smile that seemed a cross between beatific and satanic. Oh, he looked filled with the spirit, beaming with the spirit; he talked of peace, sweet peace, and asked everyone to pray that President Reagan and Gorbachev would reach an arms-control agreement. He spoke about God, about his faith. His eyes glittered; they seemed bizarre and messianic and so strong as to almost frighten.

Wright's appearance lasted only a few moments. Yet there was a connection he made in those moments. There was power in those moments. Foley, Jesuit trained, and Coelho, the almost-priest, watched and then fell silent. It had stilled them.

"That's powerful," Coelho finally said. "And that audience wants to believe, unlike *Meet the Press,* whose audience is cynical."

"It shows them that Democrats are Christians, too," Foley added.

When the show ran, Russell Long watched it. Long, retired now after thirty-eight years in the Senate, the son of Huey Long, knew something of wildness and power. He turned to his wife and said, "This is the beginning of a great speakership."

George Miller saw Wright's appearance too, and said, "I like

Schuller. He tries to bring out the best in people. Still, it's such a conservative audience. Wright moved into that with that damned smile—" He laughed, shook his head. "It was the most remarkable performance I've ever seen!"

Wright seemed almost to be going from peak to peak. The candidates for the 1988 Democratic presidential nomination—the media dismissed them as "the Seven Dwarfs"—were all faltering, and some members of the House began to think seriously of drafting Wright for the presidency.

But there was a hollowness to Wright's moment of triumph.

His control was already fraying. The GOP leadership had started a bitter attack. Gingrich's campaign against him was about to burst onto front pages. Even within the Democratic Caucus there was discontent. Deep undercurrents were in play. If those undercurrents happened to merge, they could form a powerful whirlpool which could suck him under.

On the surface, only ripples had showed so far. The GOP task force which was developing responses to Wright's control of the House had decided, said Cheney, "to attack targets of opportunity, fight a guerrilla war." Its first attack: Cheney himself leaked the minority report of the House Iran-contra committee before the majority report was released, to make sure the GOP views got good play in the press. "I wouldn't have done that except for the reconciliation vote," he said. Then, with no advance notice, Republicans offered a motion to instruct trade conferees to disregard the Gephardt amendment. Gephardt wasn't even in Washington. That violated legislative courtesy on two counts—the lack of warning, and fighting over a provision when its chief sponsor could not defend it. Republicans had lost the initial floor fight 218–214; this time they lost 239–175.

There was a message: the normal rules of legislative courtesy and fair play no longer obtained. And Newt Gingrich took a "special order," to use C-SPAN TV exposure to accuse Wright of committing a criminal act—violating the two-hundred-year-old Logan Act, which prohibited interference by private citizens in foreign policy. For an hour he berated Wright, drove home his themes. And he was gearing up his other, more personal offensive.

Wright had power and power polarizes; it divides the world into court jesters who identify their interests with it, enemies who work against it, and those who use it or oppose it for their own interests. And always power is tested. Wright was about to be tested in a way O'Neill had not been.

O'Neill had come under attacks as a symbol of Democratic policy; Republicans had called him and that policy "bloated and out of control." But no one had accused him of personal wrongdoing. That wasn't the way the game was played. Traditions and personal feelings kept O'Neill safe from personal attack. Gingrich had briefly toyed with the idea of a campaign against O'Neill, had called him "corrupt" and vowed to drive him from office. But he quickly dropped his idea. He had to live in the House, eat in its dining rooms, ride in its elevators, sit in the cloakroom and on the floor. If he became an outcast, if the entire House turned on him, his daily life would become impossible, painful, filled with contempt. If other Republicans distanced themselves from him, made snide anonymous comments to the press about him, the press, too, would dismiss everything he said. But, Gingrich said, "The intensity of the distrust and dislike of Wright is radically different than it was of Tip."

Inside the House, the reconciliation vote and Wright's aggressiveness in Central America had rubbed raw traditions of the House which protected him, and every other member, from personal attack. Republicans weren't going to defend Jim Wright. Gingrich observed, "Two things were explosive. Reconciliation and his meeting with Ortega, particularly the symbolism of meeting him on Veterans Day. That drove respectable Republicans like Cheney off the wall. I'd have gone forward anyway but it would have been much more difficult."

To the GOP leadership, Gingrich had become useful. Recognizing how useful, he noted disdainfully, "They were quite willing for *me* to do this. No one asked me to stop."

Outside the House, Wright faced even greater antipathy. Conservative activists had seen O'Neill as an incarnation of Democratic control of the Congress, to some extent just a figurehead. Wright was more than that. Wright had marked himself not only as an enemy of conservatives but as a threat. Wright's Nicaraguan involvement had created a hostility that went deeper than any of Gingrich's accusations. Congress, and congressmen, have few institutional defenders. The presidency has a legion of them. Wright had awakened that legion. That added a higher pitch to Gingrich's resonance. It alerted them to his message.

Coelho's media strategy was a good one, but it could not match Gingrich's intensity and focus.

You just keep pounding away, he had said. *There comes a point when it just takes off, or it dies.*

From Canetti's *Crowds and Power: The crowd needs a direction. . . . it will accept any goal. . . . Crowd crystals are the small, rigid groups of men, strictly delimited and of great constancy. . . . The crowd crystal is constant. . . . Their role must be familiar; people must know what they are there for. . . . Individual crowd crystals precipitate crowds. . . . Crowd crystals may, for a time, withdraw into the background, lose something of their edge . . . [but] the return of the moment when they are needed is as certain as the appearance of new crowds.*

All through the summer and fall Gingrich had been working. Back in July, just before forcing the floor vote demanding that the ethics committee reopen its investigation of St Germain, he had maneuvered Common Cause's Fred Wertheimer into joining in the attack, writing him twice. Eight days after the second detailed letter asking him to call for an investigation of several House Democrats, including Wright and Coelho, Wertheimer had written the ethics committee and attacked it for having "abdicated its responsibility." He did demand that the committee investigate members on Gingrich's list, except Wright and Coelho.

Since then Gingrich had patiently prepared for a long-term campaign against Wright. The day Congress recessed for the summer, a supporter had sent him a memo saying, "The vote on reopening the ethics investigation of St Germain . . . strikes a rich vein that can be mined for Party advantage in regaining Congressional numbers and influence." When Congress returned from recess, Daniel Swillinger, an attorney and ally, wrote: "*What is your strategy for the ethics issue over the long-term?* [italics his] i.e., how often should [Pennsylvania Republican Congressman Robert] Walker offer his [ethics] resolution? What Democratic members should have FEC and ethics filings scrutinized? Is there a better way than filing a complaint [with the ethics committee]?"

With reporters, Gingrich portrayed himself as concerned with corruption. In his freshman year in Congress he had attracted media attention by seeking the expulsion from the House of Democrat Charles Diggs, who had been convicted of financial misdeeds (and ultimately resigned), and he had later called for the expulsion of two members who had had sex with teenage pages. But Van Brocklin, who began working virtually full time on investigating Wright beginning in April, said, "Other than that, I don't think Newt did anything with ethics until St Germain and Wright."

Gingrich sent a copy of Swillinger's memo, as he did with other things, to Joseph Gaylord, who ran the GOP House campaign committee. And he began to execute his long-term strategy for turning the press to his purposes.

In September and October, he tried to sell his theme to people like Norman Ornstein, the single political scientist most often quoted by the media on Congress. He also contacted media heavyweights such as ABC's Ted Koppel; Jason McManus, the editor-in-chief of *Time* magazine; and the editors of CBS's *60 Minutes*. To Ben Bradlee, editor of *The Washington Post,* he complained that the *Post* had missed a major story on House corruption, particularly on St Germain. Bradlee wrote a note saying, "Dear Newt, You are right. How's that for an upfront confession of error? . . . *The Wall Street Journal* owns that story. Despite my heroic efforts, the *Post* reporters are very reluctant to swing in after someone else has broken a story. We should go after it, and we will." Bradlee, and soon thereafter *Post* editorial-page editor and *Newsweek* columnist Meg Greenfield, were among those who received Gingrich's file of negative stories on Wright. Greenfield was a favorite of Gingrich's; he advised colleagues to contact her and use his name.

Gingrich's packet was only one of many which media figures received every day from people wanting them to publicize their cause. But Gingrich was a member of Congress, an articulate and highly intelligent one. He was more persistent. What he said was more disturbing. His material was read by his targets, not screened out by a secretary.

While he sowed seeds among heavyweights, he simultaneously pursued an alternative route. Story ideas travel in two directions, from national to local, and the reverse. If a story appeared often enough in different local media, eventually national reporters would pick it up. Then, when something national did appear, it would rekindle local interest, and yield another story, or perhaps an editorial. And local markets were easier to crack; a congressman, even an out-of-town congressman, was a bigger deal locally than in Washington. "I'm trying to create a resonance out there," he explained. "When something moves on the wire there will be echoes."

As relentless as Wright was in exercising power, Gingrich was more relentless in pursuing it. He built a network of resonance in every possible public outlet. Chase Manhattan Bank chief executive Willard Butcher had made a speech on ethics. Radio commentator Paul Harvey had talked about it on the air. Owen Frisby, a lobbyist for the bank, sent Gingrich a transcript of Harvey's remarks. Gingrich wrote to Frisby and Butcher asking, "Let me know what you think of the pattern of ongoing corruption in the U.S. House of Representatives."

The Reverend Schuller, naively assuming Gingrich and Wright were "Christian brothers" despite political differences, wrote Gingrich a note referring to Wright's appearance. Gingrich sent back a blistering letter condemning Wright and reciting his allegations.

Wherever Gingrich traveled for a speech—and he traveled often around the country—he would talk about corruption in the House, and the corruption of Jim Wright. He told his audiences to write letters to the editors of their local newspapers, to call in on talk shows, to demand answers from their local congressmen in public meetings, *What are you doing about Jim Wright?* And he told people to write Common Cause.

He sought out local political and investigative reporters or editorial writers, and urged them to look into Wright. Perhaps the local paper would write an editorial condemning the way Jim Wright ran the House, or, better yet, about corruption in the House, or about Wright himself. Perhaps local reporters would raise the issue with local congressmen. Perhaps they would write about Wright's affairs.

Gingrich both repeated his now-old line, "Jim Wright is the most corrupt Speaker in the twentieth century"—the comment had an authoritative, academic precision to it that lent it credibility—and escalated it. Typical was a story in the *Miami Herald,* which ran the same November week that Wright seemed so triumphant. It was a perfect example of how he used the media.

Gingrich had given a speech to a local Republican group, which in advance had called Tom Fiedler, the paper's political editor, and arranged an interview. That much was routine. But it was not routine for Gingrich to come to the paper, come to Fiedler. "You almost always go see the person you're interviewing," Fiedler said. "I think he had another meeting with the editorial board. That's why he came here."

According to the paper's records, Gingrich didn't have such a meeting. He simply went to see Fiedler, and attacked Wright personally, on the record, in words that would violate House rules if voiced on the floor.

Fiedler's story quoted Gingrich's now-routine comment that Wright was the most corrupt Speaker in the twentieth century, and some variations: " 'Wright is so consumed by his own power that he is like Mussolini. . . . We have overwhelming evidence that this is a genuinely bad man . . . money laundering [on his book] . . . a genuinely corrupt man.' " The story also said that "Wright, according to published accounts, used his influence to block federal investigations into the lending practices of friends and supporters." That statement was false. The article added, "Gingrich said his charges are based on numerous news accounts." Many of those news accounts Gingrich had generated.

The *Miami Herald* was arguably the best paper in the South. After Fiedler wrote his story, his national editor did not want to run it. It included no news, only Gingrich's quotes. The editor asked why the paper should allow itself to be used by a member of the minority party who naturally wanted to undermine Wright. Fiedler later recalled, "I said that congressmen did not say such things about other congressmen, much less about the Speaker. The fact that one congressman would attack the Speaker, the brutality of the quote, that was a significant part of the news value."

It was all of the "news value." Gingrich's charges were headlined and circulated throughout Florida, and in a limited way in Washington through the Knight-Ridder bureau; other editors and reporters read it. It created resonance. As journalistic ethics required, Fiedler called Wright's office for a response, and quoted an aide weakly insisting that Wright "has had no personal gain from his duties."

The number-one fact about the news media is that they love fights, Gingrich had said. *When you give them confrontations you get attention.*

Gingrich's aide Van Brocklin immediately added this *Herald* story to the clip file as further evidence of Wright's corruption.

Gingrich said, "My technique is simple. If I can get the news media focused, he will become so expensive for the Democratic Party, it will keep him out of the chair [of the 1988 Democratic Convention]."

Even if his effort failed, raising the issue deflected attention from the "sleaze factor"—the criminal convictions of former Reagan aides Michael Deaver and Lyn Nofziger and former deputy Defense secretary Paul Thayer, the acquittal of former Labor secretary Raymond Donovan, and the ongoing ethics problems of Attorney General Edwin Meese. On November 30, Gingrich wrote Iowa GOP congressman Tom Tauke and suggested, "An Iowa-focused effort the first week or ten days of January on whether Jim Wright is too corrupt to be chairman of the Democratic National Convention would be *very helpful*" [his italics].

The national press would be swarming over Iowa in early January, getting ready for the presidential caucuses a few weeks later.

As Coelho had predicted, most major publications were preparing stories about Wright. Two *Washington Post* reporters were working on a story. Two *Los Angeles Times* reporters were working on a story. *Business Week*, *Newsweek*, *The New York Times*, NBC, and a host of regional papers were doing pieces. Coelho's hoped-for message might get out, but almost all the stories would also include a quote from Gingrich on Wright's ethics, helping Gingrich build resonance. And a magazine called *Regardie's* appeared in late November; Gingrich would give it readership far beyond that which was usual. Wright had thought that setting up his blind trust would moot references to his finances. He was wrong.

The *Post* story focused on Congress and policy; it described him as "a political lone ranger." It spoke of his emergence as "Washington's number-one Democrat" and the "dramatic shift" in the role of the Speaker. It added that "as of last week Wright appeared to be succeeding beyond all expectations." But it raised questions about his isolation.

The day after the *Post* story, *Newsweek* arrived. This was the piece for which reporters had dug deep into Fort Worth, deep into Wright's personal finances, deep into city council memos—"They probably got them from me," Gingrich's aide Van Brocklin said. "I talked to them several times and gave them what I had." By now she had become a clearinghouse, a central locus to whom Wright's enemies—like Assistant Commerce Secretary Orson Swindle III, who resented Wright's earmarking for Fort Worth economic development money he controlled—sent damaging information.

The title of *Newsweek*'s story read, "Jim Wright: Pork Barrel Politician as Statesman/A Speaker Dogged by Questions of Impropriety." It portrayed Wright as powerful but also devious and sinister: "Wright's drive for statesmanship is clouded by continuing questions of conflicts of interest . . . a series of questions about dubious connections between Wright's private interests and public office."

Yet for all the innuendo, the story noted that "reporters searched in vain for a possibly illegal quid pro quo" for any of the favors Wright did for people, and reporter Mark Miller later conceded, "If we had found any evidence of Wright benefiting improperly, we'd have printed it. We didn't. But there was the appearance of impropriety."

The most damaging story, though, appeared in *Regardie's,* a local Washington magazine run by Bill Regardie. Regardie wore open-necked shirts and gold chains, ate "power lunches" at Duke Zeibert's, and tried to use his magazine to get attention and shake Washington up. Normally, it had no impact on, and little readership among, those who dealt in power. But Gingrich would distribute copies of this story to every member of the House and to the national press corps.

The story was entitled "The Speaker and the Sleaze/The Story of How Two Good Old Boys from the Lone Star State—One Who Loved Power and One Who Loved Money—Tried to Corrupt the Thrift Industry." The "sleaze" was Donald Dixon, the operator of the Vernon Savings and Loan; he had five airplanes, $2 million a year in income, a mansion on the California beach paid for by the S&L, and a yacht which was the sister ship to the former presidential yacht *Sequoia* docked in Washington (which Coelho used for fund-raisers), while 96 percent of his S&L's loans were in default.

The story wove Dixon's and Wright's histories together, implying that they were old conspirators: "The story of Wright and Dixon is a story of greed and selfishness, of the abuse of power and wealth, of the perversion of democracy . . . of [Wright's] old-fashioned venality, financial murkiness, conflicts of interest, oily opportunism, and abuse of power. . . . Wright and Dixon have much in common. . . . The Justice Department is trying to figure out what they both were up to."

But Wright did not know the man, nor was Wright being investigated. He had no social or business or political relationship with Dixon. Dixon had never even made a campaign contribution to him, although he had to the DCCC. A later investigation which searched for a connection discovered only that Wright had been introduced to Dixon once at a DCCC fund-raiser, but Wright did not remember him. At Coelho's request, Wright had spoken to Dixon, once, on the telephone. Wright had then called Ed Gray, the head of the Federal Home Loan Bank Board, reciting the routine boilerplate language every congressman uses to protect himself—*I don't know anything about the merits. I'm just telling you what he told me, and I wonder if you could check into it*— and repeating to Gray Dixon's story.

That was the whole of Wright's involvement with Dixon. *Regardie's* played it differently. The writers, William Adler and Michael Binstein, based their story on one key meeting between regulators and Wright which had occurred on February 10 that year. They portrayed it inaccurately, misstated verifiable facts, and skirted with the legal definition of plagiarism by copying without attribution, and distorting, information from other stories. They also recited virtually every allegation of improper behavior that Gingrich had ever made against Wright.

The story reported that Wright "summoned" the regulators to the meeting. Actually, the regulators had requested it, to lobby Wright on their position, and even asked Bob Strauss to set it up. *Regardie's* also said that regulators "wanted to shut down Vernon S&L but needed Wright's help to do it," that Wright had instead demanded that they "extend forbearance . . . to Donald Dixon's Vernon S&L." Yet the only time Dixon or his S&L had been discussed was, briefly, when a regulator raised Vernon to explain why they had taken control of it months earlier. A state regulator was acting as its chief executive officer, physically occupying Dixon's old office and making all decisions. They did not ask Wright about closing it, nor did Wright ask for forbearance for it or any other individual S&L.

The magazine's editor, Brian Kelly, later conceded that the story had distorted the relationship between Wright and Dixon, and privately apologized to another writer for lifting and distorting information from his story about Wright. Gingrich was not quoted in the piece. But for months his charges against Wright had been circulating, creating an atmosphere—*atmosphere was resonance, wasn't it?* Without this atmosphere, would Kelly have demanded radical changes in the story before printing it?

Gingrich made good use of the article, circulating it to the Washington press corps. He also sent it and his other material to Republican National Committee chairman Frank Fahrenkopf, suggesting that, in the official GOP publication *First Monday* which was distributed to GOP activists and political reporters, "a four-page middle section [on Wright] quoting public sources would be very powerful, would arm our partisans with the facts, and would have a significant effect on the news media."

Coelho had aimed his media strategy at the year-end wrap-up stories. Now, even if his strategy worked perfectly, at best it would amount to damage control. Wright had a problem, and it was serious.

The title of *The Wall Street Journal*'s year-end summary read: "Wright's First Year Yields Successes but His Integrity Continues to Be Questioned." The story credited him with legislative victories but quoted Gingrich calling him "a genuinely corrupt man," and referred to allegations in *Regardie's*. Gingrich promptly began saying that one of the most respected papers in America, *The Wall Street Journal*, was calling Wright's ethics into question.

Publications were now quoting other publications, and Gingrich was quoting both, trying to build a self-sustaining reaction. Members, themselves often victims of distortions, give relatively little credence to personal attacks appearing in the press. But a certain tremor, a certain low-pitched vibration, was beginning to be felt in the House. Even that was uncomfortable; if it increased it could become dangerous.

A thin line divides innocence and arrogance. A small child has both. The child believes the world centers on the self, and refuses to recognize limits on what one can expect and demand from it. As one matures, innocence and arrogance become distinguishable.

Innocence itself divides into two kinds, one depending upon experience and one depending upon expectation. The role of experience is self-evident. But people can remain innocent, regardless of their experience, their expectations; they can, like the small child, face the world openly and remain vulnerable to it. Most men and women, usually because of pain and failure they have suffered, lose this kind of innocence and accept the limits of the world. Some do not. Some continue, even if naively, to hope.

Arrogance assumes that one can do almost anything, either because one can get away with it or—when it resembles and is a kind of innocence—because what one does must be all right. Part of the corruption of idealism, the corruption of power, stems from the blurring of innocence and arrogance, and the confusion of expectation and demand.

As that affirmation which Wright had carried around in his pocket until the paper wore away said, *If they think they do not like me, it is because they do not know me.* That was innocent in its expectation, arrogant in the demand it placed on the world to understand him. And he expected it to understand him on his own terms. Yet the world judges on its own terms, and is not so understanding.

Appearances were important; public trust in institutions depended on appearances. At the very least, Wright's insensitivity to appearances had justifiably called public—and media—faith in him into question. Wright had given Gingrich something to work with. The press was wondering, *Is there something more?*

In early December, Wright held a meeting to talk about the press. Invited were Charles Conconi, a gossip columnist at *The Washington Post* who was a friend of Wright's wife, Betty; Joseph Canzeri, who had handled embarrassments for Nelson Rockefeller and whom Conconi had suggested; Kirk O'Donnell, the former O'Neill aide who now ran the Democratic think tank Center for National Policy; Wright's two aides Marshall Lynam and Phil Duncan, who were most familiar with his Fort Worth and personal affairs; and newly hired press aide George Mair. Conconi's presence was a likely conflict of interest.

Wright wanted to respond to the allegations. He was advised to ride it out. O'Donnell pointed out that O'Neill had had similar problems his first term as Speaker. The *Boston Herald* had embarked on a crusade to get him. *The New York Times* had put his financial transactions on the front page. Then the stories had disappeared. Speakers were simply targets. He should go after inaccuracies hard but otherwise keep his eye on the big picture. Don't act as if it were getting to him. The charges had no substance. The media would stop reporting them. A response would just create another round of stories, give the press a chance to repeat the charges. Gingrich was just looking for a confrontation. They argued that his 1984 confrontation with O'Neill, his ninety seconds on all the network news shows, had made him.

The advice wasn't what Wright wanted to hear, but he took it.

No one in the room had understood Gingrich's determination and sophistication about the media.

Meanwhile, the House roiled.

The House didn't feel right. One could walk down the corridors, walk onto the floor, and sense uneasiness, restiveness, even anger. It wasn't anything one could isolate and say, *There!* But members seemed more into themselves; on the elevators they nodded at one another instead of talking. They came to the floor for votes and left quickly, instead of lingering. There was less mixing in the chamber of Republicans and Democrats. Cheney had always enjoyed talking with Foley on the floor, but had not talked to him since the reconciliation vote.

The continuing resolution, which combined in one bill all appropriations bills to run the government for the next year, set off more sparks. House Democrats, and Wright, were using it to seize power once more. In theory, the budget agreement should have allowed the C.R. to pass easily with a bipartisan vote. Theory did not mesh with reality.

The collision came over the fairness doctrine, which required broadcasters to give equal time to differing political opinions. Earlier in the year the Federal Communications Commission had revoked it. Democrats feared that that would allow conservative owners of small-town radio stations to attack them nonstop. In June, Congress had passed a bill writing the fairness doctrine into law. Reagan had vetoed it. Congress lacked the votes to override it, so House Democrats stuck it in the C.R.

That amounted to overriding a veto without the needed two-thirds vote. Republicans were infuriated. It was one more indication of Democrats', and Wright's, willingness to use power. "You think the President is going to sign this kind of continuing resolution?" Michel demanded on the floor. "Of course not!"

There were partisan games. Just after the reconciliation vote, Republicans had run full-page newspaper ads around the country entitled "Hall of Shame," accusing Democrats of voting for a tax increase to raise their own pay—the automatic cost-of-living raise. Now came revenge. Democrats knew Republicans would vote against the C.R. rule because of the fairness doctrine. To embarrass them, Democrats included a provision which killed the pay raise. Thus a vote against the rule was a vote *for* the pay raise. "I love it," Coelho laughed. Jim Chapman was singled out to get his name attached to the amendment; leading the fight against a pay raise helped back home and Wright owed him.

Democrats voted for the rule 299–14; Republicans voted against it 163–7. And they passed the C.R. 248–170, with twenty-three Republicans voting yes, twenty-one Democrats voting no.

It seemed like old times, with Wright in firm control of the House. But it wasn't old times.

Seventy-nine Democrats wrote Wright a letter complaining about Rules Committee restrictions on amendments. *Seventy-nine!* Yes, the moderates and conservatives from the South had signed the letter. But so had Mike Lowry, chairman of the liberal DSG, from Washington State. And Pat Williams had signed. *Pat Williams.* People like that signing a protest letter to the Speaker? *Something wasn't right.* The whole feel of the House was wrong, sour, distasteful.

The letter threatened Wright more than anything Gingrich had done. His office, the brass balls in their box on his desk, all the Speaker's Rooms were useless without votes; that was power. *The only thing that counts up here is votes. Everything else is bullshit.*

As disturbing as the letter itself was the fact that the discontent had not been sensed or communicated in some less formal way than a letter. It indicated a dangerous separation between the leadership and the membership. That gap had to be closed. Wright wanted every single member who had signed the letter contacted, wanted to know why each had signed, what it meant.

The immediate spark for the letter was welfare reform. Again. Tom Downey still wanted a closed rule, which prohibited any amendment except a Republican substitute. A closed rule would block a vote on a proposal sponsored by Tom Carper and backed by Stenholm and most of the MacKay group, halfway between Downey's bill and the GOP's. Downey feared it could pass. Ways and Means routinely got closed rules; Rules went along with Downey.

The justification for giving Ways and Means' closed rules was based on the importance, and possible unintended consequences, of tax balls. If the House passed an amendment on taxes which had not been thoroughly examined, it might inadvertently damage business, whole industries, even the economy. But welfare reform was not a tax bill. In one of MacKay's meetings, an Armed Services member complained, "My committee handles complex, technical legislation too. But we faced two hundred amendments. Downey led the way demanding them on arms control. Why the hell does Ways and Means get none? What makes those people think they're gods?"

Bonoir and Martin Frost, both on Rules, reported to Wright that the members were just fed up, and particularly resentful of Ways and Means' privileges. Wright listened, reassured. Maybe he could turn even the restiveness to his advantage. He nodded, then said, "If Ways and Means is going to claim the right to hunt in the king's forest, it has a responsibility to look after the king's deer. These members get on Ways and Means and think they have become lords of the Earth."

If his Rules Committee was going to give Ways and Means a closed rule, then Ways and Means had a responsibility to give him legislation he liked. *It was the old English concept again, of "King and Commons" against the nobles and the middle class.* He was king; if needed at some future time, he could direct the Caucus against Ways and Means.

For now he tried to make both Ways and Means and the Caucus happy. Coelho sat Carper and Downey down in his office, and Downey offered to shave $1 billion off his bill. But if he did, how many votes could Carper promise? Carper promised only his own. That wasn't enough. No deal. But Downey would still cut $500 million from his bill.

The pressure was not released. The bill was scheduled for December 10. But the count was close. Wright declared, "I don't want to go unless we're going to win. Steny, what do you figure?"

Steny Hoyer was running the whip task force. "We're close but we're not there yet."

The leadership pulled the bill from the schedule. It was the third time. Republicans grew even more frustrated; they literally could not win. If Democratic leaders weren't confident of passing a bill, they simply pulled it from the schedule until they could pass it. Wright got on the phone to ask for votes. Downey brought Bill Clinton, the Arkansas governor who had chaired the National Governors' Association welfare reform task force, in for lunch with twenty southern Democrats. Buddy Roemer, still in the House though just elected Louisiana governor, convinced state colleagues to support it. Other governors called their members.

Even Russo suddenly reappeared in the task force meetings. No one said anything about his vote on reconciliation, about his absence from earlier task force meetings. On the surface it was as if he had never been away. But history lay under the surface: *the past is never over, it isn't even past; forgive and forget but always remember.* "This is the last big vote of the year," Russo said. "Let's get these guys."

The House remained tense. Wright was its focus, his control its issue. Republicans erupted in bitter hostility on December 10. While the GOP Conference was meeting to discuss welfare reform, Dick Cheney interrupted and angrily announced he had just learned that Democrats planned to extend the life of the Iran-contra investigating committee through 1988. He was furious, and called it "outrageous, pure electioneering" to embarrass Republicans during a presidential election year. (Actually, Democrats wanted the extension because the White House was withholding delivery of promised documents; a bipartisan compromise was easily worked out—later.) The Republicans in the Conference were furious. Suddenly Gingrich rose. "I'll offer a privileged motion to investigate the Speaker!"

Such a vote would lead the news on every network. It would spark a whole round of print stories, of weekend television commentaries. Gingrich was announcing just how rough he intended to play.

It was his first, calculated semipublic testing of the waters among GOP colleagues, not an emotional outburst. Would his colleagues turn on him? Isolate him? No one shouted, "Let's do it!" But neither did anyone tell him to shut up. *Maybe Wright deserves it. Maybe the son of a bitch deserves it.* Gingrich would proceed—but on his own schedule.

When the House convened, before Republicans realized Democrats had meant nothing sinister by their Iran-contra committee action, Republicans immediately moved, and voted 167–0, to adjourn.

Wright was the House's focus, his control its issue. Even the Democratic Caucus seemed to be trying to shake free. Wright struggled to reassert control by both soothing and threatening it.

He did favors: Arms-control activists sought his help and he immediately did help, telling Bill Chappell, the Appropriations defense subcommittee chairman, to keep the Midgetman missile program alive. (Midgetman was a missile which moved away from the strategic doctrine most conservatives preferred.) The reassurance was more subtle.

He reassured: Lou Harris had given Wright some new poll numbers, excellent ones for Democrats. Wright cited those numbers to colleagues in meetings, on the floor, relaxing on a sofa in the cloakroom. At the same moment the GOP Conference was erupting in outrage, Wright and Coelho cited the poll to the regular December 10 whip meeting and congratulated the fifty members present on having won every single vote of consequence that year.

There was something almost desperate in his recitation of these numbers. They were his answer to the protest letter signed by seventy-nine Democrats. On the question "Which party do you prefer to handle the deficit?" two years earlier the GOP had led 52 percent–37 percent; now Democrats led 47 percent–40 percent. On cutting unemployment, the GOP had led 46 percent–44 percent; now Democrats led 55 percent–

36 percent. On inspiring more confidence, the GOP had led 52 percent–38 percent; now Democrats led 52 percent–36 percent. Republicans still led on maintaining a strong defense, but Democrats had narrowed even that margin. *See?* Wright now seemed to be saying. *See? I'm doing all right.* One colleague noted, "Wright's a pretty clever guy. This poll he's carrying around with him and showing everyone, he's using it to quiet the restiveness."

And he threatened: South Carolina's Butler Derrick approached him with an idea. Derrick was angry that only a few weeks earlier Lindsay Thomas had gotten a seat on Appropriations, a plum assignment; now Thomas was balking at supporting welfare reform. Members fought hard to get appointed to good committees, but once on a committee they were automatically reappointed. Derrick suggested that all assignments be made tentative for a member's first term on a committee; only after it would reappointment become automatic. Such a change would shift tremendous power to the Speaker, back toward that of Joe Cannon. Cannon had seen his power, and the power of future Speakers, stripped from him in a rebellion against his autocracy, and soon resigned.

Wright liked the idea. Earlier he had complained, "You get good Democrats going on committees like Ways and Means but they play golf with lobbyists, go to dinner with them, go on vacation with them. All of a sudden they're not good Democrats." (He was right. An aide to one Ways and Means member said, "He thinks one or two lobbyists are the only people who understand him. That matters a hell of a lot more than a campaign check.") Derrick's proposal would give a Speaker two more years of control. He would raise it at a Steering and Policy meeting. It was a tough, hardball move, and would leave no doubt the leadership was determined to maintain discipline.

Wright convened the meeting and Derrick made his suggestion.

A debate quickly erupted over what constituted "party policy," the standard by which members would be judged. One man suggested that since procedural votes determined who controlled the House, all votes on rules should be party votes.

"That's crazy," another man whispered to a colleague. Hadn't seventy-nine Democrats from all across the party just sent Wright a letter complaining that rules were too restrictive already?

"Why do we need this?" Rostenkowski demanded.

"Members of your own committee have deserted the leadership at key moments," Wright replied. Russo was sitting directly in front of him.

"Mr. Speaker," Norm Dicks protested. "Just this morning at the whip meeting you were telling us that we haven't lost a single vote the leadership cared about this year. Why then is all this necessary?"

To show how tough the leadership was.

Wright appointed a task force to study Derrick's idea (it would never report). But after the meeting word of the proposal spread quickly across the floor. The rumor alone served Wright's and Coelho's purpose: it was warning enough that the stakes were being raised. If someone wanted to rebel, the leadership would respond in kind. In theory, it wasn't a bad idea—the carrot and the stick. But was this the time to threaten the stick?

That Thursday, while word of the Steering and Policy discussion spread, so did word that Gingrich had threatened to demand an investigation of the Speaker.

Friday Wright hosted one more lunch in the Speaker's Dining Room. The meeting was about power. Wright was worried that his could erode. While tourists and members crowded into the Members' Dining Room across the hall, he sat down with a dozen colleagues, his closest staff, and Kirk O'Donnell. The men in the room were loyal to him, yes, but were not simply loyalists. John Dingell, Barney Frank, Dave McCurdy, Marvin Leath, Bill Hefner, Beryl Anthony, and Steny Hoyer were there, among others. Each had his own agenda, and among them they supplied much of the backbone of the House.

Wright wanted the meeting intimate, did not invite Foley, Coelho, or Bonior, and asked everyone to keep the lunch confidential. First he reviewed the details of his involvement in the savings and loan issue. That mattered: reassurance would filter through the House that no surprises were coming, nothing would explode in members' faces later if they supported the Speaker now. Then he asked how badly the press stories were hurting him.

There was an awkward moment, followed by a rush of reassurance. "No one's talking about it, Mr. Speaker, not on the floor, not in the cloakroom." "Everyone knows it's politically motivated." "For God's sake, don't let it get under your hide." One member even declared, "If the ethics rules are a problem for you, we'll change the damn ethics rules!"

That comment was not well received. But the consensus was, Do nothing. The press was writing the same story over and over and over as it was. They would have to stop. Any response just gave the press a new reason to write the story. It was nothing.

Brian Donnelly and Pat Williams disagreed. They warned that the charges could become a real problem, although this very meeting indicated he was heading the problem off. They were isolated even in that view.

Others dismissed it out of hand. One of the attendees commented later, "Frankly, I was appalled that the Speaker called the meeting. He raised it to a level it should not be at."

Another attendee said after the meeting, "The way to handle this is to gut Gingrich. Do it once and do it right and leave him hanging out there for all to see."

While everyone advised Wright to do nothing, Gingrich acted. The following Wednesday, Gingrich sent out a "Dear Colleague" to every member of the House, proposing an investigation of Wright, and including the *Regardie's* story and a five-page collection of negative quotes from *Newsweek, The Wall Street Journal, The Washington Post,* and other papers. He also held a press conference and released the "Dear Colleague." At the press conference he attacked Wright viciously, particularly on his savings and loan involvement and his book, and demanded that the House Committee on Standards of Official Conduct, the formal name for the ethics committee, investigate Wright.

A member of Congress calling for an investigation of the Speaker of the House was news. For Gingrich, it created another, major opportunity to recite the accusations and create doubt about Wright.

Gingrich's press conference and "Dear Colleague" added a chill to the House. MacKay said, "*Regardie's* has to make you wonder. There are other things. Stenholm agreed to support the budget in return for help on cutting appropriations. He was screwed. I felt we were all doing pretty well until July or August, but since then I've been finessed. I'm not sure how. Never have I seen as much difference between what I'm being told we've done this year up here—how great it's been, how much we've accomplished—and what my constituents say back home. If more people than I feel this way, he's in trouble."

Others did feel that way. One Wright ally said, "People tell Wright no one's talking about this. That's true, but only because it's an unwritten rule about not making negative comments about colleagues. These backbenchers, a lot of them are more moral than the guys making all the speeches. They sit there saying nothing, but if a problem comes up they'll get you."

Another Democrat, already an enemy of Wright, complained, "Wright doesn't let these guys play. He's got his fucking agenda. That's it. The leadership's got to understand, these guys have to play. In a democracy you should be allowed amendments on the floor. If someone ever decided to fuck Wright he's in trouble. There's so much unrest it's unbelievable."

Wright sat at breakfast after Gingrich's announcement with a cool anger, an anger reflective of pain. "If I'm attacked I want to respond," he said. "If colleagues had heaped opprobrium on Gingrich, I'd be satisfied. But they haven't. The only way he'll stop is pressure from his colleagues."

His instinct about collegial pressure was right. Gingrich was sensitive to it, alert to it; he did not want to destroy himself. But among Republicans he had become a big man. He was taking on Wright and Wright had rammed bills down their throat and usurped the role of secretary of State.

"I've watched colleagues' body language toward me," he said. "It's actually improved. If I had gone after O'Neill this hard, I would have been a social outcast. . . . Wright should get a solid 'A' for performance. As a technician of power, he's done a great job. The downside is, he's a loner still. There's no deep body of affection for him. Being a loner eliminates a safety net of both information and goodwill."

Some members had in fact jumped to Wright's defense. Others believed the best strategy was silence, that Gingrich wanted a confrontation.

Yet it was not Gingrich who seemed isolated, but Wright. It hurt him. It burned in him. He *would* act. His staff had recently decided to prepare a white paper to answer all the charges in detail. But that would take a month, and he had just watched a segment on *Good Morning America* about the criminal trials of Reagan intimates Mike Deaver and Lyn Nofziger. Three times a Republican had thrown Wright's name into the conversation, and the Democrat had not responded. Wright wanted to take the floor to respond.

"Find me parliamentary justification in the *Regardie's* story to claim a point of personal privilege," he told his senior staff at breakfast. They had been there for over an hour; the coffee in the thermos-like pots had turned cold. Wright's voice was cold, too, and definite. A point of personal privilege would give him one hour of floor time. "You tell me not to respond to Gingrich? I'll respond to the story, not to him. My colleagues have not been given the information with which to defend me. You folks talked me out of writing a letter to *Regardie's*. You'll try to talk me out of this."

There was something, again, innocent about his desire. To him the floor was sacred. He often spoke of one incident when a member had questioned another's word, and Rayburn, red-faced and bull-necked, had spat, "The chair never questions the word of a member!" It was almost as if Wright thought if he spoke on the floor his colleagues, Republicans as well as Democrats, would crowd around him afterwards, saying, *Oh, Mr. Speaker, we're so sorry, how could we have ever doubted your integrity?* He was Speaker of this entire institution, not simply leader of House Democrats. He knew there was a fury out there on the floor; he wanted to lay his hands on the members with words, let those words sink into the very seats, let those words calm the fury, and resurrect all his power.

"Mr. Speaker," an aide said, "we *will* try to talk you out of it. Not one member is talking about this crap. They don't give it any credence."

"Mr. Speaker, please. If you must do something, do it in a Caucus, not the floor. Please, not with cameras, television, reporters."

All day long staff and colleagues told him, don't make an issue, the stories would go away. At least wait until the white paper was finished and they had all the facts, marshaled definitively, to rebut things once and for all. Finally Wright agreed. But he would write a letter to the editor of *Regardie's*.

Even that move most of his advisers opposed. *Just let the damn thing lie.* When one friend of Wright's mentioned to Coelho that, regardless of what people were telling Wright, members were asking about it, Coelho said, "If the stories stop will they be asking about it in six weeks?"

But Gingrich would do everything he could to keep the stories coming. Now the world knew he was going after Wright. More than ever his office acted as a clearinghouse. Anyone with anything negative about Wright contacted it, from Fort Worth, from anywhere in the government, from anywhere in the country. Van Brocklin then called investigative reporters with the leads to check out. Gingrich said, "I talk routinely with investigative reporters. They call me and I call them."

The House at night, in the cold of December. Lights shining on the Capitol make the white marble luminescent. The great white dome atop Capitol Hill visible for miles. One stands close to the buildings and feels the cold radiating from the immense, thick sandstone columns. One stands there and feels the chill, the chill of power. Great large blocks of stone and marble, cool even in summer. Yet the building so lit up that it simultaneously has the homey feel of a Christmas tree, and, always alive, always people about, as vibrant as Times Square but different from there, too. Here everyone—cops, chaplain, staff, members—knows everyone. As cold and impersonal as history, yet home.

Wright needed peace. Events swirled and eddied around him, threatened him, threatened his power. Gorbachev had arrived for his summit with Reagan. At the White House state dinner, Dobrynin had told Wright that if the United States complied with the Central American peace agreement, the Soviets would withdraw all heavy weapons from Nicaragua, down to the level of police pistols. Wright had raised the question with Gorbachev the next day; he had confirmed that he would speak to Reagan about the issue. Wright had just sent a memo to Shultz asking him to pursue it. Peace. That's what he wanted. Peace.

He was planning a trip with his wife, Betty, and several members to the Holy Land for Christmas. Christmas and peace. In the afternoon, after the lunch talking about his difficulties, he called one member to invite him and his wife. The member declined. He wanted to be with his kids.

History? another member observed. *You hope what you do matters to someone, helps someone, but this history stuff is crap. Who will remember any of this in fifteen years, much less one hundred and fifty? History? History is your children.*

Wright looked out the window for an instant, this man who wanted so much to root himself in time, tracing backward to find his lost Irish ancestors, and forward. Then he said softly to the member who wanted to stay home with his kids, "You're absolutely right. I lived in dread the children would grow up and not know me. Thank God it's not that way."

But Wright had a different view of what history was.

CHAPTER 20

Wright had no peace. The priorities he had fought for all year were being written into law in the continuing resolution, the C.R., which appropriated $600 billion, and in reconciliation, which raised taxes and cut entitlements. He and the President would meet in their final collision of the year. He could not allow the House to cool, and rebuild his power. At stake *was* power. Both the House and the White House were trying to seize it.

The House was demanding that the already-vetoed fairness doctrine be included in the C.R. If it became a tiny part of the mammoth C.R. and the President signed it, Congress would in effect have overridden a presidential veto without the required two-thirds vote. The action marked a new reach for power by Wright and the Congress and could set a precedent.

The White House was reaching for power, too. In the final confrontation of the budget summit, Jim Baker had demanded that OMB chief Jim Miller pass judgment on the legislation implementing the agreement. Wright had angrily refused and had issued his own demand—that the agreement stipulate that implementation be by "the regular legislative process." The White House had agreed. At the time, Foley had remarked, "I was frankly surprised that Baker caved in so readily."

The reason: the White House was reaching a private agreement with Senate Democrats. To guarantee passage of the Senate reconciliation bill, Democratic senators had agreed to use OMB "scoring"—OMB would define what constituted savings—instead of allowing the Congressional Budget Office, CBO, to do it. In the budget summit, CBO figures had been used throughout.

It was a major concession. Numbers could dictate policy. The Senate had given the Executive Branch authority over legislation, authority comparable to that which Wright had rejected. And OMB was as partisan as any arm of the administration. In some ways it differed from the White House speech-writing department only in that OMB's rhetoric was written in numerals, not letters. Early in the year, Miller had publicly proclaimed that the White House budget cut the deficit to $108 billion, while OMB's own internal documents put it at $135 billion. By contrast, CBO was nonpartisan and objective; it had to be, since it had to satisfy both Democrats and Republicans.

While House Democrats and the White House confronted one another over their respective power grabs, contra aid was evoking even more bitterness. Even before Wright's involvement in the peace plan, contra aid had generated intense emotions on both sides. To the White House and to House Republicans, the issue now also symbolized Wright's usurpation of power, his ascension in Washington.

The Senate C.R. included $16 million of "nonmilitary" aid, which could be spent on anything except buying weapons and ammunition. (It would pay for delivery of weapons into Nicaragua from Honduran stockpiles.) It also retained "expedited procedures," which made a future request for more aid "privileged," bypassing the Rules Committee and guaranteeing the White House a floor vote at whatever time seemed most propitious.

In mid-December, just as both sides readied for a confrontation, Reagan and Wright met in the Oval Office, along with other senior officials. They were discussing the summit with Gorbachev, who was about to depart. Wright suggested to Reagan that Gorbachev's offer to limit military assistance to the Sandinistas alleviated U.S. security concerns. Hadn't the time come, therefore, for the United States to support the Central American peace process and talk to the Sandinistas? National Security Adviser Colin Powell steered the conversation away before Reagan answered.

Powell knew that something was about to break. While Gorbachev was still in Washington, Elliott Abrams was arranging for a Sandinista defector named Roger Miranda to start giving press interviews. Nicaraguan defense minister Humberto Ortega, brother of President Daniel Ortega, announced what Miranda was about to reveal—that the Sandinistas had contingency plans for an army of 600,000 equipped with sophisticated Soviet weapons.

The announcement exploded in the Congress, instantly rearranging the political forces surrounding contra aid and putting liberals, and Wright, on the defensive. Mickey Edwards, a key House Republican, told one Democrat, "You don't understand. We're going to see the Senate language in law if it takes bringing the government down and three vetoes."

The Senate language could destroy the peace process. The Sandinistas had consistently stated that they would not comply with the peace treaty until military aid to the contras ended. The Senate language allowed continued delivery of stockpiled military equipment. That meant the Sandinistas would not comply, which would allow contra supporters to blame them for the breakdown of the peace process when, on January 15, the five Central American presidents met to assess progress. In turn, that could help Reagan pass a major new request for contra aid.

House Republicans had not had one victory all year. *But by God, they were going to win this one.*

Welfare reform was moving toward a final confrontation as well. The Democratic whip organization had contacted every one of the seventy-nine signatories to the letter complaining about not allowing amendments. That show of concern, Wright's personal involvement, and Downey's agreement to a new committee-backed amendment (it dropped the bill's five-year cost from $6.2 to $5.7 billion) had cut Democratic "nos" to thirty-one with a dozen undecideds. But members still grumbled. The rule was still the tough vote, since only the committee amendment was to be allowed.

On Monday, December 14, the welfare reform whip task force met in a small room down a half-secret corridor on the Capitol's first floor, under the Speaker's Lobby. Coelho's staff had added Christmas cookies to the usual vegetables and dip. The task force planned each detail. Though Speakers rarely made floor speeches, Downey wanted Wright to close debate on the rule; that would lock in the commitments members made to him personally. Steny Hoyer told the task force, "Stay after your people on the rule. We'll have the entire deputy whip organization cover the doors and fan out on the floor during the vote. We need the hand-holding." A White House Christmas party for members was scheduled Tuesday night. "People are mad at being in this week anyway," another member warned. "If you make them miss that party they'll be furious." To avoid running late and conflicting with it, they would vote on the rule Tuesday and wait until Wednesday for the bill itself.

The last detail was the pace of the vote itself. Sometimes, if a member walked on the floor and saw the vote total swinging one way, the member—there's protection in being lost in a crowd—got swept along with the momentum. Republicans usually voted first and took an early lead; that gave them the satisfaction of being ahead at least for part of the vote. This time the leadership decided to close off even that opening. On Tuesday, the first tally displayed on the electronic monitor, less than a minute after the vote began, showed the rule ahead 34–0.

But it was deceptive. Quickly it narrowed. Every vote mattered. Walter Jones of North Carolina rolled onto the floor in his wheelchair, voted no and started to leave. Russo shouted, "Walter!" and ran over to him. Quickly Coelho and others surrounded his wheelchair, blocking the exit, asking him to switch if they needed him. Wright worked the floor himself, talking to members, talking to members. Suddenly the clock showed 0:00; the fifteen-minute minimum for the vote had expired. Democrats led 153–150.

Republicans mockingly yelled, "Regular order!" *If you can hold the vote open, damn you, then why don't you cut it short, too?*

But the outcome had been decided. Jones was allowed to leave. The rule passed 213–206. Republicans voted no by 170–0. The next day welfare reform passed 230–194. It had been much harder, and more bitter, than that final count hinted at.

It was also the final item on Wright's agenda for the 100th Congress. The trade bill had passed the House. The highway bill was law. The Clean Water Act was law. Insurance against catastrophic illness had passed the House. The Farm Credit bill had passed the House and in a few days would become law. The first housing bill in Reagan's presidency had passed the House and would soon become law. Two homeless bills were law. Now welfare reform had passed the House.

It was a remarkable record. If everything became law, and the bills seemed well on their way to it, the 100th Congress would be the most productive since Lyndon Johnson created the Great Society. And the legislative accomplishments did not include the fact that Central Americans might achieve peace.

But under the pressure from Gingrich, under the press scrutiny of Wright's personal life, with the hostility of the White House and the foreign policy establishment, Wright's and the House's accomplishments slipped by unnoticed. The members wanted to get home for Christmas. That was what they were thinking about. Wright had promised they would recess for the year early, as early as late October, certainly by Thanksgiving. Now they might not get home for Christmas at all. The press did not seem to notice the accomplishments either.

At the regular whip meeting Wright smiled at his colleagues and said, "Let us hope we have no further opportunity to wish each other Merry Christmas." Fifty members cheered. Then he read a column in *The Washington Post* by David Broder proclaiming Foley a master statesman. Members whistled and cheered again; Foley blushed. Wright led the applause enthusiastically. Although he longed for approval, he was not envious of Foley. Truly he was not. But he was bitter. *Why did no one write such things about him?*

Congress passed a two-day C.R. to keep the government operating until midnight Friday—one week before Christmas.

Suddenly the pace picked up; the days, even the hours, became denser, more packed with activity, frantic. Hundreds of issues, thousands of pages of legislation had to move.

Wright stepped back, partly because of the overwhelmingly large number of issues coming to a boil at once, partly because, like a child burned, he thought twice before going so near the fire again. He had been wounded; he would lie low and heal. It was only a few days since Gingrich's press conference, and the stories attacking his integrity haunted him; he awoke at night in the dark hours and wrote responses which he never made public, or simply lay awake thinking. He was tired. His concentration strayed. He became more the judge, the arbiter, letting colleagues work out details. Besides, delegation was a sign of strength, so long as he remained in charge. Wasn't it? Even on Central America, after privately castigating the Sandinistas for the 600,000-strong army idea, telling them it made no difference whether it was a contingency plan or not, Wright stepped back.

He delegated handling the negotiations with the Senate over contra aid in the final C.R. to Bonior, Coelho, and members of the relevant Appropriations subcommittee. In a meeting in his office with them,

Wright rejected one liberal's insistence on holding tough for no aid, saying, "That's not sustainable on the floor."

The vote count had changed since the talk of an expanded Sandinista army. He had already included contra aid in several short-term C.R.'s, covering September 30 to December 18. Now he suggested extending humanitarian aid until February 29, roughly $6 million, then having an up-or-down vote. He did not want to fight now. Republicans would accept this. And something, positive or negative, would have happened in the peace process by then, enough to determine the outcome.

Bonior objected, arguing, "The CIA says the contras already have enough money to last to spring. Deliveries of weapons and ammunition are at the highest rates ever. What you say is what the White House wants—drag this out, drag this out, meanwhile the contras keep getting money without a floor vote."

"House Republicans see a different conspiracy," Foley countered. "They see the Sandinistas delaying things while aid is cut off and the contras wither and die. I'd like to know where Arias is now."

"That's what people are asking on the floor," said another member. "Where's the Speaker, and where's Arias?"

Where was Wright? He remained silent, uncharacteristically silent.

After a moment, he told Bonior, David Obey, the relevant Appropriations subcommittee chairman, and Intelligence chairman Louis Stokes to work something out and get back to him.

Later, they proposed $5.5 million in humanitarian aid—only food, clothing, and medicine—and an end to expedited procedures, an end to guaranteeing a vote for the President at the time of his choosing. Wright approved it, but when Bonior, Coelho, and Obey tested the liberals' response at an anti-contra-aid task force meeting, members erupted.

"It's like the old story," George Miller said with a weary bitterness. "We've established what we are. Now we're just bickering over the price."

Another colleague demanded a separate vote on contra aid. Without at least that, he warned, "It will look like the leadership is caving in to the Senate, and we'll lose the C.R. That is not a strategy."

Coelho tried to fend off the attacks: "No one in this room is more concerned than Dave Bonior. Every time we make progress, some goddamn Sandinista screws things up."

Then Obey snapped, "To be blunt, I don't appreciate negotiating this son of a bitch, bringing it out, then have you all pose for holy pictures while I vote for it. I'll bring it down myself."

"This is a goddamned point of principle!" one member shouted at Obey, jabbing his finger angrily at him. To some liberals, the issue was complicity in murder. They would not have blood on their hands.

Wright wanted peace. He would have no peace. His ambitions and goals would not allow it. He was quickly drawn back into the vortex. His power drew him back in. And he never stopped thinking about maneuvering forces to advance his agenda. Public Works chairman Jim Howard gave him an opportunity.

Howard organized a chairmen's lunch with Wright. Whitten and Rostenkowski were not there. The chairmen complained that Whitten constantly used his Appropriations Committee to infringe on their authority. One said, "It's like a pack of monkeys in the San Francisco Zoo. Except the monkeys at least have a pecking order." Another demanded, "It's getting worse. There must be some way to make it more painful for them to do it."

They were Wright's barons and they sat in baronial splendor around the great long tables in the Speaker's Dining Room. Wright wanted them happy; perhaps sometime in the future he could turn these barons against another powerful one. *A prince should make himself the leader and protector of smaller neighboring powers, and he should endeavor to weaken those that are strong,* Machiavelli wrote. Wright listened carefully, then proposed appointing members of their committees to House-Senate conferences on appropriations bills. They liked the idea, and knew that Whitten and others on his committee hated it. Then Wright added, "I have noticed a diminution of authority in your committees in favor of Appropriations, Budget, and Ways and Means." *Ways and Means.*

But Wright's power was limited. He told Michel, "If there is a dime of contra aid in the C.R., it will need Republican votes to pass."

It was the first time in his speakership that he needed Republican votes.

The fight, now with the Senate and the White House, over reconciliation was intensifying too. Wright called a meeting of Dingell, Rostenkowski, Gray, and the leadership in H-201. They had just discovered that the Senate Budget Committee was allowing OMB to score savings, and that Bentsen had agreed to it to pass his bill.

"I had a conversation with Jim Baker downtown and we didn't need telephones," Rostenkowski grunted. He shook his head, straightened his arms, like an animal stretching itself. "To Bentsen's credit, Jim Miller wanted to be in the room and he refused. Bentsen and I have to stop passing paper and sit down, eyeball to eyeball, without staff, and settle things."

Dingell angrily quoted the summit agreement, which called for "consultation" when there was a discrepancy in figures. "That is different from allowing them to do the scoring. It's a question of who's running this, Congress or OMB?"

In one program alone OMB was demanding $1 billion more in cuts than would have occurred under sequestration's across-the-board axe. Dingell's father had co-sponsored the Social Security Act; in Wright Texas populism still ran strong. His anger stirred. He hissed, "So OMB wants to get this out of the hides of the poorest people, and have more asset sales at bargain prices to enrich private speculators."

There would be no yielding on this. This was not simply Jim Wright's fight. The chairmen and the Caucus were united behind him. Wright knew that. One could almost feel him grow stronger. He continued with a wry understatement: "If the Senate understands our righteous indignation and we have the better side of the argument, they'll be shored up."

That was the way most issues in Washington were decided: by a combination of logic—the better side of the argument—and strength. The Democratic majority of the House was asserting itself. If the Senate cooperated, good. But the House *would* assert itself. Wright recalled that George Washington had come in person to the Senate chamber with an Indian treaty to ask for the Senate's advice and consent, and the Senate had refused to consider the matter with Washington in the chamber. Washington had left and never returned to either chamber, for any reason. "Does Congress do for Jim Miller what it would not for George Washington?" he asked.

Later that day a meeting between House and Senate leadership aides reflected those same tensions. They got together in S-207, on the Senate side of the Capitol but only a few doors down the corridor from H-201. A short time earlier it had been packed with over a hundred men and women for a memorial service to a respected and popular former Senate aide named Bill Pursley; the Senate, like the House, took care of its own. It was a large room and now was empty. In the middle of it was a lonely table, and the leadership aides sat in dim light around it like characters in a minimalist, abstract play. Perhaps *No Exit*. Christmas cookies and cider masked friction. The House listed item after item after item on which it would refuse to yield despite White House veto threats. Exasperated, a Byrd aide interrupted, "The question is, how many times can we stick it to OMB?"

"As many times as we can," a House staffer shot back.

House and Senate leaders and key committee and subcommitee chairmen sat down in H-201 to try to resolve differences. They began with a forced Christmas conviviality. But the conviviality masked conflict. Earlier, the House contingent had met privately and agreed to insist on the prerogatives of the Congress regardless of what the Senate said. House Democrats were fighting for supremacy, Senate Democrats for survival. Now Wright asked for the current status of the situation.

Henry Waxman observed, "The Senate feels bound by some agreement negotiated with OMB which the House was not involved in. That agreement does not bind the House or the Congress."

The senators conceded Waxman's point. The problem centered on OMB's claim that CBO figures fell $3.2 billion short of cuts required in Medicaid and Medicare. If the administration had made those demands in the budget summit, there would have been no agreement. Waxman insisted, "I can't believe this is an honest difference on numbers. They're cooking the numbers to force their policy on us."

Dingell said bluntly, "I have concluded they are liars. And CBO's numbers were used throughout the summit. Only on the last day was 'consultation' proposed if OMB and CBO disagreed."

"May I play devil's advocate?" Chiles, the Senate Budget chairman, said. "In Gramm-Rudman, we made OMB the final scorer of sequestration. Here we are saying we've done enough to avoid sequestration. Who scores that? OMB. So why should they not score the conference?"

That wasn't a problem, Rostenkowski told him. Congress could simply stipulate that these bills vacated sequestration. Wright agreed.

The House was steamrolling Chiles. He sat there, his arms folded, pursing his lips; his staff director slipped a note to him. Chiles looked at it, then said, "We've embraced OMB figures where they gave us more savings."

"It's a good idea in those places," Dingell replied.

Then he, this big rough Pole from Detroit, leaned forward and spread himself out, his elbows and forearms seizing space at the table, and stared at Chiles.

Chiles flushed and fell silent.

Wright and Rostenkowski weighed in again. With Dingell, they weighed heavily. Very heavily. This was not a negotiation. This was a demand, a confrontation. One side would lose. The room grew tense.

Bentsen argued that Reagan would veto the bill, and everyone wanted to go home for Christmas. But shifting the argument was a sign of weakness, proof that the Senate had no rebuttal.

"Do you really think they'd veto over this, Lloyd?" Wright asked. "I don't. I don't trust these folks. They have insinuated themselves in a remarkable way into the legislative process, almost insisting on a line-item veto. I understand the elderly would be better off under seques-tration than under OMB's assumptions."

"That's correct, Mr. Speaker," a senator conceded.

The Senate began to crack. Byrd said nothing. Bentsen agreed to use CBO figures on Medicare, and look again at Medicaid. They had been arguing for an hour, an intense, draining hour. The meeting broke up. Dingell hunched forward and whispered to Wright.

Chiles interrupted. "Mr. Speaker, we still must contemplate nego-tiating with the administration at some point."

Wright and Dingell ignored him. It was as if he had not spoken, as if he were invisible. Chiles sat rigid, then refolded his arms and sat uncomfortably, as if determined to wait them out. But their contempt became almost a physical thing; they talked on.

After a long moment, Chiles rose and headed down the hallway the few feet to the door dividing the Senate and House sides of the Capitol, pushed it open, and disappeared, back home in the other body.

It was the weekend before Christmas. Everyone wanted to get home. Abruptly, issues started falling away, resolved. The tax bill came first. Rostenkowski and Bentsen sat down, alone, for six and a half hours and agreed on a tax bill Wright could endorse. It included several major provisions—an attack on tax breaks defense contractors enjoyed, and two antitakeover provisions—opposed by the White House and not in the Senate bill. Rostenkowski compromised too: he had sworn not to credit faster collection of corporate estimated taxes as part of the tax total set by the summit agreement because it did not raise new revenue. He relented, and agreed to count half of it toward the total.

Other members were taken care of. Kansas Democratic congressman Dan Glickman was angry over limited, high-priced flights between the Dallas–Fort Worth Airport and Wichita, and wanted to require more flights from Love Field, the old Dallas airport. A Wright aide told an Appropriations aide, "We *don't* want this." But they wanted Glickman happy. The American Airlines lobbyist offered to cut one fare between D-FW and Wichita by more than half if that would pacify Glickman. *Free market? Why would American want that? Deregulation? Hell, it was like the railroads in the nineteenth century, before regulation.*

Elsewhere, with members demanding to go home, the time had come to start using brute force. The Budget Committee had the authority to settle most issues, but rarely exercised it, preferring to let the committees of substantive jurisdiction reach compromises. But Public Works chairman Jim Howard walked out of the reconciliation conference. While a Budget staffer hummed the tune "Rawhide" ("Rollin', rollin', rollin', keep them dogies rollin', Rawhide!"), Budget members settled Howard's problems for him. So did Appropriations, which learned that Howard had organized the committee chairmen's lunch to complain about their committee. Howard wanted a host of new public works projects he and his committee colleagues wanted taken care of; Appropriations staff killed those in his district, and funded everyone else's.

And the floor was getting crazy. Wes Watkins offered an amendment exempting the leopard darter minnow from the Endangered Species Act. The exemption would have waived certain environmental restrictions in his district. He declared that rivers there were so clean you could go skinny-dipping in them. Claudine Schneider, an attractive Rhode Island Republican and an environmentalist, worked the doors hard and asked members if they would rather go skinny-dipping with Wes or her. Laughing, they chose her, 273–136.

Foley sat in Wright's office, half-punchy from hours upon hours of meetings. He raised his gaze to the ceiling, touched his fingertips together in a pose of saintliness, and said, "And a light appeared unto them and angels appeared unto them and the angels said, 'Adjourn this place.' And a voice said, 'Yea, how shall we do this thing?' And, lo, the angel said, *'Roll 'em!'* "

Friday afternoon, December 18, a dozen members crowded into Wright's office to decide on a final contra-aid strategy. They had been disappointed with Senator Christopher Dodd of Connecticut, blaming him for the failure of Senate Democrats to control the issue. The final plan Senate liberals had proposed in effect would have let the Central American democracies decide whether contra aid would continue.

"That was idiotic," one member complained. "How the hell can you vote to let foreign governments decide U.S. foreign policy? We've got to find a new senator to work with, someone we can trust."

Now they were waiting for Hawaii's Daniel Inouye, who, like Obey in the House, chaired the key Appropriations subcommittee on foreign operations. He entered, sat in a high-backed armchair opposite Wright, who was behind his desk, looked around and saw no other senators, and said, "Why am I here?"

"It's like the time the Texas Rangers sent one man to quell a riot," Wright chuckled. "When he showed up people asked how come they only sent one Ranger. 'There's only one riot,' the Ranger said."

But Inouye did not know this issue. It had been dumped on him, and he was ignorant of even the most important details. His ignorance marked a difference between House and Senate.

In the House members do business, involve themselves intimately and substantively in issues; staff matters, but knows its place. Because there are 435 members, each individual vote matters less, and members form more alliances, move more in blocs. Information flows horizontally, from member to member; that gives power to a member who is considered both trustworthy and knowledgeable.

The Senate's legislative workload is the same as that of the House, but it is spread among only one hundred. And there are more demands on senators' time: they have a larger number of constituents to see, more press requests for interviews, more invitations to embassy dinners. Fewer senators know a subject well. As a result, senators delegate more to staff, listen more to them, allow staff to speak for them, know less substance. Information flows vertically in the Senate, from staff upwards. Each senator also tends to operate more independently than House members. Encased in armor, lifted by crane atop a horse, protected by layers of staff lieutenants who point him toward the battlefield, each senator is a thing unto himself or herself. Since a single member has less impact in the House—because there are 435, rather than 100 —House members must make more alliances. Like nobles in a court they maneuver, armed but unarmored, naked to a stiletto, operating on their own rather than through staff, engaged more intimately in every aspect of policy maneuvering.

Still, Inouye's ignorance startled the House members; it seemed unusual even for a senator. He did not know that existing law ended military deliveries to the contras on December 31. Delivery of military aid was not a detail. It was the issue. Cutting off military aid was the key to getting Sandinistas to comply with the peace accord. The Sandinistas had said so over and over. And a few days made a difference. January 15 was the date the Central American presidents would assess Nicaragua's compliance. Finally Inouye confessed, "All I know is what Ted Stevens tells me."

The members jerked erect. Stevens was a pro-contra Republican. *And he was Inouye's adviser?* But forget that. Now, now was what mattered.

Inouye listened to their compromise proposal closely. It affirmed the existing cutoff of military aid deliveries on January 1, but extended humanitarian aid for two months.

"I can't speak for the conferees, but I can buy it," Inouye said.

"If you can do that," Obey replied, "we can get out of here."

The White House got wind of the deal. It didn't like it. At 6:00 P.M. Howard Baker called Wright. Could he support extending deliveries of military aid until January 17? That was two days after the Central American presidents met to assess compliance with the peace agreement, but Wright was willing at least to explore it. Half an hour later, amid the hors d'oeuvres and drinks at Wright's Christmas party in his ceremonial office, Bonior learned of Baker's proposal from a Wright aide. He froze, then asked coldly, "Is that a deal?"

"A conversation. Not a deal."

One could see the muscles of Bonior's neck grow rigid. He was angry, turned away, and snapped, "I'm getting fed up."

At nine that night the contra-aid conferees met. It was only a few hours after Inouye had sat in Wright's office. But Inouye rejected the House proposal. The House members were stunned. *I can't speak for the conferees but I can support it. That's what Inouye had said.*

The meeting lasted well past midnight and broke up in anger, without progress. House Democrats were furious with their Senate colleagues. They were also isolated. The White House, Senate Republicans, House Republicans, and now Senate Democrats, at least the ones who mattered, were against them.

By then, the authority to operate the government had expired. Technically, government buildings could not open Saturday. It was less than a week to Christmas and members were *here,* instead of home.

One member had a few beers in Bullfeathers, a bar two blocks from the House office buildings, around the corner from buildings whose apartments were filled with members, and complained, "I just talked to my daughter. She's three years old. She was crying, 'When are you coming home, Daddy?' I started yelling at my wife, 'You put her up to this!' She knew it would get me." The member suddenly slammed the table with his fist. "Goddammit. I'm pissed!"

At Anton's, a restaurant on the same block, a sixty-three-year-old committee chairman had had more than a few and was telling anyone who would listen, "I'm tough as nails and you better listen to me like you never listened before."

Anton's was hopping. Two labor lobbyists almost got into a brawl when one of them called the son of the president of the other's union a "lying scab." Seven years earlier the son had testified against the first lobbyist's union president. They stood up, belly bumping belly, until a third man pushed them apart. Then all three sat back down and had another drink.

It was the Christmas season.

Saturday.

At breakfast the key contra-aid negotiators gathered to plan strategy. It could just as well have been 5:00 P.M. The House had become a world unto itself, without day and night, with hour after wearying hour of negotiations. They sat around the large round table that Wright used for his daily breakfast staff meeting in the Members' Dining Room. Wright was not there; Foley, Coelho, Bonior, and the conferees from the Appropriations subcommittee discussed the situation. It was not good. They were going to lose this.

House Republicans wanted to fight. Gingrich was reportedly telling colleagues, *Just stand fast,* Wright would cave in to save his scheduled

Christmas trip to the Holy Land. *Just stand fast. By God, Republicans would win one.* And several liberals had told the leadership they didn't care what was happening on the floor, at six-thirty Monday night they were getting on an airplane. They had no-refund tickets with their whole family for vacations.

"We've got to talk to the liberals. Get them to understand."

"You can't ask for their votes if there's military aid."

"Not their votes. Their understanding."

It was the first time all year that House Democrats could not dictate at least the outline of a final agreement. The members sat around the table glumly, silently, recognizing their sudden impotence. Just then Agriculture chairman Kika da la Garza walked in. "Where's John Mack?" he asked, squinting at the people around the table, then asked, "What are we doing?"

Embarrassed, Mack said, "Ask the majority leader."

Foley chuckled. "He knows where the power is."

"The Senate just passed the farm credit bill 85-2." The House had passed it the day before. It was another of Wright's initiatives; he had forced a reluctant de la Garza to move. Now de la Garza was beaming and the members applauded. They had accomplished something anyway.

A few hours later the contra-aid negotiators briefed Wright. He warned, "We've got to go back to the basic position of the Sandinistas, that they'll comply with the peace accords after military aid ends. The Central American presidents meet—when, the fifteenth? Pushing the cutoff to the seventeenth forces the Sandinistas into a position of total capitulation and loss of their dignity, or not complying."

Wright had earlier seemed receptive to Howard Baker's suggestion of the seventeenth. He was no longer.

"Republicans feel invulnerable, partly because you're going to Israel," Bonior said. "They think you want to get out."

"Would it help you negotiate if you said the Speaker had to cancel his trip and he was really furious, obstinate, willing to stay here to Christmas through three vetoes if necessary?"

Bonior nodded. "That would be very helpful. And we need a counteroffer to the seventeenth."

"Suppose I said January 7 and not one day later."

"I'd just say the seventh," Foley warned. "They might take you seriously about 'not one day later' and this could blow up."

Republicans were so convinced of his force and willfulness that they believed they could not even deal with him, that they had to fight him. What irony. Such a view was so foreign to the Congress, and he was the constitutional head of the Congress. Had relations deteriorated that much? He had changed the speakership and the House, all right.

"Dave," Wright asked, "how many Democrats do we lose if we extend military aid ten days into the new year, then cut it off before the meeting?"

"Between one hundred and half the Caucus."

Wright shook his head in a kind of sigh. The negotiators left. Wright, alone, sat at his desk. It seemed almost as if he could feel the reins of power slipping away from him. For a moment he hunched forward and rubbed his eyes. This wasn't the way he wanted the year to end. This wasn't the triumph he had envisioned.

Early that evening, wearily, Wright headed toward Byrd's office to try to wrap up disputes over economic issues with Hill leaders, Jim Baker, and Jim Miller. They talked for two hours and the Republicans interrupted to caucus. Then they talked for two more hours. They settled nothing. At ten-thirty Saturday night Wright stood outside his H-209 ceremonial office. "Damn Miller," he growled.

Rostenkowski came down the hall from the same meeting, equally frustrated. "Hell. I didn't know why I was in there. I could get some work done. My problem is, I don't want to finish tonight and have all that hanging out there."

The Sunday papers would report any deals, and opponents could swarm all over and kill them. Wright walked into H-209, sat down, and returned a phone call to an old friend who asked if it was all right if he supported Dukakis for President. *Whoever you want. Gephardt. Gore. Anybody. As long as it's a Democrat.* Then Byrd called, asking him to return. Wearily he started back down the hall.

At midnight Saturday the contra-aid negotiations ended. The deal was complicated. It provided $14 million in aid. Deliveries of military aid would cease January 12, just before the Central American presidents assessed compliance with the Guatemala accords. But if Reagan stated that a cease-fire had not been reached because of Sandinista bad faith, military deliveries would resume on January 19 and continue until February 3. On that day, the House would vote on a new Reagan contra-aid proposal. The Senate would vote the next day. Both houses had to pass it for it to become law.

The early, fixed date for a vote was a victory for contra-aid opponents; Republicans had given up the "expedited procedures" which allowed them to pick a time for a vote when events made passage most likely. But if they won, the President could ask for still more aid in July. Breaking requests into smaller packages, rather than one big sum, improved the chances for passage.

After reaching final agreement in a members-only meeting, the House Democratic negotiators sat down in a conference room off Byrd's office and briefed their aides. Then, one by one, each member said he would vote against the deal he had just agreed to. They sat rigid, their expressions fixed and cold and defeated. It was late. Most of them went home.

Word of the agreement was already spreading. Peace activists around the country started barraging the Hill with phone calls now, after midnight, overwhelming the switchboard.

The leadership gathered in Wright's office to explain the agreement to him. He listened coldly, knowing the reception it would get in his Caucus, knowing that it mocked all he had worked for, knowing that members would go home thinking bitterly about this. Then he said, "It's okay with me. I don't have to vote for it. You do."

Sunday.

Bonior's floor aide Kathy Gille was driving back into work. With Obey and other staff she had worked until 3:00 A.M. writing language to implement the contra-aid agreement. Now she thought of all they had tried to accomplish during the year in Central America. How hard they had worked. How hard they had tried. She was worn out by the hours and hours and hours of work, barely able to stay awake to drive. There was more work today. *For what?* She wondered if instead of bringing peace they had destroyed any chance of peace. Suddenly, driving along, she burst into tears.

In H-209, a lobbyist pleaded with Wright's senior aides, "If it's not in the bill I could lose my job." They refused. Later a secretary said she felt sorry for him. "Never feel sorry for those guys," one man said. "We just guaranteed his salary for the next two years."

LTV, a company with a major plant just outside Wright's district, had a serious problem with Ways and Means. A desperate LTV lobbyist called everyone in Wright's office looking for help; he was told, *The*

Speaker does not want to get involved. But then Martin Frost, in whose district the plant was, asked for help. Wright's staff would do for Frost what they would not do for a lobbyist. He pointed out two words in the reconciliation bill which he wanted changed. Frost had beaten Rostenkowski in a major floor fight three years earlier, and Ways and Means staff said Rostenkowski would change the wording only if Bentsen's staff suggested it, and Wright personally asked him to do it. *Prince to prince.* Bentsen's people agreed. Then Wright called Rostenkowski. "Danny, I sure would appreciate it. Several thousand of those workers live in my district. Thanks, Danny." It was done.

Rick Brandon, the Senate Budget Committee staff director, pulled Mack aside in a hallway and suggested allowing the President to delay his budget submission to Congress. Current law required it January 6, but OMB could not meet that deadline because the numbers for the current year were not settled yet. "No," Mack said. If OMB had played straight, sure. But they hadn't. Brandon, backed up by a Byrd aide, insisted. *"No,"* Mack repeated. They stood, their faces close, staring at each other, Mack smiling, smiling, smiling, all the deep recesses of him churning. Finally Brandon dropped his eyes. Another House staffer snapped, "If they're six weeks late, we'll hit them hard in the press for being six weeks late. They did that to us. *Fuck 'em.* What are you guys? Republicans?"

In Wright's office, he, Foley, and Coelho reviewed a White House version of language implementing the contra-aid agreement. Bonior had removed himself; he couldn't support the agreement and his further involvement would compromise him with the anti-contra-aid task force.

Coelho read the White House draft and observed, "Their rewrite does not mention, not one word, the Guatemala accords."

"They don't want to make peace, and don't want to make a statement to support peace," Wright observed, his voice ice-like. "Apparently they're going on the theory that they have the votes to ram whatever they want down our throats."

It was a new experience for Wright. He would insist on new House-written language detailing the agreement just reached and would win on this point. It was small and bitter solace. He tried to put the best face on it, insisting, "There *is* a window there. It's up to the Sandinistas."

On the floor was a one-day continuing resolution to allow the government to operate Monday. For the first time members were learning exactly what the contra-aid deal was. Liberals huddled in angry groups among the rows of chairs. Russo pounded a fist into a palm and waved his arms. In the back of the chamber Bonior and George Miller talked quietly, leaning against the brass rail behind the last row of seats. Meanwhile the debate proceeded. *VVVVOOOOOOTTTTTE!* members called. *VVVVVVOOOOOTTTTE!* Mike Lowry, chair of the liberal Democratic Study Group, took the floor. Angry, his intensity burned through his words. "Vote this down!" he demanded, arguing that doing so would force a new contra-aid agreement, or at least a separate vote on contra aid. Then Miller spoke: "When members return, we've got to get rid of this C.R. process. It's disenfranchising the members of the House!" Republicans cheered wildly. *This was supposed to be a democracy but Wright wasn't letting members vote.* The one-day C.R. passed 207–178. Fifty-seven Democrats voted no.

The feeling wasn't good. A man who had worked in the House for twenty-five years worried, "Members are always mad when they're stuck here close to Christmas, but I've never seen them as angry as this. Never. The best thing Wright's got going for him is the six weeks off when they finally get out."

Wright and Coelho went down the list of those fifty-seven Democrats. Coelho predicted on the final C.R., the one which would carry until the next fiscal year, "It won't be too bad. I think we can keep it under a hundred."

"Just as long as a majority of the Caucus supports it," Wright said. That was all he cared about now. That a bare majority of Democrats vote yes.

All day long Wright got reports, made phone calls, talked to Byrd, Rostenkowski, Dingell. At eight-thirty Sunday night he went home. But the proceedings went on.

The fairness doctrine was about to be dropped—Senate Democrats were going to side with the GOP—until Dingell made a phone call to Byrd. Dingell's committee had jurisdiction over all that dirty-burning West Virginia coal. A Dingell ally reported, "Suddenly Byrd couldn't imagine why anyone wouldn't want to be fair."

Mack told an Appropriations staffer, "The fairness doctrine is *in.* They won on contras. Fairness is *in.*"

Monday.

Monday morning of Christmas week seemed almost normal. Wright had his usual breakfast with his usual staff at his usual table. He turned to a page-one *Post* story on House Republicans and studied it. It included attacks on him, among them Gingrich's now-routine charge of unethical behavior. But it went deeper. GOP congressman Bill Frenzel said, "Republicans have been reduced to the status of nonentity under the Wright regime." Lott complained, "This has been basically a useless year. It's been very frustrating, very difficult, very partisan." Henry Hyde complained, "There's a feeling that the White House has set [House Republicans] adrift."

"I don't want to make their life miserable," Wright commented. "I don't want them to feel they don't have a dialogue with me, that they don't have input. As long as they don't expect us to cave on policy."

He decided that next year he would kill them with kindness, starting with a luncheon to honor Bob Michel. He would invite whomever Michel wanted. Let them speak plainly and privately to him. That's what he would do. Kill them with kindness. He had always *made* friends. *Gone out actively and made them. He would do it again.* And all would be well.

But bipartisanship was short-lived. An aide informed him Republicans were still demanding that the fairness doctrine come out of the C.R. *As long as they don't expect us to cave on policy.*

"Then we'll see them New Year's," Wright declared.

There was one other major conflict to be resolved, a confrontation of House and Senate Democrats. Wright convened one last meeting in H-201. His role was arbiter. Members and senators had argued for hour after hour after hour. A decision had to be made. That—not the imposition of his own will—was the Speaker's traditional role: to bless agreements and settle disagreements.

The issue was Medicare. Henry Waxman and several senators went back and forth for another hour, each side presenting its case to Wright.

Finally, Maine senator George Mitchell complained, "This is no way to legislate. It's a very important program. You don't do this in two hours or three hours before you go to the floor."

"Look," Wright said to Waxman, "I think you're right. But this is a philosophical difference and we're not going to resolve it at this late date. We've got to go to the floor. We'll extend the status quo for one year. Lloyd and Danny have given absolute commitments to examine it next year."

Then Wright looked down the table, looked at the members on each side of him. His voice bitter with a deep bitterness, he said, "We have sat here quibbling over whether this additional burden is put on the elderly because too many Democrats are afraid to act, and too many Democrats let this administration cut taxes on rich people. The burden has shifted in this country on who pays. The elderly and the poor are paying and it's wrong. I'm sixty-five as of tomorrow. I have one more quarter to play in my life. I want this back."

Finally the train started moving. But discontent ran deep.

Reconciliation was ready to go to the floor. It would pass, but contra aid and the fairness doctrine were creating a serious problem with the C.R. Republicans were insisting they would vote no unless fairness came out. They had won on contra aid, their first victory of the year; now they wanted another win. They had leverage; Wright needed their votes. Most Democrats wanted the C.R. to pass so they could go home, but because of contra aid did not want to vote for it. And some Democrats, led by Russo, Lowry, and Robert Mrazek, truly wanted to defeat it. They were organizing to do so.

All year Wright, personally and through Coelho's whip organization, had squeezed. Unrest had built up. *This is supposed to be a democracy, isn't it?* one member had asked. In theory, members wanted the strong leadership. But members wanted something else too. O'Neill would put his arm around a member and just listen to his problems. That took time. Wright had spent all his time working on his own agenda, instead of sitting on the floor listening to colleagues' wants—*Jim, can you talk to my chairman and help me get this damn thing moving?* That lack of personal attention had combined with the pressure he had exerted to create the sour feeling.

The last few weeks had exemplified the unrest. First came the reconciliation vote, then Wright's confrontation with Shultz, the disappointing budget summit, and suddenly the ethics charges. Seventy-nine Democrats had signed that letter asking for amendments on welfare reform. They didn't get it. Wright had responded by threatening to increase his power over committee assignments. They weren't getting a separate contra-aid vote now. The leadership was using the procedural control on them that it used on Republicans.

A few days after the reconciliation vote, a Democrat had gone up to Russo on the floor and said, "You should have told me you were starting a revolution. I might have signed up."

Now Russo went to him: "Remember that revolution you asked about? It's starting now."

At most whip task forces, twenty or so members, sometimes many more, worked. For the first C.R. task force, only four appeared. And the count showed only seventy-one Democratic yes votes.

"The liberals are arguing a no vote kills contra aid," Coelho said. "They're wrong. It goes back to the Senate. They'll add more contra aid. The more there is, the more GOP votes. There are eighty now. How's that help us?"

Who runs this place? Democrats or Republicans? We need to show them who still runs this place.

One member shook his head. Looking over the "no" after "no" after "no" on the whip count, he said, "This thing has the smell of death about it."

Meanwhile, the fairness doctrine was still deadlocking the C.R. conference. All day, Democrats and Republicans went back and forth on it. Early Monday evening, Michel, fuming, called Wright to insist he order it dropped. With liberals voting against the C.R. over contra aid, with Republicans serious about killing the C.R. if Democrats did not yield on fairness, this was the chance House Republicans had waited for all year—the chance not to ask or plead or reason, but to demand.

Rank-and-file Democrats were adding pressure of their own. One friend of Eddie Boland, a conferee, told him, "You're what, seventy-five years old? How many more Christmases you got, Ed? Don't you want to spend it with your kids? I do. Switch your vote and let's get out of here."

Wright, Foley, and Coelho gathered once again to figure out a way to keep fairness in the bill. They couldn't. At 8:00 P.M., more than twelve hours into the workday, Wright called Michel to say fairness would likely come out. Michel replied that the President would wait a day to sign the bill so OMB had time to review it.

"Do we need their permission to vote?" Wright spat.

Half an hour later, the reconciliation bill—thousands of pages—lay in boxes on a cart in the Speaker's Lobby. It was too heavy simply to carry into the chamber. Ways and Means staff wheeled it in.

Wright, Foley, and Coelho could not push to pass the C.R. Anti-contra-aid activists would not *be* pushed. The leadership did not even ask how they were going to vote, much less ask them to vote yes. Early that afternoon Wright had been talking in the cloakroom to two members who were trying to kill the C.R., working against it "in a blatant way which," one member said, "would never have been tolerated under Tip." Wright talked with them about Christmas, their kids, their families, their plans. He said nothing about the C.R. *For the first time all year, the pressure was off.* But the bill had to pass.

At 9:00 P.M. Coelho had run out of steam and knew it. He walked into the Appropriations Committee room.

Appropriations was a special committee, a remnant of the old days. Staff could proudly show off ledgers containing hand-written records of bills dating back to the Civil War. The chairman's offices, at one end of the Speaker's Lobby opposite Wright's ceremonial office, had once been the Speaker's office.

It was one of the least partisan and most cliquish committees on the Hill, and was the only committee in the Congress without a staff person assigned to handle the press—they didn't talk much to the press—and its hearing room had little space for audience or reporters. The senior committee staff had worked for the committee for at least seventeen years; most had been there much longer. The chairman, Jamie Whitten, came from rural Mississippi. He spoke with a thick alluvial drawl; when he wanted people to understand him they did, but other times even fellow southerners could not make out his words. He could mumble opponents into submission, and only the year before did he finally allow a microphone into the hearing room. Yet the committee did not live in the past; it kept computerized records of how members voted on its bills, cross-referenced with their special requests for spending in their districts. The committee had so much power that its subcommittee chairmen, the "College of Cardinals," had to submit to Caucus election, just like chairmen of other full committees. Most members did not like to cross the committee.

Now Coelho asked Whitten to gather the cardinals, and then told them it was their bill. Did they want it to pass or not? If they did, he was here to help. But they would have to work.

No leadership had ever, *ever,* used the Appropriations Committee like that before. The committee was too proud, too powerful, its traditions too old and grand and separate from the leadership, to involve it like that. Its chairmen's office had once been the Speaker's office. And who was Tony Coelho to ask? Christ, Whitten had served in Congress longer than Coelho had been alive.

But Coelho handed out worksheets with names of all House Democrats, and asked them to get yes votes from members who did not have a good reason for voting no. That was all. "Each of you have done things for people," Coelho said. "Some of them have told us they're voting no or are undecided. Tom Bevill, can't you talk to this guy? He's from your state. Bill Lehman. This guy's from Florida. They don't have a real reason to vote no—they don't care that much about contra aid."

One cardinal picked up the phone, dialed a number, hung up, and announced, "I got him. It cost me $3 million but I got him."

A colleague laughed. "Hell, at that rate it's pretty cheap."

Coelho remembered the way to get one member and told an aide, "Have that defense lobbyist—you know the guy—call him."

Then the others got on the phone. This process these men understood intimately. Commitments started coming.

Leadership staff watched, shaking their heads. "My God, these guys are effective, and do they have long memories!" one aide later said.

At ten-twenty the House passed reconciliation with its tax increases and entitlement cuts, 237–181. Michel, Lott, and Cheney voted for it, along with forty-one GOP colleagues. The GOP leadership believed that was enough to demonstrate bipartisanship. One hundred thirty Republicans voted no.

Jamie Whitten took the floor to announce a final meeting of the conferees on the C.R.—to drop the fairness doctrine. He promised, "We will see you later."

The House recessed until midnight.

Michel's aide Bill Pitts walked into H-209. His voice had an edge as he asked Coelho, "How many votes you got for the C.R.?"

"I'm giving you seventy-five. Hell, you won everything. You pass it."

"I'll lie too. We've only got sixty-five GOP yeses."

"Then we're going down. Give us the votes."

"Give us the chair."

* * *

Five minutes into the morning of December 22, the House reconvened. Foley announced that it was "the sixty-fifth anniversary of the birth of our distinguished Speaker. . . . Our warmest congratulations and best wishes." The few members on the floor applauded and sang "Happy Birthday."

At 12:56 A.M. the rule passed. Appropriations aides rolled in a cart carrying the continuing resolution. It weighed thirty pounds, and the pages filled boxes and boxes. Just then the White House called Mack with an urgent problem. Buried in the bill was a provision requiring the State Department to close the Palestine Liberation Organization's office. It had to come out. *Too late now, partner,* Mack replied. Members packed the floor. There was nothing else to do, nowhere else to go, no one waiting with appointments. Not at one-thirty in the morning two days before Christmas Eve. The members wanted to vote and get out.

Within ten minutes after the debate started—the bill was scheduled for one hour of debate—members began shouting, *"VVVOOOTTTE! VVVOOOTTTE!" Vote and get out.* No one was listening to the debate. *VVVOOOTTTE!* When Jack Brooks got up and asked for unanimous consent to insert remarks in the record as if spoken—instead of actually giving his speech—wild applause erupted.

Republican Silvio Conte began by complaining, "We are going to have one vote on a conference report of over two thousand pages which not one member has read or understands." But a moment later he added, "That concludes my participation in the ritual flogging of the process," then read a poem he had written: "The Senate had dawdled/ At the pace of a snail/And the House had responded/With a long anguished wail./Is there any one person/Who can rescue our cause?/ The answer was clear/'Twould be old Santa Claus . . . /On Whitten, On Natcher,/On Michel and Wright/On Conte, On Foley,/Let's finish tonight . . ."

Members clapped and cheered and laughed. Yet the chamber was serious, the members tense. The bill spent $600 billion. Yet members debated only the $14 million in contra aid.

Robert Mrazek closed debate in opposition. He stood there tall, awkward, a grim and Lincolnesque figure but strangely eloquent. "It is one-thirty-five in the morning and I guess we are all looking forward to adjourning soon. My family is many hundreds of miles away and I miss them deeply." His words echoed in the chamber, within the members. He spoke of sitting across from men of good faith for hours negotiating this package, spoke of the fact that "I wish I could tell the members that I had some clear-cut view on how to deal with this issue," but did not. Yet he had to oppose it. *Wasn't this the best of politics? Wasn't this why one got into politics? To do something one believed in?* "As much as I would like to see my family, the greatest Christmas blessing I can think of, in my view the greatest message that we could deliver on this night, a few days before the birth of Jesus Christ, is a message that says there is hope for peace in Central America, and that we are going to try to find an avenue that will allow that initiative to be strengthened."

No member of the leadership spoke in favor of the bill. None wanted his fingerprints on it. When Conte said he had no further requests for time, the chamber cheered. It was 2:00 A.M. when they started to vote.

It went slowly, slowly. Though virtually every member was already in the chamber, after five minutes fewer than 150 members had voted. The tension built. Democrats were hanging back, forcing the Republicans to vote yes. If they wanted contra aid, they had to pass it. After ten minutes only half the House had voted, and the C.R. trailed. Lowry burst into bitter laughter, raised his hand and pointed at the Republicans, and declared, "They have to vote for it!" Coelho was laughing, too, patting Lowry's stomach. Russo and Schumer were laughing—suddenly it seemed half the two hundred Democrats were laughing. Republicans had voted no all year, hated continuing resolutions, complained about the process almost daily, and now they had to vote yes. Even Wright enjoyed it. Sitting at the rostrum, leaning over talking to Mack, he smiled at the spectacle of the minority having to produce votes for a change, having to take the responsibility of governing for a change. Oh, there was bitterness in this. This was not the best of politics.

And maybe, just maybe, this thing would go down.

Rostenkowski was sitting in his H-208 office, across the hallway from the outside entrance to the Democratic cloakroom—the only other way into it was from the floor itself—having a beer with a colleague, one of them leaning over the long, felt-covered oval conference table, the other leaning back, his feet up. They were watching on the closed-circuit TV that sat in every office and covered the floor. After a few minutes they got up and started to head for the floor to vote. Then

Rostenkowski's colleague said, "Wait a second. This is getting interesting."

He pulled on his beer. They sat down. The vote total mounted. With three minutes left it was 147–152, against.

"Hey, Danny, if you vote no, you might bring some guys with you. Here's your chance to fuck Wright, send him down in flames. Nobody would blame you either. You always voted against the contras."

Rostenkowski thought for a second, then shook his head. "No, I'm not gonna do it."

If he did Wright in, it would be a clean fight. The chairman of Ways and Means owed the Speaker of the House that much. He rose, walked onto the floor, and voted yes.

Time expired. The vote stood at 209 for, 205 against. But a few members were left. The chamber was absolutely still.

"Mr. Sundquist? Mr. Sundquist votes no." 209–206. "Mr. Owens of Utah? Mr. Owens of Utah votes no." 209–207. "Mr. Slattery? Mr. Slattery votes no." 209–208. *One vote.*

The chamber was still. But there were no more votes. Democrats had voted against it 128–116, Republicans for it 93–80. George Miller was holding up a man who was so drunk he needed holding to stand. Lowry shook hands and—literally—jumped in the air and kicked up his heels.

"The ayes have it and a motion to reconsider is laid upon the table," Wright announced.

It was not as close as it seemed. Another half-dozen members in each party would have voted yes if needed.

The House had one more issue. A final compromise on a housing bill had just been worked out with the Senate. Debate lasted a moment, even that moment interrupted—*VVVVVVOOOOOTTTE*—by—*VVVVVVOOOOOTTTE*—shouts. In one minute and fifty-eight seconds 320 votes were cast, and within a few more minutes, all the votes were cast. The bill was approved 391–2. Before the fifteen-minute minimum for a vote expired, the chamber had emptied. At 3:15 A.M. the House recessed.

Jim Wright left the floor and went not to his office but to that of Appropriations, where earlier that night he had for a while watched the College of Cardinals work. Most of those subcommittee chairmen were men of his generation, some even older: not only Whitten but colleagues like Eddie Boland of Massachusetts, seventy-five years old, O'Neill's old roommate; and William Natcher of Kentucky, seventy-eight years old, who came to Congress the year before Wright and who had been so instrumental in Wright's winning the majority leader race, who had never missed a vote, not ever, not even a vote to approve the previous day's journal, not even a quorum call, in his thirty-four years.

Wright went there to sign the bill, before it went to the White House. Coelho came in also, and the two of them and a couple of top aides and the Appropriations staff sat around the big conference table, identical to the one in Rostenkowski's room, the kind of table that looked perfect for big-stakes poker. Wright started telling stories of the House, warm, funny stories. He was sixty-five years old as of this day. Coelho, a generation younger, told some stories too. The others listened. They sat there for an hour and a half, well into the morning, before Wright and Coelho went home.

On the drive home, in the brittle, cold December night, Wright thought about all the dreams of his youth, about all he had done and all he had tried to do. All his life he had worked to achieve such a position as he now had. All his life. He looked back with pride at what he had accomplished in his first year as Speaker. Who had ever had such a first year? Ever?

Yet the year had not ended on a good note.

Earlier that day in the cloakroom, a supporter had said in a friendly tone—not an attack, as if in it together with him—"Mr. Speaker, we sure had a hell of a great start but it's a fucking disastrous end."

Wright's face had turned red and he had stormed away.

Now, in the last major vote of his first year as Speaker, Speaker of the 100th Congress, a majority of Democrats had voted against him. It was not as though they had rejected his initiative. But it was a terrible symbol. It wasn't the way he had wanted the year to end. Without the Caucus he had no power and he needed power. *I've got one quarter left to play,* he had said. *I want this back.*

After Wright and Coelho left, Mack and the Appropriations staff remained. They told more stories, drank more beer, laughed, told more stories. At six-thirty in the morning they stepped out onto the balcony. It was cold, well below freezing, but they did not feel the cold. They moved forward to the marble balustrade, stood in between the huge, thick marble columns. From there, from the summit of Capitol Hill, they looked down. Directly beneath them were magnolia trees, in leaf all winter; the treetops did not quite reach them. Straight ahead down the mall was the single spire of the Washington Monument. Directly beyond that lay the Lincoln Memorial. On either side lay the massive government buildings, Pennsylvania Avenue, Independence Avenue, Constitution Avenue. The whole city stretched out beneath them. The sun had not yet risen but there was light in the sky, and light from the city burned in the gloaming. Half a dozen of them stood out there on the balcony, shivering, silent and into themselves, cold yet warm, not wanting to go back inside.

Barely an hour after Mack and the Appropriations staff finally went home, in the dawn of the new day, workmen started emptying the suite of H-209, where Mack and other staff sat, and H-210, the ceremonial office, of furniture and stacking it in the corridor outside. They tore out the rug to expose the beautiful, old tiled floor that lay directly under the Revere chandelier. This was the old part of the Capitol, and Wright was restoring it to its former glory. Wright had moved into these rooms a year ago almost to the day, but only now was he changing the Speaker's Rooms into a place fully his own. He hadn't gotten comfortable in them yet.

PART VI
POWER
PLAY

It is far better to be feared than to be loved if you cannot be both. The prince must nonetheless make himself feared in such a way that if he is not loved at least he escapes being hated. . . . In republics there is more life, more hatred, a greater desire for revenge.

—Machiavelli, *The Prince*

CHAPTER 21

The first congressional session with Jim Wright as Speaker of the House had achieved his goals. The $90-billion, five-year highway bill was law, over the President's veto. The $20-billion, five-year Clean Water bill was law, over the President's veto. Legislation to help the homeless was law. An overhaul of the Farm Credit System was law. A housing bill was law—the first one passed in Reagan's presidency—and included new initiatives for low-income people. The budget summit, mediocre as it was, represented a victory of Wright's priorities, and, since it was a two-year agreement, it removed the budget and taxes from the new year's debate. The trade bill had passed the House. Catastrophic health insurance had passed the House. Welfare reform had passed the House. Central American governments trusted and confided in Wright more than in any member of the administration; proper or not, he had at least as much influence in Central America as the White House.

The *National Journal* and the *Congressional Quarterly* recognized Wright's success. Those two magazines were read closely by Washington insiders—who paid $455 a year for the former, $885 for the latter to track power and policy. The *National Journal* observed that Wright "may have set new standards for congressional activism. . . . Many Democrats, convinced that their party had lacked direction in recent years, were eager for strong leadership. Wright fit the bill." *Congressional Quarterly* reported "a dramatic shift in the balance of power in Washington." After analyzing key congressional votes, it concluded that Reagan's success rate had dropped from 65 percent in O'Neill's last year as Speaker to 12.5 percent in Wright's first.

The general-interest press did not look so deeply, and portrayed a different, more familiar Congress. *Newsweek* titled its congressional wrap-up story: "A Failure of Responsibility/Once Again, Congress Buckles to Special Interests," and predicted, "The second session promises to be even more contentious and unproductive than the first." *Business Week* entitled its piece "The Democrats Go Home Licking Their Wounds," and quoted Gingrich calling Wright "the most corrupt and destructive Speaker in the history of the country." (The phrase "most corrupt . . . in history" sounded too partisan and strident and undercut Gingrich's credibility; he soon returned to his more academic-sounding and precise "least ethical Speaker in the twentieth century.")

One member asked a reporter he was friendly with, "Why are you on Wright's ass?" The answer: "Because I don't think he's honest."

Gingrich's campaign was taking a toll.

Wright had another problem. Most Democrats felt they had an open channel of communication to Foley and others felt that way about Coelho, especially younger ones whom Coelho, as DCCC chair, had helped elect. Members had gotten into shouting matches with O'Neill, had told him exactly what they thought. They were careful around Wright. Coelho worried, "He does not consult. He says, 'I meet with members all the time,' and he does, but he has not built the infrastructure of personal relationships needed to govern."

Wright felt the vibrations in the web of his power and worried about them. His goals now were to allow the House to relax, soothe Republicans, and cool the press. The three goals were related. Particularly the last two were related. If Republicans felt they were being fairly treated, Gingrich would become isolated among his GOP colleagues. Collegial pressure could well stop him: if not, his pariah status would cause the press to dismiss him.

If Wright succeeded in calming things, his power could take root and deepen. Presidents came and went. Wright would remain. Rayburn served as Speaker for seventeen years. *If he ever consolidates his power, he will be a very, very formidable man,* Gingrich had said long ago. *If he survives this ethics thing, he may become the greatest Speaker since Henry Clay.* But if Wright failed to calm things, at best he would be constantly off-balance, unable to consolidate power.

At worst . . . what? The threat to his power could become serious. Deadly serious.

A few days before Christmas recess, Wright had said, "I'll kill the Republicans with kindness next year."

It would be difficult. The first vote of the year, one week after the House reconvened in late January, would be on contra aid, the single issue which most aroused passions. Whatever tone that vote set would likely continue through the rest of the Congress. But Wright would do what he could.

Earlier he had decided to host a luncheon in Michel's honor immediately after Congress returned. Now he formally invited Michel, explained his desire to listen to GOP complaints, and said, "I discern frustrations and strong feelings on your side. I want to alleviate that as much as I can short of sacrificing my responsibilities to the majority."

Michel was receptive to improving relations with the Democrats. And Gingrich was making waves which threatened him, too, which brought his leadership into question. Dealing with Gingrich was very delicate for Michel: Gingrich was useful at times, jabbing at Democrats while the GOP leadership distanced itself. Michel lacked the power to contain him anyway. But Michel now believed Gingrich had gone too far in his campaign against Wright. Unrelated to Wright's overture, he had had senior GOP staff prepare a study of past Speakers who had been accused of unethical behavior. Every one—Henry Clay in 1825, James Blaine in 1872, M. C. Kerr in 1876, and Samuel Randall in 1879—had allowed a Speaker pro tem to appoint a special investigating committee which exonerated them. Power had been part of those games too. During the recess, both Michel and Wright and their top aides went to Palm Springs for a week of sun and golf and honoraria as guests of tobacco and billboard advertising lobbyists, who often worked together. Bill Pitts handed Mack a copy of the report.

The implication, though unsaid, was clear: Wright should hand Michel the gavel and Michel would appoint a special investigating committee, then hand the gavel back. In a few weeks, at most a few months, the issue would end. Gingrich, who was ignorant of Michel's maneuver, would be cut out. "What's wrong with Bob appointing a committee which exonerates Wright?" a Republican close to Michel asked. "Get this thing behind him. For Gingrich to bring a resolution to the floor and force a vote is not the way to go about it. It would lose, of course, but some Republicans would vote for it. That would be bad."

Wright wanted to do it, but his attorney William Oldaker objected. Oldaker pointed out that the ethics committee had not existed in the nineteenth century. A special committee, even one appointed by Michel, could be lambasted as an effort to circumvent the ethics investigating process and whitewash Wright. It was not at all inconceivable that Gingrich would attack Michel, and try to generate press attacks as well. Wright had to let the opportunity pass. The ethics issue festered.

And his effort to fight back in the press exploded.

Soon after becoming Speaker, long before the first negative story had appeared about him and the savings and loan crisis, he had started looking for public relations advice. He was particularly interested in ways to get his message out into the country, and his aide Marshall Lynam brought in former Texas journalist Dean Reed, a public relations consultant, on a part-time basis. Reed had several ideas. One was to become a source for muckraking columnist Jack Anderson. Anderson did not attack his sources. Wright refused to go that route. Reed had other ideas as well, some of which were followed, but he soon disappeared. His chief legacy: bill-signing ceremonies Wright sometimes held before sending legislation to the White House. Bill signing by the Speaker was strictly a ministerial function. Previous Speakers had made nothing of it, but Wright occasionally scheduled ceremonies to raise the stature of the speakership and create press focus on major legislation. (The ceremonies aggravated the Republicans, who saw it as further evidence of Wright's ego.)

Meanwhile, Wright's wife, Betty—who considered his staff at best mediocre—began looking for another press aide. She asked Mallick to help. The résumé of George Mair cropped up. He had been a public relations executive and the publisher of an Alexandria, Virginia, newspaper. In his mid-fifties, considerably older than most Hill aides, he had charm and Hollywood contacts, and was a man of the world. There also seemed an insidious kind of cynicism about him: one got the sense that he understood things like money and Hollywood and glitter perhaps too well. Those things were not the world of power or politics, of the deep forces that stir a whole society into motion or conflict.

In the spring, Wright had asked Mair to write a few speeches. The speeches had left Wright unimpressed, but Mair had other suggestions. One was for him to ghostwrite an autobiography—he pointed out that O'Neill had gotten a million-dollar advance on his. Wright never gave him a firm go-ahead, but Mair approached publishers. He also maneuvered for a full-time job through Betty. His chief argument was to attack the rest of the staff as incompetent. Betty, who agreed, listened.

It took Mair more than six months, but he did get a job when Matthew Cossolotto, who would later strike back, left. A Phi Beta Kappa graduate of the University of California at Berkeley, Cossolotto was a speech writer who was unhappy. He had worked for Wright for several years but a second speech writer, hired when Wright became Speaker, earned almost $15,000 a year—40 percent—more than he. Cossolotto blamed Marshall Lynam for the discrepancy. He considered Lynam his intellectual inferior anyway, and showed it. To make room for Mair, Lynam told Cossolotto he had a new job—on the Foreign Affairs Committee. Cossolotto, who had been looking himself, reported there for work, announced angrily, "You mean I don't have an office?" and soon quit, fuming over his treatment.

Mair's title was "chief press officer" but neither of Wright's other two press aides—Charmayne Marsh, Wright's "press secretary," and Wilson Morris, his "director of information"—reported to him; they did not in fact communicate with him at all. Mair operated independently on several projects, trying, for example, to get the Public Broadcasting Service to conduct a tour of the Capitol with Betty playing hostess, as Jacqueline Kennedy had done in a tour of the White House. He set up meetings for Wright with editorial boards—the editors and senior reporters—of major newspapers; Wright's staff had often suggested he do that, but no one had ever arranged such meetings. Mair did. Other suggestions included setting up an 800 line which reporters could call for a current, recorded quote from Wright on issues of the day, and having Wright author a nationally syndicated column to get his views out. Mair also had one specific duty: counteracting negative stories.

Another duty was to fight negative press. Many stories written about Wright contained glaring inaccuracies. They had appeared in one story, been read by other reporters and gone into their clip files, and been repeated as fact. They had become "factoids." This was particularly true of stories about his savings and loan involvement. Mair began a concerted effort to correct them. Unknown to anyone else, he also began writing private letters complaining to publishers and senior editors about reporters.

Disciplined letters which focused on specific inaccuracies or concrete examples of unfairness could have had a positive impact and influenced future coverage for the better. Mair's letters were different. As he later explained in a memo, he had been trying to intimidate reporters by creating problems for them with their bosses. Even in that, his letters failed. To *Newsweek*'s editor-in-chief Richard Smith, he wrote a three-page, single-spaced letter which said, "In a way, I feel sorry for *Newsweek*. . . . I know *Newsweek* is in a circulation and advertising fight for its survival and that you're having to hype your sagging publication with stories on bra museums, angels of death, and seminude female movie stars. . . . The piece is awash with unsupported innuendo. . . . Why is [Wright's] smile labeled 'unctuous' rather than 'friendly'? . . ." He accused *The Wall Street Journal* of "sly-wink" innuendo, adding, "I know you have been suffering budget cuts . . . but are things so desperate that *The Wall Street Journal* cannot do it's [*sic*] own research? Are you reduced to relying on the unproven allegations of a Washington flak real estate magazine [*Regardie's*] . . . and the vague and partisan insults of demoralized Republicans?" He accused two *Los Angeles Times* reporters of "plagerism" [*sic*] and of not interviewing Wright. Both reporters interviewed Wright and there was no plagiarism. There were other letters, to other publications, calling other people names also.

Ironically, Coelho had included the *Los Angeles Times* story in a group of clips he had planned to give Wright to prove that their year-end media strategy had worked; despite its hard edge, it prominently featured the substantive points the leadership had wanted to make. Coelho had also planned a media-based counterattack on Gingrich.

On January 18, *Washington Post* reporter Tom Kenworthy wrote a story about the letters. Its impact was immediate. Coelho did not give Wright the memo and canceled the counterattack—the press would have ignored it.

Several colleagues, including Coelho, urged Wright to fire Mair. Mair hung on. *Jim's as hard a man to help as I know,* Bob Strauss had said.

Betty defended Mair and demanded to know if her husband was going to let the press decide who worked for him. She hated the press. Mair fought back, too, claiming that he had purposely misspelled words in copies of the letters he had given others on the staff. Since the misspellings appeared in the press, that meant another aide must have leaked the letters. Betty and some members of the staff believed him. (The letters were not leaked. Kenworthy heard a rumor—not from

Wright's staff—that they existed. He then called reporters likely to have received them and collected the letters, which included the misspellings, from them.) Now, on top of writing the letters, Mair was spreading poison throughout the staff. But Wright still would not fire him. Mair would not quit. Trust within the staff disintegrated. And Mair stayed on.

Wright mended fences with the particular reporters Mair had attacked, inviting them to lunch, apologizing, and having a waiter enter with a tray and ask, "Who gets the crow?"

But only a half-dozen reporters were at the lunch. Dozens of senior Washington journalists—reporters, columnists, editorial writers—viewed Wright with a new disdain. They would be less willing than ever to give him the benefit of the doubt. He needed that benefit of the doubt.

The same day Wright was eating crow, *The Wall Street Journal* ran a one-paragraph story in its "Washington Wire" reporting that the Teamsters union had bought one thousand copies of Wright's book *Reflections of a Public Man*. Brooks Jackson had tripped over the information while reviewing Teamsters political expenditures. It began to make sense that Carlos Moore, the book's publisher and a former Teamsters lobbyist, had proposed the book to Wright, offered a 55 percent royalty, and been confident of a profit himself. (The Teamsters played serious enough politics that four days before George Bush was inaugurated as President, he met with six union officials about to stand trial for racketeering.)

The small item about the book, compounded by Wright's press fiasco, energized Gingrich. Wright seemed more vulnerable than ever.

The Mair episode itself was damaging, and so was its timing: it occurred as Congress reconvened, precisely as House Democrats held their annual weekend retreat at the elegant Greenbrier resort. Rank-and-file members shook their heads in disbelief. They all knew the press, knew how stupid the letters had been. It did not set a good tone for the second session of the 100th Congress, particularly given the antagonisms with which the first session had ended. Wright had made himself an issue again.

For now, though, members quickly shifted their attention from Wright back to contra aid. The vote was barely a week away. Both sides had been maneuvering over it since the C.R. passed.

In the first week of January, less than ten days before the Central American presidents met to assess Sandinista compliance with the peace accords, National Security Adviser Colin Powell, Elliott Abrams, and other senior administration officials visited Costa Rica, El Salvador, Honduras, and Guatemala. They "urged" those governments to condemn Nicaragua for noncompliance. They accompanied that urging with a threat: the administration would have little interest in giving additional economic aid to Central America if the contras lost support.

As a counterweight to that visit, on January 14, the day before the presidents' meeting, Foley and Coelho—Wright stayed away, distancing himself from involvement—hosted a lunch with the Central American ambassadors.

Foley warned them bluntly that simply setting a new deadline for compliance would not be enough to end contra aid; something much more substantive had to come from the presidents' meeting.

Coelho had an even blunter message: Powell and Abrams represented only part of the U.S. government. Congress appropriated money and decided who got aid, not the White House.

House Democrats and the White House were clashing over who controlled foreign policy. Each side had constitutional authority: the Constitution reserved foreign policy to the Executive Branch, but the appropriating power lay with the Congress. In the *Federalist Papers,* James Madison had dismissed theories of a strict separation of powers, and argued instead for a "blend." But there was no blend.

Bonior missed the luncheon. He was in Costa Rica, demanding significant concessions from Ortega. Make them or contra aid would pass, Bonior warned. On *Meet the Press,* Arias echoed him: "The future of more aid to the contras is entirely in Daniel Ortega's hands."

On the eve of the presidents' meeting, Ortega yielded and announced an immediate end of the state of emergency, direct face-to-face contact between Sandinistas and contras in the talks mediated by Obando, a promise of amnesty immediately upon reaching a cease-fire agreement, and the release of prisoners to the United States if a cease-fire was not achieved.

A few days later, Ortega invited official American observers to monitor Nicaragua's compliance once contras laid down their arms, and wrote a personal letter to Reagan. He renounced his own past statements and those by other Sandinistas that they would not yield power even if they lost elections, and offered to shrink the army and expel

Soviet and Cuban advisers. *If only the United States ended contra aid.* Conservatives were unpersuaded, and pointed out that even as Ortega was sending the letter, another Sandinista official announced they would not give up power regardless of election results.

Military aid to the contras had stopped flowing on January 12. On January 19, Reagan certified that Sandinista bad faith was responsible for the lack of a cease-fire. Military aid started flowing again. On February 3 the House would vote, up or down, on the issue.

Wright had pulled back. After his meeting with Ortega and Obando in November, he had confronted Reagan and Shultz. But even then he had told them he did not expect to play a role in the next contra-aid vote. He had later sent ripples through a meeting of House activists— heads had turned to look at Bonior—by saying the same thing. In mid-January, on David Brinkley's show on ABC, Wright had been asked about a possible administration proposal to put military aid in escrow and replied, "It is worthy of consideration."

That had sent ripples through the Caucus too. Then—alone, without any leadership colleague—searching for a proposal he could support, searching for bipartisanship, even more, tired of fighting, he went to the White House to see Howard Baker and Colin Powell. He walked out. One senior House aide worried, "Wright's scared to death. I don't know what he'll agree to."

But Powell insisted that any proposal include military aid, and the Sandinistas had said repeatedly that any military aid would destroy the peace process. For an hour and a half they went back and forth, back and forth, over and over the same ground. Wright wanted out, all right, but at what price? He could not just bend his knee. He could not. Finally he decided, *They think they've got the votes. There's no point in talking anymore.*

There was no deal. But Wright remained in the background. He did not attend a formal meeting of the Caucus on the issue. He declined invitations to Sunday TV shows. He resisted efforts to have him make the closing floor speech.

Then Wright hosted his luncheon for Michel. It was large, too large and awkward for the candid get-off-the-chest comments Wright had wanted. Cheney did complain about the reconciliation vote. Wright said that he had done everything possible to win. Perhaps too much. The decisions to proceed, to include welfare reform, to create the second legislative day, had been his. Perhaps he had been wrong. He hoped to do better in the future. Cheney considered his comments gracious and hopeful. But events would soon dwarf the impact of his words.

A few days earlier, twenty Democratic moderates led by David McCurdy had written the White House asking for concessions in the contra-aid package in return for support. They had been rebuffed. Now, as Wright returned from the luncheon, he found them encamped in his outer office, demanding to see him.

Politicians generally dislike simply voting no; sometimes their plays resemble a shell game. To justify a no vote, they generally like to be able to point to something similar that they support. Here, without an alternative to vote for, they would have difficulty voting against Reagan's plan. In this case an alternative did more than provide political cover; it also made policy sense to keep pressure on the Sandinistas. They wanted a commitment from him to put together a Democratic contra-aid proposal.

Wright had tried to work out a final agreement with the White House. He had tried to remain in the background of this confrontation. Now he was being pulled back into it. He agreed. He would delegate the effort to put together a Democratic proposal, but publicly, inevitably, it would become his plan. He was in the background no longer. He and the White House were at war again.

A week earlier, Wright had called the idea of holding military aid in escrow "worthy of consideration," upsetting liberals. Now his aide Wilson Morris told *The New York Times* that the escrow idea "is a built-in incentive to the contras not to agree to a cease-fire. . . . We're dead set against the proposal."

The administration plan called for $36.25 million to cover four months, including $3.6 million in escrow for military aid if no cease-fire was achieved, as well as another $20 million to replace aircraft if they were shot down. On an annual basis it was more money than the contras had ever received, and if it passed, the White House could make another aid request with a guaranteed floor vote after July 1.

But the White House had ignored advice from Hill Republicans regarding what could pass. Elsewhere, the White House was blundering too. John Murtha, the Democratic leadership loyalist who was also pro-contra, told Reagan, "You've got to get rid of Elliott Abrams. Members don't trust him. He's killing you on this." But Abrams stayed. Reagan wanted to make a nationally televised appeal for people to contact their congressmen on the issue. His aides decided against a prime-time appeal, choosing instead an afternoon speech; they did not want him to highlight his appeal and then be defeated.

Tuesday, February 2, a whip task force gathered in mid-afternoon in H-324, the Thomas P. O'Neill Room where the regular whip meetings were held. The smell of victory, the excitement of it, pervaded the room.

As the meeting was about to begin, Reagan was making his televised address for contra aid. The TV was on. None of the major networks, only CNN, carried his speech live. "What a slap," one member said. How far Reagan had fallen.

The next day the House defeated Reagan's plan 219–211. From the Speaker's Rostrum, Wright looked down on the floor. To his left, Republicans milled about angrily. To his right, Democrats laughed, less with the pride of accomplishment than with derision. The center aisle dividing them seemed so wide. He had never wanted this. This was not the House he had envisioned. Rayburn had had no home but this, no family but this, no children, no wife except for a few secret weeks. Wright had those things, but this was his home too.

After the vote, Russo, grinning, went up to Foley and shook his hand. A colleague commented wryly, "He's kissing ass—I should do more of that myself."

It was a sign that Wright had reasserted control over the Caucus. Even Russo did not want to be out in the cold anymore. Or was the Caucus finally controlling Wright?

On February 4, in a meaningless vote, the Senate approved Reagan's plan. Immediately, House Democrats started to put together their own proposal. If it passed it would mark the final ascension of Jim Wright. He would have not only defeated the administration's foreign policy, but would have substituted his own. Ironically, for the one moment he wished to remain in the background, the Caucus had thrust him forward, raised him high.

Bitterly Republicans looked up at him.

Bonior led the group trying to put together the proposal. He had to produce a package which would not alienate liberals, give political cover to conservatives, and content the twelve Republicans who had voted against the President. It was difficult.

Michel made Bonior's job more difficult. He knew that if the Democratic alternative were the only option, it would likely pass. He was determined not to cede control of Central American policy to Wright. If House Republicans produced a plan of their own more palatable to Democratic moderates than the one the White House had offered, those Democrats would have a difficult time voting against it. That would make it hard, very hard, for Wright's proposal to pass; perhaps it would make it impossible. Perhaps, finally, Republicans could bring Wright down—not Gingrich's way, but the proper way, with votes, on the floor.

Michel visited Wright in his office, alone. This was between the two of them. When the House had voted on the President's plan, Democrats had had no chance to offer an alternative. Now, unless Wright demanded it, Rules would not let a second Republican plan on the floor. Michel asked him to do so.

Wright could have refused. The Republicans had just had their vote. By rights, the next vote should be the Democrats' turn. But Wright was almost desperate to reach out. He had always gone out and consciously made friends, over all those years in all those towns. And making things easy for Michel would in turn make things easy for himself. Michel left with what he considered a commitment for a vote.

Meanwhile, intensity increased. Pro-contra groups were running full-page newspaper ads accusing moderates, mostly in conservative southern areas, who had opposed Reagan of selling out to the communists. Wright had wanted the Democratic package on the floor by mid-February. It wasn't ready. At a whip meeting a southerner pleaded, "Don't leave us hanging out there."

Each day that passed the House grew more bitter.

On February 19, Gingrich held another press conference. He announced that within a few weeks, he would file formal charges against Jim Wright, demanding an ethics committee investigation.

In late February, Bonior's group finally agreed on a package: a total of $25 million in humanitarian aid (food, clothing, and medicine) for the contras and children on both sides of the war. It also stipulated that if the House Intelligence Committee certified that the Sandinistas were undermining chances for a cease-fire, the House would vote promptly on more contra aid.

Bonior briefed Wright in his office with the rest of the leadership. Wright liked it, liked the money for innocent victims. Maybe it would bring peace. He began to quote Lincoln's second Inaugural Address: "Fondly do we hope, fervently do we pray, that this mighty scourge of war do speedily pass away." Then Foley quoted the next line: "Let us strive on to finish the work we are in—" and Wright quoted the next: "to bind up the nation's wounds, to care for him who shall have borne the battle, and for his widow, and his orphan—to do all which may achieve and cherish a just and a lasting peace, among ourselves and with all nations." As Wright and Foley went back and forth, line to line, chills went up the spines of those present. They had one week to the vote.

The next whip meeting was packed with members, more than had come in months; even members who were not whips came. An extra row of seats was not enough. Members crowded the back of the room, stood in the aisle, squeezed staff into corners and crevices.

There was good news to begin with: five anti-contra church groups were endorsing the Democratic plan. That meant that the grass-roots peace activists around the country—intense people who set up picket lines in front of members' homes—recognized political reality; if this plan failed a GOP package could pass. Liberals would be forgiven for supporting this plan.

But that good news did not calm anyone. A southerner rose and complained he had heard that the Republicans expected a vote on their plan first. "The next vote has got to be on our proposal," he demanded. "I can't have several votes in a row against contra aid."

Another southerner—who served on the task force which produced the package—seconded that: "I'm taking heat. It's hurting."

"Why give Republicans another vote?" said a third. "Why give them two bites at the apple?"

"They've already had two bites! We didn't get a vote against aid in the C.R. Then the President's plan. Are they getting three votes in a row without us getting one?"

"It's time to worry about Democrats!"

"What's the procedure?" a member asked.

"It has not been decided yet," Bonior replied.

Republicans were putting together their package. It was politically astute, and included aid for children and no outright lethal aid, only logistical support. The total was $36.25 million for two months; after that, it guaranteed a floor vote, bypassing the Rules Committee, on another White House proposal. If the GOP plan was voted on, it might pass. *If it passed, the Democratic Caucus could explode.* Republicans believed they would get a vote. A Republican close to Michel said, "We have Wright's word on it."

Parliamentary procedure was crucial. Procedurally, an amendment to a bill is voted on first; if it passes, then the vote for final passage is on the bill *as amended.* The amendment can change anything from one word to every word—a complete substitute—in the bill. Republican substitutes for Democratic proposals usually come to the floor as a "substitute in the form of an amendment." If this Republican proposal was voted on first and passed, then the Democratic package would disappear without being voted on. Conversely, if Democrats made the GOP plan the main bill, and the Democratic proposal became the substitute, then the Democratic plan would be voted on first. If it passed, the Republican package would be erased without ever being voted on. Only if Republicans defeated it could they get a vote on their plan. Several Democratic moderates had said they had to vote yes on the next contra-aid package that came up, whatever it was.

The Rules Committee declared that the Democratic package would be an amendment to the Republican bill. The next vote would be on the Democratic plan. Leaving the Rules Committee, a furious Michel hissed, "They screwed us."

Later, Wright recalled, "I did say to Michel, 'Here's what I intend to do' and intended to give him a vote. I did not interpret that as a pledge. What I promised was an 'alternative under the rule.' " But he conceded, "I can understand how Michel would have thought he had a commitment."

The word "alternative" was important. That meant only that Republicans would get some undefined opportunity for a vote. Republicans insisted that Wright had promised Michel a "substitute under the rule"; a *substitute* had a specific parliamentary meaning—it meant an amendment. A substitute would be voted on first.

Wright believed he had kept his word to Michel. Michel believed he had broken it. But even if Wright had not given Michel a commitment, he had said he intended to give Republicans a vote. When the Speaker of the House says he intends to do something within his power to do, was that not good enough?

Michel was outraged, absolutely infuriated. The entire Republican Conference was infuriated. *Wright would do anything to win.* No matter how many luncheons Wright hosted, he had just driven that point home again. *You can't deal with Wright. He just takes what he wants. All he understands is power.*

Michel returned to his office and immediately released perhaps the harshest formal statement he had ever made: "Seldom in my tenure in Congress has the Democratic majority exercised such abuse of the legislative process as they have in the procedures which have been forced upon us for considering the contra-aid proposal. The Rules Committee's action in effect denied the bipartisan coalition's proposal for effective contra aid any real chance of passing or even being voted on. In over thirty years as a member of this institution, I have kept my word. I expect others to do the same."

O'Neill had had his critics but had been a rock. Even Rayburn, mythological Rayburn, had been called cautious and even timid in juggling factions within the Caucus. But Rayburn, short, thickly built, almost troll-like, had been a rock. One key to Wright's victory in the majority leader race had been the sense, *You can count on Wright.* Michel, his own reputation solid, was calling him a liar.

The only thing you have in politics is your word, the saying went. *If you don't have that you have nothing.*

Just before the vote, Ortega announced that he was dismissing Cardinal Obando as a mediator and that his government would sit down directly with the contras. That was what the White House had called for all along, but now suddenly it was demanding that Obando continue to play a role. *This is getting tiresome,* Wright thought. *Maybe this vote will resolve the issue finally.*

On the morning of the vote, Thursday, March 3, Democrats believed they would win. They were confident of erasing Michel's plan, of collecting a few GOP votes on final passage, and keeping almost all Democratic moderates. At breakfast, John Mack predicted that even Charlie Stenholm would support final passage of the Democratic package. When Wright chortled, Mack offered to bet. Wright took the bet, but was more interested in moving on and commented, "We'll see if there's life after the contras."

He was planning a mailing of 50,000 letters through the DCCC to Democratic activists—not so much to raise money as to try to create a cadre of activities attuned to his message. One idea the letter would push would be rebuilding the infrastructure; he hoped to build support for it for the future, in the next administration. Already he had sent a letter about trade to economics reporters, and he would soon talk to Foley about an omnibus, bipartisan drug bill. Two years earlier Congress had passed one under Wright's direction, and perhaps another bipartisan bill could demonstrate that Wright remained able to work with the minority.

But bipartisanship had collapsed. That day, March 3, was the regular Thursday whip meeting. Foley announced that he had asked Republican permission to convene the House at ten o'clock so that members could get out early and catch flights home for the weekend. They had refused, inconveniencing themselves just to spite Democrats. They would not now cooperate on anything. And they had just pulled surprise parliamentary tactics, part of their guerrilla war on the floor.

One member suggested changing House rules for the next Congress to prevent some of the GOP tactics, requiring, for example, a day's notice on certain motions.

"That's a good idea," Coelho replied. "We'll look into that."

More squeeze on the minority. Less room for them to maneuver. More power for the leadership. If the Republicans tried to screw around, they deserved it. Screw them.

"I'm tired of their attacking the Speaker," another member said angrily. "This rule is fair! Why should the Republicans get three votes in a row?"

Wright said, "I made a commitment to many of you in this room that you'd get a vote, before making a commitment to Michel. I know procedure. How could I have done that if I promised him a substitute? Michel knows what I said to him, that he'd have 'an alternative under the rule.' He's got that."

A few hours later the House convened in a mood which vacillated between sullen and bitter. In debate over the rule, GOP whip Trent Lott asked rhetorically, "Is there any honor and trust left between us?" Michel declared, "We were promised a fair shot at a substitute. We got a shot, all right, a shot to the head."

No Republicans voted for the rule. The debate over the bill was equally vicious, especially over the money intended for children who were war victims. Republicans claimed it would be given to Danny Ortega to distribute. It was not true; an international agency would distribute the aid. Stenholm had told Republicans that he would be with them on the first vote, but had not decided on final passage. He'd rather send the contras something than nothing. Now, in debate, Stenholm repeated the charge that the Sandinistas would control the money for war victims.

As Stenholm spoke, Wright stiffened. Their history went back a long way, back to Wright's supporting his primary opponent in 1978, back through all those times Stenholm had refused Wright's requests for help when Reagan was flying high, back four months earlier to reconciliation. Wright had stood naked before him, had asked for his help. *I somewhat prostrated myself before him and he pissed in my face,* Wright had said.

Wright was on the floor, not in the chair, and stalked to a microphone. Would the gentleman yield? he asked.

Stenholm was glad to yield to the distinguished Speaker from Texas.

For all the courtesy, Wright's words were like furies: he said Stenholm was either "just lying or he doesn't understand it."

The floor was still. It was an extraordinary statement to make in public, much less in the well of the House. Stenholm, one of those men who always stood straight, as if one's posture indicated one's character, drew himself even straighter. "I am not lying," he said.

Nor did the hostility in the chamber cool. As Mike Lowry was finishing his speech, halfway through reading a letter written by a Nicaraguan child, the gavel banged down—he was out of time, his speech a few seconds short of its emotional peak. In such circumstances a member asks unanimous consent for a few more seconds and it is routinely granted. Lowry looked up from the well and saw enemies. Republicans were enemies. *He could not bring himself to ask them for anything.* Instead he demanded that the chair grant him thirty additional seconds because noise among the Republicans had disrupted him. The chair refused. "Unanimous consent!" shouted Democratic colleagues. Lowry hesitated again, then, with no recourse, said, "I ask for unanimous consent for an additional thirty seconds."

Republican Mickey Edwards said coolly, "I object."

"Objection is heard," announced the chair. The chamber was cold with a cold silence. The chill went through every member on the floor.

The Democratic "amendment" passed 215–210. Only three Republicans voted for it, and thirty-seven Democrats voted no—a mix of liberals who opposed any aid and conservatives who wanted more.

Stenholm voted no. So did Pennsylvania Democrat Austin Murphy, whom the House had recently reprimanded over an ethics issue—diverting federal resources to his former law firm and other charges—and who was opposing everything the leadership wanted in retaliation. The Republican proposal was erased; the Democratic "amendment" had become the bill. But there was one more vote.

"The question is on final passage of the bill," the chair declared.

A handful of liberals had warned the leadership they would vote yes first, to kill the Republican plan, but would vote no on final passage. Final passage would actually send aid to the contras, and they would not do so, would not have blood on their hands. To pass this bill, Wright needed Republican help. Coelho told Bill Pitts, "We don't have the votes. You'll have to pass it. All we need is ten, maybe not that many." *But Pitts was Michel's man.* He would not help Wright, not now. John Murtha, the pro-contra Democrat, scoured the Republican side of the chamber, arguing with them, *If you care about the contras, you should support this plan. The contras are begging for the money. They've been lobbying for this rather than nothing.* The Senate would pass a much harder line aid package, and Republicans would have a shot in conference of getting something they liked. As the vote started, the leadership had three liberals who had promised to support the plan if their votes would make a difference.

Those three members watched the count and voted late. But Stenholm voted no, and Stenholm took at least three other conservative Democrats with him. Only five Republicans voted yes. The three liberals would not make any difference. The leadership came up two votes short of their mattering. They voted no.

In total, forty-five Democrats voted no. Twenty-six wanted no aid, eighteen wanted more, and Murphy. The Democrats had put together by far their most cohesive vote ever on Central American policy. It had not been enough.

Wright stood at the rostrum. With a sour look and a voice trying to hide disgust, he announced, "The yeas are 208, the nays are 216, and the bill is not agreed to."

The outcome had nothing to do with policy. Nothing to do with the contras. It was personal. Personal between Stenholm and Wright, and personal between the Republicans and Wright. Republicans cared about contra aid perhaps with more intensity than they cared about any other single issue. They argued that two years earlier they had voted down a compromise package, and ended up with $100 million in military aid. It could happen again. But this situation was different. And they had killed contra aid.

That night Alfredo Cesar, one of the contra leaders, called Wright's office complaining about the loss. *Why is he calling us?* an aide growled. *He should be complaining to Michel.*

After the vote Michel called Reagan, who was in Europe. Reagan congratulated him. It was personal between Reagan and Wright too. Later that evening Michel said, "They could have won that. It was the procedure that did them in. [We] were incensed."

That same night, Cheney had dinner with a group of lobbyists. He was furious—furious. A well-connected Democratic lobbyist asked what message he could take back to Wright to restore comity. Cheney was implacable: "There isn't any message. We want his head."

Immediately after the vote, Wright hardened. The criticism had hurt him. He searched inside himself, went into himself, and emerged. He seemed thicker, denser, stronger, deeper. Surface had gotten him into trouble; trying to maneuver, trying to keep both Michel and the Caucus happy. There would be no more of that. Frustrated but firm, solid, he lashed out and reached elsewhere for power.

Did they accuse him of trying to run American foreign policy? All right then. He would run it. And it might be time to further his structural goals inside the House as well.

He told his staff to get a telegram out to Ortega, warning him of the consequences of any aggressive action against the contras. Then he asked, "What about other legislation? It's March already." But there was little to be done. "It's because of Ways and Means," Wright snapped. "That committee has too damn much jurisdiction. The same people are in conference all the time—" on trade, catastrophic health insurance, and welfare reform, each a major bill— "while too many able people in the House are sitting around doing nothing. We'll have to get together with the parliamentarian about referring bills to that committee. Rayburn once referred a tax bill to Public Works."

Rostenkowski had voted against the contra-aid bill.

Then, less than two weeks after the vote, events in Central America seemed to sweep suddenly out of Wright's control—the Sandinista army crossed into Honduras to attack contra bases there. It was only a few days before the contras and Sandinistas were scheduled to sit down, face-to-face without an intermediary, in cease-fire talks.

The State Department and White House trumpeted this invasion almost gleefully.

Reagan asked for an emergency meeting with the bipartisan congressional leadership. They gathered in the Cabinet Room, just off the Oval Office. As they began, there was a "photo op," a photographer allowed to take a picture, and Reagan and Wright smiled, but as soon as the photographer exited the edge in the room sharpened. Administration officials demanded a new vote, and support for military aid.

Wright refused. Both Sandinistas and contras had been in constant touch with him and his staff. He trusted his information, and information was power. The contras had asked him to do nothing which would jeopardize the scheduled cease-fire negotiations. The administration had to have that same intelligence; it was ignoring it. He replied that he would allow a vote only on the kind of humanitarian-aid package just defeated, and would do that only if the White House guaranteed that two-thirds of the Republicans would support it.

"We're not interested in a humanitarian-aid package anymore," Cheney said.

Shultz concurred. He insisted that this was a significant invasion. Wright replied that Sandinista foreign minister Miguel D'Escoto had told him that no Sandinistas were in Honduras.

Michel banged his fist on the table. "This is an outrage! that you would take the word of a foreigner over the Secretary of State."

"No, Bob," Wright replied calmly. "I know when George Shultz says something it's true or he believes it to be true. Both statements could be accurate. They could have crossed the border and withdrawn."

The meeting broke up in disharmony. Wright was immovable, perhaps implacable. Republicans saw him blocking the foreign policy of the United States.

The administration launched a withering onslaught to sell its position. And *The Washington Post* reported, "Administration officials swarmed over Capitol Hill to brief lawmakers on what they described as a large-scale Sandinista invasion of Honduras. . . . Lawmakers were being given the hard intelligence information to justify reversal of the House vote . . . cutting off lethal aid." TV news broadcasts carried pictures of the jungle, stories about the Sandinista invasion.

Then the White House took a dramatic step: it sent 3,200 American troops to Honduras. It was a public relations maneuver, but a hardball one. With American troops on the ground, refusal to vote more contra military aid would make congressional Democrats look as if they were jeopardizing American lives. *Democrats would have to yield.*

Wright stood firm. It was an enormous gamble, based on information coming to him from Central America. D'Escoto, the Sandinista foreign minister, had called and insisted his country was serious about reaching a cease-fire. *They are worried about the Russians cutting off aid,* Wright thought. *That has to be a new factor, on top of all the others.* Then— ironically, while Wright was talking to D'Escoto—Alfredo Cesar, one of the contra leaders, called and reported that he and his colleagues would attend the cease-fire talks despite the incident in Honduras. That news was crucial; it convinced Wright that the contras too were serious. He grew angry, certain that the administration knew this, certain that the administration was trying to manipulate events to pass military aid to destroy chances for a cease-fire.

At his next daily press conference he declared that there was no justification for sending troops. His aides handed out copies of the Iran-contra committee report detailing "intelligence misrepresentation for policy purposes" about a minor Sandinista incursion into Honduras several years earlier, which the White House had exploited to get votes. Wright was as much as calling the administration a pack of liars.

Meanwhile the House floor erupted. In a one-minute Coelho blamed Republicans for deserting the contras: "We now know the truth. The Republicans abandoned the contras to the politics of cynicism!"

He had touched a nerve. Robert Dornan, a California conservative, responded in a one-minute and raged at "the radical and liberal leadership in this House." His minute expired but he continued talking. Gary Ackerman of New York was the Speaker pro tem, his first time ever in the chair. He banged the gavel, banged the gavel. *The gentleman's time has expired.* Dornan raged on. Ackerman was confused, did not know what to do, banged the gavel to no avail. Finally he ordered Dornan's microphone cut off. It remained on inside the chamber, but the C-SPAN coverage went silent. *Now the Democrats were cutting off free speech in the House! It was an incredible abuse of power, one more example of the corruption of power. Now they weren't even allowing Republicans to speak!* The next day the House by 381–0 approved a resolution that television coverage would be independent of the control of House officers.

Wright still stood firm. There was no vote on military aid. The contras and Sandinistas sat down across from each other, face-to-face, in Sapoa, Nicaragua.

Six days after the United States denounced the Sandinista invasion of Honduras and sent American troops there, the contras and Sandinistas agreed to a sixty-day cease-fire during which their negotiators would seek a comprehensive peace agreement.

Wright immediately endorsed it.

The *Washington Times,* one of the most conservative, pro-contra papers in America and a bitter enemy of Wright, reported that the contras "walked away from [the negotiations] with nearly everything they asked for."

Despite that assessment, Mickey Edwards initially denounced Wright's embrace of the agreement as "embarrassing and outrageous. . . . The whole process has gone backwards because of Wright's stupid meddling."

Democrats had always considered Edwards a responsible legislator, someone they could work with. Now his words, dripping with hatred, signified the depths of enmity in the House. He hated Wright. Grudgingly, Republicans did come to support the agreement. They had to. There would be one more vote on contra aid, a bipartisan package consistent with the cease-fire accord. As part of the agreement, Wright gave a written pledge—an insult that Republicans demanded it in writing—to schedule another vote on more aid if the President requested it. One week after the cease-fire announcement, by a 345–70 vote with only five Republicans voting no, the House approved $47 million in humanitarian aid to the contras. But the House was sullen that day.

Wright had won. The issue anyway; he had won the issue. But issues come and go. Power was the constant. Power was what mattered over time. It was power which determined the direction of the country. His power was being assaulted.

CHAPTER 22

Early in March, Newt Gingrich paced back and forth in his Rayburn Building office late into the night, past midnight, plotting strategy with several allies against Jim Wright. He usually worked like this, pacing, restless, thinking out loud, sitting for an instant and then jumping back to his feet; he had a stand-up desk and found it hard to keep seated or work seated. It was especially hard today; Gingrich's campaign against Wright had just suffered a setback. And for the first time it had been driven home to Gingrich that he could destroy himself in this obsession.

The setback had been dealt by Bob Michel. Gingrich now had to plan his next step. With him, Van Brocklin recalled, were herself; Daniel Swillinger, the attorney who had been helping him for months dig up dirt on Democrats; several other lawyers; and two writers for the *Washington Times*, Tony Snow, editor of the editorial page, and Terrence Jeffrey.

This meeting was far from Gingrich's first move of the year.

He had never relented from his campaign against Wright, either in the media or elsewhere. On February 17, he again wrote David Gergen, editor of *U.S. News & World Report,* and the former communications director of the Reagan White House. On February 25, he appealed to the competitiveness of Abe Rosenthal, executive editor of *The New York Times,* as he had earlier to *The Washington Post*'s Ben Bradlee, writing, "I'm just puzzled why *The New York Times* hasn't taken on the issue of corruption in the House like *The Washington Post* and *The*

Wall Street Journal have"; subsequently he flew to New York to meet with the *Times* editorial board.

He had recently raised the issue of Wright with Attorney General Ed Meese, consumer activist Ralph Nader, and the organizers of conservative causes. To each, phrased with different degrees of subtlety, he made a different appeal: to Meese, who was eager to divert media attention from his own ethics lapses, for an investigation; to Nader, for help cleaning up corruption; to—one of many such appeals—James Taylor, a conservative who ran America's PAC, for help circulating petitions calling for an investigation of Wright.

He had also repeatedly pressured Common Cause's president, Fred Wertheimer. Common Cause was key: Gingrich needed its nonpartisan credibility. In a February 16 letter to Wertheimer, Gingrich noted that "In your July 29, 1987, letter to [ethics] Chairman Dixon"—this letter came eight days after Gingrich's own letter to Wertheimer—"you stated that, 'The Ethics Committee has abdicated its responsibility. . . .' Your silence in this [Wright] matter weakens the cause of honest government." The language was a veiled threat. For someone who knew Gingrich, and Wertheimer was coming to know him, it was not difficult to imagine oneself becoming a Gingrich target. Common Cause was nonpartisan; being attacked by one party as favoring the other could devastate it.

And on February 19, Gingrich had again called a press conference and announced that he would file his ethics complaint against Wright in March.

Then Michel had acted. Shrewder and more manipulative than his salt-of-the-earth image, and careful, a careful man, he tried to keep the forces within the GOP Conference balanced. And at his core he was a legislator. If he had little use for Wright, he did not want the White House destroyed. He had sat down with Gingrich in his office and, while not telling him to stop, had made clear that this was serious business. Gingrich was talking about investigating the Speaker of the United States House of Representatives, second only to the President in power. That was precisely Gingrich's point, he replied.

But Gingrich agreed when Michel asked him to allow some people to examine his allegations. Michel then talked to GOP members Robert Livingston and James Sensenbrenner and asked them to review what Gingrich had. Several lawyers who were also GOP House aides, led by Hyde Murray, an institution man, would help them. It was to be done in utmost secrecy. No leaks, no discussion with other members. Neither was a friend to Wright. Livingston, a former prosecutor from suburban New Orleans, was one of the strongest advocates of contra aid in the House and was offended by Wright's involvement in Central America. He had also served on the ethics committee where he had developed a reputation as unforgiving. Sensenbrenner, from Wisconsin, was conservative, confrontational, and a fighter with a hard edge. That edge had been honed during six years as an official GOP "objector" (monitoring Democrats' "unanimous consent" requests on the floor). He had also led some of the GOP protests over the seating of Democrat Frank McCloskey after his disputed 1985 election—an event which Gingrich considered "seminal" in developing GOP recognition of the "corrupt in the Lord Acton sense" way Democrats ran the House.

Gingrich gave Livingston and Sensenbrenner a fat file, approximately seven inches thick. But everything in the file was newspaper clippings, and they all covered the same handful of charges. Some of the stories specifically stipulated that no evidence of anything illegal had been uncovered. Many of the charges, even if true, did not violate House rules. Livingston, Sensenbrenner, and the three lawyer-aides spent several weeks reviewing Gingrich's evidence and reached a unanimous conclusion: Gingrich had nothing of any consequence.

Michel asked them to tell Gingrich. They gathered in Michel's fine, old office. Gingrich argued that the repeated stories—some of which he had helped shape—painted a compelling portrait of a man who should be investigated. Wasn't there one hell of a lot of smoke? Livingston and Sensenbrenner agreed that there was smoke. But this wasn't an issue of appearances—of whether Wright had done something embarrassing or was not above reproach. It wasn't about whether Wright had done something for which editorial writers and columnists could or should castigate him. *You don't just go around investigating people because they did something that wouldn't look good on the front page of* The Washington Post. *You needed a solid reason.* When that standard was applied, Gingrich's file fell well short.

"What about a grand jury?" Gingrich asked. Going to the ethics committee was analogous to going to a grand jury. "Isn't there enough to go to a grand jury?"

Unanimously, the lawyers agreed there was not. Later Livingston said, "This was serious. Sometimes you try to do the right thing."

Gingrich returned to his office angry and disturbed. "It was disheartening," his aide Van Brocklin said. Even as hostile as Republicans were toward Wright, if he filed charges the ethics committee would likely vote 12–0 to dismiss them. *Then where would he be?* His credibility would be destroyed. His entire existence depended on the media attention to him. He would be destroyed. Wright was the route to power. *Jim Wright is the symbol of Democratic control of the House,* he had once said. *I don't think he's a Mafia don. He's a symbol of the machine.* But Gingrich had to take care. He called the late-night meeting. What would he do now? He and his allies reviewed what they had.

Swillinger, the attorney, picked out the strongest point in their case, that Wright had failed to disclose adequately the activities of Mallightco, his closely held partnership with Mallick. They planned to hit that hard.

The two *Washington Times* writers, Snow and Jeffrey, talked about Wright's Fort Worth activities. Their presence was unusual. It was one thing for a paper to investigate someone, then trade information with a source. It was another thing for journalists to sit in a meeting with a politician to help plan a strategy. Participation in such a meeting would have been grounds for firing at most newspapers, but Snow seemed to be coordinating his efforts with Gingrich, dispatching Jeffrey and another investigator to Fort Worth. Just after Gingrich's last press conference, Snow had run editorials on successive days attacking Wright, helping to build support for filing charges; one had been titled "Taken to the Laundry," accusing Wright of using his book to launder campaign contributions.

Three things came out of this late-night meeting. First was an intense effort that lasted several months to dig up new, damaging material on Wright. Swillinger looked into allegations about Wright's involvement in a sex scandal with teenage pages several years earlier, but was forced to report in a memo, "This whole episode appears to be a dead end." Van Brocklin looked into federally funded projects in Fort Worth, going so far as to investigate the fact that Wright's friends had several reserved parking spaces in a garage partly built with federal funds. (Gingrich demanded an explanation from the federal agency overseeing the project, and received a copy of a lease for the spaces.) Gingrich himself investigated whether Wright had ever been promoted to a general in the air force reserve—that and its pension could make a good story. (Wright had not been.)

The second decision made in the meeting was that Swillinger and other attorneys would proceed to draft an ethics complaint, seeking to focus and tighten it as much as possible to meet some of the objections Livingston and Sensenbrenner raised. Van Brocklin made sure the attorneys had all available material.

The third decision: to launch an even more aggressive media strategy. *The crowd needs a direction . . . It will accept any goal . . . The crowd crystal is constant . . . [and] serves to precipitate crowds.*

In the two weeks following this session, Gingrich initiated a blizzard of direct and indirect press contacts. He wrote to Assistant Attorney General William Weld, "May I suggest, the next time the news media asks about corruption in the White House, you ask them about corruption in the Speaker's office." A similar letter went to George Bush.

He contacted conservative columnist George Will, a strong Reagan supporter, and appealed for his help: "It is frightening to take on this much power, and the ability of the Speaker to protect himself is awesome." Gingrich was stroking his ego, implying that Will had the courage to confront Wright, and used the same sentence in letters to other major media figures.

He wrote conservative columnist James Kilpatrick and said bluntly, "Our goal is to establish a news media focus . . . so that members will realize that a public accounting of Wright's personal and financial dealings is necessary."

He contacted *Washington Post* and *New York Times* reporters and editorial writers, and columnists he believed were receptive to charges of corruption. He contacted the Ethics Resource Center, and several PACs, including Free the Eagle, Citizens for the Republic, and Citizens for Reagan. They would gather petitions calling for an investigation of Wright, and keep the issue alive, make it a priority, among grass-roots conservatives, who were urged to take action themselves. *Resonance.*

He also sent out a "Dear Colleague"—members of the press and Common Cause also got the letter—including copies of stories from *The New York Times* and *The Wall Street Journal* about the indictment of Thomas Gaubert. Gaubert, the former finance chairman for the DCCC, had co-chaired Wright's November fund-raising dinner and was one of the men for whom Wright had spoken to savings and loan regulators. The indictment dealt with unrelated charges, and Gaubert was later acquitted. Gingrich wrote that the "attached articles . . . are further proof that allegations of unethical and questionable conduct against Speaker Jim Wright need to be investigated."

Gingrich even contacted Illinois Democratic senator Paul Simon, who had a reputation for being rigidly honest. Simon wrote back commending Gingrich's "guts," and suggesting they work together on campaign finance reform.

The nationally known media figures he contacted did not write columns in response to his importunings, but several contacted him. Gingrich persisted in his dogged strategy of generating stories in smaller papers, kept up his visits to cities and reporters around the nation: in Nashville, both the *Banner* and the *Tennesseean;* in Seattle, the *Times;* in Orlando, the *Sentinel;* in Sacramento, the *Bee;* in Las Vegas, the *Review-Journal;* in Boston, the *Herald,* and others. *Resonance.* He was building resonance. The national columnists were grand-slam home runs, but he could get where he wanted with singles.

Lastly, he continued pounding on Wertheimer and Common Cause. A copy of each new clipping was sent to him. Every few weeks Gingrich wrote to him. Finally, after Gingrich's February 16 letter, Wertheimer wrote back on February 18. Gingrich's letter was addressed "Dear Fred" and signed "Newt." Wertheimer's letter was addressed "Dear Representative Gingrich" and signed with his full name and title. "It was pretty cold," Van Brocklin said. "Basically he told us they weren't going to do anything."

On March 11, Gingrich wrote him, again. He called. His staff called Wertheimer's staff. No call was returned. Gingrich placed a call a day for several weeks. None were returned. That did not matter. Van Brocklin explained, "It was an intimidation tactic. We were saying, We're not going away; you'll have to deal with this." Quietly, unknown to Gingrich or Wright, Wertheimer began to explore demanding an investigation. Meanwhile Gingrich kept the pressure up. After Livingston and Sensenbrenner told him he could not justify an investigation, he reemphasized the media: "We worked on the assumption that if enough newspapers said there should be an investigation, Common Cause would have to say it. Then members would say it. It would happen."

The Democratic leadership had not been totally dormant during all this. In December, Foley had spoken to Michel and Cheney—not Lott—about Gingrich's activities, not threatening, simply asking, "Is this what the House is coming to? This kind of vituperation?"

Foley's comments had registered with Michel, but not with Cheney.

Foley believed that "Cheney was deeply angry over the contras." Coelho agreed. Shortly before the October reconciliation vote, he had said, *I trust Cheney.* Now he said, "Cheney's changed. I don't know anyone on the Democratic leadership side who feels they can trust him anymore, or that they have his confidence. Cheney was the hit man for the White House on the contras. The Speaker totally outmaneuvered him. Since then he's been out for vengeance."

Wright had been preparing a defense. On December 18, Marshall Lynam called a staff meeting (Wright was not present) in which it was decided to compile a "white paper" covering the stockyard project in Fort Worth, for which Wright earmarked federal redevelopment funds; the savings and loan issue; the ten-year-old oil investments; the book; and Mallightco, his partnership with Mallick.

By January 15, the white paper was finished. Wright's attorney William Oldaker absorbed it into his own fact-finding, which had also started more than a month earlier. Within a few more weeks, he had rebuttals to Gingrich's likely charges, backed up by sworn depositions taken in repeated trips to Fort Worth. For the moment, Wright's people felt reasonably well protected on the facts.

By mid-January, Beryl Anthony, the DCCC head, had prepared a formal complaint about a PAC Gingrich ran which had raised $217,000 but had given only $900 to candidates. He filed it with the Federal Election Commission, and asked the Postal Service to investigate possible mail fraud. People around Wright believed those problems would keep Gingrich busy. But filing the complaint neither intimidated Gingrich—he simply denounced it as a smear—nor discredited him. The Speaker of the House was a much bigger story than a junior member of the minority. The complaint caused barely a ripple; the overwhelming majority of reporters Gingrich continued to contact were unaware of it. The media game continued.

Back in December, Wright's staff had dissuaded him from going to the floor by arguing that he should wait until they researched and checked all the facts. Now those facts would soon be available. Wright wanted to go to the floor again. *The floor was sacred,* he believed. *And this should be on the floor, for the question of his ethics most of all concerned his colleagues.*

On February 1 the first of what would become an ongoing series of meetings began with people Wright respected from inside and outside the House. The next discussion would come three days later, although sometimes weeks would intervene between meetings. The same exact group never formed twice, but people attending included, from outside the House, Bob Strauss and John White, both Texans and both former Democratic National Committee chairmen; Kirk O'Donnell, the former O'Neill aide who headed the Center for National Policy; and Oldaker. All four were attorneys. Also at the meetings were Wright aides Lynam, Phil Duncan, and Mack and several members: Foley, Coelho, John Murtha, Jack Brooks, and occasionally others, such as Martin Frost, Barney Frank, and, later, David Obey.

Brooks was the single member personally closest to Wright and knew the House; Murtha, because of his pro-contra position, was the single leadership loyalist with good links to Republicans. In addition, Murtha had both served on the ethics committee and been investigated by it; he was cleared over the Abscam bribery scandal in 1980, refusing money himself, although he was tape-recorded saying his colleagues "expect to be taken care of." He was also very close to two members of the ethics committee, Alan Mollohan and Joseph Gaydos. (Once a lobbyist offered Murtha a $1,000 honorarium to speak at a breakfast; Murtha declined—he was near his limit—but offered to speak for free if they invited Gaydos and gave him $2,000.)

They sat down in H-201. It was late afternoon; coffee and cookies were set up on a table in a corner. The room was familiar to everyone present; they had all seen the mounted longhorns, the collage of personal photographs of Wright, family, and friends many times before. Wright called the meeting to order.

The first issue was Michel's suggestion of appointing a special committee to investigate Wright. The group dismissed that alternative for the same reason Oldaker had: it could be attacked as evading the ethics committee. But, as before, Wright wanted to deal with the question. "I believe I should go to the floor," he said.

"Tip made Gingrich a big man by going after him," one man said, referring to the bitter floor exchange in 1984. "If you respond to him it will only make him bigger. He'd welcome the confrontation."

"I don't have to respond to Gingrich," he replied. "I can respond to some of the stories."

But the group argued that Gingrich could spark a confrontation anyway. And the floor just escalated the entire issue, created front-page stories, guaranteed coverage on network news and Sunday talk shows.

Everyone—*everyone*—echoed that opinion, Foley, Coelho, Murtha, O'Donnell, staff. Everyone.

O'Donnell said, as he had before and would again, that the press itself should be responded to. No inaccuracy should go unchallenged. But at this time, as the controversy over his aide George Mair's attacks on reporters was erupting, Wright could not take on the press.

And a response could create new problems. What if Wright went public and made a mistake in something he said? After all, some of the accusations concerned events which had happened a decade earlier. Others were very complicated. Any mistake, no matter how minor, could destroy his credibility. If any new accusation, any new detail, surfaced after he went public and he had not covered it already, that, too, could destroy his credibility.

The consensus was that the issue would go away by itself. A response would only delay its disappearance. Coelho himself had had a minor problem over the use by his campaign and the DCCC of Dixon's airplane and boat. After news stories appeared, he had paid $48,000 for that usage to the corporate remnant of Vernon Savings and Loan. Coelho issued a simple statement. "All they got out of me was three sentences," he said. The stories died away quickly.

"The key is to keep your attention on the legislative agenda, Mr. Speaker," a member said.

That also was unanimous, and it was advice Wright agreed with.

Stories in the national media did die away in early March. The "swirling group of advisers," as one participant called the group, turned away from a media response and focused on a legalistic strategy geared toward the ethics committee. Oldaker took several technical steps to strengthen Wright's position, then suggested a preemptive strike against Gingrich by asking the ethics committee for an advisory opinion on several issues, and phrasing the questions so that the answer had to be yes. Asking the questions would not preclude a future investigation, but, having issued an advisory opinion, the committee would have a difficult time reversing itself. Oldaker was a partner in Charles Manatt's law firm, and Manatt, a former chairman of the Democratic National Committee, had helped get Julian Dixon, the committee chairman, elected. Oldaker knew Dixon and had talked to him about it. Dixon had not discouraged him.

Oldaker discussed his idea privately with Wright, who wanted him to proceed. Wright hoped that would clear any cloud in advance of the Democratic National Convention. Oldaker then raised it in a March meeting with the advisers. Wright was not present, and the others argued Oldaker out of his idea. The members, knowing the glacial pace of the committee, believed nothing would happen quickly enough to kill the issue before the convention. Thus they ran the risk of creating a new round of stories, and new issues, for nothing. Wright did not find out for months that Oldaker had not proceeded.

But that exhausted the suggestions of the advisers. No other alternative strategies were reviewed.

For weeks, the group gathered, sometimes weekly, sometimes two or three weeks lapsed between meetings. They were called in reaction to new, negative stories, rather than to plan a strategy to pursue. There was no agenda. Not a single meeting ended with an agreement, *All right, this is what we're going to do. Now let's do it.* Wright rarely attended, yet even in his absence, he dominated the meetings; they focused on keeping him from going to the floor, keeping him constrained.

Tension had developed as well among "the swirling group." Murtha and Coelho despised each other. That went back to what Murtha considered Coelho's disloyalty to O'Neill; Murtha saw him as a maneuverer and spread stories of a California mafia of Coelho, ethics chairman Julian Dixon, and committee member Vic Fazio, who had run Coelho's campaign for whip. He wondered out loud whether Coelho was maneuvering to get Wright. Wright and Coelho both heard of it.

Still, as winter moved into spring, Wright's advisers thought they were gaining control. Coelho got a copy of Wertheimer's letter to Gingrich and the advisers interpreted it as Van Brocklin had: Common Cause would not act. They also knew Livingston and Sensenbrenner had dismissed Gingrich's charges as lacking substance, and believed that would isolate Gingrich among his colleagues.

This combination of confidence, lack of direction, and belief that no one considered Gingrich's charges credible meant that no worst-case scenarios were ever discussed, no contingency plans developed, no explorations made to insure that Wertheimer was satisfied. No one considered the need to do anything which would guarantee that he and Common Cause stay out of it, such as a private explanation of both the politics and the facts.

Gingrich had a clearly defined road he was following. Wright's swirling group had no direction, except to contain Wright. After every meeting, people would go to him individually and reiterate the old advice: *This will go away. Your going to the floor would only bring it back to life.*

Finally, in addition to the charges filed about Gingrich's handling of PAC funds, his Georgia GOP colleague Patrick Swindall was soon to be indicted for a scheme to launder drug money. Gingrich seemed on the defensive. Wright's advisers believed that they had finally contained Gingrich.

But Gingrich was still dropping pebbles in the pond. He continued to crisscross the country making speeches. In them he said, "Prominent, reputable newspapers and magazines have printed a series of charges, each involving serious allegations of House ethics. Despite these printed charges, there has been no investigation." Citing *Newsweek, The Washington Post,* and *The Wall Street Journal,* and other publications, he would urge people to "write your congressman . . . letters to the editor . . . go to public meetings . . . and call radio call-in shows and raise the issue." And, Gingrich urged them, "Write Common Cause."

In Washington he was busy, too, aggressively seeking out journalists, for example calling up Richard Cohen, who covered Congress from an institutional basis for the *National Journal,* inviting him on an hourlong early morning walk, and trying to sell him the more complex element of the story, the kind which Cohen would be interested in— not the personal corruption of Wright, but the corruption of power in the House. Cohen's stories were read by insiders and serious reporters. It was all part of the resonance Gingrich sought.

At the end of March, a small trade magazine called *Banker's Monthly* reprinted the *Regardie's* story, but split it into two parts. The first part ran and Marshall Lynam learned of it. He and Bob Strauss immediately flew to New York and confronted the editor. Several people had publicly pointed out inaccuracies and distortions in the *Regardie's* story. *Banker's Monthly* had made no effort to contact Wright's office. Reckless disregard for the truth could make a publication vulnerable to a libel suit. Strauss threatened a lawsuit. (Lynam later denied any threat had been made; Strauss acknowledged it.) The magazine agreed to delay publishing part two for a month and give Wright one full page for a rebuttal, to run opposite the story.

One of the story's co-authors immediately called reporters. Suddenly newspapers were filled with stories about Wright's efforts to strong-arm the press. Gingrich circulated another "Dear Colleague" and created still more stories by demanding to know whether House funds paid for Lynam's trip to New York, and who was paying Strauss. If he did it for free, weren't his services an illegal gift from a lobbyist? In a lengthy special order, Gingrich said, "We have seen a press person paid by the Speaker's office who . . . has been writing threatening letters to various magazines and newspapers. We now have the example of the chief of staff of the Speaker of the House and a famous attorney-lobbyist flying to New York and threatening to sue a magazine unless it censored itself . . . because they are printing an article critical of him. . . . Every reporter on this Hill has an obligation to their profession to engage directly and actively in insuring that the country knows what is going on."

By spring, Gingrich estimated he had given out copies of his thickening file of clippings to between 150 and 200 reporters. He was creating resonance. Several thousand reporters worked in Washington. All had seen stories raising questions about Wright's eithcs. Their attitude was expressed by a reporter for a major California newspaper: "There's one *hell* of a lot of smoke."

Gingrich's office was holding damp leaves to a flame, spreading the smoke. When a newspaper anywhere in the country ran a negative story, a local conservative activist forwarded it to Gingrich's office, where it went directly to Van Brocklin; anything faintly new, any new rumor or accusation, was again relayed to reporters. *The Wall Street Journal*'s Brooks Jackson said, "She'd call and say, 'Have you seen this? I'll fax it to you.' 'Fine,' I'd tell her. They had a very good clipping service. I would guess I initiated or received twenty phone calls from Gingrich himself, one every ten days or two weeks for months. She'd call more often. Sometimes she'd call me once a week."

Brooks Jackson was not the only recipient of her calls. "She'd call and say, 'This is really hot stuff,'" Ron Hutcheson of the *Fort Worth Star-Telegram* said. "But she was a fount of misinformation."

Misinformation or not, reporters paid attention. Jackson again: "One thing they certainly made sure of was that there was more than one reporter working these things. They had a little creative tension going."

Gingrich himself was contacting Wright's enemies, digging up anything negative he could from people like Eddie Chiles, a Fort Worth oilman who had owned the Texas Rangers and who had served as political godfather to Jim Bradshaw, Wright's 1980 opponent. In late April, Gingrich even contacted Henry Kissinger, Gerald Ford, and Richard Nixon. They would add immense weight to his charges, if he could interest any of them. He wrote Fred Friendly, the former CBS news executive who headed the Columbia University School of Journalism. Early in May he started recontacting people he had already pitched the story to, beginning with David Gergen, editor of *U.S. News & World Report.*

But nothing was appearing in the Washington papers, and the national press seemed quiet. On April 13, Betty Wright even defended George Mair, saying, "I don't know if he's responsible for it, but the stories have stopped."

They had stopped. In Washington.

But Wright's office knew of the activity. Reporters were calling up constantly, seeking information or reaction quotes.

There was a sense of a gathering storm. Gingrich said, "One day the Phoenix paper would write something, the next day Minneapolis." He had visited the Phoenix paper; his aide was from Minneapolis and had talked repeatedly to editorial writers there. In addition to talking about ethics, Gingrich repeatedly pointed out that Wright had assaulted the press in the George Mair and *Banker's Monthly* episodes, that the press had a responsibility to take this man on. Gingrich said, "It was as if they had this big stack of information"—the stack he had supplied— "on a table and the editor would point to it at random one day and say, 'Let's do something on Wright.' I think over forty papers had called for an investigation by [the middle of May]."

Every story went to Wertheimer. *We worked on the assumption that if enough newspapers said there should be an investigation,* Gingrich had said, *Common Cause would have to say it. Then members would say it. It would happen.* And forty papers meant forty cities, read by sixty or seventy members.

His efforts were like vibrations on a pane of glass; at first, they had no visible effect, but as the vibrations increased in intensity, grew higher and higher pitched, the glass threatened to shatter.

Keep your focus on legislation, the advisers had told Wright. Legislation was moving well. Even as Republicans exploded at him over Central American policy, the budget proceeded through the House more smoothly than it ever had. The budget summit agreement the preceding November had already settled all major issues, and, for the first time since the Budget Committee was created, the committee produced a truly bipartisan plan. When the budget reached the floor—the same day the contras and Sandinistas reached a cease-fire agreement—it passed 319–102, with a majority of Republicans voting for it. Later the Senate passed its budget; the conference bogged down because of hostility between House Democrats and Chiles, but it, too, finally reported out a bipartisan budget.

By April both George Bush and Michael Dukakis had locked up their respective parties' presidential nominations. Congress still had legislative business to conduct, but virtually all of it involved working things out in conference—and political maneuvering.

The key issue remained trade. House Democrats had been working on it for more than three years. Wright considered the trade bill the centerpiece of the 100th Congress, clearly a Democratic initiative, and a political weapon.

By the middle of April only the final maneuvering over the bill remained. Conferees had settled every question except purely political ones, over which the White House threatened a veto. The more purely political a decision is, the more it is a leadership call. The Senate disliked a House provision requiring foreigners to disclose investment in the United States. Wright yielded and agreed to drop it.

That left a provision requiring large companies to provide sixty days' notice to workers before they closed a plant or instituted massive layoffs. A major study done by the administration itself concluded that early notice was the single most important factor in helping both workers and communities adjust to massive layoffs; it also noted that West Germany, Japan, and other international competitors had such laws. Yet the White House threatened a veto over the plant-closing provision.

Rostenkowski wanted to drop it. Ways and Means had put immense effort into this bill, over two Congresses. The idea of that effort all going up in smoke over a side issue—one that came out of another committee—frustrated him. It was, again, the choice between a solution, although maybe not quite as much as his colleagues wanted but still a good bill, and an issue.

But other Democrats wanted the provision in. If the administration accepted it, they had a major, substantive victory. If Reagan vetoed it, they had a hell of an issue going into the presidential election.

Polls gave the plant-closing provision overwhelming support, roughly

80 percent support. The members wanted it. At a whip meeting one demanded, "Plant closing's got to be in. This is a giant issue in my state. If it comes out, I'm off the bill."

Wright wanted it in too. He was tired of giving in. *Can we pass a bill before Reagan vetoes it?* he had once snapped at Michel. The House leadership sat down with Byrd, Bentsen, and Rostenkowski. Plant closing was in.

The bill passed the House 312–107, after defeating a Republican motion to delete the plant-closing section by 253–167, and passed the Senate, 63–36, three votes short of the margin needed to override a veto.

In early May, Wright staged a media event by signing the trade bill— a ministerial function which he had to perform before sending the bill to Reagan—in Statuary Hall, the grand room of giant marble columns, ringed by marble and bronze statues of men like Henry Clay, William Jennings Bryan, Sam Houston, and Ethan Allen, the room which had once served as the old House chamber. Workers who had been thrown out of their jobs without notice told their stories to the press. Democrats milked it for everything they could get, and watched Republican colleagues squirm.

The bulk of Wright's legislative agenda for the 100th Congress was finished, or well on its way to completion. Most of his initiatives had already become law. The only issue left was Wright himself.

On May 6 and 7, Wright hosted a retreat at Coolfont, a West Virginia mountain resort not far from Camp David, to think through July's Democratic National Convention. Gingrich's first goal was to so embarrass Wright that he would be forced out as chairman. He was determined to hold on to the chair. Although the convention was DNC chairman Paul Kirk's show, Wright expected to perform more than a ceremonial role. *If something could be controlled,* Wright believed, *then control it. If something could not be controlled, then plan how to be flexible.*

In November, Kirk and the senior Democratic officials who were handling the convention itself had met with Wright in his office, and began planning how to use logistics to get their message out, to force the attention of the camera onto the stage. Wright's staff had remained in constant touch with convention officials. Now at Coolfont, Wright's guests were Kirk; Donald Fowler, who was in charge of planning the convention; Michigan governor James Blanchard, chairman of the platform committee; former DNC chairmen Charles Manatt and John White; Kirk O'Donnell, representing Dukakis; Budget chairman Bill Gray, representing Jesse Jackson; and pollsters, media experts, and other Democratic officials and activists. No convention chairman in the past had held such a session.

It was not an elegant resort. Only Wright liked it. They spent most of the weekend discussing how best to present their message. News coverage was one problem. To try to control it, they would set up a bull pen which would include governors, senators, and House members; each would be primed with the thought of the day, and Michael Berman, a lobbyist and former Mondale aide, would try to feed them to the networks for interviews. That would cut down on reporters seeking out their own story. O'Donnell, pollster Peter Hart, and media consultant Robert Squier had already held several meetings on how to keep the networks focused on the podium. Professionals used to packaging entertainment would try to make events each night both visually attractive and newsworthy. "This is a four-night miniseries," Fowler explained.

Wright didn't like glitz. "One caveat," he warned. "We are Democrats. If we don't have something to sell, then we should get out of the damn business. You can package this for entertainment, but if there's nothing inside, nobody's going to buy it. In 1972 we had a telethon, told people why they should send money, and we made money. In 1983 we had a telethon, very glitzy and entertaining, and it didn't even pay for the damn telecast."

Over two days they tried to anticipate every detail: how to handle demonstrations; possibly allowing Jesse Jackson's delegates a floor victory so they would leave happy; writing the rules so that the convention chairman, Wright, could suspend floor activity if it stretched embarrassingly into prime time. Blanchard, in charge of the platform, said, "I don't anticipate trouble. I've talked to a lot of people and they're all willing to give. It's a sign of how badly they want to win."

But they could not control everything. When a DNC official suggested asking politicians to allow the DNC to write their speeches, Wright just laughed. White observed, "Let's not kid ourselves. There will be five thousand politicians, all looking for a camera. Some of this can't be scripted."

The meeting ended late Saturday afternoon. Everyone departed for

Washington immediately, except Wright. This meeting had been a respite for him. Away from everything. Pointing toward the future, for
a change. He liked it out here, in West Virginia, in the mountains, not
far really from where his race for majority leader had started so long
ago. He walked down a country path, around a pond, and he walked
slowly. He was in no hurry to get back.

Sunday morning *The Washington Post* ran a lengthy story investigating
Wright's ties to the savings and loan industry. It was by far the most
detailed, authoritative account of Wright's actions to appear, written
by Charles Babcock, the same investigative reporter who had broken
the damaging story on Wright's book. The story indicted the campaign
financing system which, largely through Coelho's DCCC operation, had
given high-flying S&L operators access to senior politicians.

But it exonerated Wright of any misconduct, of doing any favors for
campaign contributors. It looked as if the negative stories impugning
Wright's ethics were finally behind them.

Monday morning Wright's staff was exuberant.

Gingrich had been in constant touch not only with Brooks Jackson,
the *Wall Street Journal* investigative reporter, but with the paper's editorial writers. Jackson was a journalist, not an ideologue, and would
investigate anyone with equal ferocity. The editorial writers at the *Journal* had agendas.

Unlike editorial writers at most newspapers, they did not simply sit
back and analyze events of the moment. The *Journal* mounted editorial
campaigns.

They created issues and kept them alive. They pounded and pounded
and pounded on the same theme. They did not let go. Like Wright and
like Gingrich, they had an agenda. In that, they were akin to crusading
newspapers of an earlier day. The repeated theme of the editorials, in
the largest-selling newspaper in the country—a truly national newspaper, delivered daily to the most influential people in communities
throughout the nation—could have impact. Ten years earlier, then–
Journal editorial writer Jude Wanniski successfully crusaded to make
supply-side economics acceptable, ultimately converting Jack Kemp to
the idea, and, through Kemp, Ronald Reagan.

The *Journal*'s editorial writers, like those at the *Washington Times,* were active "allies," as Gingrich called them. Gingrich talked particularly to *Journal* editorial writer John Fund. Van Brocklin said, "During some periods I would talk to him every day."

Brooks Jackson recalled, "I would talk to Newt and I might say something, or he would say something, and two or three days later I would see the same idea, even the precise same phrase, on our editorial page."

Gingrich and Fund had read the *Post* Sunday piece. For Tuesday, May 10, Fund wrote a *Journal* editorial. "The timing was somewhat a reaction to the *Post*," he said, adding that his complaints about Wright were "a policy difference primarily."

His editorial had nothing to do with policy. It was entitled "Where's the Investigation?" It echoed Gingrich's speeches, focusing on Wright's book, his interference with S&L regulators, his press secretary George Mair, and his efforts to prevent *Banker's Monthly* from reprinting the *Regardie's* story. It compared his situation to Ed Meese's, and went on for several thousand words, reciting almost every allegation made against Wright, taking up by itself the entire space allotted for editorials that day.

The equation of power had changed.

Democratic leadership staff talked to Republican leadership staff, saying that they had compiled dirt on several Republicans, including Michel, Lott, and Guy Vander Jagt, chairman of the House GOP campaign committee. Another Democrat wanted to file charges against Michel. If this thing continued, those charges might be filed. "Do what you have to do," a GOP aide replied.

Wright once again met with the same swirling group of advisers down the hall from his office in H-201. Once again he wanted to go to the floor. Once again, unanimously, his advisers argued for silence. Wright was angry. He had been getting that advice for months. *Look where it had gotten him.* But he took it one more time.

Eight days after the *Journal* editorial demanding an investigation, Common Cause's Wertheimer wrote a letter to ethics committee chairman Julian Dixon. A copy of the letter arrived in Wright's office by messenger at 10:00 A.M., shortly before its release to the media. It addressed two issues. "Whether or not the published reports of Speaker Wright and his book royalties present serious ethics questions appears to depend on a central issue that has not been explored—whether, and if so in what way, Speaker Wright's campaign committees were involved in the financing, printing, distributing, or selling of his book." It was asking, bluntly, whether the book was a scheme for converting campaign funds to personal use. The letter also inquired into whether "he sought to obtain special treatment in connection of the regulatory activities of the Federal Home Loan Bank Board for . . . party campaign contributors."

Daily, for several weeks at a time, phone messages to him and his staff had come in from Gingrich and Van Brocklin. The calls kept coming, relentlessly coming. So did the newspaper editorials. There had been the veiled threat in Gingrich's letter, *Your silence in this matter . . .* the prospect that Common Cause itself could become a target. "I think," Gingrich said, "Wertheimer may have intuited that the next phase was a *Wall Street Journal* editorial saying, 'Why Is Common Cause Afraid of Jim Wright?' "

On ABC's Brinkley show Wertheimer said that Common Cause acted because Wright had not answered the charges in the press. Later he said, "We raise things if there's a question in the public arena that needs to be resolved. These things are out there, in the public arena." He insisted that the *Journal* editorial had no effect on his action, that he and Philip Heymann, an assistant attorney general under Carter with whom Common Cause often consulted on ethics issues, had decided to proceed before it appeared. He dismissed Gingrich's contacts with him as "a couple of letters and one phone call."

A man who sometimes cooperated with Wertheimer said, "I think Fred started worrying about his money people."

The letter Common Cause sent to the ethics committee asked for an investigation, conducted by an outside counsel, of Speaker of the House Jim Wright.

It was a front-page story in *The Washington Post, The New York Times,* the *Los Angeles Times,* the *Boston Globe,* in every major paper in the country. NBC, CBS, ABC, CNN, the MacNeil/Lehrer show, Ted Koppel's *Nightline* all headlined it. Brooks Jackson revealed in the *Journal* that John White, Wright's friend and former party chairman who had become a lobbyist, had bought one thousand copies of Wright's book. Jackson had earlier revealed that the Teamsters had bought one thousand copies. That made two known purchases in one-thousand-book lots. Roughly twenty thousand books had been sold. Reporters wondered about other bulk purchases. Editorial writers attacked relentlessly. *The New Republic* recited a long list of charges, including having supported the Vietnam War—in which his son fought—because the army bought thousands of helicopters made in Fort Worth.

Wright's office immediately released a statement denouncing Common Cause for allowing itself to become a "handmaiden" of a partisan political attack. But Common Cause had too much credibility for the press to agree and it made Wright look defensive.

The group of advisers formed and began meeting almost daily. Usually Wright attended only for a few minutes. He was tired of it. The advice was always the same. He wanted to go to the floor. They wanted him to stay silent. Both in the meetings and, if he was not present to hear their arguments, privately, one at a time, they pressed their advice on him: *do not go to the floor*. "Tip made Gingrich important," one man said. "Why make him more important?" And the ethics committee requested indirectly that he stay silent.

But so much energy and time went into convincing Wright not to go to the floor that no alternative media strategy was ever discussed. Even now no strategy was coming out of the meetings. Even now no plan surfaced.

Betty was calling Craig Raupe night after night until he said, "Betty, you're calling out of hysteria." Furious, she stopped. Wright's staff withdrew into a bunker mentality. People close to Wright were blocked from getting to his senior staff. Even Raupe had difficulty getting to them and complained, "At some point the inner circle has to be able to get through—I'm not talking about getting to Jim, just to the top three staff." Raupe started spending half his time around Wright, and joined the advisory group.

The advisory meetings did conclude that Common Cause's letter would force the ethics committee to investigate him. Wright was urged to write a letter to committee chairman Julian Dixon of California, pledging cooperation. He did, on May 24.

That same day, Reagan vetoed the trade bill. Wright turned to that, determined to continue to perform his role, continue to exercise his power. Indeed, it was a relief to return to substance. Within a few hours of Reagan's veto, Wright convened the Democratic Steering and Policy Committee, which immediately passed a resolution declaring it official party policy to vote to override it. Later that afternoon the House did override it by 308–113, with only one Democrat voting no.

He watched the vote mount and surpass three hundred with his lips pressed together. *This is the best answer I can make,* he thought, his heart suddenly beating fast, shaking hands, giving and accepting congratulations, the smile back again, behind the smile a mixture of bitterness and satisfaction.

Gingrich did not stop. He continued to circulate, and release to the press, "Dear Colleagues," and made sure the issue would remain alive through outside groups. Judy Hughes, chairwoman of the National Federation of Republican Women, wrote to assure him, "The Federation's 160,000 members are ready to aid you in your battle against Speaker Wright." The Conservative Campaign Fund operated from the same address as Citizens for Reagan, under the same director, Peter Flaherty, and Flaherty worked closely with Gingrich. He sent a mailing to all Republican House candidates saying, "We write to encourage you to make . . . House Speaker Jim Wright a major issue in your campaign. Should Wright appear in your district, you face an opportunity to turn an honor for your opponent into an embarrassment." GOP member William Broomfield wrote him a note saying he was "amazed" at how well he had generated media response.

Gingrich also tried to keep Wright an issue in presidential politics. Immediately after Common Cause's letter he issued a press release, repeating all his charges and asking, "Does Mr. Dukakis agree with Common Cause that there is sufficient reason for a formal investigation of the Speaker? Will he allow Speaker Wright to chair the Democratic National Convention if he is under investigation?"

While the House was overriding the veto of the trade bill, a reporter asked George Bush about Attorney General Ed Meese's continued ethics problems with the Wedtech Corporation. Others involved with Wedtech had already been sentenced to prison, and an independent prosecutor was about to announce that Meese "probably had violated" the law. Reagan confidants Michael Deaver and Lyn Nofziger had already been convicted of criminal activity. South Carolina Republican governor Carroll Campbell—a former House member and classmate of Gingrich—had publicly advised Bush to attack Wright.

Bush, who then trailed Dukakis by sixteen points in the polls, snapped, "You talk about Ed Meese. How about talking about what Common Cause raised about the Speaker the other day? Are they going to go for an independent counsel so the nation will have this full investigation? Why don't people call out for that? I will right now. I think they ought to."

He cited other House members who should be investigated. All were Democrats, all were on Gingrich's list.

That night, May 24, Republicans attacked Wright from a different angle. Cheney had organized a "special order," an hour's time when the House was not in session, over C-SPAN to condemn the way Democrats ran the House. Several GOP members had worked for weeks preparing it. One after another, Republicans got up to complain about the Democrats' and Wright's exercise of power. A few days later influential *Washington Post* columnist David Broder wrote an article entitled "How About a Little Glasnost for the House?" and repeated many of the points made in the special order.

At the first whip meeting after the Common Cause letter Wright told his colleagues, "Let me share some things with you because you're family. About a year ago the right wing started a concerted effort to make me look bad. Gingrich has spent pretty much all his time at it and has a staff person full-time on it. No one paid any attention until last week and the *Wall Street Journal* editorial." He defended his action with the savings and loans—his colleagues could understand that one, all right—and his book, arguing that David Stockman and Donald Regan got advances in the millions while he "didn't get one penny in advance. Wertheimer didn't come by to see me, didn't have the courtesy to ask me anything. I could have explained everything with great specificity. As Bill Gray puts it, this game is called 'Sack the Quarterback.' We won the first eight games of the year, now they'll do anything to beat us. They're really hurting with the Meese scandal. They're thirsty for something. They're out to hurt our party by tarnishing my reputation. I assure you, there is no reason to apprehend that I did anything dishonest."

David Obey stood up. "Mr. Speaker, *The Wall Street Journal* is after your economics, not your ethics. Newt Gingrich is after your effectiveness, not your ethics."

Wright's colleagues rose and gave him a warm, standing ovation. They meant it. For now.

Early in the morning on May 26, reporters milled in the hallway outside the sergeant at arms' office, waiting for Gingrich to arrive. A few feet away, across the corridor and behind closed doors, was where Wright had breakfast every morning. The mood there was somber, the only conversation the ordering of eggs. Marshall Lynam walked in and said, "The vultures have gathered outside, I see."

Gingrich walked into the office with his papers. It resembled an old-fashioned bank, with a marble-topped counter and a row of barred teller windows behind which tellers cashed checks for House employees. He pushed open a gate, sat down at a desk, had his papers notarized, then, with a Capitol policeman trailing him, walked down to the terrace level of the Capitol to the ethics committee. There the corridor was packed with media. He walked inside, closed the door—the policeman kept the press outside—and handed his charges to a receptionist, who stamped them with the date and time of receipt. It seemed almost anticlimactic. Then he walked outside and held a press conference.

A few days earlier, Ted Koppel had said to Gingrich that he seemed isolated, that no Republican had joined him. The next morning during a quorum call Cheney had walked up to Gingrich and said, "You're not alone."

Now he released to the press a letter signed by seventy-one Republicans urging "further inquiry into the activities of Speaker Jim Wright." *Seventy-one Republicans.* Wright had inflamed them, had beaten them and beaten them, had taken charge of Central American policy, had used the Rules Committee to manipulate the floor. Anything seemed fair now. Wright had made his bed, now let him lie in it. The entire leadership except for Michel signed: Lott, Cheney, Jerry Lewis, Mickey Edwards, Guy Vander Jagt, and Lynn Martin. Livingston and Sensenbrenner, the two Republicans who had looked into the charges for Michel, did not.

That same day the DCCC's Beryl Anthony put out a press release; earlier he had complained of a Gingrich-run PAC. Now he detailed Gingrich's 1977 book deal; several wealthy friends had formed a limited partnership and taken tax deductions to pay him $13,000 to write a novel which he never produced. In 1984, he did publish *Window of Opportunity,* a political tract. He received a standard royalty, but political supporters again set up a limited partnership, this time raising $105,000 to promote the book while paying his wife more than $10,000 to administer the partnership. Anthony had had the information for months, holding it for release until Gingrich acted. Perhaps it would have discredited Gingrich if he had been acting alone. But with Common Cause involved, the story about Gingrich's book made barely a ripple in the larger one. *It had gone beyond Gingrich now.*

On the floor that day, Republicans echoed Gingrich's charges in a different way, by attacking both Wright's control of the House and his Central American policy. A routine bill authorizing funds for intelligence activities was being voted on under an open rule. Cheney and Henry Hyde offered an amendment loosening restrictions on CIA support for the contras. It was a surprise tactic, and surprises like that violated legislative courtesy. A Democratic leadership aide said, "It went beyond a surprise. They said this would not come up. They flat lied about it."

Hyde on the floor said, "Nothing has been more painful in my congressional career than not to inform Mr. Stokes [Chairman Louis Stokes] of this amendment."

Democrats beat the proposal by one of the widest margins they had ever achieved on contra aid, 214–190.

Half an hour before Wright's May 26 daily press conference, an hour after Gingrich filed charges, a surreal air suffused Wright's ceremonial office. Amidst the furor, Wright was calm, drawing into himself. *Peace. As if there was one place inside himself where he could get away from this.* He smiled—*if they think they do not like me, it is because they do not know me*—then talked of reports given him that the contras and the Sandinistas seemed to be nearing an agreement. *That was real peace. He had helped end killing. That was something he had done, and could cling to.* He crossed fingers on both hands and said, "Wouldn't it be great if they actually worked something out?"

Outside the door the press waited, a huge throng of reporters today. They were joking, laughing. There was an excitement too. The flush of the hunt. One aide turned to a page and said, "At one minute to ten"— when Wright routinely left to open the House—"start dragging him out of here."

Wright nodded. "Let them in."

Reporters flooded the room, crowding around the desk where Wright sat, forcing the stenographer who kept a record to elbow for room, pushing aides back against the walls, resembling, for the first time in his speakership, the press entourage which followed the President. Yet the reporters hesitated, seemed suddenly subdued. This was something awkward, even dirty for all of them. Wright began as if the day was

routine, as he began every day, announcing that day's legislative schedule. The first question dealt with appropriations bills. Then the prodding
began. It quickly intensified. "What about these charges, Mr.
Speaker?" "What about lobbyists buying the book, Mr. Speaker?"
"What about helping these savings and loan people, Mr. Speaker?"

"Sarah," he said slowly to Sarah McClendon, his voice tired but
patient. It was like speaking to small children who could not understand
a thing no matter how carefully or patiently explained, who could not
understand what it was like being this man, who could not know him,
know his power, know what was required to accomplish anything—a
weave of thousands of acts, most of them gentlenesses, some of them
deals, and some few of them absolute cold ruthlessness. Nor could they
know his sensitivity to the slightest trembling in, at the farthest corner
of, the web of power, and yet he had been entangled in this web himself
and by himself. Still, if he was entangled in this web he was not yet
trapped in it. "Sarah, I make these calls for constituents a thousand
times a year. Every congressman plays an ombudsman role. Forty percent of my mail is requests for my help."

Then a reporter asked how he felt about Gingrich.

"I feel the way a fire hydrant feels toward a dog."

He smiled. His lips pulled back from his teeth. It was ten o'clock.
He rose and walked out to convene the House. He was smiling from
ear to ear now. That same smile that grated on everyone, that people
had told him since 1954 to stop doing, that people had told him for so
long and so many times that they had stopped telling him. That mask.

The Washington Post's Charles Babcock had a new story: Matthew
Cossolotto, the former Wright aide who had been moved aside to make
a place for George Mair, had helped Wright put together his book
Reflections of a Public Man, possibly on government time. Wright returned Babcock's call from his car while on his way to visit his old
friend Napoleón Duarte, president of El Salvador, who was in Walter
Reed Hospital with cancer. Duarte had been there for days and yet
Wright had not gone to him; that alone signified how his own problems
were consuming him. Now, for over an hour, he sat in the parked car
outside the hospital talking to Babcock. He seemed desperate, pleading, as if the world was closing in. Why? What had he done? He pointed
out that his net worth was less now than when he entered Congress
thirty-three years earlier: "The reason is my obsession is not trying to

make money. I appeal to you to try to recognize that through any and all of this what I've tried to do is give my time and efforts to being a good congressman."

I appeal to you . . . The Speaker of the House was pleading. And he considered the story a betrayal by Cossolotto; the betrayal more than the story itself had hurt him. A man close to Wright commented, "He's the lowest I have ever seen."

Every day something else appeared. Every morning Wright's driver picked him up and Wright would read the paper going to work. Now he would start reading, throw the paper on the floor, and sit silently, silently through the twenty-minute ride, staring out the window. *If they think they do not like me, it is because they do not know me.* He still believed that. He still believed that.

Every morning he came in determined to launch a counteroffensive. His advisers continued to urge him to remain quiet. The whole strategy now was dealing with the ethics committee, which was asking him, indirectly, to say nothing publicly. One member of the committee would go to a colleague on the floor who would go to Mack. Or Murtha would hear something.

"Why don't you just bring the committee the hell in here and exercise what pressure we do have?" Raupe suggested.

"Are you crazy? I can't even appear to do that," Wright replied.

He asked the committee to hear his rebuttal—his attorney had prepared a solid document—before they decided whether to proceed. The committee never responded to his request. He waited, waited, waited. The stories continued. On June 8, *The New York Times*'s lead editorial, entitled "Speaker Wright's Ghostly Ethics," called for an investigation. He saw it and his expression froze. *What did they know about him? What did they know about any of it?*

Gingrich meanwhile sent out a fund-raising letter for a PAC requesting help in his "difficult and politically costly fight." He sent out several such letters over the year and raised $1.9 million. Wright was a powerful enemy, a negative icon to rally against. Gingrich asked not only for money, but for people to deluge the ethics committee with demands for an investigation of Jim Wright.

Wright was Speaker still. He would not be distracted, would still go to battle. At this moment of weakness, Wright took on Rostenkowski and Dingell, the two great bulls of the House, who for the moment gave up goring each other to form an alliance against him. The issue was procedure: one year earlier, Wright had promised Rules chairman Claude Pepper that he could bring to the floor a bill establishing a long-term health-care program. Before Wright made that commitment, Dingell and Rostenkowski had protested strongly. The Rules Committee was not supposed to write substantive legislation; their committees had jurisdiction over the issue, and this marked a terrible precedent. Wright had given Pepper permission anyway, as much out of sentiment as anything; Pepper, born at the beginning of the century, a senator under Roosevelt before entering the House, had waited fifty years to offer this bill.

Now it was coming up. Rank-and-file Democrats did not want to vote on the issue; it was a bad vote, offending a powerful constituency if they voted no, and subjecting themselves to attack as big spenders if they voted yes. And for what? There was no chance whatsoever the bill would become law.

Despite angry protests from the Caucus, despite the fury of Rostenkowski and Dingell, despite the fact that Wright needed a united Democratic Caucus now more than ever, Wright let Pepper proceed. *He was Speaker of the House and would not be distracted. He had never wanted to sit in the chair—he wanted to do the job. He had given Pepper his word and he would keep it. Whatever Michel accused him of, he kept his word.* Pepper brought his bill to the floor. Rostenkowski and Dingell mounted an intense and personal campaign against it, and the leadership sat the fight out—Wright had only promised Pepper could get a vote, not that the leadership would back it. Pepper lost a vote on the rule, preventing consideration of the issue, by 243–169.

That same day the Senate fell short of overriding Reagan's veto of the trade bill. Immediately, Wright began talking with House and Senate leaders and chairmen about the next step. He suggested stripping out the plant-closing provision from the rest of the trade bill, passing both, and sending both to Reagan. It was an obvious move; Bentsen immediately picked up on it. At the next whip meeting Rostenkowski also agreed: "Pass trade first. Then send Ronald Reagan the plant-closing bill right around Labor Day, if the Senate ever does anything, while we're marching with our labor friends."

Wright intended to use the plant-closing bill as a weapon against Republicans in the election. Once again he convened Steering and

Policy and made it official party policy to support it. He planned a bill-signing ceremony for the Democratic National Convention.

As he maneuvered over trade, the peace talks in Nicaragua neared a climax. Alfredo Cesar, a contra director and their chief negotiator, had been meeting secretly for three months with Paul Reichler, an American attorney who represented the Sandinistas. Cesar visited Wright and said the deal was virtually done, and that he could guarantee a majority of the contra directorate would approve it. It was a good deal: Cesar was rumored to be planning to run for president of Nicaragua and would not agree to something that killed his chances of winning. The only obstacle was Enrique Bermudez, the military commander. Cesar then briefed Elliott Abrams, and, afterwards, called Wright back to report that for the first time Abrams had told him no military aid would be forthcoming and to cut the best deal he could.

It gave Wright something to hold on to, something which made all his pain worthwhile. He talked about it on June 9 at breakfast and held up his crossed fingers. It was a relief to talk about it.

Then he turned back to his own problems. "I want to get my side out. I am ready to start a counterattack. I'm tired of waiting. We've prepared this damn document, now I want it told."

His staff still objected, one of them warning, "You may raise questions the ethics committee has not thought of. Wait for them."

"I've been listening to that counsel for a year. Where has it put me? My enemies have been maligning me. I want to get my side out, in detail. I hire all these former journalists, think they know the press, ask them what to do, and get this advice, and it does not work. I wanted to take the floor last year on a point of personal privilege. 'No, no, don't do that,' everyone told me. 'This story will die.' Well, it didn't die. There is only one way through this. Straight through it. I don't want to hang back anymore."

Later that day his advisers were still telling him to remain silent until everything had surfaced. "Right up to the time he did it, I don't recall a single piece of advice, not one, to go public," said one man who had attended virtually every meeting. But this time Wright overruled them. He had had enough.

On Friday, June 10, he began a three-day media blitz. That day he would have three separate press conferences, the regular daily briefing,

THE AMBITION AND THE POWER · 629

one off-camera to cover all the questions in lengthy detail, and one where he would give shorter answers geared for television. At night, he would get twelve minutes on *MacNeil/Lehrer* by himself, and on Sunday he would appear on two of the three network interview shows.

The main press conference was held in H-324, the room of the whip meetings, the Thomas P. O'Neill Room where O'Neill had held his last press conference as Speaker. Seventy reporters filled rows of chairs. Wright and his attorney William Oldaker sat at the front of the room behind a long table. Behind them, off to the side, sat Foley, while Coelho presided over the House. Wright distributed a twenty-three-page statement with fifty pages of documents—canceled checks, notarized statements, and newspaper clips—backing up his claims. He was calm, dressed conservatively and powerfully for television with red tie, dark suit, and white shirt, his voice grave but confident.

Gingrich had asked the ethics committee to investigate four specific charges: first, whether Wright had acted improperly in 1980 in writing the Department of the Interior on behalf of a company in which he owned more than fifteen thousand dollars' worth of stock; second, whether in 1979 Wright was invited to invest in proven oil wells as a payoff by a wealthy Fort Worth oil family for whom he lobbied Egyptian president Anwar Sadat; third, whether the 55 percent royalties on Wright's book were improper; fourth, whether the book served as a vehicle to convert campaign funds to personal use. Common Cause had also requested an investigation of his pressure on savings and loan regulators.

Wright's rebuttal was detailed and specific. He had never owned stock in Texas Oil and Gas, the company for which he had written a letter. The accusation was based on an inaccurate newspaper story, which was later retracted. For the more complicated charges, he relied on the prepared documents. He ran through questions about Matthew Cossolotto's time spent on the book—Gingrich actually defended him on this charge because he had done exactly the same thing himself. And Wright had written everything in the book; Cossolotto had simply helped compile and edit old speeches and newsletters.

At one point, as he was droning on, Oldaker handed him a note telling him to cut his answer short. Wright glanced at it, then read it aloud, and snapped, "People have been telling me things like that for a year. Now I'm going to take the time and go through this in detail."

He continued, pouring out detail after detail, burying the reporters with facts upon facts. The blood lust seemed to drain out of them. They trickled out one at a time.

Shortly after Wright's press conference, the ethics committee announced it had decided to conduct a preliminary inquiry into several areas: Wright's possible lobbying for people and companies with whom he might have invested; whether campaign funds had been used to finance the book; his savings and loan involvement; and whether Matthew Cossolotto improperly worked on the book.

On its own, the committee added one more area of inquiry—one which Gingrich had never even raised: Wright's use of a condominium in Fort Worth owned by the Mallick family for several years, first for free, and then for $21.67 a day when he was in Fort Worth. House rules outlawed accepting gifts worth more than $100 from anyone who had a "direct interest" in legislation. Within forty-five minutes Wright's office issued a rebuttal pointing out that Mallick had no interest in legislation; that Mallick actually benefited from the rent because he would have kept it vacant, as he did other apartments he owned for investment, and received nothing had the Wrights not used it; and that the ethics committee counsel had approved the arrangement. ("That's a change, to see them react that quickly and that well," commented a reporter in the press gallery.) It seemed a non-issue, a throw-in. Reporters ignored it.

But neither they nor Wright knew that the ranking Republican on the committee, John Myers of Indiana, had pressed for the inclusion of the charge. The ranking member on this committee, the only committee in the Congress divided equally between Democrats and Republicans, had almost as much power as the chairman. Nor did the reporters realize that earlier, in anticipation of an inquiry of Wright, Myers had pressed to become the ranking member. Floyd Spence, who preceded him, had fallen ill; he had wanted to stay on, and after surgery did recover, but Myers and the Republican Conference pushed him aside. Spence had a reputation as an institution man, and as being almost nonpartisan.

The investigation would proceed. Robert Livingston, one of the two Republicans who had examined and dismissed Gingrich's complaint, later said in a tone of disgust, "If it wasn't for Common Cause, there wouldn't have been an investigation. If Gingrich hadn't manipulated the press and got all those stories, there wouldn't have been an investigation."

After his series of press conferences, Wright sat in H-210 behind his desk. A *New York Times* photographer entered the room and an aide brought Wright the four books he had written for established New York publishers. Wright wanted a picture, to put his book *Reflections of a Public Man* in context.

Wilson Morris, the aide involved in Central American issues, walked in and abruptly told the photographer to leave. There was a real problem now. What had looked like a peace agreement between the contras and the Sandinistas was blowing up. "I just got a call from Cesar," he said. "He's worried."

Wright listened stolidly, staring straight ahead, his face blank. He could do nothing now. He sat there, suddenly impotent, a man whose power availed him, now, nothing, himself under attack. All this time he had consoled himself with the thought that he had brought about peace, a real peace that could create a democracy. *Now would he not even have that?* His head turned to the side, away just for an instant, away from everything for an instant. A sudden, intense emotion flashed through him; it was more sudden than could be expressed, no more than an instant's tic of a facial muscle, so sudden it could barely be felt, so sudden he could not even know if it was rage or pain or both.

Foley walked in and sprawled on a sofa across from the desk. Wright said nothing about Nicaragua and Foley observed, "You did very, very well. You were confident and that's important. The questions ended up being, 'Doesn't it *look* bad?' That's a hell of a lot preferable to the alternative. The book is the only thing the press is still focusing on some. The rest, they're yawning. Don't give an inch on chairing the convention. I was asked if you should consider stepping down. I said, 'Absolutely not.' Your confidence and demeanor are important. Continue to say you did nothing wrong."

The press flared up one more time, over the book. A front-page Sunday *New York Times* story detailed its evolution: Carlos Moore in 1984 had first wanted to compile a book of photographs of Wright, but Wright had declined, saying if there was to be a book it would have to say something. Moore had then suggested compiling some of Wright's old speeches and newsletters. Wright had agreed. Moore said he made almost $40,000 from the book, compared to Wright's $62,000. If true, it cleared Wright of using the book to convert campaign funds to personal use. But the story also quoted several people who had made bulk purchases of the book. Gene Payte, a Texas friend who had bought one thousand books, said, "I was just trying to make a contribution to Jim's income. And I couldn't give him any money. There are rules against that. So I bought this book." Gene Wood, another friend who bought one thousand dollars' worth of books, said he did so "to help Jim."

Oldaker told Wright not to make any comment about those purchases. But in his next daily press conference, Wright volunteered a list of others who had bought large quantities, without even notifying any of them that he was releasing their names. Bob Strauss bought one thousand copies. Another old Texas friend Bernard Rapoport bought one thousand. John Silber, president of Boston University, bought one thousand. The New England Life Insurance Company bought two thousand dollars' worth, and an executive there told *The Washington Post* that they had bought books in lieu of giving an honorarium for a speech. Rules limit the honoraria members can accept; they do not limit royalties.

A *Wall Street Journal* headline declared, "New Data Bolster Theory Wright Book May Have Been Route for Improper Gifts."

Gingrich's aide Van Brocklin told reporters that Wright had written into House rules on outside earnings an exemption for royalties, implying that Wright had planned his book arrangement far in advance. Wright had had nothing to do with the exemption; Democrat Morris Udall and Republican John Anderson, both authors, were responsible for it. But the charge was repeated as a fact in story after story.

The next day, Ronald Reagan declared, "I think it is proper that there is an investigation going forward. . . . I think that everyone would feel that it was more proper if it was done by an investigator outside— an appointed investigator." Bush was also telling reporters, "I want to see Michael Dukakis join me—he seems to be talking about ethics all the time, and why doesn't he just get in there and join me in suggesting we have an independent counsel for the House?"

The President of the United States, seconded by the Vice President of the United States and his party's presidential nominee, had both made aggressive comments. The story stayed alive.

The Dukakis campaign grew nervous. Kirk O'Donnell had joined it at a senior level, and he assured other campaign officials that Wright would not be an embarrassment. Still, when a *New York Times* reporter asked campaign manager Susan Estrich whether the campaign wanted Wright to chair the convention, she replied, "That's a position Paul Kirk has given him. We welcome [Wright's] cooperative attitude."

The mood of the House had soured too. Brian Donnelly, a Wright supporter, observed, "This incremental thing is deadly, things coming out one at a time. That's killing him. At first there was a visceral defense of him against a partisan attack. Now people clam up. No one's accusing him, but other than the real loyal types and the Texans, no one's defending him either. If someone mentions 'Jim,' members raise their eyebrows. That's not good."

In the regular whip meeting, where three weeks earlier members had warmly, sincerely supported him, now when a Wright loyalist gave a technical explanation about one question, one member in the back of the room shook his head. "That's not the issue," he said softly. "The issue is selling lobbyists the book."

But just when it seemed everything was unraveling, the unraveling stopped. There was no next story, no next break.

A man close to Wright told a member, "I don't think there is anything else. If there is, it's something I don't know about."

"Then Jim's all right," he replied.

Reporters continued to press, to cull sources and documents, to dig and dig and dig. They turned nothing more up. Gradually, the press pulled back. The day the ethics committee decided to investigate, a *New York Times* story detailed Republican plans to use Wright to defuse the political damage caused by Ed Meese and the more than one hundred Reagan administration officials who had been forced out under a cloud, several of whom had gone to prison. The story quoted GOP consultant Roger Stone—himself once the subject of a *New Republic* story entitled "State of the Art Sleaze"—saying Wright "symbolizes the Democratic Party. That makes him all the more inviting as a target." The *Times* also ran a front-page story quoting Gingrich that several of the charges were included "out of curiosity . . . I don't expect them to be actionable items," adding that Gingrich and his attorney believed the case was "not particularly strong," and that they had no evidence of any wrongdoing but simply wanted the issues explored.

Two weeks later, a *Newsweek* story on congressional ethics quoted Wright's claim that he had broken no rules. *Newsweek* concluded, "That's true." The magazine also reported that Minnesota Republican senator David Durenberger had written a book published by a friend and declined all royalties—but accepted $100,000 to " 'publicize' his *oeuvre*." It cited several other members who appeared to have conflicts of interest, such as Norman Lent, ranking Republican on Energy and Commerce, whose wife lobbied for NYNEX. Wright's book seemed to be a loophole and the story asked, "What are loopholes for, after all?"

The press wasn't for Wright, but no longer was it trying to get him.

When a *Washington Times* headline charged "Shadow of an Unsolved Murder Hangs Over Wright," a reference to the 1948 murder of a political opponent, Wright was outraged until one staff member said, "Even if you did it, Mr. Speaker, I don't see the problem. It doesn't violate House rules." Even Wright cracked up.

But the investigation would proceed. One senior ally warned him, "You don't want the committee to name an outside counsel. You don't want that. You don't want *me* as the outside counsel."

The history of outside counsels indicated they took a prosecutorial approach, rather than a fact-finding one. And the ethics committee, set up to protect members, could become more deadly than a public trial. While the investigation was analogous to a grand jury in theory, members would not sit through testimony; they would rely on the counsel's summary of it. And the press mattered; the press was certain to headline any hint of wrongdoing. To the press, an indictment was as good as a guilty verdict. And to a politician, perception was virtually reality.

Almost a year earlier Gingrich had said, "What I really want is to get some aggressive people with subpoenas poking around. He's been in politics or thirty years and he's from Texas." Gingrich's implication was that Texans had always mingled money and politics, that Wright had come from an earlier time, with different standards, and that something would be found.

The House had changed in Wright's years in it. In the days before television and jets, Rayburn had called the House "a selfish, sourbellied place, every fellow trying for fame . . . ready at all times to use the other fellow as a prize pole for it." The House had not changed from that description; those aspects had only intensified in the preceding twenty or thirty years, as the House reforms gave each member more power, as television and PACs made each member independent of his party. It was a different place now. O'Neill had run out of colleagues to play cards with; one by one his friends had gone away, or died away. Rostenkowski's good buddies had left the Congress. Ethics didn't change—not really, everyone knew what was right and wrong—but they became formalized, written down more precisely. Tip O'Neill once said that in the old days, "If someone wrote a check for a campaign contribution you looked at him funny." A man who had worked for Lyndon Johnson as essentially an errand boy recalled, "There would be just stacks of bills, thousands, maybe tens of thousands, of dollars, and you'd run an errand and take some 'gas money.' "

Times had changed. Wright wasn't one of the dinosaurs, like Tip whose nickname itself conjured up images of a different era. But he wasn't one of the new breed either. He was trapped between them.

The Republicans on the committee demanded an outside counsel and added the stipulation that whoever was hired should have no ties to Washington. That meant no understanding, no tolerance, of the city's ways. The Democrats, who were not about to expose themselves to charges of a whitewash, agreed. A new process had begun now, with its own pressures. The media were focusing intently on the committee, and especially on the Democrats. They had already been condemned for whitewashing St Germain. And committee Republicans? They suddenly had power.

In the middle of June, Wright and Dixon met privately in H-201, the room where so much had happened in Wright's speakership. It was their second private meeting, a few days since the first. Dixon informed him of the decision to hire an outside counsel. Wright asked, "Why not Richardson Preyer?" Preyer, a highly respected former judge, was also a former Democratic member. "Or if you want a Republican, how about John Anderson? Someone who knows the institution and what the rules are."

Dixon replied, "It can't be a former member. But don't worry. We'll get somebody who will be professional."

It was Wright's last conversation with Dixon.

Still, Wright believed there was nothing out there to find. He was confident of it.

There had been searing experiences in Jim Wright's life, the death of his infant child, his 1948 failure to win reelection to the state legislature, and the 1961 loss in his try for the Senate. Each had changed him, hardened him some, created a thicker shell, a more impenetrable mask. And the years he had spent in the wilderness, long painful years while his ambition rotted—that had been a searing experience too. Even as majority leader, under Carter, before the frustrations of the Reagan presidency, he had written in that private journal, *I've seldom felt quite so despondent about this job. I seriously—truly more seriously than ever before—contemplate retiring.*

So now Wright had another searing experience. It was his most searing. For all his ambition, for all the goals for which he used power, perhaps more important to him was his reputation, what people thought of him. Once he had wondered privately, *Is it an insatiable thirst for approval that drives me?* Reading stories that said others considered him a loner had always pained and angered him. *If they think they do not like me, it is because they do not know me.* His colleagues, he had believed, knew him. His colleagues, he had believed, were his friends. But six months earlier, he had said with a quiet, pained anger, "If my colleagues had heaped opprobrium on [Gingrich], I would be satisfied. But they have not."

He felt isolated, as if a distance had opened between him and his colleagues. That distance was more dangerous to his speakership than any investigation. Much more.

His daughter Ginger talked to him soon after the ethics committee decided to investigate him. He had never believed it would come to that. He had believed they would look at Gingrich's complaint and dismiss it out of hand. Didn't they have the guts to do that? Were they too worried about the press? They would not even hear his rebuttal before deciding. Didn't they have the guts to hear his side either?

Ginger asked him how he was doing.

"Fine," he replied, giving her that mask of a smile. Then he remembered. This was his daughter, his flesh. A long moment later he said, "Did you ever see the movie *High Noon*?"

It was a tale of public service, he believed, of responsibility to public service and family, the whole thing an allegory to him. *I'm not going to let the pygmies think they've run me off*, he thought. *I'm not going to quit under fire. Any more than Gary Cooper left town when Frank Miller was heading for the village.* He was certain that, like Gary Cooper's character, he had been targeted because he had carried out his responsibilities. He also believed that, as in the movie, those he had stood up for, his colleagues, had left him out there all alone to be butchered. *All those people he had wanted to believe were his friends. His friends.*

His daughter knew. "The scene where he took off his badge and threw it on the ground?"

She had the right scene. He was sensitive to that scene, sensitive to the depth of it, sensitive to every subtlety of it.

"He didn't throw it," he corrected her. "He dropped it."

CHAPTER 23

Something had changed in Jim Wright. The relentless scrutiny, the invasive questioning by the media, more invasive and personal than anything he had before experienced, and the sense of isolation (oh yes, that) had rubbed thin his shell and abraded the coating of the self-containment with which he had held himself in check for decades. With his loosening, the House became more chaotic. There were other things, of course, over which he had and could have no control—the presidential race, the Senate, the tactics of the campaigns—but he had anchored the Congress before. He himself seemed less an anchor now. For the remainder of the 100th Congress, the House would be tense, as tense as he, threatened by his and its private explosiveness.

On the surface, things moved well for him. The budget summit agreement and general condemnation of the continuing resolution meant that this year appropriations bills would be handled individually. By June 30, the House had passed all thirteen appropriations bills. It was the first time since 1960 that this had happened that early. And in 1960 the fiscal year had begun July 1; now the fiscal year did not begin until October 1. That day he held a major, formal press conference in the Rayburn Room whose announced purpose was to celebrate that and the other legislative achievements of the Congress. The real purpose was to try once again to shift attention from himself to the substantive achievements of the 100th Congress. This time he seemed to succeed.

When Wright entered the room he was surrounded by a crowd: the majority leader, the whip, the chief deputy whip, Chairman Dingell, Chairman Rostenkowski, Chairman Brooks, Chairman Whitten—all big-shouldered, large, tough men—other chairmen, thirty other members. They provided a show of force, of support, of power; together they represented the institutional weight of the Democratic Party and the Congress. Wright spoke of all their accomplishments. Bill after bill he cited, impressive legislation, and Congress had not yet finished. The questions came and came, but not one addressed ethics or Gingrich.

On July 13, a week before the convention, Michael Dukakis, ahead by fifteen points in the polls, came to address the Democratic Caucus. He arrived with all the fanfare of a President: the caravan of cars and Secret Service escorts, the throng of tourists waiting in the Capitol plaza to glimpse him, the crush of people lining the corridors of the House waiting for a chance handshake. Wright had planned for the entire House leadership to greet him, outside in the plaza, for the cameras. Foley suggested that Wright greet him alone, let the picture be just the Speaker and the presidential nominee. *There's no cloud over you, Mr. Speaker. Show them so.* It was a signal of Foley's loyalty and respect.

That same day the House passed the plant-closing bill by a veto-proof margin; the Senate had done the same the week before. The House passed the trade bill that day too, by 376–45. Whatever happened to the Democratic presidential nominee, the Congress, the institution the Democrats and Jim Wright controlled, was moving forward.

At the Democratic convention, too, Wright's problems were a non-story. The group Citizens for Reagan, which coordinated its activities with Gingrich ("They're allies," Gingrich said), tried to generate media attention as the convention convened by filing a complaint identical to Gingrich's with the Federal Election Commission. The media ignored it. Commentators had speculated that Wright would hand the gavel to someone else during prime time, but he did not. If Wright was inconspicuous on the platform, it was only because producers did not bother to train cameras on him.

In Fort Worth, Republicans were not running a candidate against him. They could not beat him, and did not want his organization energized to get out the Democratic vote, which could help Dukakis carry Texas. He was no longer the center of attention. Only a few weeks after the most intense press scrutiny Wright had ever endured, perhaps more intense than any congressman or senator had ever endured, the press had moved on.

During the convention Wright sat down with a confidant for a private breakfast. "The ethics committee's hired an outside counsel," Wright said. "They'll announce it next week. I think the whole thing will be over in mid-September. Next year I'm going to sit down with *Wall Street Journal* people and get them to understand me."

They were sworn enemies, his confidant replied. It was a waste of his time.

But Wright was insistent, insistent that he could make friends.

He seemed free.

On August 2, between the Democratic and GOP conventions, the White House announced it would allow the plant-closing bill to become law without Reagan's signature. (Polls reported that Republicans alone supported the bill by 62–25 percent.) The same day the Senate passed the trade bill 85–11. Soon after the GOP convention Reagan signed it with ceremony and claimed credit for it.

By then the presidential race occupied the front pages. Wright used the respite to begin wooing the press, increasing the frequency of his on-the-record press lunches and off-the-record informal dinners and barbecues at his home. From the end of June through the end of the year, he tried to host a small group of journalists at least once a week, sometimes twice a week. He invited reporters from NBC, CBS, and ABC, from CNN, PBS, and radio commentators, reporters who appeared on the televised talk shows, reporters and editors from *Time, Newsweek, The New York Times, The Wall Street Journal, The Washington Post,* the Texas press, the *Los Angeles Times*. At the lunches in the Capitol he was often joined by Foley. A journalist could still be critical of someone with whom one had shared a meal and a joke, but it was harder to be snide, or personal. When, inevitably, he was asked about ethics, he replied as he did to Jim Lehrer of *MacNeil/Lehrer:* "It's clear I've done nothing wrong, except possibly to have been stupid."

His tone with the press changed too. Earlier, he had patronized them, even been disingenuous. Once a reporter asked, wouldn't a regulator pay more attention to a phone call from him than from the average congressman. "I don't know the answer to that," he replied. Of course he knew the answer. Now he became more candid, more relaxed, no longer seemed to watch every word he said. It was not a conscious change in strategy. It was a change from within, part of that abrasion of self-control.

The outreach and change in tone helped. Nothing indicated that more than a Jack Anderson column. Anderson had earlier been among the most critical of Wright. Now an Anderson column lauded him. Granting access had made the difference. And as a direct result of one lunch, the *National Journal*'s Richard Cohen ("Foley said something which made me think," Cohen noted) wrote an op-ed piece for the *Los Angeles Times:* "The Democratic-controlled Congress has produced an array of major legislation . . . What has been startling has been the skill and success rate with which congressional Democrats have taken control of the program . . . A key difference this time has been Jim Wright's aggressive style."

Wright read it, then said, "It's finally sinking in with the press that this has been a productive Congress. The most productive in twenty-five years or so. You can sense it in the tone of the stories, a word here, a paragraph there. Finally it is sinking in."

Everything seemed back on track for him. Then, one week after the Democratic convention, the ethics committee announced the hiring of Richard Phelan as special outside counsel; a Democrat from Chicago. Phelan resigned a seat as a Paul Simon delegate to the convention in advance of the announcement. Simon had a reputation as a purist—and had written Gingrich a letter commending his "guts." The Democratic label caused Wertheimer to write a letter to the committee demanding that Phelan be assured of independence, and generated attacks by Gingrich.

In fact, there was a story behind Phelan's hiring, and it did not portend well for Wright. He had not been recommended for the job, but had sought it. There was only one reason to seek such a job: to use it to build a reputation, and one did not build a reputation by declaring people innocent. John Myers, the ranking committee Republican, checked Phelan out. "I heard he was *very* ambitious," Myers later said.

Though Phelan was a past Chicago Bar Association president, Rostenkowski's people knew nothing of him. A Wright aide said, "We received two pieces of intelligence on him. He's got an incredible ego and he plays to win."

Wright still told friends he believed the committee would report by the middle of September. Exonerating him, of course.

Meanwhile, the presidential race had grown bitter. Democrats at their convention had made Bush into a joke, had laughed at the chant

"Where was George?" The Bush campaign was responding, and responding viciously. In early August, Reagan commented on the rumor—false—that Dukakis had sought psychiatric treatment, elevating it to front-page status. A day later at the regular whip meeting, Gephardt—he had disappeared from Congress while seeking the presidential nomination but was back to being a member of the House again—said, "They go after the Speaker, and they go after Dukakis. They're desperate, they're trying everything."

Wright still rankled at the memory of Bush's comment two months earlier that he should be investigated. Coincidentally, the weekend before Bush made it, Wright had been hosting a press barbecue; a reporter had called Bush a "wimp," and Wright had jumped on him, defending Bush and attacking the press for spreading a lie. Ever since Bush's remark, Wright had avoided him. His pride demanded that he confront him if they crossed paths, but he did not want to confront him. Once he was attending a dinner at the Italian ambassador's when Bush entered. Wright slipped out of handshake range, away to another part of the room. His wife said, "I'll bet we're at the same table." They checked; they were. Betty feigned illness and they left.

August 10 was the annual members-only dinner at the House gymnasium. Wright walked in and Bush was there. A former House member, Bush still played racquetball with his close friend Mississippi Democrat Sonny Montgomery. Montgomery greeted Wright and urged him to come over and say hello to the Vice President. Wright refused and moved to the buffet table. Bush came over to him. Wright turned, saw him, and, his insides roiling, stiffened. *He had no choice.*

Members sensed the tension and backed away from the table, leaving the two of them alone, surrounded by empty space, like characters on a stage.

"George," Wright said, "I'm not feeling kindly toward you. You took a cheap shot at me. And I had just been defending you."

"When did you defend me?" Bush snapped. "You damn well didn't defend me at your convention."

"Well, George, you don't have any complaint about what I said. You don't find me attacking your integrity or your honor."

"You and I just see it differently."

The exchange was over in a moment. Wright took his plate and sat down, his insides churning. Bush walked away. They were two men who remembered what others said about them. Politics was personal to both of them. Wright was angry, tense, his movements with his fork were jerks. It should not have come to this. He had known Bush for a quarter of a century, since before Bush entered Congress. He had praised Bush publicly several times in the past and Bush had thanked him for it. And he was Speaker of the House. Bush could be President of the United States. How could they let something personal come between them? It bothered him all night.

The next morning was a Thursday, and Montgomery's prayer breakfasts were on Thursdays, directly across the hall from where Wright ate each morning with his staff. At 8:00 A.M., earlier than he usually arrived, Wright walked into the prayer breakfast and Montgomery immediately came over to him.

"You know, Sonny," Wright said, "I feel badly about some words I had with George last night."

"George said the same thing to me," Montgomery replied. "He feels badly about it too."

Wright picked up on the comment instantly. He could end this thing before it became serious. He could end it right now. "If you'll excuse me, Sonny, I'm going to go call George right now."

He climbed the stairs to his office and dialed the White House himself. Bush got on the phone immediately.

"George, if you're President and I'm Speaker, we've got to work together," Wright said.

"Jim, I'm very glad you called. I did not mean to be personally offensive."

"There's no need to go into it."

The conversation was over. As negative as the campaign got, Bush did not mention Wright again.

The Bush campaign held back nowhere else. It penetrated and divided the House; its progress could be tracked within it, in the mood, in the growing defensiveness of Democrats, in their growing frustration.

Dukakis had vetoed a Massachusetts bill requiring students to recite the pledge of allegiance. The Supreme Court in a famous ruling decades earlier had declared such laws unconstitutional, but Bush had made the veto into an issue. To dramatize it a House Republican abruptly demanded that the House recite the pledge—a ploy to make the network news and drive home the God-and-country symbols the GOP wanted to claim as its own. The chair ruled him out of order.

While the floor swirled with angry members, Wright spoke spontaneously: "I think it is very important that all of us recognize that the pledge of allegiance to the flag is something intended to unite us, not divide us. I think all of us and each of us in his heart of hearts would subscribe to the belief that patriotism knows no political party. . . . Judge Learned Hand said it well: He said that 'society is already in the process of dissolution where neighbors begin to view one another with suspicion or where nonconformity with the accepted creed becomes a mark of disaffection.' Let that not be the epitaph of this civilization."

Suddenly both sides of the aisle erupted in a standing ovation. Network newscasts ran sound bites of his speech, and of the ovation; it was the first wholly positive publicity he had received in months, perhaps since he became Speaker.

But even that small triumph had a bitter taste. On a party-line vote, the House upheld the ruling of the chair. Immediately afterwards the leadership and representatives of Dukakis's campaign gathered in H-210. Democrats could not afford to be branded as opposing the pledge of allegiance, they argued; the symbolism was more important than the legalities or the principle. After that, a Republican and Democrat alternated in leading the House in the pledge of allegiance.

The House of Representatives itself had been made into a prop for George Bush's campaign. At the next whip meeting, one member solemnly declared, "It has come to my attention that two members in this room have been seen not actually reciting the pledge, but only mouthing the words."

The meeting exploded in laughter. But the joke was no longer on George Bush, as it had been at the Democratic convention. It was on all of them.

Members began moving away from Dukakis's campaign. The 100th Congress turned back on itself. And it ended as it began, with controversy created by, swirling about, Jim Wright.

On September 13, at a dinner at the Hyatt Regency honoring Foley, the conservative group Citizens for Reagan distributed "Foley for Speaker" buttons, carried "WANTED" posters of Wright, and handed out fliers charging him with blackmail, money laundering, and influence peddling. Marshall Lynam got word of it and called a union lobbyist, who sent out counterdemonstrators. The confrontation between the pickets got physical; there was pushing and shoving. Afterwards, several anti-Wright demonstrators reported to Gingrich, who was sitting at a table outside Bullfeathers, the Capitol Hill restaurant.

Again furious, ready to erupt, Wright wanted to go the floor. Foley calmed him: "Jim, five people saw those fliers. Millions will see your floor comments."

The next day, Wright finally testified before the ethics committee, almost to the day when he had expected the committee to be finishing its investigation. But there was an ominous note. Chairman Julian Dixon had earlier ruled that Phelan, the outside counsel, could not ask questions. Only members could. When Phelan found out, he had exploded, had said, "It's an outrage!"

He had already shown aggressiveness in questioning other witnesses. But now the House had put him in his place. Nobody cared how large his ego was or about his bar association presidency. He was just staff now. Wright testified and ignored him. Then, after his testimony, Wright urged the committee to act promptly, adding that he had restrained some Democrats from filing charges against five Republicans, including Michel, Lott, and Guy Vander Jagt, the GOP campaign committee chairman. It was both an appeal and a warning. *A lot of what I do isn't calculated in some arcane sense, but a lot of what I say is calculated in ways in which I have only a vague sense myself,* he had once observed.

Phelan, angry and measuring, watched him.

Two days later, on Friday, September 16, Wright was in his ceremonial office at noon, soon to leave on a 12:50 P.M. flight to Fort Worth. Rostenkowski walked in. Earlier Ways and Means had voted to go to conference with the Senate over a textile bill; that would kill the legislation because of lack of time. At a whip meeting, a Ways and Means member had blamed the leadership for not exploiting defense procurement scandals for the campaign: "When this leadership wants something to happen, it happens." Wright had snapped, "The leadership wants Ways and Means to accept the Senate amendments on the textile bill." Passage could make a difference in two House races, possibly in a governor's race. Reagan would veto it, and Congress couldn't override the veto. So what difference did accepting the Senate amendments make? Now Wright and Rostenkowski argued over it. Finally Wright asked point-blank whether he would do it or not.

"I'll think about it," Rostenkowski replied. *Maybe he would do it,*

but he'd be damned if he'd give Wright the satisfaction of saying so then.
He turned on his heel and walked out.

Wright steamed. Was it a sign of his slipping control? Was Rosten-kowski trying to take advantage of weakness? Already there had been other signs of slippage. The whip meeting the day before had had members at one another's throats. Pat Williams had demanded action on the minimum wage, complaining, "We can't get a vote on that. The polls show 78 percent support. Next Congress, let's return to the heart of the Democratic Party." That had angered other members, who had responded in kind. Wright was frustrated, tense.

Outside the door were contra leaders. They weren't on Wright's schedule. A chain of circumstances had placed a meeting they had arranged with Coelho and Bonior in this room. Wright had only a few minutes before leaving for the airport, but he stayed. Enrique Bermudez, the contra military commander, Alfredo Cesar, and a few others walked in.

Things had not gone well in Nicaragua over the past several months. In June, Bermudez had purposely destroyed (he publicly admitted doing so) the peace agreement the Sandinistas and Cesar had reached. Jaime Morales Carazo, for a time the chief contra negotiator, had then accused Bermudez of sabotaging the talks because of his "devotion and submission to foreign interests"—the Reagan administration. A month later, after widespread demonstrations, the Sandinistas had accused the American ambassador of inciting violent demonstrations, expelled him, arrested thirty-nine demonstrators, and briefly closed, then allowed to reopen, the opposition press.

Wright was convinced the administration had funded the demonstrations to provoke a Sandinista overreaction, and that stupidly the Sandinistas had done just that. The only good thing from his perspective was that despite the breakdown of peace negotiations the cease-fire was holding. Now, Friday, September 16, Cesar and Bermudez explained a new peace proposal they wanted to offer the Sandinistas on Monday. It was an obvious ploy, including provisions certain to be rejected. That was not good-faith bargaining. With clipped words, Wright said, "I have condemned the Nicaraguan government. I will not tolerate an effort to disrupt the peace process by them. We are doing everything we can to free the prisoners, to convince them to do so as a good-faith gesture."

But he continued, his words a contained fury: "Don't try to provoke the Sandinistas for public relations purposes. Don't depend on the CIA to pull your chestnuts out of the fire anymore. That won't happen again."

On Monday the contras canceled their scheduled meeting with the Sandinistas. The next day, at Wright's regular press conference, a reporter asked Wright, "Several sources said you characterized the incarceration of ten thousand people as 'CIA provocation' and said you are not willing to . . . [assist] getting the opposition leaders out of jail because they may go out and do more agitation. This is ten thousand people we're talking about."

Wright was startled. For the first time in almost two years of daily press conferences, he asked the reporter to identify himself.

"Pete Barber of the *Washington Times*."

"The several sources whom you cite were not present at the meeting or else they were not listening. I said I was encouraging the government of Nicaragua to release the prisoners, and anyone who heard anything different was not listening or inventing something because of their ideological inclination. That is a false story."

A false story. People were lying about him. He grew angrier, furious. *All year and the year before the administration had conspired to destroy the chance for peace. They had lied to him, used him, set him up. Now someone had leaked a distortion of what he had said to the* Washington Times? *Trying to get him, taunt him? He wanted to strike back, hurt them. Hurt someone.*

For a moment he was out of control. A moment of chaos, of unraveling. *Hurt them. Turn the press on them.*

"I did say that we had received clear testimony from CIA people that they have deliberately done things to provoke the government in Nicaragua . . . and I did not believe that it was a proper role of our government to try to provoke riots or antagonize the governing officials, but I thought we should be using the influence of the United States to encourage the peace process, not discourage it."

Clear testimony from CIA people? If Wright's source was testimony that had been given to the Intelligence Committee, *that was secret.*

Wright's photograph graced the cover of *Congressional Quarterly* once again, with the tagline "Wright's Latest Firestorm."

The Sandinistas blared Wright's comments in headlines in Nicaragua. Reagan accused him of violating secrecy rules. Henry Hyde called his statement "appalling . . . Sandinista propaganda . . . God help Americans down there, that's all I can say." A gloating Elliott Abrams derisively told *The Washington Post,* "Obviously the contras have mishandled him right from the start. Maybe they should have set up a savings and loan."

Bonior tried to rebut the accusations by documenting that Wright had not breached security. In August a United Press International story had detailed a $10-million CIA program funding opposition groups; the story included a State Department quote that the program was the idea of the ambassador whom Nicaragua had expelled. CIA agents had given World Court testimony several years earlier. There were a dozen other public statements, stories in *Newsweek,* in the *Philadelphia Inquirer.* It was all in the public domain.

And if secrecy had been violated, Bonior argued, the State Department had done it. The contras had gone from Wright to see Abrams's assistant Dan Wattenberg, who reportedly orchestrated the leak. State had put Wright's private, diplomatic conversation with the contras in the public domain.

"The whole thing was a setup by the administration to try to deflect attention from the fact they are trying to sabotage the peace talks," Bonior told reporters. "It changes the complexion of this completely."

Foley argued, "This is not really an issue of what the Speaker said or didn't say. This is about the Speaker's role in the disputed policy in Central America."

But this incident was different. Every mistake Wright had made in the 100th Congress had been a considered one. He had taken risks, but had considered the risks. For the first time in his speakership, he had been truly reckless, had done something which he immediately recognized as a mistake, wished he could retract.

The day before he made the statement, he had played golf with Michel at the Speaker's Golf Tournament, a fund-raiser. Each had invited the other to his respective event. O'Neill and Michel had not exchanged such visits. The invitations were part of their joint effort to smooth relations. The day after Wright's comment, Cheney and Michel decided to ask the ethics committee for a formal investigation.

The issue wasn't Wright's comment, or even his role in Central America. It was power. Raw power. The Republicans had sensed weakness. They were exploiting it. Bob Michel was going for his throat.

* * *

Wright sagged under the weight of the attacks. It was the first time Michel had lent his name to any charge against him. Michel, whom Wright had such high regard for. Michel, whom Wright considered a friend. Michel, whom six years earlier Wright and O'Neill had kept in Congress, when he had a tough, tough reelection race and barely won, and they had blocked money from going to his Democratic opponent. To demand a formal investigation without giving him an opportunity to back away from the statement? Without even giving him the courtesy of speaking to him first? That was a deep wound. He had thought Michel was better than that. At breakfast, around the familiar round table, his staff glumly pointed out that he had revealed nothing, he hadn't heard any CIA testimony, and, besides, the press was a bunch of hypocrites, it had made heroes out of those who leaked the Pentagon Papers. He talked softly about the moral imperative of speaking out against immoral acts, wanting to convince himself. Then he shook off his own and his staff's rationalizations: "The question is one of trust."

He should not have said what he had said. Even so, for the White House to have gone after him the way it did—even if Bush did not . . . For Michel and Cheney to have demanded a new investigation . . . And he had been set up. The muscles around his jaw worked.

"I can't unsay it, or apologize for it," he declared. He used a four-letter word once every six months but now, as if deciding that he had had enough, he suddenly hissed, "I won't allow them to put me on the defensive. I'm tired of these chickenshit bastards taking every fucking thing they can and throwing it at me."

Wright struggled to turn the media focus to the policy, to the fact that the United States government was inciting the internal opposition in Nicaragua. And, again, he wrote ethics committee chairman Julian Dixon, pledging cooperation if the committee did investigate him. He was weary of such letters.

He had in fact not attended any Intelligence Committee hearings about the issue, although the committee counsel had briefed him. He had cited information in the public domain. But he had overstated the CIA's role: the United States was helping provoke demonstrations, but indirectly. Wright asked Democrats on Intelligence to back him up with the press, even if they spoke completely off the record. Each member of Intelligence refused to help him. He felt isolated again.

Still he did not pull back. Rostenkowski had agreed finally to accept the Senate amendments on the textile bill. Reagan had vetoed it. Although there was no chance the Senate would override the veto, the House might. Wright saw a final chance to beat Reagan—Reagan, whose administration was tormenting him. He was Speaker of the House. What was the point of being Speaker if he was not going to perform as Speaker? On the floor he pushed for votes, pushed hard.

That antagonized Rostenkowski again: before the vote Mack had told him, "We ain't got a dog in this fight." *Couldn't Rostenkowski rely on anything? Where was Wright? You had to know where he was.* Rostenkowski complained, "He reprimanded McCurdy, challenged Synar, told Kennelly she was on Intelligence because he appointed her, told Panetta he might not be chairman of the Budget Committee—he voted one way, then switched when he got a last-minute release. He threatened five members with committee assignments."

The vote was 272–152 for Wright, but that fell short of the two-thirds needed. Wright lost.

"Who's Wright's best friend?" Rostenkowski demanded. "Who are they? I want to know. People know who I have dinner with. I used to be very close to Jim Wright. He's a loner. That's one reason he's got a problem. I think the situation's terrible, embarrassing to the House. Members have talked to me about running against him. But I don't think I can beat him."

"Danny loathes Wright," said a Ways and Means Democrat. "He just loathes him."

But even Wright's ally Pat Williams conceded, "There's nothing vocal really, but there is an undercurrent. Occasionally someone says, 'Holy shit, why doesn't he keep his mouth shut.' There's a nervousness about Jim going over the edge and taking them along. Members grumbled about Tip. They'd say, 'I wish he'd stop slapping backs and learn something about the damn issue.' There's always grumbling. But this is worse."

Dixon and Wright's attorney Oldaker had a close relationship. They talked. Oldaker later told an intimate that Dixon asked him, "How long do you think Jim plans to remain Speaker, Bill?" A few days later Dixon told him, "I'm not sure Jim's the right person to have as Speaker at this time."

*   *   *

The pressure. The pressure driving Wright inward. The few members rallying to him. The isolation growing. The separation between him and the Caucus. And from Michel, with whom he had always believed he could work.

Yet the Congress functioned. On September 29 the Senate approved a compromise on welfare reform by 96–1. The next day the House concurred, 347–53. Bipartisanship finally arrived.

On September 30, literally seconds before midnight, the Senate passed the final appropriations bill, before the new fiscal year began October 1. Reagan signed it the next day. It was the first time since 1948 that all thirteen appropriations bills became law at the start of the fiscal year.

The only major legislation left was a drug bill. That, too, was Wright's initiative. In the spring he had made that a priority and left it to Foley to work things out. It passed the House in late September, and it, too, was bipartisan. Wright commented, "It's too volatile not to be."

In the middle of October Wright went home. There is a special relationship between most members and their districts. In many ways it is almost a feudal relationship; the members feel responsibility for their people; their whole district is their home. They are proud of their districts; proudly, like a proud host, they show off their districts to visitors. Driving through their cities, most members talk constantly— this neighborhood over here had a 22 percent unemployment rate but a UDAG grant to that development over there helped cut it to 16 percent; that high school over there in the last five years had sixty- seven poor kids go to college on Pell grants. *The only blood oath I ever swore was to my constituents.*

For Wright, who according to a ten-year-old study had brought more federal dollars per capita to his district than any of the other 434 districts in the nation, it was like that only more so. He could cite unemployment statistics by census tract, and in each neighborhood, almost each block, he could name someone he knew, someone he had helped. Each time Wright went home, each time, like Antaeus, he returned to, in touch with, the earth that gave him strength and sustenance. He could bend down, dig his fingers in the soil, see what he had planted, rise up stronger and renewed.

On October 11 in Fort Worth, ten thousand people filled the Will Rogers Coliseum to salute Jim Wright. It was not a fund-raiser, not an election event (he was unopposed), simply a tribute billed as a "Thanks, Jim" party, organized by H. Ross Perot, by Carlos Moore—the press noted that—by Wright's staff. A dozen colleagues took time out from their reelection campaigns and came. Mario Cuomo, governor of New York, came. William Clements, the Republican governor of Texas, came. It was a vast hall with a great long stage flanked by huge caricatures of Wright, dressed as a cowboy about to draw his six-guns. A well-crafted seventeen-minute tape recounted all he had accomplished, and especially all he had meant and still meant to Fort Worth. For several hours the two governors, members of Congress, and local supporters praised him.

Ten thousand people were there. That was The Washington Post's *count. Some said more. People kept coming and coming and coming, sneering at a couple of isolated demonstrators, Gingrich's allies. Ten thousand people. Jim Wright had made a difference in thousands of people's lives. Wasn't that what it was all about?*

When Jim Wright spoke he began by quoting Saint John: " 'I know your works, your tribulations, and your poverty, but you are rich.' . . . Sometimes I think I am the richest one of all. No, not in material wealth. . . . If my net worth at age sixty-five is no better than it was at thirty-one, it is because I've wanted other things. And wealth was never important to me. But this is important: how many people in life do you know who've been allowed to do in life exactly what they've wanted to do? . . . Thanks to you I am . . . As Speaker of the U.S. House of Representatives I have received more free advice, more harsh criticism in the past year than in all my previous life combined. But I also have been able to do more good for more people in the past year than in all my previous life combined—thanks to you. Yes, I am rich . . . in what may be the most precious commodity of all—I'm rich in friends!

"I love this town and want it to succeed. I love this country and want it to fulfill its promise. I am a populist and an egalitarian. I believe in the brotherhood of man and woman not as an abstract theory but as a reality. When I was very young my father taught me not to look down on anyone—and never to let anyone look down on me. That is my heritage. It is Texas, the heritage of the plains. I think it is quintessentially American. . . . I am continually amazed that a politician of any prominence, target of repeated journalistic bombardment, can retain any friends at all. . . .

"Peace is not passive. Peace must be waged by deeds of goodwill. . . . There are some in our government who do not want a negotiated peace. They want the war to resume in a vain hope of a military settlement, bought by our money and other people's blood and established upon the graves of more innocent victims of both sides. Because I have persisted in continuing the quest for peace and orderly democracy, they have turned the full fury of their anger upon me—with sneak attacks upon my integrity . . . with a concerted effort to destroy my credibility as a person and effectiveness as a leader, to destroy my influence and thus to intimidate others into timid compliance with their plans. Their attacks have not succeeded. Those who know me, home folks and colleagues, are *not* impressed by the phony charges. After sixty-five years of living and giving, my reputation is fully intact."

It was a remarkable speech, a personal speech. It came from a man at bay and under attack, explaining himself, justifying himself, searching for approval. Later he said, "It was the only thing I've done in months where I said exactly what I wanted to say." As he spoke on, interrupted by laughter and cheers at all the right places, he grew stronger, talked of what he must do, of what America must do. As he finished, the applause, loud, loud, cheers and more cheers for him, people standing, clapping, shouting, rolled through the coliseum. These were his friends.

Three days later, suddenly in the middle of the night and without warning, Craig Raupe died. Wright and he had talked often all through the 100th Congress, much more often than Raupe, who understood the demands on Wright's time, had expected. Raupe, his friend for forty years, alive with energy, never quite grown up, seldom impressed by anything, a man who knew almost everything about the House and everything about Wright and loved him anyway, had always been there for him.

At the whip meeting three weeks before the election, one member complained that people were distancing themselves from Dukakis, in some cases even more than they had from Mondale, and insisted, "I want to know, is the leadership in touch with the campaign?"

"Yes," Coelho answered.

"That's good enough for us!" shouted a voice from the back.

Members held their sides they laughed so hard. Nothing could have better expressed the state of Dukakis's chances.

Yet nothing so frustrated Wright as listening to Democrats already pointing fingers at the Dukakis campaign instead of trying to help. Four years earlier a Hill aide had said something negative about Mondale to Wright at a campaign event. "He whirled on me," the aide recalled. "It was scary. I was so spooked I left and got drunk."

Wright was tired, tired of everything and especially of fighting a Republican President. He wanted a Democrat. There were things he wanted to do. He had little leverage over the Dukakis campaign but used what he had, bringing in Kirk O'Donnell and other senior Dukakis officials for a blunt talking-to. In Martin Frost's Dallas district was a huge LTV Aerospace plant; before a Dukakis visit to it, Frost had recommended to his advance people that he use a workers' gate, and warned them to avoid another gate for executives where Dukakis could be ambushed. The advance people decided the executives' gate offered a better "visual" and brought Dukakis to it; he was drowned out by jeers. Wright had heard of a dozen examples of similar arrogance around the country. It wasn't too late, he insisted. But they had to change. They had to reach out, actively get their message out.

But by now no one was receptive. A few days later, Jesse Jackson addressed the Caucus. Bentsen had a week before, and, like Bentsen, he pleaded for members' involvement, pleaded for their campaign organizations to help. If the Dukakis campaign had isolated itself, "So what?" Jackson asked. "If you're not plugged in, plug yourself in! Plug yourself in!"

These men and women were hard professionals, rarely moved by pleadings, at least not when their names were on the line too. It was cold business. Members wanted no one else's problems.

It was into October, late into the election cycle. The House had done its business, and was waiting for the Senate to act on the drug bill, the only legislation which remained.

For a change House liberals hoped Senate delays would bail them out. To secure bipartisanship, Wright had allowed Republicans free rein on drug-bill floor votes. Liberals had gagged on one GOP-sponsored amendment after another—the death penalty for drug-related murders, limiting the exclusionary rules for evidence. "Liberals used to stand up and fight these things," one Republican said. "They used to blow them away." Few stood up and fought now. One after another, the House had passed them. No one wanted to be labeled soft on drugs, soft on crime by an opponent. But delay was unlikely to save liberals. The Democratic leadership in both bodies did not want to adjourn without passing the drug bill, not in an election year when prison furloughs became an issue in presidential politics.

So members waited for the Senate, as usual, and the leadership held the last whip meeting of the year, of the 100th Congress, the last Thursday gathering for doughnuts, fresh muffins, fresh fruit, and coffee. There was no legislative strategy to discuss. They talked briefly about the presidential race. GOP vice-presidential candidate Dan Quayle had just foundered badly in his debate with Bentsen.

Coelho urged them to put out the message: "The public is nervous about him. Pound it home! Quayle! Quayle! Quayle!"

"And Bush's judgment," added a member.

"No!" Coelho replied. *K-I-S-S!* Keep it simple, stupid! Don't confuse the press or the public with two messages. "Just Quayle!"

Another member, who had attended the Bentsen-Quayle debate, reported, "All you read about spin control by the Republicans is true. After the debate they were all over the press. It was important that we were there to talk to our local media, and it's important that we do the same in California"—for the last Bush-Dukakis debate.

Suddenly that was it. There was no more business to discuss.

It seemed that every member in the room simultaneously realized they were, except for a few final votes, finished. For an instant, it seemed that every member in the room reflected on what they had accomplished. No Congress in decades could even approach the record of the 100th Congress. It had addressed in major initiatives the environment, international trade, health care, the social fabric, economic infrastructure, civil rights. And it had brought peace. All of Wright's agenda had passed, all of it. Every law carried the policy stamp of House Democrats. It was a remarkable record. Everyone in the room seemed to come together. They laughed and cheered. *They had governed. Whatever happened between Bush and Dukakis, Congress—especially House Democrats—had governed. They were all proud of that. They were proud of that.*

The moment passed. Members were leaving. They had things to do.

"Thank you all for your help!" Coelho shouted after them. Hardly anyone remained to hear him.

On October 14 the Senate passed a drug bill. There was no time for a formal conference, but for a week key committee and subcommittee chairmen and the joint bipartisan leadership met, surrounded by aides. For hour after hour they sat in H-324, the whip meeting room, the Steering and Policy room, formally the Thomas P. O'Neill Room, and hashed out arguments. October 17 passed, October 18, October 19.

Already the 100th Congress had outlasted the betting pools on adjournment. In the Senate press gallery, no one had picked later than October 19. House leadership staff had done no better. The money in both pools went to charity. While waiting for resolution of the drug bill, other legislation had time to pass. The bill making "technical corrections" to tax reform passed, and Rostenkowski included all the "transition rules" he wanted, all the giveaways which had been stripped from reconciliation the year before. A credit-card bill passed, requiring banks to disclose more information about costs of credit. The Veterans Administration became a cabinet department.

Abruptly, at 7:00 P.M. on Thursday, October 20, the gathering in H-324 recessed. The most senior members reconvened in H-201 and asked Wright to help finally settle the bill. In a three-and-a-half-hour meeting, half a dozen issues dropped away, including the ones most objectionable to civil libertarians. Several issues still remained when Wright briefed reporters, who had been waiting, bored, in the Rayburn Room the entire time. At ten-forty-five he left to have dinner with a friend—Betty was in Fort Worth—and then go home. Betty had gotten fed up with Washington, fed up with the attacks in the press on her husband, had wanted to get away.

At dinner Wright talked about what he had hoped to accomplish when he became Speaker—to reverse the direction and priorities of the Reagan years. He was proud of what the 100th Congress had done. The scope and import of its legislation had exceeded that of every Congress since the 89th, more than twenty years earlier, and the 89th had had a President, Lyndon Johnson at the height of his power, just elected in a historic landslide, pushing, pulling, and cajoling Congress to act. In the 100th the President had resisted most of the congressional initiatives every step of the way. "Reagan was the counterrevolution," he said. "I wanted to get the revolution going again."

The drug bill dragged on through the next day. All day. Members went back and forth over the remaining issues. Finally they too were compromised or dropped. It had passed midnight and become Saturday, October 22.

But members were still in their offices, or in their nearby apartments, or in the restaurants a block away, within range for their beepers, which finally went off. Slowly but happily they trickled into the chamber, and voted to pass the compromise bill 346–11, then went home. The Senate, where there wasn't a quorum to be found, accepted the compromise by voice vote. On the House floor the leaders of both parties and their floor staffs gathered. Wright sat in the chair, sat there with pride and dignity. In a final, formal ceremony of procedure, the 100th Congress wound down.

"Mr. Speaker!" Foley announced. "I offer a privileged concurrent resolution and ask for its immediate consideration."

"The clerk will read the resolution," Wright said.

"That when the House and Senate adjourn on Saturday, October 22, 1988, they stand adjourned sine die."

"All in favor?"

"Aye!"

"Opposed?"

Silence.

"Without objection, a motion to reconsider is laid upon the table."

Michel rose to confirm that members of the 101st Congress be paid allowances, beginning the last two days of November.

Then Foley announced, "Mr. Speaker, your committee"—Foley and Michel—"appointed to join a committee of the Senate"—Byrd and Dole—"to inform the President that the Congress is ready to adjourn and to ask him if he has any further communications to make to the Congress has performed that duty. Mr. Speaker, the President has directed us to say that he has no further communications to make to the 100th Congress. He has also stated to us that he wishes to communicate to members of both parties that he feels it has been an extremely productive and useful Congress."

Michel said, "Mr. Speaker, I concur with the majority leader's report. There will be no minority report."

Wright said, "I am quite sure that all members of the House join in wishing to the President and Mrs. Reagan a most happy and joyous remainder of this year and a happy and joyous life in retirement from this enormous office. . . . Does any member have anything in the way of business to come before the House at this time? If not, the House will stand in recess subject to the call of the chair."

At 1:34 A.M. he banged the gavel. The House recessed. He surveyed the chamber a final time. The galleries were empty, the chamber, the rows of thickly cushioned chairs, empty. Directly across from the Speaker's Rostrum, almost at eye-level, was the bas-relief sculpture of Moses; from the chair, in a view unlike that from any other point in the chamber, Moses stared coldly and piercingly into one's eyes, as if decreeing a forbidding standard.

Wright climbed down from the rostrum. Foley and Michel and Coelho were shaking one another's hands, congratulating one another, and Wright joined them. Then they and their aides, joking, happy with what they had accomplished, stepped out from the chamber into the Speaker's Lobby, lined with portraits of past Speakers, Rayburn's portrait at the door Wright always went through, and turned toward H-209, crowded with seven desks including Mack's in a corner, just a few feet away at the end of the lobby. Beer and trays of hors d'oeuvres were laid out, and soon pizza came in. It was already two in the morning. Wright lingered for a while, swapping stories, smiling, looking back with pride. Finally he left. Foley sat down in a secretary's chair, leaned back, and held court, trading stories and philosophizing.

At 2:54 A.M., the House reconvened with Foley in the chair as Speaker pro tem. The doorkeeper announced "a message from the Senate." A senior Senate clerk bowed deeply from the waist and declared that the Senate had passed without amendment the concurrent resolution providing for the sine die adjournment of the 100th Congress.

"Mr. Speaker!" Coelho called out. "I move that the House do now adjourn."

By voice vote in the empty chamber full of echoes, the motion was agreed to.

Foley banged the gavel at 2:55 A.M., Saturday, October 22. The 100th Congress was over.

In the Rayburn Room, down the winding hallway that snaked past the Speaker's Rooms around the outside of the chamber, the lights went out. Workmen picked up the phones there marked "MEMBERS ONLY" and put them away for the year. Lights in hallways throughout the Capitol dimmed. The Capitol seemed suddenly, abruptly, empty.

PART VII
THE
FALL

*From the nobles, if hostile, [a prince]
has to fear not only desertion but even
active opposition. The nobles have . . .
foresight and are astute, they always act
in time to safeguard their interests, and
they take sides with the one whom they
expect to win. . . .*

*Everyone sees what you appear to be;
few experience what you really are. And
those few dare not gainsay the many. . . .
In the actions of all men, and especially
of princes, where there is no court of appeal one judges by the result.*

—Machiavelli, *The Prince*

CHAPTER 24

The press finally recognized the achievements of the 100th Congress. It adjourned for a change to almost universal praise. Yet the press would not recognize Wright's contribution. David Broder of *The Washington Post* applauded "all the good things [the 100th Congress] did. . . . It clearly left an enduring mark in many fields. . . . [Its record marked] a significant achievement for any Congress at any time." Then Broder asked, "How can a body of 535 individual, egotistical political entrepreneurs be so effective . . . [with] a President whose impulses in many instances are opposite those of Congress?"

His answer was not Wright, whom he dismissed as "brand new to the job and [he] did not have the power. . . . The answer has to lie within the membership . . . many individuals, Republicans as well as Democrats, backbenchers as well as committee chairmen."

Broder's logic did not support his conclusion—the same members he credited for such successes in the 100th Congress had served in the 99th Congress. The only changes: Democrats controlled the Senate and Wright was Speaker. Yet the respected, nonideological, reasoned Broder, who wrote encomiums to Foley, would give Wright nothing.

There is a sort of conventional wisdom that develops in Washington based on a comfort level, the comfort that comes of predictability and acceptance of the way things work. Wright made people uncomfortable. He had tried to change too much and was too unpredictable. There was more weight to him now, more hardness, and yet more of an edge, with something ungainly about him. Nothing in Washington is more respected than judgment—another word for balance, perspective on the ways of the city. His seemed questionable. Not only in the press, but at Georgetown and McLean dinner parties, where people of the permanent establishment raised eyebrows and understood one another. Wright, the Speaker of the House who had served thirty-four years in Washington, was not quite accepted.

The election was Tuesday, November 8. Thursday morning Wright, the constitutional head of the Legislative Branch, called George Bush, the President-elect, to congratulate him. Bush thanked him, then said, "I remember your comment that we have to work together. I thought I'd come see you and talk about it."

"I'll come see you, you name it. Any time, any place."

"No, no. I want to come see you. I'll come up there."

It was a gesture each understood. A few days later, the two had lunch, alone in Wright's office. They sat at the small round poker table Wright used for intimate conversations. Bush said, "I want you to know I respect you and the House as an institution. I won't have any part in anything at all that impinges on your honor or integrity."

Bush's words soothed Wright's wounds. Wright was tired of fighting. He longed for the kind of relationship Rayburn and Eisenhower had shared. That had been impossible with Reagan, a man he held in contempt. But Bush? They came from the opposite ends of America, in every sense: Bush, a child of privilege and wealth, has such natural grace that those who meet him hope he likes them. Of him, one Reagan administration official who has known him for thirty years said, "A lot of people think they're closer to him than they are." And for all his personal grace, he never seemed quite sure of what he believed in, other than a vague *America,* or what he wanted. Wright had known want as a boy and lacked personal grace, consciously worked at the simplest social skills. But his rootlessness had nothing to do with belief. *I have one more quarter to play,* he had said. *I want this back.*

Still, maybe a good relationship was possible with Bush. Bush seemed open to him, accepting of him. They talked for two hours, each seeking areas of agreement, areas where they could help each other, areas of bipartisanship. Perhaps this relationship could become fruitful. Neither mentioned taxes.

Soon after the election Gorbachev came to New York. Wright had a hunch, based on his conversation with Gorbachev, that he would offer or even unilaterally declare a dramatic scaling down of forces. He talked to Bush again about this. His hunch proved correct.

Bush, in his Inaugural Address, turned and looked pointedly at Wright, who with Betty sat close by on the platform, and said, "To my friends—and, yes, I do mean friends—in the loyal opposition—and, yes, I do mean loyal—I put out my hand."

For his first weekend retreat to Camp David as President, Bush invited Wright to join him. Though the retreat was canceled because of illness, Washington took note of the invitation.

Publicly, Wright pledged "full cooperation" with Bush, noting that as far as Bush's talk of the environment, education, day care, and the like was concerned, "we truly look forward to working with him. . . . I think I owe it to him not to preempt him but should wait for the program he offers."

Then he added, "Of course, Congress has a responsibility to develop a legislative agenda and we will do that in due course."

A few kind words from Bush could make a difference in both style and substance, but did not alter fundamental disagreements. Wright had already begun preparing his agenda for this Congress. The dry hard poverty of the Southwest, the hatred of the "interests," was alive again in him. On December 13 he sent out a barrage of letters, telling members of the Joint Economic Committee to investigate the concentration of economic power, the availability and cost of housing, education, and health care, the distribution of the tax burden. Each study would become ammunition in a war to redirect the government. Simultaneously, he asked several members to concentrate on campaign-reform legislation, wrote once again to every member of Ways and Means about the need for taxes, wrote a more personal note to Rostenkowski, wrote Dingell about legislation monitoring foreign investment.

He was still pushing, still determined. But now he was alone, more so than when he first became Speaker. His colleagues then had been ready for confrontation: now Democrats told him to go softly. The Senate leadership in particular did not want confrontation. Byrd, who had recognized that his colleagues no longer wanted him as Senate majority leader, had stepped down to chair the Appropriations Committee. George Mitchell of Maine replaced him. In many ways similar to Foley, Mitchell was cautious. He told Wright they simply did not have the votes on taxes. The warning was clear: if Wright got out front on taxes again he would isolate himself. Ironically, his only strong support came from Rostenkowski.

It frustrated him. Members of both parties had delayed major action on the deficit, waiting for two years for the new President. The election had sent mixed messages. Several states, including generally conservative ones such as Mississippi, Virginia, and South Carolina, had recently embraced tax increases to pay for initiatives in education or transportation; now Colorado, South Dakota, and Arkansas rejected efforts to make it harder to raise taxes. The accounting firm Arthur Andersen polled businessmen, almost 90 percent of whom voted for Bush; even among this group, 44 percent wanted taxes raised. The so-called National Economic Commission, cochaired by Bob Strauss and former Reagan cabinet officer Drew Lewis, had been created to provide bipartisan political cover for a deficit solution including both cuts—perhaps even Social Security cuts—and tax increases. An opening seemed to exist.

Bush declared the deficit the number-one national problem but had campaigned against raising taxes. He could not so quickly abandon his promise. Republicans on the National Economic Commission would not embarrass him; ultimately, the commission could not even agree upon a report.

Despite—or because of—the successes of the 100th Congress, despite—or because of—Bush's overtures, as Wright entered his second term as Speaker, in January 1989, he felt more constrained than in his first.

And hanging over everything was the ethics investigation.

Wright had expected the committee to finish back in September. Early that month, his attorney Bill Oldaker had objected to outside counsel Richard Phelan's efforts to probe beyond the original six charges, deep into the relationship between Wright and George Mallick, his former business partner. Phelan had found no specific reason to expand his investigation, and at first Julian Dixon, the chairman, sided with Oldaker. But John Myers, the ranking Republican, urged him to give Phelan his way. Then came Wright's CIA comment. *How long do you think Jim plans to remain Speaker, Bill?* Dixon had asked Oldaker. *I'm not sure he's the right person to be Speaker at this time.* Dixon allowed Phelan to go forward. He and his staff started interviewing Wright's most bitter political enemies, even interviewing the Texas Ranger who had investigated the 1948 murder of a Wright opponent. To investigate the 1985 purchase of Wright's book by the Teamsters, Phelan subpoenaed union records back to 1963.

The Teamsters refused to comply with the subpoena. Its attorney was Stanley Brand, a former House counsel. He believed in confronting the committee at every turn. The committee disliked him. But his clients did well. Now the committee backed down and reissued a limited subpoena.

The committee had no direct jurisdiction over Mallick, a private businessman. Like the Teamsters, he could have fought the subpoena. Possibly the committee would have backed down again. But Oldaker was representing him, as he was several other witnesses close to Wright including his staff. That gave him the opportunity to sit in on depositions, and learn the direction in which Phelan was going.

Unlike Brand, Oldaker preferred to work things out with the committee, not to fight. His clients had done well also. With the disarming, easygoing demeanor of a man who could walk into a room filled with strangers and flop down on a chair and be comfortable, he was a partner in Manatt, Phelps, a law firm headed by former Democratic National Committee chairman Charles Manatt. He had been a senior adviser to Senator Joseph Biden's aborted 1988 presidential campaign, as well as general counsel and treasurer of Ted Kennedy's 1980 campaign. Before that, he had been general counsel at the Federal Election Commission. He had a good personal relationship with Dixon, and he and Mack had decided to play the inside game with the committee, to cooperate totally. Rather than fight the subpoena, he had Mallick comply. Wright's office tried to contain Phelan another way: by leaking a story to *The New York Times* about how far afield he was ranging. It did not work.

Then, as Oldaker was reviewing records before turning them over to the committee, he discovered that Mallightco, the company Wright and Betty had formed with Mallick and his wife, Marlene, had supplied Betty with a company car beginning in 1983. On the facts, the car seemed *de minimis*. A 1979 Cadillac, Marlene Mallick had bought it new, driven it for a year and a half, then sold it in mid-1980 for $10,575 to Mallightco. The Mallicks and Wrights owned equal shares in the company so each owned half the car. The car stayed in Fort Worth for three years. Betty was working for Mallightco part-time at $18,000 a year from 1981 through 1984. In 1983 she took the car to Washington and kept driving the car after taking another job. Mallightco still owned it and paid the upkeep; although the Wrights owned half the company, and thus paid half the upkeep, it seemed questionable from a tax standpoint. A bigger problem was Mallick's credibility. He had not mentioned the car, not to Oldaker in hours of preparation, not to the committee when he testified about Betty Wright's compensation. Mallick had been a terrible witness anyway. Myers, one of three members who listened to his deposition, said bluntly. "Frankly, I think [this testimony] is going to be viewed by a lot of the members with enormous skepticism." Now Mallick seemed to have hidden something.

Oldaker told Wright about the discovery in Marshall Lynam's office, across the reception area from Wright's own. He exploded, hurling a book against the wall. "Goddammit!" he shouted. Then he turned to business: "How big a problem is it?"

"In a technical sense it's not very big, but as far as Mallick's credibility is concerned, it matters, yes."

Oldaker ran into Dixon soon afterwards at a fund-raiser in California for Senator Lloyd Bentsen and told him about the car. Dixon listened, then said, "We can still keep it inside the committee"—meaning either a letter saying Wright had shown bad judgment but broke no rules, or at worst a formal letter of reproval, which avoided a floor vote. But he added, "It may cause other problems with Betty's employment."

From the first questions Phelan had asked, it was clear he would try to build a case that her salary was a gift. On the law, Wright seemed impregnable on that issue. Oldaker knew Phelan would not be able to find any evidence that she had not worked, and dismissed the warning: "That's not relevant."

As the fall progressed, Dixon seemed to agree. He was never explicit, but indicated to Oldaker and Mack that only the car itself and the use of Mallick's apartment might cause problems.

In October, before the 100th Congress adjourned, Gingrich ally Robert Walker had, on the floor, fought procedures which Michel had agreed to. One longtime House employee had commented, "That's got to be humiliating to Michel. It's a public announcement that he's not running things." On December 5 the Republicans held their organizing caucus and new leadership elections. Trent Lott had left the House for the Senate. It was a sign of GOP frustrations that the second-ranking Republican would do that. Dick Cheney replaced him, and Cheney had moved closer to Gingrich. Michel's protégé Lynn Martin was defeated in her quest for the number-three leadership job. And two Gingrich allies were elected to lower-level leadership posts; it was the first time any of his group had penetrated the leadership. The GOP Conference sent one more message. Routinely ranking members of committees are unanimously reelected. But a core group of Gingrich allies, who believed Myers was not aggressive enough in going after Wright, voted against keeping him as the ranking member of the ethics committee.

The key to leadership is listening, Michel had said. He knew the history of GOP regicide. His predecessor John Rhodes had stepped down as leader to avoid a challenge, but stayed in the House; Gerald Ford had overthrown Charles Halleck as leader; Halleck himself had unseated Joe Martin, the last Republican Speaker. Michel listened. Already House Republicans had hired, at $250,000 a year, former Reagan White House political director Ed Rollins, a gut-fighter, to head their campaign committee. Michel had also proclaimed "Project 92," a new effort aimed at attacking Democrats more aggressively and winning control of the House. There were other signs he was listening too. For thirty years, Hyde Murray, the minority counsel, had been a senior GOP aide. He had helped Livingston and Sensenbrenner examine Gingrich's complaint against Wright six months before, and had agreed there was nothing to it. Now Gingrich's allies wanted Murray fired. Jim Leach, a moderate GOP member from Iowa, told the press, "If the most principled and respected of congressional staff are to be dismissed for respecting too stringently the traditions and rules of the House, the message would appear to be chilling."

Two years before, a Michel intimate had defended him, saying, *There are some things you have to do to keep control.* Michel neither protested Murray's firing nor fought to keep him.

And Michel released to the press his speech to the GOP conference. In it he attacked: "Let Jim Wright know that this is our House, too. . . . I'm asking each one of you today to use every last ounce of your talent, every ounce of your energy . . . to count in your subcommittees and in full committee, count on the floor and in the media." He went on to talk of ethics: "The record of enforcement in this House is a national disgrace. . . . The reputation of this institution has been smeared."

Then he said something remarkable. He announced that if a Democrat ran for Speaker against Wright, Republicans would support him. They could elect a coalition Speaker. It was a bizarre comment; no Democrat was even considering running. But such a combination had stripped Joe Cannon of his power in 1910.

After the press headlined Michel's comments, Michel called Wright. Wright did not return the call. A few days later they met at an event, and Michel said he really did want to talk to him. The two went to Michel's office where Michel insisted the media had misinterpreted his point. Wright was not appeased; too many things had happened. He believed Michel had impugned both his integrity and his patriotism. Wright left, still angry, later saying, "I'm tired of this horseshit."

Yet Gingrich was frustrated. Nothing explosive had surfaced in testimony, and ethics committee staff and members were spreading the word that Wright would be exonerated, except perhaps for minor technical violations. In mid-January, Gingrich said, "I hear Wright's going to get off. That doesn't end it. I'm engaged in a long-term struggle. The House is sick and Wright's the symbol."

Almost simultaneously, the conservative columnists Evans and Novak printed an item that Charles Pashayan would vote to let Wright off, giving him a 7–5 bipartisan majority. People in Gingrich's office talked about mounting a campaign to pressure him. Soon two conservative groups launched a letter-writing campaign in his district.

Anticipating that Wright would escape the committee without a crippling scar, Gingrich began his next stage of attack by saying that anything less than a vote to censure would be a whitewash. He intended to demand that the committee release Phelan's entire report. That would give the media something to pore over.

As the Congress convened, conservatives struck another blow at Wright's power. Both the American Enterprise Institute and the Heritage Foundation, two conservative think tanks, had embarked on similar projects when he began dominating policy in late 1987 and early 1988: books attacking Congress. Now they were released: AEI published *The Fettered Presidency*; Heritage, *The Imperial Congress*. Both were collections of essays; AEI's was edited by Gordon Crovitz, an editor of *The Wall Street Journal*'s editorial page, and Heritage's was edited by Gordon Wood, a House GOP aide.

Both studies condemned congressional activism and accused Congress of intruding on and usurping Executive Branch prerogatives; the studies were launched with major publicity efforts in the hope of influencing coverage, of planting questions in reporters' minds about the propriety of congressional initiatives. AEI held a press conference with political media celebrities; Gingrich signed a fund-raising letter for Heritage praising the book and damning Wright.

Bush's victory marked the fifth for his party in the last six presidential elections. It was also the first time since 1960 that the party of the winning presidential candidate had lost seats in Congress. The election supported an idea much discussed in Washington, that Democrats had become the party of the Congress, Republicans the party of the White House. If Democrats were going to rule the Congress, then conservatives would put Congress on the defensive. Every aspect of Wright's being, personal, institutional, and political, was under attack. There was no respite. Gingrich had created the ethics charges. But Wright had generated malevolence toward himself. And there was power behind the malevolence.

On December 13, the same day Wright's letters went out on the legislative agenda, the Commission on Executive, Legislative, and Judicial salaries recommended a 51 percent pay increase—from $89,500 to $135,000—for members and judges, and comparable raises for senior administration officials. Two years earlier, the commission had recommended the same salary structure; it had inflated the figure, anticipating that Ronald Reagan would slash it. White House aides warned the commission that this time Reagan would likely endorse its recommendations. But the commission was trapped; it could hardly recommend less than it had two years before.

The raise was needed, the commission said; new graduates of the best law schools were making more in their first year than federal judges. The best people in the private sector, if they had children approaching college age, could no longer afford to halve their incomes to join the Executive Branch. Members needed the raise just to bring their salaries into line, after inflation, with what they had been fifteen years earlier.

The public did not want to hear the arguments: a broad array of people, from conservatives to Ralph Nader, excoriated it.

On New Year's Day, a Sunday, Michel, who had just won an uncomfortably close election, and Dole both denounced the 51 percent pay-raise proposal.

But Reagan formally proposed the 51 percent raise January 9. It would take effect automatically on February 8, unless both houses voted against it. Dole said, "The Senate isn't going to duck the issue"—it would vote. Senate majority leader Mitchell agreed. As it had two years before, the Senate would leave the responsibility for passing the raise to the House.

Tony Coelho and Vic Fazio, who also served on the ethics committee, had already formulated a strategy: to follow "regular procedure"—a euphemism for avoiding a vote, as the House had two years earlier. Critics anticipated that strategy and were already condemning it, and aiming at Wright. Wright had the power to schedule a vote.

Months earlier, Fazio had begun the search for political cover to justify the raise. Ethics legislation seemed the only possible cover. He, Coelho, and Common Cause's Wertheimer were developing a reform package to be put on the floor soon after the raise went into effect. The package would include a ban on honoraria. House members could accept 30 percent of their income in honoraria. Senators allowed themselves 40 percent.

Wright, like many of his colleagues, considered a 51 percent raise too much. And the public hated it. Eighty-five percent of the public opposed it, according to an ABC–*Washington Post* poll. Wright looked at the figures one morning at breakfast and said, "It's one thing to vote against that sentiment as a matter of conscience. It's another to line your own pockets."

Of the plan to avoid a vote, he worried, "Maybe we could get past the deadline without a vote. But it would not be possible to avoid one for the entire Congress. The vote could only go one way, to give back the raise. Then you've got the worst of both worlds, all the opprobrium and none of the money."

He offered his own plan to the pay task force: drop the raise to 30 percent and at the same time ban honoraria. They could sell that as no raise at all, just an improvement in ethics. It would also help the House, where few members collected the maximum, and hurt senators, most of whom collected the higher limit. Wright wanted members to vote on the proposal but reasoned, "If you can't vote for that, how can you vote to withstand giving it back later in the year?"

The task force argued with him. Coelho insisted that Wright's idea would lose just as surely as a vote on 51 percent. The public didn't care whether the raise was $4,500 or $45,000. They just didn't want congressmen to get a raise. So they might as well go for the bigger amount. No one supported Wright. No one. He fell silent. Members left confident that he had given a commitment to block a floor vote.

Yet he was unsatisfied. Coelho, Fazio, and most members of the task force came from one of the two coasts or were senior members of the House. Members from the middle of the country were seriously concerned. He knew members wanted the money. He knew they did not want to vote. But he also knew they did not want to lose the next election. More than one member had told him the pay-raise issue could beat him. Coelho had given him a rough whip count supporting the strategy of blocking any vote, but less than a hundred members had responded. That made no sense. Out of town or not, members were reachable. In 1987, Coelho told one Wright aide, "I'm not going to let Foley step up to Speaker uncontested." He had not been threatening Wright, but clearly had his own ambitions. After that—on welfare reform—Coelho had seemed to pursue his own agenda; it had almost destroyed Wright's speakership. Wright wondered whether there was some middle ground the membership might support. Was he starting a new Congress not trusting his own whip? Was he so isolated from the membership he could not himself reach them? The pay raise could splinter the leadership, do what Republicans had failed to do. At breakfast he thought out loud of running another whip count but dismissed it, saying, "I'd do it if I could pick the whips doing the counting."

There were other tensions. Pressure had been exerted indirectly on the ethics committee to bring the investigation to a close. Phelan had stopped interviewing witnesses several weeks earlier. Why couldn't the committee finish?

Phelan said he hadn't finished writing his report. Myers resisted. Dixon backed them. Privately, Myers said he didn't want the committee to act until after the pay-raise vote.

On Thursday, January 26, several pay-raise opponents conceded that they probably could not force a House vote before the deadline. The next day Bush, keeping some distance from it, tepidly endorsed the raise. Coelho and Fazio believed they were over the hump; the raise would go into effect.

But a network of call-in radio hosts had formed; they were fanning public flames and organizing a new kind of Boston tea party. Tens of thousands of letters containing tea bags poured into Congress. The level of contempt, of outrage, rose higher and higher; the combination of hypocrisy, cowardice, and the size of the raise was enraging the public. Every member of Congress became a target of contempt and fury. But Wright was the biggest target.

It was he who could schedule or block a vote. All that week Wright was saying, "The buck stops here." Yet he was depressed. No matter what he did, he would lose and the House would lose. Some of his advisers believed the 51 percent raise was Reagan's final slap at him. There was a large issue at stake here—power.

Republicans were moving closer and closer to Gingrich's idea that the best way to take control of the House was to destroy it. Lee Atwater, Bush's campaign manager, was the new chairman of the Republican National Committee. His first mailing of the year had attacked the Democratic Congress. Now, although both Reagan and Bush had endorsed the pay raise, although Michel and Cheney were privately cooperating with Democrats to get it, Atwater put out another mailing condemning the raise and Hill Democrats. The issue could drive a wedge between Democrats and their core constituency. How did a 51 percent raise, to $135,000 a year, sound to a lower-middle-class worker?

Wright tried again to sell colleagues on his compromise plan. No one supported it. He was concerned: "This isn't going to blow over. It will last all Congress. It's bad for the party and bad for the institution. I wish I knew what the membership really wants."

He was also growing angry. Each day the pressure rose, and so did the hypocrisy level. Senators Herbert Kohl, who had just spent $6 million of his own money to win his seat, and John Heinz, heir to the fortune that bore his name, condemned the raise. House colleagues publicly attacked him for blocking a vote, and privately urged him not to allow it. One member held a press conference in his district to announce that he was sending Wright a strong letter of protest. Immediately after the press conference, he called Wright's staff and told them to make sure the Speaker never saw the letter. *All these colleagues wanted him to take the heat for them now. Where had they been when he had needed support a few months before?*

That weekend a Fort Worth columnist called him a "double-dealing rattlesnake." On Sunday, Bentsen, whose net worth was measured in tens of millions of dollars, appeared on ABC and added his condemnation of the raise. *Bentsen's running for President,* he thought bitterly.

Wright was now alone in Texas. But he had a plan. He wrote out a poll to distribute to members of both parties listing several options and asking for a confidential reply. It warned that if a majority asked for a vote, "there will be a vote."

Monday morning he started to send it out. "The members won't like it," one aide warned. Wright reddened, slammed his fist on the desk. Mack tried to talk him out of it. *What about Foley, Coelho, Fazio?* Wright knew what they thought. He turned to a secretary and told her to send out the poll.

The poll rocked the House. Wright told reporters that the survey would show that blocking a vote was "the collective decision of the membership, not something Bob Michel or I am imposing on them."

On substance, the poll confirmed his instincts. Fifty-six percent of the respondents said they honestly believed the raise was too high; 54 percent said they would "support a vote to reduce the 50 percent raise to 30 percent" and ban honoraria; 57 percent said they did not want a vote on the raise before it went into effect. But virtually every member was publicly calling for a vote.

One basic function of the leadership is to provide members with political cover. Rather than protecting members, the poll exposed them. Now even the minority whose public utterances comported with their private sentiments looked like liars. Others became liars when local reporters asked them how they had responded. And they were lying because Jim Wright put them in that position. By exposing them, he had done precisely the opposite of what the leadership is supposed to do. And he had done this thing on his own, without discussing it with the leadership. That was unforgivable.

Opponents of the raise seized on the poll as a sign of weakness and redoubled their efforts to block it. Proponents read it the same way. They were furious.

Wednesday was the weekly Texas delegation luncheon. In the Speaker's Dining Room, at home with his closest colleagues, Wright explained that he had felt compelled to survey the House, that a whip count had been incomplete. He did not say he distrusted it. Then he talked about his plan. The raise would go into effect on schedule. The day after it took effect, the House would vote to roll it back to 30 percent, then have another vote to eliminate honoraria.

Wright had planned just to feel out his colleagues' reactions. But word of his proposal spread quickly, too quickly. In mid-afternoon, Jack Brooks told Foley and Coelho. They were stunned and angered. It was his second unilateral action in three days. Even Foley, loyal Foley, was angry and hurt.

The House roiled. Some believed Wright had broken a commitment to block a vote. On Thursday, hoping to quiet the uproar, Wright hosted a lunch in H-324 for the pay-raise activists—the leadership, Rostenkowski, Dingell, almost two dozen others including Fazio. It was members only. No one else, not even Wright's closest staff, was allowed in the room. Wright invited his colleagues to tell him what they thought. They did, bitterly. Wright had to leave early—a head of state was waiting and he was already late. Downey shouted at him and he shouted back. After Wright left, the room was silent briefly, then one man erupted. "Son of a bitch!"

Later Ways and Means Democrats caucused to discuss taxes. But the only subject was Wright. "Who's he talk to?" one member demanded. "Doesn't he talk to anybody?"

That weekend House Democrats made their annual retreat to Greenbrier; waves of reporters descended on them, far more than had ever before gone to the Greenbrier. This was news. The deficit might not be, but this was. Radio call-in hosts across the country gave out the Greenbrier's phone and fax machine numbers. The lines were jammed. Back in Washington on Monday, February 6, the House held a pro forma session. Conservative Republican William Dannemeyer let it be known that he would force a vote on adjournment—if the House adjourned, it might not meet the next day, and therefore no vote could block the raise. Pay-raise opponents made plain that that procedural vote would count as if it were on the raise itself. In a meeting shortly before the House convened, Michel and Cheney warned that Republicans would vote against adjourning. So would they. Democrats reacted angrily, accusing them of breaking a commitment to help pass the raise. Two years earlier, in the same situation, Republicans had cooperated in blocking a vote on adjournment. Connie Mack had failed to get the necessary support to demand a recorded vote. This time Dannemeyer succeeded. By 238 to 88, the House voted to stay in session.

Wright came onto the floor and stood in the well of the House.

"Mr. Speaker," he smiled, a now-weary smile, addressing Foley who was in the chair, "I take this time to acknowledge the will of the House which always is supreme in the House of Representatives. Now the majority has spoken and the majority will speak even more emphatically tomorrow in keeping with the traditions of this institution, the very best traditions of this institution. The majority will rule."

The next day the House rejected the raise by 380 to 48.

Probably Dannemeyer would have forced a roll call on adjournment no matter what Wright had done, killing the raise anyway. But Wright had intervened, had made himself a lightning rod. And the poll had been a bad mistake, a serious misreading of his role as Speaker. On the floor the hostility toward him was almost tangible.

At three-thirty on the afternoon the House rejected the raise, Wright called his sister Mary. She understood him, loved him, supported him.

"It hurts too much," he said. "They need someone tough enough to take the criticism. I'm not."

He was talking about quitting. She tried to buoy him up, quoting some mail she had just gotten about how important it was to have someone like him stand up to the Republicans. He laughed bitterly, then said, "I have no power, no base of operations."

He had never cared about being Speaker for the sake of being Speaker, but only for the power it gave him to work his will.

Bush had just proposed a cut in the capital gains tax, claiming it would raise money. The idea drove Wright wild. He was convinced it would lose revenue, and give another major tax cut to the wealthy. Now he tried to get Mitchell to join him in calling for a tax on the wealthy. But Mitchell would say nothing. Wright was alone. He told Foley he would probably just serve out this term, and then Foley would be Speaker.

Wright was not the only one disheartened. Coelho had had almost as difficult a 100th Congress as Wright. He pushed as hard, with infinitely less authority. In January he told Martin Franks, who had worked for him at the DCCC, that he would probably leave Congress after one more term. Now his relationship with Wright had deteriorated further. After the pay-raise controversy, he told another friend his mind was made up. He would leave at the end of the 101st Congress.

A few days later, the House Republican Conference of all GOP members met in a large Rayburn Building room. Wright was weak now, weaker than he had ever been. Gingrich had prepared a resolution demanding that the ethics committee release all the evidence it had collected, including even raw, possibly inaccurate testimony. Before the resolution was presented, Myers spoke briefly and urged his colleagues not to vote on it, that it would make the process transparently political. He assured them they would be "pleased."

Every indication until then had been that Wright would not face a serious problem. But Myers had a sense of what was coming.

On Valentine's Day, one week after the pay-raise vote, Wright received his only good news in weeks. The five Central American presidents who had signed the peace accords reached a new agreement. The Sandinistas agreed to release all political prisoners, except for a few dozen men convicted of serious atrocities; they also gave new guarantees of political and press freedom, moved up the date of presidential elections—something the Reagan administration had demanded—and made plans to allow international observers. In return, Honduras agreed to force the contras out of its territory, which meant disbanding them. A *Wall Street Journal* editorial responded with an attack on Wright over Central America. It made no mention whatsoever of either the new peace agreement or the Sandinista concessions; instead it stated that Central American refugees were flooding the U.S. borders because of Wright's intrusions into policy.

In Washington, the Senate was considering the nomination of John Tower—a former chairman of the Senate Armed Services Committee that was now passing judgment on him—as secretary of Defense. Paul Weyrich, a New Right leader, first raised questions publicly about his drinking and womanizing. Tower's colleagues had no liking for him. *Time* magazine began a story about his crumbling nomination with an aphorism: "Morality is simply the attitude we adopt for people we don't like." Addressing the National Press Club, Tower warned, "character assassination" could lead to "a new and rather ugly phase in American politics."

But the media competed unceasingly to break the latest rumor based on a secret FBI report, which itself included raw, unchecked, and possibly inaccurate data. The fight became politicized, partisan. John Glenn, respected, middle-of-the-road, the astronaut and Ohio Democratic senator, said that although there was no smoking gun, there was a lot of smoke, and he would vote against confirmation.

The mood of Washington had turned foul. And, one Democrat worried, "I think members are rooting against Jim. The pay raise was serious."

On February 21, Phelan filed a 476-page report with the ethics committee.

CHAPTER 25

Richard Phelan went to elite Jesuit Chicago high schools and for a while wanted to be a priest; instead he decided on Notre Dame and Georgetown Law. At Quigley they taught duty and service. An attorney friend said, "A lot of his character was formed in that background." A profile in *The American Lawyer*, published before the investigation began, quoted John Jiganti, a president of the Chicago Bar Association, as saying, "He carries with him a strong moral fervor." The profile also described him as "supremely egotistical," noting that in his firm he was known as "the Presence." He was someone who "likes to throw out theories—occasionally wild ones—while associates search for case law to support them," and who "had the best intuition about what would be persuasive and what would not."

He was self-confident, even smug, his self-confidence bred of success. He founded and built a sixty-lawyer firm; it disdained the lucrative but tedious work of most law firms and did nothing but litigate. Litigators attack. They go to war. Winning is what it's all about. Moral fervor and confidence are useful for a litigator. They perform. They learn to believe, and hate the other side, like method actors becoming their characters. Phelan was suited to that. Tall, at fifty-two he still had a Huck Finn look that came from a lock of now-gray hair that regularly fell onto his forehead. Thin, almost reed-like, his deep voice and assertiveness made him seem more substantial than he was. His most striking physical feature was a long, handsome, expressive face, a trained face. Lines had worn into it, lines of Irish charm disguising an iciness, lines which could shift in an instant from fellowship to scorn, lines which could communicate sincerity, incredulity, and good humor to a jury.

He had grown bored litigating. He had money, $500,000 or more a year. It was clear to his fellow Chicago lawyers that he wanted something more. He wanted recognition. "I know one thing he likes is publicity," observed John Satalic. William Harte, who knew him well, said, "He's driven to be accepted in his profession. He does a lot of bar politicking." Fred Bartlit, Jr., a prominent attorney, said, "What drives him? Obviously not money. He's driven by a desire to be recognized as a top lawyer craftsman. Dick's a craftsman. He wouldn't do anything he couldn't prove."

But for all his ability and drivenness, perhaps because of it, there was something uneven about him. His reputation in general was favorable, but among a powerful group of insiders there were questions. For several years he tried unsuccessfully to join the American College of Trial Lawyers. He had once worked for Philip Corboy, a well-connected trial lawyer—four former associates became presidents of the Chicago Bar Association. Rumor was that Corboy blocked his admission. Later Corboy explained, "I had some dealings with him with ethics involved, but I won't discuss them."

Phelan asked William Harte to visit Corboy. As a favor to Harte, Corboy said he would not object to Phelan's admission. In 1985, Phelan became president of the Chicago Bar Association. He seemed to perform well. But after his term expired, he applied for a state supreme court judgeship. A review panel of the same bar association of which he had just been president did not rate him as highly qualified. It was a blow to his prestige. "When I see how easily the top rating is given out, I was frankly surprised he didn't get it," said Bartlit.

The blow made Phelan more determined for recognition, more restless. In late 1987, Phelan decided to take a sabbatical beginning in the fall of 1988 from the firm he had founded and dominated. He dove deeply into Democratic senator Paul Simon's presidential campaign, raising over $100,000 for him and becoming a delegate to the Democratic convention.

When the ethics committee decided to hire an outside counsel, it laid out several guidelines. The counsel should have no connections to Washington. The Republicans wanted someone with no understanding or tolerance of Washington. Democrats, afraid of whitewash charges, went along. Another guideline, John Myers said, was "not to hire anyone active in either party."

Morris Leibman, a Chicago attorney whom Corboy called "a legend around here for insiders," was asked to recommend someone. Despite the committee guidelines, Leibman said, "There was some emphasis on getting a Democrat."

Leibman submitted seven names; Phelan was not among them. But Frank McGarr, who was of counsel to Phelan's firm, was. McGarr didn't want the job. Phelan did and reportedly began a campaign behind the scenes for it. Myers investigated him and later said approvingly, "I heard he was *very* ambitious."

" 'Very ambitious'? That's the understatement of the century," observed Harte, who had earlier helped boost Phelan.

Myers suggested Phelan to Dixon, and they interviewed him along with other attorneys. Then Myers and Dixon wrote down several names. Phelan, who desperately wanted the job, who could make himself pleasing, who immediately offered to resign his delegate slot to the convention if named, was the only one on both lists. They selected him. Myers said later, "I didn't tell Julian [Dixon] this at the time, but I liked the fact that Phelan was a Democrat. That would protect us later from being attacked as partisan."

There was a history to this. On May 27, 1988, conservative activist Paul Weyrich had sent Gingrich a memo assessing possible outside counsels. Gingrich had sent the memo to all ethics committee members, inadvertently even Democrats. They had been outraged. Hiring a Democrat prevented the memo from becoming an issue. But it had to be the right Democrat. The memo talked about "paying the other side back" and recommended hiring someone who has "the prosecutorial mindset you want [and] understands the creative 'edge of the envelope' legal rationales that will be needed to bring Wright down."

The twelve members of the ethics committee were regarded as generally decent, honorable men, not inclined to hang colleagues. Only five were lawyers, but all were insiders; five of the six Democrats served on Appropriations, a usually bipartisan committee. So did Myers.

The committee had vast power. It served as investigator, grand jury, prosecutor, jury, judge, and appeals court. None of the rules of evidence for a court applied. Committee rules allowed it to "adopt special procedures deemed necessary to a particular matter." In other words, it had no rules. The United States was said to be a government of law and not men; the ethics committee exercised power through men and not law. This was not accidental. The House gave the committee such power and flexibility so it could protect members. The presumption was that it would do so.

But investigating the Speaker of the House, particularly this Speaker under these circumstances, altered the presumptions. Since the committee had six members of each party, the ranking Republican had more real power than on any other committee in the Congress. And Republicans entered the investigation with definite views of Wright; they were not favorable views. Hank Brown had handled the GOP welfare reform bill and had been outraged by Wright's use of power. Larry Craig was a member of Gingrich's Conservative Opportunity Society. Charles Pashayan, a new appointee to the Rules Committee, was well aware of Wright's past use of it. All the Republicans were being pressured by Gingrich, who had almost at once attacked Phelan's selection.

The media pressure was greater. The media would scrutinize every action of the committee, especially of the Democrats. One of Dixon's closest intimates warned Mack, "If you want to understand what drives Julian, read the morning papers."

Dixon was sensitive to any criticism. Late in 1987 the committee recommended that the House reprimand Austin Murphy. Before the floor vote, Murphy asked the Rules Committee for additional debate time to make his case. Dixon fought his request. One member told Dixon, "Murphy's no Rhodes Scholar. You're talking about the man's career. What's wrong with giving him another thirty minutes?" Dixon had exploded at him for questioning his judgment. The two men had not spoken since. The ethics committee had been castigated over its handling of St Germain. Dixon did not want to go through that again. And nothing focused the media on the committee, and him, so much as the investigation of Jim Wright.

Black but no radical, Dixon was a strong chairman when he chose to be. Quiet and solid, a large-shouldered man, he could balance competing forces. He had to; his district had almost equal numbers of whites and blacks, along with many Hispanics and Asians. He was rumored to be interested in running for the post of Los Angeles supervisor, which a California colleague called "one of the best jobs in politics. You've got power, perks, and money."

John Myers seemed as Republican as his background as a small-town banker, a Mason, an Elk, a Lion, and a leader in a congressional prayer group. He had a ready smile and always seemed the gentleman. Like most members, he had an ego. Before Reagan's election Myers had been chief deputy whip, but he was not one of the new breed of Republicans. In 1980, he had explored running against Lott for whip but realized he would only humiliate himself, and had dropped out of the leadership, taking a seat on the ethics committee, a seeming backwater, grunt job. He was not openly bitter about losing his leadership position, but he spoke of it. It rankled him. He was sensitive, very sensitive. One Reagan administration official said, "John always struck me as funny because he was truly nice and cordial, and yet I remember one or two times over trivial slights he showed a real meanness that was kind of shocking."

It had been nine years since he was forced out of the leadership, out of any chance for the spotlight. The Wright investigation was his chance to regain it. He had let Michel know of his displeasure about suggesting to Wright that he appoint a special investigating committee, to bypass ethics. He had helped push Floyd Spence, who fell ill, out of his position as ranking member on ethics the previous spring. This was Myers's chance to shine, to use power. And the McCloskey-McIntyre election dispute, which had created deep GOP bitterness, had occurred in his old district.

One House insider said, "Dixon's much stronger and smarter than Myers. You can't compare the two." Yet Myers seemed to be the driving force in the investigation. Dixon had declined to subpoena Wright's wife or his tax returns. The committee had never done either, to any member. But he had allowed Phelan, without any evidence of wrongdoing, only curiosity, to expand the investigation into Wright's entire life. Perhaps he was only fulfilling his first responsibility: to protect the integrity of the House. Perhaps he was only ensuring that no one could criticize the committee for not being thorough. But there were other things. Committee rules required exculpatory material to be given immediately to the respondent; Phelan accumulated thousands of pages of evidence but did not turn over one page to Oldaker. He was waiting for Dixon to force him to do so. Dixon never did. Dixon was a strong chairman. If he chose to be.

When several committee Democrats put pressure on Dixon to finish the investigation by mid-January, do whatever he had to do but do it,

Myers had balked, saying that he wanted to wait until after the pay raise. One committee member warned Mack, "We've lost control of the committee."

The process gave Phelan extraordinary power.

The first stage of the proceeding was analogous to a grand jury. If the investigation gave the committee "reason to believe" that Wright had violated any rules, it would issue a "statement of alleged violations," in effect an indictment. The next stage would be the "disciplinary hearing," a trial in which the standard of proof rose to "clear and convincing evidence." That would be followed, if he was found guilty, by a hearing on sanctions.

Unlike grand jurors, no member heard all the testimony. Only two or three times in seven months did more than three members listen to a witness. The committee would rely on Phelan's summary of it. This made little difference if he presented the facts impartially, which was his proper role. If he played the role of a prosecutor, however, if he carefully selected the evidence he presented, no one would be able to rebut him. Only he had the facts.

Like all good litigators, he knew how to play up to a jury, and over a period of months he worked to build trust. He told the members how impressed he was with the Congress and with them, and marveled at their wit and intelligence. With Joe Gaydos, a Pennsylvania Democrat, he joked about Notre Dame, their mutual alma mater, and talked football. With Thomas Petri, a Wisconsin Republican, he traded information on vacation areas around the Great Lakes. He ate lunch almost daily in the Members' Dining Room. Like the members, his family was back home, and he routinely took committee members out to dinner at some of the most expensive restaurants in Washington. The House paid for it; many of the dinners went on his personal expense account. His most frequent guest was Chester Atkins, a Massachusetts Democrat. Once, standing outside the Supreme Court, directly across from the Capitol, the two were robbed at gunpoint.

To prevent leaks, there were only twelve copies of Phelan's report, one for each member. They had to read its 476 pages in the committee office, and sat around as in a study hall, turning to each other and saying, "Look at page 223. What do you think of that?" And they were stunned.

Phelan charged Wright with 117 violations of House rules, in and beyond the six areas of the investigation: Wright's pressure on savings and loan regulators; several oil investments in the 1970s; the use of his book as a vehicle to convert campaign funds to personal use and the possibly improper employment of an aide to work on it; and Wright's use, for free and at reduced rent, of an apartment owned by his former partner George Mallick. Gingrich and Common Cause had raised the first five issues. The apartment had been added by the committee; Myers, after receiving letters from conservative activists, had argued for it. The apartment count involved sixty-three of the 117 violations, most related to the charge that Betty Wright's salary and benefits were gifts.

If Phelan's report was a fair, impartial representation of the facts, then Jim Wright would be driven from his speakership in deserved disgrace.

A litigator is both impresario and actor. He creates a world, tells a story with characters like a play, for an audience. He deals with words, not facts, in ways that not even writers do, turning words inside out, upside down, using them to create an image. Images embed themselves in the mind; facts do not. Phelan painted a portrait of the Speaker of the House which no member and no journalist and no citizen could accept.

Phelan's report and his later oral argument demonstrated a clash of culture. In Congress, one's word is one's bond; neither good lobbyists nor respected colleagues distort their arguments—otherwise their influence quickly evaporates. Upon request they will even give their opponents' strongest case against them. *I want the facts, untwisted,* Coelho had said. If a lobbyist twisted things just once, *I won't take his calls, won't answer his mail, and will tell his clients they're not being well represented.*

In Phelan's culture of the courtroom each opponent presents only one side. They omit facts, play with facts, give facts a one-sided interpretation. Phelan brought the adversarial system he was accustomed to inside the Congress, where it did not fit—particularly since his role in theory was to be impartial.

Yet Phelan was not manipulating the committee. He was being manipulated by it, or at least by the Republicans, who had demanded that whoever was hired as counsel have no connection to Washington. An outside counsel who understood Washington might not only have shrugged at some things that outraged Phelan, but he would have been under pressure to be impartial. Phelan was not.

On point after point after point, Phelan simply dismissed—often without mention—evidence or testimony which exonerated Wright, and presented as fact testimony, even when contradicted by other evidence, which condemned him. Sometimes he not only ignored testimony but distorted it, usually with half-truths.

The portrait. He charged, for example, that in the February 10, 1987, meeting with savings and loan regulators, "Wright made it plain that he viewed the outcome of the [Thomas] Gaubert matter to have been extremely unsatisfactory. . . . Wright was not simply seeking impartial consideration of Gaubert's claim, but a change in the Bank Board's regulatory response to Gaubert. Such use of Wright's influence is a violation of House Rule XLIII, clause 1."

Phelan had testimony from at least three witnesses, one of whom had no connection to Wright at all, that Gaubert's name was not mentioned at that meeting, and no such pressure was exerted. A balanced report would have cited conflicting testimony. Phelan simply ignored the testimony which contradicted his charge.

The portrait. He argued that Wright accepted improper gifts from Mallick, in effect laundered through a "sham" company, Mallightco. Mallick and Wright had each put up $58,000 to start the company and each owned half of it. One gift was a Cadillac, which Betty Wright used for four years. Once in his report Phelan concedes that Mallick sold the car, used, to the company for $10,575, making the Wrights half-owners of it. But elsewhere in his report and repeatedly in his oral arguments, Phelan said that Mallick "donated" or "gave" the car to Mallightco. Nowhere did he mention that Mallick used the car for three years, after selling it to the company and before Betty began using it. It was only a detail, but he was drawing his portrait with details. There were a hundred such—misstating a crucial date, dismissing one witness's testimony as hearsay when it was not, first saying it "is reasonable to assume" a Wright aide did something (which she did not do), then stating it as a fact—any one of which could be considered insignificant or accidental but every one of them pointed in the same direction.

And some things were not details. Phelan charged Wright with accepting $5,000 in unreported and illegal gifts in the form of reduced interest. In his oral presentation he told the committee flatly, "Mrs. Mallick went out, borrowed $150,000, turned around, loaned it to Mallightco, and then Mallightco, at 3.5 percent less, lends it to Mrs. Wright."

Phelan was telling less than half the truth. Marlene Mallick took out an adjustable-rate loan for $150,000 at 13.5 percent and loaned it to Mallightco, which loaned $75,000 back to her, and $75,000 to Betty Wright at a fixed rate of 13.5 percent. (The money was used for an oil investment; for tax purposes they invested as individuals rather than as a company.) For seven months both the Mallicks and Wrights paid the same interest rate. Then the Mallicks' adjustable-rate loan was raised to 17 percent, and, briefly, to 20 percent. Wright continued to pay 13.5 percent. Over the first two and a half years of the loan, Wright's fixed, lower rate amounted to a $5,000 subsidy from Mallick. But the loan lasted eight years; for the next five and a half years, as interest rates fell to as low as 7.5 percent, Wright's fixed rate exceeded Mallick's. He subsidized Mallick, more than erasing the "gift." Phelen in both his report and oral argument made no mention of this fact. He simply stopped calculating the "gift" when market rates dropped below 13.5 percent. It was another part of Phelan's portrait. (Gingrich's ally Larry Craig and Hank Brown—was it memories of welfare reform or was it just Brown?—would still vote against Wright on this charge; the other ten committee members rejected it.)

Not everything in Phelan's report was so distorted. Wright had done things that needed explanation under any standard. But Phelan accepted no explanation for anything in the report.

Democrats, having heard few witnesses, had difficulty disputing Phelan's facts. If, for example, they had not heard testimony (or remembered it in detail from six months earlier) about the February 10 savings and loan meeting, they had no reason to doubt Phelan's conclusion about Gaubert. Members could identify lapses in Phelan's reasoning without knowing the facts; they might wonder why Phelan stopped calculating a "gift" of interest at a particular time. But they had to find such weaknesses themselves. They could read the depositions if they wanted, but there were thousands of pages. Their source of information was primarily Phelan himself. He had spent months developing a relationship of trust.

And Republicans did not want to dispute Phelan's findings; they liked them. In good faith, Republicans already had an image of Wright; it was of an abusive man, greedy for every bit of power he could grab.

They could accept Phelan's portrait. There was something else, too.

When the investigation first began, Phelan had been restrained, back when Dixon had refused to let him cross-examine Wright. At first Dixon had agreed with Oldaker and refused to let Phelan expand the investigation. But from the first, Phelan had had solid support from the Republicans. They had threatened to boycott their own questioning of Wright because of Dixon's ruling, and Myers had pressed Dixon to allow the expansion. Then, after Michel and Cheney had filed ethics charges against Wright over his CIA comment, after Myers had pushed him, Dixon had seemed to lift all controls. *How long do you think Jim plans to remain Speaker, Bill?* Dixon had wondered. It was already clear where Phelan was heading. Dixon let him go.

A lobbyist explained, "Sometimes you'll talk to a member and he'll say, 'Give me your arguments.' That usually means he'll vote with you. You never know why. Maybe it's because of a contribution. He can't tell the press that. When he asks for your arguments, he's asking for reasons to justify his vote."

Reasons are both weapons and armor. They do not necessarily convince, but they can be used to attack and defend. Phelan was giving Republicans reasons to justify voting against Wright.

Phelan's deputy Michael Howlett, a partner in his law firm and whose family was part of the Daley machine, ran into a Chicago business executive, shook his head in disgust, and said, "We're doing a dirty thing here."

The Republicans had their justification. And the Democrats?

There was so much Phelan accused Wright of. So many different things. Such a pattern. Under the best interpretation, Wright had gone right up to the edge of the line of the rules and danced along it. The committee was charged with protecting the integrity of the House; appearances were relevant.

And the report was going to become public.

That was certain. Dixon and Myers had decided. The press would devour it. Reporters stood or sat in stakeouts outside the committee rooms, stalked committee members and staff, asked what was in the report. Details were slow in coming, but the fact that it devastated Wright was already in the press.

The report would generate headlines for weeks. Committee members, especially Democrats, would be measured against it. How could they justify not voting against Wright? They could not charge partisanship. Phelan was an active Democrat. And they did not love Wright. Fazio was furious over the pay raise. Furious. How many on the committee would actively fight for Wright, argue for him, work colleagues on the floor, call Phelan a liar? Republicans and Phelan's report put their integrity and the integrity of the House at issue. They needed reasons to support Wright. Very good reasons.

At least one committee Democrat sent a message through Jack Brooks to Wright that the issue of his wife's work troubled the committee. But Dixon indicated to Oldaker and Mack that the only problems were the car and the apartment. Dixon never explicitly said it, but it was the message received. Mack and Oldaker trusted Dixon.

Perhaps Dixon was misreading the committee, or perhaps a not-yet-public problem of his own clouded his judgment: his wife had invested less than $15,000 in a business two years earlier, and had already received over $150,000 in dividends from the investment. Dixon would later have to amend his disclosure forms when the press began to ask questions, and the investment raised other ethics issues besides disclosure.

For Wright, though, the car and the condo meant either a letter citing no rules violations but acknowledging bad judgment and the appearances of impropriety, or at worst technical violations and a formal letter of reproval. Wright's people planned their strategy accordingly.

Beginning in late 1988, his new press aide Mark Johnson prepared a memo. Thirty-one years old but experienced and respected in the national media, Johnson had worked for Coelho and in Gephardt's presidential campaign, then for Texas Air and its chairman Frank Lorenzo. He made money but hated the job, and left when Wright promised him total access to his office and the authority to speak for him, to be quoted by name. No aide had ever had such authority before. In early December the staff met to review his memo.

It began with the heading "TACTICS: DAY ONE," the day the committee reported, and described the scenario of a press conference, then "Spin Control: identify spinners (Members, Strauss, [Richard] Moe, [Robert] Shrum, [Kirk] O'Donnell, et al.), develop list of editorial writers, political columnists to be called, prepare talking points. In addition: Foley, Coelho, Bonior, Gray, Panetta, Aspin, Don Edwards, Pat Schroeder, other media favorites to go to press conference and talk to press after . . . Coelho call [Dan] Rather, identify other good relationships . . . Foley call . . .

"Make Other News: Same day . . . Wright issue policy statement. Must be important enough to attract coverage. . . . Goal is to put substance behind spin. . . . Accepting invitation [to Sunday interview shows] would only keep the issue alive."

From there it laid out plans for the following days. Everything was premised on a worst-case scenario of a letter of reproval. In February the staff still operated with that premise.

But after Phelan filed his report the game had changed. John Murtha, who served on Appropriations with six ethics committee members, met in H-201 with several Wright advisers including Oldaker and said, "I think we lost four Democrats."

The meeting broke up in anger and disbelief. Later he said the same thing at lunch in the Members' Dining Room. Reports of his comment roared through the House and shook it. Murtha went to Mack and Wright and, though making no specific recommendation, implied that they look for some accommodation with the committee. Wright angrily refused. *Goddammit. He was innocent.*

Oldaker asked Dixon for a chance to rebut Phelan's oral presentation. It was highly unusual, but the committee really had no rules. Dixon was playing a careful game, protecting himself if Wright survived, protecting the committee from charges of unfairness. Dixon agreed. Still, he would not allow Oldaker to read Phelan's report. Or see the evidence on which the charges were based. Or contact the witnesses for information about their testimony. Or present any evidence. His only knowledge of Phelan's case would come from the notes he took of Phelan's oral argument.

On February 27 the committee convened in executive session in an empty Rayburn Building hearing room. Outside in the hall, reporters lounged about, made jokes, and waited for anyone to emerge to give them some hint of the proceedings. Inside, the twelve members sat at a raised dais. Before them, where witnesses usually testified, was a podium with a microphone, which separated Phelan and Oldaker. They sat twenty-four inches apart, flanked by assistants at long tables. The rows of chairs, normally filled at committee hearings, were empty. The two tables reserved for the press were empty. There were only the members, the attorneys, and the microphone.

Phelan would go first, speak for several days, and be questioned by members, while Oldaker remained silent. Then Oldaker would speak, followed by Phelan's rebuttal. The arguments would last until March 14. After they ended, Oldaker would play no further role in the deliberations. Phelan would continue his formal and informal contacts with the committee, continue to be part of the proceedings, continue taking committee members to dinner, continue to answer their questions about the testimony and evidence.

Now Phelan would give them reasons for their vote.

In his opening statement, Phelan said, "I wish the American public knew what I know about this committee . . . and I wish the American public understood and wasn't so cynical about every single politician. I don't feel that way." He was one of them: "I can assure you that after seven months of living and eating in the Members' Dining Room and spending time with all of you that I hardly feel 'outside' anymore."

Then he began his attack, painting his portrait of Wright by condemning his relationship with Mallick: "When I approach the question of Mr. Mallick it shakes me a little." He portrayed Mallick as a fat spider, spinning a web of gifts around Wright, years of gifts, trapping him, Wright the willing recipient, and concluding, "In Chicago we call it having someone in your pocket."

Phelan would spend his entire first day of oral argument on Mallick, and would emphasize it again in his rebuttal of Oldaker. The issue was Mallightco. Capitalized in 1980 with $58,000 each from Mallick and Wright, it doubled in a year. In late 1980 an accountant told Mallick to create deductions for it. Betty Wright was already working for Mallick part-time for $18,000; he also gave her and several other employees, including his lawyer and bookkeeper, a rent-free apartment. In 1981 she switched payrolls to Mallightco at the same salary and benefits and began looking for investment opportunities. The Texas economy was booming and Mallightco doubled again, to over $400,000 in assets. It became a cash cow; both Wright and Mallick not only collected dividends—the Wrights also had Betty's salary—but loans. At one point, Wright owed it $85,000; Mallick owed it $47,000. Mallick also sold the company his wife's car, which stayed in Fort Worth while he continued to use it. Mallightco made a profit every year and paid dividends to Mallick, who ultimately sold his share in it, at a bargain price to his daughter, for almost double what he had put into it.

But Phelan called the company "an artifice, a sham, a conduit to provide the Speaker and his wife with . . . cash dividends and salaries and apartments and condominiums and loans . . . all in violation of the rules of gifting of this House of Representatives. . . . Over the course of some ten years some $160,000 worth of gifts were funneled through this corporation to the Wrights."

He portrayed every single thing Mallightco did as a gift to Wright, even arguing that a $40,000 stock purchase on margin amounted to a gift to Wright of Mallick's credit: "I submit to you that [Wright] probably could not have margin stock on that basis without the credit of someone else."

Phelan's comment made little sense. Mallightco made the purchase, not Mallick. And either Phelan did not understand margin or he was using more innuendo to impugn the relationship, hoping some members did not understand it. In margin, one's credit is irrelevant; buyers pay half the stock's price in cash and use the stock itself, which the broker physically keeps registered in "street name," as collateral.

The key issue, however, was Betty Wright's employment. If her job was a sham, then four years' worth of salary, six years' worth of rent, and, Phelan argued, even the car of which she owned half were gifts.

"There is not one shred of paper, not one memorandum, not one decision, not one investment, not one transaction, not one phone call that can be tied to Betty Wright," he insisted. He was correct; there was no documentation. "This is a case of a person who is on a payroll who isn't doing anything . . . a ghost payroller. . . . This person, as far as we can see, did absolutely no work whatsoever and played no role."

Betty Wright's job was to look for investment opportunities. Mallightco did not make a single investment as a result of her research, and Mallick in his testimony had made only vague references to opportunities she had examined. Phelan stated, "Mallick testified Betty Wright studied [investments] . . . but that she played no role in the decision to invest."

Phelan mocked her research: "They were going to buy a chain of banks. They were going to invest in the motion picuture *Annie*. They were going to invest in Nigerian oil. They were going to invest in bulgur wheat cakes to feed the Third World. They were going to invest in paint pigmentation. They were going to buy 175 acres of land. Do they think we are non compis mentis? I mean this corporation cannot on its own afford to buy or invest in any of these things. . . . It has $100,000 in capital and they are talking about buying a chain of banks? That insults my intelligence. I am about ready to laugh out loud. . . . They can't meet their own payroll. . . . They had to borrow from Mallick to pay Mrs. Wright's salary in 1983 and 1984. . . .

"I asked [Mallick's assistant] Pamela Smith how much time Mrs. Wright spent over the four years she worked at Mallightco. . . . She answered . . . perhaps a dozen days over four years Betty Wright [was] working on clearly identifiable projects."

(It was another distortion and a major one. He had asked her, "Can you give the chairman of the committee how much time that Mrs. Wright may have spent . . . Hours? Days? Weeks? Months?" Smith had replied, "On an average month we would see Mrs. Wright five to seven days a month, and she would be in our offices working," and that she had also worked in Washington and New York. Smith then gave specific examples which Phelan added up to reach his "dozen days" on "identifiable projects.")

And again: "The best you can say is that for a dozen days over four years she supposedly worked on some clearly identified projects. Is twelve days' worth of work worth $72,000? And we are not talking about a [merger and acquisition] person in New York. . . .

"We concluded that there was no evidence to show that there was any benefit conferred on Mallightco of whatever value by Mrs. Wright. . . . [Her] salary was a downright, outright gift paid through Mallightco to the Wrights. . . . These years, 1979, 1980, 1981, 1982, 1983, 1984, we believe that all of these [things] were gifts, they were not reported, they were from someone with a direct interest in legislation, made to James C. Wright, Jr."

His rhetoric was overpowering the evidence.

The issue of "direct interest in legislation" was crucial. If Wright were found simply to have accepted gifts from a friend—even $100,000-plus—he might survive. The committee might still only issue a letter of reproval, requiring no floor vote. Over time, he might rebuild his power, depending on how the media and Republicans played it. A new scandal was beginning to break, linking billions of wasted dollars, and millions outright stolen, with well-connected Republicans and the Department of Housing and Urban Development. The media might move on to this more serious business, and Republicans might choose to drop the subject of ethics in self-defense.

But gifts of over $100 were prohibited from anyone with "direct interest" in legislation. If Mallick had such an interest and Wright accepted gifts, that went to the heart of the integrity of a public official—accepting personal favors from someone who benefited from one's power.

House rules exempt from the gift prohibitions a member's accepting gifts from "a close personal friend"—Mallick and Wright had been friends for a quarter century—but Phelan never addressed that exemption. He did give four reasons to demonstrate Mallick's "direct interest." In August 1986, Billy Bob Barnett, owner of the giant saloon Billy Bob's, part of the Fort Worth stockyards area, was in trouble. His business was nearly bankrupt, and he approached Mallick to talk about a deal. In December they formally agreed: as a finder's fee for raising $27 million in private financing, Mallick would get 17 percent ownership. Mallick failed to raise the money and in February, barely six weeks after signing papers, he and Barnett dissolved their relationship.

The stockyards area was depressed, and for years Wright had been pouring federal dollars into it. That year, too, Congress earmarked several million dollars for a flood-control project that benefited the area. Phelan argued that Mallick's involvement in the project gave him a direct interest in the flood-control money.

The second issue was savings and loan legislation. In October 1986, Wright had asked Mallick to prepare a report on the S&L industry. Mallick had also co-signed a loan his son took out from a thrift to build a shopping center, and was ultimately sued for $1 million. Phelan claimed that Mallick's son was in default on the loan while Mallick was writing the report. (It was another false assertion; the report was finished eight months before any default.)

These two reasons, even if accepted by the committee, dated Mallick's direct interest at the earliest as August 1986. Ninety-five percent of the $160,000 in "gifts"—primarily Betty Wright's salary and benefits—occurred before then.

Phelan had to convince the committee that Mallick had a direct interest from the beginning of Mallightco. The rules used the term "direct interest' to distinguish the interest of the general public from that of those intimately involved in the legislative process. All doctors are concerned with Medicare legislation; unless they lobby actively on the issue, they are not deemed to have a direct interest. All taxpayers are interested in taxes; unless they lobby actively they do not have a direct interest. House rules defined people with a direct interest in legislation as: a lobbyist; anyone employing a lobbyist; anyone running a PAC; and anyone who "has a distinct or special interest in influencing or affecting the outcome of the legislative process which sets [him] apart from the general public."

Phelan's legal argument rested on Mallick's wealth; he was rich, though not super-rich. As a developer, at the peak of Texas real estate values he had a net worth of $7 million; in the late 1980s it fell to $1.5 million. Phelan argued that in those early years, "Matters pending before Congress could have had an enormous impact on Fort Worth real estate and its economy in general. As a result, Mallick was interested in legislation affecting taxation of real estate, interest rates, the oil and gas industry. . . . These facts compel the conclusion that Mallick had a 'direct interest in legislation.' "

"Real estate . . . interest rates . . . oil and gas . . . economy in general": Phelan seemed to describe precisely the interests of the general public. He offered no evidence that Mallick ever lobbied on any issue.

The fourth reason he gave for Mallick's direct interest appeared nowhere in his published report. But it was the core of his argument, and he pressed it in his oral argument. Mallick gave Wright gifts. Therefore, he must have been scheming to take advantage of him. He must have had a direct interest.

"That is the reason he is giving," Phelan said. "Because [he has] a direct interest in legislation. I can tell you that I think all along that [Mallick believed] the time would come and this"—the stockyards renewal—"was the time."

When it came time for questions, Democrats objected angrily.

Alan Mollohan, his tone sarcastic but intense, concerned: "You would suggest that Mr. Mallick [beginning in 1979] was laying a groundwork for some unspecified, unkown relationship in the future?"

"Yes, sir."

"But you didn't have any facts to substantiate that, did you?"

"Well, I don't know what would be more important to a real estate developer in Fort Worth, to his future—"

"You didn't have any information to suggest his past relationship was anticipating any specific legislative interest, did you?"

"Neither he nor any of the other witnesses said that they were giving gifts in order that Speaker Wright would be our prisoner futurely, no."

Even some Republicans were troubled by his reasoning. Thomas Petri: "Was there any evidence that Mallick actually ever got anything specific of a monetary value from the federal government?"

Phelan: "We didn't find that he had economically benefited . . . [but] it offended me. To suggest that Mallick did it because he was a good guy and Wright was his best friend—this is a tough, hard-nosed businessman. I have to presume and assume that he certainly assumed he would economically benefit."

Democrats again, with Fazio: "Other characters who have come before this committee, there has always been a quid pro quo. Not only is there no quid pro quo, there apparently isn't any effort on Mallick's part that would have brought a quid pro quo."

Phelan: "There isn't any quid pro quo."

Gaydos warned: "We're getting into a dangerous area here where you're going to penalize someone for being involved in a local problem, and then attribute to him a legislative interest."

Everything Wright had done with the stockyards he would have done even if Mallick had had no involvement. No one disputed that.

Gaydos had another problem. Betty had worked directly for Mallick in 1979 and 1980. Phelan conceded that she did real work then. Gaydos noted, "Here is a woman employed by Mallick and no questions are asked, she transfers to a new corporation, and she is then supposed to be in a position whereby she is getting paid for doing absolutely nothing. Why bother to transfer her?"

Since the Wrights owned half of Mallightco and paid half her salary to themselves, transferring her from Mallick's own company in effect cut her pay 50 percent. That bothered Atkins too: "You ascribe her first job [with] Mallick as bona fide employment. In her second job with Mallightco you suggest that it was not bona fide and you ascribe 100 percent of it as a gift. Do you think that is fair in light of the fact that she did appear to have done work? . . . Mallick had limited education and enormous amounts of money, who has now [through Wright] a ticket into society. . . . It seems to me it is not a unique relationship in the business world, having those kinds of relationships, and they turn out to be very profitable and useful."

As Democrats questioned him, Phelan banged his fist against the podium. His voice rose with conviction. His finger jabbed the air. It was his jury performance. He believed. But he carefully never grew angry, never offended, always mixed argument with unction. When

Fazio probed him, Phelan said, "That's an excellent question! You would have made a hell of a lawyer, Mr. Fazio!" With Gaydos, who like Phelan went to Notre Dame, Phelan joked, "We're number one, right?"

One almost got the sense it was a game to Phelan, the most exciting game he had ever played. In a superficial sense he understood the stakes, but only as they affected him. He was unaware of the rumblings of large things below; he was like a small boy sitting on his father's lap with his hands on the steering wheel, thinking he was driving the car. The members were shrewder than he: not more intelligent, probably less, but shrewder about the world with a deeper understanding of it and of the use of things. One member said, "Phelan was frankly naive."

Republicans tried to rescue Phelan with their questions. Hank Brown changed the subject to an investment in gemstones, then concluded, "I know we are not looking for areas to expand this investigation, but that struck me as one where that might be warranted." He complained that Phelan had not cited Wright for a violation for listing his acquisition of one investment in April 1979, when he had actually acquired it that February. *Brown hated Wright.* Returning to direct interest, Brown asked, "Would you say his activities and his interest here were enough to 'set him apart from the general public'?"

It was a key phrase according to the rules. Phelan declared, "No question about it."

At the end of the first day of Phelan's presentation, Oldaker was pleased. He knew Phelan's report had had a serious impact. But now, under questioning, Phelan's reasoning seemed to collapse. Oldaker hurried over to Wright's office to report. It had been a good day.

The next day was the book. The most important was whether the book had served as a vehicle to transfer campaign funds to personal use. There was clear evidence that had not occurred, yet Phelan tried to leave a shadow over Wright, saying, "When looking at the original charge . . . we remain unable to prove or disprove [it]."

The portrait. And Phelan made other charges.

Roughly twenty thousand books were sold. Ninety percent of them were sold to people who bought one thousand dollars' worth or more. Most of the bulk purchasers were lobbyists and trade associations. Without question, Wright had exploited his office for personal gain. Wright had testified, and repeatedly stated publicly, that the publisher,

Carlos Moore, sold the book, not he, implying that therefore he was not responsible for who purchased it. Moore did sell books—two thousand copies to the Teamsters, for example, and in bulk to Wright's friends in Texas. Wright personally sold no books. But his staff did, in bulk, to lobbyists.

Yet royalties were exempt from House limits on outside earned income. The book seemed entirely within the rules. Indeed, before going forward with it in 1984, Wright had checked with Oldaker, who wrote him a letter approving it. Other members of Congress had written books, although they had generally used mainstream publishers, and lobbyists routinely bought large quantities. Wright had exploited a loophole, yes. It was a major embarrassment, yes, and raised questions about his judgment. But ethically it seemed no different from accepting an honorarium. When a politician made a speech and collected a $2,000 fee, he was exploiting his office, too.

Phelan searched for a way around the House rules. Wright had written—not ghostwritten—three other books published by mainstream publishers, and had written for such magazines as *Harper's*. Still, Phelan decided to argue that his book was not really a book, and that his royalties were profits from a business venture. That meant that 100 percent of the income violated House limits on outside earnings, which could not exceed 30 percent of his salary. To make his case, Phelan argued that Wright's 55 percent royalty was totally unique. But another publisher, Mack Williams, had testified that he had offered Wright a 50 percent royalty. Phelan told the committee that Williams had offered Wright half the net proceeds, which equaled a 25 percent royalty, not half the gross. That was not the truth. Williams had offered half the gross.

Perhaps Phelan was employing a tactic, offering the committee a straw man to knock down, while making it more receptive to a less wild theory almost as damaging. Phelan argued that Wright used the book to violate outside-earnings limits by converting honoraria to royalties.

The very first book transaction seemed questionable; Southwest Texas State University sent him a $3,000 check for a speech. Federal law stipulated that members could keep no more than $2,000 from any individual honorarium (one can accept more; Rostenkowski demanded at least $5,000, giving the excess to charity). Though the books had not yet been printed, a Wright aide endorsed the $3,000 check to Moore netting Wright $1,650 in royalties. Moore later sent the school three thousand dollars' worth of books. Clearly the university was paying him for a speech by buying books. On half a dozen other occasions over a three-year period, when Wright was near honoraria limits, his staff or Craig Raupe suggested to groups to whom he was speaking that they buy books intead of paying an honorarium.

Phelan quoted a phrase in the rules, that "real facts control," to claim the purchases were really honoraria. But the words "real facts" were inserted to prevent members from claiming that earned income, which was limited, was actually unearned income, which was unlimited. Yet the royalties were specifically exempted from the earned-income limits. The exemption was total and complete.

Granting Phelan's argument required a case-by-case examination of the real facts. If a book purchase occurred independent of a speech, there was no violation. And Oldaker was certain Phelan was misquoting testimony. When Phelan talked about the testimony of Gerald Cassidy, a lobbyist, Oldaker sat up. He had been briefed on that testimony; either he had been lied to about what Cassidy said, or Phelan, when he quoted Cassidy, was lying to the committee.

Oldaker sat silently for a moment, steaming. Phelan was trying to blur the distinction between royalties and honoraria, and his possible misquote contributed to that blurring. He could not interrupt Phelan or object to anything he said. But later, as the committee was about to recess, he raised a "point of inquiry" and asked to be allowed to review the deposition. It was his first complaint in two days of listening to Phelan.

Angrily Phelan reacted. "There is a suggeston here that I am misinterpreting something."

"Gentlemen," Dixon interrupted, "we are all getting tired."

The committee adjourned.

The next morning was Phelan's final day of argument. Dixon rejected Oldaker's request to see the deposition, saying that if the committee later charged Wright, "clearly a respondent would be entitled to any [relevant] material . . . [which] shall be made available for inspection at reasonable hours."

Then he turned to his colleagues and said, "I would say to each member of the committee, we should look at our report to see if in fact the statements that are made are correct."

He was going to use Phelan's report to check Phelan's accuracy.

Phelan began this day with an old oil investment. Wright had purchased a share in an exploratory well. Phelan argued that it amounted to a gift worth $80,000 because oil was discovered in June 1979, raising the value of the well. Wright did not pay for his investment until October, and paid only what his share had been worth before the oil strike. (Oldaker later argued that Wright had made a commitment in some ambiguous correspondence in February and April. Wright had also publicly declared his ownership as of April 1979. He was not billed for the investment until September, at the same time the other investors were, and he paid for it within two weeks of being billed.)

Then came the savings and loans. They would spend most of the day on it.

Donald Dixon was the savings and loan operator on whose behalf Wright had made one phone call, sparking Jack Anderson columns, *Newsweek* stories, the *Regardie's* story, sparking Gingrich's entire campaign. Phelan said about Dixon, "We don't find . . . any problem."

Yet Phelan charged Wright with using "undue influence" on four other occasions: pressuring Ed Gray and his successor to fire two aides, and to favor two individuals. Phelan had no evidence to show that Wright was acting improperly. So he reversed the argument, said that Wright's actions and intent made no difference, and that the sole judge of Wright's actions was the regulators themselves.

"The point is, what is in the minds of those persons at the Bank Board?" Phelan insisted, defining undue influence. "Whether they were reasonable in their assumptions, whether they were correct in their assumptions, I don't think is an issue. Right or wrong, reasonable or unreasonable, that is what they acted on and that is what they did."

Again: "Whether it is true or not, it doesn't make any difference. It is what is the impression given the agency."

Phelan was holding Wright accountable not for his intentions, not for his actions, but for what someone else thought were his intentions. The law used a "reasonable man" standard, an objective criterion, to judge by. But Phelan said, "Whether they were reasonable in their assumptions, whether they were correct in their assumptions . . . right or wrong, reasonable or unreasonable . . . true or not . . . I don't think is an issue."

Phelan had been aggressive. Perhaps too aggressive. He had offered plenty of reasons to destroy Wright, but his reasoning had often been exposed. Now it was Oldaker's turn. Oldaker began:

"I need not tell you that you have in your hands the life of Jim Wright. What you decide could well make a determination as to how history is going to view this man. This man has served his country as a public servant for forty years. He volunteered for the service the day after Pearl Harbor. He was elected to Congress in 1954, at the age of thirty-one, and has been reelected seventeen times, six times unopposed. In 1987, as you all know, he became Speaker. There is not a blemish on his record. And there is not one allegation in this entire case that he broke the law. He is not accused anywhere of perjury, bribery, or any of the other pernicious acts that bring congressmen down."

The members stirred. *It sounded like he was saying let Wright off because he was Speaker, that he had done nothing really so bad.*

Oldaker next complained that the investigation of Mallick was supposed to have been limited to Wright's use of an apartment: "But it has gotten somewhat larger. I also thought that this committee . . . would not go on fishing expeditions. Suddenly all of Jim Wright's entire life back to 1949 was an issue and it wasn't just the condo. It was everything. I would suggest to you that Mr. Phelan always intended to look at those things."

Members stirred again. *Was he saying that Phelan had found something but it shouldn't count because he shouldn't have looked?*

Finally, Oldaker talked about gifts: "We have two types of gifts . . . benign gifts. . . . You could accept those benign gifts in any amount of money, without limit. Then there are pernicious gifts, from lobbyists, foreign agents, people who have a direct interest in legislation. . . . If Mr. Mallick doesn't have a direct interest in legislation, what we are talking about is moving all of the things that were disclosed by Mr. Wright on [his financial disclosure] form from one place to another. Mrs. Wright's salary. Disclosed? Yes. It is on the form. It is disclosed. We think she was paid a legitimate amount of money. . . . For assumption's sake, credit Mr. Phelan, you move salary to gift. The public knows the same thing, right?"

Oldaker seemed to be saying that it did not matter whether Betty's salary was disclosed as income or a gift, as long as it was disclosed. *Did he really mean that Betty didn't work? Was that what he was saying?* And disclosing $100,000 as salary when it really is a gift does not tell the public the same thing. Not the same thing at all. His own point about the disclosure devastated him. *And he was saying that accepting*

gifts was all right. Was he saying Wright had accepted all these gifts?
One member looked at Phelan and saw him smiling.

But disclosing $100,000 as salary when it really is a gift is not the
same thing. His own point devastated him. *And he was saying that
accepting gifts was all right. Did he really mean that Betty didn't work?*

Oldaker made his final point on her job: "You have a member's wife
here. Mr. Phelan is saying she isn't worth anything, nothing, zero. That
is what he said. Zero." He quoted a 1977 explanation of the new rules
which said that a spouse's work "is a judgment which will not be made
by me or anybody else in this House. It will be made by the IRS."

Did other members, Oldaker was saying, whose wives were lobbyists
or sold real estate or—like Dixon's wife—profited from special deals,
did they really want their wives investigated?

Fazio listened intently, and later said, "Oldaker seemed to be conceding Phelan's facts that Betty hadn't worked."

Before Oldaker's rebuttal, Atkins had told Phelan that Betty Wright
"did appear to have done some work," that her employment did not
seem "a unique relationship . . . [that turned] out to be very profitable
and useful for the business." The next time Atkins spoke he mockingly
suggested, "If Betty Wright worked . . . five days a month on Mallightco, plus car and condominium . . . would it be roughly [equal to]
$90,000 [annually]?"

Oldaker was treating this case as though Wright were an average
member. He was making a cozy argument, insider to insider. It was an
argument that could not withstand media scrutiny. Every member recognized and Phelan recognized how intense the media coverage would
be. Oldaker did not.

Later he did quote Pamela Smith's testimony that Betty had worked
"five to seven days a month," contradicting Phelan. But Oldaker never
played impresario, never painted a benign portrait of Mallightco, never
insisted fiercely that Betty Wright had worked. He brought out powerful
legal points, but he was no warrior addressing a jury. His defense rested
not on the facts but on rules of evidence: "There is no one in the record
who has testified, not one piece of evidence, that would suggest she
didn't work. There is only evidence in the record that she did work."

Phelan had in fact produced no evidence that she had not worked;
he had only impugned evidence that she had. Phelan was shifting the
burden of proof, forcing Oldaker to prove Wright's innocence. Oldaker

argued that even if members disbelieved Mallick, they were only at zero. They needed evidence to make a charge. Legally he was on unassailable ground. He cited a Supreme Court decision supporting him. Pashayan read it overnight and told him, "You're right."

But this was not a court. This was a jury, a jury of politicians.

Oldaker took this line almost casually, unworried about Betty's employment, defending instead against specifics, especially the apartment. Mallick provided free apartments to several employees, and the IRS had agreed that he required them to live in his apartments; it was a condition of employment, thus not taxable income. Wright had therefore never reported the apartment on his disclosure form as income. He had been too clever. The other employees had lived full-time in Mallick's apartments. Defending the apartment as a condition of employment, when Betty spent three-quarters of her time in Washington, twisted Oldaker into knots. He then argued that the apartment was not a violation anyway, since the rules allowed unlimited personal hospitality.

Oldaker was worried about what he regarded as more serious charges on savings and loans and the oil investment. He believed that Wright could survive as Speaker if charged on other counts, but not on these. The oil well charge he rebutted forcefully, then moved on to the savings and loan issue.

The standard Phelan wanted to hold Wright to—of charging him with a violation based not on what he did or intended to do but on what Gray, a personal enemy, thought he intended to do—seemed absurd. Yet Myers said, "What other standard would you use?" He would vote against Wright on two of the four S&L counts.

Pashayan had contempt for Gray, observing, "I know him well enough to know I don't want to know him well," and adding that one strange response to Wright "was pure Ed Gray." Yet Pashayan would vote against Wright on that same S&L count.

What was happening here?

A third Republican, Thomas Petri, observed, "The savings and loan scandal is an enormous one. It is hard to imagine the numbers, 50, 150 billion. . . . I am concerned about this Congress and this committee. This is going at some point to be in the public arena. It is going to be reviewed and discussed. Not only the Speaker's performance—our performance. Here we have maybe one of the largest evident financial dislocations certainly in this century."

Petri wanted a scapegoat. The press was watching. The press was a driving force even inside an executive session of this ethics committee. In three days Petri did not ask Oldaker a single question about the facts regarding the S&L's. Five of the six Republicans, including Myers and Petri, had voted to protect the S&L industry against the regulators two years earlier. Petri would vote against Wright on all S&L counts.

On the book, Oldaker argued the rules. Oldaker's position was that, first, royalties were flatly exempted. Nothing else mattered. Second, he claimed the book purchases were independent of the speeches, arguing that Wright gave over two hundred speeches a year as it was; 90 percent were for free. Wright would have spoken to the handful of groups, when he supposedly converted honoraria to royalties, whether they bought books or not. If he had truly been evading the limit, he would have collected much more money. Perhaps the royalty exemption was a loophole. Perhaps the rules should be changed. But the rules were written so that *royalties were exempt*.

But he was losing the committee. There seemed to be just too many charges. Too many. He was defending and defending. He challenged Phelan's accuracy, asked members to read the actual depositions, but the members stopped listening. "The thing just went on for days," said one member. "Hour after hour for days."

Details could not hold members' attention. Only a story could, a theme. Phelan, the impresario, had planted a forest; Oldaker was defending the trees. His opening statement was remembered. *He seemed to be conceding Phelan's facts about Betty*, Fazio had said.

In Phelan's final rebuttal of Oldaker, he pounded home his theme. Betty Wright did no work! Her salary was a gift! He repeated Atkins's calculation of her salary and benefits as being worth $100,000 a year, then said unctuously, "I just want the committee to know that the thoughtful creative person who thought of that was Congressman Atkins."

Chairman Dixon called on each member of the committee one final time and came to Atkins.

"I have no questions," Atkins responded.

It was over.

There was a last technical argument. Phelan had stated in his report and in his first day of argument that his standard of proof was "clear and convincing evidence." A committee aide pulled him aside and told him that he only had to reach a "reason to believe" standard that a rule had been violated at this stage. (By comparison, to indict, a federal grand jury must be thoroughly persuaded of the truth of the charge.) The "clear and convincing" standard would obtain for the trial stage.

Oldaker argued that the higher standard of proof be used. He was certain that he would win then, but feared the committee might find "reason to believe" Wright had violated some rules, in effect indicting him.

Guilty or innocent, the ensuing press frenzy could destroy him.

"Mr. Phelan's case won't get any stronger," Oldaker insisted. Phelan had spent ten months and $2 million examining Wright. Oldaker had neither cross-examined witnesses nor offered evidence. Oldaker's case would get stronger. And Phelan had claimed to meet the higher standard.

But now Phelan retreated, saying, "I was wrong."

At ten-thirty in the morning on March 15, the committee finished hearing the arguments. Later Dixon and Myers agreed to use "reason to believe."

Wright's daughter Ginger Brown stopped off in his office. She asked how he was doing. He chortled. "How am I doing? I wonder." There was a tightness in his chest that never released him now, made him feel like gasping for air. It shamed him that his daughter read these things in the paper about him. He hadn't violated any rules. He hadn't. And yet . . .

He told her about the pressures he had felt a decade earlier. In his journal at that time he had written of leaving Congress. They had had so little money. He had begun to explore the edges of the rules.

"We were just greedy," he confessed. "Damn it."

Myers began to squeeze. Suddenly he had power, and he squeezed. He wanted to make Phelan's report public even before the committee voted on the charges. Its release would create a firestorm in the media that would incinerate the committee if it protected Wright. Democrats balked. The committee had never released any information in advance of voting. It had never released any investigative material which raised charges it had rejected. Wright intended to fight the release of any such material this time.

For now, the committee kept the report private. But leaks began.

The most damaging was an accusation which the committee would dismiss, that Wright "attempt[ed] to destroy the distinguished career of a dedicated public servant because of a rumored sexual orientation"—that Wright had tried to get Joe Selby fired because he was homosexual. Wright had flatly denied it. The *Washington Times* broke the story.

On Sunday, March 19, Barney Frank, a homosexual member, appeared with Gingrich on an interview show. Frank had supported Wright, had even occasionally participated in the strategy meetings in H-201.

Wright watched from his home. Gingrich predicted that Wright would be gone in June. Frank answered hypothetical questions about Foley as the next Speaker, instead of predicting Wright's survival. Then, asked about releasing the report, he said, "I think Newt is correct. I think the report ought to be made public."

Wright was stunned. For a moment he did not react at all, feeling a cold coiling in, then gripping, his belly. Although he did not know precisely what was in the report, he knew it could destroy him. Half dizzy, weak, he called his sister Mary and began to read to her the Eighty-ninth Psalm.

> *You spoke to Your faithful ones in a vision*
> *and said, "I have conferred power upon a warrior;*
> *I have exalted one chosen from out of the people . . .*
> *No enemy shall oppress him,*
> *no vile man afflict him.*
> *I will crush his adversaries before him,*
> *I will strike down those who hate him . . ."*
> *Yet You have rejected, spurned,*
> *and become enraged at Your anointed . . .*
> *You have dragged his dignity in the dust.*
> *You have breached all his defenses,*
> *shattered his strongholds.*
> *All who pass by plunder him;*
> *he has become the butt of his neighbors.*
> *You have exalted the right hand of his adversaries,*
> *and made all his enemies rejoice . . .*
> *You have brought all his splendor to an end,*
> *and hurled his throne to the ground . . .*

Oldaker met with John Murtha, Jack Brooks, and Kirk O'Donnell. Murtha warned that things were not going well, that they should prepare a strategy for a worst-case scenario. Oldaker disagreed. He was the one who had been in the room. He said, "We won't lose any Democrats. We may pick up a Republican." There would be no worst-case planning.

He had given the committee a 108-page briefing book. Only two pages covered Betty Wright's employment.

Finally, in HT-2, on the terrace level of the Capitol, the committee met to deliberate the future of Jim Wright. In the great, vast building, the terrace level was the least visited. Its corridors were wide and high enough to drive a small truck through, dark, wide, worker-ant corridors, the home to electricians and carpenters, to the unused jail, and to the catafalque. Now they were thick with reporters. The members were tense, under pressure. The pressure was increasing.

Just as Oldaker was finishing his rebuttal, Ed Rollins, the new campaign chief for House Republicans, promised to make Wright "issue number one" in the next election. If he survived as Speaker, every Democrat in the House would have to defend against charges of corruption and double standards.

Almost simultaneously, the Senate rejected, on a partisan vote, John Tower's nomination as secretary of Defense. Bush immediately nominated Dick Cheney to be secretary of Defense. Within minutes of learning Cheney was leaving, Gingrich began calling colleagues. He was asking for votes to replace Cheney as whip—the second-ranking Republican in the House. Cheney's confirmation came swiftly, and the whip election was a lightning campaign of ten days. Forty-eight hours before it, *The Washington Post*'s Babcock revealed an unusual publishing arrangement of Gingrich's. He received a standard royalty for his 1984 book *Window of Opportunity*, but supporters put $105,000 in a limited partnership to promote it. They took tax write-offs and paid his wife, Marianne, $11,500 as general partner. A conservative book club bought his book in bulk.

Democrats demanded that he identify his limited partners and threatened to file ethics charges against him. He was stunned that Democrats now despised him, and frightened by it. As sophisticated as he was about abstractions, he was naive and insensitive to the personal. Now the story did not even affect his election as whip. Michel actively supported Ed Madigan. Gingrich beat him, 87–85. Gingrich's supporters included moderates such as Sherwood Boehlert, a friend of Wright's. They were fed up with the treatment House Republicans had received, and doubted Michel's ability to change things. Michel's listening had done him little good. No one had to say anything. Pressure on committee Republicans intensified.

But the most important pressure came from the press. Several weeks before any committee vote, *Newsweek*'s Eleanor Clift wrote that "most Democrats think the Speaker will be ousted." She simply stated it, without quoting—not even on an unattributed basis—a single member or a single aide. Her story also raised questions about "wispy skeletons that might or might not be in [Foley's] closet." "Wispy" and "closet" were code words easy to decipher. If Foley, a press favorite, could be subjected to such treatment, Wright would be eviscerated. How would the press treat the committee if it exonerated him?

Soon Myers made a public, on-the-record comment that the entire report would be made public. The pressure intensified. The *Washington Times* and *Wall Street Journal* printed new stories daily based on leaks. Wright's enemies began offering unrelated information to reporters. The *Journal*'s Brooks Jackson joked, "I had to put one anonymous caller on hold for another anonymous caller. That's the first time that's ever happened. Wright's weak now. They sense that and they're going after him."

Expectations increased that the committee would recommend a reprimand of Wright—a formal floor vote of the whole House. No Speaker could survive a reprimand. The pressure on the committee increased; if it did not call for a reprimand, it would have to explain itself.

In the deliberations, member after member in private, here, among colleagues, talked often and openly about the press. Myers talked of it constantly. So did Petri. And so did Fazio, a former journalist. *The Wall Street Journal* wrote an editorial demanding that they hold Wright to the highest standards. The committee would be measured against Phelan's report. *This is going at some point to be in the public arena,* Petri had said. *It is going to be reviewed and discussed. Not only the Speaker's performance—our performance.* Myers chorused, *The integrity of the committee and the Congress is at stake.* "Integrity" was a code word for the opinion of the press.

On April 4, just as they began voting, Brooks Jackson broke a story—

prompted by a perfectly timed leak—about Mallick's co-signing the S&L loan his son had defaulted on, which led to a $1-million lawsuit. Didn't that give him a direct interest in S&L legislation? The network newscasts that night repeated the story, and noted that Phelan was charging Wright with accepting over $100,000 in gifts from Mallick.

As the committee debated the charges, over and over Myers pressed home the standard of proof, arguing, "We're only talking about 'reason to believe.' How can you say there isn't reason to believe? We can always drop the charges when we get to the next stage, 'clear and convincing.' "

At one point Phelan said, "This is like shooting fish in a barrel."

While the press churned, Wright sat at breakfast reading the day's clips, and calmly, his voice even, raised a question about a story containing three factual errors: "Three weeks ago I asked you to form some means of response to correct factual errors. I'm not talking about reporters who say I have no friends, or that I'm poor on television. I'm talking about hard facts. Has anything been done?"

"No."

"Is there a reason not?" Calmly, so calmly he spoke. There was pain in his calmness. "Do one of you feel it's a bad strategy?"

No one answered for a long moment.

"We'll set that up today," one man finally said.

"History will not record me accurately," he said. Still in him was the lonely call of history. It seemed all he had left.

He could focus on little but the ethics committee and the media. Earlier he had tried and failed to move legislation as he had in the 100th Congress. And he had lost control of the minutiae of the speakership. The hundreds of appointments to boards and commissions went unmade, though his staff suggested action. *He could not focus.* Yet he had one more triumph. The Central Americans had moved toward both holding new Nicaraguan elections and disbanding the contras without input from the new administration. Jim Baker, newly appointed secretary of State, desperately wanted another agreement on humanitarian aid to the contras to sustain them.

On March 2, Baker held separate meetings with House and Senate Republicans and Wright, who was still the key to the issue among House Democrats. Over the next two weeks came more meetings. Senate

Democrats, after rejecting Tower, wanted to show bipartisanship. They accepted Baker's terms; they also wanted an agreement before St. Patrick's Day, when they left for a two-week recess. Wright refused Baker's offer. He filled himself with the issue, desperate for something to take his mind off ethics, desperate to accomplish something substantive, something worth doing. He pressed Baker to give the Appropriations Committee unofficial veto power over further contra aid, if the administration or the contras seemed to act in bad faith. On March 24, Baker agreed, setting off a storm among conservatives and even public criticism from White House counsel Boyden Gray for allowing an erosion of Executive power. *But Wright had brought peace. That was all he cared about now. Not power.*

On Friday, April 7, Wright made a speech on foreign policy. It was a strategic decision, an effort to shift the media focus away from his ethics to substance. The effort failed. No major paper reported on his comments. But the speech itself was strong and solid. It was Wright at his best. The applause was loud and sustained and sincere. Afterwards one man grabbed his hand, shook it firmly and warmly, and said, "You know, Mr. Speaker, that applause isn't just for the speech."

"Thank you," Wright replied, hearing the applause, his smile tight, like an animal showing its teeth.

Finally, in the first and second weeks in April, the ethics committee voted. The first charges were the most serious and concerned the savings and loans. Democrats unanimously supported Wright; Republicans split. Wright won on three of the counts by a 9–3 vote, and on the fourth by 8–4. The oil-investment charge was dropped by a 6–6, party-line vote.

Suddenly there was breathing room. *The Washington Post* broke the story of the dismissal. The story was leaked to counteract negative stories in *The Wall Street Journal*. Suddenly, it seemed Wright would get a slap on the wrist and would survive. *Newsweek*'s "conventional wisdom" feature said so. The remaining charges seemed either *de minimis* or weak.

Oldaker had begun briefing small groups of members on the issues in H-128, Rayburn's old Board of Education room. Wright controlled the room but it was far enough from his main offices that no one would connect anyone in the area to him. When Oldaker explained the "direct interest" issue to the members, they grew angry—imputing it to Mallick at all seemed strange, but back-dating the interest to 1979 seemed absurd. Nor did they like questions being raised about a member's spouse. Members were getting angry, truly angry. On Friday, a Wright aide enthused to a friend, "God damn I'm euphoric. I haven't felt this good in months."

But on Monday, April 10, Wright's office got word that CBS was about to report that the committee had charged Wright with thirty violations of House rules for accepting $100,000 in gifts, and with *perjury*. CBS did not check with Wright's office. *This was news.* Immediately Mark Johnson called the producer. They argued. Finally, less than fifteen minutes before airtime, the producer agreed to drop the mention of perjury. That night Wright, Oldaker, Mack, Lynam, and Phil Duncan stayed until 2:30 A.M. searching for a way out. They found none.

There was no perjury. And the committee had not acted. But it would. Myers, then Pashayan were repeating and repeating, "We're only talking about 'reason to believe.' How can you say there isn't reason to believe? Let's just go forward to the trial and find out."

Mollohan responded: "We spent $2 million on Dick Phelan and half a dozen investigators. Witnesses were unchallenged by Wright's cross-examination. Wright didn't present any evidence. If Dick can't prove it now he'll never prove it."

But the press was watching them, Myers repeated. *They had the integrity of the committee to think about. The press was watching.*

"Goddammit!" one member erupted. "Enough about the press!"

Then Phelan weighed in. In theory, he and his deputies were supposed to be called into the room only to answer specific factual questions, and then leave. But he spent more and more time inside the room, pounding home his arguments. Dixon was chairman. He was the one to control Phelan. He allowed it. "Betty Wright did zero!" Phelan snorted, his face twisting into disdain, holding up thumb and forefinger to form a circle. "Nothing! Zero!"

Phelan had misled the committee repeatedly. And the committee knew it. Once he told Republican James Hansen that Wright had not reported certain benefits from Mallick on his disclosure form. Wright actually had reported them—but as income, not as a "gift," which Phelan claimed it was. The next day Hansen had complained, "Contrary to the impression I got, this was reported." Then Hansen asked about other similar benefits: "You mentioned yesterday [these] were not reported?"

"That's correct," Phelan had recalled. "They were not reported."

But they had been reported, again as income rather than a gift. Phelan had lied, gotten caught, then had told the same lie again. Oldaker had pointed out the lie. Why did the Committee trust Phelan? Was his personality overpowering them? Or didn't they trust him? Were they just using him? Were they just asking for reasons before they voted?

The members reviewed Mallick's testimony. It was so vague. What had Betty Wright done? Mallick did not cite a single investment Mallightco had made based on her advice. He had said only that she had "assisted" him, but had never said how. Phelan had no evidence to support his charge about her, but Oldaker himself had seemed to concede Phelan's facts. The committee was not a court. It was charged with protecting the integrity of the House.

Reason to believe. Let's find out the truth in the trial. We've got the integrity of the committee, of the entire Congress, at stake here. What will the press say? And, unsaid, *What if we drop the charges and Phelan goes on the talk shows taking shots at the committee?*

The Republicans were a block. They had waited a long time for power. Thirty-four years since they had decided who would be Speaker. Myers had waited his entire career to exercise power. Dixon had ceded it to him. All six Republicans were voting against Wright. How could the Democrats stand against them, with a Democratic outside counsel, and that report? There was a sense, too, that on the savings and loans maybe Wright had gone a little overboard, that they had protected him on that. And there were so many charges. There was just so much. In isolation, each was easy to dismiss. But all of them? *Who on the committee fought for him, pulled colleagues aside for him, called Phelan a liar for him? Maybe Mollohan. But he stopped listening to him half the time. Oldaker himself had said that unless Mallick had a direct interest, these would be "benign" gifts, acceptable if reported. He had seemed to concede Phelan's facts. This was still a technical violation, since Wright had reported them under another heading.*

By a vote of 10–2, the committee decided that there was reason to believe that Betty Wright did no work. In total, it charged that her salary, the apartment, and the car amounted to $145,000 in gifts. (Logic failed in the amount; the committee called her entire $18,000 salary a gift from Mallick, but the Wrights owned half the company and paid half her salary, and also paid for half the car.) They had looked at the portrait Phelan had painted, and they had recognized Wright in it. For all he had done for two and a half years.

They came to direct interest.

Pashayan reiterated the standard of proof: *reason to believe.*

Just before the vote Chester Atkins asked for the Democrats to caucus. Members snorted in disbelief. A caucus? Now? They refused. Atkins came over to Bernard Dwyer. Dwyer rarely said anything. The stockyards bothered him. The request for it in the appropriations bill had come late in the process from John Mack. Mack always made his requests late, after all the other deals were cut; that way he avoided members demanding his help in exchange for helping Wright. But in this case that meant Mallick was talking about getting into the stockyards at the time the request came through. *It was only "reason to believe."* Dwyer wanted to find out more about the stockyards in the trial.

"How are you going to vote, Bernie?" Atkins asked.

"I'm going to vote against the Speaker," Dwyer said quietly.

Atkins was closest of the members to Phelan; the two had dinner regularly. He also understood the politics of ethics. As a state senator, he had chaired an investigation of a Massachusetts scandal soon after Watergate, and had maneuvered it into the chairmanship of the state ways and means committee. There he had earned the nickname "Billy Bulger's butler" for his willingness to do the bidding of state senate president William Bulger; establishing his independence from party leadership would help him live down that nickname. Frank Phillips, a *Boston Globe* reporter who had covered him, said, "He's an opportunist. As an inside player he's done some outrageous things, and in the outside game he portrays himself as a reformer." Andrew Dabilis, another *Globe* reporter, said, "When I heard about Atkins's vote, I thought Chester figured out the winning side and wanted the light to shine on him brightly."

The committee voted, tense. This issue went to the very essence of government ethics, accepting favors from someone over whom one has power. One after another after another, the Republicans voted that Mallick had a direct interest. Dating back to 1979.

So did Dwyer.

So did Atkins.

Eight to four against Jim Wright. The room fell silent.

One member of the committee sat thinking, *Jim Wright cannot survive this. Not this.*

While the committee voted, Bill Alexander, the man who a dozen years earlier had told Wright that he had won the majority leader election, filed an ethics complaint against Gingrich for his book.

The ethics committee also charged that on seven occasions in three years Wright violated honoraria limits by converting them into royalties; one vote was 7–5, with Dixon joining the Republicans.

As word filtered out of the committee about the votes, Wright asked to testify again. Committee rules stipulate that the accused has a right to respond to charges against him. None of these charges had even existed when he testified before. He had answered the charges made by Common Cause and Gingrich. Every one of them had been dismissed. Every one.

Wright's old supporter and friend Bernard Rappoport, a wealthy man who had bought a thousand books, came by. They had fought the wars together for so many years. "My father was an old Jewish radical," Rappoport said. "He told me three things. Never loan anyone your books. Always look after your reputation. And never lose your sense of outrage."

Wright laughed. His entire body was tense, electric with the energy of outrage. One could feel the physical force of the current running through him. It was as if his body tingled.

Leaks were killing him. Now, on Wednesday, April 12, Wright, Oldaker, Mack, and Johnson decided to preempt the committee with a response. Otherwise the media would be filled with nothing but reports of the votes. The House needed reassurance too.

Thursday morning was the regular whip meeting. Wright looked nervous as Foley went through the routine of the schedule. The members sat on edge as well. Then Wright rose and took a step toward them. "I want to speak to you about something in the nature of personal privilege," he said. "I know you're all concerned."

The room was absolutely still.

"I love being Speaker but there are things more important than being Speaker—" His voice broke, and he stopped, then continued. "One's personal honor and reputation. My wife's integrity. When I met her she was a career woman, an intelligent woman . . . working on the Public Works Committee. . . . After we were married she turned down raises and promotions to avoid the appearance of conflict of interest. When I became majority leader she quit, to avoid the appearance of conflict of interest." His voice broke again. "It's an insult to Betty to imply she did not work to earn this money. I have proof that she worked to earn this."

He told them he had asked to appear before the committee and rebut the charges, that he hoped to convince the committee to reverse itself. But if not, he would be asking for their help on the floor.

It was his first mention that the House might vote to reprimand its Speaker. Yet he seemed so strong, so solid, so determined, filled with conviction. His colleagues were mesmerized by his force. As he finished, the whips applauded, stood, applauded long, long riveting applause. At that moment, they would have stood with him against any charge.

Late that afternoon, in the Rayburn Room, he planned a statement. Rostenkowski had scheduled his flight back to Chicago. Wright called him and asked him to come.

"Of course I'll be there," Rostenkowski had said.

Now one hundred and fifty reporters squeezed into narrow folding seats. Twenty-seven television cameras waited for him.

Wright walked in accompanied by the men who embodied the power of the House of Representatives. Rostenkowski, Dingell, Brooks, Foley, Coelho, Bonior, all beside him. Dozens of other members filled the area behind the microphones, overflowed into a crowd against the wall. The press stopped counting. Almost a quarter of the Caucus. And no Republicans. Beneath the great, grand, full-length portrait of George Washington, Wright made his defense.

There were only three issues, he declared: whether his wife had worked, whether Mallick had a direct interest in legislation, and whether his book had violated House rules.

He made his statement, took no questions, and left.

"That was very strong," one national reporter said.

Oldaker negotiated furiously with the committee to allow Wright to testify again. Committee rules stipulate that the respondent can answer charges against him. None of the charges now being made had existed when Wright testified earlier. Every charge raised by Gingrich and

Common Cause had been dismissed. Phil Duncan, one of Wright's senior aides, said, "I can't conceive of their not letting the Speaker of the House testify."

The committee had already allowed Oldaker to respond, which went beyond normal committee procedures. But Oldaker had presented an argument only, not new facts, not testimony. Wright asked to testify; testimony was evidence.

Dixon and Myers refused his request.

Although there were only three issues, the committee formally charged Wright on five counts: three for accepting gifts in the form of his wife's salary, the car, and Mallick's apartment; one for accepting gifts from someone with a direct interest in legislation; and one for converting honoraria to royalties.

But Dixon and Myers also decided to charge him with sixty-nine violations of House rules. (Twenty-two accrued to the car alone, even though Wright owned half of it.) The committee did not discuss the decision to cite Wright sixty-nine times, but Myers later said, "It was discussed by the chairman, myself, and Phelan. We were aware of the impact it would have."

They were also aware of the impact the committee report language would have—not Phelan's report, but the committee's own report, which Phelan was helping to draft. The language was harsh, calling Wright's book "an overall scheme" to evade income limits. Phelan and the staff counsel Ralph Lotkin had written language even more damning. Democrats objected and the language was removed. Dixon said to Phelan, "When you've got a man down, you don't let him up, do you?"

On Friday, April 14, Wright walked through the reception area outside his office into Lynam's, where Oldaker was.

"They say the committee is charging me with violating House rules sixty-nine times," he said softly. "That's not true, is it, Bill?"

"I'm afraid it is, Mr. Speaker."

Wright was very still for a moment. Then, silently, he walked back past Lynam's secretary, past the reception area, past his own secretary, and sat down at his desk. All his years of service. *For what? For what? For what?*

On Sunday, April 16, the committee delivered to Jim Wright a statement of his alleged violations.

CHAPTER 26

Monday morning, April 17, the ethics committee held a press conference in the Rayburn Building. The networks covered it live. Three hundred reporters packed the hearing room. Outside in the halls were more who could not fit. Around the corner dozens of junior reporters were already in line for a copy of Phelan's report. *This was news.* At a table in front of the dais sat Dixon, Myers, and Phelan, with the other members of the committee shoulder to shoulder in a row behind them. With a few exceptions, they believed Wright had already lost the moral authority which undergirds leadership. Innocent or guilty, he had lost that. Now they wanted to make that loss clear to Wright.

Dixon began, speaking in a calm, careful, even tone. He announced that the committee was charging Jim Wright with sixty-nine violations of House rules. The reporters seemed stunned. *Sixty-nine violations. Wright couldn't be innocent of all of them.* Every headline and every lead sentence was already written. It did not matter that he went on to say there were five counts. Then Dixon said something even more explosive, something not raised in the oral arguments.

He explained that the committee had learned of another possible violation too late to investigate it thoroughly (actually, they had learned of it in November, five months earlier) and might later add it to the charges: Mallightco, while Wright's interest was in a blind trust, had paid $9,000 for what Phelan called a "nearly worthless" oil well, then the same day sold it for $440,000.

Reporters were not disappointed with this press conference.

The slow, long, grinding process had begun. The political process, the calculation of the good of the party, of the institution—and of one's own interest—had begun. And the inevitable processes of the press had begun. Reporters would pore over Wright's life, would cover him, explore and invade any opening, rip at it, strip back its edges.

To survive, Wright had to stop this process.

Wright had already written the committee, declared his innocence, and requested an immediate hearing, as early as that afternoon. He was ready. Phelan had had ten months and should be ready. To call a hearing, all Dixon had to do was bang the gavel. But Dixon and Myers waited two days—*in politics that can be a very long time; an hour is a long time to lie bleeding on the ground*—before replying that they required a formal "admission or denial of the alleged violations," that "prior to a disciplinary hearing, a respondent has the opportunity to inspect the evidence which . . . is material to the preparation of a defense," and that Phelan and Oldaker should meet to discuss the format of the hearing.

Within an hour Wright sent Dixon a notarized denial of guilt, reiterated his desire for an immediate hearing, and requested access to the evidence. Oldaker wanted it badly, confident that it would reveal major discrepancies between it and Phelan's characterization of it. Such evidence is automatically provided to criminal defendants.

Dixon had his own procedural powers. He had Phelan answer Wright's letter. Phelan said Wright's denial of guilt was not a denial. It was a motion. The committee would have to rule on it before Phelan could even discuss a hearing with Oldaker. He was playing a lawyer's game—dispute everything and delay, delay, delay.

Oldaker replied by letter and insisted that committee rules called for no such procedure. Finally Phelan met with him, but refused to move toward a quick hearing. They had words. Fuming, Oldaker reported to Mack: "You know what that son of a bitch said? 'It's not in my interest to have a quick hearing.' You know what else he said? 'This case will be decided by the editorial pages of the nation's newspapers.' "

If it was, Wright would be destroyed. Editorial writers universally acclaimed the committee. *The New York Times:* "The ethics committee has already done itself proud. . . . Its judicious demeanor to date augurs well for a fair trial in the politically tense days ahead." *The Washington Post:* "The panel confounded its critics and did the job right. . . . If [Wright] steps aside . . . for Tom Foley, the party will survive nicely:

it could even end up ahead." *The Baltimore Sun:* "The committee won't win brownie points with colleagues, but will win brownie points with history." David Broder added a column praising Dixon. *The Wall Street Journal* applauded, too, while complaining of Wright's escape on the savings and loan charges.

More commentary followed in the next few days. Meg Greenfield, editor of *The Washington Post* editorial page and a *Newsweek* columnist who was friendly with Cheney and Gingrich, declared Wright's speakership "over," even if he somehow managed to retain his title. *Time* magazine columnist Hugh Sidey, a conservative and defender of the White House, called for Wright to resign. And liberals were appalled by Phelan's charge that he had tried to fire a regulator because of homosexuality. *New York Times* columnist Anthony Lewis, a former Supreme Court reporter who cared deeply about due process, called Wright's actions "disgusting" and wished him good riddance.

Wright had succeeded in the 100th Congress with attention to detail, with unrelenting focus on a goal. The essence of his power had been his will, his subjectivity. The world had yielded to him. Now he had no focus. The world was overpowering him. He was becoming a kind of object, something to be examined and invaded and tossed about by others.

Yet Wright's case was so strong. His wife had worked. Mallick had wanted to buy a limited partnership in the movie *Annie;* she had traveled to New York and met the producers, then vetoed it. The investment would have lost at least $25,000. Mallick had wanted to invest in an energy project in West Virginia run by James Ling, the founder of LTV. She had vetoed it. The project ended in disaster. Mallightco would have risked $100,000, and lost possibly all of it. She had negotiated the private sale of a stock which had yielded a $14,000 profit.

They did not have only Mallick's word. Over the weekend Wright's staff had feverishly collected several sworn affidavits from people who had dealt with his wife professionally. They stated that she had brought their investment ideas to Mallick's attention and investigated them actively over extended periods. She had had lengthy discussions about investing in a small, experimental Texas vineyard. A banker cited five separate meetings in Dallas over several months with her and Mallick about their participation in a syndicate which would buy several banks. A developer recounted that she had introduced him to Mallick and that the three of them had explored several joint projects over a two-year period, decided on one, but canceled it because they failed to prelease the space. There were other affidavits, reciting other investments, and more would be coming in later. Phelan had found no record of any of these projects because Mallightco was a small, informal company. There were no memos; communication between her and Mallick, the only two involved, had been oral. Her notes had been destroyed in the five to eight years which had passed.

Mallightco had invested in none of the proposals for one major reason: the Texas economy and oil prices were then collapsing. So she stopped working for Mallightco and went to work for the Pacific Institute, at double her Mallightco salary.

The direct-interest charge was weak to begin with; it was sustained primarily by the claim that Betty Wright's salary and benefits were gifts. If Wright demonstrated that his wife had worked, the direct-interest charge disintegrated entirely.

Even on the book, Phelan's legal case seemed flimsy. He based his interpretation of the royalty exemption on two things: First, he quoted Senate debate on Senate ethics rules, arguing that this debate had influenced House rules. That was unlikely in any case; in this case it was impossible. The Senate debate had occurred seventy-seven days after the House committee wrote the House rules. Second, Phelan quoted draft language of the royalty rule which would in fact have prohibited Wright's bulk sales. But that draft had been rejected in favor of a total exemption. Phelan was holding Wright responsible for rejected language that was never published.

If they could get a quick hearing, before the press really got into it, they could win this thing.

Tuesday morning, the day after the committee's announcement, Wright spoke to the Democratic Caucus. He had wanted it open to the press, to have them hear him speak from the well of the House. But he had not pressed the point and the Caucus was not opened. Two hundred and twenty-three of his colleagues listened closely in the House chamber. There was no joking in the aisles, no pounding of the gavel to bring order. There was silence, except for the standing ovation when he entered.

"I'm not going to get emotional," Wright began, referring to the week before when he had spoken of his wife. "I'm going to give you a frank and forthright statement. I owe that to you. You are the ones to whom I owe the most. You have given me the greatest gift within your power to give, and I owe you a standard of conduct and a standard of leadership of which you can be proud. I love being Speaker. But let me make one thing clear. If circumstances of any type should ever make it impossible for me to be not only a respectable Speaker but a genuinely effective Speaker, then I would no longer want to be the Speaker."

He was reassuring his colleagues that he would not cling desperately to his position. In return he only wanted a chance to clear his name. The members did not stir. They were intent. Then he rebutted the charges one by one, in ten minutes offering more details on his wife's employment than had ever been given the committee.

"If you should be talking to the Lord," he concluded, "please explain to him that he seems to have a case of mistaken identity. He seems to have confused me with Job. Please tell him I'm not Job. I don't have his patience, I don't have his strength of character. I don't have his stamina. . . . There are two groups of people whose opinions mean the most to me. They are my constituents, some who have known me all my life, and my colleagues, who work with me day-to-day."

He meant those words. Then he told them, "I've never done anything to dishonor you. And I never will."

The standing ovation went on and on, ended only when he left. Then member after member rose. All defended him. Not just Wright loyalists. Louis Stokes, a black man close to Dixon and one of the most respected members of the House, told the Caucus that the committee had almost had to charge Wright based on Phelan's report and the "reason to believe" standard, but that it meant nothing. Ed Jenkins, king of the backbenchers, spoke, and his words carried weight. Barbara Kennelly, Sam Gibbons, all spoke in support.

Yet there was not the emotional rallying of the week before. Each member listened, went inward, thought his or her own thoughts. It had gone beyond the facts now, beyond guilt or innocence. They would not plot against him. They would wait, silent.

After the Caucus, reporters swarmed in the Speaker's Lobby, and their questions were a bad omen for Wright. William Choyke of *The Dallas Morning News* caught Jenkins and asked, "Do you think it's proper for Wright to be addressing the Caucus? If you were on the ethics committee, wouldn't you be upset?"

An hour later Wright held his daily press conference. It was no longer routine and was often canceled. But today he used it to talk about his wife's work. Reporters jammed his ceremonial office, one of the largest turnouts ever, spilling into the adjacent room. He repeated the details he had given his colleagues. The staff made copies of the affidavits available.

His presentation had an impact. But not enough. The next morning a *New York Times* news story—not an editorial—concluded that Phelan's report, and the charges which were dropped, "illustrated . . . how far a congressman can go in insider deals and arm-twisting without either breaking the law or earning the condemnation of his colleagues. . . . It suggests, too, how all the more grievous Mr. Wright's acts had to be for the committee to act against him."

Wright read it at breakfast and observed, "It's kind of hard to win this thing if every time I land a blow the referee hits me in the back of the head with a two-by-four."

It was an observation made without rancor. He understood the world. There was blood in the water. The press had the scent.

He believed the only way to stop it, to stop the public and his colleagues from reading stories about his venality, was to attack Phelan. Phelan had distorted so much. But the public and his colleagues did not know that. Publicizing discrepancies was his only chance to survive. It would give him personal satisfaction, too. *To feel his fists crack against bone, against skull, against ribs. And it was the only way he could win this thing. People believed Phelan. That liar. He had to make them not believe him.* "The most important thing," he told his staff, "is to discredit Phelan's report."

But when the staff started working on the project, Mack and Oldaker countermanded Wright's order.

It was a sign of the erosion of Jim Wright, and not the first. Before Oldaker's oral argument, his staff had hidden news from him that he was in trouble, both fearing to act as messenger and fearing that he would act injudiciously and hurt himself. Everyone except Mack feared him, feared his explosiveness. In a December meeting, he had talked of complete exoneration. Aides had known there would be no exoneration but had not known *this* was coming. No one had confronted him then with that reality. They had feared him, and they had patronized him. He had had to learn from other sources. There was also a certain arrogance that came from Oldaker, Mack, and Lynam, regarding the rest of the staff. Phil Duncan suggested planning for a worst case. They refused.

Mack and Oldaker were making decisions, and they still trusted Dixon. They had to. They needed him to get a quick hearing. Dixon had hired Phelan and the committee had relied on him. Dixon was sensitive to any criticism, especially in the press. They feared that attacking Phelan would antagonize Dixon and the entire committee. They focused on a legal strategy and believed that substantive legal victories would bring the media and the members in line. Others involved—mostly Texans, especially Jack Brooks, Martin Frost, and Charlie Wilson—agreed. Mark Johnson, his new media adviser, believed that the best story was no story. All indications were that the public was reacting with a yawn. That meant members were not under pressure. Raising the profile of the story raised the possibility of public interest. Frost told Wright, "You're a client. You have to act like a client. Let your lawyer talk for you."

But already there were signs of friction not so much among those advising him as between himself and his advisers. He had begun a search for a new attorney, a litigator, a warrior, for the trial stage. Wright wanted to make his case publicly and often. Those to whom he had delegated his defense were still playing the inside game.

Once Wright had been a rock. *You can count on Wright.* Once he had controlled everything by acting. Now he did not control his staff. Now he was disconnected from them, and disconnected from the floor. Not because he did not know what was going on there, but because he did know. The floor was moving away from him.

While Wright foundered, a budget deal with the White House was being worked out. It was not as it had been in the 100th Congress. He exploded at his staff for not telling him that Leon Panetta, now Budget chairman, had been waiting for him. He did not even have the power to keep a colleague waiting. He needed every margin of goodwill.

A week after the ethics committee action, the White House and congressional leaders reached a budget agreement. It papered over the deficit for another year and relied on an overoptimistic projection from OMB to meet the Gramm-Rudman target. At the White House ceremony announcing the accord, Wright said, "This is not a heroic agreement."

But he did not resist. He had no power to resist. It was a far cry from the last time he had gone to the White House to announce a budget deal.

The press would devour whatever came into its path. On April 25, Gingrich held a press conference to explain his own book transaction. It was more than a month since Babcock's story; Gingrich had had plenty of time to coordinate answers from his limited partners, who included such major players in conservative politics as Joseph Coors, owner of the beer company. Still, several limited partners told reporters they had given $5,000 with no intention of making a profit, while receiving a tax write-off. By Phelan's standards their investment was a gift to Gingrich. And Coors employed lobbyists, which automatically gave him a direct interest in legislation. Reporters attacked Gingrich, scoffed at his explanations, and his wife, who had been paid $11,500 as general partner, stormed out in tears.

But the focus of the press was Wright. Perhaps he had not violated House rules, but perhaps he was not innocent either. *We were just greedy,* he had told his daughter. He had done some things impetuously that showed bad judgment, and considered other things that approached the edges of the rules. *Washington values judgment more than anything.*

The media's power was not a new thing. Two centuries earlier, Edmund Burke had declared it more powerful than Parliament. Five centuries earlier, Cardinal Thomas Wolsey had warned, "We must destroy the press, or the press will destroy us."

After reporters saw the affidavits about his wife's work, they did retreat on that issue. But no national publication investigated and declared that she had or had not worked, interviewing people who had given affidavits and others. Only the Fort Worth paper did. Its reporter Ron Hutcheson later said, "I'm convinced Betty worked. It's not even an issue with me."

The press simply shifted to other issues. And it would not be distracted. The most important issue seemed the Sabine Lake oil deal, which *The Wall Street Journal* called "potentially more serious" than anything with which the committee had charged Wright.

The first thorough story about Sabine Lake ran in *The Washington Post,* shortly after the committee reported. Babcock—the investigative reporter who broke the stories on Wright's book, Gingrich's book, and, a week earlier, on a questionable junk-bond purchase by Coelho— wrote it. Babcock was dogged but unprejudiced. Phelan's report had already puzzled him because it lacked an appendix of supporting documents. Every other investigative report in his experience had included one. Phelan offered his interpretation but no documents. So Babcock called the people Phelan quoted about Sabine Lake, and decided that Phelan had mischaracterized the deal. There was nothing wrong with it.

Phelan's representation—that Mallightco bought its share in a "nearly worthless" well for $9,000 and sold most of its interest the same day for $440,000—distorted the truth. Mallightco had actually committed $99,000 in January to drill an exploratory well. As was standard practice, it had not paid its share immediately but was fully liable for $9,000 for its share of the mineral rights, and $90,000 for drilling costs. The well was drilled and reserves worth $80 million to $120 million were discovered. The well shot up in value. In May, Mallightco found a buyer for its interest. Before it could transfer title, it executed its commitment, technically buying and selling the well in one day. But it had put $99,000 at risk before reserves were discovered, and sold its share afterwards. (The deal was actually structured as a complex loan.) Nor was the tract "nearly worthless" when sold. Investors could not extract the reserves through the first well, but, after Mallightco sold, they spent nearly $3 million more drilling other wells to get at them. A year later they were planning to try again.

Babcock's story was buried in the middle of the paper and ignored. The Fort Worth paper later published a special section on Sabine Lake, written by a team of reporters. They, too, concluded that the deal was an honest one, that in fact the area could develop into a major oil field. Already Exxon had several highly profitable wells there.

But *The New York Times* front page blared "Profits from Dry Well Pose Tough Questions for Wright." A subhead announced, "The property was sold for a one-day profit of nearly 4,000 percent."

And the *Times* and the *Journal* competed to "move" the Sabine Lake story, to hunt down each thread to a conclusion. They investigated campaign contributions from the Jaffe family, from whom Mallightco bought its interest and who arranged its sale. They had made no contributions to Wright, but had to other Democrats, and they had other businesses which sought federal contracts. Both papers implied that the Jaffes did Wright a favor, a favor worth hundreds of thousands of dollars. But if Sabine Lake was a legitimate transaction, the favor was worth nothing.

Babcock's story on Sabine Lake did not distract his media colleagues. Few saw the Fort Worth story. Discrepancies in Phelan's report that were surfacing did not distract the media either.

David Obey had chaired the committee which wrote the House rules a decade earlier. He had a reputation as a reformer, but defended Wright. In an op-ed piece in the *Post,* he accused the committee of misapplying them to both Mallick's direct interest and the book.

Harold Sawyer, a lawyer and former Republican member of that same rule-writing committee, wrote a lengthy letter to Phelan, analyzed his legal reasoning, and excoriated it. Sawyer stated that Wright broke no rules, and concluded that "any qualified lawyer" would have advised him that his book transactions were allowed. Unsolicited, he sent a copy to Wright, whose office gave it to the press.

Reporters paid little attention to Sawyer or Obey. But perhaps the most serious question raised about Phelan's facts involved Gene Payte, a wealthy friend of Wright's. The committee had charged Wright with accepting an unreported gift from him because he had paid for one thousand books but received no more than five hundred. The money for unreceived books was the gift. This raised two issues.

First, Payte had paid the publisher Moore, not Wright. And Phelan said that Wright had received royalties for only 16,800 books, while Moore sold 21,200. Phelan conceded that Moore, who was under financial pressures, had never paid Wright $17,000 owing to him. If there had been a gift, it was to Moore.

The second issue went beyond logic. Payte read Phelan's report, which said, "Payte testified that he only received between three hundred and five hundred copies of the book" rather than one thousand. He exploded, then issued an affidavit saying, "I did not so testify. . . . I stated not once but three times that I believed 1,000 books were delivered. . . . I received all of the 1,000 books which I purchased."

Myers had asked if Payte had received only "three hundred to five hundred books." Phelan had attributed to Payte as a statement something that was actually a question asked by Myers.

Payte faxed Wright's staff the affidavit. They debated what to do with it. Some wanted to keep it quiet, for fear of angering Dixon. Wright said, "I want that out."

But it did not go out. Wright could not control even his own staff.

They thought they knew better than he. Two days later, Saturday, Wright called an aide at home and demanded that it be released. Without any planning to maximize its impact, it went to *The New York Times*, which ran a story on it. But no one else picked it up.

Dixon and Myers promptly wrote Payte and threatened to find him in contempt of Congress if he continued to make public comments about his testimony because it had been given in executive session.

Payte reacted with outrage. They had distorted his testimony entirely, and now were threatening him with contempt of Congress for correcting it. He sent a copy of Dixon's letter to Wright's office, which gave it to the press.

Other papers had not picked up on the original *Times* story, and even the *Times* ignored the committee's effort to intimidate Payte. In Wright's mind it was a turning point. He had always believed the press was more sensitive to First Amendment rights than to anything else. Now it was ignoring an effort by the Congress to silence a citizen. He began to worry that nothing would turn the press.

The press already had its direction. Perhaps if someone gathered all the known distortions in the report, all the evidence contradicting it, together and released it simultaneously, it could change that direction. It seemed that every day at breakfast Wright told his staff to do that. But Oldaker and Mack were still trying to work the committee, and feared that attacking Phelan would boomerang. The processes of the press ground on. *And Wright had still not hired a litigator.* The man of action did not act. He was not willing this thing to a conclusion. The criticism was too personal. It stung too much. He withdrew.

On April 28, *The Wall Street Journal*'s Brooks Jackson uncovered a plane ride by Wright in a corporate jet several years earlier that had never been paid for. The company had never sent a bill, and Wright's office immediately paid for it.

The next issue of the *Journal* had another story, this time by David Rogers: as majority leader Wright had made a comment in the *Congressional Record* favorable to the Pacific Institute, endorsing its motivational videotapes. Wright believed in the product, had even had company chairman Lewis Tice address House Democrats one year at the Greenbrier. But his wife worked for the company. Without question, his endorsement was improper. Angry, defensive, he insisted he had done nothing wrong, that everyone did it. He was smearing all his colleagues. It was a minor story with major impact. Colleagues moved away from him without sympathy. In a private meeting even loyalist Robert Torricelli snapped, "I don't do it."

Wright had still not hired a litigator. He seemed paralyzed.

By now reporters were poring over every facet of Wright's life. Everything. Stories that might not have been written at all in normal circumstances appeared on the front page. And all the stories pointed in one direction: that Jim Wright was venal.

And no national reporter examined the accuracy of Phelan's report. Clear evidence had surfaced that Betty Wright had done real work. Phelan's legal reasoning on the other two issues had come under heavy attack. Even the facts of the book charge had come into question. And witnesses who had testified before the committee had in effect accused Phelan of lying about their testimony. Yet reporters ignored it.

Richard Dunham of the *Dallas Times-Herald* did write a page-one story questioning Phelan's report. "It was a pretty lonely feeling out there," he said. "No one else was doing it. We did positive stories and negative stories. The negative ones were picked up by A.P. The positive ones died."

"There is a tendency to move in a herd," said Thomas Kenworthy, the *Post*'s lead House reporter. He knew of several discrepancies in Phelan's report, and, sitting in the press gallery office, a door removed from the House chamber, said, "I can't see the direct-interest charge. . . . I thought about investigating the report, but . . . the committee seems to have faith in it. What's Phelan's motive to screw Wright? Why would the Democrats on the committee go along?"

But his most important reason for not examining Phelan's accuracy was the process: "The story's very competitive. It's intense. None of us like to get beat. If someone's driving this story, it would be Al Hunt."

Hunt was bureau chief of *The Wall Street Journal*. Kenworthy would not take time away from looking for conflicts of interest in Wright's legislative history, or covering Wright's chances for survival for fear of being beaten. And the *Journal* was on this story. Brooks Jackson could already claim credit for St Germain's reelection defeat, and now focused on Wright's activities outside Congress. He disapproved of Wright, whose 1977 conversion of campaign funds to personal use bothered him. Jackson did not accept Wright's justification that he was reimbursing himself for having personally paid campaign debts a dozen years earlier. He said, "That is not appropriate behavior. . . . If I'm harder on him than other reporters, so be it."

David Rogers, the *Journal*'s chief congressional reporter, drove the stories on Wright's legislative history. He was spending hours reviewing it. He said, "I was unimpressed with Phelan's work on direct interest."

But he never questioned Phelan's accuracy because "I always thought [the case] would go to trial and balance out. . . . Phelan wasn't available. You couldn't ask him how come he was so sloppy with the interest rate thing. It was daily journalism. You couldn't get a quote. Wright was much more exposed to reporters' questions. . . . [And] I didn't feel I had the time to go off and do a thorough piece on other things. We had to stay competitive. I felt I had to keep up with everyone else."

There was another thing. He said, "It frustrated me that Phelan didn't tighten his case more. My role almost was to tighten his case for him. . . . It was the natural role for a reporter."

It frustrated him that Phelan had not made a better case? His role was to tighten the case? It was a natural role for a reporter? Or was there something personal in the media's attitude toward Wright?

Perhaps there need not be anything personal. The process itself, the forces within the press, were inexorable enough. An ethics committee Republican watched the press swirl about Wright and observed, "Editors are assigning reporters and giving them budgets, and reporters want Pulitzer Prizes."

A fury was out there. The press had a direction. It would accept no other.

Canetti: *They are not a multitude and have to make up in intensity what they lack in actual numbers. . . . The truest and most natural pack is that from which our word derives, the hunting pack. . . . [It] is out for killing and it knows whom it wants to kill. . . . The proclaiming of the goal . . . is enough to make the crowd form. This concentration on killing is of a special kind and of unsurpassed intensity. Everyone wants to participate, everyone strikes a blow.*

The House recoiled. It distanced itself from Wright. Members watched with sympathy or horror. Or satisfaction. But they only watched. *Wright was on his own.*

And the House shook him off. On April 26, the House defeated the leadership's attempt to pass an appropriations bill. Democrats were split, Republicans opposed. It was inconceivable that Wright would have lost the vote in the 100th Congress.

Republicans gave no quarter. They gloated. Mickey Edwards, who so hated Wright over the contras, gloated. "Democrats should help us govern or get out of the way," he said. Few comments could sting Wright more. Edwards was laughing at his speakership. *They're not colleagues,* Cheney had said. *There's no comity left.* One of Wright's few GOP friends said, "I'd like to help Jim. I think awfully well of him. But I told Mack that if this thing goes to the floor, not to count on any Republicans. The pressure is just too much. The big thing is, if the Democrats can stay united, they can win this thing."

Democrats were not united. Resentment over the pay raise lingered. *Son of a bitch,* one member had said, after Wright left that meeting so private even Mack could not attend. Uneasiness over his unpredictability lingered. *There's always grumbling but this is worse,* an ally had conceded after Wright's CIA comment. And all those hours and days and weeks he had not spent on the floor, leaving it to Foley or Coelho or Mack to take care of his colleagues' needs, using his time instead to work his will, reify his beliefs, all that was coming back now. *All he's got is his fucking agenda,* a Democrat had complained. Now one Democrat said, "Let him hang."

Still, older Democrats supported Wright; the younger ones stood apart. The class of 1974 seemed a dividing line. It had entered the House seventy-five new Democrats strong. Many had gone to college in the sixties and grew to maturity distrusting the government because of Vietnam and winning election after Nixon's resignation and Ford's pardon of him. The new members had taken power instantly, providing the votes for the reformers to end seniority and transfer authority from chairmen to the Caucus, directly and in the person of the Speaker. They had made a science of reelection; they had had to, since so many of them came from traditionally Republican districts and ran more scared than machine politicians. So they had built personal machines attuned to themselves. They did not want to be out on the defensive.

It was a class of little tolerance, as intolerant and matter-of-fact as the television camera. Politics, and power, have always been cold, colder than other professions perhaps because the occasional betrayal betrayed all the heat and warmth of the crowds and handshakes and laughter and working together. But it had always been intimate. Brutus had stood as close to Caesar as a whispering lover. Now even murder had lost that intimacy. Murder was done by moving away, by isolating, by leaving a colleague bleeding. Messages were not delivered face-to-face but sent through unattributed quotes in the newspapers. Death was as intimate now as ten seconds on the news.

Some loyalists did rally around. The Texans. Legal and members groups merged to keep the Caucus informed of events, of new legal strategies, of explanations for each new story in the press, to give the Caucus something to hold on to. Because it was slipping away. David Nagle organized a group of about fifteen who met regularly and kept their distance from Wright purposely, so they could be seen as independent. Jim Moody came around. Bonior worked to help him. People like Donnelly were trying to build support to keep Wright as Speaker even if reprimanded, and warned colleagues that the ethics committee had become "a Gestapo." Dingell was a rock. The dinosaurs and the institutionalists. And the great, old enemy and older friend—Rostenkowski, who had warred with Wright for so long—looked about him at the new younger members with their fancy haircuts and their media-savvy staffs, all of them outsiders to the institution, and raged, "Those jerks! Those sons of bitches!" Rostenkowski told Wright he was with him.

But there was no cohesion. The leadership did nothing. *This was personal.* Coelho's whip organization was dormant. He gave Wright advice on the media, and reports from the floor. But one of his aides gave damning quotes from "a Democratic leadership aide" to the press. Foley sat in the cloakroom, in his own reasoned way making Wright's case. He was totally supportive, defended him in the media, did everything he was asked. But this was a personal thing. Wright was on his own. Whenever the rare positive story appeared some member circulated it with a "Dear Colleague." But members had to be asked. "Isn't that something?" one Wright aide said. "Nobody volunteers."

Wright would not ask. Forty years ago, in that one election he had lost by thirty-eight votes, he had learned that everyone wanted to be asked. He had used that knowledge to win the majority leadership post. But he would not ask now. *This was too personal.*

Outside the House, lobbyist J. D. Williams, who had given Wright the idea a dozen years earlier to convert his campaign funds, organized a group of lobbyists to help sustain him, and raise money for his legal costs, which were over $500,000. But that got in the papers and they were asked not to meet again.

One new supporter, thirty-nine-year-old Robert Torricelli, from New Jersey, was one of the new breed of television-savvy sophisticates. He was short, intense; his eyes had a way of sparkling that indicated he had a sense of the absurd. He rarely played internal House politics, instead concentrating on substantive committee work. But after defending Wright with a good legal analysis in a small member briefing in April, Wright had asked him to join the formal legal team. Torricelli had immediately accepted. Only a member can speak on the floor; without being said it was clear that if the charges came to the floor, he would defend Wright.

He believed he was really being asked to help achieve an orderly transition to a new Speaker. He believed that Wright recognized that too.

Time had slowed. Each day seemed interminable. Finally Oldaker and Dixon—not Phelan—talked. Wright needed a hearing. Almost two weeks had passed. Dixon was carefully never going so far that he could not retreat if things changed. He and Oldaker reached an agreement: Wright would waive his rights to all motions, get the evidence against him, and Dixon would schedule a hearing in two weeks. Oldaker wrote Phelan, outlining the tentative discovery agreement and promising not to "discuss" testimony with witnesses. Phelan wrote back—waiting two days—"Your letter indicates only that you . . . will not 'discuss' testimony with witnesses. . . . The Committee requires that, in order to approve early discovery, you and your client agree not to 'contact' those witnesses." Delay, delay, delay. Oldaker prepared a letter waiving rights to motions and gave it to Wright to sign.

But Wright had lost confidence in Oldaker. Clark Clifford, a great dean of the Washington establishment, adviser to every Democratic President and many Republican ones since Truman, had begun advising him, along with his protégé and partner Robert Altman. Before signing the waiver, Wright called Altman, who advised him not to waive anything.

Oldaker was angry. Later that day, he, Altman, and House counsel Steven Ross sat in the ceremonial office and argued in front of Wright. Altman and Ross insisted that the motions were important, and he shouldn't have to waive anything to get what the rules entitled him to anyway. Oldaker retorted that it didn't matter what the rules said. The committee wasn't going to give him the testimony without the waiver.

The motions were worthless anyway. The committee had already voted. They weren't going to reverse themselves. While lawyers argued legal points, the press would be destroying Wright. They needed to end this thing as quickly as possible.

Wright listened. All his life decisive, now he vacillated. There was doubt in him. With some amazement he was watching events unfold, watching himself be buffeted about. He had always believed he could control things. *He creates himself when he acts,* Gingrich had observed. Action defined his control. Two years earlier he had risked his speakership in a moment, against unanimous advice, when he joined with Reagan on a peace plan. He had, in a moment, decided to create a second legislative day. He took another step toward becoming an object. He was afraid to act, afraid to make a mistake. A paralysis had seized him. There still was no concentrated review of Phelan's report. He had already interviewed several litigators but had not made a decision. He needed to move forward. Instead, he hesitated to close off any possibilities, any chances. Waiving the motions closed off a possibility. He told Oldaker to prepare the motions Altman suggested.

That weekend Wright said, "A pimp has more due process than I do."

Wright was walking through the Rayburn Building to a meeting. Gingrich was ahead of him in the corridor. They could not avoid each other. As they walked past, Wright, his smile fixed on his face, said, "Hey, Newt."

Gingrich did not reply. He just looked disdainfully at Wright.

A Harris poll concluded that a solid majority of Americans believed Wright should remain as Speaker unless found guilty. That was very good news.

Yet the distance between him and the Caucus grew greater daily. There was a nervous shrinking back. "Who's defending Wright?" said one friend. "Outside of the Texans, nobody. The closest is when you walk through the Speaker's Lobby—you can't even walk through, it's like a pack of wolves—reporters ask, 'What are you gonna do? What are you gonna do?' 'Can I see the evidence first?' you say. That's the closest to a defense."

Jim Wright's grip on the House had let go. There was no longer the digging in, no longer the tight willful focus with which he had held all the forces of the House together.

When he walked onto the floor, into the cloakroom, members stiffened. There was an awkwardness. They could not talk about his difficulties with him. But what else could they talk about with him? A smile. A broken sentence of conversation. Even these politicians, so skilled at charming even one another although the charmed could see through the charmer, so skilled at saying nothing, they could do nothing but smile and cough. Even those who wished him well, even they . . . what could they say? They were waiting for him to go away. He was no use to them anymore.

The *Post*'s Kenworthy wrote a story which began with an unattributed quote from a member that Wright was like a cancer victim going through the stages of denial, rage, and acceptance, that he was near the end of the rage period.

At breakfast, the waiter started to leave before Wright finished his order. "Goddammit! Come back here!" he snapped. Almost in the same breath he apologized, then turned to his staff. "I've said I want Phelan's report rebutted. It has not been done. Now I say, do it!"

"Yes, sir, but Mack and Oldaker don't think it's a good idea."

"Goddammit!" He slammed his fist on the table. "This is my life! If they don't want to do it, then they come to me and tell me why not. They're worried about attacking the committee and meanwhile the public thinks I'm a sleazy son of a bitch. I can't expect my colleagues to go out and explain everything."

He had never been like this. Not in the middle of the Nicaragua business. Then a calm had held him, an inner certainty. Now everything was uncertainty. He left breakfast and headed for his office. Everything was out of focus. *I feel like a zombie,* he thought. He could not focus. *I can't think too deeply or it will overpower me.*

The staff still did not make the report a priority.

A few days later in a speech, he quoted John Adams, saying that the nation was "a government of laws and not of men," and cited the constitutional protection against ex post facto laws.

It was a plaintive cry.

But the principle he had cited about governing through law, not men, was true. If Wright had broken no rules, it should not matter how close to the edge he went, or how often he went there.

Or should it? The ethics committee was a jury, and a politicized one at that. It was no court. Only five of the twelve were even lawyers. *The ethics committee's first charge was to protect the institution.* Within the rules or not, Wright had used the book as a vehicle to profit from his office. *Wright had already said he owed his colleagues a standard of conduct of which they could be proud, that if he could not be a respectable and effective Speaker, he would no longer be Speaker. Still, there was nothing to the other charges at all. Was the book really so bad?* He had exploited a loophole.

On May 4, *The Washington Post* ran a four-thousand-word story on John Mack's assault sixteen years earlier on Pamela Small; he had hit her with a hammer, exposing her skull, had slashed her throat with a knife. It had been a horrible, heinous act. He had never contacted her to apologize.

Still, the sheriff who had handled Mack's case had said that Wright should be commended, that Mack was special. The *Post* mentioned none of that. It had learned of the story two and a half years earlier, when anonymous letters had gone out to many Hill reporters. Leonard Downie, the managing editor, had declined to pursue it. Two years earlier *The Fort Worth Star-Telegram* had run a long piece, interviewing the victim and recounting the crime although focusing on Mack's rehabilitation. Mack had then offered to resign. Wright had refused it. His office had waited nervously to see how other publications reacted. The Associated Press and *Washington Times* had run small items. *Post* reporters told Wright's aides they would do nothing. The story died. Mack had stayed.

Now Downie decided to run the story. Small had worked at the *Post* and a close friend wrote the story, a fact the *Post* did not reveal. An editor justified the timing by saying the victim had never before allowed her name to be used, but *Post* reporter Paul Taylor later told the *Columbia Journalism Review,* "Vengeance was clear in the story. . . . The *Post* was the willing vehicle for [Pamela Small] to exercise her vengeance."

Although many House members and staff had already known that Mack had a criminal record, few knew the details. Women in the House were shaken and outraged.

Dozens of newspapers picked up the *Post* story off the wire. The networks broadcast it. For the first time, the public was aroused about

Wright. *Mack, the convicted felon, could not vote. But he was getting almost $90,000 in taxpayers' money.*

Mack had been hired at $9,000 a year. He was a teenager when he committed the crime. Wright had given him a second chance. That did not matter. *This was news. This was a hot story.*

The day after the story on Mack, *The New York Times* broke a story on Wright's investment in Jewell Enterprises, a nursing home company. An old friend had invited him into the deal and promised the chance for a large profit: the company was planning to go public. Company executives were eager to have him invest. His name helped attract others. To buy his shares, Wright borrowed $100,000 from a bank close to Jewell's owners.

But soon Wright became displeased. Because of Jewell's accounting practices, he had to pay taxes on $26,000 he never received. He told a company executive that he was getting out. To pacify him and several other angry investors, the executive paid them enough to cover their taxes, and made some interest payments for Wright. But not all investors were paid, and the company was going bankrupt and should not have paid anything. In the end, Wright lost his entire $100,000 and repaid most of what the executive gave him. But he had never reported the payments.

Stories accused him of getting favorable treatment and violating disclosure rules. His retort: he lost $100,000, more than half his net worth. What kind of favor was that? What was there to report?

What he cared about was legislation. The bill raising the minimum wage was in conference. Bush had vowed to veto it. Wright had argued with senators over the issue and even won. *He had plunged himself into it, into any respite.* What good did it do? The press cared nothing of substance anymore. He was the story. An aide reported to Wright a discussion among Democrats of how best to turn the issue to political advantage. Wright snapped, "These people who want to be clever are losing sight of the poor bastards out there trying to live on that wage. Our goal is the maximum amount we can get, the soonest we can get it to them."

The Mack story did not go away. It resonated in the House and the country. One member said, "My wife's asking me how I can support someone who's got John as his top staff person."

The air went out of the Texans who had been defending Wright. Charlie Wilson, always voluble, stood in the Speaker's Lobby giving monosyllabic answers to reporters' questions.

Wright sighed. "My friends tell me they're now hearing questions about me when they go home." Wright had wanted to clear his name, and then probably leave. He understood politics. Now sometimes all he wanted was a way out.

That same first week in May the ethics committee held three days of closed hearings into the Sabine Lake oil deal. At the end, Dixon said, "I'm convinced there was value there"—that Mallightco had sold its interest at a fair price, that the deal was an honest one.

Oldaker still trusted Dixon; "Julian was afraid of a neutron bomb on Sabine Lake and didn't want to proceed until that was resolved. Now that they know nothing's there I think things will move quickly."

Yet Dixon continued to indicate to reporters that the committee might still charge Wright with violations over Sabine Lake. What was he after? Dixon could convene a disciplinary hearing simply by banging his gavel. But it would expose Phelan and the committee's weaknesses, and rip the House apart. *The first charge of the ethics chairman was to protect the institution.* There was no movement toward a hearing. Perhaps Dixon did not want one.

Three weeks had passed since the committee brought its charges. An infinity of hours, an infinity of stories. Finally—finally—Wright chose a trial attorney, Stephen Susman of Houston, rated one of the ten best trial lawyers in the nation by *National Law Journal.*

Sunday night, May 7, Susman and Oldaker met with Wright in his office. This night Wright was enthusiastic. He was desperate enough to hope. Susman was enthusiastic too. Oldaker warned, "There's an Achilles' heel, Jewell. Normally we could explain it and it would go away, but in this atmosphere it will cause a firestorm."

Wright grew angry at the negative thought.

Immediately Susman began to play the press. One of the highest-paid attorneys in the country, he said he had planned to work pro bono, but decided to charge Wright what the committee was paying Phelan: "If Jim Wright can give thirty-five years to his country. I can give thirty-five days."

It wouldn't be that long.

* * *

On Tuesday, May 9, Wright called a morning staff meeting. Everyone came. It was the first formal staff meeting he had called in his entire speakership. As he spoke he grew angrier and angrier.

"If we don't turn the course this week, it is my judgment that they will have destroyed us," he said.

He had one priority: discrediting Phelan's report. And he wanted it their priority: "I wished this done three weeks ago. If we do not get this done by the end of the week, I think I'm through."

Finally, his entire staff began poring over the report, comparing it to the little testimony they did have. Yet Wright was suddenly a distant figure. Susman was in charge now. A day later, senior aides went to him and asked him to pull them off researching Phelan's report. He did. He needed them to call all the buyers of bulk books who had not testified. Phelan's staff had started doing that, and Susman wanted no more surprises.

The next day Susman ran through a dozen ideas with Oldaker and the staff. *Did you do this?* Susman would ask. *No,* Oldaker would reply. *Did you do this?* Susman would ask. *The Speaker didn't want that done,* Oldaker would reply. *Did you do this?* Susman would ask. *No,* Oldaker would reply. With each answer Susman's tone hardened.

That day, Wright and the attorneys attacked Phelan. They had to separate the committee from him, give the committee a reason to reverse itself. At a press conference, Torricelli scorned Phelan's legal "scholarship." Oldaker attacked Phelan's distortions. Susman, asked what Phelan's motive was, replied, "Lawyers like to win."

Wright himself was supposed to say nothing. He could not keep silent. Reporters found him in a corridor and he said of one specific charge, "That is just not right, that is inaccurate, that is a lie. . . . [Committee members] were rendered totally dependent on Phelan."

But Wright and his attorneys offered too little evidence of their charge. It was just name-calling. The press immediately sought responses from the committee.

Dixon declared, "I think [the attacks on Phelan] are totally inaccurate, totally wrong, and an exercise in bad judgment by his attorneys."

Committee members grew angry. Fazio had read the affidavits about Betty Wright's work and later said, "Between them and the higher standard of proof we would have reversed ourselves on that."

Even so, he flared at one Wright aide. "If you think Phelan wound us around his finger, why did we drop so many charges?" And the media was filled with unattributed quotes from members saying the attack on Phelan was a mistake. He was sacrosanct. The committee was sacrosanct. Media commentators were unanimous: the attack on Phelan was disastrous.

The afternoon of the attack on Phelan, Mack went to Wright. Wright's office was disordered. His desk had never been clean. Now mounds of papers covered it. He could not focus, could clear nothing from his desk. But he focused now on Mack. Both knew what Mack was about to do.

"I want to thank you for giving me a chance, Mr. Speaker. I'm so grateful to you. I owe you everything."

Coelho came in. He was Mack's friend, real friend, the one member who had publicly defended him. The Republican campaign committee had already gone after him in his district for it. He sat tensely, as if himself exhausted with nervous tension.

Mack continued, telling Wright he had to resign for his family and both their sakes. They had done everything together for ten years. Everything.

Wright quietly thanked him—everything they had shared, everything—credited him, told him, "What you did you did yourself."

Mack hesitated, then said, "I love you, Mr. Speaker."

The next morning at breakfast, Wright asked the status of the supplemental appropriation. It was the kind of question Mack answered. There was no Mack. The table fell silent. It was Thursday, the day of the regular whip meeting. Mack did not attend. It was empty without him, his seat behind Jim Wright, facing the rows of members. Empty.

Later, in Wright's office, Mark Johnson asked if he was considering all his options. It was May 11.

"Yes," he said softly. All his options. They both knew what that meant. His voice was very soft. "Yes."

Wright thought often of the institution now. In a way it was all he thought about. About how it had changed. Whether he was the cause. He was not the only one who thought about the institution.

Michel's aide Billy Pitts heard Mack was leaving. Pitts had worked in the House almost twenty years. His father had had his job before him. He sat in a chair Rayburn had used, had had his wedding ceremony performed by the House chaplain in the House. Pitts told a Democrat, "This place sucks."

Long, long ago, in the heat the way Texas gets hot, Wright had started in politics, giving those speeches for Colonel Ernest Thompson, who was running for governor. He had been only fifteen then, standing up before the crowds, feeling the sweat on his chest and arms and back and face, fire in him, feeling the surge of approval back from the crowds. *It's heady wine. You never get used to it.*

He liked the heat. He liked getting into a car that had been in the summer sun with the windows rolled up, liked leaning back against the burning seat, liked letting the heat pour into him, envelop him, relax him, force his muscles to let go. It was sensual. His voice was sensual, expressive. There had always been something in him that he had wanted to express, to let the world see. He painted. He wrote. He made oral history tapes. He kept a journal. He wanted to show the world himself and have it applaud.

What had driven him all these years? A haunting search for friendship? *Is it an insatiable thirst for approval that drives me?* he once asked himself. Always he had been the new boy in a small town, making himself agreeable and smiling, putting on his mask, retaining his dignity with his temper and boxing. He was instead isolated, shunned. Ambition? He came from that family where even his sisters had been taught to compete, to shoulder aside a place for themselves in the world of men—how remarkable that was in small-town Texas in the 1930s. His ambition lay shattered. His vision of America? That vision was a complex, personal mixture of bitter Texas populism, basic Christianity, and Main Street boosterism. He had no power to bring it about.

Everything in him had burned at a high heat, under those layers of self-control. His power had come from his heat. There are different kinds of power—for example, the power that comes from enduring, a power which was not his. His power had come from action. He had created possibilities by acting. He had controlled by acting. His actions had forced others to react to him. Action defined his control. Action pierced to the center of things; while others maneuvered around the edges of an issue he had gone to the center. *Were you for peace or not? Let's stop playing games. Let's find out, then go from there.* Two years earlier he had risked his speakership in a moment, against unanimous advice, in joining with Reagan on a peace plan. He had, in a moment, decided to create a second legislative day. Two years earlier his willful, relentless focus had bent the Congress to his will. He had manipulated every detail to advance his agenda. He had a wildness but it was almost never reckless. He had understood what he was risking; he had had courage.

He had seen possibilities. It was what could be so unnerving about him. To some extent, it was that element of him that made others uneasy, and allowed the ethics committee members to convince themselves that Phelan was right. Phelan's portrait of him—manipulative, acquisitive, ruthless—did not ring so untrue.

All politicians have some of those attributes in their nature. But most are charmers; they treat whoever is with them at the moment as if he or she is the only person in the world. With Wright, those to whom he was speaking often had the sense they were fitting into a puzzle he was solving. *It was like chess and Ping-Pong,* he had said. *I have goals and pursue them, sometimes in ways so arcane I don't understand them myself.* He could look at someone and seem to see through him and on both sides and into the past and future. The papers reported that no one had told him he had no chance to survive. They speculated that Clark Clifford may finally have made that point to him. But he had known from the time Barney Frank had called for the release of Phelan's report. He had as much as told the whips that while the committee was voting. There were still moments when he believed he could survive, when he talked of remaining Speaker for years, but he knew it was not possible. First he had wanted exoneration, and then he would leave. That's what he had been fighting for. More and more he wanted not even that.

At all those moments when he had acted and defined the world he had been alone. He was alone now.

But he no longer acted.

This was too personal, too painful, to do anything except withdraw. *I feel like a zombie. I can't think too deeply or it will overpower me.* So now there was a vacuum. His lawyers and advisers and staff flowed into that vacuum, replacing his intense focus with a diffuse indirection. For he was apart. Perhaps their strategy was better than his, but he never followed it. And he never required them to follow his.

A friend asked him how he was. *How was he really, in his heart?*

"Pagliaccio," he replied. "The clown. Walking around in a clown suit. A smile on my face. Entertaining the world. Crying inside."

He had been pure action. That was the essence of his power. All that was left of his power was his mask.

He withdrew more than ever into his office. The lawyers would take hours of his time, especially Altman. Yet they never seemed to accomplish anything. He would spend time with Johnson, reviewing some quickly dated media strategy. Coelho would come in. Often he would be alone. He would try to write a defense of himself, and stop after one paragraph. He would try to focus on policy—meetings on appropriations, on Social Security, where everyone paid him formal deference as if nothing were wrong—and shift from topic to topic. He would review a draft of a speech an aide had written, make notes on the first page, and then put it aside. He would talk on the phone to his family.

By now Rostenkowski was visiting Wright in his office often. Just two years before, Wright had threatened his chairmanship. That had taken guts. Rostenkowski wouldn't have done that if the roles had been reversed. Rostenkowski knew there weren't many around like Wright. He respected him, went on tirades against the committee and Phelan. The day Mack left he collected signatures from twenty-six chairmen demanding that their colleagues not prejudge Wright. They had warred, but had also warred side by side. They would talk for thirty minutes, sometimes an hour, talking about the institution. Rostenkowski had served two years under Rayburn. They talked of him some. Wright smiled and laughed, remembering. He thought of Rayburn a lot now, and of Rayburn's House. They talked about their old colleagues, whatever happened to them, about what the House used to be and what it had become. This new breed, they didn't have much meat to them. They didn't have the kind of arms you could grab and sink fingers into muscle and feel the muscle tense. There weren't many you wanted to have beside you in a war anymore. And Rostenkowski told Wright, "If you leave, Jim, don't be surprised if I retire." His voice cracked for an instant, and his eyes watered. "Don't be surprised if I don't run again."

Brooks visited Wright too. An older rival than Rostenkowski. He was always chewing on some raggedy cigar. Brooks knew Rayburn, all right. That was part of why they had been rivals. Wright loved the institution he had first served in. He still loved it, but it had changed so. There would be only three warriors left soon, Brooks, Dingell, and Rostenkowski.

His legal team formally argued a series of motions before the committee. Phelan was ordered to turn over certain documents and any exculpatory material. Committee rules required exculpatory material to be handed over as soon as it is discovered. Of the thousands of pages Phelan had gathered, he gave Oldaker two pages of exculpatory evidence. He was laughing at Oldaker. He had the votes. And the committee scheduled a hearing on a motion to dismiss the major charges. But tension had surfaced between Wright's attorneys. Altman annoyed those close to Wright with his constant references to "Mr. Clifford," while addressing Wright as "Jim," never "Mr. Speaker." Susman called Wright "Jim" too. He seemed to have contempt for Oldaker, but never himself mastered the details of the case, and never asked Oldaker for a complete briefing on what he had done. And Susman and his assistant Neil Manne had their own media adviser. Ironically, Susman and Oldaker agreed on only one thing: that the motion was a waste of time. They had to proceed with it because they had said they would. At one point, when Wright quoted Altman, Susman replied, "Let me tell you something. Altman's a zero."

On May 13, Coelho answered all the questions raised a month earlier in the story about his $100,000 junk bond purchase. He had committed to buy the bonds on April 10, 1986, but did not then have the money. Thomas Spiegel purchased the bonds in his own name. Spiegel was the highest paid savings and loan executive in the country and a friend of Drexel Burnham's Michael Milken, also a friend of Coelho's. Several weeks later, the bonds were transferred to Coelho's name. He paid the original purchase price, although the bonds had appreciated roughly $4,000. That raised the issue of a gift from someone with a direct interest in legislation.

In addition, Coelho had borrowed $50,000 of the purchase price from Spiegel's S&L, but had not disclosed the loan. His accountant took responsibility for all the errors. And Coelho was now disclosing every detail of the transaction himself. Still, in this climate it could be serious. When he found out the loan had been unreported, he told a friend, "I'm resigning, right now."

His friend had dissuaded him for the moment. But Coelho had seen the press play Mack. He was watching Wright.

Rumors spread among Hill insiders that Babcock was researching more stories about him. Members began to speculate that when Wright left the speakership—by now it was not a question of "if"—Coelho might not run for majority leader.

Republicans were jubilant. They had another target.

The daily press conferences were canceled. The corridor outside Wright's office, which had always been open, became closed to the press. To avoid the reporters packing the Speaker's Lobby, he began going into and out of the chamber through the cloakroom door, opposite the Rayburn Room. Other members did too. So reporters began to stake out different spots in the Capitol. They tracked Wright through the halls. Wherever he was scheduled to be, a gaggle of reporters gathered. Not people who knew him, knew anything of the House, but people with microphones shouting questions that they did not want answered. He was exposed. More so than any person in the Executive Branch, much less a President. There was no insulation, no protective layer anymore. A camera crew in the plaza trained a telephoto lens on his office window. Reporters, and cameras, were planted outside his home. When he awoke in the morning and looked out he saw them, with their folding canvas chairs, watching him, their telephoto lenses trained on him, boom microphones swinging toward him. When he and Betty went out to dinner, a man on a motorcycle with a walkie-talkie kept pace, directing the vans with cameras. Once Wright stopped his car, went over to him, and said, "We're going to the restaurant on the next block. Now how about just staying back here and giving us some peace for a moment." He had become hunted, a hunted object. It was the media's deathwatch.

On May 16, Wright, Oldaker, Torricelli, and Johnson met and discussed reality. Even if they forced the committee to reverse itself on the gift and direct-interest charges, it would not back down on the book. And it would probably recommend a reprimand. That meant a floor vote. Wright and Torricelli discussed the chances of overriding a recommendation to reprimand. Torricelli told him frankly that he doubted they could do it.

It was a somber statement. No one had said anything like that to Wright before, but he seemed to share the opinion himself. Softly he said, "Why don't you find out what the committee's thinking?"

Later that day Torricelli, Fazio, and Dixon met in Dixon's office. They talked for an hour and a half.

Fazio had hardened against Wright since the initial votes. The whole committee had. Whether rules had been violated or not, he blamed Wright's judgment for having brought them all to this. There was no forgiveness in him. But neither was there vindictiveness.

They thought the committee would likely drop the gift charges relating to Betty's job, as well as the direct-interest charge. Torricelli told them the Speaker was certain of his case there. The committee would not back down on the books, but perhaps a decision on the books could be postponed. History would record no legal judgment. Wright would retain all the amenities of a former Speaker, and depart in an orderly manner. And he would resign.

Later Dixon called Oldaker and said, "Why did you send Torricelli to see me? I don't trust him."

He didn't trust Wright either, and feared if the charges were dismissed Wright would refuse to resign. He brought his colleague Louis Stokes in as a buffer.

A clean sweep. Republicans began to whisper about a clean sweep.

If Republicans targeted Coelho as they had Wright, and the press complied, they might destroy him. And suddenly there were rumors about Foley. A year earlier, *Newsweek* had talked of questionable stock dealings. His stockbroker had made a speculative and successful investment for him, although he had also lost money on similar speculations. But a month earlier *Newsweek* had talked about "wispy skeletons" which might be "in his closet."

That rumor had come most likely from a February police raid of a homosexual prostitution ring which had serviced several politicians. (Reagan and Bush administration officials were involved, but neither Foley nor any other Democrat.) A senior House Democratic aide—he did not work for Wright but was loyal to him—began to spread a rumor that Foley might be implicated, hoping to buy time for Wright. Gingrich's aide Karen Van Brocklin began to call reporters and push the story on them.

*   *   *

There was no organized movement in the Caucus to oust Wright. Members feared vengeance from Texans, from Rostenkowski, from Dingell. On the floor, Tim Penny sat next to a man close to Wright and said, "My mind's open on his guilt or innocence, but he's got to go as Speaker." The man replied, "Tim, you're entitled to your opinion. No one will hold that against you. But if you're seen as trying to bring about his leaving, there are people who will cut your balls off the rest of your time in the House."

But on May 18, Philip Sharp, an Indiana Democrat, said, "It's time for a leadership change."

He was the first. It resonated through the House. How long would it be before others said the same thing? How long before other Democratic members joined in?

At ten-thirty that morning, the eighteenth, Wright and his legal team met to discuss the motion they would argue the following Tuesday, and decide whether to ask the committee to televise it. Earlier, all advice had been to stay away from television if at all possible. Now, convinced that their only chance was to show the public that the facts were on their side, they decided TV would benefit. Committee rules prohibited television out of courtesy to the respondent, but they were sure that if they asked, the committee would agree. Just then they got the news: the committee had decided to televise the proceedings. It was one more indignity, one more indication that the committee had its own agenda. Then Susman said, "What do you really want, Jim?"

Wright pressed his lips together for an instant, his voice carefully controlled. "I want to preserve my reputation, as much as that is possible. I want to leave with some degree of dignity. I want to keep my pension. I want to preserve the amenities of a former Speaker. I would resign if they'd drop direct interest."

Torricelli said, "There's a very narrow opening to work something out."

The stories had never stopped. Now they escalated. On Friday, May 19, the *Los Angeles Times* reported that the IRS was starting a criminal investigation of Wright. Oldaker talked to a senior IRS official, who told him, "You'll be happy to hear this. I checked. The story's wrong. There is no investigation, civil or criminal."

Oldaker quoted the denial. It made no difference. That weekend commentators agreed that the IRS story had finally killed Wright. There was no charity in them. A columnist wrote that soon, like the Cheshire cat in *Alice's Adventures in Wonderland,* he would fade away to nothingness, leaving only the grin behind. On *Inside Washington, Post* reporter Juan Williams snorted, "He's just looking out for himself, for his own behind."

On *The McLaughlin Group,* the host asked when Wright would resign. The group responded: "Wednesday!" "Thursday!" "Tuesday!"

On both shows the journalists still talked about "sixty-nine violations."

The conversation between Torricelli and the committee continued. That weekend Wright talked to his son, James Claude Wright III, in New Mexico and told him, "I just wish I could get out."

On Tuesday morning, May 23, Wright was almost trembling, smiling weakly. Yet he wanted to appear himself before the committee. It had never heard him on these charges. The public had never heard him. As he began to weave words together to form his own defense, the rhythms of his voice reached out and for an instant it seemed possible that *Yes. Yes. You can win.*

But Susman and Wright's aides dissuaded him from appearing. The committee could be offended. He might open himself to cross-examination. The committee might even refuse to allow him to speak. Susman suggested that Betty appear. Wright called her, then sent his driver to pick her up. Susman and the other attorneys left for the arguments. Wright turned on the television.

For the purposes of the motion, Wright's attorneys agreed to Phelan's facts; they claimed that even if those facts were correct, they failed to justify the charges. The committee convened in a committee room in the Rayburn Building. Row after row of seats were packed with several hundred reporters. Susman began. Within his first few moments one of the supervisors of the House press gallery leaned forward and whispered to a reporter, "This guy's *good.*"

At the noon break, Susman was surrounded by reporters. He had become the star and stood broad-shouldered, good-looking, with big hands, his shirt soaked with sweat, looking almost like a boxer between rounds.

But in the afternoon, after more argument, the committee members began to ask questions. The members seemed, even most Democrats, protective of Phelan. And the Republicans bored in on Susman, hostile. He did not know several answers but would not defer to Oldaker. By late in the afternoon, Susman sat frustrated, slumped backward, his legs outstretched, his arms crossed, angry. And then it was over.

Still, Phelan had convinced few reporters on the key charge of Mallick's direct interest. "Pretty tortured reasoning," said William Eaton of the *Los Angeles Times*.

"I had reserved judgment until this," said Richard Cohen of the *National Journal*. "Phelan doesn't have much of a case."

Kenworthy of *The Washington Post* said, "I couldn't see direct interest before. I see it less now."

"Phelan showed his vulnerability," *The Wall Street Journal*'s Rogers said.

But the reporters had been taken aback at the vehemence of the committee, their hostility toward Susman. David Holmes, who ran the House Periodical Press Gallery, turned to one of his gallery's reporters and shook his head almost in disbelief. "I was shocked. You wonder what they were listening to. I've heard the phrase 'hanging judge' for a long time. Now I've seen it."

Wright, Betty, and his attorneys watched the news. The networks quoted Phelan saying, "He accepted $145,000 in gifts!" "That's a lie!" Wright stormed. "That's a lie!"

The others in the room said nothing. Then they counted votes, based on the questioning. No Republican would be with him. Atkins would not switch. Dwyer seemed more amenable to change, but not enough to count on. No one in the room believed that if they proceeded to trial Wright would get a fair hearing. Torricelli called Stokes and asked him to talk to Dixon and see where the votes were.

Could they trust Dixon, though? Oldaker had had a more than professional relationship, a real relationship, with him, had relied on him, trusted him. But no longer. "You don't know where he is. You can't count him anywhere."

"Julian was against me from the start," Wright said. No one disagreed.

The next morning at nine o'clock the group gathered again. The lawyers. Clark Clifford. Altman. Torricelli. Oldaker. Susman. His assistant Neil Manne. Mark Johnson. They argued whether to talk to the committee. Clifford thought no: "Tell them to do what they have to do."

"Take it to the mat," Susman agreed. "It's not time to get out of Dodge yet."

But Torricelli, Oldaker, and Johnson thought the possibilities had to be explored. Wright had already in his own mind decided to resign. If he could do it cleanly, go out with his head high, he would spare himself . . . well . . . everything.

Finally Wright said, "Listen to what they have to say."

Torricelli started down toward the ethics committee meeting room, but it was ringed by reporters. He sent a note in to Phelan, who met him on the steps of the Capitol's west front, deserted, empty of tourists, looking down on the mall. It was bright, sunny, with a hint of a breeze.

"You don't have the votes," Phelan said bluntly. "Yesterday didn't help."

"The Speaker's willing to resign."

Phelan offered to drop the charge of Mallick's direct interest prior to 1986, covering the period of Betty's employment, and not rule on anything else. In return, Wright would announce his resignation the next day, effective the following day, and appoint a Speaker pro tem.

"That's not acceptable," Torricelli snapped. "That will be rejected out of hand. But I'll take it to him."

Torricelli repeated the offer to Wright. Wright exploded. *No outsider would dictate to the Speaker of the House when and how he would leave.* He intended to preside over the election of a successor and leave in orderly fashion, with dignity. There was a constitutional issue as well. The Speaker was a constitutional officer. If he resigned, any appointment of a Speaker pro tem also lapsed, leaving no constitutional head of the Legislative Branch. Wright could not leave the Congress in that disarray.

Clifford, Altman, and Susman started to argue again over whether he should even be talking to the committee. An intern entered and said Phelan was calling. Wright jerked erect. "That son of a bitch!"

Torricelli went outside, picked up the phone, and agreed to meet at two-thirty. The ethics committee broke for lunch.

The staff had finished, finally, preparing a seventy-two-page document detailing "errors, distortions, and fallacies" in Phelan's report. It cited dozens and was still incomplete. They had never gotten access to the evidence against Wright, promised by Dixon even before the statement of alleged violations was issued, and so could not check Phelan against most of the witnesses.

"If we had gotten this together earlier," said Phil Duncan disgustedly, "maybe it would have done some good."

Even now it was not distributed to the press.

At two-thirty Torricelli and Phelan sat down. Phelan made it plain he controlled the committee. Staff, not the chairman, controlled the votes. He patted his pocket and announced, "I've got Atkins's proxy right here."

Phelan's second offer was better: the committee would drop the direct-interest charge today. Wright would announce tomorrow his resignation, effective the following Wednesday or Thursday.

Phelan also made a threat. If Wright refused, the committee would deny the entire motion and open an investigation into Jewell and Sabine Lake. That meant a long delay, possibly months. Wright would be even more isolated, even more hunted. Sharp had already called for his resignation. Others would follow. Republicans might force a floor vote declaring the speakership vacant. It would be a final humiliation.

Torricelli reported Phelan's proposal. Wright refused. He would announce his resignation on the floor of the House, the House he had served in for almost thirty-five years. The House he had led. He would not be bullied into this by anyone, much less by Phelan.

The demand for an almost immediate announcement made no sense. But the problem was trust. Dixon feared that if charges were dropped, Wright might try to remain Speaker. Fazio approached Torricelli on the floor and told him to have Foley meet with Wright, then with Dixon to reassure him. Torricelli returned to Wright's office. It was filled with lawyers. There were too many lawyers. This was House business now, not legal business. He suggested getting Foley and Coelho in.

At three-thirty in the afternoon, the leadership met for the last time. The Speaker, the majority leader, the whip. For a moment Wright thought of the 100th Congress, of all they had accomplished. The room was full. Lawyers and the leadership and a few close aides. The painting of that Texas church under the brooding sky was behind Wright now: others, not he, looked at it.

The leadership had one final piece of business to conduct. Foley and

Coelho were somber, formal, but reassured him. "Whatever you decide, we'll support you, Mr. Speaker."

Both believed the right thing was for him to resign and spoke for it in their own ways. But they were outraged at the idea that Phelan was dictating it to him. He should do it with dignity. He was right to want the House in session. It would recess in a few hours for Memorial Day. They discussed whether to bring it back early and decided that wasn't necessary.

Altman interjected, "Mr. Clifford believes strongly that Jim should fight."

He began to argue all over again. Each time Altman said "Mr. Clifford" and "Jim" the members and Wright's staff stiffened. Coelho shook his head. Staying could hurt Wright badly. If Democrats followed Sharp's lead and called for him to resign it would humiliate him. Altman protested. Suddenly Coelho began to shout at him, shout that there were too many lawyers, that they knew nothing of the House. The room was tense.

Wright decided. *He was not plea-bargaining, dammit. He was not negotiating away the speakership. That damn well had to be clear.* But if this thing could be worked out with dignity, it should be done.

Foley went downstairs to his office. Dixon joined him, and Foley explained what the Speaker was thinking. The language was coded. *This is what the Speaker would probably do if this happened.* But it wasn't a "deal."

It was late and getting later. Dixon called his committee together and briefed them. Myers didn't like it but Republican James Hansen said, "That sounds reasonable."

But these discussions were going on and on. Atkins seemed to be balking too. It had gotten complicated. Too many messengers. Too many buffers. It was late in the afternoon. They recessed, then reconvened.

"There's nothing solid," Dixon said. "We can't get a definitive statement on what the Speaker will or won't do. The Speaker wants to be able to say he's not negotiating a deal. So do we. As far as I'm concerned, we're going on recess for Memorial Day."

But the press said Wright was negotiating a deal, leaving it to Myers to say, "I don't think it behooves a member of Congress or is appropriate for a member of the committee on ethics to make deals."

*   *   *

Texan Michael Andrews told the press, "The Speaker's support is deteriorating with every passing day." Wright had gotten Andrews on Ways and Means over Rostenkowski's objection. His quote was a short step from calling for his departure. Stenholm, who had supported Wright until now, said, "Some rules, if not broken, were bent severely. It's coating all of us." Michel was fiercer, calling his affairs "a blot on the institution."

Resign. Resign now. For the good of the party. For the good of the House. Why haven't you resigned already? End this for all of us.

A *Washington Post*/ABC poll revealed that the public by 60 percent to 33 percent believed Wright should not resign.

That night on ABC's *Nightline,* Susman's assistant Neil Manne said there was no deal, that Torricelli had been free-lancing. Furious, Torricelli called Mark Johnson at midnight and demanded that he call Ted Koppel immediately and set him straight. The next day Torricelli exploded at Susman. It was another culture clash. An attorney had to be willing to sacrifice himself for his client, perhaps even lie for him. Susman exploded back: "You're a congressman but you're also a lawyer. If there's something you can say to protect your client, you say it. So what if what you tell them isn't exactly right."

The next day Wright was rocked and bitter. "I should have listened to Clark Clifford," he said. "I should not have sent Torricelli over there at all."

It was Memorial Day weekend. The House would not reconvene until Wednesday, May 31. He and his wife needed to escape. They were going to the mountain retreat of a friend, Bob McCandless, in the Shenandoah Valley. To escape the press they had to drive into Washington, in the opposite direction from their destination, into the Rayburn garage where the press could not follow, walk through the labyrinthine corridors, switch cars, and exit from a distant place. Reporters besieged Mark Johnson, demanding to know where he had gone.

But finally Wright had peace. He talked to his son and a daughter and sister all gathered in New Mexico. His son, James III, wanted him to fight. Even his sister Mary, who as long ago as November had wanted him to give it up, just walk away, now said fight. His daughter Ginger said if he did she would quit her job and help him. Friends in Fort Worth wanted him to fight.

Friday afternoon Coelho called him to inform him that he was going to announce his own resignation from Congress. They did not discuss the decision and Wright was not surprised. He had sensed it earlier, when Coelho had sat in his office when Mack resigned. *John. Now Tony. And, soon, himself. What was this? Were they all such evil people?*

That night Coelho gave his story exclusively to *The New York Times;* only that paper, he believed, had shown any balance in its coverage. Only a few days before, a *Los Angeles Times* headline had inaccurately charged he was the target of a Justice Department Investigation. He knew Babcock was researching more stories on him. Republicans might force an ethics investigation of him. He said, "I will not be the vehicle to do damage to those institutions and the causes I hold dearly. My family is important to me. the cause of epilepsy is my primary concern. . . . June 15, which is my forty-seventh birthday, will be my last day in Congress."

Coelho had often talked of quitting, just as he had talked of challenging Foley for Speaker. It would be the former, not the latter.

Suddenly Coelho became a hero. Selfless. Sacrificing himself for the good of the party. In contrast to Wright, who was prolonging the agony of the House and of the party.

Wright was not much more than commuting distance from Washington but it seemed another world, filled only with the smells of fields, the view into the clean distance. It was warm. In the eighties. In the foreground was a barn, some hay. Behind them he counted range after range of ancient mountains, so ancient that the world had worn them down to little more than hills. He counted within his view five distinct rings of mountains and imagined the five sets of valleys between them. There was not a sign of men in them, not that he could see, except for the barn immediately before him. He thought for a moment that for all one's ambitions, all one could do was change the foreground a little. He had done that already. He felt at peace, his decision made.

On Tuesday, May 30, he held his usual breakfast with staff but left quickly. He met with lawyers. He met with staff. He had a private lunch with a friend in H-201. At breakfast he had seemed calm, his decision made. Now his movements were jerky, uncertain. His friend had never seen him like this. "The press is a herd," Wright said. "If I could find some way to get in front of the herd and turn it around. . . . But I can't."

For a moment, with an edge to his voice, he talked about all the comments of how "selfless" Coelho had been.

If he demanded a trial, the committee would go after him with new fervor. They would look at his entire life. *Phelan* would look at it. It might take months, months more of this.

After lunch, Charlie Rangel called and told him he had to fight this. Wright said how could he, he had no support.

"How do you know?" Rangel replied. "You got anybody counting? How do you know what support you have? Who should I talk to? Marty Frost? Foley? Who?"

No one. There was no one to talk to. It was too late for that. Rangel had waited to be asked. No one had asked. Wright knew members wanted to be asked. He had learned that in 1948. But he wouldn't ask for this. This was too personal. And it was over now.

The next day he would speak on the House floor. It was what he had wanted for a year and a half. To take the floor and explain himself.

The next morning he added cream to the skim milk for his cereal and wolfed it down. His hand was almost shaking. Abruptly he left. For the first time, perhaps ever, he shouldered his way through the reporters staked outside the door with no comment of any kind. He was alone, spent the day alone.

By mid-afternoon the press gallery was full, crowded, more so than anyone could ever remember. There was, even in this age of non-smokers, stale cigarette smoke in clouds in the room. There was constant paging for reporters over the loudspeaker. Every phone booth was full. The press gallery was full.

All the galleries were packed solid with people waiting. This was history. It was ninety degrees outside, and tourists in shorts who had planned their trips months in advance wandered through the Capitol with guides, impervious to the moment. The rules were waived to allow press photographers to take pictures.

No speaker in the nation's history had been forced from office. But all the forces Jim Wright had unleashed in the 100th Congress, all the forces in himself, had brought him to this point.

The lights of the House were turned up; the networks were televising it live. Claude Pepper, born at the beginning of the century, had recently died, and the House now voted 397–0 to allow his remains to lie in state in the Capitol Rotunda. After the vote not a member left the chamber.

Wright strode to the well of the House, where he had spoken so many hundreds of times. "Mr. Speaker," he said to Foley, Speaker pro tem, who was in the chair, "I ask that I may be heard on a question of personal privilege."

"The distinguished Speaker is recognized for one hour."

"For thirty-four years," Wright began, "I have had the great privilege to be a member of this institution, the people's House, and I shall forever be grateful for that wondrous privilege. . . . And you, my colleagues—Democrats and Republicans—I owe a great deal. You have given me the greatest gift within your power to give. To me the Speaker of the U.S. House of Representatives is the grandest opportunity that can come to any lawmaker in the Western world. . . . I would hope that I have reflected credit upon the people of my district, who know me best, and upon the people of this House who, next to them, know me best."

Democrats applauded, and scattered Republicans. Michel did not. The GOP leadership sat together, occupying one row, Gingrich next to Michel. None of them applauded. Wright reviewed the accomplishments of the 100th Congress, and then said, "I love this institution. I want to assure each of you that under no circumstances, having spent more than half my life here, this House being my home, would I ever knowingly or intentionally do or say anything to violate its rules or detract from its standing. All of us are prone to human error. . . .

"For nearly a year I have ached to tell my side of the story. True, the questions to which I have to respond keep changing. But today silence is no longer tolerable, nor, for the good of the House, is it even desirable.

"So without any rancor or bitterness, without any hard feeling toward anybody, I thank you for indulging me as I answer to you, and the American people, for my honor, my reputation, and all the things I tried to stand for all these years."

Now, finally, with his audience the American people, and not the media, he told his story for an hour. He spoke extemporaneously. He mopped his brow. He wiped the sweat from his face. And he was compelling. He spoke of the charges against him and made his case, inserted into the *Congressional Record* statements of people who affirmed his wife's work, of Obey and Sawyer and others on the technical issues.

There was an intensity in him, a riveting intensity which reached through the television, this man who was such a bad television performer, and seized hold of people. This voice, so gently urgent. And he pleaded for the House.

"When vilification becomes an accepted form of political debate, when negative campaigning becomes a full-time occupation, when members of each party become self-appointed vigilantes carrying out personal vendettas against members of the other party, in God's name, that is not what this institution is about. . . . All of us, in both political parties, must resolve to bring this mindless cannibalism to an end. There has been enough of it.

"I pray to God we will do that and restore the spirit that always existed in the House."

And now he told the story that epitomized the House to him, of decades earlier when Cleve Bailey had protested to Rayburn that his colleague Chet Holifield had not been in the chamber during a close vote, and therefore his vote should not be counted. "Speaker Rayburn grew as red as a tomato and I thought he was going to break the gavel when he hammered and said, 'The Chair always takes the word of a member!' . . . Cleve Bailey came down and abjectly, literally with tears in his eyes, apologized for questioning the word of a fellow member. We need that."

He smiled. *That smile that was so unkind to him and which he could not rid himself of.* He put his hands on his hips.

"Have I made mistakes? Oh, boy. How many!"

But in his pettiest, angriest, and smallest moments, he had not lacked courage. Advisers had told him just before the speech not to mention Mack. They said it would spoil his moment, that people did not understand Mack, that he should talk only of himself in this. *But what did the world know of John? What did the world know of either of them?* He talked of Mack, talked of America giving a person a second chance. He stopped, wiped sweat from his face, cleaned his glasses, smiled. Then he closed.

"If I have offended anybody in the other party, I am sorry. I never meant to. . . . Are there things I would do differently if I had them to do over again? Oh, boy, how many may I name for you?

"Well, I tell you what. I am going to make you a proposition. Let me give you back this job you gave me as a propitiation for all of this season of bad will that has grown up among us. Let me give it back to you. I will resign as Speaker of the House effective upon the election of my successor, and I will ask that we call a Caucus on the Democratic side for next Tuesday to choose a successor.

"I do not want to be a party to tearing this institution up. I love it. . . . Then I will offer to resign from the House sometime before the end of June. Let that be a total payment for the anger and hostility we feel toward each other. . . . God bless this institution. God bless the United States."

The House was absolutely still. Then came the applause. A crowd of colleagues surrounded Wright as he walked up the aisle, off the floor, out of the chamber.

From the press gallery reporters tried to storm down the stairs. The police blocked them. For a moment at least, the hallways outside the House chamber and the Speaker's Lobby belonged to the members.

Back in the corridor outside Wright's office twenty members—there were 259 Democrats in the House—gathered for this man who from the time he was a boy had worked not to be the outsider. Wright was in his office, joking, a weight off him; he opened his arms and said, "Hey, everyone says I don't have friends like Tip did. But I've got 'em. Look here."

He clasped everyone's hand, went down the line with words for each except when there were no words, Wright the only one without tears.

"You were a great teacher," said a California member, tears in his eyes. A dozen years before, he had deserted Phil Burton and voted to elect Wright majority leader.

"Well, thank you." He laughed, an easy graceful laugh. "You were a great pupil."

The phone rang. It was Rostenkowski. Wright sat in his secretary's chair, put his feet up on the desk, and leaned back. Here was a colleague.

"Hey, Danny. . . . Hell. I feel liberated. . . . . Oh, Lord, yes. . . . The institution certainly has. . . . I remember when you came up here, Danny . . ."

That was a long time ago.

As Claude Pepper lay dying, he asked that Jim Wright give the eulogy, then called the Library of Congress to make sure it sent him background material. Pepper, first elected to Congress in 1936, knew what Wright believed in. They believed in the same things. The eulogy was Wright's last act as Speaker. The New Deal was over.

A few days after Pepper's funeral, Tuesday morning, June 6, the Democratic Caucus met. The members filled the House Chamber, packed the Democratic side. Beneath the murmur of conversation was a somberness. Caucus chairman Bill Gray gaveled them to order and recognized "the distinguished Speaker of the House."

Jim Wright rose to a standing ovation and nominated Tom Foley as Speaker in a brief speech. He finished to a standing ovation as well, then sat in the front row next to Jack Brooks and other Texans.

The seconding speeches came, Coelho cheerful and lauding Foley, once his rival; Lee Hamilton, so much like Foley, seconded him, too, followed by others. There were no other nominations. Foley was nominated by acclamation, and Gray called upon "Speaker Foley" to address the Caucus.

Foley was not Speaker yet. He corrected him, paid tribute to Wright, to his 100th Congress, then spoke about himself, about why he was a Democrat, about his sense of public service.

The Caucus ended. Members left the chamber. There was no special cluster of colleagues that formed around Wright; as he walked up the aisle members shook his hand, but that was all. They barely slowed his progress.

It would not be long before the House convened to elect the new Speaker. The galleries opened and people began to fill them, some eager to witness a small moment of history, some just tourists. A few members lingered on the floor. Doing business. Life moved on.

Jack Brooks still sat in the front row, talking with one member. Others sat elsewhere, talking, their feet up, doing business, oblivious to the galleries; this was their House. The seats were large and comfortable, soft enough to sink into, firm enough to give support. The carpet was plush, comfortable under foot. In a week would come the election for majority leader and whip. Bonior was running for whip, and speaking intently to a colleague, he later declared that Wright would "always be my speaker." He lost. Henry Waxman and Bill Gray, two other candidates for whip, spoke in a back row; Waxman would soon drop out and support Gray. After the reconciliation vote, the dividing line in Wright's speakership, Waxman had dismissed the Republican fury, saying, "Most members are interested in the future. That's what I'm interested in."

But the past does not leave this place. If victors look to the future, the defeated remember the past. There is a permanence to the floor. An immortality of place. Twenty years from now on some vote some member will think, *That son of a bitch, I remember what he said about Jim Wright,* and send some ambition spinning. And what future Speaker will not remember Jim Wright, all that he accomplished and all that happened to him?

Life moved on. *The Wall Street Journal* continued its long series of editorials insisting that the real problem was not Wright but the imperial Democratic Congress and the reelection rate of House incumbents. It was Gingrich's theme, his long-term struggle.

Republican National Committee communications director Mark Goodin gave the press a memo entitled "Tom Foley: Out of the Liberal Closet." It compared his voting record to that of Barney Frank, a homosexual. The memo's implied message was clear. It went too far. Republican National Committee chairman Lee Atwater first defended the memo, then accepted the resignation of the aide. Gingrich ordered his staff person Karen Van Brocklin, who had called several reporters to push the story, not to speak to the press.

Gingrich declared that he had "a list" of Democrats to investigate.

But his plans to paint the Democrats as the party of corruption broke apart over a scandal in the Department of Housing and Urban Development. Billions of federal housing dollars had gone improperly to or through favored Republicans; tens of millions had simply been stolen.

Gingrich himself faced an ethics committee investigation of his book arrangement, and of possible violations of campaign spending laws. Workers on his staff had taken unpaid leave to work on his reelection. Upon their return, he had doubled their salaries for a month or two months, then rescinded the raises, which appeared to compensate them for the time spent on his campaign. Phelan's firm, though not Phelan himself, conducted the investigation, and declined to charge Gingrich with any violations. The Ethics Committee concurred.

Of Phelan, attorney friend Fred Bartlit had said, "He wouldn't say anything he couldn't prove. No trial lawyer would say 'she worked a dozen days in four years' when the testimony said 'five to seven days a month.' It's too easily discredited." Bartlit also said, "Dick doesn't have any political ambition."

In the summer of 1989, Phelan tried to raise $4 million to run for governor of Illinois, telling the *Chicago Tribune*, "Media is the whole game." He fell short of his fund-raising goal and ran instead for president of the Cook County Board, saying that he had no ambition for higher office. Later he backed away from the statement. He spent nearly $2 million (including $800,000 of his own money) for the 1990 Democratic primary, mostly on television ads.

Shortly after Wright resigned, ethics chairman Julian Dixon amended his financial disclosure form to reveal that his wife, Betty, had made "over" $150,000 in less than two years on an investment of less than $15,000. The investment was in a business seeking the gift-shop concession at the Los Angeles airport; her being black allowed the company to claim minority ownership, strengthening its chances of getting the concession. Johnnie Cochran, a Dixon friend, chaired the airport commission which oversaw the granting of the concession. Cochran, a lawyer, had been paid $175,000 by the ethics committee to investigate St Germain. Both Dixon and Cochran insisted there was no connection. Dixon and Myers both said they saw no reason to investigate. Dixon's wife also ran a small business; she sold gift items, often in bulk to lobbyists—things lobbyists could give away, for example, at a trade association meeting.

* * *

Thursday, June 29, was Jim Wright's last day in the Congress. He had been asked to address the weekly, members-only prayer breakfast and did. It was the largest turnout they ever had, almost 20 percent of the House. As he finished, the sound of applause rippled outside into the corridor; like some soothing liquid it flowed across the hall, filling the Members' Dining Room and the private place where he and his staff had breakfasted for so many days over so many years, flowing around the corner to the sergeant at arms' office.

There was a whip meeting. He did not go. It was a heated meeting. The new leadership, Speaker Tom Foley, majority leader Richard Gephardt, whip Bill Gray, sat in the front and fended off the membership.

"Where's the direction?" one member demanded. "What the hell are we doing?"

At noon, Wright walked out of his office, the Speaker's office. On the Capitol steps there was a final stakeout of reporters.

Less than fifteen minutes after Wright's departure, workmen began tearing up his office, reconfiguring it for Foley's furniture. Change would come quickly: the corridor outside the office, always open before, would be closed. It would take on a stately feel, like the West Wing of the White House, with a sedate, dark blue rug and Early American furniture. The same sedate rug was laid in the elevator that serviced the area. A policeman blocked tourists from even getting off the elevator on the floor. The Speaker's office was painted blue as well. There was a different, calming stability to the corridor; it had become a place to speak in measured tones.

In August 1987, as Gingrich was launching his campaign against Wright, he said, "If Wright survives this ethics thing, he may become the greatest Speaker since Henry Clay."

In March 1989, Wright told his daughter, "We were just greedy. Dammit."

What had Wright actually done?

Betty Wright did real work for Mallightco. No reading of the affidavits, from witnesses the committee never heard, could yield any other conclusion.

The car? It was six years old when Betty Wright left Mallightco's employment. The company should not have paid for it the next few years, but the Wrights owned half the company, and Mallick had benefited from the car when it was years newer. The apartment was more questionable. It seemed less a gift than a benefit which should have been considered and reported as income. It was insignificant, except that Wright had put his shoulder against the edge of the law and the rules and pushed until he bent back a place for it.

Clearly Mallick had no direct interest in legislation.

But there was the book. Those who actually wrote the royalty rules—members of both parties—agreed that the book did not violate any rules, that Wright had found a loophole. Wright certainly did that. He used his book to profit from his office. Perhaps he had seen it as a gray area. If one could accept honoraria from lobbyists, which was profiting from one's office, what was wrong with selling them large numbers of books? The principle—taking money from lobbyists—was the same, wasn't it? Once a member did that, the only issue was whether the member had sold himself, too. No one had ever accused Wright of doing that.

And yet didn't the public rightly demand more? Hadn't Wright himself demanded more in those early years in politics? Hadn't Wright himself agreed that the Speaker of the House should be held to a higher standard than his colleagues? There were those who believed the book alone was enough to cost him his speakership. There were others who dismissed it as an absurd charge, in normal times worth no more than one embarrassing and quickly forgotten editorial. But these weren't normal times, and Wright as much as Gingrich had created the abnormality.

In some ways it was the very pettiness of his activity that damaged him the most. It demeaned him, made him seem a small man, a conniver. There was smallness in him.

But there was largeness, too. His ambition was large, his vision of his role was large, and what he was willing to do to achieve those things was large. He had risked destroying himself to achieve his goals. He had warned Rostenkowski that if he thwarted him, he would try to unseat him as chairman. That had established his power.

He had used that power to drive his agenda through the 100th Congress, and make it the most productive in decades. He had risked that power when he had disdained the Caucus and joined with Ronald Reagan in a peace initiative. Then he had battled against the weight and power of the presidency and seized control of policy toward an entire hemisphere.

A few days before he left Congress, Arias wrote him a letter crediting and thanking him for bringing peace to Central America.

Shortly before that, John Myers had sat in his office, talking about the ethics committee. He was justifying his votes to charge Wright with using undue influence on the savings and loan regulators, and asked, "Suppose instead of 'undue influence' the charge was 'abuse of power'? Wouldn't you vote for it then?"

Was that why Myers had voted against him? For abusing power? How many other times did Myers vote against him for abuse of power? How many other Republicans voted against him for abuse of power? Was that why Myers had found someone like Phelan, antici-pating the result? The ethics committee had the same number of Re-publicans as Democrats. Phelan and the press made Republicans more than equal.

Wright was not charged with abuse of power. Whether he did abuse it or not, though, he had used it. And the committee used its power too. The Democrats did not rally to him. No Democrat on the com-mittee worked his colleagues in the off-hours, talked to them on the floor, took them to dinner, called Phelan a liar. Dixon particularly but other Democrats, too, did not so much kill him as let him die, let events take their course—and let Republicans and Phelan control events. Dixon did not step in to seize control and stop it.

One thread connected all of Wright's life—hubris. Years ago, as mayor of Weatherford, he had coerced the gas company to service the poor areas, though he had no authority to do so. He had first plunged himself into financial difficulty with his prideful assumption of his cam-paign debt, his prideful eagerness to assume that financial burden per-sonally. That was hubris. His insensitivity to appearances as he struggled to climb out of debt was hubris too. It was hubris, and the admixture of arrogance and innocence in him, to demand that others see the world his way. In each of these things, and in his ambitions, was his sense that rules did not apply to him.

Gingrich had said, "He creates himself when he acts. That's very threatening to a system governed by rules."

Gingrich was correct. Wright did act, and created new realities in doing so. Pushing the limits of his own personality, himself on edge, he put others on edge and seemed to personify the chaos not of what is possible—politics is the art of the possible—but of what might become possible. The hubris and chaos represented also the elements of greatness in him. There was power in him, and will, and the willingness to use power.

There had been no Speaker like him in this century. He was a throwback, perhaps to Thomas Reed, that three-hundred-pound giant of a man who once took the House by the throat, shook it, and transformed it. Or perhaps his true precursor was Henry Clay, who had dominated foreign policy and advanced his "American Plan" of national development.

In his last days in the House, Wright thought constantly of Rayburn. At every turn of the corridor, in every corner of the cloakroom, there was Rayburn, that short, squat, powerful body and hairless skull, confiding a lesson in him, inviting him to the Board of Education for a drink, and lonely. But even Rayburn had let the House alone, had chosen carefully his few moments of decisive battle, had waited until those battles had been forced upon him. Wright had not.

Jim Wright had a brief, shining moment in the sun. He was alone, soaring above his colleagues, above the Congress, above the White House, his will his wings. He soared above the moment. For a moment.

Then there is W. H. Auden's "Musée des Beaux Arts":

> In Brueghel's Icarus, for instance: how everything turns away
> Quite leisurely from the disaster; the ploughman may
> Have heard the splash, the forsaken cry,
> But for him it was not an important failure; the sun shone
> As it had to on the white legs disappearing into the green
> Water; and the expensive delicate ship that must have seen
> Something amazing, a boy falling out of the sky,
> Had somewhere to get to and sailed calmly on.

METHODOLOGY AND
ACKNOWLEDGMENTS

I first met Jim Wright several months before he became Speaker, when I wrote a profile of him for *The New York Times Magazine*. It became immediately apparent that his concept of the speakership was radically different from that of his recent predecessors. It seemed to me that his efforts to push his own view of the world on Washington, and to reorder the balance of power there, would make a perfect vehicle for a book exploring how power is exercised—how Washington really works. I asked him to cooperate. In fact, I asked for something I believed he would not grant: access to private meetings so that the book would truly reflect an insider's view of power.

In a two-hour discussion on his sixty-fourth birthday, December 22, 1986, his senior staff argued against his cooperating while I explained exactly what I hoped the book would do. I made clear he would have no financial stake in the book, no editorial control over it, and would not even get to read the manuscript prior to publication.

He agreed to my request. Two weeks later he was formally elected Speaker of the 100th Congress.

His cooperation meant that I had daily, routine access to virtually all meetings in which Wright participated (the basic rule of thumb was that if staff was allowed to attend, so was I). Other members of the Democratic leadership also granted me access to many of their private meetings, and several other members of Congress invited me to theirs as well, even when their purpose was to defeat Wright. Most of the events related in this book I personally observed.

The guidelines for using Wright's quotes were these: First, nothing

.he record. Second, any policy-related comments could be
ind attributed. Third, derogatory personal comments about
colleagues could be quoted but not attributed without permission.
Fourth, nothing at all would be revealed prior to 1989, either in print
or in conversation. The guidelines for using quotes from other members
of the House Democratic leadership were similar. Quotes of members
not in the leadership were cleared with them—if a member preferred
that a quote remain unattributed, it remained so. No quotes were
changed.

I did not witness everything in the book and the text does not differentiate between those comments which I did and did not hear. In
cases where the quotes came from reporting, my interviews were conducted often within minutes of a meeting, almost always within hours.
In most cases, but not in absolutely every case, quotes were confirmed
with more than one person. When I say someone "thought" or "believed," that person told me those were his thoughts. The ethics committee operated in executive session, but I obtained transcripts covering
many of its proceedings. Quotes from inside the committee came from
the transcripts.

In addition to observing meetings, I conducted more than two
hundred formal interviews with over sixty of the 435 members of the
House, and with many aides, lobbyists, and reporters. Equally important were the hundreds, perhaps thousands, of brief conversations in
hallways when I asked someone, "How should I interpret that?" or
"Why did you do this?" All interviews followed normal journalistic
ground rules.

There are many people to thank. Most of all, of course, I thank
Speaker of the House James Claude Wright, Jr. I also thank then–
majority leader, now Speaker, Thomas Foley; former majority whip
Tony Coelho; and chief deputy whip David Bonior for their tolerance
and assistance. Former congressman Buddy MacKay was exceptionally
helpful. Then–Budget Committee Chairman, now whip, William Gray
III also helped, as did Republican congressman Newt Gingrich, who
was as candid with me throughout the 100th Congress as Jim Wright
was. I also thank for his tolerance Republican leader Robert Michel.

They gave me an opportunity the like of which few writers have ever
had, and if the book fails to live up to that opportunity, it is a failure
of my talent.

I also want to thank three people who contributed much to the House, and loved it: Craig Raupe, Dick Conlon, and Jim Howard. All three were friends. All three died during the 100th Congress.

Jim Howard, from New Jersey, a chain-smoking, old-time-style chairman of the Public Works and Transportation Committee, was a school principal inspired to run for Congress by John Kennedy and civil rights and was elected in 1964. Howard and Wright had a special relationship. At one point when Howard asked Wright for a favor, a leadership aide said, "It's the kind of thing where Howard complains, 'The Speaker never does anything for me,' and everyone else in the House complains, 'Doesn't he ever tell Howard no?' "

Dick Conlon spent twenty years as executive director of the Democratic Study Group. He contributed mightily to making the House a small-'d' democratic place. There is a saying in Washington that people come to do good and stay to do well. That did not apply to Conlon, who never lost his passion. He died suddenly, in a sailing accident. At his memorial service—it packed the largest committee room in the House—one congressman remarked, "Dick would have liked this. The staff got seats and the members have to stand. And he outdrew Phil Burton."

Craig Raupe shared with me many insights into the House, into Texas politics, and into his close friend and former boss Jim Wright. They were as close as brothers for forty years. Craig became my friend, too, the kind of man who made you feel cheated because you had not met him earlier, did not know him longer. There is a saying in hockey— "He doesn't pick his spots." It's a compliment about players who will run up against anyone. Raupe didn't pick his spots. He always told everyone exactly what he thought.

And I thank Margaret Anne Hudgins Sullivan, whom I love and whose careful reading, insights into character, and literary knowledge make me seem deeper than I really am, and Rose Fulford Hudgins.

My editor, Dan Frank, I thank for his confidence, and also for his occasional terror, which in turn shook me out of lethargy. He was blunt when bluntness was required, and entirely supportive. As any writer knows, when you start out across the ocean in a small boat, it's nice to know you're not totally alone.

My agents, Ann Sleeper, even though she abandoned me for Isabel, and Raphael Sagalyn, took up my cause with some ferocity.

Victoria Meyer went beyond the call of duty to help.

I thank also several people who read parts of the manuscript. Most

onymity, probably for good reason, but Richard Cohen did
having his name associated with this book.

Kirk O'Donnell and Gary Hymel both shared their intimate knowledge of the House. More important, they are both trusted in the House,
and their endorsement of me meant that congressmen who would not
normally have talked to me, at least not with candor, did.

Jim Wright's staff honored me with their trust also, especially Char-
mayne Marsh, Kathy Mitchell, John Mack, Wilson Morris, Mark John-
son, Marshall Lynam, Phil Duncan, Steve Charnovitz, Peter Robinson,
Ben Procter, Michael Grisso, Lorraine Miller, Scott Lawson, Janice
Joyner, Angela Jones, Richard Orndorff, and Anne Page. Nicholas
Masters and Steven Champlin were also exceptionally helpful, as were
Werner Brandt, Charles Mellody, George Kundanis, and Kathy Gille.

Mary Connell and Ginger Brown shared intimacies, trust, and their
friendship.

The Everett McKinley Dirksen Congressional Center in Pekin, Illinois, came through with support precisely when most needed. I thank
the people there. James Witt at the Rayburn-Dirksen Institute at the
University of West Florida also lent assistance.

David Montgomery, Washington bureau chief of the *Fort Worth Star-
Telegram*, lent background material, and Stewart Fleming, U.S. editor
of the *Financial Times*, offered routine use of his library and Xerox
machine. The work of political scientist Robert Peabody proved helpful
in Chapter 1.

A note on this edition. All major figures in the book—including but
not limited to former Speaker Jim Wright, Speaker Tom Foley, former
Democratic whip Tony Coelho, Republican leader Robert Michel, and
Republican whip Newt Gingrich—were contacted prior to this printing
and offered the opportunity to correct anything they regarded as a
factual error. Those involved directly in the ethics investigation, including the ethics committee chairman, Julian Dixon, and ethics committee outside counsel, Richard Phelan, were also given this
opportunity. There is no dispute about the facts in this book.

Thanks.

John M. Barry

INDEX